"Value-packed, accurate, and comprehensive..."
—*Los Angeles Times*

"Unbeatable..."—*The Washington Post*

LET'S GO:
ROME

is the best book for anyone traveling on a budget. Here's why:

No other guidebook has as many budget listings.

In and around Rome, we found 38 hotels or hostels for under $27 a night. We tell you how to get there the cheapest way, whether by bus, train, or plane, and where to get an inexpensive and satisfying meal once you've arrived. There are hundreds of money-saving tips for everyone plus lots of information on student discounts.

LET'S GO researchers have to make it on their own.

Our Harvard-Radcliffe researchers travel on budgets as tight as your own—no expense accounts, no free hotel rooms.

LET'S GO is completely revised every year.

We don't just update the prices, we go back to the places. If a charming *trattoria* has become an overpriced tourist trap, we'll replace the listing with a new and better one.

No other budget guidebook includes all this:

Coverage of both the city and daytrips beyond; directions, addresses, phone numbers, and hours to get you in and around; in-depth information on culture, history, and the city's inhabitants; tips on work, study, sights, nightlife, and special splurges; detailed city maps; and much, much more.

LET'S GO is for anyone who wants to see Rome on a budget.

Books by Let's Go, Inc.

Let's Go: Europe
Let's Go: Britain & Ireland
Let's Go: France
Let's Go: Germany, Austria & Switzerland
Let's Go: Greece & Turkey
Let's Go: Israel & Egypt
Let's Go: Italy
Let's Go: London
Let's Go: Paris
Let's Go: Rome
Let's Go: Spain & Portugal

Let's Go: USA
Let's Go: California & Hawaii
Let's Go: Mexico
Let's Go: New York City
Let's Go: The Pacific Northwest, Western Canada & Alaska
Let's Go: Washington, D.C.

LET'S GO:

The Budget Guide to

ROME

1993

Kayla Alpert
Editor

David Thorpe
Assistant Editor

Written by
Let's Go, Inc.
a wholly owned subsidiary of
Harvard Student Agencies, Inc.

ST. MARTIN'S PRESS
NEW YORK

Helping Let's Go

If you have suggestions or corrections, or just want to share your discoveries, drop us a line. We read every piece of correspondence, whether a 10-page letter, a velveteen Elvis postcard, or, as in one case, a collage. All suggestions are passed along to our researcher/writers. Please note that mail received after May 5, 1993 will probably be too late for the 1994 book, but will be retained for the following edition. Address mail to:

Let's Go: Rome
Let's Go, Inc.
1 Story Street
Cambridge, MA 02138

In addition to the invaluable travel advice our readers share with us, many are kind enough to offer their services as researchers or editors. Unfortunately, the charter of Let's Go, Inc. and Harvard Student Agencies, Inc. enables us to employ only currently enrolled Harvard students.

Editor	Kayla Alpert
Assistant Editor	David Thorpe
Contributing Editor	Margaret Meserve
Managing Editor	July Belber
Publishing Director	Paul C. Deemer
Production Manager	Mark N. Templeton
Office Coordinator	Bart St. Clair
Office Manager	Anne E. Chisholm
Researcher-Writers	Alexis Averbuck
	Kristin Kimball
	Margaret Meserve

Sales Group Manager	Tiffany A. Breau
Sales Group Representatives	Frances Marguerite Maximé
	Breean T. Stickgold
	Harry James Wilson
Sales Group Coordinator	Aida Bekele
President	Brian A. Goler
C.E.O.	Michele Ponti

ACKNOWLEDGMENTS

Oh yes, I see that those of you who think I overpack, overspend, and under-sight-see are not laughing anymore (...but wait, are the jokes that bad?). It's true though. I could never have written this budget of a travel guide without the assistance, guidance, love, and respect of a great number of people (not to mention the last-minute national strikes in Thailand).

Gossip hydrant, wardrobe consultant, cookieboy, the stripes-to-my-gingham, and oh yeah, assistant editor, Master Thorpe honed my bad jokes into well-written bad jokes, versed himself in arcane historical subjects, and coped with my fits of hair-splitting, emotionalism, panicdom, and run-on sentences. He organized, collaborated, pampered, and accessorized well beyond the call of an assistant's duty. Finally, his unwavering commitment to Broadway Musicals about Rome...well, it made me just cry. I respect you, **David Q. Thorpe**! Can you hear me? Yeah, you.

Take away the jokes, the vulgar innuendoes, the title page, and this is **Margaret Meserve**'s book. More than anyone on the road or in the office, Margaret never hesitated in her enthusiasm and sheer dedication to the Rome guide. From day one, she infused this book with her knowledge, insight, and passion about Rome, braving the heat of the Forum, pushing past thousands of tourists at the Vatican, sniffing out the only store in Rome with Froot Loops, and even coming straight from the Boston airport to our office to perfect every section and turn of phrase.

No sooner had **Alexis Averbuck** geared herself for the jungles of Thailand, than she was artfully dodging mopeds and Romeos. With high-school Spanish, last-minute instructions, and a truly uncommon eye for bedspreads and tablecloths, Alexis hit the *pensione*, *piazze* and *pizzerie* with pure enthusiasm, meticulousness, and spirit. The Italian textile industry thanks you as well. We seized **Kristin Kimball** from the jungles of the far East only to have her test more mattresses, inspect more toilets, and schmooze with more hotel proprietors than should ever be done in a young life.

The Back Room of the office...just so rich. Managing Editrix, **July** not only provided format expertise and grammatical know-how, but also unwavering support for our libelous remarks, conspiracy theories, and shameless puns. **Al Marash**, a most swell best friend, wrote the superb film section. Riff afficionado, stereo despot, animal-noise orchestrator, hairball, and still such a great guy, **Mike Vazquez** can mooch my home-cooking anytime he like. That is, if **Elijah Siegler**, fellow gourmandizer, Yenta, A.R.T. subversive, and snarf victim, doesn't get there first. **Muneer** wowed us with the longest eyelashes in the office and with his cheap Indian food. I am deeply honored and moved that **Nell Eisenberg** named her baby crocodile skull after me. **Jane** gave the office some much-needed style and discipline.

Those brave souls who crossed the border to our room deserve some credit. **Chris Capozzola** was cartographer extraordinaire. Fire Island has never seen a Conga dancer or apple-babka connoisseur quite like **Bart** "That's no home perm" **St. Clair**. Thanks to **Geoff Rodkey** for his true appreciation for all things classic. **Becca Knowles** is just so cute, perky and demure, especially for hiring **Pat LaRiviere** who whipped up the hilarious timeline. Workaholic **Mark Templeton** deserves fame, fortune, Farrah, or at least a week's vacation. **Andrew Kaplan** heroically withstood my computer unfriendliness and my Sally Jesse imitations and is a great big friend. Many *Grazie* to **Amy D.**, **Steve B.**, **Bunny L.**, and fellow Capricorn **Zach S.** for their invaluable help.

My passion for things Roman is not without its sources. To **Vincenzo Amato** and other *amici-* **Stefania, Ghigo, Cinzia, Donatella,** and the rest-for putting up with my faltering grammar, Americanisms, and pitiful Vespa driving, I give a big "Cerchi Rogna?!". I'm eternally grateful to **Elena R-Stockel** for making me a part of her family (and for taking me to the best ceramic warehouse in Italy). Through the falafel stands of Paris, hairdressers of Rome, and any number of plumbing disasters, **Ann Celi** has been *sconvolgente*. **Lauren Gwyn** and **Jen Rubell** take the fire from the passion of the road. **Francesca Müller** has lovingly seen me through every meal, term-paper crisis, flea market, and one ignominious Quest For Thighmaster. To fellow Hervé Villechaise devotee and hapless pawn of the moisturizing cream industry, **L. Courtney Wechsler**, I need never ask "Ai Capito?" Despite a life-long addiction to her feather pillow and pricey Italian shampoo, **Nichola Consuela Conze** is my model for adventure. Finally, my brothers **Jordan** and **Seth** have inspired me by their own courage and support. I really owe everything to my amazing **parents** (including one round-trip airfare to Rome-and several outstanding American Express bills); I couldn't have picked any better.

—KSA

Mille grazie to Miss Alpert for not letting a little thing like work get in the way of the fragrant summer roses we stopped to smell so often: the endless parade of boyfriends, the long weekends on Fire Island, the sentimental classic movies on rainy, mid-week afternoons, the merciless gossip, the embarrassingly frequent trips to Urban's and the Harvest. Thanks for making a dream come true: my name in lights around the world and the opportunity to write for a living (however brief the opportunity and meager the living). Most of all thanks for making *Let's Go:Rome* truly collaborative.

Thanks also, counter-clockwise, to the eclectic **back room**: Mike for being cool; Alex for admiring my clothes and letting me feed him cookies, Munerva for forcing me to eat Indian food all summer, Eliahu for sneaking me into the A.R.T. and knowing Elvis Costello's solo album, Jane for dressing flawlessly, Nell for introducing me to Mayla and her way of life, July for patiently manage-editing and remaining on the side of free speech and warranted anarchy. In the rest of office, Mark Templeton and Chris Capozzola put up with my hapless questions.

Chello to the cultured and artistic residents of Porter Park: Justin, Jonathan, Nora and Andrew; living there was more fun than hanging out at the Peach Pit and Shooters *combined*. Visitors that brightened my day and sometimes took me to the Cape: Ed, Abigail, Lev, Chris, Joe, and last but not least James R. A cross-country wave to my oldest pals Gab and Jen.

Hi Mom!

—DLT

About Let's Go

A generation ago, Harvard Student Agencies, a three-year-old non-profit corporation dedicated to providing employment to students, was doing a booming business booking charter flights to Europe. One of the extras offered to passengers on these flights was a 20-page mimeographed pamphlet entitled *1960 European Guide,* a collection of tips on continental travel compiled by the HSA staff. The following year, students traveling to Europe researched the first full-fledged edition of *Let's Go: Europe,* a pocket-sized book with tips on budget accommodations, irreverent write-ups of sights, and a decidedly youthful slant.

Throughout the 60s, the series reflected the times: a section of the 1968 *Let's Go: Europe* was entitled "Street Singing in Europe on No Dollars a Day." During the 70s *Let's Go* evolved into a large-scale operation, adding regional European guides and expanding coverage into North Africa and Asia. In the 80s, we launched coverage of the United States, developed our research to include concerns of travelers of all ages, and finetuned the editorial process that continues to this day. The early 90s saw the introduction of *Let's Go* city guides.

1992 has been a big year for us. We are now Let's Go, Incorporated, a wholly owned subsidiary of Harvard Student Agencies. To celebrate this change, we moved from our dungeonesque Harvard Yard basement to an equally dungeonesque third-floor office in Harvard Square, and we purchased a high-tech computer system that allows us to typeset all of the guides in-house. Now in our 33rd year, *Let's Go* publishes 17 titles, covering more than 40 countries. This year *Let's Go* proudly introduces two new entries in the series: *Let's Go: Paris* and *Let's Go: Rome.*

But these changes haven't altered our tried and true approach to researching and writing travel guides. Each spring 90 Harvard University students are hired as researcher-writers and trained intensively during April and May for their summer tour of duty. Each researcher-writer then hits the road for seven weeks of travel on a shoestring budget, researching six days per week and overcoming countless obstacles in the quest for better bargains.

Back in Cambridge, Massachusetts, an editorial staff of 32, a management team of six, and countless typists and proofreaders—all students—spend more than six months pushing nearly 8000 pages of copy through a rigorous editing process. By the time classes start in September, the typeset guides are off to the printers, and they hit bookstores world-wide in late November. Then, by February, next year's guides are well underway.

A NOTE TO OUR READERS

The information for this book is gathered by Let's Go's researchers during the late spring and summer months. Each listing is derived from the assigned researcher's opinion based upon his or her visit at a particular time. The opinions are expressed in a candid and forthright manner. Other travelers might disagree. Those traveling at a different time may have different experiences since prices, dates, hours, and conditions are always subject to change. You are urged to check beforehand to avoid inconvenience and surprises. Travel always involves a certain degree of risk, especially in low-cost areas. When traveling, especially on a budget, you should always take particular care to ensure your safety.

CONTENTS

Contents

LIST OF MAPS

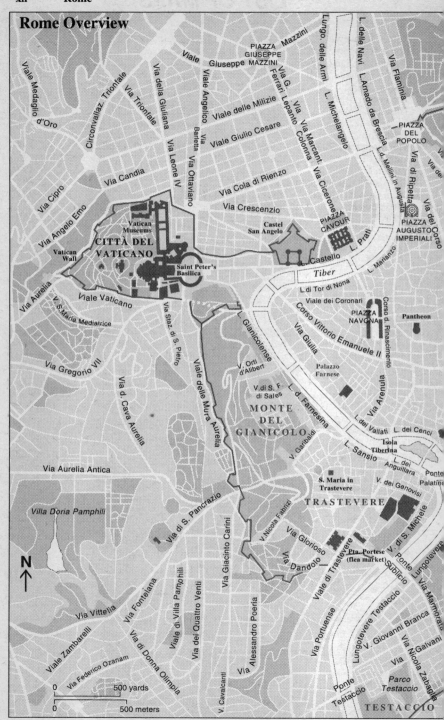

Rome Overview

LET'S GO: ROME

General Introduction

*For every traveler who has but a mere modicum of
style, the only useful guidebook will be the one
which she herself has written.*
— *Waven Q. Tresses*

Unfortunately, if you haven't had the pleasure of writing your own travel guide,
you'll have to trust us. The best way to start your vacation is beforehand; you don't
have to plan your every move, but doing a little background reading on Rome might
make your sight-seeing more meaningful. You need not bury yourself in *The Rise and
Fall of the Roman Empire*—our own General Introduction is a healthy enough dose and
offers suggestions on further reading and interesting films. *Let's Go:Rome* begins with
practical information, from advice on packing and ways to get cheap flights to a list of
English-language bookstores and how to buy a condom. The second section of the
General Introduction offers you an unusual glimpse into the city's history and way of
life. We follow with a comprehensive listing of budget accommodations and restaurants. The Sights section navigates you through the city's numerous *piazze*, churches,
and monuments, starting from the *piazza del Popolo*, the traditional entrance to the
city, through the Historical Center, to some of the outlying areas, up to the Vatican City.
Our maps are inserted in the areas to which they pertain (look in our Table of Contents
for the list of maps). The Entertainment section details nightlife, cultural events, festivals, sporting events, shopping, and much more. We have also devoted some space to
escaping the city, with day-trips to Lazio (the province around Rome) and to neighboring provinces. The amount of things to see and do in Rome can be overwhelming, but
(we can never say it enough) one of the best things to do in the Eternal City is nothing.
Escape from the hordes of tourists at the Colosseum, leave your *Let's Go* behind, and
kick back in a *caffè* for a few hours. Use our guide as a starting point for your own explorations; the best discoveries may be those you make yourself. If *Let's Go* is the bible
of the budget traveler, healthy skepticism may serve you better than blind faith.

Planning Your Trip

A Note on Prices and Currency

This book was researched in the summer of 1992. Since then, inflation may have
raised prices as much as 10%. Hotel prices are changed every year in January. The exchange rates were compiled in September, 1992. Since rates fluctuate considerably, be
sure to confirm them before you go by checking a national newspaper.

The surest way to have a successful trip is to plan ahead. Read up on the places you'd
like to visit beforehand; dig into a book on ancient history, leave a novel set in Rome
next to the toilet, or rent the video of *Roman Holiday* to get you in the mood; definitely
talk with friends who've been there. Make a loose itinerary of places you want to see,
and daytrips that interest you. Tourism is one of Rome's biggest industries, and you
should have no trouble finding lots of information. Take the time to write to some of
the organizations listed below in the Useful Organizations section and get details about
upcoming events, festivals, entertainment, local excursions, or anything else that floats
your boat. Keep in mind that Rome is one of the most expensive—and least English-
speaking cities—in the world, so doing some extra work beforehand could save you

money, time, and early signs of aging on the road. Make your hotel reservations in advance; many places do not require a deposit, but you should call to re-confirm a few days before arriving. Lost souls can receive a blessing from the Pope by writing ahead to request tickets for a papal audience. Consider exploring some of the countryside and ancient monuments beyond the city limits, or even staying at a regional farmhouse through the *Agriturist* program (see Alternative Accommodations below). Organize your itinerary and plan your budget before you go, but always allow for leisure time, adventure and misadventure, the occasional budget-breaking meal, and of course, inflation.

Attempting to see all the Roman monuments, churches, and museums in four days, or even in two weeks, will sap both your sightseeing energy and your social time. Fortunately, many of the more noteworthy monuments, *piazze,* and fountains lie closely together in the historic center *(Centro Storico).* Piazza Navona is a three-minute walk from the Pantheon, and only ten minutes by foot from the Vatican. Still, don't go crazy trying to stake out every Renaissance church you studied in Art History 101. Stroll around the city, look up at the various bell towers, and peek into the atriums of various residential *palazzi* as you wander. One of the most rewarding aspects of any Roman holiday is meeting Italians. Go back to the same *caffè* or bar several times, strike up conversations with people at restaurants and shops. Romans love to talk, even if it means gesticulating their entire life story for non-Italian ears. If you make an effort to be polite and friendly, so will most people you meet; any attempt to speak Italian, however bungled, will almost always be enthusiastically received.

If you are planning to stay in Rome long-term, whether you are a student, a businessperson, or a crazed Gore Vidal fan, make some arrangements and contacts before you go. Write to your embassy for English-speaking organizations, contact a real estate agent, and try to get in touch with your long-lost Italian cousin Ghigo. If you want to study at a program in Rome, try to find someone who's been in the same program and ask them for details; once there, make an effort to branch out from the other Americans to meet some Italian students. The initial complications of moving, learning a new language, and dealing with the city's municipal ineffectiveness are worth the infinite splendor of living in Rome.

Useful Organizations and Publications

The mounds of information available to travelers can seem overwhelming. Give yourself time to think about your trip so you won't get lost in the whirlwind of tourist-office pamphlets and brochures. Don't be shy about asking a tourist office for information—it's their job and they'll be happy to help you—but remember that their mission is to lure you to Rome, not to assess objectively the virtues of a particular sight you're interested in. Choose your information carefully and develop a clear idea of what you want to see. Finally, leave some free time in your schedule to wander and explore.

Tourist Offices

Centro Turistico Studentesco Giovanile (CTS), via Genova, 16, 00184 Roma (tel. (06) 467 91, fax (06) 467 92 05). With 90 offices throughout Italy, CTS provides travel, accommodation, and sight-seeing discounts, as well as information for students and young people. Sells the *Carte Verde* for discount train fares, the International Student Identity Card (ISIC) and International Youth Cards (FIYTO card). Branch offices in London and Paris.

Italian Cultural Institute, 686 Park Ave., New York, NY 10021 (tel. (212) 879-4242); 496 Huron St., Toronto, Ontario, M5R 2R3 (tel. (416) 921-3802). The Italian government's cultural agency abroad. Information on Italian art, music, literature, and current events, including the occasional concert, exhibition and lecture series. Consider calling them even if you don't bother writing anywhere else—they're friendly and helpful (though very busy in summer). Other offices in Los Angeles (tel. (213) 207-4737), Chicago (tel. (312) 822-9545), San Francisco (tel. (415) 788-7412), Washington, DC (tel. (202) 328-5590), Montréal (tel. (514) 849-3473), Ottawa (tel. (613) 236-0279), and Vancouver (tel. (604) 688-0809).

Italian Government Travel Office (ENIT), 630 Fifth Ave., #1565, Rockefeller Center, New York, NY 10111 (tel. (212) 245-4822); 500 N. Michigan Ave., Chicago, IL 60611 (tel. (312) 644-0990); 360 Post St., San Francisco, CA 94108 (tel. (415) 392-6206); 1, pl. Ville Marie, #1914, Montréal, Que. H3B 3M9 (tel. (514) 866-7667); 1 Princes St., London, England WIR 8AY (tel. (01) 408 12 54). Write for their detailed (and indispensable) guide *Italia: General Information for Travelers to Italy* and for regional information.

Enjoy Rome, via Varese, 39, Roma (tel. (06) 445 18 43). A new agency offering accommodation services, bicycle itineraries, discounts galore, and innumerable other services.

Italian Embassies and Consulates

U.S.: Italian Embassy, 1601 Fuller St. NW, Washington, DC (tel. (201) 328-5500). Consulate General, 12400 Wilshire Blvd., #300, **West Los Angeles**, CA 90025 (tel. (310) 820-0622); other consulates or embassies of Italy at 2590 Webster St., **San Francisco**, CA 94115 (tel. (415) 931-4924); 500 N. Michigan Ave., #1850, **Chicago**, IL 60611 (tel. (312) 467-1550); 630 Camp St., **New Orleans**, LA 70130 (tel. (504) 524-2271); 100 Boylston St., #900, **Boston**, MA 02116 (tel. (617) 542-0483); 535 Griswold St., #1840, **Detroit**, MI 48226 (tel. (313) 963-8560); 690 Park Ave., **New York**, NY 10021 (tel. (212) 737-9100); **student office**, 686 Park Ave., New York, NY 10021 (tel. (212) 879-4242); 421 Chestnut St., **Philadelphia**, PA 19106 (tel. (215) 592-7329); 1300 Post Oak Blvd., #660, **Houston**, TX, 77056 (tel. (713) 850-7520).

Canada: Consulate of Italy, 3489 Drummond St., Montréal, Que. H3G 1X6 (tel. (514) 849-8351); Embassy of Italy, 275 Slater St., Ottawa, Ont., K1P 5H9 (tel. (613) 232-2402).

U.K.: Embassy of Italy, 14 Three Kings Yard, London, W1 (tel. (071) 629 82 00); Consulate General of Italy, 38 Eaton Place, London, SW1X 8AN (tel. (071) 235 93 71); Consulate General for Scotland and Northern Ireland, 32 Melville St., Edinburgh, EH3 7HA (tel. (031) 220 36 95, for passport/visa inquiries (tel. (031) 226 36 31); Italian Consulate in Manchester, 111 Piccadilly, Manchester, M1 2HY (tel. (061) 236 90 24).

Australia: Embassy of Italy, 12 Grey St., Deakin, A.C.T. 2000, Canberra, G.P.O.B. 360 (tel. 73 33 33).

New Zealand: Embassy of Italy, P.O. Box 463, 38 Grant Rd., Wellington (tel. 473 53 39, fax 472 72 55); via Zara 28, Rome 00198 (tel. (6) 440 29 28, fax (6) 440 29 84).

Budget Travel Services

Compagnia Italiana Turismo (CIT), 544 Broadway #307, New York, NY 10012 (tel. (800) 248-8687); 1450 City Councillors St., Montréal, H3A 2E6 Quebec (tel. (514) 845-9101). New York office sells rail tickets wholesale; Montréal office specializes in individual and group tour packages. Other branch offices in Chicago, Los Angeles, and Toronto.

Council on International Educational Exchange (CIEE/Council Travel), 205 E. 42nd St., New York, NY 10017 (tel. (212) 661-1414; for charter flights (800) 223-7402). Publishes books on educational, volunteer, and work opportunities throughout the world. Sells the International Student Identity Card (ISIC), FIYTO and ITIC cards. Pick up or write for their free annual *Student Travel Catalog* (postage US$1). **Council Travel** is the budget travel subsidiary of CIEE, located at the same address (tel. (212) 661-1450). Sells Eurailpasses, travel gear, ISIC, FIYTO and HI/IYHF cards. CIEE has branch offices in Paris, Bonn, Dusseldorf, Tokyo, and throughout the U.S. Address mail inquiries to the New York office.

Educational Travel Centre (ETC), 438 N. Frances St., Madison, WI 53703 (tel. (608) 256-5551). Flight information, HI/IYHF cards, and Eurailpasses. Write for their free tour and flight information pamphlet *Taking Off.*

Federation of International Youth Travel Organizations (FIYTO), Islands Brygge 81, DK-2300 Copenhagen S., Denmark (tel. (31) 54 60 80). Issues the International Youth Card (IYC). Free annual catalogue lists over 10,000 discounts available to cardholders.

International Student Travel Confederation (ISTC), ISIC Association, Gothersgade 30, 1123 Copenhagen K, Denmark, (tel. (31) 93 73 77, fax (31) 93 93 03). **US**, CIEE/Council Travel Services (see address above). **Canada**, Travel CUTS (see address below). **U.K.**, London Student Travel, 52 Grosvenor Gardens, London WC1 (tel. (071) 730 34 02). **Ireland**, USIT Ltd., 7 Anglessa St., Dublin 2 (tel. (01) 77 81 17). **Australia**, SSA/STA, 220 Faraday St., Carlton, Melbourne, Victoria 3053 (tel. (03) 347 69 11). **New Zealand**, Student Travel, Courtenay Chambers, 15 Courtenay, 2nd floor, Wellington (tel. (04) 85 05 61). Issues the ISIC.

Let's Go Travel Services, Harvard Student Agencies, Inc., Thayer Hall-B, Harvard University, Cambridge, MA 02138 (tel. (617) 495-9649). Managed by the same folks who produce these books—well, not really, but at least we've met socially. Sells Eurailpasses, American Youth Hostel memberships (valid at all HI/IYHF youth hostels), International Student and Teacher ID cards, International Youth cards for nonstudents, maps and travel guides (including the *Let's Go* series), discount airfares, and a complete line of budget travel gear. All items are available by mail.

STA Travel, 17 E 45th St., New York, NY 10017 (tel. (800) 777-0112); 48 E. 11th St., New York, NY 10003 (tel. (212) 986-9470); 7202 Melrose Ave., Los Angeles, CA 90046 (tel. (213) 934-8722); 74 Old Brompton Rd., London SW7 3LQ, England (tel. (071) 937 99 21 for European travel, (071) 937 99 71 for North American travel, (071) 937 99 62 for the rest of the world); 222 Faraday St., Melbourne, Victoria 3053 (tel. (03) 347 69 11); 10 High St., Auckland, New Zealand (tel. (09) 309 99 95); other offices worldwide. A worldwide youth travel organization that provides ISIC cards, HI/IYHF memberships, railpasses, insurance, bargain flights, and travel services.

Travel CUTS (Canadian Universities Travel Service), 187 College St., Toronto, Ont. M5T IP7 (tel. (416) 979-2406), with offices in Victoria, Vancouver, Halifax, Edmonton, Saskatoon, Winnepeg, Ottawa, Montréal, and London. Offers student rates on both domestic and international travel. Sells ISIC, HI/IYHF, and International Youth cards as well as Eurailpass and Eurail Youthpass. Arranges adventure tours and work abroad. Their newspaper, *The Student Traveler,* is free at all offices and on campuses across Canada.

Organizations that sell the IYC in Rome include:

CTA, via G. Marcora, 18, Roma (tel. (06) 584 04 46).

EAS (Experience America Society), piazza di Spagna, 12, 00187 Roma (tel. (06) 678 45 65).

ATG, via dei Barbieri, 3A, 00186 Roma (tel. (06) 687 55 38 or 687 70 41). Also at via de Amicis, 4, 20123 Milano (tel. (02) 89 40 50 75) and via San Bragio, 14, 35100 Padova (tel. (049) 895 07 94).

CTS, via Genova, 16, 00184 Roma (tel. (06) 467 92 71).

ETLI, Youth Section, via Leopold Serra, 19, 00153 Roma (tel. (06) 554 38 33).

Hostel Associations

To stay in the Italian youth hostels affiliated with **Hostelling International (HI),** formerly **International Youth Hostel Federation (IYHF),** you must often become a member of HI/IYHF. (The IYHF recently decided to change its name to Hostelling International (HI). The same blue triangle symbol will be used as the HI/IYHF mark of approval. However, some national branches of the network have not yet changed their names to include the words Hostelling International; they may be changing them in the future, so watch out for such discrepancies, and always look for the blue triangle if in doubt.) In most countries, membership cards are available while you wait from certain budget travel agencies. The cost varies by country (in the U.S., US$25, under 18 US$10, over 54 US$15), and membership is good through the calendar year. The HI/IYHF affiliate in Italy is **Associazione Italiana Alberghi per la Gioventù (AIG),** via Cavour, 44, 00184 Roma (tel. (06) 487 11 52 or 474 67 55, fax (06) 474 12 56). Membership cards are available in Italy from major hostels, AIG offices throughout Italy, and student travel services. AIG hostels vary in the strictness with which they observe membership requirements; a number of hostels not affiliated with the AIG exist as well, and do not require HI/IYHF membership. Specific requirement information is included in individual listings of hostels throughout the book. Buying a card before you leave home avoids problems (as not all hostels requiring cards sell them); they can be purchased through any of the HI/IYHF affiliates listed below. For a listing of the one youth hostel in Rome, see Accommodations below.

U.S.: American Youth Hostels (AYH), 425 Divisadero St. #310, San Francisco, CA 94117 (tel. (415) 863-9939).

Canada: Canadian Hostelling Association, now **Hostelling International—Canada (HI—C),** 1600 James Naismith Dr., Gloucester, Ontario, K1B 5N4 (tel. (613) 748-5638).

U.K.: Youth Hostels Association (England and Wales), Trevelyan House, 8 St. Stephen's Hill, St. Albans, Herts, AL1 2DY (tel. (07 27) 552 15).

Australia: Australian Youth Hostel Association, Level 3, 10 Mallett St., Camperdown, NSW 2050 (tel. (02) 565 16 99).

New Zealand: Youth Hostels Association of New Zealand, P.O. Box 436, Corner of Manchester and Gloucester St., Christchurch 1 (tel. (03) 79 99 70, fax (03) 65 44 76).

Books

Forsyth Travel Library, 9154 W. 57th St., P.O. Box 2975, Shawnee Mission, KS 66201 (tel. (800) 367-7984 or (913) 384-3440). A mail-order service that stocks a wide range of European city, area, and country maps, as well as guides for European train and boat travel. The sole North American distributor of the Thomas Cook *European Timetables,* a compilation of European train schedules (US$24.95, US$4 shipping). Write or phone for a free newsletter and catalog.

John Muir Publications, P.O. Box 613, Sante Fe, NM 87504 (tel. (505) 982-4078, fax (505) 988-1680). Publishes over 75 books on travel and environmental explorations, including the *Kidding Around* series of itinerary planners for the junior traveler, and several books by veteran traveler Rick Steves, including his *Europe through the Back Door* (US$17.95), which explains how to avoid tourist traps, and an Italian phrasebook (US$4.95).

Travelling Books, P. O. Box 77114, Seattle, WA 98117 (tel. (206) 367-5848). Provides a mail-order service from their extensive catalogue of books, maps, language aids, and sundry accessories. The catalogue, which includes travel tips and information, is free.

Superintendent of Documents, U.S. Government Printing Office, Washington, DC 20402 (tel. (202) 783-3238, fax (202) 275-2529). Open Mon.-Fri. 8am-4pm. Publishes *Your Trip Abroad* (US$1), *Safe Trip Abroad* (US$1), *Health Information for International Travel* (US$5), and "Background Notes" on all countries.

Wide World Books and Maps, 1911 North 45th St., Seattle, WA 98103 (tel. (206) 634-3453). Publishes a free catalog listing the most recent guidebooks.

When to Go

Swarms of tourists converge on Rome in July and August, which means scaling the walls of booked hotel rooms and sharing your first experience of the Sistine Chapel with 4000 other tourists. Hotels legally charge more in the high season, and their rooms are populated by lemming-like tour groups. While the tourist industry opens in the summer—the Tourist Office extends its office hours and the youth hostel opens—Romans abandon ship for their own vacations, particularly in August, when the exodus is known as *Ferragosto*. Easter seems to be the hot time for a pilgrimage to the Vatican, though they don't even sponsor an egg-hunt; there are however a couple of processions featuring the Pope. The time to see Rome at its most authentic is in the early fall or late spring; the weather is temperate, there are few tourists, hotel prices go down, and you can attend the autumnal olive and wine harvests in Lazio or the springtime flower shows in the city. Though winter in Rome is relatively mild, *caffè,* restaurants, and the general population move indoors. Piazza Navona is just not the same when you're standing in three inches of slush.

Weather

Rome's summers are hot and dry with temperatures often above 24°C (75°F), cooling with the afternoon *ponentino,* a west wind that rises from the Tyrrhenian Sea 15 miles away. The winters are fairly mild, with temperatures averaging 7°C (45°F). Snow rarely hits Rome, but the city gets chilly from the *tramentino,* a stormy wind from the north. The spring and fall are the rainy seasons, with temperatures around 14°C (57°F). Check with IAMAT (see Health, below) for more specific information.

Holidays

Holidays are listed below so you'll know when the city shuts down or parties down. Plan your trip accordingly—remember that in August, compared to the rest of year, the Italian *Ferragosto* will make Rome seem like a ghost town. Be particularly aware of holidays, both legal and religious, when planning your itinerary; you can curse these days, when banks, shops, and almost everything else shuts down, or you can get into the spirit. The only official holiday specific to Rome (besides the daily 3- to 4-hour lunches) is June 29, the feast day of Saints Peter and Paul. Rome and the rest of Italy officially closes on the following dates: January 1 (New Year's Day); January 6 (Epiphany); Easter Monday; April 25 (Liberation Day); May 1 (Labor Day); August 15 (Assumption of the Virgin); November 1 (All Saints' Day); December 8 (Day of the Immaculate Conception—that's the conception of Mary, not Jesus, of course); December 25 (Christmas Day); and December 26 (feast of St. Stephen). Check out our section on festivals (see Entertainment: Festivals below) to plan your trip to coincide with the snail banquet in San Giovanni or the artichoke festival in Ladispoli.

Documents and Formalities

Passports

You will need a valid passport both to enter Italy and to reenter your home country. As a precaution, carry a photocopy of it showing the number and date and place of issue. **Keep this separate from your passport.** Leave a second copy with a loved one at home. Consulates also recommend that you carry an expired passport or an official copy of your birth certificate in a separate part of your baggage, either of which would be necessary to reissue your passport in case of emergency. You can request a duplicate birth certificate from the Bureau of Vital Statistics in your state or province of birth. It's also wise to carry a few extra passport-type photos. If you lose your passport, notify the local police and the nearest consulate immediately.

Remember that your passport is a public document and may not be withheld or used as collateral without your consent. Don't worry if a hotel proprietor requests your passport when you check in; hotels must register tourists with the police (see Visas below). Your passport should be returned within two or three hours. However, if you surrender your passport before seeing your room and then change your mind, the proprietor must give you your passport back.

If your parents or grandparents were born in a member country of the European Community, you may be able to claim dual citizenship with that country. This double citizenship will give you access to EC citizenship, and consequently, greater ease in acquiring work in Italy, even if your dual citizenship is with Ireland or the United Kingdom. Male applicants should beware: claiming Italian citizenship will obligate you to military service.

U.S. citizens can obtain a 10-year passport (US$65) or, if under age 18, a 5-year passport (US$40). Apply at any U.S. Passport Agency office or at one of the several thousand federal and state courts and post offices that accept passport applications. All travelers to Italy, including infants, must have a passport in their name. If you fall under any of the following categories, you must apply in person (although parents may apply on behalf of children under 13): if you are applying for your *first* passport; if you are under 18; if your current passport is more than 12 years old, or if it was issued before your 16th birthday. With your application, you must submit proof of U.S. citizenship (a certified birth certificate), proof of identity (an unexpired document with photo and signature, such as a driver's license), and two identical 2 x 2 inch photographs (most camera stores take passport photos).

To renew your passport by mail (US$55), you must submit a previous U.S. passport issued not more than 12 years ago and have been at least 16 years of age the first time you applied for a passport. Submission of the old passport fulfills the requirements of proof of citizenship and identity; you need only to enclose two recent, identical 2x2 inch photographs and the application along with it. The passport office normally requires three to four weeks to process an application, but it is wise to apply *several months in advance,* especially during the busy period from February to July. You should also be aware that some countries forbid entrance if your passport is due to expire in less than six months, and that returning to the U.S. with an expired passport sub-jects you to an US$100 fine.

Rush service is available for travelers who are willing to pay a fee for express mail service and can prove (with an airplane ticket) that they are departing the country with-in five working days. If your passport is lost or stolen, report the loss to the nearest U.S. embassy or consulate and the local police immediately. For more information, call the U.S. Passport Information's 24-hour recording (tel. (202) 647-0518) or contact the Washington Passport Agency, 1425 K St., Washington, DC 20524-0002 (tel. (202) 647-0518, recorded information (202) 647-0518).

Canadian citizens may apply for a five-year passport in person at one of 26 regional offices or at the Passport Office, Promenade du Portage, Plâce du Centre, Hull, Ontar-io; by mail at the Passport Office, Department of External Affairs, Ottawa, Ontario K1A 0G3; or, outside Canada, at the nearest Canadian embassy or consulate. Appli-cants should submit evidence of Canadian citizenship verified by a "guarantor" (a pro-fessional who has known you for at least two years), two identical passport photos co-signed by you and the same guarantor, a completed application (available at passport and post offices, and travel agencies), and CDN$35. The Passport Office recommends that you apply in winter, if possible. Expect a 5-day wait if applying in person, 3 weeks if applying by mail. No rush service is available. For more information, refer to the pamphlet *Bon Voyage, but...*, free from the passport office.

British citizens should apply in person at a local passport office. You must present original copies of your birth certificate; two identical, recent passport photographs, signed and countersigned by a qualified person; a completed application co-signed by that same person, and a copy of your marriage certificate (if applicable). The fee is £15 and your passport is valid for 10 years, five years if you are under 16. The process takes four to six weeks. Family passports may be issued, but children aged 16 and up require separate passports. Rush service is available upon proof of need for immediate depar-ture. Applicants should count on at least a month of processing time, and more during the busy season between February and August.

Irish citizens should pick up an application at a local guard station or request one from one of the two passport offices. If you have never had a passport, you must send your birth certificate, the long application, and two identical pictures to Passport Of-fice, Setanta Centre, Molesworth St., Dublin 2 (tel. (01) 711 633) or Passport Office, 1A South Mall, Cork, County Cork (tel. (021) 272 525). To renew, send your old pass-port, the short form, and the photos. Passports cost IR£45 and are valid for 10 years. Apply for a passport as soon as you know you will need it, though rush service is avail-able.

Australian citizens must apply for a passport in person at a local post office, where an appointment may be necessary; through a passport office; or through an Australian diplomatic mission overseas. A parent may file for an applicant who is under 18 and unmarried. With your application you must turn in proof of citizenship, proof of your present name, two photographs, and other forms of identification. Proof of citizenship can be an Australian passport valid for more than two years and issued after November 22, 1984, a birth certificate, or a citizen certificate from the Department of Immigra-tion. The photographs (45mm by 35mm) must be identical, not more than six months old, and signed as instructed in the application. Other ID includes driver's license, credit card, rate notices, etc. Application fees are adjusted every three months; call the toll-free information service for current details (tel. 13 12 32 or (008) 02 60 22). There is also a departure tax -when a citizen over 11 years old leaves the country.

Applicants for a **New Zealand passport** must contact their local Link Centre, travel agent, or New Zealand Representative for an application form which they must com-plete a mail to the New Zealand Passport Office (address below). Completed applica-tion forms must include (1) evidence of New Zealand citizenship (such as a previous New Zealand passport or an original birth or citizenship certificate), (2) two identical photographs correctly certified, and (3) the appropriate fee. For an application lodged in New Zealand, the fee is NZ$56.25 for adults and NZ$25.30 for children under 16 years; for an application lodged overseas, the fee is NZ$110.00 for adults and NZ$49.50 for children under 16. Children are required to have separate passports and their names can no longer be endorsed in the passport of their parents or guardians. Childrens' passports have a maximum validity of five years. Those children whose names are already endorsed in their parents or guardians' passports will be able to travel using such documentation until they reach 16 or until the passport expires, whichever occurs first, but only when accompanied by the passport holder. The standard processing time is 21 days, but urgent applications will be given priority. A New Zealand citizen who is overseas may send or take his/her passport application to the nearest New Zealand Embassy, High Commission, or Consulate which is authorized to issue passports. Unless the passport is urgently required, the application will be processed in New Zealand. For more information, contact the **New Zealand Passport Office**, Documents of National Identity Division, Department of Internal Affairs, Box 10-526, Wellington.

Visas

A visa is a stamp placed on your passport by a foreign government that permits you to visit that country for a specified purpose and period of time. Tourists from the United States, Canada, Great Britain, Ireland, Australia, and New Zealand do not need a visa to visit Italy for three months or less. If you wish to remain longer and can prove that you are a bona fide tourist with adequate means of support, you may obtain a one-time three-month extension from any local police station *(questura)*. The Bureau of Consular Affairs warns, however, that visa extensions are granted infrequently. If you intend to travel for more than three months, your chances for a long-term visa are better if you apply before your departure. Travelers from countries other than those listed above should check with the Italian Government Travel Office or the nearest Italian Embassy; Italy does require visas from citizens of many countries in Asia, Africa, and the Middle East.

Entrance to Italy as a tourist does not include permission to study or work there. To apply for a student visa, you need a letter of acceptance from the institution you will be attending and either a statement of financial support from your parents or a letter from your bank or accountant confirming that you have sufficient financial resources. To obtain a work visa, you must submit a written promise of a job that no available Italian can fill. Fluency in English is often a sufficient stipulation.

Italy requires foreigners to register at a local police station *(questura)* within three days of arrival in the country. Hotels (a blanket term including all the now-obsolete classifications like pension, hostel, and even campground) are responsible for registering their guests—that's why hotel owners have to take your passport for a few hours when you check in. If you aren't staying in such a public accommodation, the responsibility technically becomes yours and you must go to the nearest police station to register. The U.S. Department of State provides two cheap pamphlets (US$0.50), *Americans Abroad* (not to be cofused with Mark Twain's 18th-century travelogue) and *Foreign Entry Requirements,* and the helpful *Your Trip Abroad* for US$1. Send a check to the **Consumer Information Center,** R. Woods, Consumer Information Center—2B, P.O. Box 100, Pueblo, CO 81009 (tel. (719) 948-3334). You can get a visa (and more information) from the nearest Italian embassy or consulate; Americans can also get information on visa requirements from the Bureau of Consular Affairs, 1425 K St. NW, Washington, DC 20524 (tel. (202) 647-0518). If you're in a rush for your visa, you can also try **Visa Center, Inc.,** 507 Fifth Ave., New York, NY 10017 (tel. (212) 986-0924). Service costs varies with passport requirements but averages US$10-15.

Student and Youth Identification

The **International Student Identity Card (ISIC)** is the most widely accepted form of student ID and is often required for student prices on flights, trains, and clubs. Cardholders qualify for over 8,000 discounts, including reductions on museum admission, theater tickets, movies, and transportation. Make a habit of presenting it and asking about student discounts wherever you go. Ask: *c'è un sconto studentesco?* (CHAY oon SCON-toh stoo-dehn-TEHS-coh). The annual *International Student Travel Guide* lists some of the discounts available with the ISIC card. Pick it up when you apply or write to CIEE for a copy. When issued in the U.S., the card provides repatriation insurance of US$3000, medical/accident insurance of US$3000, plus US$100 coverage of per-day, in-hospital care for up to two months. To apply for the card (US$14), you must supply current, dated proof of your full-time student status (a letter on school stationery, signed and sealed by the registrar, or a photocopied grade report); a 1½ x 2 inch photo with your name printed on the back; and proof of your birthdate and nationality (a photocopy of your birth certificate or passport). The card is valid for 16 months, from September 1 through the end of the following calendar year. However, you cannot purchase a new card in January (when your old one expires) unless you were a student during the most recent fall semester; *if you are about to graduate, get the card now.*

The same organization has also recently introduced the **International Teacher Identification Card (ITIC),** which is supposed to earn the educators of tomorrow's youth the same discounts that those youth are racking up across Europe. The card, however, still draws blank stares from most of the European tourism industry; it might not be worth your investment. Young-looking teachers have sometimes been known to apply for the ISIC on their school's stationery.

Some of the student travel offices who issue the ISIC are **Council Travel,** 205 E. 42nd St., New York, NY 10017 (tel. (212) 661-1450); **Let's Go Travel Services,** Harvard Student Agencies, Thayer Hall B, Harvard University, Cambridge, MA 02138 (tel. (617) 495-9649); and **Travel CUTS,** 187 College St., Toronto, Ontario M5T 1P (tel. (416) 979-2406).

With the increase in the use of phony ISIC cards, many airline and other establishments may request double proof of student status; student travelers may want to bring a along a school picture ID or signed statement from their school registrar as well as the ISIC card.

Anyone under 26 can take advantage of the **International Youth Card** (US$10 without insurance, US$15 with; in the U.K, £4; in Canada CDN$12) issued by the Federation of International Youth Travel Organizations (FIYTO). Also known as the FIYTO card, the International Youth Card (IYC) gets you discounts on international and intra-European transportation, accommodations, museums, restaurants, cultural activities, and tours. When applying, you must include your passport number, proof of birthdate, and a passport-size photograph with your name printed on the back. Further information can be obtained in the U.S. by contacting CIEE (see Budget Travel Services above), Travel Cuts in Canada or many Youth and Student Travel Offices in Europe. Purchase of the card includes discount guides published by FIYTO. For further information, write FIYTO at Islands Brygge 81, DK-2300, Copenhagen S., Denmark (tel. (31) 54 60 80).

International Driver's License

All foreign drivers in Italy must be in possession of both an **International Driver's Permit** and an **International Insurance Certificate,** (also known as a green card), which certifies that you have liability insurance. If you've held a U.S. driver's license for at least a year, IDPs are available for US$10 from the **American Automobile Association (AAA).** Contact your local AAA office or call their main office at 1000 AAA Dr. (Box 75), Heathrow, FL 32746-5063 (tel. (407) 444-7000). Specific inquiries about the IDP should be addressed to **AAA Travel Agency Services** (mail stop 100), Heathrow, FL 32746-5063 (tel. (407) 444-7883). For CDN$10, you can get a permit from the **Canadian Automobile Association (CAA),** 2 Carlton St., Toronto, Ont., M5B 1K4 (tel. (416) 964-3170). Applicants must hold a valid license, submit two passport-sized photos, and proof of age (drivers must be 18 years of age or older). You may obtain a green card through your own insurance company (if your policy applies abroad), or through rental and travel agencies.

Customs

Customs is not the nightmare that you've been led to believe. Unless you're bringing back a Lamborghini, a kilo of cocaine or a barnyard animal, chances are you'll go straight through the green line and on to the baggage claim. Head directly for the customs officer who most closely resembles Wilford Brimley, and avoid undersexed hairless Nazi types with something to prove. The duty and exemption information that follows is truly bewildering, but applies most closely to those who will be in Italy for a longer period of time. If you will have been away for more than a month, you'll find it harder to convince customs officials that you have nothing to declare; sending things home is the best way around this hassle. Travelers who visit Rome for a short period of time have often been seen throwing away their receipts and enjoying their vacation, rather than keeping a running tally for the pure pleasure of the customs officials. Before you leave home, record the serial numbers of all valuables you take on your trip (especially any that are produced or sold in Europe for less than in your home country) and, if possible, carry receipts to prove that you did not buy them abroad. A customs agent at your point of departure may be able to stamp or certify your list of serial numbers. If you are bringing prescription medicine across the border, be sure the bottles are clearly marked and have the prescription ready to show the customs officer. If you are bringing prescription medicines home from Italy, try to get your prescription and the labels on the bottles translated into English to prevent the condescending stares of dubious border control agents.

Non-residents may import Italian or foreign banknotes and bearer securities up to 20 million *lire* before declaring the amount to customs. You can export up to 20 million as well; check with the tourist offices or the embassy for further details. Portable radios may require a small license fee upon entering Italy. Except for the currency limit, few export restrictions apply except on antiques and precious art objects, which require the authorization of the Sovrintendenza delle Antichita e Belle Arti, Ministero dei Beni Culturali e Ambientali.

Upon returning to your home country, you must declare all goods acquired abroad and pay a duty on any articles exceeding an established value or quantity. Holding onto receipts for purchases made abroad will help establish values when you return. Keep in mind that those delish Bacio candies you buy at duty-free shops abroad are *not* exempt from duty when you return. "Duty-free" means only that you don't have to pay taxes in the country of purchase.

U.S. citizens may bring back US$400 worth of goods duty-free; the next US$1000 is subject to a 10% tax. All items included in your duty-free allowance must be carried with you—none may be shipped separately. Goods must be for personal or household use and may include up to 100 cigars, 200 cigarettes (1 carton), and 1 liter of wine or liquor. You must be 21 or older to bring liquor into the U.S. If you stay abroad for less than 48 hours, or if you have claimed any part of your US$400 exemption within the previous 30 days, you are eligible for an exemption of only US$25, including 50 cigarettes, 10 cigars, 150ml (4 oz.) of alcohol, and 150ml of perfume. All items included in your allowance must accompany you. The exemptions of persons traveling together may be combined. The first US$1000 above your exemption will be taxed at a flat rate of 10%.

You may mail unsolicited gifts back to the U.S. duty-free if they're worth less than US$50 and do not contain liquor, tobacco, or perfume. Write "Unsolicited Gift," with a description of the price and nature of the gift, on the outside of the package before mailing. If the parcel is worth more than US$50, the Postal Service will collect the duty and a handling charge from the recipient. Spot checks are occasionally made on parcels' mark the price and nature of the gift on the package. If you mail home personal goods of U.S. origin, mark the package "American goods returned." For more information, request the brochure *Know Before You Go,* available from the U.S. Customs Service, 1301 Constitution Ave., Washington, DC 20229 (tel. (202) 566-8195). You can also receive this brochure for 50¢ by writing R. Woods, Consumer Information Center, Pueblo, CO 81009; request item 477Y. Foreign residents residing in the United States are subject to different regulations; ask for the leaflet *Customs Hints for Visitors (Non-residents)*.

Canadian citizens may bring back CDN$20 worth of goods after a 24-hour absence, any number of times per year. After 48 hours, you may bring back goods valued up to CDN$100. Written declaration may be required. After seven or more days, once per calendar year, you may bring back goods valued up to CDN$300. Only the 48-hour and seven-day exemptions may include alcohol (40 oz. of wine or liquor, *or* 24 12-oz. bottles or cans of beer) and tobacco (200 cigarettes, 50 cigars, and two 200gm containers of loose tobacco). The age at which you may import liquor varies by province. Keep in mind that medicines containing codeine—available over the counter in Canada—may not be as legal in your country of destination. Values above the exempted limits are taxed at about 20%. You may also send gifts up to a value of CDN$60 duty-free, but you cannot mail alcohol or tobacco. Before leaving, list the serial numbers of all your valuables on a Y-38 form at a Customs Office or your point of departure. Write to the **Canadian Customs and Excise Department,** Mackenzie Ave., Ottawa, Ont. K1A 0L5 (tel. (613) 957-0275) for the booklet *I Declare/Je Déclare*. Another helpful booklet, *Bon Voyage, But...*, is available from the department of External Affairs (tel. (613) 996-2825).

British citizens may claim an exemption of up to £32 of goods. If you are over 16, you may include tobacco (200 cigarettes or 100 cigarillos or 50 cigars or 250g of tobacco) and alcohol (2 liters) of still table wine, plus 1 liter of alcohol over 22% by volume or 2 liters of alcohol not over 22% by volume). You must be 17 years of age to import alcohol into the United Kingdom. If you have obtained these goods in the EC (of which Italy is a member), the amount which you can import increases by about 50%. Direct questions to Her Majesty's Customs and Excise Office, Custom House, Nettleton Rd., Heathrow Airport, Hounslow, Middlesex TW6 2LA (tel. (071) 382 54 68).

Irish citizens may import a maximum of IR£34 per adult traveler duty-free (IR£17 per traveler under the age of 15). You may bring in 200 cigarettes or 100 cigarillos or 50 cigars or 250g of tobacco, and 1 liter of alcohol over 44 proof or 2 liters of alcohol under 44 proof. You must be 17 years of age to import these items. You may import as much currency into Ireland as you wish. For more information, write Division 1, Office of the Revenue Commissioners, Dublin Castle, Dublin 1 (tel. (01) 679 27 27).

Australian citizens are allowed an exemption ("concession") of AUS$400, including 1 liter of wine, beer, or liquor, and 250g of tobacco or 250 cigarettes. Australians under 18 receive a concession of AUS$200 and may not import alcohol or tobacco. Before leaving, register new or expensive items on the appropriate form available from any local Customs office, and have the list stamped at Customs before departure. You may mail back personal property as long as it's at least 12 months old (no infants, please). You may mail back unsolicited gifts duty-free as long as the are legitimate gifts. Exports of more than AUS$5000 (or its equivalent in *lire*) without permission from the Reserve Bank of Australia is prohibited. For more information, request the brochure *Customs Information for All Travellers* from a local office of the Collector of Customs or from an Australian consulate abroad.

Citizens of New Zealand may bring in NZ$700 worth of duty-free goods as long as the goods are intended for personal use or as unsolicited gifts. Travelers 17 or older are allowed 200 cigarettes (1 carton) or 50 cigars or 250g of tobacco or a mixture of all three not to exceed 250g. You may also bring in 4.5 liters of beer or wine and 1.125 liters of spirits or liqueur. Persons traveling together may not combine individual concessions. The *New Zealand Customs Guide for Travelers* and *If You're Not Sure About It, DECLARE IT* are both available from any customs office. For more information, contact **New Zealand Customs,** P.O. Box 29, Auckland (tel. (9) 77 35 20).

The U.S. customs service has proclaimed that "a vital part of customs's role is screening out items injurious to the well-being of our nation." The U.S., Canada, U.K., Ireland, Australia, and New Zealand all prohibit or restrict the import of firearms, explosives, ammunition, fireworks, plants and animals, lottery tickets, obscene literature and film, controlled drugs, or other harmful items.

Money

For many tourists, especially students, the admirable pursuit of a bargain becomes an ugly, unhealthy, even destructive, fixation. Some of the more odious symptoms include staying in the sleaziest motels, eating the most unsavory food (or not eating at all), and skipping the most magnificent monuments. Sadly we report that many travelers spend years living on an extremely tight budget to save enough money to go abroad, only to skimp on their travel once in Rome. When you hit the budget travel doldrums, devote a little cash to cushioning the shocks. Force yourself to go for one more elegant meal after days of picnicking. Spend the night in a quiet *pensione* with a private terrace after weeks in a hostel. Sit down for a *cappuccino* in piazza Navona or at the Pantheon—such a mini-luxury break might cost you L6000 at most, but you'll feel like Charo, not Charlie Brown. And for crying out loud, pay the L10,000 entrance fees for the Vatican Museum and the Forum—it's so worth it. Consider spending two weeks staying in the Historical Center in Rome rather than four weeks south of the train station. For the same money, you could spend two weeks enjoying yourself—the Italians and other tourists will appreciate your company more, and you'll return home happier and well-sated.

Currency and Exchange

The Italian monetary system is based on the *lira* (plural: *lire*). The smallest denomination of Italian currency is the L10 coin (although these are becoming as rare as they are worthless; the L50 coin is now the more common lowest denomination), and the smallest note is the L1000 bill. Decades of skyrocketing inflation are responsible for these counterintuitive and astronomically large bills; American and Canadian travelers have the happy luxury of acquiring some sort of rough conversion merely by dropping the thousands. You'll find that Italians do the same in conversation; your purchase may cost *dieci* rather than 10,000. Before leaving home, most people buy about US$50 worth of *lire* to save time and hassle upon arrival, but the rates you encounter at the airport or train station in Rome will often be better than those you got at home (albeit the worst you'll find once you're in Italy). See Once There: Money below for the addresses of banks with the lowest exchange rates.

When exchanging money, look for *"cambio"* signs and shop around. Avoid exchanging money at luxury hotels and restaurants as well as train stations and airports; the best deals are usually found at banks such as the **Banco d'Italia** or the **Banco Nazionale del Lavoro**, where the rates are far more favorable, although you should expect to pay a commission of 1-2%. Changing currency is best done in the morning; banking hours are usually Monday through Friday, 8:35am-1:35pm with an extra hour in the afternoon (usually 3-4pm, but this varies). Remember that unless a percentage rate is charged, you will lose a fixed chunk of money each time you convert. To minimize your losses, exchange large sums at once, but never more than you can safely carry around. It also helps to plan ahead: if you are caught without *lire* at night or on a Sunday, when banks and exchange bureaus are usually closed, you may be forced into a particularly disadvantageous deal. Hold tight to your wallet whenever you change money, and make sure that no one is following you. Beware of street money-changers, who will give you counterfeit money. Count your money discreetly inside the *cambio*, never out on the street, and make sure you are not followed after changing money.

Traveler's Checks

No part of your trip is likely to cause you more headaches than money—even when you have it. Carrying large amounts of cash, even in a money belt, is unwise. Traveler's checks, which can be replaced if lost or stolen, are far safer. Although not all Italian establishments, including banks, accept traveler's checks, your peace of mind will far outweigh any occasional inconvenience. American Express is probably the best-known and most widely recognized traveler's check today. Buying American Express traveler's checks will also grant you access to some of the services at their offices (i.e. mail—see Staying in Touch below) for free even if you don't carry a card.

Don't forget to write.

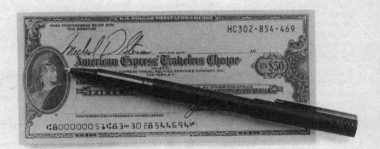

Now that you've said, "Let's go," it's time to say, "Let's get American Express® Travelers Cheques." Because when you want your travel money to go a long way, it's a good idea to protect it. So before you leave, be sure and write.

None of the major companies listed below supply traveler's checks in *lire,* so buy checks in your home currency—changing money from one foreign currency to another will cost you dearly, but there are numerous other hassles when you try to cash Italian currency traveler's checks (i.e. only the banks that issued them will cash them). Aussies and New Zealanders may be better off by buying dollar or pound traveler's checks; the teller at the bank in the small town in Lazio may not even know where New Zealand is, no less what its exchange rate is. Buy mostly in large denominations but also get a few smaller checks. While large notes spare you long waits at the bank, small notes minimize your losses if you just need a little cash to tide you over a few days before departure. Given the tendency for Italian exchange to charge flat commissions, changing small checks generally serves to make bad rates much worse. If you're forced to change in a small town, grit your teeth and change a reasonable amount of money—you probably won't lose more than a few thousand *lire.* If you change five US$20 checks in five different places during your trip because you can't bear a rotten exchange, you will end up spending L20,000 in extra commissions.

In the event of theft or loss, red tape and delay will complicate even the best of circumstances. If you need replacement checks, showing receipts will speed up the process dramatically. Keep receipts in a safe place, far away from the checks themselves, and leave a list of check numbers with a responsible and easily reached individual at home. To protect yourself from clever thieves who take just one or two checks from the middle of the pile to escape detection, record the number of each check as you cash it. That will make it easier to identify exactly which checks are missing if some do disappear.

Most banks and many agencies sell traveler's checks, usually for face value plus a 1-2% commission. Consult your bank or phone book for the nearest vendor. All of the following agencies operate affiliated offices in Italy from which you can obtain replacement checks or emergency funds.

American Express, in the U.S. and Canada tel. (800) 221-7282; in the U.K (0800) 52 13 13; in Australia (02) 886 06 89 and (008) 25 19 02; collect from elsewhere (801) 964-6665 for referral to offices in individual countries. Available in 7 currencies. American Express has also introduced a new option *Checks for Two,* in which either of two specified individuals can cash a check without the John Hancock of the other cosigner. There is an extra fee for this service; it's definitely not cheaper than each of the two of you buying your own checks. Offices cash their own traveler's checks free. A free list of all offices is available at any Travel Office. For more information, write: American Express Company, Traveler's Check Division, Salt Lake City, UT 84184-3406. Rome office listed below, under Once There.

Bank of America (WorldMoney), in the U.S. tel. (800) 227-3460, collect from elsewhere (415) 574-7111. Available in U.S. dollars only. A commission rate of 1% per US$100 is charged for non-bank members. For more information, write: Bank of America, P.O. Box 37010, San Francisco, CA 94137.

Barclay's, in the U.S. and Canada tel. (800) 221-2426; in the U.K. (202) 67 12 12; collect from elsewhere (212) 858-8500. Affiliated with Visa. Available in U.S. dollars, British pounds and German marks; Canadian dollars available in Canada. Charges a commission rate of 1%. To report lost checks call (800) 227-6811 in the U.S.; collect from elsewhere (415) 574-7111.

Citicorp, in the U.S and Canada tel. (800) 645-6556, collect from elsewhere (813) 623-1709. Available in U.S. dollars, British pounds, German marks, and Japanese yen. Charges 1-1½% commission. Checkholders are automatically enrolled in Citicorp's Travel Assist Hotline (in the U.S. tel. (800) 523-1199, collect from elsewhere (215) 244-1740) for 45 days after purchase and may avail themselves of the World Courier Service which guarantees hand-delivery of traveler's checks anywhere in the world.

MasterCard, in the U.S. and Canada tel. (800) 223-9920, collect from elsewhere (609) 987-7300. Available in 11 currencies.

Thomas Cook, in the U.S. tel. (800) 223-7373, collect from elsewhere (609) 987-7300. Affiliated with MasterCard. Available in 11 currencies.

Visa, in the U.S. and Canada tel. (800) 227-6811; in London (071) 937 8091; collect from elsewhere (212) 858-8500. Available in 13 currencies. Commission depends on individual bank.

If You've Lost Your Checks

Dont't Panic. First of all, look around you and look through all of your things. If you're sure that they're gone, look for the receipts. Take a deep breath and head for a pay phone. If you use American Express checks, head to the office or call their toll-free number (an English-speaking operator is on-call 24 hours; see Once There, below, for details.). If the office is open, the staff will ask you which checks you have cashed, which checks were stolen, and will want to see lots of identification. They usually issue you new checks on the spot (or if by phone, the next working day). If you use another company's checks, you will need to call that company in the States to make arrangements (see our Telephones section below on how to make an international call). If your checks were stolen, you will speed the process if you file a police report at the nearest station.

Credit Cards

In this day and age, no one should travel in Europe without a credit card. They earn great exchange rates, allow you to minimize the amount of easily stolen cash you carry, and are invaluable in emergencies of any kind. They can also be thoughtlessly abused; just because you're not seeing the money doesn't mean you're not spending it, and you should keep to the same daily budget you would have set yourself on without a credit card. Although most low-cost establishments (especially *pensioni*) in Rome do not accept credit cards, most banks offer you instant cash advances from your **Visa** or **Mastercard** at an excellent exchange rate. Many credit card companies, including **American Express,** can give you a top-secret personal identification number (PIN), which allows you to use the increasing number of automated teller machines (ATMs) throughout the city, accessible 24 hours a day. Check with your issuing bank about conversion charges, interest rates, and ATM locations. This infusion of cash might be your most convenient source of money for several days (Sending Money below outlines the difficulties in getting money from home). Be forewarned that the transatlantic connection is still a major obstacle often preventing successful transactions, and some ATM machines only have instructions in Italian. Credit cards are accepted in many restaurants, most stores, travel agencies, and in the train stations. If you want to make a major purchase of any sort in Rome (hiking gear, for instance), you might save a substantial amount of money by charging: in calculating the bill, credit card companies use gracious exchange rates you can only dream about encountering in person.

American Express has its own office in Rome, at p. di Spagna, 38 (tel. 72 82 or 676 41; for lost or stolen checks tel. 167 87 29 99 toll-free, 24 hrs.), just to your right as you face the base of the Spanish Steps. The office is chaotic at times, but fairly efficient and everyone speaks English, offering an assortment of useful services to cardholders. They will honor a personal check of up to US$1000 every seven days (the first US$200 in cash, the rest in traveler's checks). They will also wire to replace lost or stolen cards. American Express's free "Purchase Protection Plan" insures against loss or theft of any item bought with the American Express Card within 90 days of purchase. Cardholders or checkholders can use the American Express office at p. di Spagna (or at any location throughout Italy) as a mailing address for free; others must pay L2000 to pick up mail. American Express offices are much more reliable for holding mail than Italian post offices. Messages can be left in the office in a stamped envelope for L2000. Perhaps the greatest bonus for holders of U.S.-issued cards is Global Assist, a 24-hour help line that provides information and monetary aid in cases of personal medical emergency or document loss. You can also send urgent messages home through this service. *The Traveler's Companion,* a list of full-service offices throughout the world, is available at American Express Travel Offices. A great map of Rome is also yours for the asking and the office also offers guided bus tours (see Touring Tips, below).

While many of these services are also available to holders of other cards, primarily **Visa** or **Mastercard,** it varies according to the bank which issues the card (Citibank, Chase, Signet etc.); check with your individual bank before going abroad.

If your income is low and you are not a student, you may have difficulty acquiring an internationally recognized credit card. However, if a family member already has a card, it's easy to get an extra one. American Express will issue a second green card for

US$30 per year (US$35 for a gold card); bills go to your loved ones. Check with your individual issuing bank for details on obtaining an extra Visa or Mastercard.

Convenient as they may be, credit cards require extra vigilance. Lost or stolen cards should be reported *immediately,* or you may be held responsible for forged charges, so write down the card-cancellation telephone numbers for your bank and keep them in a safe place separate from your cards (maybe with someone at home that you can call). Always be sure that the carbon has been torn into pieces, and ask to watch as your card is being imprinted; an imprint onto a blank slip can be used later to charge merchandise in your name, eventually resulting in a pitched battle with your credit card company.

Sending Money

The easiest way to get money from home is to bring an **American Express Card.** American Express allows cardholders to draw cash (up to US$200 in local currency) from their checking accounts at the office in Rome or any of its full-fledged offices, and many of its representatives' offices, up to US$1000 every 21 days (no service charge, no interest). With someone feeding money into your account back home, you'll be set. The next best approach is to wire money through the instant international money transfer services operated by **Western Union** (tel. (800) 225-5227) or **American Express** (tel. (800) 543-4080). The sender brings cash into one of their offices or calls and charges it to a credit card; the receiver can pick up the cash at any overseas office abroad within minutes (American Express fee about US$25-35 to send US$250, US$70 for US$1000; Western Union US$50 for US$1000). To pick up the money, you'll either need to show ID or answer a test question. Not all American Express offices are authorized to receive wired money; while the Rome office definitely does, you should check with other offices directly or call American Express. The simplest and stodgiest route is to **cable money** from bank to bank. Find a local bank big enough to have an international department; bring the address of the receiving bank and the destination account number. Usually both sender and receiver must have accounts at the respective institutions, making this a viable option only for those who are spending a long period of time in Rome and have already established a bank account. Transfer can take up to a few days; the fee is usually a flat US$20-30. Outside American Express offices, avoid trying to cash checks in foreign currencies; they draw stares of confusion and usually require weeks to clear and a US$30 fee to clear.

Finally, if you are an American in a life-or-death situation, you can have money sent to you via the State Department's **Citizens Emergency Center,** Bureau of Consular Affairs, CA/PA, Rm. 5807, U.S. Department of State, Washington, DC 20520 (tel. (202) 647-5225 or, in an emergency after business hours, (202) 634-3600). For a fee of about US$25, the State Department will forward money within hours to the American Embassy in Rome (or the nearest consular office), which will then disburse it according to instructions. The agency prefers not to send sums greater than US$500, but will enclose a message upon request. The quickest way to get money to the State Department is through Western Union or by dropping it off at any State Department office if your American counterpart is near one.

Value-Added Tax

The Value-Added Tax (VAT) is a form of sales tax levied in the European Economic Community. VAT is generally part of the price paid on goods and services. In Italy, the amount varies from item to item, averaging out at 19%. At certain large stores, visitors from outside the EEC can request exemption from the VAT on merchandise costing L625,000 or more. Ask for an invoice when you make your purchase and present both the certificate and goods to a customs officer upon leaving the country. Once you leave the country, you can claim a refund from the store by mail as long as it is still within 90 days of the date of purchase. Payment by credit card may speed up the processing of the refund check.

Bargaining

Bargaining is somewhat common in Rome, but use discretion. It is appropriate in dealings at markets, with street vendors, and over unmetered taxi fares (a practice to avoid, but still, always settle your price *before* getting into the cab). Haggling over prices is out of place most everywhere else, especially in large stores. Hotel haggling is most often done in uncrowded, smaller *pensioni* or for *affitta camere* (*Let's Go* mentions when such activity is common). Even if you speak no Italian at all, memorize the numbers. Let the merchant make the first offer and counter with one-half to two-thirds of her his bid. Never offer anything you are unwilling to pay—you are expected to buy if the merchant accepts your price. Ask yourself whether bargaining over one or two dollars is worth all the added hassle.

Packing

Pack light. Leave your ultra-hydrating placenta eye cream, your lucky bowling ball, and your overstuffed feather pillow at home. Separating extras from essentials is crucial for maximum comfort and sanity. The convenience of traveling light far outweighs the disadvantages of a limited wardrobe—no one's likely to notice you've worn the same two outfits for the last six weeks. Lay out everything you think you'll need, pack only half of it and bring twice as much money. Leave expensive jewelry and watches at home; save room for gifts and souvenirs. The more you have to lug around, the less you'll be able to zip about town. Invest first in a money belt or, even better, a neck pouch that will tuck securely *under* your clothing. A fanny pack that goes around the outside of your waist marks you as a tourist and is just begging to be ripped off; besides, it's not very flattering, even to the best of figures. Guard your money, passport, and other valuables here and keep it with you *at all times*.

Luggage

Determining which type of luggage best suits your needs is critical. Consider a light suitcase if you're going to stay in Rome for a long time. Those who wish to travel unobtrusively might choose a large shoulder bag that closes securely. Choosing a model with expandable rather than hard sides is key.

If you're planning to cover a lot of ground by foot, bus, or thumb, a sturdy backpack with several compartments is unbeatable. Packs come in two varieties—external frame and internal frame. Each type has its own advantages. Internal packs are sturdier and more compact. Because they mold well to the back and maintain a lower center of gravity, internals are easier to carry over rough terrain. And the straps usually zip away out of sight, helping to reduce damage in airline baggage compartments. The main advantage of external frame packs is their ability to lift weight off the back, allowing greater ventilation (of prime importance if you plan to hike in summer) and better weight distribution (which may provide greater comfort over long distances). For normal loads, when the pack functions primarily as a suitcase, an interior-frame model will be less cumbersome and easier to transport. A front-loading pack, in contrast to a top-loading model, will free you from groping for hidden items in the bottom of your pack. Whichever type you choose, don't buy a cheap pack. Bargain backpacks have bad zippers, shabby construction, and—worst of all—wimpy straps that will maul your shoulders after a week of hard traveling. A good internal frame pack usually costs US$90-300. Try out several models at a good camping store—packs, like clothes, fit different people differently. When you find one, fill it with weights in the store and take it for a spin. When packing, put all your gear into the pack, then simulate Italian conditions by walking to the nearest cathedral a few times and up and down a dozen flights of steps to make sure you can manage the weight. To minimize tottering, place heavy items up against the inside wall near your center of gravity, and lighter items toward the bottom and top.

No matter what kind of luggage you choose, a small daypack is indispensable for plane flights and sightseeing. You can tote lunch, some bottled water, your camera, *Let's Go* and other valuables, and a stock of toilet paper to counter its sporadic absence in Italian restrooms. Label every piece of baggage with your name and address and purchase a few small combination locks for the baggage (these tiny padlocks pass through two zippers, holding a bag shut); in a pinch you can put a safety pin through

the zippers just to make things a little harder for a potential thief. Knife-wielding overnight train robbers won't be dissuaded, but lazy kleptomaniacs may bypass your belongings for more permeable packs.

Sleeping bags are useful for both the serious camper and the budget traveler in winter, when many hostels and *pensioni* save fuel at the slight expense of their patrons'
health and happiness. When shopping for a sleeping bag, primary consideration should
be given to the climate of your intended destination (check the brief temperature table
at the end of the General Introduction, or request the climate chart from IAMAT, see
Health below). Down-filled bags are fluffy and warm, but expensive (US$150-400)
and impractical (they're useless when wet). Cheaper bags filled with synthetic insulation (like Quallofil) dry faster, retain their insulation even when soaked, and are lighter
and more durable (US$100-175). Unless you are traveling in the Italian Alps in the
winter, a synthetic bag will suffice for Italy (see Camping section below for further details on sleeping bags).

Clothes and Shoes

Climate should be the primary consideration in paring down the ranks of your traveling wardrobe. Dark-colored items will not show the wear and tear they're bound to suf-
fer, but light colors will be cooler and more comfortable in hot weather. Natural fibers
usually beat synthetics. Especially during Rome's summers, cotton or cotton blends
keep you cooler and happier, and are easy to wash in the sink.

No nation outdresses Italy. This is not only the country that brought you Armani and
Gucci, it's the country that buys most of that absurdly expensive fashion. Any attempt
to compete or blend in will likely prove futile (and financially irreparable), but do bring
appropriate clothing for visits to Italy's art-encrusted cathedrals and churches, where
shorts, skirts above the knee, and sleeveless and cut-off shirts are usually forbidden—
some of the more famous churches employ clothing guards to keep the immodest away.
While casual American fashion is the rage among young Italians (especially Levi's
jeans), most *ragazzi* don't wear army surplus shorts, Notre Dame sweatshirts, or grubby tank tops even on the hottest days of summer. You will fit in better with a light pair
of khaki pants or a long loose skirt and a plain t-shirt. If you maintain a neat, conservative appearance, you'll fare better when dealing with hotel owners. Women travelers
may further avert some harassment by eschewing miniskirts and tank tops (see the
Women Travelers section below for further details). In any case, if you want to attend a
papal audience in Rome, women will need to wear a dress and keep their arms and head
covered, and men will need a tie and jacket (for both genders, garments should be dark
or subdued in color).

Footwear is not the place to cut corners. Lace-up walking shoes provide better support and Italian social acceptability than running or tennis shoes. Again, check the climate—for the rainy fall or spring, you may want to buy a pair of good waterproof shoes
with a strong grip. If your plans include Alpine forays, good hiking boots are essential.
Try light-weight boots instead of the traditional leather ones. The former are more
comfortable, less expensive, and can be just as rugged. With these light-weights your
foot can breathe easier, and therefore you will too, especially if hiking during summer.
But be forewarned: many lightweights that feel nice and cushy in the store will be falling apart after only a few weeks on the trail—look for durability when shopping. Italy
is the place to invest in that perfect pair of leather sandals for beach posing; otherwise,
toss some light shoes into your luggage for evening strolls, beachcombing, and club-
hopping. Be warned; those of you with larger feet may have trouble squeezing into the
tiny Italian-made shoes. *Break in your shoes before you go.* Sprinkling talcum powder
on your feet and inside your shoes and wearing two pairs of socks helps prevent chaf-
ing and blisters, while moleskin will protect any blisters that do develop. Bring lots of
socks: grungy or worn socks promote blisters and youth hostel ostracism.

Sundries

One pocket of your backpack should be devoted to sundries—a flashlight, Swiss
Army knife, first aid kit, travel alarm, water bottle, safety pins, some cord, and a needle
and thread. All kinds of toiletries are available in Rome, so you won't need extra tubes

of toothpaste. Contact lens solutions, while widely available in exactly the same brands, are prohibitively priced, so try to bring as much as you'll need. Laundry services in Italy are absurdly expensive and inconvenient. Washing clothes in your hotel sink is a far better option. A mild liquid soap (available in camping stores) can serve as anything from dish detergent to shampoo, or buy a bottle of great Italian detergent, *Presto,* at any *alimentari.* Don't forget a plug for the sink; often a rubber squash ball is just the right size to stop the drain, or you can buy a stopper at a hardware store. A mess kit will also be extremely useful, since feasts are easily and readily purchased at the market. Carrying a metal plate (one with high sides that can double as a salad bowl) may look silly when you're packing, but tossing the ingredients of a fresh mozzarella and ripe tomato salad in your lap will look even sillier.

Camera equipment is expensive, fragile, and heavy. The less you bring, the fewer your worries and back ailments. All kinds of films are available in Rome, though black and white film is a little trickier to find, and the farther you go from tourist centers (like near the Vatican), the lower the prices will be. Despite disclaimers to the contrary, airport X-ray equipment often fogs film—the higher the speed, the greater the likelihood of damage: 100-speed film is less of a crisis. Resist the pleas of personnel to send your camera and film through and have it hand-checked. For extra heavy protection, purchase a lead-lined pouch and stash your rolls in it.

Your favorite electrical appliances will require an electric converter. Voltage is either 125 or 220v AC throughout Italy, although hotels often offer 110v. Check before plugging in or you could zap your appliance into oblivion. Since Italy's prongs are not flat but round, U.S. and Australian gadgets need an adapter, available in Italy or from most travel stores. The **Franzus Company,** Murtha Industrial Park, P.O. Box 142, Railroad Ave., Beacon Falls, CT 06403 (tel. (203) 723-6664, fax (203) 723-6666) publishes the free and illuminating pamphlet *Foreign Electricity Is No Deep Dark Secret* (which contains, among other things, a voltage list for countries other than Italy) and sells a variety of adaptors and converters (Italian adaptor US$3.50, kit of 1600wt converter and 4 adaptor plugs US$27.50).

Insurance

The firms listed below offer insurance against theft or loss of luggage, trip cancellation/interruption, and medical emergency. Bear in mind that most policies do not insure items against theft, only against loss or damage by an identifiable third party. However, beware of unnecessary coverage. Check to see whether your homeowner's insurance (or your family's coverage) provides against theft during travel. Homeowner's policies will generally cover theft of travel documents (passports, plane tickets, rail passes, etc.) up to US$500.

If you have health insurance in your home country, chances are any additional travel insurance you purchase will only cover any expenses your own coverage does not, and may not be worth the investment. University term-time medical plans often cover summer travel. Medicare's foreign travel coverage is limited, and is valid in Canada and Mexico only. Canadians are protected by their home province's health insurance plan; check with the provincial Ministry of Health or Health Plan Headquarters. Buying an ISIC, International Teacher ID or Youth Card in the U.S. provides $3000 worth of accident and illness insurance and $100 per day up to 60 days of hospitalization while the card is valid. CIEE offers an inexpensive Trip-Safe plan with options covering medical treatment and hospitalization, accidents, baggage loss, and even charter flights missed due to illness; STA offers a more expensive, more comprehensive plan. American Express cardholders receive automatic car-rental and flight insurance on purchases made with the card. (For addresses for CIEE and STA, see Useful Organizations—Budget Travel Services above.)

Remember that insurance companies usually require a copy of the police report for thefts, or evidence of having paid medical expenses (doctor's statements, receipts) before they will honor a claim. Have these written in English, if possible, and make sure that you return home within the specified time limit to file for reimbursement. Always carry policy numbers and proof of insurance. Note that some of the plans listed below offer cash advances or guranteed bills. Full payment in cash is virtually the rule at most Italian hospitals. If your coverage doesn't include on-the-spot payments or cash transferrals, then budget for emergencies.

Travel Assistance International, 1133 15th St. NW, #400, Washington, DC 20005 (tel. (800) 821-2828). Medical and travel insurance up to $30,000. Frequent Traveler plan offers $15,000 coverage for up to 90 days of travel during a single calendar year. Short-term plans available.

Access America, Inc., 6600 W. Broad St., P.O. Box 90310, Richmond, VA 23230 (tel. (800) 234-8300). A subsidiary of Blue Cross/Blue Shield that offers travel insurance and assistance. Covers everything from trip cancellation/interruption to bail money to emergency medical evacuation. 24-hr. hotline.

The Travelers Insurance Co., 1 Tower Sq., Hartford, CT 06183 (tel. (800) 243-3174 or (203) 277-2138). Baggage, trip cancellation/interruption, disruption/default, accident, and emergency medical evacuation and assistance coverage.

Travel Guard International, 1145 Clark St., Stevens Point, WI 54481 (tel. (800) 782-5151). Offers a comprehensive "Travel Guard Gold" package, including free medical evacuations and repatriation of remains. The ScholarCare program is tailored to students and faculty spending time abroad.

Edmund A. Cocco Agency/Globalcare Travel Insurance, 220 Broadway, #201, P.O. Box 780, Lynnfield, MA 01940 (tel. (800) 821-2488). Coverage for travel, accident, sickness, and baggage, as well as on-the-spot payment of medical expenses. Services include legal assistance, emergency cash transfers, and medical transportation. Protection against bankruptcy or default of airline and cruise tickets is also offered.

Wallach and Company, Inc., 107 West Federal St., P.O. Box 480, Middleburg, VA 22117-0480 (tel. (800) 237-6615, fax (703) 687 3172). Optional trip cancellation, accidental death, and baggage protection plans. 24-hr. worldwide emergency assi*stance*.

Health

Don't cut corners on health—few things are as disappointing as a trip ruined by illness or accident. The basic advice: eat well and avoid exhaustion. Follow a reasonable itinerary to prevent physical and psychological anxiety. Don't be too anxious to embrace all the local customs—watch the caffeine intake; one person's 10 cups of espresso a day is another's poison. Protein is an excellent source of sustained energy, and fluids are essential. Italian water is safe to drink unless marked *acqua non potabile* (water not suitable for drinking). Don't bother investing in overpriced bottles of water; there are plenty of safe, cool water spouts throughout Rome. If you do buy water, do it at neighborhood *alimentari* and markets (where it will cost less than L1000) rather than at tourist-targeted minimarts (where it will cost L3000 if you're lucky).

Like the rest of southern Italy, Rome scorches in the summer, with the added effects of urban heat-trapping inventions like pavement. Be wary of over-exertion and heatstroke. Drink plenty of non-alcoholic fluids, don a sun hat, and stay indoors during peak sun hours (10am-2pm). Heatstroke can occur even without exposure to the sun; symptoms include headache, flushed skin, excessive sweating, and fever. Experts recommend getting out of the sun immediately, covering yourself with cold, wet, towels, and drinking fruit juice or salty water (to ward off dehydration). Churches and atriums are generally cool places to escape the heat, especially since many restaurants and *pensioni* do not have air conditioning. People with asthma and/or allergies should be aware that Rome often has visibly high levels of air pollution, particularly in summer.

If you're planning on spending a lot of time beneath the open sky, cancer-causing UV rays can penetrate cloud cover, so use sunblock, even on cloudy days; they are also stronger as altitude increases. Biking or driving through farm country in Lazio and elsewhere can summon allergies that you didn't even know you had. If you're worried about any of the above, see your physician before leaving; in any case, you should check with her or him and make sure your inoculations are up to date. While no shots are necessary to enter Italy, staying up to date is a wise idea. Typhoid shots remain good for three years; tetanus for ten. You might think about joining **International SOS Assistance** (tel. (800) 523-8390). Members receive emergency medical care, including transportation to hospitals or appropriate care units. Weekly (US$40), monthly (US$80) and annual memberships (US$275) available.

Even if you are in good health at home, you can never be sure how your body will react to the stresses of traveling in a foreign country. It's a good idea to include a small **first-aid kit** among your traveling accessories. You can make one at home, or purchase a ready-made one from a hardware store, and stock it according to your needs. Items you might want to include are bandages, antiseptic soap or an antibiotic cream, a thermometer in a sturdy case, a Swiss army knife (with tweezers), moleskin, sunscreen, insect repellent, aspirin, a decongestant, something for motion sickness, an antihistamine, and a remedy for diarrhea. However, pharmacies in Rome do carry all kinds of medicine, some even at prescription strength, and the many well-trained pharmacists, even if they don't speak English, are generally willing to help.

If you wear glasses or contact lenses, take an extra pair or a prescription with you, and make arrangements with someone at home to send you a replacement pair in an emergency. If you wear contacts, you should take along a pair of glasses to rest tired eyes, especially in Rome where the pollution can cause discomfort and difficulty. Bring extra solutions, enzyme tablets, and eye-drops—the price for lens solution in Italy can be exorbitant, and under-cleaning your lenses risks serious eye injury.

Travelers with a chronic medical condition requiring medication should consult their physician before leaving. Always carry up-to-date prescriptions and/or a statement from your doctor, especially if you will be bringing insulin, syringes, or any narcotics into the country. Carry an ample supply of all medications, since matching your prescription with a foreign equivalent may be difficult. It's a good idea to carry medication with you on flights, in case your baggage is misplaced. If you are have diabetes, contact your local **American Diabetes Association** office, where they can assist you in obtaining an ID card. Request a copy of their information sheet which includes ways to state that your condition, as well as a guide to requesting help in several European languages.

Travelers with medical conditions that cannot be easily recognized (e.g., diabetes, allergies to antibiotics, epilepsy, heart conditions) should consider obtaining a **Medic Alert Identification** tag (US$35 for a steel tag, US$40 for silver, US$50 for gold). This internationally recognized emblem identifies the medical problem and provides the number of Medic Alert's 24-hour hotline. Attending medical personnel can call this number to obtain information about the member's medical history. Write to Medic Alert Foundation International, 2323 North Colorado St., Turlock, CA 95381-1009 (tel. (800) 432-5378).

Local health units called *consultori* counsel women on reproductive rights, contraception, the availability of "morning-after" pills, and abortion laws and procedures. For more information, see Medical Services, below.

Before leaving home, you may wish to join the **International Association for Medical Assistance to Travelers (IAMAT),** 417 Center St., Lewiston, NY 14092 (tel. (716) 754-4883); in Canada, 40 Regal Rd., Guelph, Ont. N1K 1B5 (tel. (519) 836-0102); in Australia, 575 Bourke St., 12th floor, Melbourne 3000; in New Zealand, P.O. Box 5049, Christchurch 5. Along with a variety of useful brochures (*How to Adjust to the Heat, How to Adapt to Altitude,* and the moving epic, *How to Avoid Traveler's Diarrhea*) members receive an ID card, a chart detailing advisable immunizations for 200 countries and territories, and a worldwide directory of English-speaking physicians who have had medical training in Europe or North America. Membership is free (a donation is requested) and doctors are on call 24 hrs. for IAMAT members. Those donating $25.00 or more to IAMAT will also receive a packet of 24 World Climate Charts detailing climates, seasonal clothing, and sanitary conditions of water, milk and food in 140 cities around the world.

If you're concerned about being able to locate English-speaking doctors in Rome, consult the hospitals and first aid centers listed in the Practical Information section of Once There, or ask at English-speaking embassies and consulates. Throughout Italy, American Express and Thomas Cook offices can help you find English-speaking doctors. Remember that First Aid Service *(Pronto Soccorso)* is available in airports, ports, and train stations. Finally, at every drugstore *(farmacia)* in Italy, there is a list of pharmacies open all night and on Sundays.

Further useful health information is also available from a variety of sources. Write the **Superintendent of Documents,** U.S. Government Printing Office, Washington, DC 20402 (tel. (202) 783-3238) for *Health Information for International Travel* (US$5). **The Pocket Medical Encyclopedia and First-Aid Guide** (US$4.95) might also be helpful. Write Simon and Schuster, 200 Old Tappan Rd., Old Tappan, NJ 07675, Attn: Direct Order Dept. (tel. (800) 223-2348).

Travelers with Specific Concerns

Women Travelers

The natives are quite friendly. Often spotted on neon vespas, brandishing mirrored ray-bans and sporting quite a bit of hair gel, these Romeos show a remarkable interest in your birthplace, your destination, and your desire for a pair of saliva pajamas. While the constant barrage of queries and catcalls can become annoying, sometimes plain offensive, take it in stride. Italian males consider flirtation both an art form and a game; most comments should not be taken seriously. Women, whether alone or in groups, can avoid most harassment by adopting the attitude of Roman women: walk like you know where you are going, avoid eye contact (sunglasses are indispensible), meet all advances with silence and dignity, and, if still troubled, walk or stand near older women or couples until you feel safe. If you can, tell a police officer that you are being followed. A walkman with headphones clearly signals that you are not listening (but be careful—purse-snatchers and pickpockets will take note of your musical oblivion as well; you don't necessarily have to have the music on). Wearing tight or suggestive clothing can attract unwanted attention, but so can attire that is perfectly modest but obviously American (sweatshirts, college t-shirts, sneakers, Bermuda shorts, even jean jackets). If you are physically harassed on the bus or in some other crowded space, don't talk to the person directly (this only encourages him); rather, use body language, like a well-aimed knee or elbow, to make your point. Stepping hard on toes works admirably. Again, if you sense real trouble ask the people around you for help. With luck, you may get the satisfaction of seeing your tormentor get an indignant, rapid-fire Italian tongue-lashing. When traveling on Italian trains, avoid empty compartments, especially at night. Look for compartments with nuns for maximum safety. For more detailed advice, the *Handbook for Women Travelers* is available for £4.95 from Judy Piatkus Publishers, 5 Windmill St., London W1P 1HF England (tel. (071) 631 0710). Memorize the emergency number (113 or 112) and keep enough money handy for emergency telephone calls and bus or taxi rides.

Budget accommodations occasionally mean more risk than savings. Avoid small dives near Termini Station in favor of university dormitories or inexpensive *pensione* in the center. Centrally located accommodations are usually safest and easiest to return to after dark. *Let's Go* notes individual accommodations that are particularly safe or unsafe for women. Some religious organizations also offer rooms for women. For a list of these institutions, contact the city's archdiocese or write to the tourist office. Also helpful is the **Associazione Cattolica Internazionale al Servizio della Giovane,** which runs hostels for women throughout Italy. Their main office is at via Urbana, 158, 00184 Roma (tel. (06) 482 79 89).

All this need not discourage women from traveling alone. Don't take unnecessary risks, but don't lose your sense of adventure either. A series of recent travelogues by women outline their voyages; check a good library or bookstore for these and other books: *Nothing to Declare: Memoirs of a Woman Traveling Alone and Wall to Wall: From Beijing to Berlin by Rail* by Mary Morris (Penguin); *One Dry Season* by Caroline Alexander (Knopf); *Tracks* by Robyn Davidson (Pantheon); and *The Road Through Miyama* by Leila Philips (Random House/ Vintage).

Gay and Lesbian Travelers

Unlike other major Western European capitals like London and Paris, Rome is not the site of a particularly large, visible, or in-your-face gay and lesbian community. Only a few Italian cities (Bologna, Milan, Turin) have managed to outgrow the prevailing cultural silence surrounding homosexuality. Gay and lesbian tourists from North America may be frustrated at the lack of gay identity in Rome. Many Italian men who might be defined as gay elsewhere would never call themselves gay; for example, tops are considered straight, while bottoms are considered gay. However, there are some signs that the sexual is becoming political: Italians elected their first openly gay candidate for Parliament in 1992, and of course, Ilona Staller (also known as "La Cicciolina," or lil' dumplin), the breast-baring soft-porn actress, remains a popular delegate to the same body. While Rome may lack a widely-politicized gay and lesbian community, Italian governments have historically been hands-off when it comes to the sexual behavior of its citizens: according to a law passed in 1898, sexual acts between members of the same sex are legal for those above the age of consent (16).

This is not to say that you can't have good time. Some Italian traditions work in your favor: holding hands or walking arm-in-arm with someone of the same-sex, especially for women, is common. You may be astonished by how openly affectionate Roman men are with one another, especially compared to their high-fiving, shoulder-punching American counterparts; remember, however, that this homosocial ease hasn't translated into tolerance for men or women who *really* want to express their affection for one another. Rome can be a considerable tease; the visual clues gay men use elsewhere, such as a modicum of style, are used to great effect by Roman men, straight and gay. Italians invented that "Euro" look that got you teased in high school.

There are only a handful of openly gay bars, and none of them get started before 11pm. As with the rest of Roman nightlife, gay nightlife happens outside, particularly in piazza Navona (around via della Pace), Trastevere, and other popular strolling places. See our Entertainment section below for more information on cruising, beaches, and clubs, or write to the addresses below for more comprehensive information. The national gay organization is affiliated with the recreational branch of the Communist party, ARCI, which organizes social events, movies and sports. Write to **ARCI-gay**, p. di Porta Saragozza, 2, PO Box 691, 40100 Bologna (tel. (051) 43 67 00) for more information on gay and lesbian life in Italy. *Babilonia* (Casella Postale #11224, Milano 20110), a national gay magazine, is published monthly and is available at most newstands. Women's organizations and lesbian groups are often one and the same in Italy. The best source is the **ARCI-Coordinamento Donne** is located in Rome, at via F. Carrara, 24 (tel. (06) 35 791), whence they publish the bi-monthly newsletter *Bollettino Associazione Lesbiche Italiane*. The following sources should prove helpful in planning your trip; before ordering any publications, try the gay and lesbian sections of your local bookstores.

Italia Gay/Europe (US$12.95). Three quarters of this 291pp. guide is devoted to Italy, the other quarter to big cities and popular gay vacation spots in Europe, including Amsterdam, Barcelona, Ibiza, Prague, Copenhagen, and Brussels. Mostly in Italian, but the sprinklings of English will help you locate discos, outdoor cruising spots, and gay and lesbian associations throughout Italy. Available from Giovanni's Room (see below) or write to Babilonia Edizione, Casella Postale #11224, Milano, 20110 (tel. 569 64 68 or 57 40 47 88, fax 552 134 19).

Spartacus International Gay Guide (US$27.95) provides over 1000 pages of information for gay men, covering almost every country in the world. Order from 100 E. Biddle St., Baltimore, MD 21202 (tel. (301) 727 5677), or Bruno Gmünder Verlag, publisher, Worldwide Sales and Distribution, Luetzowstrasse 10, P.O. Box 30 13 45, D-1000, Berlin 30, Germany (tel. (030) 254 98 200).

Giovanni's Room, 345 S. 12th St., Philadelphia, PA 19107 (tel. (215) 923-2960) is an international feminist, gay, and lesbian bookstore and mail-order house. They stock most of the publications listed here, as well as many others of interest to gay and lesbian travelers.

Ferrari Publications, P.O. Box 37887, Phoenix, AZ 85069 (tel. (602) 863-2408), publishes *Places of Interest* (US$12.95), *Places for Men* (US$12.95), and *Places of Interest to Women* (US$10). Ferrari also publishes *Inn Places: USA and Worldwide Gay Accommodations* (US$14.95).

Women Going Places, (US$14.00). A new guide carrying on the spirit of the the popular *Gaia's Guide International*, which has discontinued publication. Lists resources relevant to women travelers, emphasizing women-owned and -operated enterprises. Includes tour operators, accommodations, women's centers, helplines and bookstores. Useful for straight as well as lesbian women. Available direct from the publishers in Europe: Women Going Places at the Business Factory, 141 Praed Street, London W2 1RL; (tel. (71) 706 2434, fax 071 706 1942). In the U.S and elsewhere: Inland Book Company, P.O. Box 120261, East Haven, CT. 06512 (tel. (203) 467-4257, fax (203) 469-7697).

Senior Travelers

The freedom of retirement affords many seniors the opportunity to travel, while an assortment of discounts on transportation, tours, and museums helps make it affordable. Write the Superintendent of Documents (see Useful Publications) for a copy of *Travel Tips for Older Americans* (US$1).

Senior travelers are entitled to a number of travel-related discounts—always ask about these. **Hostelling International,** formerly **International Youth Hostel Federation,** in fact welcomes seniors; memberships are available to people over 55 at a discounted US$15. For more information, contact HI/AYH, P.O. Box 37613, Washington, DC 20013-7613 (tel. (202) 783-6161) or any HI/IYHF-affiliated hostel federation. The following organizations and publications provide information on discounts, tours, and health and travel tips for globe-trotting seniors.

American Association of Retired Persons, Special Services Dept.. 601 E St., NW, Washington, DC 20049 (tel. (202) 434-2277 or (800) 227-7737). U.S. residents over 50 and their spouses are eligible for group and individual discounts on lodging, car and RV rental, air arrangements, and sightseeing. For AARP-arranged tours and cruises call (800) 927-0111. Annual membership US$8.

Bureau of Consular Affairs, Superintendent of documents , U.S. Government Printing Office, Washington, DC 20402 (tel. (202) 783-3238). Their *Travel Tips for Older Americans* (US$1) provides information on passports, visas, health, and currency.

Elderhostel, 75 Federal St., 3rd floor, Boston, MA 02110 (tel. (617) 426-7788). Several Italian universities participate in this miniaturized-study abroad program (US$2200-2800, including airfare from New York). Available to people over 60 and their over-50 spouses, courses are offered in a variety of academic fields and last two to four weeks. Courses given in Rome include Roman history and art, modern Italian politics and the history of the Vatican.

National Council of Senior Citizens, 1331 F St. NW, Washington, DC 20004 (tel. (202) 347-8800). For an annual membership fee of $12 or a lifetime fee of US$150, members receive information on discounts and travel abroad, hotel and auto discounts, and supplemental Medicare insurance.

Pilot Industries, Inc., 103 Cooper St., Babylon, NY 11702 (tel. (516) 422-2225). Publishes the newly-revised *Senior Citizen's Guide to Budget Travel In Europe* (US$5.95) and *The International Health Guide for Senior Citizen Travelers.* (US$4.95). Postage for both books is US$1.

Travelers with Disabilities

Italians are making an increased effort to meet the needs of people with disabilities. The **Italian Government Travel Office (ENIT)** provides listings of accessible hotels and associations for people with disabilities in various Italian cities and regions. ENIT also lists several organizations in Rome for information and assistance.

When making arrangements with airlines or hotels, specify exactly what you need and allow time for preparation and confirmation of arrangements. In most **train stations,** a porter will help you for L500 to L1000 per bag. Major train stations will provide assistance as long as you make reservations by telephone 24 hours in advance. Italy's rail system is modernized, so most trains are wheelchair accessible. For more information, call Italy's state rail office in New York at (212) 697-2100.

If you plan to take a seeing-eye dog into Italy, contact your veterinarian and the nearest Italian consulate. You will need an import license, a current certificate of your dog's innoculations, and a letter from your veterinarian certifying your dog's health (See the section below on Pets).

The organizations listed below may prove helpful.

American Federation for the Blind, 15 W. 16th St., New York, NY 10011 (tel. (212) 620-2159 or tel. (800) 232-5463). Offers information, recommends travel books, and issues ID cards (US$10) to the legally blind that are useful for discounts. Write for an application, or call the Products Center at (800) 829-0500.

Directions Unlimited, 720 North Bedford Rd., Bedford Hills, NY 10507 (tel. (800) 533-5343). Specializes in individual and group vacations, tours, and cruises for people with disabilities. Also helps plan trips in the U.S.

Disability Press, Ltd., Applemarket House, 17 Union St., Kingston-upon-Thames, Surrey KT1 1RP, England (tel. (081) 549 6399). Publishes the *Disabled Traveler's International Phrasebook* (£1.75), a compilation of useful phrases in 8 languages, including Italian. Supplements also available in Norwegian, Hungarian, and Serbo-Croatian (60p each).

Mobility International, USA (MIUSA), P.O. Box 3551, Eugene, OR 97403 (tel. (503) 343-1284, voice and TDD). Provides information on travel and exchange programs, accommodations, organized tours, and more. Contacts in over 30 countries. Publishes *A World of Options: A Guide to International Educational Exchange, Community Service and Travel for Persons with Disabilities.* (US$14 to members, US$16 to nonmembers, postage included.)

The Society for the Advancement of Travel for the Handicapped (SATH), 345 5th Ave. #610, New York, NY 10016 (tel. (212) 447-7284, fax (212) 725-8253). Advice and assistance on trip-planning. Publishes a quarterly travel news letter and information booklets (free for members, $2 for nonmembers). Annual membership US$45, students and senior citizens US$25.

Travel Information Service, Moss Rehabilitation Hospital, 1200 W. Tabor Rd., Philadelphia, PA 19141 (tel. (215) 456-9600). Brochures on tourist sights, accommodations, transportation, and travel accessibility services mailed for a nominal fee (US$5).

Evergreen Travel Service, 4114 198th St. SW, Suite #13, Lynnwood, WA 98036 (tel. (800) 435-2288 or (206) 776-1184). Provides travel information and arranges tours world-wide for people with disabilities. In the U.S., their "Wings on Wheels" tours feature charter buses with wheelchair accessible facilities; they also offer tours for the blind and "lazy bones" tours for travelers who like a slower pace. They've been assisting people with disabilities for over 25 years.

Traveling with Children

Despite now having the lowest birth-rate in Europe, Italians are well known for their love of children, and you will probably encounter more cheek-squeezing than complications. Most hotels will put a cot in your room for a 30% price increase. Even the most fussbudgety of children tend to enjoy the simplest (and cheapest) of Italian foods: pizza, spaghetti *(al sugo* or *al ragù* will bring a plain, red meat sauce), and *gelato.* Even so, planning ahead and drawing up a detailed itinerary are especially useful for those traveling with small children. Remember that you may have to slow your pace considerably, and keep in mind that all the new sights and experiences are especially exhausting for kids—you may want to leave room for a mid-afternoon nap for everyone. Allow plenty of flexibility in your plans, book your rooms ahead of time and plan sight-seeing stops that both you and your children will enjoy. Inspire your kids with enthusiasm and interest in Rome ahead of time with stories about the city. Before you go, rent the film *Ben Hur* or *Spartacus* to witness Charlton Heston's notorious stint as a gladiator. Colorful scenes of ancient Roman baths, apartment houses, and the Circus Maximus set the stage for the comic adventures of *Asterix the Gladiator.*

Caffè della Palma (near the Pantheon) and Sweet Sweet Way (in piazza Navona) **candy stores** are always good for a rest stop or at least for a bribe. The **zoo** at Villa Borghese is a cool respite from ancient monuments and churches, and here you can also rent bicycles or a rowboat to paddle in the small lake. There are **boat rides** down the Tiber (see Transportation) and **horse-drawn carriage rides** around the city, originating from piazza di Spagna. The Sunday **flea market** at Porta Portese is great fun for kids with a penchant for junk. Kids also love the **caricatures** and portraits done in piazza Navona. There are puppet shows in English on Saturday and Sunday at **Teatro dei Satiri,** via di Grotta Pinta 19 (tel. 686 53 52 or 589 62 01), off Campo dei Fiori. Check out the genuine Sicilian puppet shows at the **Teatro Crisogono,** via S. Gallicano 8, off viale Trastevere. If your kids really get cranky, **LUNEUR** park is an old-fashioned amusement park, with a hokey Wax Museum, a rickety roller coaster, and other overpriced rides,sugary snacks, and carnival attractions. There are **playgrounds** at Villa Ada, Villa Celimontana, and the Euro-sculpture park by Porta Ardeatina.

Apart from the obvious, manufactured fun, kids enjoy the **Colosseum,** the **Trevi Fountain, St. Peter's dome**, the **Villa d'Este** at Tivoli, the **Monster Park** at Bomarzo, and the models exhibit at the **Museum of Roman Civilization** in EUR. For those tykes with a taste for the macabre, check out Castel San'Angelo with its **dungeons,** the spooky **catacombs,** and the **Capucin Crypt** off piazza Barberini, which is decorated with skeletons. Daytrips to nearby lakes and beaches like Lake Bracciano are also a good breather from the city.

In addition, train systems in Italy sometimes offer discounts for groups or families traveling together. There are discount Eurailpasses for groups and children (children under 12 travel at half-price, children under four usually travel free), and an Italian kilometric ticket can be used by up to five at once. For some families it may be more convenient to travel by rental car, but train will often be cheaper, reduce the fidgets, and provide a novel, absorbing experience for North American children. See the Transportation section below for more details.

Wilderness Press, 2440 Bancroft Way, Berkeley, CA 94704 (tel. (510) 843-8080) distributes *Backpacking with Babies and Small Children* (US$8.95) and *Sharing Nature with Children* (US$7.95), which present useful tips for the outward-bound family. **Lonely Planet Publications,** 155 Filbert St., Oakland, CA 94607 (tel. (510) 893-8555 or (800) 229-0122) publishes *Travel With Children* (US$11.00, $1.50 postage), a book chock-full of user-friendly tips and anecdotes; they also publish a free quarterly newsletter full of general travel advice and stories. To order from overseas, contact: P.O. Box 617, Hawthorn, Victoria 3122, Australia.

Or maybe you would just like a few moments of peace and quiet. For the frazzled or theater-going parent, there is a **babysitting service** in Rome, **A1 Circolo Dei Bambini**, 34 via Ricci Curbastro (tel. 558 29 16).

Pets

If you are bringing your cat or dog into Italy, you must have a veterinarian's certificate containing the breed, age, sex, and color of the pet, the owner's name and address, and a statement that the beastie is in good health and has been vaccinated against rabies between 20 days and 11 months before entry into Italy. Both the Italian Government Travel Office and your local Italian Embassy have these forms, which are valid for 30 days. Parrots, parakeets, rabbits, and hares also need these certificates, and Customs will examine them upon entry into Italy (cats and dogs may be examined too, although not in all cases). Bring a leash or muzzle if you have a dog; one or the other is required in public.

Specific Diets

Consult the Food and Wine sections below for general comments on eating in Rome.

Orthodox **Jewish travelers** should consult local tourist boards for a list of kosher restaurants. Also useful is *The Jewish Travel Guide* (US$10.95, $1.50 postage) from Jewish Chronicle Publications, 25 Furnival St., London EC4A 1JT, England; the U.S. and Canadian distributor is Sepher-Hermon Press, Inc., 1265 46th St., Brooklyn, NY 11219 (tel. (718) 972-9010). The guide lists synagogues, kosher restaurants, and Jewish institutions in over 80 countries. The Jewish quarter in Rome is located by the piazza Cenci, off via Arenula. There are several delicious kosher restaurants, foodstores, and bakeries listed in the Food section. Check with the synagogue of Rome (tel. 687 50 51) for more information.

Vegetarians should write the **Società Vegetariana Italiana,** via dei Piatti, 3, 20123 Milano, for information on vegetarian restaurants, foods, and stores. A vegetarian should have no problems in Italian restaurants, since the majority of first courses (*primi,* the pasta course) are meatless, and most restaurants will also supply you a mixed plate of their vegetable side dishes upon request—ask for *cortoni cotti senza carne* (side dishes without meat) or *verdure miste* (mixed vegetables). If you carry along your own dish, you'll also be well-equipped to buy from the tempting displays of fruits, vegetables, breads, and cheeses from shops on every corner or open-air markets. *Let's Go* includes some vegetarian restaurants, including a macrobiotic center near the Spanish Steps, and you can always ask for a dish *senza carne* (without meat). For more information, contact the **Vegetarian Society of the U.K.,** Parkdale, Dunham Rd., Altrincham, Chesire WA14 4QG (tel. (061) 928 07 93). They publish the international *The Vegetarian Travel Guide* (£3.99), listing vegetarian and health-conscious restaurants, guesthouses, societies, and health food stores throughout the world (be warned: half the book is devoted to the U.K.) Another possible resource is the **North American Vegetarian Society,** P.O. Box 72, Dolgeville, NY 13329 (tel. (518) 568-7970).

Alternatives to Tourism

Work

The employment situation in Rome is grim for natives and grimmer for foreigners. Work visas are extremely difficult to obtain since you must find a job that cannot be filled by an Italian. Any and all openings are coveted by herds of would-be expatriates, so competition is fierce. Unfortunately, the innocent dream of a glamorous job in Rome is illegal without a real-life visa, and stiff punishments can be an unglamorous reality. Foreigners are most successful at securing harvest work, restaurant or bar work, housework, or work in the tourism industry, where English-speakers are needed.

On the other hand, there is the cash-based, untaxable, underground economy—*economia sommersa* or *economia nera*--which makes up as much as one-third of Italy's economy. Many people find success by working their connections. Friends abroad may be able to expedite work permits or arrange informal work-for-accommodations swaps at their uncle's *trattoria* or their cousin's farm. Many permitless agricultural workers go untroubled by local authorities, who recognize the need for seasonal manpower. European Community citizens can work in any other EC country without working papers, and if your parents or grandparents were born in an EC country (hear ye, Australians and New Zealanders), you may be able to claim dual citizenship or at least the right to a work permit. (Beware: claiming citizenship in Italy obligates men to do military sevice.) Students can check with their university's foreign language departments, which may have official or unofficial connections to job openings abroad.

Whether you want to be a *rustico* or a supermodel, the following organizations and their publications may be of service.

Peterson's Guide's, 202 Carnegie Center, P.O. Box 2123, Princeton, NJ 08543 (tel. (800) 338-3282); in New Jersey (tel. (609) 243-9111). Publishes *The Directory of Overseas Summer Jobs* (US$14.95), a listing of 50,000 volunteer and paid openings worldwide. Peterson's also distributes *Work Your Way Around the World* (US$16.95), a collection of practical advice and creative job-hunting ideas.

CIEE (see Useful Addresses above). For publications and organizations with information on work in Italy, check *Work, Study, Travel Abroad: The Whole World Handbook,* compiled by CIEE (US$12.95, $1 postage).

Vacation Work Publications, 9 Park End St., Oxford OX1 1HJ, England (tel. (0865) 241 978). They just came out with the comprehensive *Live and Work in Italy* along with their standard *Directory of Summer Jobs Abroad,* a list of 30,000 vacancies in a variety of fields (each £7.95).

In Rome, check the help-wanted columns in the English-language papers *Daily American* and the *International Daily News. Wanted in Rome* (L1000) is available in English-language bookstores or from their office at via dei Delfini, 17, 00185 Roma (tel. (06) 679 01 90), or try *Porta Portese,* via di Porta Maggiore, 95 (tel. 73 37 48). *Metropolitan,* an English-language bi-monthly magazine, also has a fairly helpful classified ads section, and is available at the Economy Bookstore (see English Language Bookstores below). You can also place a free ad offering your services in *Metropolitan.*

The magazine *AAM Terra Nuova* (L6000 per issue), good for agricultural jobs, can be obtained by writing to Casella Postale 190, 50032 Borgo S. Lorenzo (tel. (055) 84 56 116). Radios will usually broadcast free advertisements.

Teaching English

Teaching English can be the most lucrative and accessible profession for young people, though Rome tends to be the most competitive market of all the Italian cities. No more than minimal Italian is necessary to teach conversation, though many language insitutes require a college degree and/or some sort of TEFL or RSA certificate or completion of a shorter TEFL training course. There are numerous English-language institutes in Rome that offer jobs through ads in *Wanted in Rome* (L1000, available in all the English bookstores) and in the Rome daily newspaper *Il Messagero*. Some schools simply post signs in stores, hair salons, or *caffè*. The language schools are listed under *Scuole de Lingua* in the Italian yellow pages, and are also listed in the English yellow pages. The best time to look is September/October and just after Christmas, when the University begins its semesters. If you want to take a TEFL course in Italy, contact International House, viale Manzoni, 57, near piazza Barberini, which offers TEFL courses, has a good bulletin board, and advertises teaching jobs throughout Italy.

Many people find it easier to teach English privately by postering their services around the University and on the community bulletin boards. A common method is to set up a small class of 4-6 students. The going rate, depending on the size of the class, is about L15,000-L35,000 per hour. There are numerous "How to Teach English" handbooks at the English bookstores in Rome, but consider buying one before you go. Another short-term option, albeit horrifying, is to be a substitute teacher at one of the American or British schools; generally, you need a college degree, nerves of steel, and a *Codice Fiscale* (tax code).

If you're interested in arranging a teaching job before you get to Italy, try the following organizations:

International Schools Services, P.O. Box 5910, Roszel Rd., Princeton, NJ 08540 (tel. (609) 452-0990). The ISS, which operates and assists English-speaking schools abroad, publishes a free pamphlet entitled *Your Passport to Teaching and Administrative Services Abroad.* The *ISS Directory* (US$29.95, $5.75 postage) can be obtained through contacting Peterson's, Inc. See below for their address.

Institute of International Education (IIE), Communications Division, Box TF, Institute of International Education, 809 United Nations Plaza, New York, NY 10017 (tel. (212) 883-8279). Publishes *Academic Year Abroad,* a directory of teaching opportunities in over 100 countries worldwide. To purchase a copy (US$31.95 plus $3.80 shipping), send a check made out to the IIE.

U.S. Department of State, Office of Overseas Schools, Room 245 SA-29, Department of State, Washington, DC 20522-2902 (tel. (703) 875-7800). The USDS will send you a list of English-language K-12 schools abroad which you can then contact directly. Also try the **U.S. Department of Defense,** 2461 Eisenhower Ave., Alexandria, VA 22331 (tel. (202) 325-0885).

Au Pair Work

English-speaking *au pairs* are becoming chic accessories to the lifestyles of the Italian rich and famous, or at least to the affluent Italian middle class. For young (mostly) women, working as an *au pair* can provide a free place to live and the opportunity to immerse in Italian family life. In exchange for room, board and a little spending money (at least L200,000 per month), au pairs are expected to devote themselves to the family's *principini* and *principesse,* and to enroll in a language class. Every situation is different; some families want the *au pair* to teach their kids a bit of English and others expect their *au pair* to do light housework. There are many advantages to being an au pair: you can get an unparalleled look into *la dolce vita,* especially since many families take their *au pair* on vacation to the Alps or to the sea; you can learn Italian; and you are exempt from getting a *libretto di lavoro* (work permit). However, keep in mind that you will be spending a lot of time with people under 4 feet tall, whose idea of a good time is tying you to a tree, and whose conversations tend towards the scatalogical. You also may find that your Italian vocabulary is that of a five year old, and that, along with your household responsibilities (like scrubbing floors and ironing underwear), you might have a hard time meeting people your own age. Make sure you understand what the family expects of you before you commit, and always try to meet with them in advance. Once there, your host family must register you at the police station, agreeing to take full responsibility for you. Proof that you are taking a language course may also be required. Check in the local newspapers, like *Il Messagero, Metropolitan,* and *Wanted in Rome* for openings, and consider placing an ad yourself. Try the following agencies and publications:

> **The Au Pair and Nanny's Guide to Working Abroad**, put out by Vacation Work in Oxford, is an invaluable source of advice and information. Available through Vacation Work (see above) for £5.95.
>
> **Agenzia Universale**, PO Box 38, L'Ufficio Postale, Tivoli 00019, Rome (tel. 271 02 42, fax 271 02 42). An agency that places au pairs throughout Italy. They have some contacts for work in the tourist industry as well.
>
> **Agenzia Cisial**, Via Gian Giacomo Porro, 18, Rome (tel. 887 05 64). Arranges au pairs to work throughout Italy. **At Your Service Agency**, 163A Gwent Street, London, NW4 4DH (tel. 081 203 6885 or 203 6862). Places British citizens with families all over the continent.

Tourist Industry

Summer positions as a tour group leader are available with **Hostelling International/American Youth Hostels,** P.O. Box 37613, Washington, DC 20013-7613 (tel. (202) 783-6161). You must be at least 21, take a week-long leadership course (US$295, room and board included) and lead a group in the U.S. before leading a trip to Europe. The **Experiment in International Living (EIL)** requires language fluency, leadership ability, and extensive overseas experience for similar positions. You must be at least 24 years old. EIL also runs an exchange program for high school students (P.O. Box 676, Kipling Rd., Brattleboro, VT 05302; tel. (800) 345-2929). If you speak some Italian, you may be able to get work with a touring company or at a local campsite. The two main campsites in Rome (the Tiber and the Flaminio) take on English help before the season begins in the early summer of each year.

Other than teaching, **long-term employment** is difficult to secure unless you have skills in high-demand areas, such as medicine (including nursing) or computer programming. If you're determined to have a glamorous international career, Eric Kocher has compiled job-hunting strategies in *International Jobs: Where They Are, How To Get Them* (US$14.66, postage included), published by Addison-Wesley, 1 Jacob Way, Reading, MA 01867 (tel. (800) 447-2226). For jobs in private industry, contact the Italian consulate for a listing of firms, or consult the *Directory of American Firms Operating in Foreign Countries,* published by World Trade Academy Press, 50 East 42nd St., #509, New York, NY 10017 (tel. (212) 697-4999). Although the three-volume set costs US$195, World Trade also offers excerpts containing lists of American firms in specific countries (averaging US$10-$15 per country).

The **Association for International Practical Training (AIPT)** is the U.S. affiliate of the International Association for the Exchange of Students for Technical Experience (IAESTE). AIPT offers on-the-job training and internships in more than 80 countries for full-time students with at least two years of university study in engineering, computer science, math, the natural sciences, applied arts, or agriculture. Apply (US$75) to IAESTE Trainee Program, c/o AIPT, 10400 Little Patuxent Parkway, Suite #250, Columbia, MD 21044 (tel. (410) 997-2200).

Volunteering

Volunteering is another good way to immerse yourself in a foreign culture. In addition to personal satisfaction, you may even receive room and board for your work. *Volunteer! The Comprehensive Guide to Voluntary Service in the U.S. and Abroad* (US$8.95), offering advice and listings, is available from CIEE (See Useful Organizations: Budget Travel Services).

Volunteers for Peace, 43 Tiffany Rd., Belmont, VT 05730 (tel. (802) 259-2759), publishes *The International Work Camp Directory* (US$10 postpaid) and a free newsletter. The organization arranges placement in 34 different countries (US$125 placement fee). Though few openings are available, you can volunteer as a camp counselor for the **YMCA** in Italy by contacting their International Camp Counselor Abroad Program (ICCA), 356 W. 34th St., New York, NY 10001 (tel. (212) 563-3441). Applicants must be over 17 and U.S. citizens.

Archeological Digs

For information on archaeological digs, write to the **Centro Camuno di Studi Preistorici,** Via Guglielmo Marconi, #7, Valcomonica (Brescia) (tel. (0364) 420 91). This research center offers volunteer work, grants, tutoring, research assistant positions, and training and apprenticeship in scientific art and editing. The **Archaeological Institute of America,** 675 Commonwealth Ave., Boston, MA 02215 (tel. (617) 353-9361) puts out the *Archeological Fieldwork Opportunities Bulletin* (US$10.50 non-members) which lists over 200 field sites throughout the world. Available from Kendall/Hunt Publising Co. (tel. (800) 338-5578.)

Study

How to dress, smoke, gel your hair, ride a Vespa, and swear in Italian are some of the *truly* useful skills you will learn from your Roman peers if you're lucky enough to study in Rome. A good place to start is *Work, Study, and Travel Abroad: The Whole World Handbook* (see Work above), which describes over 1000 study programs, and lists eligibility requirements and application timetables for each. Continue your search with the following organizations. Senior travelers should consider a course with **Elderhostel** (see Travelers with Specific Concerns: Senior Travelers).

American Field Service (AFS), AFS International/Intercultural Programs, 313 E. 43rd St., New York, NY 10017 (tel. (800) 237-4636, or (212) 949-4242). Offers both summer- and year-long opportunities in Italy for high school students, ages 15-18.

Association of American College and University Programs in Italy, Corso Vittorio Emanuele II, 110, 00182, Roma (tel. (06) 654 47 52).

Centro Turistico Studentesco e Giovanile (CTS), via Genova, 16, 00184 Roma (tel. (06) 467 91, fax (06) 467 92 05). A tourist office with connections to the Italian Ministry of Foreign Affairs and the Italian Ministry of Education, they will provide you with the information on foreign study in Italy.

The Institute of International Education (IIE), 809 United Nations Plaza, New York, NY 10017 (tel. (212) 883-8200). Publishes several annualreference books. *Vacation Study Abroad* (US$26.95, postage US$3) and *Academic Year Abroad* (US$31.95, postage US$3) describe a myriad of study-abroad programs. *Vacation Study Abroad* (US$24.95) details over 1000 summer and short-term programs. IIE also recently compiled *Financial Resources for International Study* (US$36.95, $5.75 postage), which lists 630 foundations offering grants to the cosmopolitan scholar. Available from **Peterson's Guides,** P.O. Box 2123, Princeton, NJ 08543-2123.

If your Italian is fluent, consider enrolling directly in an Italian university. Universities are overcrowded, but you're likely to make plenty of Roman friends to educate you in the less-academic matters of Rome. Italian universities are much more reasonably priced than their American counterparts; you'll save money and have a much more authentic Roman experience; credits are generally accepted at your home institution without much fuss, but ask around first. For an application, write to the nearest Italian consulate. In Rome, contact the *Segretaria Stranieri,* Città Universitaria, piazzale delle Scienze, 2, Roma. Remember that visas are required of foreign students in Italy. The following student organizations in Italy can provide you with leads and advice.

Amicizia, Casella Postale 42-PG I, 06100 Perugia (office address: via Fabretti, 59; tel. (075) 202 12). International student organization for work and study in Italy.

Ufficio Centrale Studenti Esteri in Italia (UCSEI), via Monti Parioli, 59, 00197 Roma (tel. (06) 320 44 91 or 321 89 01). National organization for foreign students in Italy.

Another option is studying at an institute run for foreign students by an Italian university. Write to the Italian Cultural Institute for a complete list of programs (see Useful Organizations). The following schools and organizations offer a variety of classes.

Centro Linguistico Italiano Dante Alighieri, via B. Marliano, 4, 00162 Roma (tel. (06) 832 01 84, fax (06) 860 42 03); via dei Bardi, 12, 50125 Firenze (tel. (55) 234 29 84, fax (55) 234 28 77). Language classes, cultural daytrips, extracurricular activities. Will find you a cheap apartment as well. Write a month or two in advance.

Italiaidea, p. della Cancelleria, 85, 00186 Roma (tel. (06) 68 30 76 20, fax (06) 689 29 97). Organizes language, arts, and culture courses throughout the year, including vacation courses at the seaside or in the mountains during summer months. Located in central Rome.

Getting There

From North America

While it is impossible to estimate particular airfares, as prices and market conditions vary constantly, a few general rules do apply. Off-season travelers enjoy lower fares and face much less competition for inexpensive seats, but you needn't travel in the dead of winter to save. Peak-season rates usually apply from late May to mid-September. If you arrange your travel dates carefully and make flight arrangements well in advance, you can travel in summer and still find low-season fares. Unfortunately, Rome (and Italy in general) is not the center for bargain airfares. If you are traveling elsewhere in Europe, consider beginning your trip outside of Italy; a flight to Brussels or Frankfurt can cost considerably less than one to Rome. However, keep in mind that saving as much as US$100-200 by flying to Milan, Florence, or even Brussels for your Roman holiday may be devoured by the round-trip train fare to Rome, and the extra hassle may not be worth it.

Have a knowledgeable travel agent guide you through the options outlined below. Nothing can replace a friendly relationship with a good travel agent when it comes to arranging successful trips and finding great bargains, so ask around and try to find someone that you both like and trust. If you don't have time to do this footwork, keep in mind that commissions are smaller on cheaper flights and some travel agents will be less than eager to help you find the best deal; it may be helpful to check with more than one agent. Check the travel section of the Sunday *New York Times* or another major newspaper for extra-bargain fares. Also consult CIEE, Travel CUTS, Let's Go Travel, and other student travel organizations.

Since inexpensive flights from Canada cost substantially more than the lowest fares from the U.S., Canadians may find it more economical to leave from the States. Be sure to check with Travel CUTS for information on special charters.

Charter Flights

In general, charter flights are the cheapest. You can book charters up to the last minute, but most flights in early summer fill up well before the departure date. Later in the season, companies may have trouble filling their planes and will either cancel flights or offer special prices. With charters, you may stay abroad for as long as you like and may often fly into one city and out of another. Charters do not generally allow for change. You must book specific departure and return dates and you lose most, if not all, of your money if you cancel your ticket. Some charter companies do allow you to change the dates of your flight for a nominal fee, however.

In addition, charter flights can be unreliable. Companies reserve the right to change the dates of your flight, add fuel surcharges after you have made final payment, or even cancel the flight. The most common problem is delay. Charter companies usually fly a single plane to and from Europe, so delays accumulate and one mechanical failure can delay all flights. If you prefer not to take the chance, regular national carriers to Italy include Alitalia, Delta, Pan American, and American Airlines. Since reservation systems are often messy, you should have your ticket in hand as early as possible and arrive at the airport at least two hours before departure. In some cases, you may get a discount for early reservations.

CIEE, 205 E. 42nd St., New York, NY 10017 (tel. (800) 222-5570), was among the first on the charter scene. Its two agencies offer service to most major European cities.

CIEE operates both Council Charter (tel. (800) 223-7402) and Council Travel (tel. (212) 661-1450) for students and teachers, with over 30 offices in the U.S. Flights are extremely popular, so reserve early. There is no Council Travel office in Rome, so you must go directly to the airline to change the dates of your tickets.

Airline Ticket Consolidators

These agencies advertise prices lower than most charters and sell unused tickets on scheduled flights. Check the travel section of major newspapers for ads. There are several discount travel agencies worth contacting. **Bargain Air,** 655 Deep Valley Dr., Rolling Hills, VA 90274 (tel. (800) 347-2345 or (213) 377-2919, fax (213) 377-18248) offers discounted flight to most European cities, including Milan. Check also with **Discount Travel International,** Ives Bldg., #205, 114 Forrest Ave., Narberth, PA 19072 (tel. (800) 334-9294; reservations (215) 668-7184); **Last Minute Travel Club,** 132 Brookline Ave., Boston, MA 02215 (tel. (800) 527-8646 or (617) 267-9800); or **Uni-Travel,** P.O. Box 12485, St. Louis, MO 63132 (tel. (800) 325-2222 or (314) 569-0900). For US$20, **Travel Avenue** will search for the lowest international airfare available and then discount it 8-25%. They are located at 641 W. Lake St., Chicago, IL 60606 (tel. (800) 333-3335).

Air Hitch, 2790 Broadway, #100, New York, NY 10025 (tel. (212) 864-2000). Travelers indicate a five-day period and a region, rather than a specific date or city, pay in advance, and receive a "flight indication" listing of three possible flights, one of which you will be booked on. East Coast to Western Europe $160, West Coast to Europe $269, and $229 to Europe from anywhere else in the continental U.S. Be warned: Airhitch is not for the clueless—read all the fine print they send you. Absolute flexibility on both sides of the Atlantic is a must.

Commercial Carriers

If you decide to make your transatlantic crossing with a commercial airline, you'll be purchasing greater reliability, security, and flexibility—usually at a higher price. The major airlines offer two options for the budget traveler. The first is to fly **standby.** Tickets may be purchased in advance on a private basis or through a ticket consolidator, but you are not guaranteed a seat on any particular flight. Seat availability is known only minutes before departure, and standby seating varies from airline to airline. Since you are not tied to a particular departure, there is greater flexibility, but traveling by a fixed itinerary will be difficult, if not impossible. In addition, standby tickets are harder to come by and may be more expensive than economy round-trip fares on certain routes.

Your second option on a commercial airline is the **Advanced Purchase Excursion Fare (APEX).** This plan provides confirmed reservations and flexible ports of arrival and departure, but you must tailor your trip to meet strict minimum/maximum length requirements, usually seven to 60 or 90 days. Tickets (often non-refundable) must be purchased three or four weeks in advance. Book APEX fares early—by June you may have difficulty getting your desired summer departure date. **Alitalia,** Italy's national airline, is geared primarily to executives and well-heeled travelers, but they do offer APEX and off-season youth fares.

Courier Flights

Anyone who travels light should consider flying as a courier. The company hiring you will usually use your checked luggage space for freight (some will give you carry on documents instead); you're left with the carry-on allowance. Restrictions to watch for: most flights are round-trip only with fixed-length stays (usually under two weeks); you may not be able to fit your love into your carry-on (single tickets only); and most flights from North America originate in New York (including a scenic visit to the courier office in the suburbs near JFK airport); most to Italy arrive in Milan. Round-trip fares from the U.S. range from US$175 to US$400. **Now Voyager,** 74 Varick St., #307, New York, NY 10013 (tel. (213) 432-1616), acts as an agent for many courier flights worldwide from New York, although some flights are available from Houston and they are planning to expand their service. You'll have better luck (and more open phone

Always travel with a friend.

Get the International
Student Identity Card,
recognized worldwide.

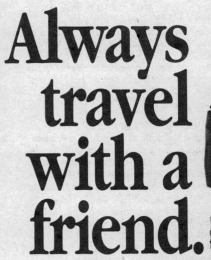

For information call toll-free **1-800-GET-AN-ID**.
or contact any Council Travel office. (See inside front cover.)

 Council on International Educational Exchange
205 East 42nd Street, New York, NY 10017

lines) going directly through the courier companies; pick up a copy of *The Air Courier's Handbook* (US$12.95) at your bookstore for a list.

From Europe

Travel agents in your home country can often give you specific information on travel within Europe, but it's simpler, and usually cheaper, to make arrangements once you arrive there. Check newspapers, travel agencies, and student travel organizations. Look into **STA Travel,** 74 and 86 Old Brompton Rd., London SW7 (for international travel, tel. (071) 937 99 62; North American, (071) 937 99 71; European, (071) 937 99 21). Also check with **Scandinavian Student Travel Service,** Hauchsvej 17, 1825, Frederiksberg C, Copenhagen, Denmark (tel. (01) 21 85 00), for student and youth charter flights.

By Plane

Budget fares are available on high-volume flights between northern Europe and Rome, mostly in the spring and summer. Carriers within Europe often offer student discounts. There are many good charter flights from London.

Air Travel Group Ltd., 227 Shepherd's Bush Rd., London W6 7AS (tel. (081) 748 13 33), acts as an umbrella organization for three services. **Italy Sky Shuttle** programs flight assignments from seven U.K. to 17 Italian airports, **Magic of Italy** offers resort holidays in choice villas and **Italian Escapades** arranges travel itineraries, books flights, rents autos, and makes motel reservations. They also operate branch offices in Manchester, Bologna, Milan, Naples, Rome, and Palermo. **London Student Travel,** 52 Grosvenor Gardens, London SW1 0AU (tel. (01) 730 34 02), offers competitive fares all over the continent, and there's no age limit for many of their flights. Also check with **Magic Bus,** 20 Filellinon, Syntagma, Athens, Greece (tel. (32) 32 37 47), which operates inexpensive flights within Europe, despite its name.

By Train

If you're traveling to Rome from elsewhere in Italy, you'll want to use the economical and efficient train system. Italy's major train lines, following ancient precedent, converge on Rome. Most major Italian cities either lie on a direct line from Rome, or can be reached with a single change. The key routes are to the north: the **Rome-Turin** route runs along the Tyrrhenian Sea through Pisa and Genoa; the **Rome-Trieste** line through Florence, Bologna, Padua, and Venice; the **Rome-Milan** line through Florence and Genoa; and the **Rome-Brennero** line through Florence and Bologna on the way to Bolzano. To the south, the **Rome-Messina** line links Rome to Naples, Reggio Calabria, and (via ferry) Sicily. The **Rome-Lecce** trains link Rome with Fùggia, Bari and Brìndisi. Going across the peninsula, the **Rome-Ancona** line connects Rome with the Adriatic, whence the main Adriatic line can take you either north or south along that coast.

Trains have a fixed price, as well as a supplement if the train you want to take is a *rapido* (an express train) or an *IC* (a deluxe train running non-stop between major cities.) Eurail cardholders (see below) are exempt from supplements but not from reservation charges (these vary according to the length of your trip). Reservations cost extra (usually under L10,000, sometimes much less), but are not always necessary; ask the booking agent. An *IC* train, while charging the same supplement price, can cut travel time by as much as a third. Reservations are required for *IC* trains and must be made at least a few hours in advance; however, the price of a reserved seat is included in the supplement; ask about *IC* train departure times and reservations at a train information booth or at travel agencies in the city from which you depart. In Rome, you can make reservations and purchase tickets at the windows in the Termini station, at a travel agent like CTS or CIT (see below) or at the reservations office *(prenotazioni)* downstairs near the Albergo Diurno. Plan ahead and treat yourself to seat reservations to avoid standing in the aisle with your backpack for several hours. Request *Non Fumare* for a smoke-free voyage. Trip lengths and prices given here are for *diretto* (direct) trains, unless otherwise indicated at the train station. From **Florence:** 2hr., L22,000;

EUROPE BY YOURSELF

WITH THE YOUTH & STUDENT TRAVEL SPECIALISTS

FROM ROME TO

	✈ return	🚂 return
Athens	$ 310	200
Cairo	$ 540	-
London	$ 215	340
Tunis	$ 260	-
Istanbul	$ 370	220
Los Angeles	$ 780	200
New York	$ 620	200

FROM LONDON TO

	✈ return	🚂 return
Amsterdam	£. 75	57
Athens	£. 133	265
Berlin	£. 126	96
Madrid	£. 124	167
Paris	£. 64	70
Rome	£. 120	170
Venice	£. 150	157
Los Angeles	£. 285	-
New York	£. 220	-

FROM PARIS TO

	✈ return	🚂 return
Amsterdam	ff. 910	488
Berlin	ff. 1480	1121
Rome	ff. 1100	1008
Madrid	ff. 1580	1042
New York	ff. 2450	-
Sydney	ff. 8425	-

Prices are valid for summer '92
Domestic and international tickets.
Discounted and regular international
train tickets. Hotel reservations. Tours
and pocket holidays worldwide.

YOUTH & STUDENT TRAVEL CENTRE

ROME	via Genova, 16 - Tel. (06) 46791
ROME	corso Vittorio Emanuele II, 297 - Tel. (06) 6872672 - 6872673
ROME	Air Terminal Ostiense - Tel. (06) 5747950
FLORENCE	via dei Ginori, 25/R - Tel. (055) 289721/289570
MILAN	via S. Antonio, 2 - Tel. (02) 58304121
NAPELS	via Mezzocannone, 25 - Tel. (081) 5527975/5527960
VENICE	Dorso Duro Ca' Foscari, 3252 - Tel. (041) 5205660/5205655
LONDON	44 Goodge Street, W1P 2AD - Tel. (004471) 5804554/6375601 Metro Goodge Street
LONDON	220 Kensington High Street, W8 7RA - Tel. (004471) 9373265 Metro High Street Kensington
PARIS V°	20, rue des Carmes - Tel. (00331) 43250076 Metro Maubert Mutualitè

rapido supplement L9300. From **Venice:** 5hr., L40,000, *rapido* supplement L13,800. From **Naples:** 3hr., L15,400, *rapido* supplement L5300.

If you're doing a lot of traveling in Europe before or after visiting Rome, consider the ever-popular Eurailpass; with the pass you can get to Italy from a number of European countries and also travel within Italy. (However, if you're traveling only in Italy, the Eurailpass is not worth it.) The Eurailpass is valid for unlimited travel in 17 European countries and also entitles you to free passage or reduced fares on some ferries and buses. If you're under 26, you can purchase the **Eurail Youthpass,** valid for one (US$508) or two months (US$698) of second-class travel. If you're over 25, you must purchase a first-class Eurailpass, ranging from 15 days of unlimited travel (US$460) up to three months (US$1260). Eurailpasses may be bought only outside of Europe and are available only to those who do not reside in Europe. Several other packages are available; for more information or to purchase a pass, contact Council Travel, Travel CUTS, Let's Go Travel Services, or a travel agent (See Budget Travel Services).

If you're under 26, you may also purchase BIJ tickets, which cut regular second-class train fares on international runs by about 50%. BIJ tickets are sold by **Transalpino** and **Eurotrain.** Neither organization has a representative in the U.S., so Americans will have to purchase tickets in Europe. If you cannot find a Transalpino or Eurotrain office, try a large student or budget travel organization such as Council Travel, ISTC, or STA Travel. In Rome, you'll find **Transalpino** at p. Esquilino, 9Z (tel. 487 08 70; open Mon.-Fri. 9am-6:30pm, Sat. 9am-1pm). There's also a booth in **Termini**, at track #22 (tel. 488 05 36; open Mon.-Sat. 8am-8:30pm; in summer also on Sun. 8:30am-5:30pm). Ferry information here as well. When you buy a BIJ ticket, you must specify both your destination and route, and you have the option of stopping off anywhere along that particular route for up to two months. The fare from London to Rome is about US$165, US$305 round-trip; from Brussels or Paris, one-way US$129, round-trip US$240; from Amsterdam US$133, round-trip US$244; from Copenhagen US$174, round-trip US$314; from Frankfurt US$107, round-trip US$213. On an overnight ride, you might want also to purchase a **couchette**, the economy version of a full sleeping berth (about US$15—very worth it, as you will not sleep a wink in a second-class seat).

By Bus

Few people think of buses when planning travel to Italy, but they are available and cheap. **Magic Bus** runs direct service between many major cities in Europe. Their main office is located at 20 Filellinon, Syntagma, Athens, Greece (tel. (32) 32 37 47), but information is available from cooperating offices in many other cities. **London Student Travel** at 52 Grosvenor Gardens, London SW1W 0AU (tel. (01) 730 34 02) operates express buses from London to destinations in Italy.

Once There

Safety

Rome is congested day and night with lost, bewildered, and distracted tourists, each loaded with cash and valuables in every pocket. The bright side is that Roman thieves, provided with so many thousands of easy targets, rarely resort to violence.

Carry all your valuables (including your passport, railpass, traveler's checks and airline ticket) either in a **money belt** or a **necklace pouch** stashed securely *inside* your clothing (both available at any well-stocked travel store). These will protect you against the skilled professionals who use razors to slash open backpacks and fanny packs. If you carry a purse, buy a sturdy leather one with a secure clasp; wear it with the strap across your chest and the purse away from the street, keeping the clasp against you. Even these precautions do not always suffice: some moped desperados carry knives to cut the straps of purses and backpacks, or you may simply find yourself being dragged behind a speeding Vespa. Your best bet is to wear your purse away from the street and keep a firm hand on it at all times. To avoid having them painfully ripped from your person, don't wear any valuable or valuable-looking jewels.

For backpacks, buy small combination padlocks and, where possible, slip them through two zippers, securing a pack shut; they barely weigh anything, and their presence will deter non-razor-handy thieves and pickpockets. In a pinch, thread a safety pin through the zippers. Never put valuables in your back pocket or the outside pocket of your daypack—nothing makes an easier target. Keep a hand on your bags at all time; when standing still, clutch them close to your chest or between your legs. Be watchful of your belongings on buses, and don't check baggage on trains, especially if you're switching lines. Never use the phrase "Watch my bag for a second?" whether or not you're asking someone from your own country. If you travel into or out of Rome by train, avoid empty train compartments, particularly at night. In case you fall asleep, secure the straps of your pack through the over-head luggage rack with a padlock. (For more on train safety, see the Once There: Transportation section below.)

Never, ever count money in public, and watch to see that you are not followed after changing money. There are as many ways to relieve a tourist of a wallet as there are gypsies in Rome. A favorite trick to watch out for is gypsy children in packs, begging for change and thrusting flat pieces of cardboard or newspaper at your waist, under which they probe pockets and unzip fanny pouches. The buggers are especially thick around the Forum and the Colosseum, where people are blindly admiring the architecture, and on crowded buses like the #64 and the #492. These kids will do anything for a buck, including pulling down their pants and shrieking. Gypsy women will also approach you, nursing their baby, in order for you to look away. Stand proud, you've seen it before, and remain alert. It's not just gypsies who pick pockets. On the bus and subway, unarmed but devious thieves may brush up against you while the inevitable crush of people is most disorienting and grope your bags and pockets. They often work in pairs—one may make an obvious grab or pinch your fanny, distracting you while a subtler hand takes the goods. Criminals may also sexually harass women to distract them. If you sense that pickpockets have closed in on you or that you are being harassed for any reason, don't be afraid to call attention to yourself or to the offending

party; most Romans are embarrassed by these criminals and will move to help you. If, on the bus, you know your wallet has been taken, alert the driver at once; he will lock the doors and drive to the nearest police station.

For a big city, Rome is relatively safe at night. Women and men will generally feel safe walking through the center of town during all but the darkest hours. Outside the *Centro Storico* (historical center), however, use caution. The area around Termini and to its south (especially near piazza Vittorio Emanuele and the Colle Oppio, notorious drug areas) and Testaccio deserve special care; walk in groups at night. Good old-fashioned bipedal mugging is particularly bad in the suburbs of Cinecitta and Centocelle. If for any reason you plan to sleep outside (an option we do NOT recommend) or simply don't want to carry everything with you, store your gear in a train or bus station locker, but be aware that these are occasionally broken into. Keep your valuables on you even in low-budget hotels where someone else may have a passkey, and particularly in dormitory-style lodging——a trip to the shower could cost you a passport or wallet. Ask the manager of your hotel or hostel for advice on areas to avoid; if you're feeling especially unsafe, look for accommodations with either a curfew or a night attendant. Women should also consult the section on Women Travelers in Travelers with Specific Concerns before arriving in Rome.

If you are robbed, always file a report *(denunciare)* with the police—you'll need it for insurance, and its helpful in case anything is turned in, which may actually happen. Inquire after **lost property** at the lost property office, **Oggetti Rinvenuti,** via Nicolo Bettoni, 1 (tel. 581 60 40; open Mon.-Sat. 9am-noon). Also try Termini, at track #1 (tel. 47 30 66 82; open 7am-11pm). Check your embassy as well, since cash-drained wallets are often returned there. One last chance: **ACAT,** via Volturno, 65 (tel.469 51; open Mon.-Fri. 9am-noon and 2-5pm).

If you are ever in a potentially dangerous situation anywhere in Italy, call the EMERGENCY ASSISTANCE NUMBER—113 or 112. 113 is the Public Emergency Assistance number for the State Police, and usually has an English interpreter on hand; 112, the Immediate Action Service of the Carabinieri (the military police) should be your second choice. 115 is the nationwide telephone number for First Aid *(Pronto Soccorso)*, and 116 will bring the ACI (Italian Automobile Club) if you need urgent assistance on the road.

Drugs

Travelers should avoid drugs altogether. A "zero-tolerance" law was passed in 1990; possession of any amount of narcotics or even "soft drugs" (i.e., marijuana) is now illegal. The law is strictly enforced and sentences for violations are stiff; travelers have been jailed for possessing as little as 3g of marijuana. Your government is relatively powerless in the judicial system of a foreign country. All foreigners are subject to Italian law. Consular officers can only visit the prisoner, provide a list of attorneys, and inform family and friends; they cannot repatriate you to a prison in your home country and they cannot reduce your sentence.

Even if you don't use drugs, beware of the person who asks you to carry a package or drive a car across the border. For more information, write for the pamphlet *Travel Warning on Drugs Abroad* from the **Bureau of Consular Affairs,** #5807, Department of State, Washington, DC 20520 (tel. (202) 647-1488).

Staying in Touch

Mail

The postal system in Italy has justly drawn snickers from the rest of Western Europe, and now ranges from barely decent to deplorable. Aerograms and airmail letters from Italy take anywhere from one to three weeks to arrive in the U.S., while surface mail—much less expensive—takes a month or longer. Since postcards are low-priority mail, send important messages by airmail letter. Letters and small parcels rarely get lost if sent *raccomandata* (registered), *espresso* (express), or *via aerea* (air mail). Stamps *(francobolli)* are available at face value in *tabacchi* (tobacco shops), but you should mail your letters from a post office to be sure they are stamped correctly. Overseas letters are L1150; overseas postcards are L1050. Letters and postcards within Europe are L750 and L650 respectively.

Make sure anyone sending you mail in Rome from North America plans on it taking at least two weeks to reach you. Mail from home can be sent to a hotel where you have reservations. The **American Express** office will hold mail up to thirty days for card or traveler's check holders. Have the sender write "client's mail"on the envelope with the office's complete address. Letters addressed to the post office with your name and the phrase **Fermo Posta** (General Delivery) will be held at the post office of any city or town for pick-up. Address letters like this: Name; Fermo Posta; p. San Silvestro, 19; Roma 00186. It's also a good idea to have the sender capitalize and underline your last name to ensure proper sorting. Before giving up on a letter as lost, however, check under your first name too. You must claim your mail in person with your passport as identification, and you may have to pay L250 per piece of mail. In major cities like Rome, the post office handling *Fermo Posta* is usually efficient and open long hours (though they close at noon on Saturdays and the last day of the month, and are also closed on Sunday). Since a city may have more than one post office, write the address of the receiving office if possible.

Rome's **main post office** is located at the p. San Silvestro, 19 (tel. 6771), between p. di Spagna and the Corso. Its postal code is 00186. Stamps are at booths #22-24, *Fermo Posta* at booths #58 and #60. Currency exchange (no checks) is at booths #25-28. Stamp machines and computer information in English are located in the lobby. (Open Mon.-Fri. 8:20am-6:50pm, Sat. 8:20-11:50am. *Cambio* open Mon.-Fri. 8:20am-5:30pm, Sat. 8:20-11:50am.)

If you need to get something to or from Italy with celerity, both **Federal Express** and **DHL** operate in Italy, as do several of their Italian competitors. Shipments from North America to anywhere in Italy are guaranteed to arrive within 48 hours; shipments (up to 500g) from Italy are guaranteed anywhere in the world within two days. The cost from the U.S. to Italy for under 220g of documents is about US$25; shipping anything but documents usually involves filling out a commercial invoice. Contact either company for more information. **Federal Express**: for delivery to Rome, call (2) 268 602 92—the telephone code is (2) because the Milan office handles calls for Rome. In the U.S., tel (800) 238-5355; in Canada, tel. (800) 463-3339. Other regional offices: London, tel. (71) 622 93 93; Sydney, tel. (2) 317 66 66; Auckland, tel. (9) 275 39 80. In Rome, **DHL** is located at via Labicana, 78B (tel. (6) 794 91), southwest of Termini near the Colosseum. (Open Mon.-Fri. 8:30am-6:30pm.) In the U.S. and Canada tel. (800) 225-5345; other regional offices in London, tel. (81) 890 93 93; Sydney, tel. (2) 317 83 33; Auckland, tel. (9) 636 50 00.

Parcels, unsealed packages under 1kg (500g for Australia), may be mailed from San Silvestro; otherwise they must be mailed from **p. de Caprettari**, near the Pantheon (tel. 654 59 01; open Mon.-Fri. 8:25am-3:20pm, Sat. 8:25am-12:20pm). Packages must be under 20kg and 200cm (the sum of the 3 dimensions) and should be tied with a single string. Parcels sealed with tape or glue will be charged at the higher letter rate. Another parcel office is at **via della Terme**; the entrance is on via Viminale (open Mon.-Fri. 8:25am-7:40pm). Other post offices throughout the city generally open 8:30am-2pm.

The generic **postal code** for Rome is 00100; specific codes are elaborations on the 00101, 00102 theme. For *Fermo Posta* at S. Silvestro Post Office the code is 00186; at American Express, 00187.

The **Vatican** runs its own postal system which is substantially more efficient and reliable, with the same prices. Check under the Vatican City section for details.

Telephones

Italian phone numbers range between two and eight digits in length. *Let's Go* makes every effort to get up-to-date and correct phone numbers, but everyone is at the mercy of the Italian phone system, which this year is undergoing yet another in a seemingly endless series of major overhauls. Rome is in the process of unifying all phone numbers to eight digits, so numbers are changing as frequently as the heads of state (see

Modern Politics below). If you call an old number, you may hear a recording of the new number in Italian, possibly even in English. For **directory assistance,** dial 12. Insert L200 if you are calling from a pay phone, which will be returned when you complete your call. Phone books often list two numbers: the first is the number at the time of printing, the second (marked by the word *prendera)* is what the number will be at some future, unspecified time. For an English-speaking operator, dial 170.

There are three types of telephones in Italy: token phones, metered phones, and modern coin/card phones. Hold-outs from the dark ages of telecommunications take only tokens (*gettoni)* which are available for L200 from machines in train and bus stations, coffee shops, and telephone booths. *Gettoni* are also accepted as L200 change, so there's no need to worry about buying too many. Instructions are posted on all phones; one *gettone* buys five minutes. You should usually deposit three or four, even if your call is local. If you underestimate, you may be cut off in the middle of your conversation. At the end of your call, press the return button for unused *gettoni.* To place long-distance calls, deposit six *gettoni* initially, and continue to feed the machine at every beep (read: constantly). For inter-city calls, deposit eight or more. Thankfully, *gettoni* phones are beings phased out, lightening the purses of Italians everywhere. If you're lucky, you won't be bothered by these lingering dinosaurs. When using them, be sure to dial slowly; they sometimes misdial and will disconnect if you treat them roughly. Expect a couple of tries and some blood, sweat, and tears to get through.

Scatti calls are made from a phone run by an operator (who may simply be the proprietor in a bar). Every town has at least one bar with a *telefono a scatti,* which can be used for international calls. A meter records the cost of your call, and you pay when you finish. Check with the operator before you lift the receiver, and remember that he or she may tack on a substantial service fee.

The third type of phone is most common, and accepts either coins (L100, L200 or L500) or **phone cards**. Cards are an attractively modern method. Buy one for L5000 or L10,000 from a SIP office or a machine, usually found near the phone. When you insert the card, a meter subtracts *lire* from it as you speak and displays the remaining value. Partially used cards can be removed and re-used. If you happen to run out in the middle of a call, you must insert another card, so buy more than one if you're planning a long conversation.

For the most part, it is not difficult to make **long-distance calls within Europe.** A person-to-person call is *con preavviso,* and a collect call is *contassa a carico del destinatario* or *chiamata collect.*

Intercontinental calls can be made from phone card pay phones. In some small towns, however, international calls must be made from telephone company offices (SIP or ASST), generally found near the main post office and sometimes in major train stations, or from a *telefono a scatti.* To place a call at a telephone office, fill out a form at the counter. You will be assigned to a specific booth. Some offices ask for a L10,000 deposit. When direct-dialing is possible, you can dial two zeros and then the **country codes** (U.S. and Canada 1, Ireland 353, Great Britain 44, Australia 61, New Zealand 64), followed by the area code and number. Calls to the U.S. cost L10,000 for three minutes and L3000 for each minute thereafter. Rates are highest on weekdays 8:30am-1pm, decrease after 6:30pm on weekdays and Saturdays from 1 to 10pm, and are at their lowest 11pm-8am, on holidays, and between 2:30pm on Saturday and 8am on Monday. Perhaps the simplest way to call long-distance is to use the **AT&T** or **MCI Direct Service;** dialing a single number will connect you to an overseas, English-speaking operator who will then dial your collect call for you (you can also use a calling card). When calling the U.S. from most major cities in Italy, you can reach an AT&T operator by dialing 172 10 11 or an MCI operator with 172 10 22. For MCI customer service call 167 87 90 73. You may want to consider getting a calling card from either company if you plan to make a lot of international calls; the cost is significantly lower. In order to receive a little card with the AT&T Direct numbers for most European countries, call AT&T at 1-800-874-4000. Beware once again that getting through often takes several tries.

Calls to Italy must be preceded by the country code (39) and then the city code. Rome's telephone code is (06). When direct-dialing, the zero should be dropped from the beginning of each city code. Italians usually yell into the phone when calling long-distance, and you'll know the reason if you attempt to call internationally. The best connections are often abysmal; don't bother hanging up and trying again, it will probably only get worse. Develop your diaphragm muscles, lose your inhibitions, and bellow if you want to communicate with your loved ones.

Telephones ASST, p. San Silvestro, 20 (tel. 679 61 91), next to the main post office. For long distance calls; foreign currency accepted. Open 8am-11:30pm. Also two offices at Termini, on ground level open 24 hrs., downstairs open 8am-11:30pm. **SIP**, in the Villa Borghese parking lot. Open 8am-9:30pm. Phone booths throughout the city. A booth in Termini across from aisle 6 (open Mon.-Sat. 8am-11pm, Sun. 9am-noon and 5-10pm) sells magnetic phone cards in L5000 or L10,000 units. These are also available at *tabacchi* and newstands arround the city. Phone cards will not work until you break off the perforated corner.

Telegrams and Fax Machines

The surest way to get an important message across the ocean is by wire service. **Telegrams** are sent from the post office and cost L815 per word, including the address. Night letters are wired and then delivered (L370 per word up to 22 words). In Rome, telegrams can be sent from the post office at p. San Silvestro during business hours, at booths #73-76.

Faxes may be sent and received at #77. At night, use the Telegraph Office (p. San Silvestro, 18, next door to the post office—tel. 675 55 30) for sending telegrams or receiving faxes. The night office is open whenever the post office is closed (Mon.-Fri. 6:40-8:25am; Sat. 11:40am-midnight, Sun. 12:01am-8:25am Mon. morning). The staff doesn't believe faxing to or from the U.S. is possible, but insist. Fees are about L10,000 a page. Elsewhere, fax service is available in Termini at the west end of the arcade (Mon.-Fri. 8:25-1:50pm, Sat. 8:25-11:50am), at Capitalexpress (see Mail, above), the Open Door bookshop (see English Bookstores, below) and increasingly, in *tabacchi* around the city. If you have difficulty with a public fax service, try asking the concierge of an upscale hotel. Explain your situation and offer to pay all charges.

Getting In and Out of Rome

By Plane

International flights touch down at **Leonardo da Vinci Airport** (tel. 659 51), referred to as **Fiumicino** for the coastal village in which it is located. This modern, well-equipped facility houses many useful services, including a money exchange (a good place to get *lire* for the train, subway, or bus) and a baggage check. After you exit Customs, you'll find a tourist office (tel. 601 12 55) immediately to your left; open 8:15am-7:15pm). The employees will provide you with maps of the city and try to find you a room. The train from Fiumicino into Rome leaves from the second floor of the arrivals wing. Look for signs for the *Treno* (not the *Metropolitana*). This new line is the fastest and most convenient way into Rome, whisking you from the international and national terminals to the spanking new **Air Terminal Ostiense** inside the city. Buy your ticket (L6000) from one of the machines on the second floor; these make change and have English instructions. (Trains depart every 15min., 6:30am-12:45am, and the trip takes 20min.) After 12:45am, blue ACOTRAL buses leave from outside the International terminal for piazza dei Partigiani, where Air Terminal Ostiense is located (L5000; departures at 2:15am, 3:30am and 5am). Two new "bullet" trains have been installed in the airport, running from Florence's Santa Maria Novella Station and another from Naples's Mergellina station. If you're headed to either of these cities, show your Alitalia ticket for a free ride; otherwise, the cost is L127,000 (more expensive than the normal train fares, but much quicker and more convenient).

At Air Terminal Ostiense there are phones, a money exchange, car rental booths and a branch of the student travel agency CTS (see below). If you arrive there on the train from Fiumicino, a series of elevated walkways takes you to either Linea B of the *Metropolitana* (you're at the Piramide stop; Linea B takes you to Termini for transfer to Linea A and the Vatican) or to any number of buses outside in piazza dei Partigiani

(#57 goes to Termini by way of piazza Venezia; #95 follows the via del Corso to via Veneto and the Villa Borghese). Both bus and subway require that you buy a ticket before boarding. Buy subway tickets in the subway station, bus tickets in the bar at the train station. If you need a taxi, a cab from Ostiense is still much cheaper than one from Fiumicino, where the fare can run as high as L70,000. Refuse all offers of special prices or flat rates and insist that your taxi use the meter.

Most charter and domestic flights arrive at **Ciampino** (tel. 79 49 21 or 79 49 41). From here take the blue ACOTRAL bus to the Anagnina stop on Linea A of the *Metropolitana* (L700; departures every 30min. from 6am-9:30pm). Linea A takes you to Termini, the Spanish Steps, or the Vatican. Ciampino is inside the Rome city limits; do not allow a taxi driver to charge you the long-distance supplement.

By Train

Termini, named for the nearby baths *(thermae)* of the Emperor Diocletian, is the transportation hub of Rome, the focal point of most train and both subway lines. Termini is bursting with multilingual information booths, currency exchanges, baggage services, restaurants, bars, day hotels, barbers, telephone offices, gift shops, and even an aquarium. Lines are inevitably long: railway information is at the front, near piazza dei Cinquecento; tourist information is inside between tracks 2 and 3. (Tel. 47 75; all lines open daily 7am-10:40pm; reservations must be made in person.)

The various stations on the fringe of town (**Tiburtina, Trastevere, Ostiense, San Lorenzo, Roma Nord, Prenestina, Stazione S. Pietro**) are connected by bus and/or subway to Termini. Be particularly careful of pickpockets in and around the station. Never keep your wallet in your back pocket; if you carry a purse, wear it across your shoulder and keep your wallet in a secure inside pocket. Always hold tightly to your luggage. Don't be distracted by Termini commotion and be firm in repelling swarms of quickfingered kids. Watch especially for crowds of children (some as young as toddlers) waving newspapers or cardboard close to you: beneath the flutter of paper, tiny fingers may be rifling through your pockets.

Luggage storage is available along track #1. (Open daily 4am-1am, L1500 per piece per day, no bicycle storage.) For items lost or stolen on the train try the **Oggetti Rinvenuti** office far down track #1 (tel. 473 06 02) or consult the **police** on the same track (tel. 481 95 61 or 488 25 88, open 24 hrs.). For theft inside the station, consult the **carabinieri** to the right of the tourist office (between tracks #1 and 2). Improve the odds against theft by using the **waiting room** along track #1 when you can. If you're the privileged owner of a phallus and want to nap between trains, you can rent a *camera riposo* (sleep room) downstairs at the **Albergo Diurno** (tel. 48 48 19; men only, one person per room; L8000 an hour, open daily 6:40am-7:30pm). Services available to both men and women include showers (L10,000), baths (L12,000), a barber, manicurist and pedicurist. Sheets, towels and soap are available for modest fees. You can store your bags as you use the services (L2000 per piece per hour).

If you're interested in traveling from Rome to other cities in Italy by train, see By Train-Getting There, above, for information on how to use Italy's efficient and fairly inexpensive rail system. Sample trip lengths and prices given here are for *diretto* (direct) trains, unless otherwise indicated at the train station. To **Florence:** 2hr., L22,000; *rapido* supplement L9300. To **Venice:** 5hr., L40,000, *rapido* supplement L13,800. To **Naples:** 3hr., L15,4000, *rapido* supplement L5300. To get to **Greece,** take the train to the port of Bríndisi (7-8hr., L43,500, *rapido* supplement L15,800), where you can catch a ferry. Information and tickets are available from **Hellenic Mediterranean Lines**, via Umbria, 21 (tel. 474 01 41; open Mon.-Fri. 9am-1pm and 2-6pm. English spoken.) Ferries leave Bríndisi at 10pm (one every two days in summer, three a week during winter). A ticket for one-way deck passage costs L65,000, except during high season (going to Greece, July 17-August 16; returning to Bríndisi, August 8-Sept. 6), when the fare rises to L105,000. Train reservations cost L4000 (the station staff will be honest about whether you need a reservation or not, and not all trains accept reservations). If you don't have a Eurail pass, Bari might make a better point of departure for Greece.

By Car

To drive in Rome (or in Italy) you need to get an International Driver's Permit before you leave the U.S. Contact AAA Worldwide Travel Department, 8111 Gatehouse Road, 5th Floor, Falls Church, VA 22042. Tourists in Italy can get by, however, with an American driver's license that has been officially translated by ACI (Auto Club d'Italia), via Marsala 14A. (tel. 494 06 40 or 494 06 49) You need to procure a medical certificate from an Italian doctor (ACI's has hours Mon.-Fri. 3:30-5pm, Sat. 12:30-1:30pm, at via Marsala 8, Room 128 on second floor). To get the translation, bring the certificate, three ID photos, a valid overseas license and a photocopy of it, a *certificato anamestico rilasciato dal proprio medico di famiglia,* and proof of residence in Italy to the office at via Marsala 14. Be advised that foreigners may only buy petrol coupons overseas or at the frontier, not inside the country. Try these two agencies for more information on driving in Italy.

Those entering Rome by car approach the city center by way of the **Grande Raccordo Anulare (GRA),** the beltway that encircles Rome. You can take any of several exits into the city. If you are coming from the north, enter on **via Flaminia, via Salaria,** or **via Nomentana.** At all costs avoid **via Cassia,** whose ancient two-chariot lanes can't cope with modern-day traffic. **Via Tiburtina** to the east is even worse. Follow the Grande Raccordo around to **via del Mare** to the south, which connects Rome with **Lido di Ostia.** When leaving the city by car, don't attempt to follow the green **Autostrade per Firenze** signs; get on the Grande Raccordo instead and follow it around; it's longer but faster. From the south, **via del Mare** and **via Pontina** are the most direct connections from the coastal road from Naples. From the Adriatic coast, take **via Appia Nuova** or **via Tuscolana** off the southeastern quadrant of the Raccordo.

By Thumb

We strongly urge you to consider the risks inherent in hitchhiking. *Let's Go* does not recommend hitchhiking as a means of travel, and the information presented below is not intended to do so.

Many more people hitchhike in Europe than in the U.S., but stop and give it some thought before you decide to do it. Not everyone can fly an airplane, but most any bozo can drive a car, and hitching means entrusting your life to someone random who decides to stop their car near you on the highway. Avoid getting in the back of a two-door car, and never let go of your backpack. Never put your pack into the trunk. When you get into a car, make sure you know how to get out again in a hurry. Couples may avoid hassles with male drivers if the woman sits in the back or next to the door. If you ever feel threatened, experienced hitchhikers recommend that you insist on being let out immediately, regardless of where you are. If the driver refuses to stop, mant people try acting as though you're going to open the car door or vomit on the upholstery.

Those choosing to hitchhike north toward Florence usually take bus #319 to p. Vescovio and #135 onto via Salaria. They get off at the entrance to the *autostrada*; it's illegal to hitchhike on the highway itself. Those hitching south toward Naples, a rather dubious proposition in terms of safety, and a downright reckless one for women, generally take subway Linea A to Anagnina (the last stop) on via Tuscolana right at the entrance to the *autostrada*. Another option hitchers recommend is to check for rideshare offers on bulletin boards at English language institutes and universities or publications.

Orientation

The best way to inspect the streets of Rome, if you wish to study as well as see them, is to break your pocket-compass and burn your maps and guidebooks...take Chance for a mentor and lose yourself.
—George Sala, 1866.

Touring Tips

Plan on getting lost, and make the most of it. Getting lost in the streets of Rome can be one of the most frustrating and enjoyable parts of your holiday. Rome's greatest treasures often lie hidden in the perplexing tangle of streets: the Pantheon emerges quite suddenly as you wind your way through narrow, cobbled streets and Bramante's Tempietto sits in the small courtyard of a lonely church. On your first morning in Rome, hop on bus #119 for a whirlwind peek and orientation tour of the historical center. An *Aquabus* down the river will cruise you through some of the major monuments.

Schedules and timetables are often unreliable, so do keep your *Let's Go* handy. It's best to call ahead whenever possible. Remember that the Roman lunch lasts from 1pm-4pm, longer than either phone numbers or heads of state, and that Romans will not work until they have digested. Use this time to visit monuments open all day and to gaze at architecture. Better yet, join the Romans for an extended lunch and take a snooze yourself. Most shops and offices are open weekdays and Saturdays 9am-1pm and 4pm-8pm; in winter 3:30-7:30pm. Nearly everything closes down on Sunday and on Monday mornings, as well as on Saturday afternoons in summer, except for a few *caffè*, restaurants, and tourist services. All museums are closed on Monday. Food shops close early on Thursday. But the seven major basilicas of Rome are open all day, every day. Smaller churches usually open with the first mass at 6 or 7am and close around 12:30pm. If no mass is planned, each church follows the divine caprices of its curate. Many churches reopen at 4pm for a few hours. Most museums and monuments close at 1:30 or 2pm. Plan your day strategically: important business (money changing, travel plans) first thing in the morning, museums and sights until afternoon, and then, if you haven't drifted into a post-prandial languor yourself, sights that don't observe siesta (the Forum, Colosseum, *piazze*, fountains, and the seven principal basilicas affiliated with the Vatican: S. Pietro, Sta. Maria Maggiore, S. Giovanni in Laterano, S. Paolo fuori le Mure, S. Croce in Gerusalemme, S. Lorenzo fuori le Mure, Sta. Agnese fuori le Mure).

Guided tours on an air-conditioned bus are the easiest and most convenient way for older travelers or those on a very tight schedule to visit the city's principal sights. **Carrani Tours**, via V.E. Orlando, 95 (tel. 48 80 51 10). Eleven different bus tours of Rome and environs (some including meals, admission to sights, or even audience or blessing by the Pope) range from L36,000 for a simple tour to L85,000 for a nighttime tour complete with dinner, wine, and strolling musicians. **Appian Line**, via Barberini, 109 (tel. 488 41 51), offers thirteen different tours of the city (also including meals, admission to sights, or encounter with pope) from L30,000 for a simple tour to L85,000 for the strolling accordions. **American Express**, p. di Spagna, 38 (tel. 676 41), offers a series of bus and walking tours daily except Sundays and holidays, at 9:30am and 2:30pm in summer and three or four times a week in winter, (L40,000-50,000, including various admission fees to museums and sights). Open Mon.-Fri. 9am-5:30pm, Sat. 9am-12:30pm. **ATAC** also offers a no-frills quickie tour (see under Buses and Trams).

Boat Tours Servizio di Navigazione Fluviale, or Aquabus (tel. 686 90 68), runs boats from the Isola Tiberina to Ponte Duca D'Aosta, with a stop at Ponte Cavour, from May through August. (L1500; a weekly pass is L6000 and monthly is L20,000.) Boarding points run down the side of the river with schedules posted. The boats run Tues.-Sun. approximately every 25 minutes. Service ends at midnight, and in September at 8pm. Bicycles are allowed on the boats.

Addresses in Rome are intriguing to say the least. In some older parts of the city, street numbers go progressively down one side of the street and back up the other, unlike in the U.S., where odd and even numbers advance together. This means that at one end of a street you may find #1 and number #100 opposite each other, with #50 and #51 anchoring the other end. Also unlike in the U.S., streets are numbered by openings onto the street rather than by lot. Thus #25 may be a *palazzo* two blocks long, while the next block may hold fifteen numbers. Don't put too much stock in gauging where a number is by deduction; call first for directions.

August in Rome

Rome shuts down at the beginning of August, and by *Ferragosto* (Aug. 15), the big Italian summer holiday, you'll be hard-pressed to find a single Roman in the city. Though the museums and sights remain open, most offices and restaurants close down completely. You won't starve during this period; a humanitarian law bars bread shops from closing down for more than one day at a time. *La Reppublica* and *Il Messaggero* newspapers each publish daily lists of open pharmacies, *alimentari*, and other essential services and businesses. Closed pharmacies usually display a list of open ones.

Useful Publications

The tourist office has free maps and brochures on Rome and its environs. The brochure **Here's Rome** is an invaluable source of information containing important phone numbers, accommodations listings, sample tourist itineraries and shopping and entertainment options. In 1992 it was unavailable, but ask, and make sure you get an up-to-date copy; ask also for **Romamor**, a brief introduction to the city. The gazeteer **Carnet di Roma** lists the month's museum exhibits, concerts and festivals in the region (in Italian and in English). The **Tourist's Yellow Pages** are also free and available at the tourist office. **Un Ospite a Roma (A Guest in Rome)** is a free pamphlet, updated weekly, listing the events, exhibits, and concerts of the week as well as vital phone numbers for museums, galleries, and emergency services. It's unavailable at the tourist office, but you can ask for it at better hotels.

Metropolitan is a new, free, English-language magazine containing all kinds of articles, reviews, helpful advice, entertainment listings, and a classified ads section. You can even put your own classified ad in for free. The magazine is available at the various English-language bookstores and the newsstand at 11 Largo Torre Argentina. **Wanted in Rome**, a highly informative biweekly English-language newsletter (published Sept.-June), contains job and housing classifieds, a calendar of cultural events, and short articles on topics of interest to English speakers (available at English-language bookstores and English-speaking institutions for L1000). **The Informer** is an all-Italy expatriate magazine on sale the Lion bookstore and the Economy Book and Video Center. The Economy Book and Video Center, via Torino, 136 (tel. 474 68 77) also publishes a bimonthly **Happenings** which lists cultural events and discussions available for English speakers; it is available in English bookstores. *This Week in Rome,* available at newsstands (L4500), is a flashy, tourist-targeted listing in English of events of interest.

Rome's circuitous streets make a map an indispensable and noisome reality for the traveler. The **Tourist Office,** via Parigi, 5, and **American Express,** piazza di Spagna, both offer excellent street maps at no charge. The Lozzi *Roma Metro-Bus* office has a good map of the city plus a booklet containing all Metro, bus, and tram routes; it is also available at newsstands and bookstores (L5000). If you plan to ride buses much, this map is invaluable—though you can get a similar one for L1000 at the ATAC booth at Termini (see Buses and Trams, below). For a thoroughly indexed street atlas, try **Rome A to Z** (sold with **Lazio A to Z**, L14,000) which includes a pocket guide of 20 bike itineraries around Rome.

Layout of Rome

In his *Early History of Rome*, Livy concluded that "the layout of Rome is more like a squatter's settlement that a properly planned city." Two thousand years of city-planning later, Rome is still a splendid, unnavigable sea of one-way streets, dead-ends, clandestine *piazze*, incongruous monuments, and incurable traffic. Getting lost is as inevitable as death and taxes.

No longer defined by the Seven Hills, modern Rome sprawls over a large area between the hills of the **Castelli Romani** and the beach at **Ostia**. The central sights, however, lie within a much smaller compass. Rome was, until recently, a city built to be covered on foot. From Termini, the central locus and arrival point for most visitors to Rome, **Città Universitaria** and the student area of **San Lorenzo** are to the east, while most of the major tourist sights slope down between the hills to the west toward the

Tiber. **Via Nazionale** is the central artery connecting Termini with the city center. At its base, via Nazionale joins the immense **piazza Venezia**, crowned by the conspicuous white marble pile of the **Victor Emanuele Monument**. From piazza Venezia, via dei Fori Imperiale leads southeast to the **Forum** and **Colosseum;** Corso Vittorio Emanuele heads west into the historic districts that fill the bend in the Tiber; the **via del Corso**, the backbone of the city, stretches straight north to the **piazza del Popolo** and the **Spanish Steps**.

The fourteen districts of Rome (called *rioni*), distinct in appearance and character, emerge from the snarl of traffic that fills these boulevards. To the north, the enormous **Villa Borghese** and **Pincio** parks border the piazza del Popolo, the high-class shopping streets centering round the **Spanish Steps**, and the (now very faded) glamour of the **via Veneto**. South of here, between via Tritone and via Nazionale, **piazza Barberini** points the way to the stunningly restored **Trevi Fountain**. The **Forum** and **Colosseum** lead out of the city towards the ruins of the **Circus Maximus**, the **Appian Way** and the **Catacombs**. From piazza Venezia to the west, the **Largo Argentina** marks the start of the Corso Vittorio Emanuele, which leads into the medieval and Renaissance tangle of alleys, towers, churches, and fountains around the **Pantheon** and **piazza Navona** (north of the street) and **Campo dei Fiori** and **piazza Farnese** (between via Giulia and the river), before crossing the Tiber to the overwhelming prospect of **Castel Sant'Angelo** and the **Vatican City**. South of the Vatican (but more accessible from the other bank than from St. Peter's) is the medieval **Trastevere** quarter, home to countless *trattorie* and the best streets for wandering in the city. Back across the river, the historic **Tiber Island** and **Jewish Ghetto** lie in ruinous calm behind the Victor Emanuele Monument. Bounding the historic city at the south is the peaceful **Aventine Hill,** crowned with gardens and monasteries, and the delicious **Testaccio** district.

Transportation

The most disconcerting thing about rush hour in Rome is that it lasts 24 hours a day. Droves of demon mopeds buzz through red lights and over sidewalks. When fired into a *piazza,* that cute little Fiat 500 transforms itself into a noisy left-armed bullet. A jaunt to the Colosseum at 3am to avoid the crowds will prove just how populated and active the city really is. On the up side, with so many Romans darting about, public transportation has developed to meet the demands. Bus and train service is surprisingly extensive, and the city is doing its best to lengthen Metro lines, despite delays caused by workmen uncovering ancient ruins with each shovelful. Be attentive while taking public transportation, however. Many well-dressed "undercover" pickpockets can razor-blade a leather bag in seconds without you feeling a thing.

Buses and Trams

Rome's bus system is an extensive, surprisingly efficient and comfortable means of getting through the city. Though the network of routes may seem daunting at first, the **ATAC** intra-city bus company (tel. 46 95 or 469 51) has ubiquitous booths and a friendly staff who can help you find your way. At the Termini ATAC booth (piazza dei Cinquecento, English spoken) you can buy a detailed map of bus routes (L1000), which you'll need unless you've already bought Lozzi's city map. Each bus stop (*fermata*) is marked by yellow signs listing all routes that stop there, key streets on those routes, and routes with nighttime service (*servizio notturno*). Nighttime routes are indicated by black shields (on the newer signs) or at the bottom of the older, painted signs; they are often different from daytime routes of the same number, and far less frequent. The abbreviation *Pass.* on the signs lists the times the bus will pass that stop during the night. You must signal a nighttime bus to stop, even if you are standing right under its sign. Routes that do not have *servizio notturno* generally stop running at midnight.

Tickets for the bus cost L800. Stamp the ticket in the orange machine at the back of the bus as you board (you may only board a bus from the front or back doors, not from the middle); the ticket is then good for any number of transfers over the next ninety minutes. If you exceed ninety minutes during your last ride, stamp the other end of the ticket to prove that it was still valid when you boarded. Bus tickets are available at newsstands, *tabacchi*, and kiosks throughout the city. The **B.I.G.** daily ticket is valid for 24hrs. on the Metro and buses (L2800). A weekly bus pass (*biglietto settimanale*) is valid for eight nights and days but not for the Metro (L10,000, sold at Piazza dei Cinquecento). A monthly pass is also available (see under Subway). Trams use the same tickets as buses. You are on your honor to stamp your ticket, and although bus inspectors used to be rare, they are becoming more frequent, often boarding a bus in threesomes between stops, eliminating all hope of escape. There is a strict L50,000 fine if you are caught without a ticket. If you don't have the cash on you, the inspectors will take you to a police station until you can arrange to pay it. Playing dumb tourist doesn't help either. Buy a number of tickets during the day, as they are difficult to come by at night. (Ticket salesmen ride the *servizio notturno* buses and will sell you a ticket on board. This service is available only after midnight.) The following is a list of useful bus routes.

> **13** (Tram) S. Giovanni in Laterano, Colosseo, Porta S. Paolo, viale Trastevere. **19** (Tram) S. Lorenzo area, Villa Borghese, via Ottaviano and p. Risorgimento. **30** (Tram) Porta S. Paolo, Colosseo, S. Lorenzo area, Villa Borghese. **23** S. Paolo Basilica, Porta S. Paolo, Lungotevere to Vatican. From Vatican past Trastevere. **27** Testaccio, Colosseo, via Cavour, Termini. **46** Vatican, Corso Vittorio Emanuele II, Largo Argentina, piazza Venezia. **56** and **60** Trastevere, Largo Argentina, piazza Barberini, via Veneto **57** Air Terminal Ostiense, via Nazionale, Termini. **62** via XX Settembre, Largo del Tritone, piazza Venezia, Corso V.E. II, Vatican. **64** Termini-Vatican (the wallet eater—watch out for pickpockets). **75** Trastevere-Termini. **81** Colosseo-Vatican. **95** Air Terminal Ostiense, p. Venezia, via Veneto. **118** Colosseo, Baths of Caracalla, Catacombs of S. Sebastiano, via Appia. **119** Pantheon, piazza di Spagna, piazza del Popolo. **170** Termini-Trastevere. **492** Tiburtina, Termini, piazza Venezia, Vatican.

Night buses: be careful at night; bus numbers and routes change, and you must signal a night bus to stop for you. Women waiting at bus stops often endure relentless ride offers and heckling.

> **20N** Porta S. Paolo (Air Terminal), Colosseo, S. Maria Maggiore, Termini. **30N** piazza del Risorgimento, viale Trastevere, Porta S. Paolo, Colosseo, Villa Borghese. **45N** piazza della Rovere (Vatican), Largo Argentina, piazza Venezia, piazza San Silvestro. **60N** Via Veneto-Trastevere. **78N** Vatican-Termini.

ATAC also offers a no-frills, three-hour circuit of the city, leaving from p. dei Cinquecento (daily at 4pm, Oct.-March Sat.-Sun. and holidays at 2:30pm; L6000). They provide a map and some explanation in Italian and quasi-English, whirling you around the city for a comprehensive peek. Otherwise, take plain ole bus #119 for an orienting glance at some of the city's more visible monuments. **ACOTRAL**, bus service between Rome and the province of **Lazio**, (tel. 591 55 51), has moved its departure points outside of the city proper to facilitate traffic; you need to take the subway to an outlying area and catch the bus from there. Take **Anagnina** (last stop on Linea A Metro) for Frascati and the Colli Albani: **Rebibbia** (last stop on Linea B Metro) for Tivoli and Subiaco: **Lepanto** (last stop on Linea A before Ottaviano) for Cerveteri, Tarquinia, Bracciano, Lago Vico, and Civitavecchia. *Let's Go* lists specific transportation information in the Daytrips section. For information, it may be easier to call CTS or any travel agent where English is spoken.

Subway

The two lines of the subway (*Metropolitana*) intersect in the basement of Termini and can be reached by the stairway inside the station. Entrances to all stations are marked on the street by a white "M" on a red square. Linea A runs from Ottaviano, near the Vatican, through p. di Spagna, p. Barberini, p. della Repubblica, and Termini, before heading to Anagnina and intervening stops in the southeastern suburbs of the city. Linea B runs from Rebibbia in the northeastern suburbs, through the university area around p. Bologna, to Termini, the Colosseum, Piramide (change here for the train to Fiumicino), and Magliana (change here for trains to Ostia and the beach) before terminating at Laurentina in EUR. The subway is fairly safe, but guard your valuables.

The majority of Rome's sights are a trek from the nearest subway stop, but for covering large distances fast, the subway beats the bus any day. (Linea A daily 5:30am-11:30pm; Linea B Sun.-Fri. 5:30am-9pm; Sat. and holidays 5:30am-11:30pm.) Tickets are L700 and can be bought in newstands, *tabacchi* or at coin-operated machines in the stations (there are bill-changers in the station but they are often broken). It is impossible to board the subway without a ticket. Trains to Ostia and the Lido beach are not part of the subway (buy an extra L700 ticket at the station of origin or at Magliana, where you change trains).

If you will be in Rome for more than a couple of weeks, consider purchasing the *abbonamente mensile*, which allows unlimited rides on one bus line (L18,000), one bus line and both subway lines (L22,000), or all bus lines and no subway lines (L22,000), and are good for a calendar month starting on the first of the month. Each pass is known as a *tessera* and is available wherever bus and subway tickets are sold. Theoretically, student *tessere* (about half price) are available only to Italian students, but a request phrased in Italian will usually procure one. However, many bus inspectors may well make you show an official Italian student ID and charge you the L50,000 fine for not having one.

Taxis

Taxis are a viable but expensive option. On call 24 hrs., they can be flagged down in the streets. Taxi stands are at piazza Sonnino in Trastevere (at the end of viale Trastevere before the bridge), at piazza Venezia, piazza della Repubblica and at piazza di Popolo. Make sure your taxi has a meter; then at least you'll know that you're being robbed legally. Official rates are L3000 for the first 660m or first minute, then L266 every 330m or minute. Night surcharge L3000; Sunday surcharge L1000. Each suitcase L500 (small parcels and lap dogs excepted). Radio taxis (tel. 35 70 or 66 45 or 49 94 or 881 77). Taxis from and to the airport cost around L70,000.

Car

We hesitate to comment on the sanity of any traveler wishing to get around Rome by car. But if the aggression of other drivers, the weaving antics of moped maniacs, and the suicide squads of pedestrians don't totally unnerve you, keeping a car in the city does guarantee a high-adrenalin trip. It also assures a high-cost one. Parking is expensive and difficult to find, and if you don't keep your eyes peeled for the little signs, you may drive into a car-free zone and incur a fine. Gas *(benzina)* costs four times as much in Italy as in the U.S. (approximately L1500-1550 per liter). **FINA** gas stations will often accept Visa cards as payment; Exxon, Shell, and Mobil will take AmEx. Rental charges are another expense: L430,000-500,000 per week with unlimited mileage. Nonresidents of Italy are eligible for discounts of up to 60%, usually only by reserving from home. Most rates do not include insurance, which is usually about L15,000 per day. Moreover, all agencies require either a credit card or a minimum deposit of L200,000 in cash. You must be over 21 with a valid international driver's license to rent. An added financial hazard awaits outside the city; if you plan to drive cross-country on major *autostrade,* make sure to budget for extremely expensive tolls. While cruising the *autostrade,* try to buy gas off the highway in smaller towns, although be aware that smaller stations may not take credit cards. The following agencies will provide more information.

TCI (Touring Club Italiano), via Marsala, 14, inside the shopping arcade. Bookshop selling maps, guides, and books (Italian) to every region of Italy. Open Mon.-Fri. 9am-1pm, 4-7pm.

ACITOUR (the travel agency run by ACI), via Marsala, 14, inside the shopping arcade. Can make reservations and help with travel plans. Operates a money change (no commission). Open Mon.-Fri. 9am-1pm and 2-6pm. Exchange open Mon.-Fri. 9am-1pm and 3-5pm.

If you're still game to rent, Avis, Hertz, Maggiore, and Europcar all operate booths on the east side of Termini. You can make arrangements at these booths or at each firm's headquarters in the city, in phone or in person. By calling the central reservation numbers you can arrange to rent a car in Rome or in any part of Italy. All firms will let you drop your rental car off in any other Italian city where they have an office. English is spoken at all locations.

MAGGIORE Reservations (Rome) tel. 854 16 20. They have a special **Junior Rate** (ages 21-26): L88,000 per day for 1-3 days and even lower rates for weekly or long-term rentals. For this information, call the general information office (tel. 854 69 56). Otherwise, open Mon.-Fri. 8:30am-6:30pm; Main Office via Po 8A (tel. 854 86 98 or 884 01 37), Open Mon.-Fri. 8:30am-6:30pm; Termini (tel. 48 37 15). Open Mon.-Sat. 7am-8pm; Air Terminal Ostiense (tel. 574 52 60); Toll-free National Number (1678) 670 67. Open Mon.-Fri. 8:30am-6:30pm.

AVIS Termini (tel. 470 12 19). Open Mon.-Sat. 7am-8pm, Sun. 8am-1pm; Main office p. Esquilino 1C (tel. 470 12 16). Open Mon.-Fri. 9am-130pm, 2:30-6pm; Fiumicino office (tel. 60 15 51). Open 7:30am-11pm.

HERTZ Termini (tel. 474 64 05); Main Office, via Veneto, 156, (tel. 321 68 31). In the underground parking garage, accessible from the top of via Veneto or from the p. di Spagna Metro stop. Open Mon.-Sat. 7am-8pm, Sun. 8am-1pm; Fiumicino (tel. 60 14 48); Toll-free National Number (1678) 220 99.

EUROPCAR Reservations (Rome) tel. 52 08 12 00. Open Mon.-Sat. 9am-6pm; Termini (tel. 488 28 54). Open Mon.-Sat. 7am-8pm; Air Terminal Ostiense (tel. 574 57 85). Open Mon.-Fri. 8am-8pm; Sat. 8am-1pm; Fiumicino (tel. 60 18 79 or 60 19 77). Open 7am-11pm.; Toll-free National Number (1678) 680 88; Open 9am-6pm.

COMPANY SERVICE Main Office, via Padova, 90A (tel. 427 28 55); Fiumicino (tel. 650 71 62); National Reservations Number (0522) 79 25 41.

Bicycles and Mopeds

Rome's many hills, cobblestone streets, dense traffic, and lunatic drivers make the city less than ideal for bikes and mopeds. In some areas, however, bikes can be a perfect way to explore the city; bike rides around Rome's parks are a welcome relief from a city of stone. There is a nine-mile bike path along the Tiber, but though Rome is trying to clean it up, it still tends to be a bit dirty and stinky. You can take your bike on the *Aquabus* to get to a cleaner path further from the center. A bike ride down the Appian Way may be the best way to see the many monuments, as well as the long stretches of countryside between them. Bicycles generally cost around L4000 an hour or about L10,000-15,000 per day, but the length of that "day" varies according to the shop's closing time. In summer, try the unmarked stands at p. di San Lorenzo at via del Corso or via di Pontifici at via del Corso, both near p. di Spagna (open 10am-1am); at p. Sidney Sonnino, off viale Trastevere; or at the Metro Spagna exit at vicolo Bottino (open 9am-11pm). Rates average around L5000 per hr. While Rome is definitely not the place to take your first moped or scooter ride, moped aficionados can rent mopeds and scooters for between L40,000 and L55,000 a day. You need to be at least 16 years old, but you don't need a driver's license. Or, take your pick of these zanily-titled establishments. **Practice safe cycling and wear a helmet.**

I Bike Rome, via Veneto, 156 (tel. 322 52 40), which rents from the Villa Borghese's underground parking garage. Bikes run L4000 an hour, L10,000 per day, or L30,000 per week; a Hertz card will get you a 50% discount. Open Mon.-Sat. 9am-1pm and 4-8pm, Sun. 9am-8pm.

Bicimania, piazza Sonnino, where viale Trastevere crosses the bridge. (tel. 780 77 55). Mountain bikes are L5000 an hour, L18,000 per day. Also rents tandem bikes. Open 9am-midnight.

St. Peter Rent, via di Porto Castello, 43 (tel. 687 49 09). Open Mon.-Sat. 9am-1:30pm and 3:30-9:30pm.

Scooters for Rent, via della Purificazione, 84 (tel. 488 54 85). Open 9am-7:30pm.

Scoot-a-long, via Cavour 302 (tel. 678 02 06) Open Mon.-Sat. 9am-7pm, Sun. 10am-2pm and 4-7pm.

Practical Information

Tourist Offices

Tourist Office EPT, in the Termini Station (tel. 487 12 70 or 482 40 78), between tracks #2 and 3. Lines can be horrendous. Open 8:15am-7:15pm. **Central Office**, via Parigi, 5 (tel. 488 37 48 or 488 18 51). Walk from the station diagonally to the left across p. dei Cinquecento (filled with buses) and go straight across p. della Repubblica. Via Parigi starts on the other side of the basilica, at the Grand Hotel. Open Mon.-Sat. 8:15am-7:15pm. **Fiumicino Office**, outside Customs (tel. 601 12 55). At any office, pick up a map and copies of *Romamor* and *Carnet di Roma e della Sua Provincia*. If you will be traveling in the region around Rome, also ask for *Alberghi di Roma e Provincia*, which lists all hotels and *pensioni* registered with the EPT. All these offices will help you find a room; they advise arriving in Rome early in the morning before hotels book up for the night.

ENIT, via Marghera 2 (tel. 4971282); as you exit the tracks at Termini, head to your right—turn right onto via Marsala, and take your first left onto via Marghera; it's 2 blocks down on the left, across the street from the right-hand end of the shopping arcade. Some information on Rome, but mostly brochures and hotel listings for the rest of Lazio and the rest of Italy's provinces and major cities. Open Mon.-Fri. 9am-1pm, Wed. also 4-6pm.

Budget Travel Organizations

Budget Travel Centro Turistico Studentesco (CTS), via Genova, 16 (tel. 467 92 79), off via Nazionale, about halfway between p. della Repubblica and p. Venezia. Branch offices at Termini (at track #22, tel. 467 92 54), at via Appia Nuova, 434 (tel. 78 80 84 49), at Corso Vittorio Emanuele II, 297 (tel. 687 26 72) and at Air Terminal Ostiense (tel. 574 79 50) are open same hours as main office (see below). ISC and YIEE cards L15,000 each. (Bring ID photo and proof of student status). *Carta Verde,* available for those under 26, for a year of 30% discounts on trains within or originating in Italy, L40,000. Discount plane, train, boat and bus reservations and tickets, plus a free map, and currency exchange. Accommodations service, including out-of-town reservations. Bulletin boards with notices for rides, companionship, special services, etc. Lines can be aggravatingly slow; if information is all you need, it's better to phone (information tel. 467 92 71). Excellent English spoken at all locations. Main office open Mon.-Fri. 9am-1pm and 4-7pm, Sat. 9-1pm. Another office at via degli Ausoni, 5 (tel. 445 01 41) open Mon.-Fri. 9:30am-7pm, Sat. 9:30am-1pm.

Enjoy Rome, via Varese 39 (tel. 445 18 43), one block east of Termini station, perpendicular to via Milazzo. A brand new tourist office with friendly, creative, English-speaking employees and a multitude of services and ideas. Hotel reservations for Rome and all of Italy. They also help with all kinds of alternative accommodations, including university accommodations, religious institutions, and short- and long-term apartments. They arrange cycling tours throughout the city and offer a discount card valid at various shops, rental agencies, language schools, and nightclubs. The lines couldn't be worse than at CTS and the employees are less harried. Open Mon.-Sat. 9am-1pm and 3-5pm.

Compagnia Italiana di Turismo (CIT), a national travel agency that can book and provide information on discount train tickets and tours. In Termini (tel. 448 16 78), p. della Repubblica, 64 (tel. 479 43 49), via Veneto, 14 (481 43 82), Air Terminal Ostiense (tel. 574 57 44); general information tel. 479 41. All offices open Mon.-Fri. 9am-1pm and 2:30-6pm.

Italian Youth Hostels Association (Associazione Italiana Alberghi per la Gioventu), HI/ IYHF, via Cavour 44 (tel. 487 11 52). Plenty of advice and a list of hostels throughout Italy. IYHA cards L30,000. Open Mon.-Thurs. 7:30am-5pm, Fri. 7:30am-3pm. **Transalpino**, p. Esquilino, 9Z (tel. 487 08 70). 40-50% youth discounts on international train tickets. Ferry information as well. Open Mon.-Fri. 9am-6:30pm, Sat. 9am-1pm. Also a booth in **Termini**, at track #22 (tel. 488 05 36), open Mon.-Sat. 8am-8:30pm; in summer also Sun. 8:30am-5:30pm.

Embassies

All embassies answer the phone 24 hrs. in case of emergency.

United States. via Veneto, 119A (tel. 467 41). Passport and consular services open Mon.-Fri. 8:30am-1pm and 2-4pm. Report stolen passports here; new passports can be issued in about an hour, for a $65 fee ($40 for minors). Bring a photo ID (or if all yours have been stolen, bring another U.S. citizen with a valid passport to vouch for you). A passport issued overseas is good for one year, and may be renewed for ten years (once back in the states) at no cost. They have a comprehensive list of American groups, from an American choir to the Republican club.

Canada. Consulate, via Zara, 30 (tel. 440 29 91 or 40 30 28) Consular and passport services here open 9-10am and 1:30- 2:30pm. Embassy, via G.B. De Rossi, 27 (tel. 8415341).

U.K. via XX Settembre 80A (tel. 482 55 51). Consular and passport services Mon.-Fri. 9:30am-12:30pm and 2-4pm; July 13-Aug. 28 open Mon.-Fri. 8am-1pm.

Australia. via Alessandria, 215. (tel. 85 27 21). Consular and passport services Mon.-Thurs. 9am-noon and 1-4pm, Fri. 9am-noon.

New Zealand. via Zara, 28 (tel. 440 29 28). Consular and passport services Mon.-Fri. 8:30am-12:45pm and 1:45-5pm.

Money

When you get to the train station, there are many *cambi*, but all with low rates and high commissions. The one by the train information booth is open 8am-8pm daily; if you arrive before or after those hours, there are automatic tellers that will change American dollars into *lire* at the current bank rate (always higher than the traveler's check rate). We recommend buying $US50 in *lire* ahead of time to save you trouble in the train station. Count your money discreetly inside the *cambio*, never out on the street, and make sure you are not followed after changing money. Beware of street money-changers, who will give you counterfeit money. Large banks like **Banco d'Italia** or **Banco Nazionale del Lavoro** have offices all around the city, or try the locations listed below.

Frama, via Torino, 21B, first left on via Nazionale (tel. 474 68 70 or 481 76 32); or Corso Vittorio Emanuele II, 106 (tel. 68 30 84 06 or 686 85 84). No commission. Open Mon.-Fri. 8:30am-1:30pm and 3-5pm, Sat. 9am-1pm.

Numismatica Internazionale, p. dei Cinquecento, 57/58 (tel. 488 50 05), in the arcade on the left side of the piazza as you face away from the station; 1.5% commission. Open Mon.-Sat. 7am-7pm.

ACITOUR, via Marsala, 14, inside the shopping arcade (no commission). Open Mon.-Fri. 9am-1pm and 3-5pm.

Thomas Cook, piazza Barberini, 21A (tel. 482 80 82) and via di Conciliazione, 23/25 (tel. 68 30 04 35). No charge for Thomas Cook traveler's checks, 2.5% commission on all others. Open Mon.-Sat. 8:30am-6pm, Sun. 9am-2pm.

Try to change enough money to last you through the weekend, but if you're out of cash by **Sunday**, try Thomas Cook, hotel desks, or the souvenir shops around the Vatican, though the rates will not be the best. Or use the automated tellers which give you Italian for American bills. Machines besides the one in Termini are located at via Marsala, 4; via del Corso, 230 and 283; via in Aquiro (between p. di Montecitorio and the Pantheon); via degli Uffici del Vicario, 78; p. San Silvestro; via di Conciliazione (leading to St. Peter's); via Veneto 7, 74 and 115 and elsewhere in the city center. Keep a $20 bill on you for emergency change at night.

American Express, p. di Spagna, 38 (tel. 676 41; lost or stolen cards toll-free 24hrs. 167 86 40 46; lost or stolen traveler's checks toll-free 24hrs. 167 87 20 00). Chaotic at times, but fairly efficient, and perfect English spoken. You'll make friends with Mary from Skokie while you wait on line; comforting for those who are homesick or new to the city.Mail held for free for 30 days. Mail can be forwarded to another address by surface mail for a L7000 fee on arrival, or by airmail with prepaid postage. The postal code for the office is 00187. Messages can be left in the office in a stamped envelope for L2000. There's no need to change checks here, as you will find the same rates and shorter lines at any of the small *cambi* all over the city. You can, however, count your money in the open here without fear of being robbed (be careful of being followed once you leave, nonetheless). Excellent maps of Rome are free for the asking. Open Mon.-Fri. 9am-5:30pm, Sat. 9am-12:30pm.

To **wire money,** try Western Union (tel. 654 76 78; in the U.S. (800) 325 6000; or use AT&T operator to call the 800 number from Italy). Money transfers usually take 24 hrs., and can be picked up at For You Travel Agency, p. Navona, 78 (tel. 686 98 01 or 686 13 17). Open Mon.-Fri. 9am-1pm and 2-6pm, Sat. 9am-12:30pm.

English Bookstores, Libraries, and Churches

Bookstores

Economy Book and Video Center, via Torino, 136 (tel. 474 68 77), off via Nazionale. Italy's largest selection of English language books, new and used, as well as books on tape. Friendly management also rents videos, buys books, and gives free maps. Open June-Sept. Mon.-Fri. 9:30am-7:30pm, Sat. 9:30am-1:30pm; Oct.-May Mon. 3-7:30pm, Tues.-Sat. 9:30am-7:30pm.

Anglo-American Bookshop, via della Vite, 57 (tel. 679 52 52). Steps from p. di Spagna. An astonishing array of titles, including academic works, books on the history and art of Italy, guidebooks to Rome and Italy, and paperback fiction. Open Mon. 4-8pm, Tues.-Sat. 9am-1pm and 4-8pm. In winter, afternoon hours are 3:30-7:30pm.

The Lion Bookshop, via del Babuino, 181 (tel. 322 58 37), between Spanish Steps and p. di Popolo. For the literature lover and Anglophile in you. Community bulletin board here as well. Open Mon.-Fri. 9:30am-1:30pm and 3:30-7:30pm, Sat. 9:30am-1:30pm; Sept.-May Mon. 3:30-7:30pm, Tues.-Sat. 9:30am-1:30pm and 3:30-7:30pm.

Open Door Bookshop, via della Lungaretta, 25 (tel. 271 69 00). A tiny shop crammed with paperbacks of all languages, and an amiable proprietor who may let you use his fax machine if you ask nice. Also rents videos. Open Mon. 4-8:30pm, Tues.-Sat. 9:30am-1:30pm and 4-8:30pm.

Corner Bookshop, via del Moro, 48, Trastevere (tel. 583 69 42). Open Mon. 4-7pm, Tues.-Sat. 10am-1pm and 4-7pm.

Esedra International Bookstore, via Torino, 95 (tel. 488 14 73), carries English and Italian books. Open Mon.-Fri. 9am-7:30pm, Sat. 9am-1pm.

All the stores listed above carry the *Let's Go* series, proof positive of their high quality. **Viale di Termini**, connecting Termini with p. della Repubblica, is lined with outdoor booksellers who often sell dirt-cheap used English paperbacks. **Via di Conciliazione**, the broad avenue leading to St. Peter's, has several bookstores selling English-language histories and guidebooks to Rome, as well as devotional materials. **Rare books and prints** (good for browsing, and cheaper than you might think) are sold in the outdoor market at piazza Borghese, south of the Mausoleum of Augustus, off via di Ripetta (open daily).

English Libraries

USIS (United States Information Service), referred to as the American Library or Bibliotheca Americana, via Veneto, 119A (tel. 46 74 24 81). Periodicals and reference material on American political and social affairs (mainly a resource for Italians to learn about the U.S.). Open Mon.-Fri. 1:30-5:30pm, Wed. 1:30-7pm.

British Council Library, via Quattro Fontane, 20 (tel. 482 66 41), between p. Barberini and via Nazionale. A font of fiction. Films and lectures in the winter. Borrowing privileges with membership (L25,000 for 1 yr.). Open early Sept.-early July Mon.-Fri. 10am-1pm and 2-6pm, Sat. 10am-1pm.

Centro Studi Americani, via Michelangelo Caetani, 32 (tel. 654 16 13), off p. Mattei in a large *palazzo* on the second floor. Borrowing allowed with deposit. June 27-July 16 Mon. and Wed. 10am-6pm, Tues., Thurs., and Fri. 8:30am-2:30pm; Sept.-June 26 Mon., Tues., Thurs., Fri. 9:30am-5pm, Wed. 3-7pm.

Academies and Cultural Institutions

American Academy in Rome, via Angelo Masina, 5 (tel. 584 61). Library open to students with a letter of introduction from an American professor responsible for their work. Occasional exhibits open to the public. **British School at Rome**, Via Antonio Gramsci, 61 (tel. 321 34 54). Library open to British students with a letter, or occasionally on application in person. Exhibits open to the public.

English Language Churches and Confessionals

St. Paul's Church (Episcopalian), via Napoli, 58, at via Nazionale. (tel. 488 33 39). Sunday Eucharist, 8:30am; sung Eucharist, 10:30am.

All Saints Anglican, via del Babuino, 153 (tel. 679 43 57). Sunday Communion, 8:30am; sung Eucharist, 10:30am; 1st Sunday of the month, sung Matins, 10:30; Eucharist 11:30.

Rome Baptist Church, piazza di S. Lorenzo in Lucrina, 35 (tel. 687 66 52). Sunday service 10am; Bible study 11am.

Ponte Sant'Angelo Methodist Church, piazza Ponte Sant'Angelo, via Banco di Santo Spirito, 3 (tel. 686 83 14). Sundays service 10:30am; communion 1st Sunday of the month.

St. Andrew's Church (Presbyterian), via XX Settembre, 7 (tel. 482 76 27). Sundays at 11am.

Roman Catholic Church of San Silvestro, piazza San Silvestro, 1 (tel. 679 77 75). Sundays and Holy Days mass at 10am and 5pm. Weekdays mass at noon.

Church of Santa Susanna, masses held in Sant'Agnese in Agone, piazza Navona (tel. 482 75 10). Sundays and Holy Days, 9am, 10:30am, and noon. Weekdays at 6pm. Confessions 5-6pm Saturdays.

St. Patrick's Church, via Boncampagni, 31 (tel. 46 57 16). Sundays and Holy Days at 10am.

English Language Confessionals: In St. Peter's, Sta. Maria Maggiore, S. Giovanni in Laterano, S. Paolo fuori le Mure, the Gésu, Sta. Maria sopra Minerva, Sant'Anselmo, Sant'Ignazio, and Sta. Sabina.

Medical and Emergency Services

Upstairs at the U.S. embassy (see address above) is the **American Citizens Services** (tel. 467 41). Contact them in any emergency. They will provide a list of English-speaking doctors and, if you are in the hospital, they will come visit you. If you have been arrested, contact them for a list of English-speaking lawyers (the embassy will visit you in prison, too). In extreme emergencies they will loan you money. The service also houses a treasure-trove of information, especially for those in Rome for a long stay. Lists of English-speaking doctors, schools, clubs and organizations. Advice on getting a residence permit and driver's license; you can get an absentee ballot here and even file your taxes. Open same hours as passport office.

Lost Property: **Oggetti Rinvenuti**, via Nicolo Bettoni 1 (tel. 581 60 40), Open Mon.-Sat. 9am-noon. **Ufficio Stranieri (Foreigner's Office)**, via Genova, 2 (tel. 46 86 28 76). English spoken. Report thefts here. Open 24 hrs. **Termini**, at track #1 (tel. 47 30 66 82; open 7am-11pm.) **ATAC**, via Volturno, 65 (tel. 469 51) Open Mon.-Fri. 9am-noon; 2-5pm. Also check at your **embassy** as wallets are sometimes returned there.

Crisis Lines: **Samaritans** via San Giovanni in Laterano, 250 (tel. 70 45 44 44). Native English speakers. Call or visit their center. Open for calls and visits 1-10pm.

Late-night Pharmacy: Tel. 19 21 for recorded listings in Italian. All pharmacies post the names, addresses and hours of neighboring pharmacies and all-night pharmacies. *La Repubblica* and *Il Messaggero* newspapers publish a list of pharmacies open in Aug., and the closed pharmacies usually post a list. The following are your best bet, especially in Aug. **Farmacia Internazionale Antonucci**, p. Barberini, 49 (tel. 482 54 56 or 487 11 95) above the p. Barberini Metro stop, near the Spanish Steps. Open 24 hrs. **Farmacia Grieco**, piazza della Repubblica, 67 (tel. 488 04 10 or 48 38 61), steps from Termini. Open 24 hrs. **Farmacia Piram**, via Nazionale, 228 (tel. 488 07 54). Open 24 hrs. **Farmacia Risorgimento**, p. Risorgimento, 44 (tel. 372 46 22).

Hospitals: **Vaccinazoni**, via Galilei, 3 (near S. Giovanni in Laterano). For shots and vaccines. Open Mon.-Sat. 9am-12pm and 3:30-5:30pm. **Rome-American Hospital**, via Emilio Longoni, 69 (tel. 256 71). Private emergency and laboratory services. English-speaking physician on-call 24 hrs. The following four hospitals/clinics are open 24 hrs.: **Policlinico Umberto I**, viale di Policlinico, 255 (tel. 499 71) near the train station. Take Metro Linea B to the Policlinico stop. A free public facility. **Policlinico A. Gemelli**, largo A. Gemelli, 8 (tel. 338 69 22). A university complex farther from the town center. **Nuovo Regina Margherita**, via Emilio Morosini, 29 (one block off viale Trastevere; tel. 58 44). Walk-in first aid. **Salvator Mundi**, viale delle Mura Gianicolensi, 67/77 (tel. 558 60 41). Expensive private clinic. English-speaking doctors guaranteed.

Medical Assistance: International Medical Center, via Amendola, 7 (one block from Termini), second floor (tel. 488 23 71; nights and Sundays 488 40 51). On call 24 hrs. English spoken. Will refer you to an English-speaking doctor, make an appointment, or send one to your hotel. Each doctor's visit L105,000. Will provide prescriptions. Mobile paramedic crew on call. Open Mon.-Sat. 8am-9pm; phone lines always open.

Dental Hospital: G. Eastman, viale Regina Elena, 287 (tel. 445 01 66). Unless it's an emergency, call in the morning for an appointment in the afternoon. Check in *Wanted in Rome* or *Metropolitan* for English-speaking dentists in private practices.

Red Cross: (tel. 51 00). Ambulance service; refreshment stand. **American Red Cross,** tel. 684 0148. Offers courses in first aid, AIDS education, and CPR in their "Have Annie Will Travel" program.

Police: Ufficio Stranieri (Foreigner's Office), via Genova, 2 (tel. 46 86 28 76). English spoken. Report thefts here. Maintains a lost and found service. Open 24 hrs. **Police Headquarters,** via San Vitale, 15 (tel. 46 86). **Railway Police**, on track #1 in Termini (tel. 481 95 61 or 488 25 88).

Emergency Lines: First Aid (Pronto Soccorso) tel. 115. **Police** tel. 113. **Carabinieri** tel. 112.

AIDS

There are no restrictions on travelers with HIV or AIDS entering the country, nor is there any obligation to report an infection on arrival in the country or if you've found you have it once here. Italians are generally very sensible about medical treatment, and the medical professionals will not pry if you get tested; do double-check that your test is confidential, or even done anonymously if need be. AIDS education is becoming more prevalent throughout the country, and you will never have any problems finding condoms *(preservativi)* at any pharmacy.

AIDS tests can be performed at any **Analisi Cliniche** (a private lab which handles all sorts of tests, from allergies to pregnancy). Simply ask for the "AIDS test" or "HIV test"-there isn't an Italian word. (AIDS is pronounced Ah-eeds in Italy.) Tests can be expensive (up to L150,000). Do not try to get a test at a hospital (they'll just refer you back to the labs). Look in the Yellow Pages under *Analisi* for the private labs or refer to one of the following.

Unione Sanitaria Internazionale, via V. Orsini, 18 (in Prati, north of the Vatican; tel. 321 50 53) or via Machiavelli, 22 (Metro Linea A, p. Vittorio Emanuele stop) Open 7am-8pm.

Analisi Cliniche Luisa, via Padova, 33 (off via Nazionale; tel. 44 29 14 06). Open Mon.-Fri. 9am-noon and 4-6:30pm.

Alessandri, viale Mazzini, 33 (tel. 321 79 99 or 323 05 04). Open Mon.-Fri. 9am-noon and 4-7pm.

Cavour, via Cavour, 238 (at Metro Linea B Cavour stop; tel. 474 39 48). Open Mon.-Fri. 9am-12:30pm and 4-6pm.

Public city hospitals, the Policlinico Umberto in particular, have services for treating AIDS patients (though no special clinics).

Gynecology, STDs, and Abortion

Analisi Cliniche will perform tests for venereal disease *(malattia venerea)* as well as pregnancy tests, or you can buy home tests over the counter at pharmacies throughout the city. These labs also do pap smears and cryotherapy.

V.D. Clinic, San Gallicano, via dei Fratte di Trastevere, 52A. (tel. 58 48 31). Small inexpensive clinic run (if you can believe it) by nuns. Crowded and chaotic. Open 8-11am.

As it is a Catholic country, Italy isn't the easiest place to get an abortion. The Vatican surrendered its right to interfere in Italian politics in the Lateran Treaty of 1929, and the anti-choice movement is fairly low-key. Because it can be difficult to find a doctor who will perform an abortion, many people consult the **International Medical Center,** via Amendola, 7 (one block from Termini), 2nd floor (tel. 488 23 71; nights and Sundays 488 40 51). They are on call 24 hrs.; English spoken. They can make referrals to English speaking doctors. Open Mon.-Sat. 8am-9pm; phone lines always open.

Ospedale San Camillo in Monteverde, Circonvallazione Gianicolense, 87 in Gianicolo (tel. 587 01). Abortion on demand is not available; women must have a gynecological exam, a discussion with the doctor, and possibly even undergo counseling. A D+C (simple abortion) runs about L600,000—the procedure is sometimes covered by insurance.

Medical Vocabulary

Here are some (possibly) useful phrases that might otherwise be rather difficult to gesticulate or act out in the middle of a pharmacy:

Malattia venerea (mal-ah-TEE-ah ven-AIR-ee-ah): venereal disease **Infezione vaginale** (infetz-YO-nay vaj-een-AL-ay): vaginal infection **Bernococcio**(bear-no-CHO-cheo): lump **Esantema**(ez-an-TAY-ma): rash **Gonfiore**(gon-FEE-or-ay): swelling **Bolla** (bowl-a): blister **Vescica** (ves-CHEE-cha): bladder **Pelle**(PELL-ay): skin **Ginècologo**(geen-AY-co-log-o): gynecologist **Ho delle mestruazioni dolorose** (O del-ay mes-trew-atz-YOHN-ay dol-or-ROSE-ay): I have menstrual pains **Ho un'infezione vaginale** (O oon in-fetz-YO-nay vaj-EEN-aal-ay): I have a vaginal infection **Prendo la pillola** (pren-doh la pee-LO-la): I'm on the pill **Non ho avuto le mestruazioni per** (due) mesi (no O av-UT-o lay mes-trew-atz-YOH-nay payr DOO-ay MEZ-ay): I haven't had my period for (2) months **Sono incinta** (di 3 mese) (so-no een-CHEEN-ta dee tray MEZ-ay): I'm (3 months) pregnant

Use your **condom sense** by purchasing and using condoms (*profilattichi*, or in common parlance, *preservativi*), available over the counter at all pharmacies and in most supermarkets. A packet of 6 costs between L10,000 and L13,000. Or bring a supply of your trusted standby brand from home, helpful for use during the flight over.

Miscellaneous Services

Community Bulletin Boards: **Lion Bookshop,** via del Babuino, 181 (tel.322 58 37); **Cinema Pasquino,** vicolo del Piede in Trastevere (tel. 58 03 622); **All Saints Anglican Church,** via del Babuino, 153 (tel. 679 43 57). Also check the area around the **University** for apartment listings, English-tutoring jobs, Italian tutors, and other services.

American/Foreign Foods: **Castroni**, via Ottaviano, 59 (tel. 361 10 29). Near the Ottaviano Metro stop, about 1/4 mile from the Vatican. Also a branch on via Cola di Rienzo. Meet up with other Americans dying for Coco Puffs, Hungry Man dinners, or just a can of strawberry frosting. American and British teas, crackers, cookies, Asian condiments, and a wide assortment of freshly made baked goods, sweets, and pastries.

Outdoor Markets: Porta Portese (Sunday 6am-noon). Clothing, bric-a-brac, antiques, watches, shoes, books. Watch your wallet. **Campo dei Fiori** (until noon). Fruits and vegetables, cheese and meat. **Via Sannio** (until noon). New and used clothing and shoes. **Fontanella Borghese** (Mon.-Sat. 9am-7pm). Antique books and prints, posters, postcards, coins, silver objects.

Laundromat: No self-service, coin-operated laundromats. Wash your clothes by hand with the miracle-working *Presto* available in any *alimentari*, or pay a bundle to have your favorite pair of Sergio Valentes and your lucky Underoos dry-cleaned. **Tintoria Lavanderia "Rita,"** p. Campo dei Fiori, 38 (tel. 687 90 96). Dry cleaning and laundry service. Open Mon.-Fri. 9am-2pm and 3-7:30pm. **Lavaservice**, via Montebello, 11 (tel. 474 31 52). Northeast of Termini. L4000 per kg. Open Mon.-Fri. 8am-5pm, Sat. 8am-1pm. **Lavanderia Acqua Secco**, via Castelfidardo, 29 (tel. 494 13 45). Around the corner from Lavaservice. 3kg for L15,000. Open Mon.-Fri. 9am-7pm, Sat. 9am-1pm.

Public Baths: **Albergo Diurno,** Stazione Termini (tel. 48 48 19), underground in the station. Follow the signs for the Metro; Albergo Diurno is through the bar on the left. Open 6:40am-7:30pm. Showers (L10,000), baths (L12,000), barber, manicure and pedicure services. Sheets, towels, and soap are available. You can store your bags as you use the services (L2000 per piece per hr.).

Swimming Pools: A free list of 62 in Rome available from the tourist office. In winter, a membership fee must be paid. In summer, daily membership is available from most pools. **Piscina della Rose**, viale America, 20 (tel. 592 67 17). Take Metro Linea B to the EUR Marconi stop. Outdoor pool. L15,000 for a full day swim; after 2pm, L10,000. Open June 1-Sept. 30 9am-5:50pm.

Beaches: The beach closest to Rome is **Lido di Ostia**, 28km away. From Termini, the trip will take you about 45min. Take Metro Linea B to Magliana and switch lines for the beach (L700 for ticket to beach in addition to Metro fare, available at any Metro station, including Magliana). From Magliana, trains every 15min. 6am-10:30pm. Get off at the last stop and take the #7 bus as far as you want (it runs the length of the beach); the further you go, the cleaner and less crowded the beach. Though once notoriously polluted, Rome's beaches have been praised in recent years. For scenic beauty, however, consider the beaches or lakes of Lazio as an alternative. Shed the trappings of civilization on the **nude beach** at Capocetta. Take bus #7 to terminus, then walk 1km on the beach before you start getting naked. See our Lazio section for more details. For gay beaches, see our Entertainment: Gay Entertainment section, below.

Long-Term Stays

Finding an Apartment

Finding an apartment in Rome is downright painful. About twenty years ago, the municipal government passed all kinds of legislation in efforts to protect tenants from being evicted. Today, many landlords are reluctant to rent out their apartments for fear of "squatters" (tenants who abuse these laws in order to stay in their apartment without paying rent for years) and therefore leave their apartments empty. However, since these laws only apply to Italian citizens, many landlords are more than willing to rent to foreigners. Still, the real estate market is extremely tight, especially in the historical center, because so many families have lived in their houses for generations. The prices have also skyrocketed; expect to pay no less than L1,000,000 for a one-bedroom in the center. Cheaper areas include the Nomentana neighborhood, as well as the area around piazza Bologna and the university. Always keep in mind that utilities are inordinately expensive in Rome, and that these bills can hike up your rent by as much as 1/4. Check the English classified ads in *Wanted in Rome* and in *Metropolitan* and get a copy of *Porta Portese* for Italian advertisements. The community bulletin boards (see above) carry advertisements for roommates, and some are posted at the University. Real estate agencies can simplify your life, and they often carry the best apartments in the center, but they often charge a hefty fee (from one month's rent to a high flat fee). Still, if you're planning on staying in Rome for a long time, it might be worth looking into. Prowl around a particular neighborhood you'd like to live in and check for "for rent" *(affitare)* signs, or ask people in the neighborhood if they know of any apartments. Check with foreign university programs as well; they often rent out apartments for their students for the year, but leave them empty come summertime. Ultimately, the best way to find an apartment is through connections—network, network, network. If you know someone who heard of someone who once had a hairdresser who lived in Rome—get that person's phone number. The following are real estate agents who specialize in finding apartments for foreigners:

Edwards Real Estate Agency (tel. 861 08 71 or 861 12 62). English, French, Spanish, and Arabic spoken. Deals with apartments and villas, furnished or unfurnished.

Lucille & Co, (tel. 332 65 854, fax 332 65 850). English spoken. Similar services to above.

Welcome Home Relocation Services, (tel. 376 69 36). Bill themselves as "leaders in quality expatriate housing." They offer all kinds of housing as well as assistance in documentation and orientation.

Students who plan on attending the University of Rome should get in touch with the following, no-frills university housing program:

CIVIS International Students' Hostel, viale Ministero degli Affare Esteri, 5 (tel. 396 29 51).

Opening a Bank Account

Anyone who's ever tried merely to change a few *lire* will attest to the horrors of the Italian banking administration; employees are snippy, computers crash at the drop of a hat, and the amount of paperwork is enough to give any Greenpeace member a coronary. In order to open a bank account in Italy you must present a *Certificato di Residenza* (which you receive from your local *commune* when you register as a resident), a passport or photo ID and a *Codice Fiscale*, the equivalent of an American Social Security number which you also get from the *commune*.

Registering to Vote in the United States

To obtain an absentee ballot, contact the following organization or call the Embassy for details. Registering and voting are generally painless; you must merely fill out all your paperwork well in advance of registration deadlines or elections. **Republicans Abroad Italy**, via Archimede, 164 (tel. 328 80 29, fax 808 89 34). Open Mon.-Fri. 4-7pm. A Republican committee of U.S. citizens in Italy. You can register an absentee ballot with them even if you're not a Republican.

Life and Times

Rome in a Nutshell

c.1,000,000-70,000BC: First human settlement in Italy.

c.2000: Italic tribes settle the boot-like peninsula.

c.1200: Arrival of the belligerent but cultured Etruscans.

c.800: World's first "Club Med"—Greeks settle in southern Italy.

753: Mythical founding of Rome by Romulus and Remus.

616: Forum and Circus Maximus laid out.

509: Romans rebel against Etruscan rule, found republic.

378: "Servian Wall" built around the city.

312: Appian Way and Aqua Appia begin.

275: Romans defeat Pyrrhus, last defender of the Greeks, seizing control of the entire peninsula.

264-241: First Punic War against Carthage for control of the Mediterranean.

219: Second Punic War—Hannibal "the Elephant Man" crosses the Alps.

167: First public library built..

149-46: Third Punic War. Down goes Carthage.

106: Birth of Cicero.

100: Birth of Julius Caesar.

91-87: Social War—tribes throughout the peninsula fight for extension of Roman citizenship rights

73: Slave rebellion led by Spartacus, put down by Pompey.

60-50: Triumverate rules Rome: Caesar, Pompey, and Crassus.

48: Still in his salad days, Caesar frolics in the sands of Egypt with Cleopatra.

45: Caesar declared *imperator.*

44: Caesar skewered by Brutus.

27: Caesar's nephew Octavian founds the empire, takes the title Caesar Augustus, and initiates the *Pax Romana* era of peace throughout empire.

4 BC: Birth of Jesus in Bethlehem.

29 AD: Jesus condemned to death.

64: Great fire destroys much of Rome. Nero a suspect.

67: Martyrdom of St. Peter and St. Paul.

79: Pompeii and Herculaneum buried by Vesuvian belch.

80: Completion of Colosseum.

98-117: Emperor Trajan rules the Roman empire at its largest.

117-125: Completion of Pantheon.

247: Happy 1000th Birthday, Rome; bacchanalia in the streets.

271-276: Emperor Aurelian erects walls around the city.

284: Diocletian divides empire into East and West.

296: Lions 31, Christians 0—Diocletian initiates persecution of Christians.

315: Constantine declares Christianity the official state religion.

326: First Basilica of St. Peter built.

330: Constantine transfers capital of empire to Byzantium, renames city Constantinople (people just liked it better that way).

411: Rome taken by the Visigoths.

455: Rome sacked by the Vandals.

476: Odoacer, chieftain of the Ostrogoths, crowned king of Italy. Rome has fallen and it can't get up.

498: Rival popes brawl in the streets.

567-751: Lombards run amok in Italy.

752: Lombards threaten Rome; Pope Stephen II appeals to Pepin the Short, king of the Franks.

778: Frankish Charlemagne vanquishes last Lombard king, takes his title.

800: Charlemagne crowned Holy Roman Emperor by Pope Leo III.

852: Walls built around the Vatican.

962: Refounding of the Holy Roman Empire, when Otto I of Saxony is crowned by Pope John XII. Emperor holds power to invest clergy with their titles.

1075: Beginning of investiture conflict between church and state over power to appoint and invest clergy.

1122: Concordat of Worms settles investiture conflict, stripping emperor of power to invest.

1309: Clement V moves papacy to Avignon, a sort of Rome away from Rome. Beginning of the "Babylonian Captivity."

1378-1417: Great Schism: two popes, one in Rome and one in Avignon.

1494: Charles VIII invades Italy.

1508: Michelangelo begins Sistine Chapel ceiling.

1534: Michelangelo paints the *Last Judgement,* the final stage of his ceiling project.

1563: Council of Trent sparks Counter-Reformation.

1600: Giordano Bruno burned at the stake for heresy.

1626: Consecration of St. Peter's.

1762: Completion of Trevi Fountain.

1773: Expulsion of Jesuits from Rome.

1798: French kidnap the pope.

1806: That's all folks. Holy Roman Empire peters out.

1808: Napoleon annexes Rome to French empire.

1849-66: French rule Rome.

1870: September 20: Italian troops enter Rome.

1870: October: Rome made capital of recently united Italy.

1922: October 28/29: Mussolini leads Fascist March on Rome.

1944: June 4: Liberation of Rome.

1946: Italian Republic reestablished by national referendum.

1957: Treaty of Rome establishes the Common Market.

1959: Fellini's *La Dolce Vita* gets two thumbs up.

1960: Rome hosts the Olympic Games.

1962: Vatican II—they're back, they're bad, and they're saying Mass in English.

1965: Vatican II dissolves.

1978: Christian Democratic presidential candidate Aldo Moro murdered by Red Brigade.

1979: Abreast of politics, porn star La Cicciolina is elected to Parliament.

1981: Pope John Paul II shot and wounded in St. Peter's Square.

1984: Marriage and education secularized by new Concordat.

1991: Honk if you're over 50—50th Italian Government collapses.

1992: New president Amato elected

1993: *Let's Go: Rome* hits the stores. Unemployed, David and Kayla seek comfort in *The Joan Rivers Show* and Barney's Columbus Day Sale.

Ancient Rome

History

Rumor has it that the twins **Romulus and Remus** were left behind by a **Vestal Virgin** who had been exposed by her jealous uncle (if the Vestal Virgins broke their vow of virginity they were buried alive). Suckled by a passing she-wolf and raised by a kindly shepherd, the forgotten twins grew up to found Rome in 753 BC. Wary of sharing power, Romulus slew Remus, initiating a grand Italian tradition of ruthless and bloody politics. The new kingdom flourished under two centuries of Etruscan rule, until reckless king **Tarquinius Superbus** raped the virtuous Roman matron **Lucretia**. Lucretia committed public suicide, and her outraged family led the Roman populace in overthrowing the Tarquins in 510 BC.

Free from foreign domination, the Romans set about establishing a republic, a quasi-democracy in which land-owning patricians (and, later on, wealthy plebeians) gathered in their Senate to make laws, hear trials, and declare war. A complex system of magistracies and administrative positions (including praetors, quaestors, aediles, and tribunes) oversaw the city's growing infrastructure: under their care Rome blossomed with fora, temples, roads, bridges, and aqueducts. From its power base in the Tiber valley, the liberated city quickly began to expand, conquering its less-civilized backcountry neighbors with unflinching efficiency. But despite popular misconceptions, the early Romans were rarely needlessly cruel. They won the voluntary submission of once-independent tribes with shrewd imperialist policy: practices like gradual enfranchisement and requiring military service from their youth instead of harsh taxation allowed the "Roman" republic to spread throughout Italy. In the two and a half centuries between the expulsion of the Etruscan kings and the **Punic Wars**, Rome managed to conquer and absorb the Etruscan Empire to its north, along with the indigenous Latin, Sabine, and Umbrian tribes closer to home. The 3rd-century BC **Samnite Wars** won the city control over the entire southern peninsula, with the exception of the (increasingly nervous) Greek cities. The Greeks invited peerless **King Pyrrhus** of Epirus to defend them; while winning a series of battles against the republic, Pyrrhus invariably failed to press his advantage, assuring his eventual defeat. The term "Pyrrhic victory" forever associates Pyrrhus's name with this sort of defeat in victory's clothing. After losing to Rome at Beneventum in 275BC, Pyrrhus quit Italy, leaving the rest of the boot open to Roman dominion.

After conquering Italy, the most important battles of the republic were the three **Punic Wars,** waged against Carthage (260-146 BC) for control of important Mediterranean trade routes, as well as for territory in Spain and Sicily. During the second of these wars, the Carthiginian general **Hannibal** unexpectedly transported his army—elephants and all—up through Spain and across the Alps. Surprising a series of Roman generals as he swooped down the peninsula, Hannibal made it all the way to the walls of Rome, but failed to breach them. His campaign petered out into a cat-and-mouse game played with the Roman general **Fabius Maximus**, who eluded the overeager Carthiginian for several years until Hannibal's army, starving and exhausted, retreated home to Africa. Pressing the advantage, Cato the Censor (of *Carthago delenda est* fame) egged on his fellow Romans and retaliated in the Third Punic War by razing Carthage in 146 BC. Roman soldiers sowed Carthaginian fields with salt to prevent the city from ever thriving again. It was during the Punic Wars that Roman leaders began to envision themselves as the rulers of a pre-eminent world power. Rome would later conquer and subjugate Spain, Sicily, Sardinia, Corsica, Greece, and North Africa; their accomplished aim was to consolidate control over Mediterranean trade and shipping and match their military dominance with economic superiority.

Traditional Roman society had been austere and religious in character. Aflood in riches from its many successful conquests, Rome became a festering swamp of greed and corruption. Yeoman farmers who formed the venerated foundation of Roman agricultural society were pushed off their land by avaricious politicians and driven into slavery or starvation. Social upheaval quickly followed; by 131 BC, slave, farmer, and plebeian demands for land redistribution led to popular riots against the corrupt patrician class, culminating in the **Social War** (91-87 BC); tribes throughout the peninsula fought successfully for the extension of Roman citizenship and the many social and economic benefits accompanying it. **Sulla**, the patrician general who had led Rome's troops during the conflict, then marched his armies into Rome (an unprecedented and heretofore socially taboo move), taking control of the city in a bloody military coup: over 1600 knights and senators were executed without benefit of trial.

Sulla's strong-arm tactics set a dangerous precedent for the republic as generals once sworn to the service of the state now amassed large private armies, funded by their own huge fortunes. The century-old conflict between conservative patricians and the more liberal-minded popular party (who advocated expanding Roman citizenship, extending rights to Italian and foreign-conquered peoples, and limiting the ancient power of the Senate), exploded in a series of blood-lettings, during which the Republican government gave way to the machinations of power-hungry warlords. In 70 BC, **Spartacus,** an escaped gladiatorial slave, led an army of slaves and farmers 70,000 strong in a two-year rampage down the peninsula (Charlton Heston set a new standard for **machismo** when he played the title role in the Hollywood version of the gladiator's antics, the homoerotic classic *Spartacus*). When the dust cleared, **Pompey the Great,** a close associate of Sulla effectively took control of the city, but soon found himself in conflict with his sometime co-ruler **Julius Caesar.** Caesar, the charismatic conqueror of Gaul, finally emerged victorious, but a small faction, fearful of his growing power, assassinated him on the Ides (15th) of March in 44 BC (as spookily predicted by a **soothsayer** in Shakespeare's *Julius Caesar*). Command of the city and its provinces eluded several would-be heirs before falling to his nephew, Octavian, who consolidated and concentrated power, assumed the title of **Augustus Caesar,** and inaugurated an imperial government in 27 BC. His reign (27 BC-14 AD) is generally considered the golden age of Rome, ushering in the 200 peaceful years of the **Pax Romana** (Roman peace). Rome gained a virtual monopoly on all Mediterranean trade, while at home the city benefited from a building boom of magnificent new constructions. Poets and authors thrived, transforming the sturdy Latin language into a tool of remarkable complexity and expression.

Like the capitoline wolf it claims as its sacred symbol, Rome continued to hunt for territorial prey as long as its power remained. But within a few years of Augustus's death, the power he had amassed began to corrode. The princes of the Julio-Claudian house proved unequal to the simple task of world government, as their minds, intoxicated by power, slipped into fevers of cruelty, debauchery, and even insanity. Dour **Tiberius** (who could apparently push his thumb through a man's skull), flaky **Caligula**, inefficient **Claudius** and sadistic **Nero** drained the imperial treasury to support their increasingly decadent lifestyles. While the behavior of many of Octavian's successors pushed the limits of credulity, the Roman war machine remained oblivious. In the 1st century, what are now Germany, Britain, Palestine, Syria, and even parts of Persia fell to the stinking feet of well-trained Roman soldiers. When Nero's inanities grew intolerable, generals from the successful legions staged a coup and took control. The soldier-emperor **Trajan** (98-117 AD) expanded the empire to its greatest size, conquering Dacia (modern Romania) and areas along the Danube River with feats of engineering and tactical brilliance. Successor **Hadrian** (118-138) preferred philosophy to war and concentrated on decorating the city with his own architectural designs, including the **Pantheon** and his own colossal mausoleum. The city clung to its status as *caput mundi* (head of the world) until the death of **Marcus Aurelius** in 180 AD. By then, the empire had grown too large to defend. Emperors, required to delegate huge amounts of money and power to their generals in the field, lay vulnerable to military coups, and the tumultuous 3rd century AD saw no fewer than 30 emperors take the throne, of which only one managed to die of natural causes. Despite occasionally enlightened administrations (of the African Septimius Severus, for example), the brutality and depravity of despots like **Commodus**, **Caracalla,** and the confused **Elegabalus,** who actually believed he was the sun, did much to undermine the stability of the Empire.

Literature: Only the Classics

As the Etruscan language remains completely opaque to modern scholars, the available Italian literary tradition begins with the ancient Romans. The Rome of Augustus, despite a government prone to banishing literary and other detractors, nurtured the greatest Latin authors of antiquity. **Virgil** (a.k.a. Publius Vergilius Maro), revered as the only Roman poet worthy of comparison to Homer, wrote a creation myth to glorify the newly imperial city. His epic poem the **Aeneid** links the founding of Rome with the fall of Troy via the wanderings of Aeneas. After escaping the sack of his hometown, Aeneas drifted to Latium, doing his famous turn with Queen Dido along the way. In Virgil's story, the oracle of Apollo tells Aeneas to "seek your ancient mother; there the race of Aeneas shall dwell and reduce all other nations to their sway." After protracted journeys around the Mediterranean and into the underworld, Aeneas settles in the Tiber valley (surprise!) where his descendents, Romulus and Remus, would found the all-conquering Rome. **Robert Fitzgerald's** blank verse translation is probably the best approach to this epic; only a brave soul would stuff the original into a backpack for train ride reading.

Ovid (see Mythology, below) was banished to Romania when he offended Octavian. Official Rome preferred **Horace**, whose martial lyrics ("Sweet and fitting it is to die for one's country") beat better time with the sentiments of Augustus. **Livy** set down the authorized history of Rome during these first years of empire. **Julius Caesar** provides a first-hand account of the final shredding of the Republic; his *Commentaries* recount his experiences on the front lines of the Gallic wars. With Caesar's close contemporary **Cicero** (bumped off by Mark Antony within a year of Caesar's fatal Ides of March), Latin prose is said to have reached its zenith: *De Republica* sets forth classical republican theories of government, while *Brutus* offers a history of Roman oratory. Earlier republican literature is often less lofty; **Plautus's** farces, for instance, can be seen as antique sitcoms. The poetry of Verona's **Catullus**, on the other hand, set a standard for passion that gave Romeo and Juliet a lot to live up to. From the post-Augustan empire, **Petronius's** *Satyricon* is a bizarre, blunt look at the decadence of the age of Nero, while **Tacitus's** *Histories* summarize Roman war, diplomacy, scandal, and rumor in the years following the death of Nero with unblinking even-handedness. His *Annals* look down from the upright Rome of Trajan's reign onto the scandalous activities of the Julio-Claudian emperors (Tiberius is a special target). Finally, **Marcus Aurelius's** *Meditations* bring us the musings of a philosopher-king on the edge of a precipice— subsequent emperors presided over the Empire's drawn out but persistent decline.

Greek and Roman Mythology

More entertaining forays into the golden age of poetry include **Ovid's** racy *Amores* and his virtuosic collection of transformation myths, the *Metamophoses*. The latter is a principal source for our knowledge of Greco-Roman mythology, a set of stories second only to the Bible in its influence on the Western imagination. When Romans plundered Greece, they even stole its gods; take your favorite Greek myths, latinize the gods' names, and *presto*, instant Roman mythology. Myths were passed from generation to generation and region to region, where they were gradually embellished and interpreted to reflect local concerns. The anthropomorphic gods and goddesses lived as immortal beings with divine power, yet often descended to earth to intervene romantically, mischievously, or combatively in human affairs, sometimes disguised as animals or humans. Traditionally, 14 major deities preside: **Jupiter** (Zeus, in Greek), king of gods; his wife **Juno** (Hera), who watches over child-bearing and marriage; **Neptune** (Poseidon), god of the sea; **Vulcan** (Hephaestus), god of smiths and fire; **Venus** (Aphrodite), goddess of love and beauty; **Mars** (Ares), god of war; **Minerva** (Athena), goddess of wisdom; **Phoebus** (Apollo), god of light and music; **Diana** (Artemis), goddess of the hunt; **Mercury** (Hermes), the messenger god and patron of thieves and tricksters; **Pluto** (Hades), lord of death; **Ceres** (Demeter), goddess of the harvest; **Bacchus** (Dionysus), god of wine; and **Vesta** (Hestia), goddess of the hearth.

Jupiter was a sexual gymnast, and Juno was equally inventive in her tricks on lovers. **Danae,** imprisoned in a tower by her father, was impregnated by Jupiter in the form of a golden shower, and **Ganymede,** a handsome Trojan shepherd, was snatched up from earth to be the cup-bearer of the gods. **Europa** was ravished by Jupiter disguised as a bull. Worse still for mortals, Juno, powerless to injure her philandering husband directly, lavished her vengeance on the objects of his affection: **Io** was turned into a cow and chased pitilessly by an enormous gadfly; **Leto**, pregnant with Diana and Phoebus, was forbidden to rest on solid ground until the itinerant island of Delos lent its tiny shore for her to give birth upon, and **Callisto**, who got off relatively easy for her dalliance with Jupiter, was changed into a bear. **Semele**, one of the few willing consorts of Jupiter, dissolved into ash when he appeared to her in his full Olympian brilliance. Both **Edith Hamilton's** and **Bullfinch's** *Mythology* are eminently readable retellings of these and other myths.

Less Than Nero

You are not the kind of person who should be here. You are sixteen years old and you're floating on this barge in the middle of a lake and this naked Spanish prostitute is dancing close to you. You start to get hot. You drink some wine. You are already drunk and you drink some more. You write some poetry and it's shit. You make people watch you read it anyway and they applaud. You are emperor of the Western world. If you want to do something, you have the right to do it.

Elected emperor at the tender age of sixteen, the handsome nephew of Caligula began a sadistic reign of terror, torture, and bad poetry readings. Nero (54-68 AD) rocked the house as highest administrator, judge, and priest in an enormous empire that extended from the Atlantic all the way to the Caspian Sea. He started out rather humanely, guided by his overbearing but well-meaning mother, and he was too timid even to sign the standard death warrants. But soon he proved to be the most vicious, destructive, and untalented teen in world history, with the possible exception of Donny Wahlberg. Nero transmogrified into a megalomaniacal monster, and ordered the cruel murder of his mother, Agrippina, as well as the death of his nineteen-year-old wife, who was found tied up in cords in a hot bath with all her veins slashed. He then married his pregnant mistress, who died from the swift kick he landed on her stomach. He even made his best buddy and advisor, the philosopher Seneca, slash his own wrists. Nero was haunted by paranoid visions; he often woke up screaming with visions of his dead mother (cf. Macbeth), and he initiated a one-man witch-hunt through his palace, managing to condemn senators, army officers, aristocrats, as traitors and various others to be beheaded. Nero may even have set the famous fire of 64 BC on purpose; he certainly took advantage of its destruction, comandeering acres of burnt-out land in the middle of the city to construct a gargantuan palace which stretched from the Palatine Hill to above the Colosseum. Nero blamed the Christians for the fire and hosted a block party with the spectacle of Christian death throes—some torn apart by dogs, others burned at the stake—serving as entertainment; Nero even dressed up as a charioteer for the occasion.

Nero was the original party animal, frequently hosting and attending extraordinarily lavish events. He arrived at picnics in the highest style, accompanied by a thousand carriages drawn by mules in silver dresses. One gossip columnist of the time reported of a famous barge-party, "Nero disgraced himself with every kind of abomination, natural and unnatural, leaving no further depth of debauchery to which he could sink." Nero was a sportsman as well, and even when he didn't feel like driving his own chariot, he played with toy ones at home. When he wasn't trying to kill those close to him, Nero imagined himself an *artiste*, shocking the conservative Roman populace by appearing on stage to read his own poems or dance his own ballets. He worked hard to improve his voice by placing lead weights on his chest in painful efforts to strengthen his diaphragm. Nero was also the first emperor to employ a speechwriter, first to bring a polar bear to Rome, and first to conceive of the idea to build a canal through the Isthmus of Corinth (eventually accomplished in 1893). Ultimately, Nero tried the patience and the coffers of his republic too severely, and the Senate sentenced him to death by flogging. Nero disguised himself and rode horseback to the home of a former servant. He couldn't bring himself to commit suicide, so he had his servant slice his neck with a dagger. He did have enough *chutzpah* to utter in his last moments, "What an artist dies with me."

Spectator Sports

When Juvenal wrote that "bread and circuses" were all that were necessary to keep the Roman populace happy, he was referring in part to the free snacks and wild, violent goings-on staged in the 50,000-person-capacity Colosseum. In order to keep the city's large numbers of unemployed occupied, emperors depended on the distracting powers of ceremonial pageantry and calculated violence of gladiatorial combats: gladiators would first ride around the arena in chariots, then walk around it, attended by slaves toting their awe-inspiring battle gear—plumes in the helmets added a dash of color. Shirtless, nipples hard from the excitement, the gladiators would make the traditional salute to the emperor (right arms swept out from across their chests) and bark out the haunting refrain "Hail Emperor! We men who are about to die salute thee!"

After the intensity of this opening ceremony, much-needed comic relief was supplied by performers: vertically-efficient men, *zaftig* women, and people with disabilities. Finally a piercing horn section announced the main attraction. The gladiators wore whatever suited their individual fighting styles: those who favored speed over strength wore almost no protective gear and carried only a net and spear to trap and then stab an opponent. Buffer gladiators wore all the armor they could and carried heavy swords and lances. Professional gladiators had a chance to test out what would work best at gladiatorial schools. While attendance was mandatory for some criminals and prisoners of war, occasionally free men would go to gladiatorial school just to get a date: the grueling practices, revolting accommodations, and occupational hazards were well worth the attention that foxy ladies bestowed on a gladiatorial victor.

Long before Brecht and 20th-century drama, gladiatorial combats broke down the fourth wall between performer and audience. The crowds exhorted the combatants to beat the crap out of each other, whipping themselves into an ear-shattering frenzy. Fallen, injured gladiators could make a sign begging for mercy. While the Emperor was mulling over his decision, the blood-thirsty crowd howled and screamed for a thumbs down. Usually the crowds were appeased. Most Romans, even the cultural elite, saw nothing wrong with these savage spectacles. The writings of Seneca, the famous tutor of Nero (go figure), proved a rare exception: "It is pure murder...the spectators call for the slayer to be thrown to those who in turn will slay him, and they demand that the victor be kept for another butchering."

The second most popular event at the Colosseum was the killing of wild, often exotic, animals. Lions, tigers, bears, crocodiles, giraffes, and camels were all released from an underground network of tunnels into a simulated forest. Professionals (*venatores*) would work the frightened animal into a fevered pitch and draw out its death as long as possible.

There was some good clean fun in imperial Rome. Over at the Circus Maximus, Romans placed wagers on old-fashioned horse and chariot races. As many as 10 horses at a time would pull chariots decorated in colors representing a particular stable. The horses themselves sparkled with jewels, pearls in their manes and flashy doo-dads attached to their armor. Crashes were common, and chariot, horse, and rider disappeared into towering clouds of dust, which of course was what the Romans liked best.

The Rise of Christianity and The Fall of Rome

The Age of Martyrs: Witnesses for the Persecution

Weak leadership and the southward invasions of Germanic tribes combined to create a state of anarchy in the 3rd century AD. **Diocletian** secured control of the fragmented empire in 284 AD, established order, divided the empire into eastern and western halves, and escalated the persecution of Christians, in a period that became known as "the age of martyrs." The persecution began in 64 when the Emperor Nero, a poetaster and dedicated sadist, needed a patsy for the immense destructive fire he was widely believed to have started. While Nero made a show of trying Christians in court, in truth the Roman people were diverted and appeased by the entertaining sight of Christians dressed in the hides of animals and torn to shreds by savage canines, or set on fire as lamps so law-abiding citzens could do a little reading before bed. The Christians who died came to be known as "martyrs," from the Greek for "witnesses," an apt term for those who experienced first-hand the full extent of Roman cruelty.

While subsequent, more tolerant, emperors turned their attention to enemies their own size, popular prejudice persisted; so did the torture and murder of Christians. The average Roman viewed Christians with hostility, perceiving them as a threat to his clearly superior way of life. Christians looked forward to a time when Christ would return to earth and Rome would be consumed by flames; converts challenged traditional Roman family values by their unwillingness to participate in rituals, particularly those dedicated to pleasure; Christian pacifism such as refusing to serve in the Roman army was interpreted (rightly) as subversive. At the same time, zealots eager to prove their fidelity to Christ were often willing participants in their own martyrdom. When you visit the Colosseum, imagine or act out the feeding of Christians to lions; Christians were also used as disposable targets for archery and scrap for wood-chopping exercises. Despite this hazardous environment, by the end of Diocletian's violent reign there were approximately 30,000 Christians gathered in Rome.

The fortunes of local Christians took a turn for the better when **Constantine,** Diocletian's successor, saw a huge cross in the wartime sky along with the letters, *"In hoc signo vincit"* (By this sign you shall conquer). Sure enough, victory followed the vision, and Constantine, combining military strategy with spiritual conversion, conquered his co-emperor Maxentius in 312 and declared Christianity the state religion in 315 AD. But Constantine hastened the end of Rome's supremacy by moving the capital of the empire east, to the newborn city of Constantinople. As city officials lost touch with their far-off imperial government, Christian bishops began to assume some traditional civic duties, like caring for the poor and hungry. Meanwhile huge armies of barbarian mercenaries broke through neglected fortifications along the empire's northern borders and descended on the city. In 410 **Alaric,** king of the Visigoths, deposed the last of Rome's western emperors and sacked the city. The ensuing scramble for power wasn't fully resolved until 476, when **Odoacer,** an Ostrogoth chieftain, was crowned King of Italy. Sacker-extraordinaire **Attila the Hun** arrived on tour in 452; despite the absence of an opposing army to greet him in Rome, fast-talker Pope Leo I convinced him to pillage elsewhere.

Art and Architecture

Given the chaos of the 3rd and 4th centuries, emperors' minds tended to focus on making war, not art, and it wasn't until Rome's late middle age that the Christian Church began to nurture household-name Italian artists. Painting of the time was mostly simple wall **frescoes** done by anonymous artisans; some from Diocletian's baths are on display at the National Museum. Christians were forced to bury their dead outside the city walls in **catacombs**; the color, composition, and treatment of subjects in the **Christian catacombs** recall Roman wall painting, with togate figures actually representing Christ and the apostles. You'll find more sophisticated early Christian work on sarcophagi and statues in the Vatican Museums. Mosaics from this period are all over Rome. Virtuosos working for wealthy patrons used *tessarae* (tiles) as miniscule as 1/32nd of an inch. The taste of Roman emperors, however, tended to run towards the gargantuan. Witness the humongous head of Constantine, located in the Palazzo dei Conservatori on the Capitoline Hill, six feet high and weighing nine tons. The tremendous size of the **Arch of Constantine**, a tribute from the Senate in 315 celebrating his victory over Maxentius, compensates for its lack of complexity and artistry.

The most significant architectural contributions of the late Empire to the city of Rome are the first official buildings of the burgeoning western Church. These new structures were used for worship and often housed sacred relics. The rise of Christianity marked the beginning of a search for new aesthetic forms. The most pressing concern was the redesign of the Roman temple to accommodate the Christian Mass. The first Christian churches in Rome lacked a unique architectural style, and simply took the form of renovated Roman basilicas, clamorous rectangular spaces supported by columns intended for raucous public debate rather than introspection. The great hall of Constantine's mother's palace was transformed into a basilica now known as **S. Croce in Gerusalemme**; on a holiday to the Holy Land, the Empress-Dowager "identified" the cross on which Christ was crucified, and had it hauled back to Rome. Constantine, who fashioned a divine bit for his horse out of the nails in the wood, is credited with building the first of many versions of the **Basilica S. Lorenzo Fuori Le Mura**, a sanctuary for pilgrims visiting the tomb of St. Lawrence. In the early 5th century, when barbarians started knocking on the city gates, the real threat to Rome's great monuments was already inside the city walls. The damage done by Alaric's sack of Rome in 410 was more symbolic than physical: in typically shameless behavior, Roman citizens continually attempted to dismantle the city's landmarks for their building materials and valuable metals.

The Middle Ages

Diocletian's bisection of the empire increased its instability; in each year during the next two centuries, at least one of the two empires was at war. The eastern Roman (Byzantine) emperor **Justinian** conquered the western division in 526 and imposed the *corpus juris,* or codified law of the empire, which served as the legal model for European nations for half a millennium. Unfortunately, much of the quarrel between the two divisions of the empire revolved around Rome; the city suffered the consequences of war like never before. By the 6th century the eternal city, once home to a million people, could support just several thousand. When the Goths slashed the aqueducts in 546 AD, they sealed the city's fate. The hills of Rome, once crowded with houses (all served by running water), public baths, and splashing fountains, were deserted as the remaining citizens crowded into the unhealthy neighborhoods along the Tiber banks. It was in these days that some of the most famous neighborhoods of Rome — Trastevere, Campo dei Fiori, and the streets around piazza Navona—were first heavily settled. In the ramshackle alleyways swarming round the river, starvation and plague ran rampant, relieved only by the periodic invasions of barbarians who made the Goths look like underpaid extras from *Spartacus.*

The struggle for Rome required a temporary friendship with the papacy for protection. Since Constantine made Catholicism the official religion, Roman nobility had gradually turned toward the church as a new means of maintaining their power and status in the increasingly unstable realm of politics. Rome owed its salvation from the turbulence of the Dark Ages in large part to the moneyed popes who kept up a decent tourist industry attracting monied pilgrims, and who invoked the wrath of God to intimidate would-be invaders. Pope **Gregory the Great** (590-604) devised new, efficient strategies for distributing food and sent the word of God via missionaries all over Europe.

Twelve Heads of John the Baptist: Pilgrims and the Relic Trade

Shortly after Gregory the Great assembled and sent out his missionaries, pilgrims began to flood back into Rome. The pilgrims came from all classes, from nobility to criminals wearing massive iron collars who had been sent to Rome for spiritual rehabilitation. The city's as yet limited number of places of Christian worship were glutted with the faithful, as were *diaconiae,* where pilgrims were given temporary food and shelter. These large numbers of spiritual tourists gave birth to the **underpaying guidebook industry;** early travel guides, dating as far back as 615, instructed their readers in the holy history of the city and how to locate its sacred relics. Among the numerous ways of extracting money from these zealous foreigners was to sell them supposedly hallowed artifacts. Pope Gregory, in order to curtail this shameless growth industry, implied that the power of relics was unknown, uncontrolled and potentially deadly (cf. *Raiders of the Lost Ark*). Undaunted, European pilgrims kept coming and were soon joined by thousands of refugees from the Middle East (fleeing the ever-expanding Muslim Arab powers); this new influx of believers gave Rome's relic collection the credibility it needed. Among other objects, these Giovanni-come-latelies carried with them the ostensible head of Anastasius, a Persian martyr, as well as the "actual" manger that cradled Jesus, put on display at the S. Maria Maggiore.

While Pope Gregory objected, after the new wave of pilgrims sacred relics circulated like so many baseball cards. So numerous were the medieval pilgrims that the routes of their pilgrimages provided a basic structure for early maps of Europe. All along these routes, bazaars, inns, and markets appeared, along with, of course, hawkers of phony relics. Not the least of these hawkers was the Church itself; at one point, churches in Italy housed no fewer than 12 heads and sixty fingers of St. John the Baptist. Disgust with the relics trade, and with the Church's involvement in it, helped inspire the Protestant reformers. John Calvin railed against the practice, while the Church of England's 39 articles consider the veneration of relics "repugnant to the word of God." The Catholic church officially releases followers to decide for themselves if they believe in ancient remains; however, the Vatican must provide a saintly relic for the altar before any new Catholic church can open its doors for worship. Because of the colorful history of the relic trade, the Vatican recently began hiring scientists to check the authenticity of its collection. In the most devastasting conclusion thus far, professional archaelogists have decided that the Shroud of Turin, alleged to be the sheet in which Jesus was buried and miraculously retaining his imprint, is in fact......PHONY!

Art and Architecture

As early as the 6th century, Pope Gregory the Great was calling for art which would edify the illiterate masses, art that would not glorify the individual or the earthly world in which she lived but rather laud the world beyond. The gaze of the Christian art which eventually emerged in the Middle Ages was fixed firmly on heaven. Viewers will be struck by the lack of proportion, the disregard for the body, the all-too-common monochromatic backgrounds, and the landscapes cluttered with obscure symbols; it may help to remember that these paintings are supposed to combine a disregard for this world with the placement (and diminution) of the individual in a larger, protective hierarchy of symbols and belief.

The first important non-Classical style introduced into Italian art was the religious and highly stylized **Byzantine.** Byzantine art made its first big splash in Rome with the mosaics of Sant'Agnese (638). Byzantine influence made its most profound impact in architecture, however, both by perfecting the blueprint of the Christian basilica and by crowning these churches with domes and vaults. The earliest Italian churches to bear the Byzantine influence are in Ravenna, notably the Church of San Vitale. In Rome, that ultra-serious architecture known as Romanesque rose to a rather extended prominence. From roughly 500-1200 AD Romanesque churches dominated Europe, and although it is often (deservedly) maligned, the Romanesque can be the most moving of all architectural styles. Romanesque churches are unmistakable due to their small, rounded arches resting on massive stone piers, creating a sense of heaviness and power. This heaviness was unavoidable; if large windows were placed in the walls, the weight of the roof would push the walls apart and the church would collapse.

When you spot a Romanesque church, check inside for characteristic Romanesque art—either distorted, stylized, Byzantine-type artwork or Classical relief sculpture in the stone of the buildings themselves—and note how little light invades the interior. The great Italian Romanesque churches include the Cathedral of Pisa, San Ambrogio in Milan, the cathedral of Massa Marittima, and San Miniato in Florence. Luckily, in Rome the 12th century saw the appearance of the **Cosmati** families who filled these grave monuments (S. Maria in Cosmedin, S. Maria in Trastevere and S. Clemente) with luminous mosaics.

Medieval Anarchy

Crimes of Papacy: Murder...Intrigue...Eight Dead Popes in Eight Years.

After a 200-year period of papal imbroglios following Pope Gregory's reign, a series of sensible rulers brought Rome the first buds of the Renaissance. When Rome was faced with the threat of invasion from the German Lombards, the pope was forced to ask for help from none other than Frankish warlord Pepin the Short, immortalized in the fabu-lousy Broadway musical *Pippin* ("Corner of the Sky," "Magic To Do"). Under Pepin's benevolent protection, **Hadrian I** repaired the city's aqueducts and restored its churches. Hadrian's successor, Pope Leo III slipped a crown on the unsuspecting head of Pepin's son **Charlemagne** on Christmas Day, 800, declaring him "Emperor of the Romans," a title later known as Holy Roman Emperor; from then on, wars were fought and Rome occasionally besieged in order to secure papal approval for the title. For the time being however, Rome rejoiced in this Carolingian *renovatio*: eye-catching Byzantine art flowed into the city, new churches were built, even the weighty bowling ball of academia resurfaced.

Peace was short lived. Charlemagne's death in 814 AD preceded another 200 years of near-anarchy. In 846, Muslim Saracens rowed up the Tiber and plundered St. Peter's and S. Paoli fuori le Mura. With the gradual weakening of Frankish power in Europe, three powers—the church, Roman nobility, and imperialist forces—engaged in a shockingly bloody and absurd struggle for control over Rome and the papal seat. Far and away our favorite tale of gore from this period is the show trial of Pope Formosus. If you think you're bitter, get this: Formosus's successor Pope Stephen VI dug up his predecessor's corpse, dressed it in ecclesiastical robes, and put it on trial. Not surprisingly, the corpse was convicted on all counts, its three blessing fingers ripped off (just in case) and the body chucked into the Tiber. Stephen was later murdered, the next pope brutally overthrown, and the Pope after that murdered as well. In the years around the turn of the 9th century, there were eight popes in eight years. Nine popes were murdered during the 10th century. Maybe not such a good time to be pope.

The first major figure to emerge in this two-century game of king of the mountain was **Alberic the Younger** in 932. The scion of a powerful aristocratic Roman family, Alberic attempted to wrest control of Rome away from the church and steer it towards a secular governmental structure or *commune*. (Alberic had no idea how mammoth this task was: the Vatican didn't officially butt out of Rome's political affairs until a nearly a millenium later, under the Lateran treaty of 1929). On his deathbed in 964, however, Alberic appointed his degenerate teen-age son John XII as pope, to combine the powers of the Church and Rome's aristocracy once more. (After his father's death, John installed a harem at the Vatican.) Brilliantly indecisive, John crowned the German monarch **Otto I** as Roman Emperor, largely for protection against Berengar, a Northern Italian ruler; panicked that he had appealed to the weaker leader, John subsequently asked Berengar for similar protection from Otto. Otto emerged the victor, controller of both the city and the papacy, but the next hundred years of Roman history were dominated by the gruesome tit for tat of Romans revolting against imperialist papal appointments and popes imposing imperialist punishments on the rebels. Deposed by Otto and then returned to power behind Otto's back, Pope John had various appendages and the breathing apparati removed from traitorous clergy. (John was murdered shortly thereafter, probably by the husband of his mistress.) Around the turn of the 10th century, Otto's violent grandson **Otto III** developed a penchant for ripping out the eyes of members of the **Crescenzi** family, the persistent and powerful nobility who would periodically storm the papal fortress, Castel Sant'Angelo.

After the Roman families and foreign powers had their turn, the late 11th century belonged to **Hildebrand,** a crusading monk whose no-nonsense reforms won him a position as Pope Gregory VII. Hildebrand was so successful at winning back loyalty and respect for the Catholic church in Europe that a German Emperor whom he had excommunicated was forced to come back to Rome begging for forgiveness. The second time the emperor was excommunicated, however, he laid siege to Rome, and Hildebrand's followers jumped ship. In 1084, the Norman conqueror **Robert Guiscard** (who had also fought on behalf of Hildebrand), remembered—a little ahead of schedule—that Rome was due for its tricentennial sacking.

The Jewish Pope (and Other Bubbameisers)

Like elections in the U.S. today, papal succession was largely determined by who could afford the position; most of the costs were bribes to secure support from other church officials. Only a handful of families, many of whom claimed a birthline back to the Roman emperors (being related to Julius Caesar is the ultimate Roman pedigree), were in a position to sponsor a pope. In 1130, the Pierleoni family won the papal seat with the election of Pope Anacletus; however, supporters of rival cardinal Innocent II took papal mudslinging to a new low by accusing Anacletus of being Jewish and labelling him the "Jewish Pope." This allegation was an indictment of the whole Pierleoni family, and was considered on the whole more damaging than the suggestion also circulating that Anacletus was having an affair with his sister.

Anacletus's great-grandfather, known as Baruch, had, in fact, been born Jewish. A wealthy and respected man, Baruch often donated substantial sums to those families seeking a papal nomination. Baruch eventually converted to Catholicism, was baptized, and married into a noble Roman family; the Baruchs, meaning "blessed" in Hebrew, adopted the name Benedictus, also meaning "blessed," but in Latin. (Other Italian Jews who converted would make similar translations of their names: the Italian last name "Sacerdoti," meaning "priest," was adopted by converting Jews named Cohn, Cohen and Coen, all of which also mean "priest.") With each successive generation, Anacletus's ancestors had grown wealthier and more influential, and more irreproachably Christian. His grandfather was one of the richest men in Rome. When Pope Urban II was chased from the Vatican in 1099, he ran for sanctuary to the home of Anacletus's father, Petrus Leonis. By this time, Petrus Leonis had become so powerful that his family essentially co-governed Rome with their off-and-on rivals the Frangipanis.

Anacletus wasn't the first prominent Christian to come from a Jewish background; there's Jesus, for example, as well as St. Peter and St. Paul. What's more, even the Jews of the 12th century wouldn't have considered him one of their own; Hebrew law had already established that to be biologically Jewish, a person's mother had to be Jewish as well. Furthermore, a Jew that converted was in the Jewish community's eyes the deserving object of scorn. The "Jewish Pope" was largely a fabrication, and in the end the case against Anacletus failed, and he managed to die of natural causes while still the Pontiff (no small feat at that time).

Despite the overwhelming evidence to the contrary, the idea of a Jewish Pope, for whatever reason, captured the imaginations of both Christians and Jews. Some history books still refer to Anacletus as the Jewish Pope (without quotation marks), pointing him out as an amusing anecdote, a symbol that *anything* could and did happen at the Vatican in those topsy-turvy, wild-and-wacky middle ages. Another recurrent legend tells of a Pope who was secretly a woman; she was supposedly unmasked and executed after she gave birth during a Papal procession. In the Jewish community in Rome, Anacletus's story became part of the community's folklore, developing into the stuff of legend. Most versions of the story portray Anacletus undergoing an identity crisis, with an inexplicable sense that he is an impostor. In one version, he is kidnapped from the family of a rabbi and raised Catholic. As a precocious youngster, he rises to the highest position in the church and then becomes obsessed by questions of his origin; after intimidating some servants into revealing the circumstances of his birth, he summons the rabbi, and via a handy birthmark, discovers he is the rabbi's kidnapped son. Determined to abdicate, Anacletus gathers all of Rome to hear a speech in which he preaches Judaism as the true faith. After delivering his address from a high tower, he realizes that he has no means of escape from the mob he has just enraged and jumps from his holy perch. In some versions, he vanishes in the air; in none of them does he die—the story simply ends. In a more eclectic account, the birthmark becomes a game of chess: Anacletus and his rabbi father realize they must be related when they both use the same signature moves, and Anacletus steals away under cover of darkness.

These stories are poignant fantasies; elaborate narrative machinery is employed to rescue a member of the Jewish community who is simultaneously the leader of its rival religion and brutal enemy, the Catholic Church. The scandal of a "Jewish Pope" and the stories that surround it captures both Christian anxiety about the inescapably Jewish origin of Christianity, and Jewish anxiety about giving birth to Christianity, the religion that would eclipse and try to destroy it.

Medieval Anarchy, Part II

Rise of the Commune, Abduction of the Pope, and a Load of Papal Bull

All over Rome you'll see streets, buildings, bridges, and *piazze* named after the city's first families: Orsini, Colonna, Pierleoni, Frangipani, Vitelleschi, Tebaldi, Savelli, Pa-

pareschi, Annibaldi. Despite foreign emperors, popes, and anti-popes, ever since the fall of the Empire, these tightly knit clans vied for control of Rome's *rioni* (neighborhoods) and their daily operation. By the mid-12th century, a new class of citizens had coalesced in Rome: large numbers of businessmen, lesser clergy and nobles, and expert craftsmen had prospered but remained disenfranchised from the political system, such as it was. Inspired by the radical preaching of reformist monk **Arnold da Brescia**, in 1143 these Romans rose against their noble superiors, looted their houses, declared Rome a republic and demanded that the church give up its temporal power. It almost worked, too, but subsequent popes were able to strike bargains with foreign emperors (mostly German) and reinstate themselves and Rome's families as rulers of the city. Brescia was tortured and hanged. However, the church faced more Republican rioting for the next 45 years.

Romans managed to win limited self-determination about the same time that King John was buying time by signing the Magna Carta in England. It wasn't until **Pope Clement III**, a Roman by birth who could claim to have the city's interests at heart, that the rebels and the papacy struck a bargain. The Church's temporal powers were accepted, members of the Senate swore their loyalty to the pope and returned seized church property. In exchange, the church agreed to recognize the city of Rome as a *commune*, with its own power to declare war or peace. This agreement paved the way for the unprecedented power of **Innocent III**. Innocent was a skilled mixture of politician and dictator. He can be credited with elevating the Church's power in Europe to its highest point yet; however, he wasn't above consolidating that power with cheap tactics such as the Bull of 1215. In it he stated his unqualified support for all of the Church's previous anti-Jewish decisions, setting a poor but *puissant* example for anti-Semitism in the rest of Europe.

After Innocent's death, the Vatican was again under assault from disgruntled German emperors and the increasingly demanding Senate; in order to break the sway of the city's noble families, strong man Senator **Brancaleone di Andalò** demolished 140 family towers and made an example of two Annibaldis by publicly hanging them. His successor, French-born **Charles of Anjou**, heralded a brief period of French dominance in Rome; in the 1260's and 1270's six French-born popes and 21 French or French-allied cardinals (about a third of the cardinals created in that period) were elected. The pope who broke the French hold over the Vatican was the much-reviled **Boniface VII**, elected in 1294. Possessing a remarkable knack for impersonations, Boniface won his papal seat by imitating the voice of God and murmuring through a hidden pipe to his gullible predecessor that it was time to step down. European monarchs were less convinced of Boniface's divine power. After he antagonized nearly every ruler in Europe with a string of excommunications, the French presence in Rome (aided by the Colonnas, only too happy to help out, since the Church had seized much of their property) kidnapped Boniface and trundled him off to the south of France. Boniface was allowed to return to Italy to die, but the **Babylonian Captivity** had begun; for most of the 14th century, popes would conduct their business from Avignon, France under the thumb of French kings.

The last notable figure in Roman history before the fresh winds of the Renaissance began to blow is one of its most eccentric—**Cola di Rienzo**. Favoring frivolous costumes, the energy and rhetorical flourishes of this self-proclaimed "Illustrious Redeemer" of Rome hearkened back to the harangues of Arnold da Brescia. A champion of Republican ideals and a fierce critic of Rome's noble families, Cola succeeded in establishing Rome (if briefly) as the capital of "Sacred Italy," with 25 cities, including Florence, Venice, and Milan, sending delegations to a national parliament. Cola's ambition got the best of him, however; the once supportive pope was disturbed by the messianic tone Cola's speeches were beginning to take, and despite his victory in a bloody battle with the unusually consolidated noble families, Cola and the Roman people obeyed a papal bull (edict) demanding that he step down.

After hearing the convincing words of St. Catherine of Siena, Pope Gregory XI agreed to return the papal seat to Rome and restore the city's greatest source of income, the papal court. Combined with a hugely successful Jubilee celebration in 1390, Rome was thus positioned to take full advantage of the cultural and intellectual prosperity of the Renaissance.

Art and Architecture of the Late Middle Ages

While church-building continued throughout the middle ages, the anarchy that followed on the heels of the Carolingian *renovatio* put an end to the artistic innovations accomplished in that period. The **Cosmati** were a group of families that enlivened humorless Romanesque churches with dazzling decorations; the term comes from the Christian name of one of these families whose signatures managed to survive into the present day. Best known for their mosaics, the Cosmati crushed precious stones from ancient ruins and pieces of colored glass to produce flawless squares, ellipses, and oblongs saturated with color. The spirit of the ruins they pilfered is reincarnated in their work, which recalls the marble inlays of the Forum. The Cosmati are also credited with looking to Muslim artists for their rich palette and arrangement of shapes, similar to those found in Persian rugs. Endowing the Roman churches of their time (S. Maria in Cosmedin, S. Maria in Trastevere S. Clemente) with royal splendor, they decorated everything from paschal candlesticks to columns, including altars, altar screens, tombs, pavements, and bishops's chairs. Particularly beautiful is **Iacopo Torriti**'s mosaic *Coronation of the Virgin,* at S. Maria Maggiore. Some Cosmati went on to architecture and sculpture. **Pietro Vassalletto** designed the beautiful cloisters at the Lateran and St. Paul's-Outside-the-Walls. Eventually in demand by patrons all over Europe, two of the more prestigious Cosmati commissions are Henry III's tomb and the shrine of Edward the Confessor, both in Westminster Abbey in London.

Florentine artist and architect **Arnolfo di Cambio** provided both S. Paul-Outside-the-Walls and S. Cecilia with sumptuous Gothic *baldacchini* (canopies). **Pietro Cavallini** was a major figure of the late middle ages; like many of the "genius" artists of the Renaissance, Cavallini was accomplished in several media, particularly mosaics (the *Life of the Virgin* in S. Maria in Trastevere) and frescoes (the *Last Judgment* in S. Cecilia).

Literature

Italy had no *Beowulf* to brighten up the middle ages, and when the silence of a millenium was finally broken, it wasn't by a Roman; nonetheless, we feel compelled to mention him. Any good Italian bookstore seems to devote at least one ceiling-to-floor case to annotated and critical editions of the works of Tuscan **Dante Alighieri** (1265-1321), one of the first European poets to eschew Latin; he is considered as much the father of the modern Italian language as of its literature. After the death of his young love Beatrice in 1290, and exile from Florence in 1302, Dante began writing his masterpiece, *La Divina Commedia,* partially as a form of personal solace. Dante peopled his allegorical journey through the afterlife with famous figures from his own lifetime; among the *Commedia's* chief charms are Dante's acid descriptions of Italian cities and their inhabitants. His lines on Rome are particularly haunting and mourn its bloody history. Of Constantine's "gift" (handing Rome over to the papacy he writes "Ah, Constantine, what evil was spawned not by your conversion but by that gift which the first rich Pope accepted from you." A good annotated version will get an interested reader through the difficulties of the Italian; for a more casual glance into the *Inferno* (and the rest of the *Divine Comedy*) Ciardi and Mandelbaum have produced the best English translations.

Renaissance

History and Politics

The no-nonsense **Pope Martin V** (a member of the powerful Colonna family) seized power in 1420, marking the beginning of the Renaissance urbanity and absolute papal rule that lasted until 1870. He wasn't much for art and architecture, but established a strong administration that made Rome the capital of a Church-controlled Renaissance state. The roads were widened and paved and buildings in the new style were erected; unfortunately, many ancient structures were demolished to provide building materials for these projects. The popes attracted scholars and artists from Florence and other parts of Italy, so by the 15th century Rome was the principal center of Renaissance culture—don't let the Florentine tourist office tell you otherwise. **Julius II** (1503-13) began an enormous building program, setting out plans for St. Peter's dome and for the whole city. He hired the architect Bramante, who demolished medieval Rome with such enthusiasm and intent that Raphael nicknamed him *ruinante*—if it ain't Bar-oque, don't fix it.

In fact, when Protestant upstart and Renaissance foe **Martin Luther** returned to Rome in 1510, he was sorely disappointed by the city's aesthetic indulgence and spiritual dissolution. He could barely recognize "the footprints of ancient Rome, as the old buildings were now buried beneath the new, so deep lieth the rubbish." He was enraged at the church's apparent equation of beauty with spirituality, and at the blatant pursuit of worldly happiness and the utter confidence in salvation. Martin Luther was revolted by the sight of Raphael's ornate *Stanze* in the Vatican, in which Christian and pagan symbols mingled, and in the buff no less. While the pope went "triumphing about with fair-decked stallions, the priests gabbled Mass," he sputtered, and went about writing the 95 theses of the Protestant **Reformation**.

After excommunicating that pesky Martin Luther, **Pope Leo X** (in power 1513-1521) asserted his interest in the humanities, drawing up his own plans for a new St. Peter's dome, putting forth **politically correct** ideals, and commissioning artists Michelangelo and Raphael. However, despite most of their profound patronage of the arts, the popes of the Renaissance were extremely detrimental to Italy's political health. Their blatant disregard for honest politicking and for the well-being of the country undermined Italy's unity and military force. To supplement their pocket money, most of these popes taxed the Romans and their country cousins like nobody's biz. Previously prosperous cities of Lazio and Umbria soon filed chapter eleven, and much of the distressed agricultural population just up and left for better regions. The popes also curried favor with all different countries—whichever suited them best at the time—extracting money from whomever they could. These fragmented alliances, leaving Rome vulnerable to invasion, soon proved fatal.

The Sack of Rome: Rome Has Fallen and It Can't Get Up

While Rome had been sacked numerous times in the past, on the morning of May 7, 1527 the city faced *the* **Sack of Rome**—an intense eight-day pillage courtesy of German warriors, Spanish marauders, and 15,000 paid Lutheran mercenaries—after Italy became a bone of contention between France and Spain. The city was then in the hands of the blood-happy imperialist troops, who stormed through the Borgo, killing everyone and everything in sight and managing to destroy thousands of churches, palaces, and houses in an amazingly short time. The troops broke down the doors of churches and convents, palaces, monasteries, and studios, hurling the contents into the street. They broke into tombs, including the one holding Pope Julius II, and ripped the jewelry from the corpses. Priceless religious ornaments were used for blasphemous mockery, and some troops launched a fake papal procession through the streets. The Holy Lance that had speared Christ's side and been presented to Innocent VIII was pilfered by a German soldier who paraded it around town. Some sporty raiders even took St. Andrew's and St. John's heads to use as soccer balls. The invaders tortured men to reveal the hiding-places of valuables or to pay ransom for their lives or the lives of their families. One report relates the horrors of one sect of torturers, who force-fed the Roman captives their own roasted testicles. Priests were made to utter blasphemies on pain of death, or to take part in profane travesties. One priest was murdered because he refused to kneel and give the Holy Communion to a donkey. They targeted convents for sexual assault; nuns were auctioned off as whores or used as gambling chips. Women of the Roman aristocracy were also dragged to the convents; "marchionesses, countesses and baronesses served the unruly troops," wrote the sieur de Brantôme, "and for long afterwards, the patrician women were known as "the relics of the Sack of Rome"". There never was an official body count, and as one Spaniard wrote, "I know nothing wherewith I can compare it, except it be the destruction of Jerusalem. I do not believe that if I had lived for two hundred years, I should see the like again." One man declared, "Rome is finished."

The pope managed to escape the sack and died ten years later of a fever, and joyous were his people. Intruders smeared his tomb with dirt, and stuck a sword through it. The pope's nephew quickly changed the name on the tomb, for fear that the pope's body would be paraded through the streets on a meat hook.

The Spaniards brought to Italy the Counter-Reformation, the Jesuits, and the **Inquisition,** which became the primary tool for suppressing Protestantism and Judaism. Inquisition victims include such noted astronomers as Galileo Galilei and Giordano Bruno. By the end of the 16th century, Spanish control over the Italian states weakened and the power of the papacy grew again. A new era of construction began under **Pope Sixtus V** (1585-90) and his architect Domentico Fontana. Lucky for us, his plans to transform the Colosseum into a wool factory providing jobs for prostitutes failed. By 1600 Rome was again a thriving metropolis facing little political unrest. Having created such havoc earlier in the century, the popes lost much of their political relevance in the play between European powers during the Thirty Years War. Rome kicked back, lit up a cigarette, and cultivated *la dolce vita* for awhile, leaving the rest of Europe to brawl.

Everything You Always Wanted to Know About the PAPACY but Were Afraid to Ask

Though the popes of the Renaissance have a reputation as being enlightened patrons of art, they also rank as some of the greediest, most destructive and power-hungry popes ever. The papacy was more of an exclusive old-boy's club among the noble clans, devoting itself to their own families' enrichment and turning a blind eye to the contemporary state of religion and society. It cost a fortune to get elected to the papacy, but once elected the popes made their money back and then some. When Church money didn't suffice, popes taxed the surrounding provinces to recoup their high election expenditures and outrageous building expenses.

Pope Paul II (alias Alexander Farnese) had four illegitimate children. A notorious stage-father, he was unscrupulous about promoting them: two of his grandkids were named cardinal while still in their teens. He also relied heavily on his astrologer (not unlike our own spiritual leader Nancy Reagan).

Pope Leo X, the greatest sponsor of the arts, was also a heavy-duty spender, and it wasn't long before he spent all his inheritance and the entire papal budget, past, present, and future. Macchiavelli's friend Francesco Vettori claimed that the pope "could no more save a thousand ducats than a stone could fly in the air." Leo hardly cared, continuing to spend hither and thither, hiring more servants (over 600) for his household, giving generous loot bags (that is, gold purses) to his party guests, and gambling the night away. He bought pricey French hounds and Icelandic falcons with which to go hunting in the country. His feasts brought back the memory of Roman times. He served up peacocks' tongues and nightingale pies, and hired third-rate performers for outrageously silly and vulgar performances. His court jester, the notorious Da Mariano, would eat ravens and carrions—beak, feathers, and all—to satisfy the sick humor of the dinner guests. The pope was quite a prankster, as was once said of him "it is difficult to judge whether the merits of the learned or the tricks of the fools afforded most delight to His Holiness." The pope played a notorious and unfathomably elaborate trick on an old, doddering priest, Barbarello. The pope assured the gullible priest that his lousy poetry was comparable to Petrarch's; the pope insisted on throwing him a grand **poetry reading**, crowning him with laurels and riding him in on a white elephant. On the special day, the pope swathed the Vatican windows in red velvet and assembled throngs of costumed peasants from common casting and a handful of trumpeters to herald the *faux poéte*, dressed to kill in a red toga with gold trim. Mind you, this is the same pope who commissioned Michelangelo and Raphael, restored important churches, brought musicians to the city, and offered his extensive library to scholars.

Art and Architecture

> ...if cleanliness is next to godliness, it is a very dis-
> tant neighbor to chiaroscuro.
> —Henry James

The succession of wealthy popes who were eager to leave their mark on the city in the form of new buildings, paintings, and sculpture gave a sagging Rome its most gorgeous makeover since ancient days of monumental glory. The Catholic Church mingled with other European powers, shared the same taste in artists, spoke the same languages, and shared aspirations of grandeur. Eager to improve the city after the sack, financed by the (naughty) sale of indulgences, and unaffected by the prudish strictures of the Protestant Reformation, the succession of popes during the Renaissance left an unrivaled legacy of magnificent churches, paintings, and sculpture. While the early stages of the Renaissance Rome were set in Tuscany, the movement soon shifted to Rome, where artists were attracted by the promise of fame and work. Hailing from Rome's secular noble families, the popes nevertheless bolstered the Church's supremacy and spiritual optimism by commissioning artists to depict conversion scenes and martydoms. This age heralded the split between science and faith, and the church condemned both Galileo and Giordano Bruno for their astronomical assertions that the earth was not the center of the universe. Philosopher and scientist **Pascal** struggled to resolve the division of human experience between the real and the imaginary, the external and the internal, the rational and the emotional; he resolved, "The heart has its reasons that the mind cannot know." Artists as well as scientists explored the possibilities of this spiritual-intellectual rift like no previous age; painters, sculptors, and architects relied heavily on subjective experience, exploiting its emotional and dramatic potential, all while employing the most advanced technical and scientific discoveries the Age of Science had to offer.

The new scientific undertandings of anatomy contributed to discovery of correct perspective and the perfection of human musculature in two-dimensional renderings. The rediscovery of Roman and Greek forms as well as the new "worldly" concerns of the Church further revitalized the interest in the human form as well as a turn to realism, exemplified in **Caravaggio**'s dramatic depictions of the mundane. In **Michelangelo**'s *Last Judgement,* Christ is portrayed as a robust, Herculean figure rather than as the piteous, half-starved medieval figure. Nudity came back into vogue, most works cautiously remaining in the spiritual realm, and pagan themes were explored with new interest. Venuses and Madonnas were painted with equal reverence and with equally good looks. **Bernini** took a walk on the wild side with his orgasmic *St. Teresa in Ecstasy,* and played up the spectacle by creating an ersatz theater around the sculpture in the church of S. Maria della Vittorio. The Church played on the viewer's confidence in the realistic, on the stirring impact of emotional drama, and on the purely theatrical entertainment in the works they commissioned, counting on all three to inspire faith in and reverence for the Church. Though the rational Age of Enlightnment was right around the corner, it was faith who played muse to the creative brilliance of this period.

The Odd Couple: Bernini and Borromini

The personality differences between effervescent, cavalier boy-genius Giovanni Lorenzo **Bernini** and dark, tempermental Francesco Castelli **Borromini** is abundantly clear in their works. Known as the "greatest European" in his day, the architect, sculptor, theatrical producer, painter, and dandy Bernini more than set the standard for the Baroque during his prolific career. Confident in the precocious genius of his son, Bernini's father, a Florentine sculptor brought his son to Rome to start work; he was immediately signed on for training and didn't stop working until the age of eighty. For

Bernini, work was pleasure, and by the end of his life, he had served every pope of his time and had shaped the cityscape more than any other artist in history. His swarthy good looks endeared him to countless patrons and fans, and he was given creative control beyond any artist's wildest fantasy. His taste for the histrionic extended beyond his lively personality, and he directed countless theater productions and pranks—including one in which he let a torrent of water flood towards his terrified audience, until it was stopped by a gate. His mastery of marble is unsurpassed, and his expressive sculptures deny the boundaries of clay and flesh.

Along with his charged **St. Teresa**, Bernini's Hellenistic **David** stands in great contrast to Michelangelo's classical version of frozen perfection. The sculpture is a study in energy, expressiveness, and concentration whereas Michelangelo's embodies the restraint and coolness of Greek figures. Unlike Michelangelo, Bernini creates a drama within the figure, implying Goliath's presence. Maffeo Barberini paid Bernini to carve his features onto the sculpture; like Caravaggio, Bernini was eager to dismiss the generic heroic ideal his predecessors (like Michelangelo and Raphael) sought to emulate. Bernini revolutionized sculpture, taking it from an epic to a temporal form, releasing it from its cold, isolated nature to one of dramatic engagement, movement, and imperfect realism.

Although architecture was in some sense only a small portion of Bernini's career, he was one of Rome's greatest architects. The oval of the *piazza* of St. Peter's was really the culmination of a life's work; he personally supervised the construction of each and every one of the Doric travertine columns (284). Only Bernini could manage to transform the overwhelming space to an inviting, even emotional square, which would, as he said, "maternally embrace" the crowds of Catholics and others in its colonnade. His churches and monuments (including the grand **baldacchino** at St. Peter's and his own favorite, the **church of Sant'Andrea del Quirinale**), exemplified his high-flown, theatrical, illusory style that came to define the Baroque.

Tortured, acutely cerebral, non-conformist, and Swiss, **Borromini** spent much of his career repudiating the prevailing zeitgeist of the Baroque, with its sumptuous illusions and ornate decoration. His surviving architectural designs, fraught with an endless series of changes and minute details, bespeak the sheer agony and intellectual integrity of Borromini's life work. Where Bernini played with illusion and decoration, Borromini sought purity (though in the most complex terms) and utilized painfully difficult geometry in creating his architectural structures. Borromini once served as a student to Maderno, and was commissioned to design some of the details on Bernini's *baldacchino*. It became increasingly apparent, however, that Bernini's style and his own were wholly incompatible. He manages to imbue his work with vigor and animation solely by the undulating movement of concave and convex forms and the play of shadow and light, unadorned with Baroque frippery or excessive ornamentation. He staunchly refused to deck his buildings with the sensational windswept statues that Bernini so loved, and insisted that the carefully (painfully) wrought structures speak for themselves. While his works don't necessarily pack the emotional punch of Bernini's, but he created an entirely new architectural vocabulary. In the **church of S. Carlo alle Quattro Fontane**, the façade appears elastic, almost stretched out of shape or distended, creating a sense of tensions and counter-pressures and fusing sculpture and architecture, Gothic and Renaissance, like never before. Eventually the complexity, tension, and pressure of Borromini's work caught up with him; he became obsessed with his calculations and machinations, and withdrew completely from society. Whereas Bernini wallowed in his fame, attending banquets in his honor all through Europe, Borromini would only be comforted by an old parish priest. Finally, a few days after burning a series of architectural plans, he put a sword through his chest and died.

Portraits of the Artists as Young Men

Michelangelo (1475-1564)

The supreme artist with the supremely tortured soul grew up amongst the stone-masons of Tuscany; "With my wet-nurse's milk, I sucked in the hammer and chisels I use for my statues," Michelangelo Buonarroti claimed. After serving as an apprentice to Domenico Ghirlandaio and attending an art academy, he was discovered by Lorenzo the Magnificent, who nurtured the young genius in the palace's court circle of artists and humanists. During this period, Michelangelo honed his knowledge of the human body after he swapped a crucifix for the privilege of dissecting corpses in the Cloisters of San Spirito. At the age of twenty-one he headed to Rome, already recruited by the pope for some minor works, to seek his fortune. His first claim to fame was a marble cupid that imitated the ancients so perfectly that admirers claimed it could be mistaken for an authentic one. He received a flood of commissions, including the profoundly sorrowful and sensuous **Piéta** in St. Peter's, which made him the leading sculptor of marble and quite a celebrity. He returned to Florence for a decade, agonizingly carving his colossal and heroic **David** out of a huge piece of inferior marble; the confidence, pride and perfection of the statue inspired Florence to make it its symbol, and they parked it outside of the town hall, instead of the *duomo*. This larger-than-life nude male figure initiated a mad rush of other sculptors, including Benvento Cellini, to try to out-do Michelangelo.

In 1502, Pope Julius II sent for Michelangelo, now almost thirty and at the height of his career, to return to Rome to build a **tomb**. The relationship that was to last eight years between overbearing, irascible, and demanding Julius II and the arrogant, intro-verted and temperamental Michelangelo was not a meeting of like minds. Julius first commissioned Michelangelo to construct a colossal tomb, which was left unfinished because Julius got carried away instead with his grandiose plans for St. Peter's. Along with the a lack of funds and relentless demands from other popes after Julius died, Michelangelo had to abandon the project. Infuriated and fed up, he fled Rome in 1504. Still, the half-finished tomb sculptures provide some insight into Michelangelo's cre-ative process. Julius managed to sweet-talk the moody artist into returning to Rome to paint the **Sistine Chapel** ceiling. Michelangelo agreed, and spent the next four years slaving over, or rather under, the problem-ridden project. First, Michelangelo had to learn how to paint frescoes before he could start. The technique is extremely difficult and riddled with complications. At one point, Michelangelo almost lost his shit com-pletely when a moldy portion of the fresco just fell to the ground. A perfectionist and type-A personality, Michelangelo fired all his assistants for being incompetent and took up even the most menial tasks himself. He threw away the pope's original pictoral design and got permission to do the whole job himself, a considerable challenge from which he never fully recovered. Michelangelo spent days lying on his back, craning his neck and head up to the ceiling until they were practically dislocated. The chapel was suffocatingly hot in the summer, and freezing in the winter, and on a daily basis, he had paint and plaster dripping into his face, causing a rash. The pope's incessant *kvetching* didn't help either and Julius sometimes climbed up on the scaffolding to prod Miche-langelo along. The ceiling was finished in 1512, four months before Julius's death, and Michelangelo escaped to Florence. Thirty years later, Michelangelo returned to Rome, greeted by the new Pope Paul II, who cried, "I've been looking forward to employing you for thirty years!" The pope commissioned the aged Michelangelo to return to the Sistine Chapel for his most important work, **The Last Judgement**. By contrast to the idealized figures, careful details and more optimistic images of the Sistine ceiling, *The Last Judgment* reveals Michelangelo's terrifying vision of the Apocalypse, anticipating the swirling colors, dark, emotional drama, bleak decor, and imperfect figures of the Mannerist period. Michelangelo continued in his architectural designs, but never paint-ed again. He died at the age of 89; to fool the Romans-who would certainly want to bury Michelangelo's body in their city- his casket was smuggled to Florence, in honor of the artists' wish to be buried there.

Caravaggio (1573-1610)

Michelangelo Caravaggio was as refined in his life as he was in his art. While his anxiety attacks drove him to introspection and isolation, Caravaggio violently vented his frustrations on other people. Often drunk, the sight of a uniform made him particu-larly irascible: 16th-century police reports reveal that Caravaggio stabbed a captain of the papal guards, went to jail for lobbing stones at a policeman, and was picked up after verbally abusing an officer who, understandably, wanted to see his permit for carrying firearms. Born in Caravaggio (near Milan), Caravaggio moved to Rome when he as around 20. Although he had plenty of work as a painter, he chose to stay in the seedy Roman underworld of prostitution and gambling. His acquaintances from the underbelly of the city appeared as holy and revered characters in his paintings: a pouty male prostitute posed for *Boy with a Basket of Fruit;* his St. Paul in the *Conversion of St. Paul* is ruggedly blue-collar-looking; St. Paul's horse, usually grandly depicted, could be any bored work horse.

Caravaggio participated in the art world on his own terms. While some clients were put off by his reputation and those of his models, Caravaggio had a fruitful relationship with the Catholic Church; Church officials recognized the raw, intense spirituality in Caravaggio's work that the Baroque Church wanted (and needed) to illustrate; his figures would "speak to the people" as it were. After stabbing and killing an acquaintance in a dispute over a ball game, Caravaggio fled Rome. He died of a fever while attempting to return to the city to take advantage of a papal pardon. Director Derek Jarman, whose own work borrows heavily from Caravaggio and other figures from the Baroque, gives a brilliant account of the artist's life in his film, *Caravaggio.*

Carnival : It's All Fun and Games Until Someone Loses an Eye

The decadent nature of Renaissance Rome welcomed back the carnival hi-jinks and horrors of ancient times that were more or less abandoned in the medieval period. Initially, Pope Paul II (1458-64) set up some races in the spirit of good, clean fun. There were races between kids, with a pair a stockings for the winner. There were races between young Christians, between middle-aged men, between senior citizens, and between buffaloes and donkeys. There was a separate race for Jews, and for this race the pope raised the winner's haul to a sumptuous bolt of fabric. Thus was born the Roman *Carnivale.*

Pope Paul II later moved to a new palace, the Palazzo San Marco, overlooking the via Lata, and thus decreed that the events take place in view of his window. These windows are visible in the facade of the **Palazzo Venezia** which eventually replaced the pope's palace. The races, or *corsi*, were then run from the palace to the Arch of Domitian (now via del Corso), which is how the street got its name. The Roman Carnival audience delighted in the most cruel and unusual races, with appalling events harkening back to the evil-entertainment days of the Empire. There was a race reserved for hunchbacks and other cripples that prompted rather insensitive heckling. In the beginning, the Jews were as enthused about Carnival as anyone else, but as the Roman sense of fun and games began to go awry, all those footraces took on a new, horrific dimension. The pope's henchmen kidnapped elder Jews from the ghetto, stuffed them with Italian pastry and made them run the course. The organizers added horses to goad the Jews on. Jews were not allowed to wear masks during Carnival, and in fact, many Romans took this time of the year as license to be extra nasty to the Jewish community, tormenting individuals, spitting, taunting, hitting and even throwing things at them. Those Jews who refused to participate cheerfully in the shameful baiting and the cruel races were promptly flogged by a man hired just for that purpose, standing by on nearby via Cavalletto.

Another race viewed with as much vicious enthusiasm and elation as the Jewish race was that of the *Barberi.* Riderless Arabian horses were wrapped in white cloth and prodded to insane speeds by nail-encrusted saddles and barbs attached to their private parts. The horses galloped wildly down the course, eventually halted by a huge white sheet strung across the road.

With these elaborations of Carnival came some more innocent festivities. Crowds donned elaborate costumes, parading around as nymphs, gods, heroes, and fairies. A tall greased pole was set up in piazza Navona for teams of men to climb up and test their machismo and strength—a contest still held during the carnival in New York's Little Italy. Streamers, ribbons, and garlands of flowers decorated buildings and benches. At the end of the day, the pope hosted a lavish banquet for Roman VIPs, and allowed the crowds of masqueraders to take doggie bags home. In one burst of drunken enthusiasm, he strewed money from his balcony to the screaming commoners below.

One of the most stylish popes, Julius II, urged the festivity to new levels of grandeur and pomp. Before the races begun, there was a grand parade of the most elegant society members festooned in embroidered capes and bizarre hats, brandishing flashy lances and antique swords. Jews were still dragged from the Ghetto and humiliated by brutal races. One contemporary account reports, "Last Monday, the Jews had the gratification of running against a strong wind, in a cold rain worthy of that perfidious people. When they arrived at the finish, they were obscenely covered with mud from head to foot."

In 1667, two centuries after the races started, the Jewish community managed to bribe the Church and Carnival administrators to let them avoid participating; the Jews offered some money as well as the promise of decorating annually the small grandstand where the judges sat. The judges suddenly managed to rack up enormous bills, charging the Jews for new and improved furniture and frippery. The rest of the Carnival festivities continued their usual wild ways.

Disease and Disaster

Along with the humanist ideals of Petrarch, creations of Michelangelo and Raphael, and licentious happenings at *Carnivale*, Renaissance Italy encountered a humiliating arrest to its achievements: namely, **syphilis**. The disease was probably imported to the continent in 1494 from either Africa or the West Indies, or from (egads!) America by Christopher Columbus's crew. French soldiers contracted the disease from prostitutes in Naples and nicknamed it the "Neapolitan disease"; in turn, the Italians called it *morbo gallico* (disease of the Gauls). In Rome, the disease spread like wildfire, infecting seventeen members of the Pope's family and court, including Cesare Borgia (illegitimate son of the satanic pope, Rodrigo; murderer; and protagonist of Machiavelli's *The Prince*), who was treated for it within two months of its first appearance.

To add to the horrors of the city's inundation by venereal disease, the Tiber produced a violent **flood** in 1495, with water gushing into the streets, surging through churches and homes, until it was suppressed by the fortified walls of the city's palaces. Many people were drowned, including the prisoners in the fearsome Tor di Nona, which overlooked the (now-called) Ponte Umberto, a stark prison that once held astronomer-*cum*-heretic, Giordano Bruno and sculptor-*cum*-jewel thief, Benevento Cellini.

The ascetic Florentine Dominican friar **Girolamo Savonarola** soon proclaimed these calamities the wages of sin to be paid by the decadent Church and inaugurated an all-out rampage on the papal and municipal excesses of Rome. He condemned the Church for its whoring and its profligacy. He warned the city of famine, pestilence, and general catastrophe if it neglected to clean up its act; he even envisioned a black cross rising from the hills of Rome emblazoned with the words, "The Cross of God's Anger". The pope (Pius III) tried to shut him up, first by a papal decree forbidding him to speak, then when Savonarola persisted, the pope offered him a cardinal post. The friar refused the official hat, claiming that one "red with blood" would be more appropriate for the corrupt position. The pope finally just excommunicated him. Savonarola persevered with a vengeance until the Florentines themselves got sick of his continual haranguing and tortured, burned, and hanged him.

Jews in Renaissance Rome

Pope Sixtus IV (1464-71) was a strong and vocal defender of the Jews; at the same time he commissioned the Sistine Chapel as a great monument to Catholicism. Nevertheless, to the consternation of the Roman Jewry, he turned a blind eye to the first major stirrings of the Spanish Inquisition. Finally, perhaps prodded on by his talented Jewish physician, he warned King Ferdinand and Isabella (reminder: the sponsors of Christopher Columbus, who is now rumored to have been Jewish) to loosen their anti-Semitic strictures. Sixtus IV even took pains (via papal edicts and arm-twisting) to silence the rampant anti-Jewish sentiment among certain monks and intellectuals, some of them recent converts from Judaism.

The Inquisition and expulsion of the Jews from Spain in 1492 sent many of them packing to Italy (a kinder, gentler nation) and to Rome to join the well-established Jewish community, where they set up shops and businesses. Many towns and cities, such as Livorno, did welcome their services as merchants and moneylenders; Jews were exempt from the ancient Church injunction against usury (loan interest), and even when their money-lending practice was threatened by law, it went underground. Shakespeare's *The Merchant of Venice* illustrates some of the prevailing antipathy toward (and simultaneous financial dependency on) Jews in 16th-century Italy in its cruel depiction of the sadistic moneylender, Shylock.

Pope Leo X (1513-22), known more for his intense patronage of the arts than his religious devotion, involved a select number of Jews in his court. In fact, he threw caution to the wind, and made a small, subversive gesture in favor of the Jews during his formal entry into the Vatican. During all popes' first procession, the Jews gathered at the Ponte Sant'Angelo with their rabbi to present their book of law to prove that they were worthy citizens; by tradition, the pope would reject the Jewish faith, voice some pre-scripted foolishness about the Jews' general unworthiness, sinfulness, and inferiority, and then begrudgingly confirm their privileges. At the inauguration of each pope, the Jews additionally decorated the popes' parade routes with elaborate tapestries and banners; this was generally the most contact with the pope that the Jews had. When the rabbi met with Leo X, the new pope uttered the prescribed indignities and disrespect with a certain amount of reluctance and shame. Leo's own Jewish court companions included the handsome musician Jacopo di Sansecondo (who also served as a model for Raphael), as well as an advisor, a physician, and one Giovanni Maria, a flautist who pleased the pope so much that he was made a count and got a healthy allowance. Following this period of papal tolerance for Jewish culture, Leo's predecessor, Julius II, also an avid patron of the arts, commissioned Michelangelo's Moses statue in a burst of respect for the Old Testament.

However, the Counter-Reformation ushered in a new period of anguish and unrest in the Jewish community. **Pope Paul IV** (1555), a Neapolitan who vowed that he "would burn his father at the stake if he were a heretic," revived the hatred and intolerance of the Spanish Inquisition once more, searching out heretics for the Church bonfire. Torture was widely practiced and some people were burned at the stake. While the Catholics' attack was aimed more directly at the Christian heretics, Jews were also regarded as enemies. In 1556 all Jews were herded into the Ghetto, a small, low-lying malarial district near the Tiber. Under the scrutiny of the Mattei family, the gates were locked at night, and during the day Jews were forced to wear yellow caps (for men) or yellow veils (for women) if they ventured beyond the dreary zone. Jews were only allowed to work in outdoor markets or rag shops, though many pursued mystical practices, such as astrology and fortune-telling to make a living; it was not unheard of for patrician ladies of Rome to get their palms read on a regular basis in the Ghetto. The walls of the Ghetto did not fall until two centuries later. For more details about the history of the Jews in Rome, see under Jewish Ghetto-Sights, below.

What a Drag Queen: Queen Christina

One of Europe's most intriguing figures during the 17th century was Sweden's Queen Christina. Christina was a Renaissance man: she eschewed the dress of women, was an expert hunter, and could ride a horse like nobody's business; fluent in many languages and exceptionally well-read, she was also a renowned art collector who possessed one of the greatest art collections ever assembled. Unpopular in Sweden for converting to Catholicism and refusing to bear the nation an heir, Christina abdicated and took off to Rome on the advice of two Jesuit priests. There, the city's greatest artists gathered around her: Allesandro Scarlatti oversaw her private orchestra, while Bernini carved sculptures for her and gave her inside information on the art market. The philosopher Rene Descartes was her private tutor, and he actually died from a case pneumonia he caught while teaching her in her drafty, unheated residence. She is buried in St. Peter's; an inscription welcoming her to the city remains on the **Porta del Popolo**.

Dysfunctional Families

The Cencis

Three hundred years after the death of Dante's beloved, Rome furnished the Renaissance with its own young and beautiful Beatrice, killed in the flower of her youth, only to be immortalized after her death by the curlicues of a great poet. **Beatrice Cenci's** father **Francesco Cenci** (1549-98), like many Roman aristocrats, perceived himself to be above the law, but was not particularly good at getting away with breaking it. When Francesco was tried by a papal court in 1594 for sodomy and extreme cruelty, the prosecutor cited a rap sheet as long as his arm that began when Francesco was eleven years old. Despite the 16th-century idea of jurisprudence that included healthy doses of torture for Francesco's accusers, he was still found guilty. After being forced to donate a small fortune to the papacy, however, Francesco was free to go. Fleeing the scandal of his trial, he took his wife and daughter to an isolated castle southeast of Rome in 1595, where he developed an unhealthy attraction to Beatrice, described in Shelley's closet drama *The Cenci* (1819) as "a creature formed to adorn and be admired." While there was apparently no physical consummation of love, he physically and mentally abused both mother and daughter.

After several years, Beatrice proved equal to her father's bullying. Beatrice had no trouble enlisting the help of her two brothers (also with no love lost for their father), as well as the services of hit man Marzio Catalano, who practiced carpentry on people's heads. Francesco was discovered one morning in 1598 in the branches of some trees (beneath a balcony from which he had been thrown) with a nail driven through his skull. Catalano was caught first and named all of his co-conspirators. Beatrice's arrest became a *cause celêbre*. Her father was singularly unpopular in Rome and Beatrice was widely seen as a woman driven to a violent act of self-defense. The Cenci murder case raised questions of domestic abuse and self-defense that are remain unresolved by courts today. The appeal for a papal pardon was heard and rejected by **Pope Clement VIII**. (Clement VIII was similarly strict two years later with **Giordano Bruno**, approving his sentence to burn at the stake as a heretic.)

Beatrice got off comparatively easy—she was beaheaded in 1599 in a *piazza* across from the Castel Sant'Angelo. Her brother, on the other hand, was tortured with red-hot instruments, put out of his misery with a mace, and then drawn and quartered for good measure. Only her younger brother Bernardo was spared the death penalty; instead he was sentenced to life in prison. Beatrice's cause has attracted the attention of an impressive line-up of famous and diverse writers. Shelley told his version of the story in *The Cenci*, which he wrote in 1819 while living on the via del Corso in Rome, while Stendhal included her in his sentimental *Chroniques Italiennes*. Beatrice's story has also been retold by the 20th-century writers Alberto Moravia and Antonin Artaud.

The Borgias

Before the Cencis, there was another unusual Roman family, the Borgias, who have also been immortalized on stage, in song, and in print. Victor Hugo airbrushed the events of Lucrezia Borgia's life in a play he wrote about her; Gabriel Donizetti made her the protagonist of one of his operas. Said to be equally captivating, her brother Cesare inspired the title character of Machiavelli's the *The Prince*. A close look at the history of the Borgia family, makes it seem peculiar that they should be cast as heroes and heroines rather than villains. All of 15th-century Europe trembled at the mere mention of this unscrupulous but unusually attractive family. While the very first Borgia Pope, Calixtus III, was harmless enough, his nephew and successor **Rodrigo Borgia** (1430-1503. His papal name was Alexander VI) was intent on founding no less than a kingdom to be ruled by his progeny, of which there were many. The pitter-patter of little feet was heard all over the Vatican in the 1470s: Rodrigo and his mistress—with whom he lived openly—had four children together; he fathered six others by other mistresses. Rodrigo wasn't all business; he outraged republican Rome by throwing bash after decadent bash. Although Rodrigo was said to be bewitchingly attractive and had no trouble getting dates, at one of his gatherings 50 prostitutes were hired to dance a ballet entirely naked. You can still see Rodrigo's insatiable appetites in his face, in the unflattering frescoes done by **Pinturicchio** in the Vatican Museums.

While Rodrigo ruled in Rome, his son **Cesare Borgia** (1476-1507) went about the bloody business of carving out a new kingdom in Europe. Cesare, who had inherited his father's comely appearance, became the original "Valentino" after subduing the Duchy of Valentois. Cesare swiped title after title from conquered nobles, ruthlessly pillaging cities as large as Urbino; Venice and Florence were certain they would be next. It could be as dangerous being Cesare's friend as it was to be his enemy. Notorious for his nonchalance while witnessing murders, he once invited four high-ranking officers to a banquet and continued munching on a drumstick while they were strangled in front of him. Historians suspect Cesare of murdering his elder brother, as well as his brother-in-law, both of whom he saw as hindrances to his power.

Rodrigo and Cesare acquired immense holdings but never managed to establish their own kingdom. Rodrigo's younger sister **Lucrezia Borgia** (1480-1519) certainly did her part to help out, marrying five times by the time she was 22, each time to a strategic purpose. Lucrezia's first (at age 11) and second betrothals were mutually dissolved. Her third marriage (at age 13) was to a Sforza, Milan's most powerful family. When the Sforzas were no longer necessary to Borgia interests, Lucrezia had no problem getting an annullment from the Church, since her father was the pope. Her fourth husband was murdered, and given her history, her fifth husband, the duke of Ferrara, was understandably reluctant. Their wedding (Rodrigo held an army to the duke's head) was one of the most extravagant European royalty had ever seen. For the trip to Ferrara, Lucrezia's considerable beauty was set off by a gold brocade cape, and her pale skin protected by a canopy held aloft, for some strange reason, by university professors. Notorious for overpacking, Lucrezia burdened some 150 mules with her trousseau, from which she produced a stunning ermine-trimmed red-velvet wedding dress.

Contrary to the way the Borgias as a family are remembered by history, Lucrezia's story had a happy ending. Her marital bliss was crowned by a brood of children. Rodrigo and Cesare, on the hand, got their just desserts; the former may have been poisoned and the latter was struck down in battle. In their heyday, the Borgias were reviled by the Roman people; it's no surprise that shortly after their deaths outrageous and often supernatural tales were spun, many of which survive today. Perhaps the most well-known is the supposed incestuous relationships of Rodrigo and Cesare with Lucrezia, of which there is no hard evidence.

The 18th and 19th Century

Il Settecento: Italian (and Especially Roman) Irrelevance

The first three-quarters of the 18th century in Rome were remarkably quiet politically, especially compared to the tumult of previous centuries. When the **Treaty of Westphalia** ended the **Thirty Years War** in 1648, its terms were less than favorable to papal power, which waned considerably afterwards. A succession of popes were either unable or uninterested in international affairs. **Pope Clement XIV**, faced with overwhelming anti-Jesuit sentiment, expelled the Jesuit Society from Rome in 1773. His successor, **Pius VI**, mishandled conflicts between the Church and the post-revolution French Assembly. Anti-clerical sentiment exploded in Paris: effigies of Pius were set on fire and a severed head landed in the lap of the Papal Nuncio as he was traveling in his coach. In Rome, envoys of the Republic replaced portraits of the pope in the French Academy with portraits of revolutionary heroes and leaders. Roused from their usual complacency, in 1793 Romans attacked a French delegation that arrived on the Corso over-accessorized in tricolor badges. After murdering one of them, the crowd spread through the streets, vandalizing the homes of French sympathizers, setting the French Academy on fire, shouting "Long live the Pope" and "Long live the Catholic religion."

France's commander-in-chief, Napoleon appeared on the scene in 1796 to refill French coffers emptied by the revolution with the treasures of Europe. Napoleon refused to depose the pope altogether for certain strategic reasons, but he brought the

Church to its knees by extorting millions in tribute and carrying off precious works of art and mountains of jewels. Romans watched 500 wagons leave the city loaded with booty; in fact, some of the most important pieces of Italian and Roman art are now found in Parisian museums. In 1798, Napoleon's successor as commander-in-chief, General Berthier stormed the Vatican, deposing the pope and establishing yet another **Roman Republic**. Although Berthier interrupted the longest reign of any pope since ancient times, the papacy returned to temporal power in Rome in 1815, as Napoleon's empire began to crumble.

Rome as Capital of the Kingdom of Italy

Among the victors of the reactionary, monarchistic coalition that extinguished the flame of French liberty was the calcifying Austro-Hungarian Empire of the Habsburgs. Demanding their haunch of Napoleon's carcass, the Austrians annexed northern Italy, including Rome. But having been given a taste of freedom by Bonaparte, the Italians began to hope for their own nation-state. By 1848, the move toward a unified Italy, known as the **Risorgimento**, had erupted in every major city in the country; underground resistance groups like the **Carbonari** and **Young Italy** organized and sabotaged Austrian institutions. Once again the focus of international politics, Rome provoked the wrath of Catholic Europe by finally voting to abolish the papal state and establish in 1849, you guessed it, another **Roman Republic**. Pope Pius IX appealed to the heads of state of Europe with great success; within three months, Rome was once again besieged by the French and another dreaded Bonaparte, Napoleon III. The resistance was led by **Carlo Mazzini** and **Guiseppe Garibaldi**, alumni of the Carbonari and Young Italy respectively. Although the former preached with revolutionary fervor, and the latter, with the aid of his scruffy Garibaldians, steadied Rome against a complacent French force, the French triumphed and reinstated Pope Pius IX.

Pius IX was interested in the advances modern science was making into early Christian history (such as the excavations of the Catacombs) and modern gadgets. He had his own train; painted white and gold, one car was specially built to house a mobile chapel. His politics, however, remained firmly medieval; this time, the military impetus for a united Italy engulfed rather than emanated from Rome. Regional Italian rulers united all of the country except for Rome and Venice, then declared Rome the capital and crowned the first Italian king, **Vittorio Emanuele.** In 1870, when the French declared war on the Prussians, there was no one to stop the Italian forces (led in part, again, by the resurgent Garibaldi) from crashing through the Vatican. There the pope "imprisoned" himself, refusing to give up his editorial control, and urging all Italians to support him; he died a lonely man in 1878. The new government set about erecting public buildings to house its ministries and new apartment buildings to house its gigantic corps of civil servants.

The Grand Tour

If you're one of the hordes of backpacking students Eurailing around Europe in the summer, consider yourself in fine historical company: 18th-century Europeans (the English in particular), first discovered the absolute necessity of making the **Grand Tour**. Before making the transition from school to employment and marriage, upper-crusty young gentlemen were sent across the English Channel to visit the glamorous capitals of the Continent, traditionally ending in a visit to the holy places of Rome around Easter. Guided by a tutor and one of the many new travel books available, these young pups were supposed to carefully inspect the ruins and monuments of European history and acquire refined continental tastes and manners. In Rome, not just any *cicerone*, or tour guide, would do, but only the amazing **Winkelmann**, a German archaeologist who specialized in Roman antiquities, and who is frequently referred to by his last name alone (see Love Among the Ruins, below).

While gentlemen were acquiring finesse and polish, they were also getting their hands very dirty. The ulterior motive behind the Grand Tour was to give the sons of England and other nations a chance to sow their wild oats, usually in Italy, and to leave them there. Tutors were known as "bear leaders" because of the often animalian behavior of their charges. Cunning English gentlemen ditched their bear leaders in time to make Carnival in Italy, where social mores were substantially more relaxed compared to home. **Robert Burns** characterized the behavior of 18th-century British tourists in Italy as "whore-hunting among groves of myrtles."

In Rome, self-indulgent British were reminded of their sins and their Protestantism by the presence of the offensively opulent Catholic church. For these tourists, Rome wasn't so much a religious Mecca as a scholarly one. Raised on Greek and Latin authors, British tourists knew the history of Rome better than its own citizens. One of the most famous Grand Tourists of the century was **Edward Gibbon**, whose visit inspired him to write the *Decline and Fall of the Roman Empire*. Less noble foreign visitors gathered in coffee shops and salons of Roman nobles—to whom they came with letters of introduction—for flirtation and cross-cultural comparisons.

There were of course drawbacks to the Grand Tour, including substantial physical hardships (and venereal disease). Getting across the Alps took a minimum of two days. Carriages had to be taken apart and carried, while the traveler swung from two parallel poles in a rope chair, as his bearers transported him on foot. **Lord Byron** mitigated the discomforts of leaving home by taking an entourage of seven servants, five carriages, and a small herd of livestock. Often a destination could prove as dangerous as the trip; among a host of other diseases, Tiber-fostered malaria, known as "Roman fever," felled the unwary and the unlucky.

Perhaps the most famous tourist to die of malaria is Henry James's fictional freebird **Daisy Miller**. James's story illustrates how the 19th-century Grand Tour belonged to the *nouveau riche* Americans, anxious (consciously or not) to imitate their English cousins. Sour old **Mark Twain** characterized this new American Grand Tour as an encounter between the "Old World" and "New Barbarians" in his satire of the Grand Tour, titled *The Innocents Abroad*. Overwhelmed by the absurdities of tourism in the eternal city, Twain's narrator feels "liable at any moment to fall prey to some antiquary and be patched in the legs and 'restored' with an unseemly nose, and labeled wrong and dated wrong, and set up in the Vatican for poets to drivel about and vandals to scribble their names on forever and forevermore."

Carnival: The Fun Never Ends

The Roman Carnival of the 18th and 19th century continued to be Europe's unrivaled party; letting off steam in the eight days before Lent, each Roman, Goethe wrote in *Italian Journey,* "has leave to be as mad and foolish as he likes, and almost everything, except fisticuffs and stabbing, is permissible." The festivities were kicked off with a fake kick to the small of the Chief Rabbi's back, who presented most of the funds for the Christian celebration, on (the involuntary) behalf of the Jewish community. The church's decked-out high officials then paraded down the Corso through crowds of Romans dressed and cross-dressed in wildly exaggerated costumes of foreign countries. People wore scary masks to prevent being injured by the pelts of hardened *confetti*. On the last night, the streets were crowded with people carrying candles: "May he who does not carry a candle be knocked senseless" were the simple rules of the last night's mayhem; Romans moshed all night long in an orgiastic effort to blow out each other's candles. "Ladies," the Baedeker guides hinted, "are advised to eschew the Corso on the chief days of the Carnival."

'Paradise of Exiles': Expatriates in Rome

*[Rome's] greatness, accomplished and destined,
lies in just the fact that she is not and never can be
exclusively Italian.*

—*William Dean Howells*

Before the Modernists took over Paris in the early 20th century, 18th- and 19th-century Rome was the uncontested favorite destination of expatriate European artists. Rome was, in **Percy Shelley's** phrase, the "paradise of exiles." **Goethe** gushed upon arriving in Rome in 1787, "Only now do I begin to live." **Zola** also wrote of the wondrous squalor of the city in his book *Rome*. Artists and intellectuals fled their homelands in order to escape everything from scandal and bankruptcy to stultifying morality and boredom. They came to Rome primarily to take inspiration from the daily encounter with the past, and the fact that Rome was quite a bargain in those days didn't discourage them either. Rome was the perfect locale for indulging in the 18th- and early 19th-century taste for "ruin poems" or "graveyard literature," in which the living take solace and wisdom from the dead of centuries past. In **Lord Byron's** wildly popular *Childe Harold's Pilgrimage* the histrionic protagonist exclaims:
Oh Rome! my country! city of the soul! The orphans of the heart must turn to thee,
Lone mother of dead empires!
Frederick Jackson Turner would later use excerpts from *Childe Harold* as inspiration for a series of Roman paintings.

Byron's friend **Shelley** cited the conducive atmosphere of Roman rubble in his introduction to the closet drama *Prometheus Unbound*, "chiefly written upon the mountainous ruins of the Baths of Caracalla." Shelley would, of course, retire to the fashionable Via del Corso. In the same productive year (1819), Shelley looked back to 16th-century Rome for the subject of his long lyric *The Cenci*, concerned with the sensational Cenci murder case. (See Dysfunctional Families-Renaissance above). The Brownings were also intrigued by foul play in the Eternal City; a 17th-century Roman murder trial is the subject of **Robert Browning's** gargantuan poem *The Ring and the Book*. In the days before monuments had opening and closing hours, historian **Edward Gibbon**, prompted by insomnia, was drawn to the Forum where "each memorable spot where Romulus stood, or Tully spoke or Caesar fell, was at once present to my eye; and several days of intoxication were lost or enjoyed before I could descend to a cool and minute investigation." Later, feeling complicated among the ruins of the Capitol, **Gibbon** hit on the "the first thought" of his classic history text and quick beach read, *The Decline and Fall of the Roman Empire*.

After extensive tours of ancient monuments during the day, most expatriates took full advantage of contemporary Rome in the evening. Most British found lodgings in the comfortable neighborhood of the piazza di Spagna, described by Tobias Smollet as the "English Ghetto." The enduring expatriate haunt was the **Caffè Grèco**, which still stands in the via Condotti (see Caffès-Entertainment, below). The Grèco was never rowdier than when American sculptor **William Wetmore Story** introduced his hell-raising friends **Hans Christian Andersen** and **Elizabeth Barrett Browning** there in 1861. **William Dean Howells**, American Man of Letters, visited Rome on his pseudo-British grand tour and published the tome *Roman Holidays and Others*. **Edith Wharton** offered her impressions of the city in *Italian Backgrounds*.

In 1765, Samuel Johnson's name-dropping biographer **James Boswell** wrote extensively of the Roman nightlife to his confidante **Jean-Jacques Rousseau**. Of one evening Boswell wrote, "I sallied forth like an imperious lion...I remembered the rakish deeds of Horace and other amorous Roman poets, and I thought that one might well allow one's self a little indulgence in a city where there are prostitutes licensed by the Cardinal Vicar." Boswell made it his project to sleep with a different woman every day. Although he was involved with a Roman *"fille charmante"* (with the added charm that she was the sister of a nun), he preferred older women: he confessed to being "quite brutish" with one *"monstre"* who charged him five shillings. Rousseau's prediction that he would contract some venereal disease came true; Boswell came down with a nasty case of crabs, long before the invention of Qwell.

Oscar Wilde was frustrated by the lack of diamonds in Rome's rough trade; but, as he recounted in a hilarious letter to a friend, tourism afforded some innocent pleasures: "I found that the Vatican Gardens were open to the Bohemian and the Portuguese pilgrims. I at once spoke both languages fluently, explained that my English dress was a form of penance, and entered that waste desolate park...The peacocks screamed, and I understood why tragedy dogged the gilt feet of each pontiff. But I wandered in exquisite melancholy for an hour. One Phillipo, a student, whom I culled in the Borgia room, was with me: not for many years has Love walked in the Pope's pleasaunce." More cerebral foreigners simply fell for the city of Rome itself. **Joachim Du Bella**y described Rome as a "mistress"; *Romische Elegien* is Goethe's sanitized title for a book he once named *Erotica Romana*. Finally, **Sigmund Freud**, on whom it was certainly not lost that "Roma" is "Amor" spelled backwards, writes of being sexually aroused by the city in an obscure psychological text, *The Interpretation of Dreams.*

No discussion of expatriate Rome would be complete without a mention of **John Keats**, who went there in the fall of 1820 to recover his failing health. Despite a glamorous *pensione* with a to-die-for view of the Spanish Steps (now the **Keats-Shelley Memorial House**—see Sights, below), Rome didn't do a thing for Keats's already-advanced tuberculosis; he died in less than three months at the age of 25. Historians seem torn between memorializing Keats and putting that great view of the Spanish Steps back on the market.

Henry James

Rome's greatest Amercian expatriate and popularizer in the 19th century was **Henry James**, who made fourteen visits to Italy, beginning in 1869 and ending in 1907. Not a few of these included stays of varying lengths in Rome. James's book of essays on Italy, *Italian Hours*, records one of his longest visits to the city. The chapter entitled "A Roman Notebook," excerpts from five months of a journal he kept while staying with friends and relatives. More readable than many of James's novels, *Italian Hours* provides characteristically erudite appraisals of the emergence of the Italian nation (unified in 1870), as well as supine social commentary: "January 21st.—The last three or four days I have regularly spent a couple of hours from noon baking myself in the sun of the Pincio to get rid of a cold. The weather perfect and the crowd (especially to-day) amazing. Such a staring, lounging, dandified, amiable crowd! Who does the vulgar stay-at-home work of Rome?" James's first novel *Roderick Hudson* is set in Rome, as is one of his most famous short stories, *Daisy Miller.* James would be joined in Rome by his brother, interdisciplinary superstar William "Billy" James. While few were as devoted to it or spent as much time there, practically every American author worth his salt recorded a visit to Rome: Washington Irving, James Fenimore Cooper, Henry Wadsworth Longfellow, Herman Melville, Edith Wharton, William Dean Howells, Nathaniel Hawthorne, Ralph Emerson, Mark Twain.

Contemporary Expatriates (I Want to Hold Your Hand in Rome....Not!)

Some 20th-century artists haven't faired as well in Rome. **James Joyce** is one of the few superwriters to have *hated* the city. He took rooms in the via Frattina and worked for pennies at an Austrian bank, longing all the while for the sights and sounds of Dublin. Sick of his daily encounters with commerce, James saw Rome as a man who earned a living by "exhibiting to travellers his grandmother's corpse." More recently, **Madonna Ciccone** couldn't justify the love of the Pope, who called her show obscene, as well as Rome's pop-music fans, who deserted her wholesale when an Italian popstar showed up on the same day at another venue.

Rome has proved kinder to the poison pen and tongue of **Gore Vidal** who set one of his early novels, *The Judgment of Paris,* there. A short segment of **Federico Fellini**'s *Roma* (1972) captures a real-live expatriate on film. Vidal's *nomifregismo* is a match for any Roman's; eating dinner at an outdoor table in Trastevere amidst the riot of Carnival, he remarks that Rome is "as good a place as any to wait for the end of the world." Since, Gore Vidal has moved to the countryside outside of Rome with his long-term companion (somewhere in Campagna, we think), complaining that Rome has lost much of its intrigue and charm of earlier days.

You're dying for her to rush down the stairs, push through the crowd, embrace Gregory Peck, and move into his studio in Rome at the end of the movie *Roman Holiday.* Although it was never meant to be in that 1953 Oscar-winning classic, **Audrey Hepburn** did return to Rome to marry an Italian and live the sweet life; she only recently moved out of Rome, tiring of its contemporary problems and fading glamour. **Anita Ekberg**, the pre-implants blonde bombshell of *La Dolce Vita*, is now a perennial favorite on the Roman talk-show circuit, bemoaning the sorry state of Rome today. Photographer **Cindy Sherman** retreated to a studio in Trastevere several years ago to shoot her "Old Masters" series of her dressed as generic Dutch and Flemish portraits. If you want to give being a famous expatriate a shot (though we have to admit that in Rome it's not what it used to be), see Living and Working in Rome.

Art and Architecture

In the late 1700s, southern Italy would provide a new direction for world art and the long-awaited reaction to the Baroque. That reaction was **Neoclassicism**; inspired by the understandable excitement surrounding the excavations in Pompeii, Herculaneum, and Paestum, Neoclassicist artists reasserted the austere values of Greco-Roman art that the Renaissance had also imitated. The greatest artists of this period weren't Roman, but came logically to Rome, the world's unrivalled source of antiquities. Foremost among the Neoclassicists was **Jacques-Louis David** (1748-1825), who studied in Rome at the French Academy. Like his contemporaries, David was interested in the legends of ancient Rome; his archetypal Neoclassicist painting, the *Oath of the Horatii* (1784), depicts the Horatii swearing to defend Rome against Alba, even at the cost of their lives.

An essential stop on the Grand Tour was a visit to the print shop of **Giovanni Battista Piranesi** (1720-1778). Piranesi was the uncontested master of etched *vedute*, or views, of Rome. These black and white depictions of monuments are sometimes maligned for their likeness to souvenirs, as well as for their sheer numbers. Rather than blandly commercial, however, studies from his four-volume series *Antichità Romane*—such as the moonlight view of the Colosseum—are hauntingly futuristic. This series of etchings of ancient Roman monuments qualified as a scholarly work: for them, Piranesi was elected to the London Society of Antiquaries and considered second only to the greatest 18th-century antiquarian **Johann Winkelmann.** Alongside Piranesi and Winklemann was Neoclassicist sculptor **Antonio Canova** (1757-1822), equally famous for his devotion to and reinterpretation of antiquity. His statue of Pauline Bonaparte in the Villa Borghese exemplifies his cool, intellectual style.

Pope Benedict XIV preferred restoring Rome for tourists to conducting Church business; for the first time, street signs appeared, as well as historical markers. He commissioned paintings for St. Peter's and mosaics for S. Maria Maggiore, which had been redesigned by prominent architect **Fernando Fuga**. Except for a few buildings (some by Piranesi) the Baroque managed to withstand the tide of Neoclassicism, as **Nicola Salvi's** Trevi Fountain, completed in 1762, testifies. The last palace built by a pope for his family is one of the largest; **Pope Pius VI** constructed the expansive Palazzo Braschi for his nephew. Pius also made a number of enhancements to St. Peter's and the Vatican museums. The tumultuous Risorgimento put a damper on construction in the mid-1800s; once the country was unified however, large-scale building took place in Rome to accommodate the new government. Many consider this the era in which the Rome that inspired endless expatriate adulation was demolished. The previously undeveloped area between Termini and the Quirinal Hill became crowded with apartment buildings, as did the area from the Colosseum to via XX Septembre, and later from via XX Septembre to the Villa Medici. A number of beautiful buildings were lost to this expansion, including Henry James's favorite, the Villa Ludovisi. The uninspired public architecture that began to fill Rome is exemplified by the frothy late 19th-century monument to Italy's first king, **Vittorio Emanuele**.

Love Among the Ruins: Johann Winkelmann

The father of modern archaeology and the son of a German cobbler, Winkelmann managed to imbue the Church with a love of Greek culture and to establish a series of strict guidelines for archaeological excavation and curation. Winkelmann was famous for his undying love for all things Greek, and while declaring "Good taste was born under Greek skies" he made sure that the Roman landscape followed suit. He actually converted to Catholicism, despite his reverence for the pagan aesthetic, and began work as a librarian after moving to Rome. After a few years of successful schmoozing and social climbing, Winkelmann established himself as a scholar and curator among the upper ranks of the Vatican, as well as serving as a posh tour guide for the aristocratic Brits abroad. Winkelman oversaw the excavations at Pompeii and Herculaneum, sponsored by the dissolute Bourbon King of Naples, Ferdinand IV, and he wrote a stunning exposé, *Open Letter on the Finds of Herculaneum*, outlining the irresponsible, even destructive ways in which the excavations were carried out. The diggers were actually prisoners of war working under horrifying conditions: half-starved and shackled together so they could hardly move. Objects were carelessly hacked out of the dirt, precious objects were broken or stolen, murals were cut from their walls, and nothing was catalogued. What objects did survive the onslaught were imperfectly "restored" and stuck in local museums or shipped out of the country as royal gifts. The letter rang out 'cross the continent and scholars henceforth supervised all archaeological digs. Winkelmann eventually became the Pope's Chief Supervisor of Antiquities, a position that confirmed him as the world's leading authority on the ancients, and he published the first comprehensive work on Greek art, *History of Ancient Art* (1764).

Like Piranesi, Winkelmann became a fixture on the Grand Tour; he was one of the few guides who could make archaeological sights interesting to skirt-chasing "milords," as the Italians called them. No prude, however, Winkelmann was known to cover for tourist friends who, overcome by the romance of the ruins, ducked behind them for a quickie. Winkelmann's illustrious career soon came to an end; on a return visit to Germany (after strangely turning down a fantasy-fulfilling trip to Greece), he stopped in Trieste. He made fast friends with an out-of-work cook who stabbed him to death. Moments before dying, Winkelmann gasped out the name of his killer to the crowds surrounding him; the murderer was hanged.

History of Music

The Italians are musical tyrants, as anyone who's studied the piano, belonged to a school band, or slaved over a cello can attest. The *piano, crescendo,* and *allegro* are there for a reason: Italians invented the systems for writing musical notation that remains today. Guido D'Arezzo came up with the musical scale, and a 16th-century Venetian printed the first musical scores with movable type. Cremona brought forth violins by Stradivarius and Guarneri; the piano (actually the *pianoforte,* which just means soft-loud, the way it plays) is an Italian invention. Even so, for Italians, vocal music has always occupied a position of undisputed preeminence. **Palestrina** and his Roman colleagues, worried that the Council of Trent might banish the use of polyphony in the liturgy, pre-empted such repression by eschewing Venetian flamboyance in favor of crystalline harmonies. At the same time, **madrigals,** free-flowing secular songs for three to six voices, grew in popularity.

The 16th century brought the greatest musical innovation in Italian history: opera. Born in Florence, nurtured in Venice, and revered in Milan, **opera** is Italy's most cherished art form. Invented by the **Camerata,** an artsy clique of Florentine poets, noblemen, authors, and musicians, opera began as an attempt to recreate the dramas of ancient Greece (which they decided had been sung) by setting their lengthy poems to music. After several years of effort with only dubious success, one member, Jacobo Peri, composed *Dafne* in 1597, the world's first complete opera. *(Dafne* has since been lost—not a great loss, according to all contemporary accounts.) A school of operatic composers soon emerged, eager to master the Camerata's new genre of music. As opera spread from Florence to Venice, Milan, and Rome, the styles and forms of the genre also grew more distinct. Much of early opera featured *stile recitativo,* a style which attempted to recapture the simple, evocative singing and recitation of classical drama. The first successful opera composer, **Monteverdi,** drew freely from history, blithely juxtaposing high drama, concocted love scenes, and bawdy humor. By charming his patroness the Duchess of Mantua, Monteverdi's jewel *Orfeo* (1607)—still performed today—assured the survival of the genre.

Contemporaneous with the birth of opera was the emergence of the **oratorio,** which sets biblical text to dramatic choral and instrumental accompaniment. Introduced by the Roman priest, **Saint Filippo Neri,** who liked to preach against a background of dramatic music, the oratorio was soon incorporated into masses throughout Italy.

Instrumental music began to establish itself as a legitimate genre in 17th-century Rome. **Corelli** developed the concerto form with its contrasting moods and tempos, adding drama and emotion to technical expertise. **Vivaldi** wrote over 400 concertos while teaching at a home for orphaned girls in Venice. Under Vivaldi the concerto assumed its present form in which the virtuoso playing of the soloist is opposed to and accompanied by the concerted strength of the orchestra.

Eighteenth-century Italy exported its music; Italian composers coined the established musical jargon, their virtuosi dazzled audiences throughout Europe. At mid-century, operatic overtures began to be performed separately, resulting in the creation of a new genre of music; the **sinfonia** was modeled after the melody of operatic overtures and simply detached from their setting. Thus began the symphonic art form, which later received its highest expression in the hands of Italy's northern neighbors. At the same time, the composer **Domenico Scarlatti** wrote over 500 sonatas for the harpsichord and **Sammartini's** creative experimentation furthered symphonic development. In opera, Baroque ostentation yielded to classical standards of moderation, simplicity, and elegance. Italian opera stars, on the other hand, had no use for moderation; many a soloist would demand showy, superfluous arias to showcase his or her skill.

To today's opera buffs, Italian opera means Verdi, Puccini, Bellini, Donizetti, and Rossini—all composers of the 19th century. With plots relying on wild coincidence and music fit for the angels, 19th-century Italian opera continues to dominate even today's stages. **Verdi** became a national icon by mid-life, so much so that *Viva Verdi* was a battle cry of the Risorgimento. Acting as altar boy at the age of seven, Verdi became so distracted by the music of the mass that a harried priest kicked him off the altar; when he returned home bleeding and his parents asked him what had happened, he replied only, "Let me learn music." The music which he wrote as a man includes both the tragic, triumphal *Aïda* and *Il Traviata,* whose "foul and hideous horrors" shocked the London Times. Be aware as you listen that much of Verdi's work promoted Italian unity; his operas include frequent allusions to political assassinations, exhortations against tyranny, and jibes at French and Austrian monarchs. Another great composer of the era, **Rossini,** boasted that he could produce music faster than copyists could reproduce it, but he proved such an infamous procrastinator that his agents resorted to locking him in a room with a single plate of spaghetti until he completed his compositions. His *Barber of Seville* remains a favorite with modern audiences. Finally, there is **Puccini,** composer of *Madama Butterfly,* noted for the beauty of his music and for the strength, assurance and compassion of his female characters. Relying on devilish pyrotechnical virtuosity and a personal style marked by mystery and incessant rumors, violinist **Niccolò Paganini** brought musical Europe to its knees and filled its ears with, in the words of Brahms, "angelic singing." One of the first musicians to make highly publicized concert tours, Paganini inspired Franz Lizst to become a virtuoso pianist; the pair here were the 19th-century equivalent of rock stars, complete with groupies.

Italian music continues to grow in the 20th century. **Ottorino Respighi,** composer of the popular *Pines of Rome* and *Fountains of Rome,* experimented with shimmering, rapidly shifting orchestral textures. **Gian Carlo Menotti,** now a U.S. resident, has written short, opera-like works such as *Amahl and the Night Visitors,* but is probably best known as the creator of the Two Worlds Art Festival in Spoleto. **Luigi Dallapiccola** worked with serialism, achieving success with choral works such as *Canti di prigionia* (*Songs of Prison*) and *Canti di liberazione* (*Songs of Liberation*); both protest fascist rule in Italy.

No single trend has emerged to characterize Italian music over the last dozen years; a look at Italy's most popular performers reveals a surprising diversity of musical genres. **Luciano Pavarotti** remains universally adored; his cathedral-filling voice draws packed audiences. (For more details on rock music, see Twentieth Century: Popular Culture below). If you are interested in experiencing the annual outdoor opera set among the Baths of Caracalla in Rome, see our Entertainment section, below.

The 20th Century

History

The 1920s *fascisti,* not the first army to invoke the Roman Empire, took their name from the symbol of authority in ancient Rome, the *fasces,* a bundle of sticks tightly wound around an axe. The tightly bound sticks represented their loyalty to one another, while the axe symbolized their belief that violence was the only way to combat the threat of Bolshevism. Mussolini had grown so powerful elsewhere in Italy that the 1922 **March on Rome** was just for show, as were the reports that 3000 fascist martyrs had died in the attempt. Like his best friend **Adolf Hitler,** Mussolini was a master of propaganda; 10 years later Rome would get a superficial facelift as German tanks were rolling into Poland. Italy declared war on an already vanquished France in order to win some of the spoils.

Rome mananaged to avoid the new destructive power that was unleashed in World War II; carefully-aimed Allied bombs avoided the population and Hitler declared Rome an "open" city when he withdrew from it. While many Jews had been driven out of the country, a sizeable number survived by being hidden by neighbors in private homes, convents, and monastaries. As word got out that the Germans were surrendering, the Roman resistance mobilized; the **Fosse Ardeatine** massacres in were terrible reprisals for a resistance bomb that exploded as German police marched along the via Rasella. For every German soldier that died, 10 Italians, including 75 Jews, were executed in the caves of the Ardeatine Way.

The Musclehead of Italy: Benito 'il Duce' Mussolini

One-time schoolteacher, journalist, political anarchist, and (believe it or not) pacifist, Mussolini was a ruthless and ambitious chameleon, a political maverick, a grandiloquent orator, and a master of manipulation. *Il Duce,* "the Leader," as he made himself known, began his political career with the militant PSI (the *Partito Sinistra Italiano*— the party of the left). He went to prison for party-related activities but eventually cut his ties to the party over the issue of World War I (he argued for Italy to enter the Great War). Mussolini traded his *Marxist Reader* for the Nationalist flag and began to attract a following as early as 1918 (he was then only 25 years old), calling for the appointment of a dictator over all of Italy. He described this leader as "a man ruthless and energetic enough to make a clean sweep," hinting three months later that he was the man. His followers were a motley crew of disgruntled anarchists, socialists, and republicans, revolutionaries looking for a cause, conservative monarchists and agitated soldiers. In 1919, Mussolini assembled army veterans and young men to form paramilitary combat groups (the *fascii di combattimenti*), also known as the **Blackshirts**. These militant right-wing squadrons (*squadristi*) waged a fierce, anti-leftist campaign for power shaped by Mussolini's taste for the theatrical. Shouting patriotic slogans, belting out nationalist ditties, and sporting the trademark black shirts of the anarchists, these groups broke labor strikes for industrialists, terrorized Socialists and Communists, raided newspapers sympathetic to Bolshevism, and forcefully established mini-dictatorships in small towns and cities while the police and the army turned a blind eye. To gain widespread support, Mussolini played on the anxieties of the middle class, whose businesses and life-savings were in peril from the rising inflation.

Seeking still more popular support, Mussolini formed the parliamentary **National Fascist Party** (*Partito Nazionale Fascista,* or PNF) in 1921, which won thirty-five seats in the Chamber of Deputies. The party platform was a list of vague concerns for financial stablility, international power and national order. Mussolini felt that the Fascist party represented an attitude and an (ill-defined) need for action, not a specific ideology. In 1922, Victor Emanuel II commanded Mussolini to form a government and serve as the Prime Minister. Thus Mussolini forged a totalitarian state in Italy, controlling every aspect of Italian life, suppressing opposition parties, regulating the press, demolishing all labor unions, and (this actually for the better) revamping the entire train system. Along with the new efficiency of the trains, the only other positive achievement of Mussolini's checkered career was the **Lateran Pact of 1929**, regulating relations between the Vatican (the Holy See) and Italy. The clergy was prohibited from joining a political party, but in certain areas such as marriage, the Vatican was granted authority. The Vatican was also allowed to operate its press. The provisions of the Lateran Pact were later included in the Italian constitution in 1948.

Mussolini was so impressed with German efficiency that he joined forces with Hitler in 1939. Mussolini relied on propaganda rather than strength in fighting WWII, and he ignominiously squandered his army in France, Russia, and Greece, until a royal coup along with the allied forces liberated Italy in 1944 and deposed *Il Duce*; the disorganization of the Italian army is humorously portrayed in the 1991 film *Mediterraneo*. Roberto Rosselini's neo-realist film, *Roma, città aperta*, depicts some of the terrible living conditions in Rome under the German seizure of the city right before liberation.

In the earlier stages of his career, Mussolini was a relentless workaholic and quite a *schlubb*. In the morning, he rose at 5am to perform violent exercises, eat a tiny breakfast (all of his meals were sparse due to his stomach ulcer), and sped through more than a dozen Italian and foreign newspapers. He fenced, boxed, swam, played tennis, and went horse-back riding all before going to the office at 8am. He didn't really derive any pleasure from these sports, but was wholly concerned with covering up the fact that he had been treated for venereal disease for years. Mussolini scorned pleasure so completely that his sexual life was limited to an occasional quickie in his office, and then he wouldn't even bother to completely remove his pants or shoes. He was a horrible dresser to boot, and barely showered; he merely splashed on a bit of Jean Naté before heading to the office. He was so worried about wasting his precious time that he got elastic shoelaces with pre-made bows so he wouldn't have to tie his shoes.

Mussolini moved his office in 1929 to **Palazzo Venezia**, from which he delivered his famous speeches with his trademark oratory style, which, though it moved some to tears, was utterly buffoonish. He would stand on the balcony, uttering his mixed metaphors, clever allusions, and fatuous speeches with the most histrionic seriousness, flapping his arms wildly, and then, from time to time, he would halt for pregnant pauses and a knowing glance at the screaming spectators below. More than anything, Mussolini loved spectacle. For all of his work-horse habits, Mussolini wasn't really cut out for the day-to-day grunt work of politics; he became increasingly restless in meetings, preferring to devote his energies to media junkets—shaking hands with farmers, hosting (useless) international delegations, or reviewing troops—all while being photographed. During the later days of his career, he kept candles perpetually lit in his office so that people would think he was working all through the night.

Part of Mussolini's drive for spectacular success was his revival of imperial images. He fancied himself an emperor in the grandest tradition and was determined to mark Rome as his empire by a series of gargantuan architectural schemes-luckily for us, most remain unexecuted. Under his aegis, the government spent more than 33,624 million *lire* on public works, excavations, and rebuilding. He plowed down many important medieval, Renaissance, and Baroque works to create the wide processional street, **via dei Fori Imperiali,** to carry him past the great monuments of empire like the Forum and the Colosseum; ironically, the constant coughing of car pollution along this street is now the major cause of the monuments' rapid deterioration (see Colosseum, below). He commissioned numerous archaeological excavations, including the Curia at the Forum and one at Largo Argentina. He even refurbished the Ara Pacis and the Augusteum for use as his own tomb. Finally, to symbolize the grand achievements of the Fascists, Mussolini envisioned a huge Forum named after himself that would make St. Peter's and the Colosseum look like day-old cabbage.

Mussolini changed his mind and instead ordered a statue of Hercules 263 feet tall, with its right hand raised in Fascist respect, its features resembling Mussolini's own. One hundred tons of metal and part of an enormous foot and head later, the project came to its appropriate close. Most of Mussolini's archaeological projects went unfinished, the outrageous sums of money were pocketed by corrupt officials, and most of his more ambitious schemes drifted into oblivion. The dreary, cement-filled **EUR** neighborhood and the destructive, trafficked via dei Fora Imperiali stand as continual reminders of Mussolini's unsettling vision, destructive course, and ultimate failure. Today, his legacy lives on through his granddaughter, **Alexandra Mussolini,** who is trying to revive the Fascist party and was recently elected to Parliament.

How Modern Italian Politics 'Work'

The end of World War II ushered in sweeping changes of the Italian system of government, but no clear leader emerged to marshal the battered republic in its turbulent early years. The Italian Constitution, adopted in 1948 and still going strong, established a new **Italian Republic** with a president, a bicameral Parliament with a 315-member Senate and a 630-member Chamber of Deputies, and an independent judiciary. The president, elected for a seven-year term by an electoral college, is the head of state and appoints the prime minister. Chief executive authority rests with the prime minister and his **Council of Ministers,** subject to legislative approval.

Within this framework, the **Christian Democratic Party** (DC), boosted by U.S. money and military aid, bested the Socialists and emerged as the consistent ruling party; however, domination by a single party has not brought Italy stability; the republic has been mired in political turmoil, with more than 50 different governments since World War II. With the exception of one brief Socialist stint in the 1980s, the Christian Democrats have flourished under Italy's "polarized centrism"—a multi-party system with most voters belonging either to the right-leaning Christian Democrats, or to one of the left-leaning parties: the **Socialist Unity Party** (PSU, though usually referred to by its old name, the PSI) or the **Democratic Party of the Left** (PDS, a much less radical version of the old Communist Party, the PCI). A small minority of Italian voters belong to one of the several centrist parties that bridge the ideological gap. Since no single party can claim a majority of voters, Italian governments are the tenuous results of compromises formed between less-than-cordial parties. Before 1989 and the domino fall of Eastern Europe's regimes, the Communists exerted a strong influence, especially in the south, and received about 30% of the vote in most national elections. Recently, while the political picture has grown more inscrutable, one thing has been certain: the revamped PDS continues to slide. In the April 1992 elections, PDS support declined ten points from its strong 27% showing in 1987.

'Years of Lead': The Postwar Era

The instability of the postwar era, in which the Italian economy sped through industrialization at an unprecedented rate, gave way to violence and near-anarchy in the 1970s. The *autunno caldo* (hot autumn) of 1969, a season of strikes, demonstrations, and riots, foreshadowed the violence that characterized most of the 70s; 20% inflation (and the corresponding devaluation of personal savings), spiraling unemployment rates, and the proliferation of terrorist groups left the Italian government at a loss to respond. With all the bullets flying, this period was known as the "Years of Lead;" the violence culminated in Rome in 1978 with the kidnapping and murder of ex-Prime Minister Aldo Moro. The thugs responsible were the leftist terrorist group, **Brigade Rosse** (Red Brigades), formed in Turin in 1970. Moro's corpse was dumped in the Jewish Ghetto. After years of public violence against judges, senators, and deputies, Moro's death shocked the government into launching major anti-terrorist campaigns that enjoyed at least mild success in restoring order.

Today, Italian politics are just as dangerous and even more scandalous. In 1979, the Radical Party's candidate **Ilona Staller,** the ex-porn star "La Cicciolina," was elected to the house of deputies in Viareggio. The buxom blonde celebrated her win by baring her breasts to the eternally grateful city in a victory parade. In 1991, Staler married American kitsch *artiste* Jeff Koons, whose major works include an enormous sculpture of himself and Ilona as Adam and Eve making it in the Garden of Eden. High on La Cicciolina's political agenda is (big surprise) legalized prostitution. In another tabloid news item, support for the Christian Democrats took a dive after the **P2 Masonic lodge scandal** broke and revealed bribes, kickbacks, and corrupt dealings between the DC hierarchy, right-wing fringe groups, and the heads of large banks.

Mafia is an Italian Word

Although the extent of **mafia** power has waned somewhat in recent years, the loosely affiliated leaders of the nebulous organization still command great control over Italy's society, politics, and economy, especially in the *Mezzogiorno* and Sicily. As the leaders of the black market, the *mafia* has become the pillar, however crooked, of the Italian economy. Some of the *mafiosi's* success stems from the cultural acceptance of their activities (in the good old days, members were regarded not as thugs, but as men of honor and strength). But today's *mafia*—with its heightened passion for drug-running and violence—inspires universal fear and resentment among Italians. The Italian parliament passed an unprecedented anti-*mafia* law in 1982, followed by the Palermo *maxi processi* (maxi-trials), the largest *mafia* trial in history. Sicily-based *La Rete* (the Network), a new political party with a strong anti-*mafia* platform, has become the most influential in Palermo—it won 15 Parliament seats in the April 1992 elections. Surrounding these elections came enormous protests in Rome (held around piazza della Repubblica), decrying the government's laxity and irresponsibility in dealing with one of Italy's most serious problems.

Really Recent Politics: Rome, the Ball and Chain of Italy

Divisions in Italy are not just between frightened citizens and organized criminals. Over the last 15 years, regional parochialism has been on the rise and northern patience with the wayward south is wearing thin. In response, regional governments have been granted more autonomy, but some northerners want more: the right-wing **Lombard League** seeks to unite the fattest part of the north and rejects especially unproductive Rome and the rest of the South. The Lombards scored a major victory in the April 1992 elections—a 9% share of the electorate up from less than 1% in 1987—with a platform advocating a new federal system which would cut off subsidies to the dependent South.

Recent Italian politics, characterized by instability, querulousness, and scandal, isn't well-equipped to attack these problems. Political participation is among the lowest in Europe. The chaos of Italian politics disillusions even its leaders. After three long years, Socialist **Bettino Craxi**, lamenting his inability to work with the Christian Democratic majority, resigned from the prime minister's chair in March 1987. After Craxi's departure, three Christian Democrats took office in quick succession. Then, following a rare, brief period of relative stability, the musical chairs of Italian politics recommenced in April 1992: Christian Democrat **Giulio Andreotti**, who had been Prime Minister since July 1989, resigned, and **President Francesco Cossiga** also announced his retirement, citing Italy's "disastrous financial situation, the prominence of bad in our society, public disservice, and institutional paralysis." In the 1992 elections, the Christian Democrats gathered less than 30% of the vote for the first time since 1946, but managed to hold on to the presidency. On May 27, 1992, after disputes over voting procedures, a fist-fight between the neo-fascists and Christian Democrats (really!), and 10 days and 15 rounds of voting that produced no majority, **Oscar Luigi Scalfaro** was finally elected Italy's new president. By the time you buy this book, anything could have happened.

On to Happier Subjects: The Death of Art and the Birth of Film

In the early 20th century, expatriate artists who had once flocked to Rome and fostered the Eternal City's art and culture began taking their inspiration from the City of Light. Nonetheless, the **Galleria Arte Moderne** in Rome houses the works of household names from around the world as well as many inconsequential modern Roman artists. Modern Roman architecture leaves something—well, everything—to be desired. City planners are still dealing with Fascist gaffes such as the **via dei Fori Imperiali**, which cuts through the ancient Imperial Fora and endangers the Colosseum with the smog of its daily traffic jams. Except for a few blocks of imaginative Art Nouveau apartment buildings around via Doria, budget-crunched Rome has had to forego the artful innovations that 20th-century architects have had to offer.

For Rome's contributions to the arts in this century, don't go to the museum—go to the movies. Years before there was Hollywood, there were the **Cines** studios in Rome. Constructed in 1905-6, Cines created the so-called Italian "super-spectacle," extravagant, larger-than-life re-creations of momentous historical events. The first "blockbuster" picture in film history was the nine-reel *Quo Vadis*, directed by Enrico Guzzani for Cines studio in 1912. The film featured real chariot races, real Christian-eating lions in the Colosseum, 5000 extras, mountainous three-dimensional sets, and a burning-of-Rome sequence that blazed the way for the scorching of Atlanta in *Gone With The Wind*.

Soon after the international success of *Quo Vadis*, the advent of World War I and the subsequent rise of Fascist government brought an end to the Italian super-spectacle. Recognizing the popular power of cinema and its possibilities for propaganda, Mussolini did create the *Centro Sperimentale della Cinematografia*, a national film school (the first outside the Soviet Union), and the gargantuan **Cinecittà studios**, both located in Rome. The presence of famous director and covert Marxist **Luigi Chiarini** attracted many of students who would themselves rise to directorial fame in the celebrated postwar wave of Italian cinema. Among these were **Roberto Rossellini** and **Michelangelo Antonioni**. When the group surrounding Chiarini started publishing a film journal, a rival publication was founded by none other than Vittorio Mussolini, the dictator's son. Mussolini himself avoided the aesthetic questions of film, except to enforce the occasional "imperial edict," one of which forbade Italian audiences to laugh at the Marx Brother's *Duck Soup*. Hail Fredonia!

With the fall of fascism, a generation of young filmmakers was suddenly free to express itself, unconstrained now by the regulations of the discredited regime. Mussolini's nationalized film industry (which lasted until 1943) produced no great films, yet sparked the subsequent explosion of **neo-realist cinema** (1943-50). The new style was characterized by the rejection of sets and professional actors in favor of location shooting and authentic drama. Such low production values, soon to shape a revolution in film, were determined in part by postwar economic circumstance, in part by the vigorous new aesthetic (itself not unrelated to economics) that was emerging. Neo-realists first gained attention in Italy with **Luchino Visconti's** 1942 *Ossessione,* a film based on James Cain's pulp-novel *The Postman Always Rings Twice*. (Hollywood would later turn the story into a film-noir classic of the same name.) **Roberto Rossellini's** 1946 tale of a Resistance leader trying to escape a Gestapo manhunt, *Open City,* was mostly filmed on the streets of Rome, just two months after the city's liberation. The neo-realist documentary style and the authentic setting led some audiences to believe the movie was actually newsreel footage. *Roma, città aperta* won world-wide acclaim for the neo-realists and holds a place in film history on par with *The Birth of A Nation, The Cabinet of Dr. Caligari,* and *Citizen Kane*. Perhaps the most famous and commercially successful neo-realist film, **Vittorio de Sica's** *The Bicycle Thief* (1948) is also set in Rome.

When neo-realism turned its wobbly camera from the Resistance to social critique, it lost its popular interest and, after 1950, gave way to individual expressions of Italian genius. Post-neo-realist directors **Federico Fellini** and **Michelangelo Antonioni** rejected logical narrative construction, turning away from the mechanics of plots and characters to a world of moments and witnesses. Fellini employed a closed system of recurring signs and symbols to create a personalized universe that pervades many of his films. In the autobiographical *Roma*, a gorgeous stand-in for the director encounters an otherwise grotesque cast of characters. *La Dolce Vita* (1960), regarded by many outside Italy as *the* representative Italian film, scrutinizes the stylish Rome of the 1950s. In this film Fellini takes up Italy's ongoing fascination with its decadent aristocracy (a theme Antonioni pursued a year later in *L'Avventura*) and questions the country's post-war love affair with U.S. culture. The film's best-known moment features Swedish starlet Anita Ekberg wading in the Trevi Fountain with a kitten on her shoulder. (When the Pope viewed *La Dolce Vita*, he promptly included it on the index of banned films.) Antonioni's Italian films include *L'Eclisse* (1962), *Deserto Rosso* (1964), and the more accessible *Blow-Up,* his 1966 English-language hit about mime, murder, and mod London. Antonioni's *L'Avventura*, the story of a group of bored young aristocrats, has been hailed as the second greatest film of all time—maybe the idea was still original back then.

Pier Paolo Pasolini, perhaps the most controversial of Italian directors, was also one of the greatest. Pasolini—who spent as much time on trial for his politics and atheism as he did making films—began his artistic career as a poet and screenplay writer. Already considered Italy's premier poet when he took over the director's chair, Pasolini brought to the screen his intensely lyrical poetic vision. Always suspicious of his own tendency to aestheticism, the ardent Marxist set his first films in Italian shanty neighborhoods and in the underworld of Roman poverty and prostitution. With *Hawks and Sparrows*, regarded by many, including Pasolini himself, as the director's masterpiece, Pasolini abandoned his preoccupation with the subproletariat and embarked upon an investigation of the philosophical and poetic possibilities of film. Pasolini is generally credited with having helped introduce the problems of structuralist linguistics to the theory of film, radically influencing the way critics, feminist film theorists, and progressive filmmakers have thought about their medium these last 30 years.

By the late 60s it was clear to international critics that there were few young directors capable of inheriting the legacy of the previous two decades. Most of the "old Leopards" were considered to have passed their creative peaks and, by the early 70s, were dying off in rapid succession. Factional disputes regarding politics led to the disbanding of the National Association of Italian Filmmakers and the collapse of the Venice Film Festival in 1968. The free-flowing U.S. bucks that had backed so many productions in the 50s and 60s were sucked back home as hard economic times hit the U.S. and inflation rose in Italy. Despite the hardship, the great tradition of Italian film has refused to choke and die. One of the most important and controversial Italian filmmakers of the 70's was **Lina Wertmuller;** her film *Swept Away* (1974), in which a rich Milanese woman is stranded on a desert island with a rampantly chauvinist provincial sailor, was an ironic approach to feminism which left many feminists fuming. Those familiar with **Bernardo Bertolucci's** *Last Tango in Paris* and *Last Emperor* should see his 1970 *Il Conformista* (The Conformist), the story of a man hired to assassinate his former teacher. Other major modern Italian films include de Sica's *Il giardino dei Finzi-Contini* (Garden of the Finzi-Continis) and **Francesco Rosi's** *Cristo si è fermato a Eboli* (Christ Stopped at Eboli), both based on the books of the same titles. In the 1980s, the **Taviani** brothers were catapulted to fame with *Kaos,* a film based on five stories by Pirandello, and *La Notte di San Lorenzo* (Night of the Shooting Stars), recounting the ludicrous and tragic final days of World War II in an Italian village. The schlocky Oscar-winning *Cinema Paradiso,* directed by Giuseppe Tornatore, is a recent invasion of U.S. by Italian cinema, along with the lite, Oscar-winning comedy *Mediterraneo*, which chronicles the bathetic experience of Italian soldiers stuck on a Greek Island during WWII.

Neo-realism has recognizably influenced most Italian films since the war, so perhaps you will want a break from a style whose founder, Cesare Zavattini, declared that "the ideal film would be ninety minutes of the life of a man to whom nothing happens." For a more **American take on Rome,** try Audrey Hepburn's first film, the delightful romantic comedy *Roman Holiday* (1953). Audrey is pretty sexy, as is her co-star Gregory Peck; the Rome they explore will leave you drooling in anticipation of your own trip. An overlooked film which destroyed Lorimar Studios but features a not-to-be-missed performance by Sandra Bernhard, is *Hudson Hawk* (1989); filmed in Rome, the plot involves Bruce Willis pilfering the Vatican's private collection. A movie best appreciated on the big screen but available at many video stores is *Belly of An Architect*, directed by British bad-boy Peter Greenaway. This mid-80s movie chronicles the personal and professional dissolution of an obsessive American architect come to Rome to supervise an exhibition on an obscure 18th-century French architect. Greenaway's painterly eye picks out and presents some of Rome's most glorious scenery in broad, almost two-dimensional tableaux. If you can resist the Eternal City after watching this flick, *Let's Go: Rome* is probably your only hope.

20th-Century Literature: Two Nobels so Far

Italy was a center of Modernist innovation in poetry. The most flamboyant and controversial of the early poets is **Gabriele d'Annunzio,** whose cavalier heroics and sexual escapades earned him as much fame as his eccentric, over-the-top verse. **D'Annunzio** was a true child of pleasure, or *Il Piacere*, the title of his novel set in Rome. In the mid- and late-20th century, **Salvatore Quasimodo, Eugenio Montale** and **Giuseppe Ungaretti** dominated the scene. Montale and Quasimodo founded the "hermetic movement" (also known as "obscure poems dropped from an airless ivory tower"), but both became more accessible and politically committed after the Second World War. Both snagged Nobel Prizes along the way. Ungaretti brought to Italy many of the innovations of the French Symbolists; his collection *L'allegria* set a trend toward increased purity of language and clarity of meaning in Italian poetry. Ungaretti was drawn to Rome to study Keats and Shelley, and during his stay he disseminated his ideas to hundreds of admiring college students.

Among a welter of great 19th- and 20th-century writers, Rome's unique contribution was the Roman dialect poets. Three of the greatest were **G.G. Belli** (1791-1863), **Trilussi** (1871-1950), and **Cesare Pascarella** (1858-1940). In his fictional history *ABBA ABBA*, **Anthony Burgess** imagines a conversation in which Belli explains the advantages of local dialects over national language: "A language waves a flag and is blown up by politicians. A dialect keeps to things, things, things, street smells and street noises, life." Writing nearly 3000 sonnets, Belli was known for his vulgar caricatures of important Risorgimento figures. *ABBA ABBA* includes English translations of Belli's poems.

The 1930s heralded in the heyday of a group of young Italian writers who were much influenced by the experimental narratives and themes of social alienation in the works of U.S. writers like Ernest Hemingway, John Dos Passos, and John Steinbeck. This school included **Cesare Pavese, Ignazio Silone, Vasco Pratolini,** and **Elio Vittorini.** One of the most representative works of 1930s Italian literature is Vittorini's *Pane e Vino* (Bread and Wine), written while the left-wing intellectual and political activist author was in exile. The most prolific of these writers, **Alberto Moravia**, wrote the ground-breaking *Gli Indifferente* (The Time of Indifference) which launched an attack on the Fascist regime and was promptly censored. To evade the stiff government censors, Moravia employed experimental, surreal forms in his subsequent works. His later works, up to the 1970s, use sex to symbolize the violence and spiritual impotence of modern Italy.

The works of the greatest of modern Italian authors, **Italo Calvino**, are unsurprisingly most widely available in English. Calvino's writing—full of intellectual play and magical-realism—is exemplified in *Invisible Cities,* a collection of cities described by Marco Polo to Kubla Kahn. The more traditionally narrative *If on a winter's night a traveler...* is a boisterous romp about authors, readers, and the insatiable urge to read, but perhaps most enjoyable for the traveler is *Italian Folktales,* Calvino's collection of traditional regional fairytales.

Most recently, **Umberto Eco's** wildly popular *The Name of the Rose,* a richly-textured mystery set in a 14th-century monastery, somehow managed to keep readers on edge while making the history of the revolutionary crisis in medieval Catholicism vaguely intelligible. *Foucault's Pendulum,* his latest, becomes rather precious in its complications, but wraps the story of the Knights Templar and half-a-millennium of conspiracy theories into a neat pocket-size package for transport.

Italian Popular Culture:
The Boob Tube and so Much More

Rome is not the center for Italian popular culture; rather it is Milan that is home to fashion, the film industry, and the more popular magazines. Poor Rome is stuck with the national TV station, **RAI.** Two hours in front of the boob tube in Rome may prove harmful to your otherwise glorious impression of the Eternal City. No doubt you will run across one of the garish variety shows that Italians inexplicably love. **Créme Car-**

amel features lightweight entertainers, such as the leggy 1991 Miss Universe (and also Miss Italia) **Pamela Prati** "singing" her favorite tune, "Tiramisù, Mi Piace!" **Fantastico!** is another one of the campy concoctions and a favorite haunt of insufferably boppy young ersatz rapper **Giovanotte** ("Muova-ti, Muova-ti!"). The strip-game-show **Corpo Grosso** is more shocking for its complete inanity (and that of its contestants) than for its unsubtle display of T&A. The inimitable "Cin-Cin Girls" have a secret number on their breasts which refers to a facile trivia question. With every correct answer, the contestant selects one of an assembly of international strippers (mostly from the Ukraine and Eastern Europe) to perform, and the entire show culminates with the contestants (male and female) doing their own sorry excuse for a strip-tease. If you're name is Brooke, Carolyn, Ridge, or Thorn, don't be too flattered if Italians exclaim "beautiful" when they meet you—it's more likely the name of their favorite soap opera character; (the Bold and the) **Beautiful** U.S. soap opera hit Italy two years ago with full force, and every Italian (housewives, students, and businessmen alike) now spends a portion of his/her afternoon break following the vicissitudes of big-haired blondes and hunky hunks dressed in Gitanos (syndication is 6 years behind).

Rock music came to Italy in the 1960s, a reflection of musical trends set in U.S. and Britain, but endowed with a unique and indigenous character that blended Italian folk songs and Mediterranean rhythms with pop beats. **Luigi Tenco** adapted the sound of be-bop to spirited folk melodies while **Lucio Dalla** produced socially conscious rock. Both rock and politics continued to grow more radical over the next decade as epitomized by the band **Area,** whose lyrics both reflected and strengthened the political unrest of the 1970s. British punk rock and U.S. hardcore found their way to Italy via bands like **Negazione** and **Raw Power**, who produced an unusually fierce, heavy-metal-damaged take on the music. (Negazione is still around, and still loud.) Although Italian discos rely primarily on English and U.S. bands, when not boogieing down to the sounds of the mid-80s, young Italians prefer the native singers and Italian lyrics of *musica leggera* (light Italian rock), as performed by **Claudio Bagliori, Bennato Edoardo,** and **Gianni Morandi.**

To get a better glimpse into Italian pop life, pick up a copy of **Moda** or **King** magazines. If you can read Italian well, pick up **Il Messaggero**, the Rome newspaper, or **Corriere della Sera,** the country's most reliable and moderate. **Il Manifesto** is the paper with the Communist slant.

Accommodations

Institutional and Student Accommodations

If you are looking for a raucous time in Rome, institutions are not the place to go. While providing affordable accommodations, most of them are inconveniently located, difficult to arrange, and curfews at the HI/IYHF hostel and various religious organizations keep you locked away from *la dolce vita*.

Hostel

Ostello del Foro Italico (HI/IYHF), viale delle Olimpiadi, 61 (tel. 396 47 09). Take Metro linea A to Ottaviano and then bus #32. Inconvenient location. 350 beds. Lockers provided, though management takes no responsibility for valuables. Three-day max. stay (extensions granted when vacancies exist). HI/IYHF card required—buy one at the desk for L30,000. For information or reservations, contact the regional office of **AIG**, via Carlo Poma, 2, 01195 Roma (tel. 372 92 95; open Mon.-Fri. 8:30am-1:30pm). Reception open 2-11pm. Lockout 9am. L18,000 per person. Showers and breakfast included.

Student Housing

Student residences in Rome (and throughout Italy) are inexpensive and are theoretically open to foreign students during vacations and whenever there is room. In reality, these accommodations are often nearly impossible to arrange. If you try your hand, get a little help first. All university towns operate a **Casa dello Studente** to which you can apply. Another useful source of information on student housing is the *Guide for Foreign Students* from the **Italian Ministry of Education,** viale Trastevere, Roma. **Enjoy Rome**, an agency with a plethora of helpful services, recently opened an office on via Varese 39 (tel. 445 18 43). They can arrange for any number of alternative accommodations, including student housing, as well as for hotel accommodation.

The **Relazioni Universitarie** of the *Associazione Italiana per il Turismo e gli Scambi Universitari* operates a low-priced-accommodations service for foreign students throughout the year in Rome and in many of the other major university towns. Discount student travel services are also available. The main office is at via Palestro, 11, 00185 Roma (tel. 475 52 65).

The **Centro Turistico Studentesco e Giovanile (CTS)** is the Italian student and youth travel organization. Their offices, located throughout Italy, help you find and book accommodations in *pensioni* or dormitories. The London, Paris, and Athens offices can reserve a room for you in Italy for the first few nights. The central office is at via Genova, 16, Roma (tel. 467 91).

In recent summers, **AIG** (the Italian Youth Hostel organization) has run a program in conjunction with Rome's universities to provide housing for tourists in vacated student quarters (late July to mid-Sept.). The centers are via Cesare de Lollis, 24/B, viale del Ministro degli Affari Esteri, 6, and via D. de Dominicus. One-week max. stay. L20,000 per person; breakfast included. Contact the tourist office at Termini or at via Parigi, 5 (tel. 46 37 48), or AIG (listed above under Ostello del Foro Italico).

Alternative Accommodations

Religious Institutions: Convents, monasteries, and religious houses offer shelter, but unless you have a personal reason for seeking such accommodations, it is inadvisable, as rooms often exceed L20,000 per night and strict curfews incarcerate you at 11pm. Guests need not attend services but are expected to make their own beds and, often, to clean up after meals. Often found in rural settings, monasteries are usually peaceful. Staying in a monastery can be an enriching option for those who seek a quiet, contemplative experience and a first-hand taste of Italian history. **Protezione della Giovane** at Termini (tel. 475 15 94; open erratically) or near Termini at via Urbana, 158 (tel. 46 00 56) can make arrangements. Also check with the **Enjoy Rome** agency (listed above). Carrying an introduction on letterhead from your own local religious leader may facilitate matters, although many monasteries will accept only Catholic guests. For more information about specific regions and a list of convents, monasteries and other religious institutions offering accommodations, write to the tourist board in Rome or to the regional offices of the area you'd like to stay in.

Country Living: For a quiet, non-religious atmosphere, stay in a **rural cottage** or **farmhouse.** Usually, you will be given a small room and asked to clean up after yourself, but you will have freedom to come and go as you please. For more information, write to the office of **Agriturist,** corso V. Emanuele, 101, 00186 Roma (tel. 651 23 42), or contact any of their offices in the region that you will be visiting.

Women-Only: The **YWCA** runs a branch in Rome with simple, safe rooms for women only. The rooms are no huge bargains, though. The address is via Cesare Balbo, 4 (tel. 46 39 17), off via Torino, west of Termini. Curfew midnight. Singles L36,000. Doubles L58,000. Triples L69,000. Quads L92,000. Showers and breakfast (7:30-8:15am) included. No breakfast offered Sunday. Tell reception by 10am same day if you want lunch (1-2:15pm, L15,000).

Last Ditch: This is really for people in dire straits, though it's still no great bargain. **Esercito della Salvezza (Salvation Army),** via degli Apuli 39/42 (tel. 49 05 58). Take bus #492 or 415 from Termini. L22,500 per person

International Organizations: You should also consider contacting international host organizations. **Servas,** for example, is dedicated to promoting understanding among cultures. Members stay free of charge in host members' homes in over 90 countries. Stays are limited to two nights, unless you are invited to stay longer. Prospective members are interviewed and asked to contribute US$45 plus a refundable $15 deposit for the list of hosts. To apply, write U.S. Servas Committee, Inc., 11 John St. #407, New York, NY 10038 (tel. (212) 267-0252).

Volunteers for Peace is a work camp organization with similar goals. VFP publishes a newsletter and an annual directory to workcamps in 30 countries, primarily in Eastern and Western Europe (US$10). Write to VFP, Tiffany Rd., Belmont, VT 05730 (tel. (802) 259-2759).

Hotels

"Everyone soon or late comes round by Rome," wrote Robert Browning, and they usually come round by summer. In July and August, Rome bulges with tourists. A huge quantity of rooms meets this demand, but quality varies significantly and hotel prices in Rome are quite often astronomical. Be prepared for prices that do not necessarily reflect quality—in other words, you will not find large fluffy towels, plush carpeting, chocolates on the pillow, and noise and temperature control even if it seems like you're paying for them. Although reservations help, they do not always guarantee that a room awaits you for the full length of your intended stay, or at the decided price, as large groups frequently take precedence over a reserved double in the minds of some proprietors. Prices vary substantially with the time of year, and a proprietor's willingness to bargain increases in proportion to the length of your stay, the number of vacancies, and the size of your group. Settle the price before you commit. Don't assume that misunderstandings will miraculously disappear on their own; knowing a few key words of Italian can greatly ease communication gaps and make your stay more pleasant (you may want to check the glossary in the back of this book for some basic phrases). Have the proprietor write down the price to make sure you know what you've bargained for.

A provincial board inspects, classifies, and registers all hotels. No hotel can legally charge more than the maximum permitted by inspection, but some proprietors double their prices at the sound of a foreign voice—remember that an official rate card must adorn the inside of the door of each room. Under this system, you are unlikely to get ripped off by checking into the first place you find, or to find an unusual bargain by

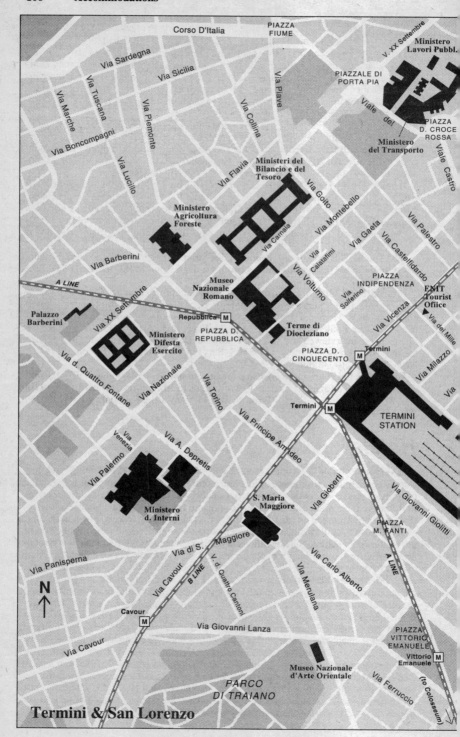

Termini & San Lorenzo

shopping around for hours. Differences between hotels of the same class are largely a matter of location and character, rather than price or facilities. In general, the most charming places are near or in the historic center, while cheaper, less charming joints lie near Termini.

Hotels in Italy have recently been classified on a five-star system. Under this system, all accommodations should be called *hotels;* be aware, however, that a number of establishments retain their old classifications as *pensioni* (small one-to-three star hotels) or *locande* (the cheapest; usually one star, if any). *Albergo* is synonymous with *hotel.*

Rates tend to be lower per person in a shared room. A room with a double bed is called a *matrimoniale* (though marriage is no longer a prerequisite). A double with separate beds is called a *camera doppia,* and a single is a *camera singola.* Showers, which are rarely in the room, usually cost L1000-2500 extra. Many rooms have a bidet or a sink, good for chilling wine, washing socks, or soaking tired feet. Some places offer only full pension *(pensione completa),* meaning room and board (3 meals per day), or half-pension *(mezza pensione),* meaning room, breakfast, and one other meal. This is rare in Rome, and more common in summertime resorts and countryside getaways. Rooms with a private bath cost 30-50% more.

Italian law establishes a high and low season for areas popular with tourists. Remember that off-season months are different for alpine regions and seaside resort areas. Rome's off-season runs October through April, though special occasions like Easter sends prices rising. If you do write for reservations, be aware that Italian law considers a booking legal once a deposit has been paid, and you probably won't be able to get your deposit back if you have to cancel. Without reservations, start looking for a room in the morning during high season, or call a day in advance. Pick up a list of hotels and their prices from the tourist office (you can also call the tourist office and have them quote rates over the phone). If you plan to arrive late, call and ask a hotel to hold a room for you. Many small hotels accept phone reservations several days in advance. Many small places don't have an English speaker, but this shouldn't dissuade a non-Italian-speaker from calling. Instructions on making a room reservation in minimal Italian are included at the back of this book, and most *pensione* proprietors are used to receiving this type of call.

In many smaller towns (and some larger ones), householders rent rooms in their homes to passing travelers, sometimes with the blessing of the tourist authorities, sometimes without. Look for *affitta camere* signs posted around town or notes in store windows. Rates are extremely variable; be prepared to bargain, but don't expect to pay much less than what a reasonable one-star *pensione* in town would cost.

The **tourist offices** in Rome will scrounge (reluctantly in peak season) to find you a room. The main office, at via Parigi, 5 (tel. 46 37 48), is the most helpful. They can also provide a booklet of the current official prices for all of the hotels and *pensioni* in Rome which are the maximum rates allowed by law. Both the **Centro Turistico Studentesco e Giovanile (CTS),** via Genova, 16 (tel. 47 99 31), and the **Enjoy Rome** agency (tel. 445 18 43) can also help you find a place. **Protezione delle Giovane,** Via Urbana, 158 (tel. 46 00 56) maintains an office in the train station and will assist women in finding convent accommodations and moderately priced rooms.

Steer clear of the many spurious "officials" swarming around Termini offering to find you a place. They will likely direct you to a run-down location charging 50% more than the going rate. Though authentic tourism officials carry photo IDs issued by the tourist office, the sneaky imposters now issue themselves fake badges and cards. It is best to avoid using any of the "officials" buzzing around Termini. Use *Let's Go* to find your acccommodations, go directly to the tourist office, or if worse comes to worst, find a place on your own by trial and error (see below). Some *pensione* proprietors will point you to another hotel if they are full.

If the queue at the tourist office extends to infinity, check your bags at the station and investigate nearby *pensioni.* It's usually not hard to find a place, several establishments often operate in a single building. During peak season, some hotels will try to charge more than the official prices, and will automatically tell the tourist office they are full. You may do better calling and bargaining on your own. There are over 300 *pensioni* in Rome with prices comparable to those listed here. Exercise caution, but don't be afraid to set out on your own. **Always insist on seeing a room first,** though some proprietors are not always amenable. Check the mattresses, the bathroom, and the water pressure; most rooms come equipped with sinks. It is crucial to check the security; test the locks (make sure your room key doesn't open the other rooms as well), ask about the curfew or when the front door locks, check how accessible the room-keys are to other guests or passers-by, and find out whether someone mans the front desk at all times. Inquire about additional costs. Some hotels charge for hot showers, heat, or for bathrooms in the room. Don't be enticed by an included breakfast; a cup of coffee and a stale roll can hike the price up by L8000 or more. In the winter, check if the *pensione* has heat or you'll be sorry. According to Italian law, you are not allowed to have unregistered visitors in your room, so don't be surprised or upset if the proprietor won't let you take your new Italian "friend" in for a nightcap.

It is illegal and ill-advised to "camp out" in the public places of Rome. Though violent crime is infrequent, dozing tourists invite trouble. If you must, sleep in groups with designated sentry watches in Termini (check your bags at the station's luggage storage room or risk serious material loss; Rome's best pickpockets hang out at Termini, waiting to prey on tired tourists) or rent a room at the **Albergo Diurno** (day-hotel) in Termini, for men only. Check at the tourist office for a list of other day-hotels. You can rent a *camera riposo* (sleep room) for L8000 an hour, open daily 6:40am-7:30pm. Services open to men and women include showers (L10,000), baths (L12,000), a barber, manicurist, and pedicurist. **Women, whether alone or in a group, should never sleep outdoors.** It is also a good idea to be careful even at designated campgrounds.

For these listings expect increases of approximately 10% for the summer of 1993.

North of Termini

There are clusters of clean, reasonably priced *pensioni* and hotels awaiting the weary backpacker within 10-15 minutes of Termini. Although somewhat run-down, this area is not particularly dangerous; all that remains of what used to be a red light district are two struggling Pussycat theaters and the occasional unobtrusive prostitute by the Diocletian baths. Keep in mind that there are a lot of other travelers looking for budget accommodations in the summer months, so it pays to book a room at least a few days in advance. Don't despair at the labyrinthine layout of the area. By foot, find via Marsala running parallel to Termini to the right of the main exit. Head north (left) on via Marsala, and it will become via Volturno. As you walk along via Volturno, you will come to intersections with via Gaeta, via Calatafimi, and via Montebello; turn right onto any of these to find rooms. (Via Calatafimi is a small bent road that connects via Volturno and via Montebello.) Take via Gaeta to get to the streets running parallel to via Volturno (via Palestro and via Castelfidardo). If you can't carry your bags another step, take bus #3 or 4 directly to this *pensione* district.

For a wholesome snack, there is a fruit and vegetable **market** on via Milazzo, between via Varse and via Palestro (open Mon.-Sat. 6am-2pm). There is another market with similar hours on via Montebello, and a few reasonable grocery and convenience stores in the area.

Pensione Tizi, via Collina, 48 (tel. 474 32 66 or 482 01 28). A 15-minute walk from the station. Take via Goito from p. dell'Indipendenza, cross via XX Settembre onto via Piave, then take the first left onto via Flavia, which leads to via Collina. More safely located than other accommodations around Termini, this family *pensione* has welcomed students for years to its comfortable rooms. Singles L35,000. Doubles L45,000, with shower L55,000. Triples L64,000.

Pensione Papa Germano, via Calatafimi, 14A (tel. 48 69 19), off via Volturno between via Gaeta and via Montebello. Mama, Papa, and the *bambini* Germano run this place with German discipline and Italian warmth. Deservedly popular with backpackers and students, reservations are a must during the summer months. Papa speaks English, and will help you find a place if he's booked. He may also try to match lone travelers with other groups to fill a room. Singles L35,000. Doubles L48,000, with bath L60,000. Triples L70,000. Reduction of 10% on all rooms Nov.-Dec. Visa/Mastercard accepted.

Hotel Home Michele, via Palestro, 35 (tel. 444 12 04). As close to Barbie's dreamhouse as you'll ever find in Rome. Knickknacks everywhere, especially those of the pink fluffy sort. It's small, so book early. Singles L30,000. Doubles L50,000. Triples L60,000.

Pensione Ercoli, via Collina, 48, above the Pensione Tizi on the third floor (tel. 474 54 54). The young, English-speaking, Sardinian management is eager to house students and families. Friendly dorm atmosphere. Rooms and bathrooms are in perfect order, but any room key opens all the doors; lock your backpack zippers, and lock the whole thing to something immobile to discourage casual inter-tourist theft. Singles L30,000. Doubles L45,000, with shower L53,000. Triples L60,000.

Hotel Gexim, via Palestro, 34 (tel. 444 13 11). A 9-room *pensione* run by a young couple who prefer guests that stay more than one night. Light, airy rooms and no curfew. Singles L38,000. Doubles L55,000, with shower L70,000. Triples L75,000. Laundry sent out for L18,000 per load.

Pensione Piave, via Piave, 14 (tel. 474 34 47 or 487 33 60). Definitely a step up from the garden variety budget accommodation, and worth the extra *lire*. All rooms have private bath, telephone, and carpeted floors. The singles have double beds and one room even has a little fireplace. English spoken. Check out at 10am but luggage can be left all day. Singles L50,000. Doubles L70,000.

Pensione Monaco, via Flavia, 84 (tel. 474 43 35 or 481 56 49), around the corner from Tizi and Ercoli. Dim, and no decor to speak of, but bathrooms and beds are spanking clean. Manager won't put up with any funny business; tipsy guests get an extra cold shoulder. Curfew midnight. One shower per day included, an extra one will cost you L2500. Singles L30,000. Doubles L45,000. Triples and quads L20,000 per person.

Pensione Albergo Mary, via Palestro, 55 (tel. 446 21 37 or 446 24 30) and **Pensione Albergo Mary 2,** via Calatafimi, 38 (tel. 47 40 371, fax 482 83 13). Sister establishments. Moderate prices, clean, and a frumpy black bird in the lobby at the original. Some employees speak a little English. Singles L40,000. Doubles L60,000, with shower L80,000. Larger rooms available at Mary 2 for L25,000 per person. Prices soften in the low season. Visa and Mastercard accepted.

Pensione Restivo, via Palestro, 55 (tel. 446 2172). *La donna simpatica* who runs the place takes great pride in the blinding whiteness of her sheets. Large, bright and quiet rooms. Singles L40,000. Doubles L60,000. Triples with bath L80,000.

Pensione Lachea, via San Martino della Battaglia, 11 (tel. 495 72 56), off p. dell'Indipendenza. *Let's Go's* biggest fan, the warm-hearted owner will ensure every comfort. Doubles L42,000. Triples L60,000. Bargaining is not out of the question if the place isn't full.

Hotel Cervia, via Palestro, 55 (tel. 49 10 57, fax 49 10 56). 21 rooms and 41 beds, so check here if you find the smaller *pensioni* full. A bit musty, but the helpful management speaks English. Curfew 1am. Singles L35,000-40,000. Doubles L60,000-75,000.

Pensione Katty, via Palestro, 35 (tel. 444 12 16).This place will never win a Good Housekeeping award. A good price, though, if it's not already full. Singles L35,000. Doubles L44,000. Triples and quads L17,000 per person.

Locanda Marini, via Palestro, 35 (tel. 444 00 58), across the hall and in cahoots with Katty. Less-than-cheerful interior is warmed by the spritely proprietrix. Practice your phrasebook Italian with her. L17,000 per person.

Hotel Continentale, via Palestro, 49 (tel. 495 03 82 or 495 26 29). A mere 2 yards from Termini, and recently renovated. Rooms have telephones and some have balconies. Breakfast included. Some English spoken. Singles with shower L50,000. Doubles with shower L50,000, with shower and toilet L80,000. Quads with shower L120,000. Credit cards accepted.

Hotel Positano, via Palestro, 49 (tel. 49 03 60, fax 49 01 78). Comfy, family-style place with clean floors and firm beds. Singles L50,000, with bath L70,000. Doubles L60,000-100,000. Triples L120,000-140,000. Major credit cards accepted.

Pensione Simonette, via Palestro, 34 (tel. 444 13 02). A tidy 16-room operation. A little Italian will go a long way with the hospitable management. Singles L45,000, with bath L50,000. Doubles L70,000, with bath L80,000. Triples L108,000.

Pensione Piemonte, via Vicenza, 34 (tel. 44 52 240), off via dei Mille and p. dell'Indipendenza. Practically a hotel. Charming, but prices are on the rise. Singles L50,000. Doubles L70,000, with bath L120,000.

Hotel Galli, via Milazzo, 20 (tel. 445 68 59), off via Marsala. Clean and close to Termini. A decent choice, especially for garage-sale art aficionados. Stay here while you look for a classier joint. Singles L35,000. Doubles L55,000. Triples L23,000 per person, but crowded.

Hotel Fenicia, via Milazzo, 20 (tel. 49 03 42), downstairs from Galli. Friendly, English-speaking management. Rooms are small but clean. Singles with shower L50,000, same price if you want to squeeze two people in. Doubles L60,000.

Pensione Roxena, via Marghera, 13 (tel 445 68 23). Bland is the operative word here, but the 11 rooms are spacious and clean. All have sinks, but shower and toilet are in the hall. Midnight curfew. Singles L40,000-50,000. Doubles L50,000-75,000. Triples L75,000. Quads L100,000.

Hotel Pensione Stella, via Castelfidardo, 51 (tel. 404 10 78, fax. 404 15 31). A smiling woman brandishing a mop keeps the place clean. Management will bend over backwards to keep you happy. Doubles L70,000, with shower L80,000. Triples L90,000.

Hotel Harmony, via Palestro, 13 (tel. 48 67 38, fax. 474 39 04). A two-star hotel that's really worth it. All rooms have clean bathrooms and large windows with nice views. Professional, English-speaking staff. A bit pricey in the summer, but the rates will fall with the mercury. Singles L80,000. Doubles L110,000. Breakfast included.

Hotel Pensione Cathrine, via Volturno, 27 (tel. 48 36 34). A stone's throw from Termini. Singles L35,000. Doubles L45,000-51,000.

Hotel Castelfidardo, via Castelfidardo, 31 (tel. 474 28 94 or 494 13 78). Completely new rooms, clean showers, and helpful management. Singles L40,000, with bath L50,000. Doubles L55,000, with bath L70,000.

Hotel Pensione Domus Mea, via Calatafimi, 31 (tel. 488 11 74). Clean, spacious, and a terrace off almost all rooms. Curfew 1am. Singles with bath L50,000. Doubles with bath L85,000.

Hotel Ventura, via Palestro, 88 (tel. 445 19 51). First-floor location is convenient, but noisy at night. Rooms are small but newly renovated. Singles L30,000. Doubles L50,000. Triples L70,000.

South of Termini

In general, the area south of the station is busier, noisier, and seedier than the one to the north, and the proprietors tend to be greedier, grouchier, and less helpful. Many places overcharge the hapless and exhausted tourist who stays one night before moving on to a better scene. However, there are decent places and great bargains to be found with a little perseverance. To avoid confusion among the crisscrossing streets, remember that via Principe Amadeo runs parallel with the west side of the station two blocks over and can be reached by taking any of the side streets that intersect with via Giolitti outside the west exit of the station. The closer you get to p. Vittorio Emanuele, the seedier the area becomes at night. Use extra caution if you're a woman traveling alone.

Pensione di Rienzo, via Principe Amadeo, 79A (tel. 446 71 31). A tranquil retreat at a reasonable price. Lovely, large rooms, most with a balcony overlooking a peaceful courtyard. The manager is a kindly gentleman who speaks English. Prices vary by season. Singles L28,000-45,000, with bath L40,000-55,000. Doubles L30,000-55,000, with bath L40,000-72,000.

Albergo Onello, via Principe Amadeo, 47 (tel. 488 52 57). A diamond *pensione* in the rough of south-of-Termini. Pretty, rustic rooms and gracious management. Singles L50,000. Doubles L75,000, with bath L85,000. Triples L90,000, with shower L110,000.

Albergo Terni/Diocleziano/Orbis/Pensione Dina, via Principe Amadeo, 62 (tel. 474 54 28). The lot of them in one building. Quality and price vary tremendously, so make sure you see what you're getting. Bottom-end prices are singles L25,000-L35,000. Doubles L50,000-L70,000.

Pensione Cortorillo, via Principe Amadeo, 79A (tel. 446 63 94). Seven rooms with wooden beds and flowers on the table. Doubles L55,000, with bath L80,000. Try bargaining.

Pensione Eureka, p. della Repubblica, 47 (tel. 482 58 06 or 488 03 34). Agreeable, and the statues and murals in the entry make you feel right at Rome. English spoken. Not exactly south of Termini; more like northwest, off the far left corner of p. dei Cinquecento as you exit Termini. Showers L2000. Self-service laundry L15,000 per load. Curfew 1am. Singles L36,000, with shower L39,000. Doubles L61,000, with shower L70,000. Triples L85,000, with shower L95,000. Breakfast included.

Pensione Pezzotti and **Hotel Cantilia,** via Principe Amadeo, 79D (tel. 446 69 04 or 446 68 75). Choose your rooms and price level in either establishment owned by the same courteous management. **Pezzotti:** Singles L40,000. Doubles L55,000. Triples L71,000. **Cantilia:** Singles L60,000. Doubles L89,000. Prices drop drastically in the off-season. Private baths, phones, balconies, and TVs.

Pensione Exedra, p. della Repubblica, 47a (tel. 488 39 12), next door to the Eureka on the third floor. Comparable in every way, with similarly unglamorous showers. Showers cost L2000 if staying for only one night. Doubles L68,000. Quads L120,000. Each extra person L28,000. Reservations only one night in advance. Breakfast included and served in your room.

Hotel San Paolo, via Panisperna, 95 (tel. 474 52 13), at via Caprareccia. Dirt-cheap but the swell proprietor, a cross between Grizzly Adams and Mickey Rourke in *Barfly*, makes up for the questionable decor. Singles L30,000. Doubles L45,000, with bath L50,000. Reservations accepted.

Albergo Teti, via Principe Amadeo, 76 (tel 482 52 40 or 474 35 83). Exceedingly comfortable, if a bit pricey. All rooms are tastefully decorated. Those with bathrooms also have a TV. Singles L40,000, with bath and TV L60,000. Doubles L65,000-L70,000, with bath and TV L80,000.

Hotel Orlanda, via Principe Amadeo, 76 (tel. 488 06 37), in the same building as Albergo Teti. Rooms are sparse but clean. One has a wooden floor and is quite charming, and the rest are the usual tile. Official curfew is midnight, but other arrangements can be made. Singles L35,000. Doubles L50,000, with bath L60,000. Triples L65,000.

Hotel Milo, (tel. 474 01 00, fax. 474 53 60), same building as Albergo Titi, and Orlanda. Two floors of immaculate, recently renovated rooms with bath, telephone, and TV. Special price for *Let's Go* readers. Singles L65,000. Doubles L100,000.

Albergo California, via Principe Amadeo, 47 (tel. 482 20 02). Not the subtlest neon flowered wallpaper we've ever seen, but the place is clean. Singles L35,000. Doubles L70,000, with bath and TV L85,000. Triples L120,000. You can check out anytime you like, but you can never leave.

Hotel Sweet Home, via Principe Amadeo, 47 (tel. 488 09 54, fax 481 76 13), downstairs from the California. Home away from home if you live in the "It's a small, small world" ride. There's also a family room available with a double bed, two twin beds and a crib. Singles L50,000. Doubles L70,000, with shower L90,000. Negotiate and haggle.

Hotel Pelliccioni, via Cavour, 47 (tel. 48 44 27). This palatable and pricey *pensione* proffers a TV and refrigerator in every room. Singles L51,000, with bath L75,000. Doubles with bath L90,000. Don't bother ordering the expensive breakfast.

Around Piazza Navona

Vecchia Roma (Old Rome) is the ideal, if increasingly expensive, base for living as the Romans do. By day, its winding cobblestone streets, hidden *piazze* and numerous *caffè* charm; by night, the area swarms with boisterous Romans and tourists alike. Most major sights are within walking distance (great for people traveling with children) and the day market at nearby Campo dei Fiori yields bounties of cheap fruit and vegetables. Unfortunately, hotel proprietors (mostly English-speaking) haven't failed to exploit their desirable location; prices here tend to be second only to those around the ultra-chi-chi piazza di Spagna. Reservations may be the only way to get a bed, especially in the summer. Most *pensioni*, unless otherwise indicated, do *not* accept credit cards.

Albergo Della Lunetta, p. del Paradiso, 68 (tel. 686 10 80, fax 689 20 28). Take via Chiavari off corso Vittorio. (If you're coming from Termini, catch bus #64 or at night #70.) An economical eden in the heart of Old Rome, this is the best value in the p. Navona area. Homey blue-flowered wallpaper, tidy rooms with armoires, phones, and desks. Muse in the central garden or the TV lounge. Singles L30,000, with bath L55,000. Doubles L60,000, with bath L90,000. Triples L90,000, with bath L120,000. Reservations recommended.

Pensione Primavera, p. San Pantaleo, 3 (tel. 654 31 09), off corso V. Emanuele south of p. Navona. A good value for its location, but not exactly luxurious. You're lucky if you can get the corner room with enough furniture for a small cocktail party, two picture-windows for people-watching, and a view of a cathedral cupola. All of the windows in this ascetic *pensione* have thick shutters that keep the rooms quiet. Doubles L65,000, with bath L75,000. Triples L90,000, with bath L105,000. Proprietor not opposed to bargaining. Prices drop in winter.

Pensione Mimosa, via Santa Chiara, 61 (tel. 654 17 53), off p. di Minerva behind the Pantheon. Will never be featured in the *Architectural Digest* hotels-of-the-world issue, but a fantastic location. A matronly woman presides over this kitschy abode, with puppy wall calendars and red checkered tablecloths in the breakfast room. Curfew 1am. Singles L44,000, with breakfast L50,000. Doubles L65,000, with breakfast L76,000.

Albergo Abruzzi, p. della Rotonda, 69 (tel. 679 20 21). Here the humble can contemplate the great; this *albergo* is located smack dab in front of the Pantheon and its noisy admirers. While the friendly cleaning staff keeps the place nice, don't expect to be smothered with attention from the other employees. Singles L45,000-55,000. Doubles L70,000-78,000. Reservations recommended in summer.

Hotel Piccolo, via dei Chiavari, 32 (tel.654 25 60), off Corso Vittorio Emanuele. Next to a bustling grocery but off the beaten path. Friendly woman proprietor, clean, quiet and comfortable, but perversely small bathrooms, even those with showers. Singles L50,000, with shower L69,000. Doubles L70,000, with shower L80,000, with bath L90,000. Quads with bath L140,000. Reservations recommended in summer.

Albergo Pomezia, via dei Chiavari, 12 (tel. 686 13 71). The recently renovated section is far nicer than the old one; all of the redone rooms have baths. Telephones, heat in the winter, matching furniture, and bathrooms Joan Crawford would praise Christina for. Curfew Sun.-Fri. 1:30am. Singles L50,000, with bath L85,000. Doubles L70,000, with bath L110,000. Triples L90,000, with bath L148,000. Prices drop in winter.

Pensione Navona, via dei Sediari, 8 (tel. 686 42 03). Take via de'Canestrari off p. Navona, cross over corso del Rinascimento, and continue straight. A very helpful Italo-Australian family runs a tight ship in this 16th-century Borromini building. The renovated section, earth-toned with matching wood fixtures, puts the older section to shame, but all of the rooms are quiet and clean and most have bathrooms. They tend to fill up with larger groups, so call ahead. They can refer you to other hotels in the area. Checkout 11am. Singles with bath and breakfast L60,000. Doubles L90,000, with bath and breakfast L95,000. Each extra person thereafter L43,000.

Albergo Del Sole, via del Biscione, 76 (tel. 654 08 73). Off p. Campo dei Fiori. A portrait of the old proprietor haunts every common space. Escape from his likeness in rooms with top-notch furniture, plush lounging chairs, and matching bedsteads and armoires. Checkout 11:30am. Singles L52,500, with shower L60,000, with bath L70,000. Doubles L75,000, with bath L90,000-96,000.

Hotel Smeraldo, vicolo dei Chiodaroli, 9 (tel. 687 59 29), off via Chiavari. These monkish cells are immaculate and unadorned except for the bidets in every room. Air-conditioning and elevator-access for a hefty L15,000 per day extra. Breakfast L5000. Singles L55,000. Doubles L70,000, with bath L90,000. Triples L90,000, with bath L125,000. Quads L110,000, with bath L145,000. All major credit cards accepted.

Near The Spanish Steps

Marxist ideologues, budget travelers, and quiet Amish types be warned: this area of Rome will not be sympathetic to your lifestyle. This is the Italian equivalent of Paris's Rive Gauche, and the Beautiful People flock here to browse through boutiques and galleries. In an area where designer silk suits, leather loafers, mini-skirts, and face lifts abound, inexpensive accommodations are scarce. The neighborhood also suffers from a lack of grocery stores and affordable restaurants. Still, for fashion victims who find themselves lingering in front of Fendi after the buses stop running, try the following *pensioni*.

Pensione Fontanella Borghese, Largo della Fontanella Borghese, 84 (tel. 687-11-55), off via Condotti after it crosses southwest over via del Corso. The area's only real bargain, and the management knows it. Singles L25,000. Doubles L45,000. Triples L52,000. Make reservations three weeks in advance.

Pensione Fiorella, via del Babuino, 196 (tel. 361 05 97), off p. di Spagna near p. del Popolo. Spruce set-up and obliging management. Curfew 1am. Singles L40,000. Doubles L70,000. Breakfast included. No reservations, so arrive early in the morning.

Pensione Parlamento, via delle Convertite, 5 (tel. 679 20 82, for reservations 684 16 97), off via del Corso on the street leading up to p. San Silvestro. Plant-crowded landing, glamorous roof-top terrace with flowers, safes in all the rooms for your jewels, and even hairdryers in some for that big hairdo *all'italiana*. High ceilings, balconies, and sketchbook views. Very amiable management who speak English. Breakfast L12,000 (don't bother). Singles L53,000, with bath L90,000. Doubles L70,000, with bath L82,000, with shower and bath L95,000. Each additional person L25,000. Reservations recommended. Increase prices 10% if using credit cards.

Pensione Brotsky, via del Corso, 509 (tel. 361 23 39). Tranquil rooms that overlook a courtyard. Color TV lounge, and candy-striped towels. Singles with bath L90,000. Extra person L30,000. Reservations recommended.

Hotel Marcus, via del Clementino, 94 (tel. 68 30 03 20, fax 683 25 67). Off via della Scrofa, Clementino is an extension of Condotti. Stairwell with stained-glass ceiling leads to this homey hotel. Relive tender childhood moments watching dubbed reruns of T.J. Hooker in the TV room. Matching wood furniture, telephones, heaters in the winter, secure double windows. All rooms with small bath. Singles L80,000-85,000. Doubles L95,000. Triples L120,000. Quads L140,000. Flash your *Let's Go* and you might get a discount.

Pensione Erdarelli/Pensione Pierina, via due Macelli, 28 (tel. 679 12 65, fax 679 07 05). Clean and centrally located. Shake your cosmic thang in the extra luggage/dressing room. Singles L72,500, with bath L92,000. Doubles L110,000, with bath L130,000. Triples L150,000, with bath L177,000. Major credit cards accepted. Breakfast included.

Hotel Pensione Suisse S.A.S., via Gregoriana, 56 (tel. 678 36 49), off p. di Trinità dei Monti. In the Swiss tradition of pricey perfection and neutral yet quaint location. TV lounge, phone in every room, tidy bathrooms, some with tubs. Singles L65,000. Doubles L98,000, with bath L128,000. Triples L165,000. Half the bill may be paid with credit cards. Breakfast included.

Across the River

The *pensioni* on the other side of the Tiber aren't the cheapest in Rome, but they tend to be quiet, clean and friendly. Those in **Ottaviano**, near the Vatican, are attractive for their proximity to popular sights and a safe, residential area. Hedonists and bohemians might prefer to stay in **Trastevere**, scene of much nighttime revelry and home to many young expatriates. Bus #64 from p. del Cinquecento and #81 from via Cavour at Santa Maria Maggiore, as well as Metro Linea A, all run to Ottaviano. Buses #75 from p. Indipendenza, 60 from via XX Settembre, and 170 from p. del Cinquecento all run from near Termini to Trastevere. One of the friendliest food markets in Rome can be found at p. di San Cosimato, in Trastevere. For those around the Vatican, there is an indoor food market at the piazza d'Unità, off via Cola di Rienzo.

Residence Guiggioli, via Germanico, 198 (tel. 324 21 13). Five of the best rooms in Rome. Beautiful antiques adorn pristine rooms. The wonderful proprietress will chat with you in Italian whether you understand her or not. Doubles L65,000; matrimonial suite with private bath L70,000.

Pensione Lady, same building as the Guiggioli, 4th floor (tel. 324 21 12). The same loving couple has been running this clean, peaceful pensione for thirty years. This explains the unintentionally campy 1960s mod decor. They prefer travelers who will stay more than one night. Singles L45,000; *matrimoniale* and doubles L55,000. Closed for 1 or 2 weeks in November.

Pensione Manara, via Luciano Manara, 25 (tel. 581 47 13). Take a right off viale di Trastevere onto via delle Fratte di Trastevere to via Luciano Manaro. Friendly management runs this homey establishment overlooking colorful p. San Cosimato in the heart of Trastevere. English spoken. Doubles L52,000. Triples L40,000. Quads L87,000. Showers L3000 each, good and wet.

Pensione Zurigo/Pensione Nautilus, via Germanico, 198 (tel. 372 01 39 or 324 20 50), same building as the Guiggioli, reception on the fifth floor. Not quite as charming as Guiggioli but very serviceable. Spacious spic-n-span rooms, fluent English spoken. Doubles L60,000, with bath L80,000.

Pensione Ida, via Germanico, 198 (tel. 324 21 64), on the 4th floor next to Guiggioli. If the rest are full, offers so-so doubles for L60,000.

Pensione Ottaviano, via Ottaviano, 6 (tel. 38 39 56 or 370 05 33), off p. del Risorgimento north of p. San Pietro. The only hostel-style *pensione* in the area. Temporary home to backpackers of all different nations. English spoken. Conveniently located, but not exactly the bargain of the century. L20,000 per person for a bunk in a shared room.

Hotel Pensione Alimandi, via Tunisi, 8 (tel. 39 72 39 48 or 39 72 39 41 or 39 72 63 00, fax 397 239 43). Take the steps off viale Vaticano down to via Sebastiano Veniero, and go straight—literally meters away from the Vatican Museum. A gorgeous place with a beautiful garden patio on the first floor and a terrace on the roof. Telephones in every room. TV lounge with electric piano and bar. Make reservations in high season, because they sometimes receive large groups. Singles L50,000, with bath L65,000. Doubles L65,000, with bath L85,000. Triples L90,000, with bath L114,000. L10,000 per extra bed. Credit cards of all flavors accepted.

Hotel Amalia, via Germanico, 66 (tel. 39 72 33 54 or 39 72 33 56 or 397 23 82, fax 39 72 33 65). Nice entry with an attractive courtyard, but the rooms are a little dingy for the price. Pastel minimalism, a few plants, and a TV lounge. Private baths to be added in the fall of '92; look for concomitant increase in price. English spoken. Singles L50,000. Doubles L80,000. Triples L106,000. Don't bother with breakfast for L12,000. Mastercard and Visa accepted.

Hotel Florida, via Cola di Rienzo, 243 (tel. 324 18 72). Clean, sparse modern rooms with telephones. Friendly management. Singles L53,000. Doubles L73,000, with bath L94,000. Triple 130,000.

Pensione Esty, viale Trastevere, 108 (tel. 588 12 01), about ½km down viale di Trastevere from the Ponte Garibaldi. Simple rooms await in an Orwellian building somewhat removed from the rowdy heart of Trastevere. English spoken. Singles L36,000. Doubles 52,000. Triples L70,000. Quad L85,000.

Camping

You probably won't catch the malaria that killed Daisy Miller, but there are still plenty of mosquitoes menacing tourists in campgrounds near the city. Though there's often little space between sites, peaceful seclusion is usually steps away. In August, arrive early—well before 11am—or you may find yourself without a spot. Rates average L6000 per person and another L6000 for the car. Many of the campgrounds are downright luxurious, boasting everything from swimming pools to campground bars, while others may be more primitive—you may want to shop around. The **Touring Club Italiano** corso Italiano, 10, 20122 Milano, publishes an annual directory of all camping sites in Italy, *Campeggi in Italia,* available in bookstores throughout Italy. A free map and list of sites is available from the **Italian Government Travel Office** or directly from **Federcampeggio,** via V. Emanuele, 11, Casella Postale 23, 50041 Calenzano (Firenze).

Camping on beaches, roads, or any flat, inconspicuous plot is illegal, but not uncommon, in Italy. Campers who don't make fires or litter will lessen their chances of being disturbed. Respect for property rights is extremely important—within sight of a farmhouse, ask permission.

Capitol Campground, via di Castelfusano, 195 (tel. 566 27 20), in Ostia Antica, is 3km from the ruins and has a swimming pool and tennis courts. Take the train from the Piramide Metro stop to Ostia Antica, then walk the 3km; or take the train to Lido Centro and bus #5 to the site. Open year round. L8500 per person, L7500 per tent. L4500 per car.

Nomentano, on via della Cesarina (tel. 610 02 96), at via Nomentana. Closer to Rome (11km away). Take bus #36 from Termini and transfer to bus #337 at p. Sempione. L8100 per person, L4000 per tent; open March-Oct.

Flaminio, via Flaminia Nuova (tel.333 26 04) is about 8km outside of Rome. Take bus #910 from Termini to piazza Mancini, then transfer to bus #202 or 204. L9000 per person, L7200 per tent; open March-Oct.

Seven Hills, via Cassia 1216 (tel. 376 55 71), 8km north of Rome. Take but #201 from Piazza Mancini. L8900 per person, L4700 per tent. Open March 15-Oct. 30.

Camping Equipment

Camping requires preparation. Spend some time perusing catalogs and questioning knowledgeable salespeople before buying any equipment. There are many reputable mail-order firms—use them to gauge prices and order from them if you can't do as well locally. **Campmor,** 810 Rte. 17N, P.O. Box 997-LG91, Paramus, NJ 07653-0997 (tel. (800) 526-4784), offers name-brand equipment at attractive prices. Open 24 hours and absolutely every day, **L.L. Bean,** 1 Casco St., Freeport, ME 04033 (tel. (800) 221-4221), has plenty of its own equipment and some national brands. Even better, though less accessible, is the northwest U.S.'s long-time favorite, **Recreational Equipment, Inc. (REI),** P.O. Box C-88125, Seattle, WA 98188 (tel. (800) 426-4840). They carry excellent equipment and clothing for nearly every outdoor activity. They also distribute the guide *Europa Camping and Caravanning* (US$13) and, like L. L. Bean, have a mail-order catalog.

Good **sleeping bags** are rated for specific minimum temperatures. The lower the mercury, the higher the price; expect to pay between US$100 and US$300. Anticipate the most severe conditions you may encounter, subtract a few degrees, and then buy a bag. Remember, the warmest bag will keep you *warm,* so don't overpurchase if you need a bag just for the summer. **Pads** to go under your bag cost about US$10 for simple foam pads and US$50 for the best foam/air hybrids. Some bags now include internal pad holders so you won't find yourself sleeping next to your pad when you awake.

Modern **tents** remarkably clever contraptions in primary colors, are self-supporting (equipped with their own frames and suspension systems) and can be set up quickly. Up-to-date versions of simpler designs are made of modern materials and have effective insect netting and integral floors. Make sure you have and use the tent's protective rain fly (dew can be quite soggy). Backpackers and cyclists will require especially small, light models; single-person tents are available from under 1kg (2.2 lbs.), two-person from under 1.4kg (3 lbs.). Two reputable U.S. manufacturers of lightweight tents are Sierra Designs and Eureka. Expect to pay at least US$95 for a simple two-person tent, US$125 for a serviceable four-person model; the lightest and most durable tents will set you back US$100-250. For the best deals, look around for last year's merchandise, particularly in the fall; tents don't change much, but prices may be reduced by as much as 50%.

Other camping basics include a battery-operated **lantern** (*never* gas) for use inside the tent, and a plastic **groundcloth** to put under the tent. If you want to do a lot of cooking, **campstoves** come in all sizes, weights, and fuel types, starting at about US$50. Bring some **waterproof matches** (and some cooking equipment) or the stove might prove useless. Sufficient equipment to cook may prove more of an albatross than a convenience—consider your eating requirements and preferences carefully. A **canteen, insect repellent,** and **Swiss army knife** are all small but useful items to throw in with your gear.

Before leaving home, you may want to write to the **Automobile Association,** Fanum House, Basingstoke, Hampshire RG21 2EA, England, for their publication *Camping and Caravanning in Europe. Camp Europe by Train* (US$16.95) is available from **Ariel Publications,** 14417 SE 19th Pl., Bellevue, WA 98007 (tel. (206) 641-0518). The **National Campers and Hikers Association, Inc.,** 4804 Transit Rd., Bldg. #2, Depew, NY 14043 (tel. (716) 668-6242) distributes travel guides for campers and sells the International Camping Carnet (US$23), required for entry to some European campgrounds.

Food and Wine

Feast During Famine

In the heyday of the Roman republic, citizens ate only two meals a day, *prandium* (a light mid-day meal) and dinner. Dinners were typically lavish, festive affairs lasting as long as ten hours, with entertainment, music, and hanky-panky considered as vital as food. Roman writers such as Petronius, Juvenal, and Martial reported the erotica, exotica and general excesses of the Imperial dinner table: peacocks, flamingos, and herons were served with their full plumage meticulously replaced after cooking. Wolves, hedgehogs, and puppies were the red meats of choice. Dormice, small rodents resembling squirrels, were kept in barrels to keep them from exercising and were force-fed to obesity for the table. According to Pliny, Maecenas was the first to serve ass's meat in the first century BC, but most epicures preferred the meat of the onager, a wild type of donkey. Elephant trunk was supposedly a great delicacy, and one emperor, Elegabalus, was just wild about camel's feet. Forks were not yet invented, and anything that could not be picked up with a spoon was grabbed with fingers; servants offering warm, scented water and napkins were in constant attendance. Wine was decanted through strainers into large bowls, and cooled in snow or warmed in hot water. The imperial cuisine was not only exotic—it was also consumed in unimaginable amounts. The Emperor Maximus reputedly ate 40 pounds of meat daily, washed down with 40 quarts of wine. Farone, the court jester to Emperor Aurelian, became the life of the party by devouring an entire sheep, a suckling pig, and a wild boar, along with 100 pieces of bread, swigging 100 bottles of wine to wash it down. These food orgies became virtual vomitoriums; after gorging themselves on slabs of meat and barrels of wine, the guests would retreat to a special room to throw it all up, and then return to the party. Naked Spanish girls, acrobats, and fire-eaters provided the visual entertainment. These feasts were *de rigeur* only among the court and the 200 other families that could afford such luxury. More decorous families forwent the vomit-inducing gluttony and the naked ladies, though spitting on the floor was commonplace and loud belching was a polite compliment to the chef. The most outrageous banquets were staged by the *nouveau riche* merchants. Trimalchio, a shipping magnate who dabbled in many of the shadier dealings of this gilded age, hosted a notorious feast featuring a boar stuffed with live birds, written up in the *Satyricon* of Petronius.

Today, meals in Rome are still lengthy affairs, continuing for hours on end as each course is savored with deliberation. (Breakfast—a gulp of caffeine and a sticky bun—is the only exception.) Accordionists wail out Frank Sinatra (L100 tip expected), corks fly off the local *Castelli Romani* wines, and a crispy *bruschetta* (a piece of toasted bread garnished with oil, garlic, and herbs) begins the meal. When you sit down, order *mezzo e mezzo* and your waiter will bring you a half liter of wine and a half liter of sparkling water. Later, the *primo piatto* (first course) arrives, usually *risotto* (rice) or pasta, often prepared *alla carbonara* (with bacon and egg) or *alla matriciana* (with bacon, white wine, tomato, and pepper). On Thursdays, many restaurants serve up homemade *gnocchi*, a doughy potato pasta, which gets its name from the dialect meaning of *gnocco* (puddinghead). Pasta and *risotto* in Rome, and even more so in the surrounding countryside, are prepared *al dente* (to the teeth), so be prepared to chew at great length. Any pasta dish served *alla carrettiera* (teamster's style) is made with tuna and mushrooms; *alla prestinara* (baker's style) is cooked with garlic and oil, and *all'arrabbiata* is "rabid," cooked with lethal, hot red peppers. Romans do not slurp their pasta, but carefully wind the spaghetti around their fork, making sure that there are no loose ends. It takes a bit of practice and patience to eat pasta as graciously as the Romans do.

Then comes the second course, *secondo piatto,* of meat or fish. Popular main courses include *saltimbocca* (slices of ham and veal cooked together), *abbacchio alla scottaditto* (tender grilled lamb of the "burnt finger"), *involtini al sugo* (rolled veal cutlets filled with ham, celery, and cheese, smothered in tomato sauce), and *coda alla vaccinara* (stewed oxtail with vegetables). Write home about trying *pajata* (veal intestine with its mother's milk clotted inside, seasoned with garlic, chili peppers, tomatoes and white wine). Seafood is often expensive; specialties include *anguilette in umido* (stewed baby eels from Lake Bracciano) and cheaper, *filetti di baccalà* (fried cod filets). The festival of San Giovanni features *lumache* (snails).

There are numerous vegetable specialities served on the side *(contorni)* or after the main course. *Carciofi alla giudia* (or *alla romana*) are crispy fried artichokes from the Roman countryside, adopted from Rome's Jewish community, and *fiori di zucca* are gorgeous zucchini flowers stuffed with cheese. Most *trattorie* feature a serve-yourself *antipasto* bar with all kinds of marinated vegetables, salads, and meats, perfect as a main course for smaller appetites and vegetarians. Even the most carnivorous gourmets will enjoy *contorni* like *fagiolini* (early-picked, tender string beans), *zucchini* (tastier than the American or English variety), *melanzana* (eggplant prepared in a variety of ways), *bieta* (swiss chard), and the more adventurous *cicoria* (dandelion greens). You can eat the latter two *all'agro* (room temperature with lemon and olive oil) or *passata in pedella* (reheated in a pan with olive oil and garlic). Salads are usually eaten after the main course, and have not received the immense degree of popularity, enormity, and variety as in the States. They do come in a few different ways. *Insalata verde* is a green salad; ask for a sprinkling of *rughetta* (arugula to Americans, rocket to the Brits), or *radicchio* to add a tasty bitter touch. *Insalata mista* is a mixed salad (note that tomatoes in Italy are often partially green). *Insalata caprese*, with tomatoes, fresh mozzarella, and fresh basil, is enough to make you an expatriate. Fresh fennel (*finnochio*) is often served in raw chunks with a salted olive oil dip as a digestive.

After hours of rumination, and long after those with non-Italian appetites are full, dessert, fruit, and *espresso* are served. Imported from Venice, homemade *tiramisù* (ladyfingers soaked in espresso, layered with sweet mascarpone cheese, a dash of brandy, and dusted with bittersweet chocolate) is an out-of-body experience. Actually, *tiramisù*, which literally means pick-me-up, is named for its rejuvenating powers; the story goes that after a passionate encounter, a man would whip up a batch to arouse his, um, sexual energy. *Zuppa Inglese* (English soup), despite its name, is actually a trifle-like cake layered with custard and soaked in rum. For the less daring, *macedonia* is a mixed fruit cup.

The *coup de grace* is a potent shot of *sambuca* (anise liqueur)—try it *con le mosche* (with flies), that is, flaming with the traditional coffee beans floating on top. *Grappa* is another post-prandial option; in its finest form, it is similar to brandy and is a doubly distilled clear liqueur made from old grape pressings. The low-grade version usually contains all kinds of fruit alcohol and sugar, but it does the job. A fitting cap to any meal is a leisurely stroll with world-famous Italian ice cream: *gelato*. (See our Appendix for a more complete list of dishes, foods, and phrases commonly encountered on Roman menus.)

Emulating the Roman smorgasbord every night will cost you an arm and a leg and a month's membership at the gym; a 10-course meal can easily cost upwards of L50,000, and the never-ending stream of starch, oil, and butter will do untold damage to your waistline. A more realistic option is to take advantage of the *coperto* (cover charge), which generally entitles you to unlimited baskets of delicious, dippable bread. Pasta is generally the cheapest and most satisfying choice on the menu and comes with plenty of moppable sauce. Huge plate-size pizzas satisfy the biggest appetites and the tightest budgets. Multi-course, price-fixed menus (referred to by *Let's Go* as *menù*), often including wine, are becoming more and more common, and are much less expensive than ordering a full feast à la carte. Still, since the government ensures fair dealing by controlling what is served, you will encounter no surprises. This may reassure non-Romans of not getting pig's feet *marinara*, but it also means the food is rather run-of-the-mill. The fixed price has been rising steadily, though you can still find a few bargains. House wine (though sometimes watered down) is often as cheap as a bottle of sparkling water. If you want water from the tap, ask for *acqua semplice* and ignore the waiter's grumbling. Whether you have one course or seven, your *coperto*, in effect, rents you a spot at a table, and the waiters generally should not (and usually won't) hassle you to leave. Linger over that house wine, bread, and *pasta al ragù*. When selecting a restaurant in Rome, keep in mind that family-run places charge less (by a couple thousand *lire*) than those with hired help. Do try to save your pennies for one final pig-out night before you leave Rome.

There are different categories of restaurants in Rome, though like most official things in the city, these don't mean much. *Ristorante* is generally the most elegant sort, with dolled-up waiters, linen tablecloths, and expensive (though not necessarily better) dishes. A *trattoria* has a more casual atmosphere and lower prices. Often, there are no menus and they just bring you what they are making. In most establishments, you can order a half-portion of pasta, which gets you a plate 2/3 full for 2/3 the price. Kosher restaurants are found in the Jewish Ghetto (see Jewish Ghetto below). If you find an original *osteria* (or *hostaria*), you'll see old locals sitting around a table, chewing the fat, playing cards, downing bottles of wine or beer. By tradition, you bring the food and they supply the booze. One notorious story tells of a proprietor on via Flaminia who was sitting outside his *osteria*, smoking his cigar, when a papal procession rode by. The proprietor was so absorbed in his own thoughts that he failed to notice all the pomp and circumstance. One of the pope's attendants, angered at the guy's disrespect, asked him what he was doing. The proprietor replied "me la fumo" (I'm smoking). The saucy Roman expression *melafumo* now means "I couldn't care less." However, these casual spots are rare and many so-called *osterie* are overpriced *ristorante* in disguise. Similarly, *trattorie* can range tremendously in price, so always check the menu. Many of the smaller, more authentic lunch spots, actually *enoteche*, sometimes sporting the sign *vino e cucina*, cater to a regular crew of workers, and are the last relics of the *osteria* lifestyle. An *enoteca* is actually a wine store (not a bar), and some have added card tables with paper tablecloths to the back room and serve simple fare in a no-nonsense way. We list some of these establishments in a separate section below (see Wine

Shops). At a *pizzeria*, you sit down to your own plate-size pizza. A well-prepared pizza is light and crispy and blackened a little around the edges, served piping hot by its creator. Look for signs that say *Forno a Legno* (wood-burning oven). Most of these sit-down *pizzerie* only open in the evening. There are innumerable pizza creations and combinations, so order exactly what you want. The most common pizzas are the *margherita* (mozzarella and tomato sauce; ask for *basilico*, basil), *napolitana* (*margherita* with anchovies), *capricciosa* (a bit of everything, olives, ham, hard-boiled egg, tomato, cheese) and *funghi* (with mushrooms). Be warned that asking for *pepperoni* will get you red peppers, not salami.

The billing at Italian restaurants can be a bit confusing. Most restaurants add a *pane e coperto* (cover charge) of about L1500 to the price of your meal, as well as tacking on a *servizio* (service charge) of 10%-15%, but it is a Roman custom to leave L1000-2000 tip nonetheless. In family-run establishments without hired servers, tipping is not expected. Before you sit down, check the cover price; cheap pasta can be sabotaged by a L3000 cover. In a *bar,* look for a sign stating either *servizio compreso* (service included) or *servizio non compreso* (not included). In the case of the latter, drop some cash into the kitty on the bar. Restaurants and stores are also required to give you a *ricevuta fiscale* (a receipt) for tax purposes. You are required by law to carry it with you until you are sixty feet out of the restaurant. There is fine for both the restaurant and the patron if you fail to do so, though such arrests are infrequent. Still, don't be surprised if your waiter comes chasing you down the street with your receipt if you forget to take it.

An alternative to a traditional Italian meal is a moveable feast. Rome vaunts innumerable picnic spots. Some of the best are the Villa Borghese, Villa Ada, the Janiculan Hill (Gianicolo), the Palatine Hill, the Botanical Gardens in Trastevere, the Appian Way, and small towns in Lazio. *Alimentari* are your best bet for standard groceries. They generally include dairy, dry goods, and deli sections. For specialty cheeses and fresh bread and meats, try the smaller *panetterie* and *salsamentarie*. These shops will either fix you a sandwich or simply sell you the ingredients; an *etto* (100g) of anything is usually enough for a sandwich. For produce, seek out the Italian greengrocers' small *frutta e verdure* shops. Food stores are open roughly Mon.-Wed. and Fri. 8am-1pm and 5:30-8pm, Thurs. and Sat. 8am-1pm. Get a taste of local produce and local haggling techniques at Rome's many outdoor markets. The largest markets are at p. Campo dei Fiori, p. Vittorio, and off Cola di Rienzo (indoors, near the Vatican). Smaller markets can be found on via Montebello and piazza delle Pace off piazza Navona. Markets generally operate Mon.-Sat. 6am-2pm, and sell a large variety of goods from food and housewares to clothing and antiques—good to remember if you're planning an extended stay and need kitchen supplies. Supermarket STANDA offers a huge selection of foodstuffs, produce, toiletries, kitchen supplies, cheap clothing, and anything else you can think of. There is one located on viale Trastevere, a few blocks down from piazza Sidney Sonnino, and one on via Cola di Rienzo, several blocks down from the Ottaviano Metro stop, and several blocks up from piazza del Popolo. They hold the standard food store hours (see above).

For easy home fixings with an Italian twist, try *prosciutto e melone* (smoked ham and cantaloupe), *bresaola e rughetta* (smoked beef and arugula/rocket) or an *insalata caprese* (tomatoes and mozzarella cheese layered with basil leaves). Vendors are usually happy to let you sample the different kinds of cheeses, olives, and meats. Don't just eat what you know; try an *etto* of this, an *etto* of that, and play with combinations. A dollop of *ricotta*, a wedge of local *pecorino* (sheep's cheese) with sliced pear, and a baggie of spiced olives are musts. Pizza is sold in slices by weight at establishments which brandish the *pizza rustica* sign. An *etto* repels a snack attack. The rudimentary pizza sold in these shops, however, is a different breed from the real variety made by hand at wood-burning pizzerie. Other favorite Roman snacks include *baccalà,* deep-fried cod fillets, and *suppli al telefono,* deep-fried rice balls with melted mozzarella in the middle which are named for the long, telephone-cord-like strands that the mozzarella makes as you pull the treat away from your mouth. *Arancini* are deep fried rice balls with mozzarella, mushrooms, and/or tomato sauce, and *crocchetti* are breaded globs of mashed potatoes.

A *bar* is an excellent place to have a quick and inexpensive bite (though take care to avoid *bars* on major tourist thoroughfares, as prices go through the roof), offering any number of hot and cold sandwiches, salads, and pastas, washed down with a *Campari.* *Tramezzini* come with all different fillings, smothered in mayo, surrounded by soft, de-crusted white bread, just like Mom used to make. Otherwise, try the rolls and pizza bread stuffed with *prosciutto,* cheese, or even omelettes; ask for it *scaldato* (heated). Sandwiches range in price from L1500-5000. A *tavola calda* (literally, hot table) and *rosticcerie* (take-out) are often cheaper than formal sit-down meals, but quality varies. Most offer a broad range of hot and cold dishes, from roast chickens, fried *calamari,* and eggplant parmesan to rice salad and sandwiches, and some have tables or counters to rest your tootsies. Stay away from the area near the train station—most ostensible "bargain" restaurants (offering dirt-cheap, fixed-price menus) are actually second-rate tourist snares which serve nothing resembling Italian cuisine. Hop on a bus to reach the university district of **San Lorenzo** or the traditional area known as **Testaccio,** on the eastern banks of the Tiber. These are the last truly untouristed restaurant districts in Rome. The areas around **piazza Navona** and **Campo dei Fiori** harbor some romantic *trattorie,* and **Trastevere** boasts the liveliest *pizzerie.* The best places fill up immedi-ately, so set out early to avoid the rush. Romans generally eat late—around 9pm. Most restaurants close for at least two weeks in August. One final tip; some say the mark of a good restaurant is the presence of voracious *carabinieri,* who take their food serious-ly, so keep an eye out for the blue uniforms.

In Vino Veritas

Italy's rocky soil, warm climate, and hilly landscape have been celebrated as ideal for growing grapes since the days of the Empire. Today, Italy produces more wine than any other country, and it is even served, slightly diluted, to children as young as six. Be-cause of Italy's political fragmentation and general disorganization, many wines have remained confined to the neighborhood of their vineyard. Even more so than the popu-larized *Asti Spumante* and *Chianti* from the North or *Marsala* from Sicily, Lazio's har-vest never travels far from the winemaker's own dinner table. While the majority of oenophiles and exporters have long neglected or even snubbed Italian, and especially Latian, wines, you can discover uncharted wine territory at humble *vigne* all through the countryside. The major wine-producing region around Rome is to the south, known as the *Castelli Romani* for the summer villas built there by bacchanalian patricians, mostly producing a fruity white wine. *Frascati* is perhaps the most well-known, inspir-ing Roman dialect poet Trilussa to exclaim, "in a mouthful there's such good humour that sings hymns and decks your heart with banners." One of the finest golden wines of the region grown on the slopes of Montefiascone, owes its name, *Est! Est!! Est!!!,* to a fussbudget German Cardinal who was traveling through the district. He sent his valet ahead of him to sample the local wines, to chalk "Est" ("it's good") on the doors of inns with satisfactory offerings, and "Est Est" if it was particularly good. When the valet reached Montefiascone, he was so enraptured with the harvest that he wrote "Est Est Est," a great piece of publicity for the wine which has since assumed this name. The Cardinal himself loved the wine so much that he stayed at the inn for several days, drinking such vast quantities that he died.

The god Bacchus was credited with having first brought the vine to the Aegean from India. The beverage caught on, and Italians became supreme wine-makers. In the high-ly efficient republic of the Roman Empire, wine was so widely produced that vineyards were occasionally demolished to check the problem of over-production, despite the fact that the Romans drank wine in mind-boggling quantities. Julius Caesar wanted to produce a wine that would wow the guests at his inauguration banquet, and ordered a "legendary" wine to be produced, created by a mixture of grapes from Southern Italy. Wines from throughout Italy are available in most wine shops and restaurants. While those on a tight budget may not get to taste the legend of Rome, there are numerous, inexpensive, local wines (often named for their towns) that are worth tippling:

Frascati - fruity, dry and clear; the most famous local white wine, often served from a long thin bottle. **Est Est Est** - the famous white wine of Montefiascone. **Colli Albani** - pale gold, fruity, and delicate; from the region around Castel Gandolfo **Colli Lanuvini** and **Velletri** - a dry white and a dry red, both good for fish and the latter, for meats and robust pastas; both hail from the area south of Lake Nemi. **Cerveteri** - offers a full-bodied red wine and a slightly bitter, aromatic white. **Zagarola** - a soft white wine, all the rage in the Renaissance. **Monte Compatri Colonna** - another local white that goes well with a plate of light pasta.

You can usually order by the glass, carafe, or half-carafe, although bars rarely serve wine by the glass. *Vecchio* means "old," and *stravecchio* means "very old." *Secco* means "dry" and *abboccato* means "sweet." When in doubt, request the local wine—it will be cheaper (typically around L3500 a liter) and best suited to the Roman or Latian cuisine. Cheap house white wine can have a particularly pungent smell from the chemical preservatives, and cheap red can give you a nasty headache. If your carafe of house wine seems a little suspicious, send it back and opt for an inexpensive bottle of wine or mineral water. Many of the more inexpensive *trattorie* don't have a wine list, and instead they just yank down one of the bottles lining the rafters. Check the date before you drink it; white wine should not be more than two or three years old, but don't worry about a particular vintage date. Most of the wines from the Roman countryside are served young and err on the sweet side. Before going, you might want to go to your local library and check out *The Wine Atlas of Italy* by Burton Anderson (Simon and Schuster, $40), winner of numerous awards including the competition for Wine Book of the Year, and packed with regional information including culinary specialties and travel tips.

Wine Shops: Dining While Wining

Enoteche (or *bottiglierie*), traditional wine and olive oil shops, have become an economical and more authentic lunchtime alternative to pricey *trattorie*. This tradition began in the days when shop proprietors whipped up bowls of pasta to share with the men who delivered barrels of the local harvest. The workers lingered over the long marble counters that are still prevalent in most shops and slurped up whatever noodles had been prepared by the *mama* of the house. Eventually, the proprietors extended their modest cooking to the customers, and word got out; laborers and others soon began flocking to these wine shops for a cheap and filling afternoon meal and a game of cards. The wine shops installed card tables, put up signs *"vino e cucina,"* and turned family members into waiters. In the 1960s and 70s, students, hippies and political activists gathered here to talk Marx and Marcuse, the latest government, alternative consciousness, and specific concerns. Today, anyone looking for substantial, inexpensive food in an informal, personable setting will enjoy the cuisine and company in these neighborhood establishments. Most of these places are open only on weekdays during lunchtime (approximately noon-3pm). Arrive early; these places tend to fill up around 12:30pm with workers in no hurry to leave, and you may be hard-pressed to find a seat even if you wait. Unfortunately, the prices have risen since days of yore and a full meal can cost upwards of L20,000, though you generally get a lot for your money. Feel the place out; some of the smaller places expect you to order at least a *primi* and a *secondi* if you're taking the place of a 300-pound construction worker with an appetite to match. Other places allow you to linger indefinitely over a salad, tipple your house wine, and kick back. Tell them how much you want, and they'll charge you accordingly. You'll have to look carefully to find these places, since most are not marked by more than a small sign or the wandering smell of garlic; explore the areas around via del Governo Vecchio and beyond...as in the winding streets behind via Tomacelli (on the way to piazza Navona from via del Corso and the Mausoleum of Augustus) to find more of these modest establishments. Most places close at least two weeks in August. Check our Wine Bars section (under Entertainment, below) for more listings.

Da Benito, via dei Felgnami 14, in the former Jewish Ghetto. You can't get more authentic than this: a tiny one-room shop lined with age-old bottles and hungry hordes of workmen. The daily menu is posted on the door, usually offering some sort of hearty dish of pasta, including the Roman Thursday special, *gnocchi*. A full meal will run you about L16,000. Get here early. Open Mon.-Sat. noon- 3:30pm.

Armando, via degli Ombrellari, 41-43 (tel. 68 30 70 62), near the Vatican, off Borgo Pio. A typical *bottiglieria* with enough outstanding *contorni* like swiss chard and *cicoria* to burst any meateater's bubble. The crepes with ricotta and spinach and the *rigatoni alla siciliana* (with eggplant and peppers) are superb. Pastas L6000-10,000. A full meal starts at L35,000. The prices are even cheaper for lunch. Open Thurs.-Tues. noon-3pm and 7-11:30pm.

Birreria Trilussa, via Benedetta, 19/20 (tel. 71 54 21 80). Behind the fountain across the Ponte Sisto from Campo dei Fiori. A dark, woody pub that hums till all hours. Beer, wine and mixed drinks (L6000-8000), plus *bruschette* (L2500), pasta (L6000-8000) and an *antipasto* spread (L7000). Open 8pm-3am.

Chianti Corsi, via del Gesù 88, near the largo Argentina. Harried waiters yelling "Arrivo!" (hold your horses!) snake their way through the crowds of politicians, workmen, and salesgirls that pack the place for the delicious lunchtime specialties. Don't come here if you've got a plane to catch or romantic nothings to whisper; the service is slow and the crowds are noisy. Happily, you can linger at length over something as small as a *minestrone* or as light as their *insalata completa* (huge salad). Full meal around L15,000. Open Mon.-Fri. noon-2:30pm.

313 Cavour, 313 via Cavour. The place has prettied itself up since its days in the 1960s as a dark, angst-ridden hang-out for bohemians, Trotskyites, and their ilk. Today, the place services Roman yuppies with unusual specials and bottles of wine removed with long pincers from the overhead shelves. Order a sampling of different dishes, such as the vegetable pies made from organically grown veggies, or the *polenta lasagna* layered with spicy spinach. Test your masculinity with the variety of quiches, like the chicken with arugula. A very full meal starts around L15,000.

Spiriti, via di Sant'Eustachio, 5. Any frugal gourmet's lifetime fantasy. Don't expect to rub elbows with rough laborers; this is a step above the average *enoteca*. Do be prepared to stand on line with Romans to try their infamous *lasagna alla carta musica*, prepared with Sardinian bread that looks like sheets of music. The combo platter includes atypical offerings, such as Greek *tabouleh* or warm scamorza cheese topped with grilled eggplant and radicchio. The whole shebang starts around L18,000. Open Mon.-Sat. 10:30am-3pm and 5:30pm-1am.

Fiaschetteria da Alfredo, via Banchi Nuova, 14 (tel. 686 37 34). Take via Governo Vecchio to via Banchi Nuova all the way to the end. Small and easy to miss. One of the last vestiges of traditional Rome. Papa Alfredo and his lovely wife go to their vineyard in the country to press the wine they serve at the old marble tables (L5000 per liter). The menu changes daily. Full meals run about L14,000. Open Mon.-Fri. noon-3:30pm and 8pm-midnight. Closed in Aug.

La Bottega del Vino, via Santa Maria del Pianto, 9, near Piazza Navona. The most sophisticated wine shop we've ever heard of. The back room opens up to candlebra, linen, and china. This is definitely a splurge, but the pay-off is fantastic. *Involtini* are smoked salmon rolled with crabmeat instead of veal or beef. Full meal costs upwards of L19,000. Prepare to spend, but order the delicious house wine to soften the blow. Open Mon.-Fri. 12:30-2pm.

Al Parlamento, via dei Prefetti, 15, take via di Campo Marzo from via del Corso. Have your morning glass of *chianti* here; they open bright and early. Small selection of dishes but lots of wine. Open Tues.-Sun. 9:30am-1:30pm and 4-8:30pm.

Trimani Wine Bar, via Cernaia, 37, near Termini Station, perpendicular to via Castelfidardo. Schmooze with the help or the local customers while partaking of their simple eats and hearty wines. Open Mon.-Sat. 11:30am-3pm and 5:30pm-midnight.

Restaurants

Piazza Navona

Authentic, inexpensive *trattorie* are easy to find in the piazza Navona area, but steer clear of the main *piazze* where the restaurants entice witless tourists with English menus and then milk them for their last *lira*. Venture into the alleys along via Governo del Vecchio to eat Italian food with real-life Italians. Many of the best places for lunch are unmarked and don't have menus: look for doorways with bead curtains or follow an Italian workman on his lunchbreak. There is no shortage of *alimentari*, *tavole calde*, and *pizzerie rustica* lining via di Ripetta and around the Pantheon. The best ice cream places surround the Pantheon.

Palladini, via del Governo Vecchio, 29. No sign or place to sit, but bustling with a Roman lunch crowd eating seçonds-old *panini*. Point to the fillings of your choice. Favorites include *prosciutto e fichi* (smoked ham and figs) or *bresaola e rughetta* (smoked meat with arugula/rocket) sprinkled with parmesan cheese and lemon juice. A hearty sandwich costs about L3500. Open Sept.-July. Mon.-Sat. 8am-2pm and 5-8pm.

Pizzeria Baffetto, via del Governo Vecchio, 114 (tel. 686 16 17), on the corner of via Sora. This unembellished pizzeria has made Baffetto a household name among Romans. Once a meeting place for 60s radicals; now you have to stand in line with Romans of all political persuasions to get your hands on the *pizza gigante*, enough to feed the entire Christian Democratic party. One of the bakers looks *exactly* like Al Pacino. Pizzas L5000-10,000. *Vino* L6000. Cover L1000. Open Mon.-Sat. 6:30pm-1am. The service is harried; sit, eat, and you're outta there.

Il Giardinetto, via del Governo Vecchio, 125 (tel. 686 86 93). Escape the hard, dusty cobblestones of the area, and dine beneath the leaf-lined ceiling of this Tunisian-run oasis. Edith Piaf's *La Vie En Rose* and soothing Barry Manilow lilt through this pastel heaven. The unobtrusive waiters allow you to take your time over the well-seasoned pastas (L7000-10,000—try the *gnochetti* or the *pasta gorgonzola*) and house wine (L8000 per liter). Portions generous enough to skip the *secondi* (L12,000-16,000). Finicky eaters take note: the *pasta primavera* is served cold. Open Tues.-Sun. 1-3:30pm and 8pm-midnight. Reservations and credit cards accepted.

Trattoria Gino e Pietro, via del Governo Vecchio, 106 (tel. 686 15 76), at vicolo Savelli. Keep your eyes peeled for the reddish wood sign that marks the location of this cozy establishment, teetering on the line between *trattoria* and *osteria*. Delve into the back room for a huge homemade array of *antipasti vegetali* (L7000). *Fregnace alla arrabbiata* L6500. *Secondi* L7000-11,500. Cover L2000. Open late Aug.-late July Fri.-Wed. noon-3pm and 7:30pm-midnight. Reservations accepted.

Insalata Ricca 2, p. Pasquino, 73 (tel. 68 30 78 81), at the beginning of Governo Vecchio. Who ever said sequels disappoint? This spin-off of the original (listed below) is just as good. Omelette cooked to order (L5500). Salads L4500 for small and L6000 for large. *Gnocchi verdi al gorgonzola* L8500. *Secondi* L7000-10,500. Open Tues.-Sun. 12:30-3pm and 6:30-11pm. Reservations recommended on Sat. Credit cards accepted.

Pizzeria Corallo, via Corallo 10/11, (tel. 654 77 03), off via Governo Vecchio. Unusual pizzas in a chic setting of green arches and a metal palm tree. Shoot the breeze with the young proprietor, Alessandro. The waiters are as zesty as the fare. Enjoy wild creations like the *foccacia scamorza fiori di zucca e alici*, a pizza with scamorza cheese topped with zucchini flowers and anchovies. Pizzas (L8000-12000). The pastas don't live up to the pizzas or the delicious antipasto spread. The homemade desserts are sublime. Cover L2000. Service 10%. Open 12:30-3:30pm and 7:30pm-1am.

La Creperie di St. Eustachio, p. St. Eustachio, 50 (tel. 68 30 74 46). Crepes equally delicious and more creative than those of Italy's snooty neighbors to the north. The salted crepes with cheese and prosciutto (L7000-9000) and the dessert crepes are served by the friendly chef. Try the obscenely rich *nutella e ricotta* crepe (L8000). Open Tues.-Sun. 5pm-2am. Closed Aug. 5-18.

Navona Notte, via del Teatro della Pace, 44-46 (tel. 686 92 78), one long block north off via Governo Vecchio. Touristy, but pretty cheap and generous portions. You'll be surrounded with psychedelia and fish tanks if you don't dine outside. The *menù* (L14,000) features fresh mussels and a choice between pizza or spaghetti. Otherwise, pizzas and pastas are L7000, salads L3000, a liter of wine L8000, and *coperto* L1500. Open Thurs.-Tues. 7pm-3am.

Campo dei Fiori

While this is perhaps the most popular neighborhood among Romans to wine and dine, with its cobblestone streets, miniature *piazze*, and the grandness of via Giulia, the area never feels too populated. The exception, of course, is the lively market at the Campo, bustling with fruit vendors, cheese sellers, oversized swordfish, and screaming Italian housewives (open Mon.-Sat. 6am-2pm). There are innumerable restaurants hidden in these streets; try via Monserrato behind and to the west of the Campo, as well as the *piazze* to the front. *Caffè,* bars, pastry shops, and *alimentari* tempt and tantalize along via dei Giubbonari.

L'Insalata Ricca, largo di Chiavari, 85 (tel. 654 36 56), off corso Vittorio Emanuele near p. Sant'Andrea della Valle. Funky modern art, innovative dishes, and an off-beat ambience are successfully combined here with neighborly service and savory, traditional *trattoria* food. Try the *gnocchi al sardi* (L6500) or request their title dish *insalata ricca,* a robust salad with everything on it (L6500, smaller portion L5000).Whole wheat pasta *integrale* L8000. Cover L2000. Open Thurs.-Tues. 12:30-3pm and 7-11pm. Open during *Ferragosto* except Aug. 14-16.

Filetti di Baccalà, largo dei Librari, 88 (tel. 686 40 18). Take via de' Giubbonari off p. Campo dei Fiori; largo dei Librari will be on your left. Be sure not to miss this busy, unpretentious little establishment located in a miniature *piazza* beneath a quaint church. The ideal spot for informal *antipasti* and wine, this self-service favorite makes an unforgettable *filetto di baccalà* (deep fried cod filet, L3200-3500). Wine L5000 per liter. Cover L1000. Open Sept.-July. Mon.-Sat. 5:30-11:30pm.

Ristorante La Pollarola, piazza della Pollarola, 24-25 (tel. 654 16 54), take l. Chiavari two blocks south of c. Vittorio Emanuele. A typical Roman *trattoria* with good eats, charming location, and tolerable prices. Outside dining in the summer. The *au rigour antipasti* (L6000) walks the party line. *Primi* (L8000-12,000). *Secondi* (L8000-18,000). House wine L 8000 per liter. Cover L3000. Open Sept.-July Mon.-Sat. 12:30-3pm and 7:30-11pm. Reservations and credit cards accepted.

Arnaldo ai Satiri, via di Grotta Pinta, 8 (tel. 686 1915), near via Baullari. The menu lists the regular Italian favorites, like a spicy *fusilli alla melanzane* (pasta with eggplant, L8000) and a great *insalata gigante* (huge mixed salad, L8000), but also dishes rarer to Rome, like fresh *gazpacho* (L5000) and the speciality of the house, pasta with cabbage cream sauce (L8000). Alight with red lightbulbs and candles, the nighttime atmosphere is a spooky cross between a bordello, a bar mitzvah, and an ecclesiastical service. Outdoor eating in summer. Open Wed.-Mon. 12:30-3:30pm and 7:30pm-1:30am.

Near the Spanish Steps

Caveat edax (let the diner beware): the high prices in this flashy district are no guarantee of quality. Although looking for inexpensive meals around piazza di Spagna is like looking for a bargain at Armani, there are a few places that don't check for gold cards at the door. Before entering the McDonald's at piazza di Spagna, stop, look at the Big Mac wrappers on the Spanish Steps, remember that you're in a culinary capital, and reconsider. Opt for a hot *panino* with mozzarella and prosciutto, a fresh salad, or a piece of *pizza rustica* at one of the many bars in this area. There's an *alimentari* at via Laurina, 36 (open Mon.-Sat. 8am-2pm and 5-8pm). You can always get that Grimace hand puppet back home.

Centro Macrobiotico Italiano, via della Vite, 14 (tel. 679 25 09), on the third floor, just off via del Corso. Membership costs L30,000 per year (which reduces as the year progresses; in the summer months, membership is only about L13,000). They do allow tourists one meal with a L2000 surcharge and a passport. Although they sell New Age books and natural cosmetics, and conduct aromatherapy and stretching classes, their focus is on food. The dishes are all fresh and, uncharacteristic to Italian cooking, contain no butter. A full meal comes to about L15,000. *CousCous vegetale* L6800. Natural *gelato*, made with soy milk and honey, L5000. Open Mon.-Fri. 10am-7:30pm.

Pizzeria Al Leoncino, via del Leoncino, 28 (tel. 687 63 06), at via dell'Arancio. Take via Condotti from p. di Spagna, cross via del Corso, then take via del Leoncino off via Tomacelli. Fast, inexpensive, and informal. The traditional, hand-prepared pizzas (L6000-8000) are baked in front of you and the hordes of Romans who love the place. Wine L4000 per liter. Open Sept.-July Thurs.-Tues. 1-2:30pm and 7pm-midnight.

Al Piccolo Arancio, vicolo Scanderberg, 112 (tel. 678 61 39), near the Trevi Fountain in an alley off of via del Lavatore, which runs off p. di Trevi. The sign says "Osteria." Unusual and delicious pastas and appetizers. Try the *fiori di zucca* (fried zucchini flowers stuffed with mozzarella, L7000), or the *carciofi al Judaica* (a whole fried artichoke). If you're lucky enough to hit this place the same day as the fish merchants (Tues. and Thurs.), order the homemade *gnocchi al salmone* (L7000) or the *raviole di pesce* (L7000). Cover L2500. Arrive early. Open Sept.-July Tues.-Sun. 12:30-5pm and 7-11:30pm. Credit cards accepted.

Trattoria Da Settimio all'Arancio, via dell'Arancio, 50 (tel. 687 61 19). A favorite for Romans in the know. Run by the same family that runs Al Piccolo Arancio. Excellent three-course meals L23,000-26,000. Try the *ossobuco* (braised veal shank in sauce, L12,000) or *abbacchio* (roast lamb, L15,000). Huge portions of fresh vegetables (L4500) and delicious *antipasti*. Cover L3000. Open Mon.-Sat. 1-3:30pm and 7pm-midnight. Closed Aug. 7-Sept. 6. Credit cards and reservations accepted.

La Cappricciosa, largo dei Lombardi, 8 (tel. 679 40 27), right off via del Corso and across from via della Croce. If the gleaming white tablecloths are too blinding outside, head indoors to the Italian-frequented portion of the restaurant. The abstract New Age paintings are as soothing as Kitaro's best work. The helpful waiters bring you *primi* (L6000-8000), pizza (*alla Marinara*, L7000) and desserts (all L5000). Open Wed.-Mon. 12:30-3pm and 7pm-1am. Closed Aug. 15-31. Credit cards and reservations accepted.

Al Vantaggio, via del Vantaggio, 30 (tel. 323 68 48), off via del Corso. Lovely outdoor dining in summer. But don't get its peach tablecloths and massive canvas umbrellas confused with those of its over-priced neighbors. Filling, elegant meals. *Menù* (L20,000) with *risotto* and roast chicken. Open Mon.-Sat. noon-3pm and 7-11pm. Closed Aug. 9-23. Credit cards and reservations accepted.

Hostaria Alle Due Colonne, via del Seminario, 122 (tel. 678 0655), near piazza di San Ignazio. A tranquil setting with a L20,000 *menù*. Otherwise, cover is L1500. Open Mon.-Sat. 7-10pm.

Trattoria La Buca di Ripetta, via di Ripetta, 36 (tel. 68 95 78), 2 blocks from p. del Popolo. An air-conditioned sanctuary adorned with wine bottles. *Pasta primavera*, L8000; *secondi* L9500-15,500. Wine L8000 per liter. Cover L2000. One of the few places open for lunch on Sunday. Dress nicely. Open Sept.-Aug. 15 Tues.-Sat. 12:30-3pm and 7:30-11pm, Sun. 12:30-3pm. No credit cards, but traveler's checks and American dollars accepted. Reservations recommended.

Ristorante da Ugo al Gran Sasso, via di Ripetta, 32 (tel. 321 48 83). Ugo's da great guy with da sassy-o name, and the *spaghetti al vongole* (spaghetti with fresh clam sauce, L8000) is jus gran. *Pasta alla carbonara* L8000. Other pastas L6000-8000. *Secondi*, L7000-10,000. Cover and service L2000. Open Sun.-Fri. noon-4pm and 7-11pm. Closed Aug. 1-20. Credit cards accepted.

Otello alla Concordia, via della Croce, 81 (tel. 679 11 78). Pretty but pricey. Quiet, plant-filled courtyard off the street. *Menù* L30,000. Cover L3000. Open Mon.-Sat. 12:30-3pm and 7:30-11pm. Some credit cards and reservations accepted.

Trattoria e Pizzeria del Pollarolo, via Ripetta 4-5 (tel. 361 02 76). Ten yards from the piazza del Popolo presides the Pizzeria del Pollarolo. Simple eats, low on ambience. *Pizza capriciosa* L9000; other pizzas range from L8000 to L12,000; *Fettucine all'arrabiata* L7000. *Ravioli* L9000. *Secondi* L8000-18000. Cover charge L2000. Open Sept.-July Fri.-Wed. noon-3pm and 7-11pm. Credit cards accepted.

Ristorante Vegetariano Margutta, via Margutta 119 (tel. 678 60 33), off via del Babuino. The place to be if you're a rich vegetarian—say, Daryl Hannah. The teak tables and tasteful earth tones may transport you to an L.A. suburb. *Gazpacho* a whopping L10,000. *Insalata Margutta* L12,000. Other salads L8000-12,000. *Secondi* L10,000-12,000. The L15,000 buffet is your best bet, offering an assortment of sauteed and marinated vegetables and pasta. Open Sept.-July Mon.-Sat. 1-3:30pm and 8-11pm. Also **Antico Bottaro**, passeggiata di Ripetta, 15 (tel. 361 22 81). Same food and even higher prices. Open Tues.-Sun. 1-3:30pm and 8-11pm. Credit cards and reservations accepted at both.

Near the Colosseum and Forum

Despite its past glory, this area has yet to discover such a noble concept as "the affordable restaurant." There are a plethora of bars and *tavole calde* around piazza Venezia, on via del Corso, and on corso V. Emanuele, though they're short on charm. If you can't take one more step from the Arch of Titus, try the following places:

Pizzeria Imperiale, largo C. Ricci, 37 (tel. 678 60 84), at the start of via Cavour opposite the Forum entrance gate (the second restaurant on the right). Recover from ruins under shady umbrellas. Pizzas (try the gorgonzola) L8000-10,000, pasta L7500-9000. Wine L8000 per liter. Cover L1500. Open Mon.-Sat. noon-4pm and 7:30-11pm.

Bar Martini, piazza del Colosseo, 3 (tel. 700 44 31), on the hill behind the Colosseum. Simple, cheap *menù turistico* (L14000) includes pasta or pizza, salad, dessert, and coffee. Sit outside for the best view of the Colosseum around. Cover L1500. Open Thurs.-Tues. 8:30am-12:30am.

The Jewish Ghetto

To the west of the roaring via Arenula, the former Jewish Ghetto has endured centuries of anti-Semitism, modernization, and tourism to remain a proud and small community. While the Jews were confined to the Ghetto in 1655, this neighborhood is becoming an extremely chic locale, with all kinds of Romans trekking over here to sample the home-cooking and stroll through the narrow, medieval lanes. Many of the best Roman dishes were actually plagiarized from this neighborhood's recipes, like the *carciofi alla romana* (fried artichoke) and the *penne al salmone* (pasta with salmon). Today, the area boasts some hearty Jewish and Roman favorites alike, though you won't find *prosciutto* on the menu; these places are all at least semi-kosher. Unfortunately, since many of these restaurants have become quite trendy, they are somewhat out of reach for the budget traveler. Still, the Roman Jews are some of the most animated Italians around and their love of food will never let your plate remain empty for a moment.

Uno, via del Portico d'Ottavio, 1E (tel. 654 79 37), around the corner from the Teatro Marcello. They have wonderful fresh anchovies with green beans and delicious and unusual kosher pastries. Fully kosher kitchen. Open Tues.-Thurs. 12:30-3pm and 7:30pm-midnight, Fri. 12:30-3pm, Sat. 7:30pm-midnight.

Ristorante Da Giggetto, via del Portico Ottavio, 21 (tel. 656 11 05). The overwhelmingly friendly proprietor insists that you eat as much (or more than) humanly possible. Sup on the fish soup then dig into the *penne al salmone* (L10,000) for starts.

Ristorante Piperno, Monte del Cenci, 9 (tel. 654 27 72). Founded in 1856, this traditional (and pricey) locale boasts of having introduced the fried artichoke into mainstream food culture. They also have *pasta ai ceci* (with chickpeas) and vegetarian *fritto misto* (Italian veggie tempura). Pastas (L10,000-15,000). Open Tues.-Sat. 12:30-3pm and 7:30-midnight, Sun. 12:30-3pm.

Trastevere

You can't say you've been to Rome without having mounged on a pizza and swilled some house wine in one of the rowdy outdoor *pizzerie* in Trastevere. Just across the river from the historical center and down the river from the Vatican, this is the site of the city's most elegant restaurants as well as the most raucous beer parlors, hopping pizza joints, and a loud bohemian population. By nightfall, the piazza S. Maria di Trastevere is packed with hippies and boom boxes as well as the monied, somewhat ruffled diners in the *piazza's* costly restaurant. Wander the streets by day or night, and stop in to one of the many *caffè*, bars, and nightclubs.

Taverno del Moro, via del Moro, 43 (tel. 580 91 65), off via Lungaretta in Trastevere. Beautiful *antipasto* spread. *Pizza quattro stagioni* L12,000. Cheesecake L4000. Bread and cover L2000. Open Tues.-Sun. 7-11pm. Credit cards accepted.

Mario's, via del Moro, 53 (tel. 580 38 09). Take via della Lungaretta off viale Trastevere, and turn right after the church. The L14,000 *menù turistico*, including drink and coffee, makes this place a steal. Pasta is consistently phenomenal (and so cheap) at L4500-6000. *Fettucini ai funghi porcini* (with porcini mushrooms) is only L6000. Cover L800. Open Sept. to mid-Aug. Mon.-Sat. noon-4pm and 7pm-midnight. Credit cards accepted.

Pizzeria Ivo, via di San Francesca a Ripa, 157/158 (tel. 581 70 82). Take via delle Fratte di Trastevere off viale Trastevere. Alas, the tourists have finally discovered this Trastevere legend (no thanks to us), but the mouth-watering pizza's still well worth the long wait and chaotic atmosphere. Pizza L8000-11,000. Cover L1000. Open Sept.-July Wed.-Mon. 6pm-1am.

Il Duca, vicolo del Cinque, 56 (tel. 581 77 06). Off via del Moro on the left as you head toward the river. A classic Roman *trattoria* on a lively nighttime street. Divine *bruschetta* (try it *al carciofo*—with artichoke paste—L2500), *lasagne*, and other pastas (L7000-10,000). Wine L8000 per liter. Cover L2000. Open Tues.-Sun. 12:30-2pm and 7:30pm-midnight.

L'Ape sul Melo, via del Moro, 17 (tel. 689 28 81). Great for lighter foreign appetites. Bistro atmosphere with a good beer and wine selection. Salads and snacks L6000-8000. 18 types of hot sandwiches (around L6000). Great desserts, including chocolate mousse (L4000). Open Thurs.-Tues. 7pm-2am.

Taverna della Scala, p. della Scala, 19 (tel 580 37 63). A quiet *trattoria* (dine inside or out). Pasta (L5000-7500), pizza (L4000-7000), wine L5000 per liter. Cover L2000, service 12%. Open Mon.-Fri. 7pm-1am, Sat. and Sun. 12:30-3pm and 7:30pm-midnight.

Hostaria der Belli, p. S. Apollonia, 11 (tel. 580 37 82). Off via di Lungaretta between viale Trastevere and p. Santa Maria. A friendly *trattoria* specializing in Sardinian cooking. *Ravioli sardi* (in tomato cream sauce, L8500), *fettucine alla sarda* (with ham and mushrooms, L8000), wine L7500 per liter. Cover L2500. Open Tues.-Sun. 12:30-2pm and 6:30-11pm.

Il Tulipano Nero, via Roma Libera, 15 (tel. 581 83 09), in pza. San Cosimato. A friendly, rowdy pizzeria—dine outdoors in the summer months. Iron palates can attempt the *rigatoni all'elettroshock* (very hot indeed, L8000), or try the interesting pizza combos. *Pizza tonno, mais, e rughetta* (with tuna, corn, and arugula, L7500) tastes far better than it sounds. Wine L9000 per liter. Cover L1500. Open Thurs.-Tues. 7:15pm-1am.

Da Giovanni, via della Lungara, 41 (tel. 686 15 14). Take via della Scala onto via della Lungara, and follow it about ½km until right before the Mazzini Bridge, or take one of the many buses that run along the *lungotevere.* A family-run *trattoria.* Simple, superior meals run about L17,000. Large wine selection (L6000-40,000 per liter). Cover L1500. Open Sept.-July Tues.-Sun. 7:30-10:30pm.

Birreria della Scala, p. della Scala, 58/60 (tel. 580 37 63). Take via della Lungaretta off p. Sonnino; follow it past p. Santa Maria onto via della Paglia and turn right at p. di Sant'Egidio. This hub of Trastevere's social scene packs rowdy Romans into enormous booths. Pulsates with live music 8-10pm. Endless menu offers 26 types of pasta (L6000-8000). Sip notoriously anaesthetic mixed drinks at the bar (L8000-10,000). Open Thurs.-Tues. 7:30pm-2am.

Popi-Popi, via delle Fratte di Trastevere, 47 (tel. 589 51 67). Right off viale Trastevere. Several clean, bright, bustling rooms; can be crowded and impersonal. Pizzas with paper-thin crusts (L6000-9000), excellent *spaghetti alla carbonara* (L7000). In summer, tables spread out under canvas umbrellas across the street. Open Fri.-Wed. 7:30pm-midnight.

The Vatican and the Borgo

The area around the Vatican reeks of "American burgers and fries," or at least, the whole idea of it which pervades the air. By night, however, the tourists depart and many *trattorie* clear out (and put out better food) by night. The streets of the original Borgo (along the Leonine Wall north of via di Conciliazione) fill with Romans heading to various restaurants, *birrerie,* and clubs, while the residential district around via Cola di Rienzo is home to some of the best undiscovered bargains in town, as well as an immense indoor food market (on the corner of piazza d'Unità).

Armando, via degli Ombrellari, 41 (tel. 686 16 02). North of via di Conciliazione. Delicious lasagne is the house specialty at L7500; the *vino bianco* is a delight after a day of museum-trudging at L6000 per carafe. Don't pass up the *antipasto.* Cover L2000. Open Thurs.-Tues. 12:30-3pm and 7-11pm.

Hostaria dei Bastioni, via Leone IV, 29 (tel. 31 98 78), off p. del Risorgimento near the Vatican Museums. A miraculous subterranean restaurant which rightly boasts of its seafood specialties. *Risotto alla pescatora* (rice with seafood sauce) L7000. Fresh fish dishes L11,000-14,000. Wine L4000-6000 per carafe. Noisy for outdoor lunch. Cover L2000. Service 10%. Open Mon.-Sat. noon-3pm and 7pm-1:30am.

Ristorante Tre Pupazzi, Borgo Pio, 184 (tel. 684 55 93). A friendly, homey spot on the Borgo's liveliest street. Pizzas L6500-8000, pasta L6000-9000. Try the homemade *agnolotti* (L7500) and the delicious *antipasto* spread (L6000). Wine L5000 per liter. Cover L2000. Open Mon.-Sat. noon-2pm and 7-11pm.

Hostaria il Mozzicone, Borgo Pio 180 (tel. 686 15 00). Two doors down from the above, this busy *trattoria* sees more tourists, but has a cool outdoor terrace and inexpensive pasta. Pasta L6000-7000. Cover L2500. Open Mon.-Sat. noon-2:30pm and 7-11:45pm.

Il Pozzetto, Borgo Pio 167 (tel. 686 45 33). A bright, bustling *trattoria* with a super-friendly staff. Pasta L5500-7500, pizzas L6500-8000. Cover L1500. Open Tues.-Sun. 12:30-2:30pm and 7:30pm-midnight.

Cucina Abruzzese, via dei Gracchi, 27 (tel. 684 58 89). The somber decor hides some of the area's best home-cooking. A pretty arbor on the street shields you from the sun. Pasta L4500-7000. Cover L2000. Open Tues.-Sun. noon-2:30pm, 7-11:30pm.

Hostaria L'Etrusco, via dei Gracchi, 12 (tel. 31 21 24). Unbelievable pastas (try the tortellini), L5000-8000. 'Nuff said. Cover L2000. Open Wed.-Mon. noon-2pm and 7:30pm-midnight.

L'Archetto, via Germanico, 105 (tel. 312 55 92). A little off the beaten path, this hole in the wall serves up piping hot pizzas (L6000), *filetti di baccalà* (fried fish, L4500) and *fiori di zucca* (fried zucchini flowers, L5000). Open Tues.-Sun. 7pm-midnight.

La Caravella, via degli Scipioni, 32 (tel. 39 72 61 61). Near the entrance to the Vatican Museums. Best for pizza. Cover L2500, pasta dishes L6000-9000. Open Mon.-Sat. noon-4pm and 7-11pm. Credit cards accepted.

Lo Stregone, piazza dei Coronari, 1 (tel. 686 87 93). Steps across the river from Castel Sant'Angelo. *Menù turistico* (pasta, meat, salad, dessert, bread, and cover) L20,000, and well worth it. Open noon-3:30pm and 7:30-11pm.

Testaccio

The oldest area of Rome, as yet unassailed by tourism, Testaccio is a stronghold of Roman tradition. This is really for people who want to get a true taste of Rome, or at least a taste of local animal parts; vegetarians and unadventurous eaters would do better elsewhere. Especially in the Mattatoio neighborhood, around the old slaughterhouses, you can dare to eat as the Romans do at restaurants that serve authentic local delicacies, such as *animelle alla griglia* (grilled calves' veins—tastiest when slightly chewy) and *fegata* (liver). The hippest nightclubs are (incongruously) located here as well, so you can boogie your oxtail-intake away. Take bus #27 from Termini or bus #92 from p. Venezia to reach this area south of the historical center.

Trattoria Turiddo, via Galvani, 64 (tel. 575 04 47), in the Mattatoio district of Testaccio (take bus #27 from Termini or the Colosseum). Locals come here to taste the food they grew up on, like *rigatoni con pagliata* (with tomato and lamb intestine, L8000), *coda alla vaccinara* (stewed oxtail, L14,000), and *animelle alla griglia* (grilled calf's veins, L11,000). Standard Roman specialties available for the weak of stomach. Vegetarians strongly cautioned. Cover L2000. Open Sept. 21 - Aug. Mon.-Tues. and Thurs.-Sat. 1-2:30pm and 7-10:30pm, Sun. 1-2:30pm.

Trattoria Al Vecchio Mattatoio, p. Giustanini, 2 (tel. 574 13 82), next door to the above. A gutsy Roman eatery. Their *tonarello sugo coda* (thick spaghetti with tangy tomato oxtail sauce, L8000) seconded by *arrosto misto di frattaglie* (a mixed grill of liver, intestines, veins and back muscles, L14,000), washed down with some extra-strong wine (L7000 per liter), will put hair on anyone's back. Cover L2000. Service 12%. Open Sept.-July Wed.-Sun. 12:30-4pm and 7:30-11pm, Mon. 1-3pm.

Trattoria da Bucantino, via Luca della Robbia, 84/86 (tel. 574 68 86). Take via Vanvitelli off via Marmorata, then take the first left. A Testaccio tavern. Indigenous pasta delights like *bucatini alla amatriciana* (L8000). Wrestle with their *coda alla vaccinara* (L11,000). Vegetables L5000-6000. Wine L6000 per liter. Cover L2000. Open Aug. 27-July 21 Tues.-Sun. noon-3pm and 7:30-11pm.

Pizzeria Ficini, via Luca della Robbia, 23 (tel. 574 30 17). Down the street from the above. For those who've lost their carnivorous nerve, a friendly, no-nonsense pizzeria. Pizzas L6000, calzone L7500, wine L6000 per liter. Don't miss the *bruschetta ai fagioli* (L2500). No cover. Open Sept.-July Tues.-Sun. 7:30-11pm.

Trattoria Lo Scopettaro, Lungotevere Testaccio, 7 (tel. 574 24 08). Noisy outside, cozy inside; along the river. The usual meat suspects; Frascati wines L7000 per liter. Cover L2000. Open Tues.-Sun. noon-2pm and 7:30-11:30pm.

Pizzeria Remo, via Romolo Gessi, 12 (tel. 57 42 76). Nothing touristy about this place, a bustling Roman eatery with heavenly pizza pies (L5500-7500). Cover L1500. Open Mon.-Sat. 7:30-11:30pm.

San Lorenzo

A five-minute bus ride east of Termini on bus #71 or 492 (get off when the bus turns onto via Tiburtina), San Lorenzo sits in the midst of the Città Universitaria. Many unpretentious *trattorie* and *pizzerie* offer grand cuisine for the university students here in an atmosphere that encourages conversation.

Il Pulcino Ballerino, via degli Equi, 66/68 (tel. 49 03 01), off via Tiburtina. A wonderful, artsy atmosphere with cuisine to match. Try the unusual *tagliolini del Pulcino* (pasta in a lemon cream sauce, L8000) or *polpeltine all'arancio* (meatballs in an orange sauce, L10,000). Cover L1500. Open Tues.-Sun. 8pm-midnight. Closed first two weeks of August.

Pizzeria L'Economica, via Tiburtina, 46 (tel. 445 66 69), on the main road of the bus route. The name says it all. The large family who runs this place cooks up some of the most vicious pizza around (L3000-5000). Or try the *antipasto* dish for an incredible L4500. Wine L4000. Crowded, with lots of outdoor tables. Go early or late to avoid waiting. Open Sept.-July Mon.-Sat. 6:30-11pm.

Pizzeria Formula 1, via degli Equi, 13 (tel. 49 06 10) in San Lorenzo, off via Tiburtina. Romans know their pizza, so when it's as good and cheap as this, expect to wait. Pizza of all varieties L5000-7000. Try the zucchini flowers stuffed with mozzarella and anchovies. Open Mon.-Sat. 6pm-midnight. It's anyone's guess really; the owner claims that the place is "sempre aperto!" (always open).

Il Capellaio Matto, via dei Marsi, 25 (tel. 49 08 41). From via Tiburtina take via degli Equi and take the 4th right onto via dei Marsi. Vegetarians rejoice! Numerous pasta and rice dishes for L7000-11,000. Sorceress's salad, with potato, shrimp, corn, carrot, and egg L8000. Numerous cràpe dishes around L6500. Chicken dishes available for flesh-eaters. Talented customers have had their napkin sketches reproduced in the menu. Uncrowded. Open Wed.-Mon. 8:30pm-midnight.

Pizzeria il Maratoneta, via dei Sardi, 20 (tel. 49 00 27), off via Tiburtina. Four young marathoners bake pizza on the run (L5500-8500). Tomatoes and marinated seafood cover half of their gorgeous *Pizza Mare e Monte* (sea and mountain pizza), while tomatoes, mozzarella, mushrooms, eggplant, onion, zucchini, and peppers bury the other half (L8500). *Antipasto di mare,* L6000. Friendly waiters manage the throngs at outdoor tables. Open Mon.-Sat. 6pm-12:15am.

Hostaria da Paolo, via dei Sabelli, 6/8 (tel. 731 42 56). Take via Porta L'Abicana off via Tiburtina and then take the third left. Working stiffs frequent this small *hostaria,* where Swiss Family Robinson decor surrounds incongrously mirthless service. Homemade *pappardelle* pasta (L6000) served up by old Paolo's unsmiling progeny. You might actually afford a full meal: *insalata,* L2500, *secondi piatto* L6000-9000. Wine L5000 per liter. Open Mon.-Sat. noon-3pm and 7:30pm-midnight. Closed most of August.

La Tana Sarda, via Tiburtina, 116 (tel. 49 35 50). Personable Sardinians rush from table to table, piling plates with delicacies. Romans rave about the *gnochetti sardi* (twirled pasta with meat sauce, L7000) and the *ravioli sardi,* filled with flavored ricotta, L7000. Cover L2000. Open Sept.-July Mon.-Sat. noon-3pm and 7-10pm.

Near the Station

There is no reason to subject yourself to the gastronomic nightmare of the tourist-trapping resturants that flank Termini; a more authentic Roman meal is only a ten-minute stroll away. Within walking distance of the train station, the following establishments provide excellent service for a largely local clientele. There is a market on via Montebello and another on via Milazzo between via Varse and via Palestro, both from around 6am-1pm except for Sunday.

Le Caveau, via Conte Verde, 6 (tel. 731 02 66). Follow via Giolitti along the train station until you hit via Cairoli. It intersects via Conte Verde about 600m down. Follow the slightly seedy path to this rambunctious hideout overflowing with happy Roman youth. Lots of loud music and 24 types of pizza (L4000-8000). Try the *gnocchi verdi al gorgonzola* (L7000). Excellent beers (L2000-4000). Open Tues.-Sun. noon-3pm and 6:30pm-midnight.

Osteria con Cucina de Andreis Luciano, via Giovanni Amendola, 73/75 (tel. 46 16 40). Take via Cavour west from p. dei Cinquecento; via Giovanni Amendola is the first intersecting street. A green bead curtain screens the entrance to this haven for ravenous budget-travelers. Inside, enjoy a good belch with the burly workmen who fill the place in the afternoon, or work the backpacker crowd that wanders in around dusk. Generous portions of standard pasta dishes L3300-3600. Huge marinated half-chicken L5000. *Pollo e pepperoni* (chicken and peppers) is L5000. Those who lack a workin' appetite can order half portions for half-price plus L300. Wine L3000 per liter. Bread and cover L1000. Open Mon.-Fri. 9am-3pm and 7-9pm, Sat. 11:30am-5pm.

Pizzeria Giacomelli, via Faà di Bruno (tel. 38 35 11), near viale Mazzini. A notorious pizzeria bursting with Roman *ragazzi*. One of the few *pizzerie* open for lunch. They'll do your pizza your way; in 3 different sizes, hundreds of garnishes, and they'll even make the crust thicker if you ask. Their monster pizza is not for beginners; it comes with everything from mini artichokes to beans to sausages. Pizzas L7000-15,000. Try one of their homemade dessert pies, if you dare. Open Tues.-Sun. 12:30-3pm and 6:30pm-midnight.

La Cantinola da Livio, via Calabria, 26 (tel. 482 05 19 or 474 39 62). Take via Piave off via XX Settembre, then take the 4th left onto via Calabria. This cozy establishment specializes in *frutti di mare*—live lobsters wait tensely in tanks by the door. Stellar cuisine and impeccable service. Seafood fresh from Sardinia daily. *Spaghetti alla Cantinola* L9000. *Scampi* L15,000. *Antipasto di mare* L10,000. Open Mon.-Sat. 12:30-3pm and 7:30-11:30pm. Credit cards accepted.

Est!!! Est!!! Est!!!, via Genova, 32 (tel. 488 11 07), to the right of via Nazionale from the station. Colorful and campy interior, with great *spaghetti alla Carbonara* (L8000) and pizzas (L8000-10,000). Wine L6000 per liter. No cover. Open Tues.-Sun. 12:30-4pm and 7:30-11pm.

Restaurant Monte Arci, via Castelfidardo, 33 (tel. 474 48 90). Take via Solferino past p. dell'Indipendenza off the east side of the station and then take the first left past the *piazza*. Boisterous waiters serve delectable *paglia e fieno al Monte Arci* (a pasta and spinach dish, L10,000) and *gnocchi* with mushrooms and asparagus (L7000). Cover L2500. Open Thurs.-Tues. noon-3pm and 7-11:30pm. Credit cards accepted.

Il Ristorante Tudini, via Filippo Turati, 5, one block from Termini on corner with via Gioberti. An appetizing reprieve from Termini fare, decorated with modish marble tables and greenery. *La pennette alla vodka* L7000, *veal scalloppine* L10,000. Cover L2000. Open Mon.-Sat. 12:30-11:30pm. AmEx and Visa accepted.

Desserts

If you have a sweet tooth, the road from Rome will lead straight to the dentist. The mere sight of glazed pastries in myriad bakery windows produces cavities, and the spectrum of the *gelato* rainbow will make every cone the most difficult choice of your life—thank heaven you can get more than one flavor at a time. Chocolate is the purist's choice but don't miss out on exotica like *tiramisù*, kiwi, and *bacio* (a "kiss" of hazelnut and chocolate). Usually you also have the option of a free dollop of heavenly whipped cream (*panna*). At the larger places, pay first and take the receipt to the counter to order. Here are some shrines along the obligatory *gelato* and pastry road to Nirvana.

Giolitti, via degli Uffici del Vicario, 40 (tel. 679 42 06), near the Pantheon off via della Maddelena. A Roman institution as venerable as the Vatican. Indulge yourself with their gargantuan 10-scoop "Olympico" sundae for L8000 and do penance on the thighmaster when you get home. The homemade *panna* is unbeatable. Cones start at L2000. Open Tues.-Sun. 7am-2am.

Fassi Palazzo del Freddo, via Principe Eugenio, 65/67 (tel. 73 78 04), off p. Emanuele west of Termini. This century-old *gelato* factory is a confectionery altar duly worshiped by many. Some heretics argue that the *gelato* here beats Giolitti's hands down. Try both and argue your calories away. Cones L1500-3000. Open Tues.-Fri. 3pm-midnight, Sat.-Sun. 10am-2am.

Gelateria Trevi di A. Cercere, via del Lavatore 84/85 (tel. 679 20 60), near the Trevi Fountain. A small, family-run *gelateria* of yesteryear, whose fare puts glitzy *gelaterie* down the street to shame. The infamous *zabaione* is the house specialty. Small cones L2000. Open June-Sept. daily 10am-1am, Oct.-May Fri.-Wed. 10am-1am.

Pascucci, via Torre Argentina, 20 (tel. 656 48 16), off corso Emanuele, east of p. Navona. The six throttling blenders on the bar have earned this place a reputation throughout the republic; they grind fresh fruit into colorful, frothy *frulatti* frappes (L2700-4000). Open Tues.-Sat. 6:30am-midnight.

Ai Tre Tartufi, p. Navona, 27. Neighboring Tre Scalini perfected the famous *tartufo*, a menacing hunk of chocolate ice cream rolled in chocolate shavings, but the tourists there have sent the price through the roof. Next door, Tre Tartufi serves up practically the same confection for L4000 (L8000 if you want to sit outside), as well as *gelato* and coffee. May well be the only place you can sit in piazza Navona and still afford a hotel room. Open Tues.-Sat. 8pm-1am.

Lucifero Pub, via dei Cappelari, 28 (tel. 654 55 36), on the street leading north out of Campo dei Fiori. Snacks and desserts in a relaxed, arch-filled nook. Indulge in a fondue, or try the sinful chocolate mousse (L5000). Cover L1500. Open Tues.-Sun. 8pm-2am.

Il Fornaio, via dei Baullari, 5-7 (tel. 654 39 47), across from p. San Pantaleo, south of piazza Navona. Throw your deal-a-meal to the wind and pig out on the myriad of baked yummies this shop has to offer, from pieces of pizza and fresh bread to cookies, cakes, and pies. Cookies (*biscottini*, L1800 per *etto*); breads (*pane siciliano*, L6500 per kilo; croissants L700 each); desserts (*mele in gabbia* L1300 per *etto*). Open Mon.-Sat. 7am-1:30pm and 4:30-8pm.

Gelateria della Palma, via della Maddalena, 20 (tel. 654 07 62), off p. della Rotonda. So many flavors, so short a lifetime. A glamorous candy selection to turn Willy Wonka green with envy. Medium cone L2500. Open 8am-1:30am.

Caffè

Caffè and *Campari* make up the fifth food group in Rome. Bars and *caffè* are scattered all over the city. Many also serve light foods or sweets, but they are generally not full-fledged hunger-quashing restaurants. See listings under Caffè-Entertainment, below.

Sights

Rome wasn't built in a day, and it's not likely that you'll see anything of the city in 24 hours either. The city teems with monuments—ancient temples, medieval fortresses, Baroque confections of marble and rushing water—crowding next to and even on top of each other on every serpentine street. No other city in the world can lay claim to so many masterpieces of architecture from so many different eras of history—not to mention the treasures of painting and sculpture secreted inside.

Accept the fact that it's impossible to see everything the city has to offer, relax, and set out to see what you can, remembering that the city is a hot and dusty place in summer (and a crowded and chaotic one year-round), likely to sap the energy of even the most hardened sightseer. Pace yourself, make time for a stop in a bar or *caffè*, and carry a bottle of water (refillable at any of Rome's corner water-spouts; you'll see Romans bending to drink from the streams). See Touring Tips in the General Introduction, above, for even more practical advice. Though you'll probably end up covering the city neighborhood by neighborhood (in the same way that we've arranged our Sights section), the following chronological catalogue may help show how the myriad monuments fit together, both in relation to each other and to the larger fabric of the history of Rome, of which they are so important a part. Do us (and yourself) a favor and read the General Introduction; the grandeur that was Rome (so evident in the splendid monuments and churches that decorate the city) hides some fairly astonishing affairs. The **ancient city** of Rome centered on the **Capitol** (Capitoline) and **Palatine Hills**, in the southern half of the modern city. These two riverside mounds remain the most famous of Rome's seven hills (the other five being the Quirinal, site of modern-day Termini; the Viminal, the next rise to the south; the Esquiline, where Sta. Maria Maggiore now presides; the Caelian, rising south of the Colosseum; and the Aventine, overlooking the Tiber south of the Circus Maximus). On the low ground between the Capitol and Palatine, the ancients built the magnificent **Forum Romanum**, the political and economic center. Close by were the **Colosseum**, the **Imperial Fora** and **Palaces,** and the riverside temples of the **Forum Boarium**. But even ancient Rome sprawled beyond its natural borders. Elsewhere in the city the majestic **Pantheon, Hadrian's mausoleum** under Castel Sant'Angelo and the rival **Mausoleum of Augustus** bear testament to the architectural ingenuity of the city's first inhabitants. Long removed from their original niches, **ancient statues** still evoke the glories of the classical ideal: the best collections are found in the **Musei Capitolini** and in the **Museo Pio-Clementino** (inside the Vatican Museums). Outside the city, pagan tombs still line the ancient **Appian Way** (the first and greatest of Roman roads), while the forbidding brick ramparts of the 3rd century **Aurelian Walls** can be seen at many points along the ancient city's perimeter. The romantic ruins at **Ostia Antica** preserve whole streets of ancient houses and stores.

When the Goths sacked Rome in 410 AD they destroyed much of the city's pagan splendor and ushered in the **middle ages,** but when they cut the city's **aqueducts,** they did its monuments an inadvertent favor. Thirsty survivors of the sacks came down off the city's hills and settled anew by the banks of the Tiber, in the elbow-shaped bend to the north of the ancient center. Though ancient monuments were relentlessly pillaged for their marble and bronze, those far from the river at least avoided being swallowed entirely by medieval construction. The new riverside neighborhoods bristled with fortified houses and towers, the tangible result of the paranoia gripping the sack-prone city. The densest concentrations of medieval houses make up the picturesque quarters of **Trastevere, Campo dei Fiori,** the **Jewish Ghetto** and the area around **piazza Navona.** Here you'll find a labyrinth of cobblestone alleys and crumbling balconied houses (many of them built from pagan marbles) alongside ancient fountains and churches.

Christianity offered a ray of hope to citizens huddling in squalor along the malarial Tiber, and the middle ages saw a boom of church building. Constantine, emperor from 306-337 AD, legalized the upstart Eastern sect and laid the foundations for the city's first great basilicas: the extraterritorial churches of **Sta. Maria Maggiore, S. Lorenzo fuori le Mure,** and **Sant'Agnese fuori le Mure** preserve their paleochristian roots.

The basilical form, borrowed from pagan administrative architecture, is marked by a long central nave divided by columns, polychrome marble pavements, and gilded mosaics in the apse over the altar. Other mosaic-studded medieval churches in the city include **Sta. Maria in Cosmedin** and **S. Gregorio** near the Capitol Hill, **Sta. Sabina** on the Aventine, **Sta. Maria in Trastevere** across the river, and **Sta. Prassede** on the Esquiline Hill.

Rome set about launching its **Renaissance** with particularly self-conscious activity. Medieval squabbling between rival cardinals and their families had led to the **Great Schism** (see Renaissance General Introduction, above), and during the subsequent "Babylonian Captivity" the city suffered untold neglect. Martin V and his successors, returning to the throne of Peter, set about cleaning up and clearing out the dilapidated city with one goal in mind: the glorification of the papacy's power. The **Vatican Palace** was renovated, a gargantuan project which included the construction and decoration of the **Sistine Chapel**, the exquisitely frescoed **Borgia Apartments**, and the **Raphael Stanze**. Construction began on a new **Basilica of St. Peter,** and several new, straight streets were carved out of the welter of medieval alleyways that snaked through the city, among them the **via Giulia** and the **via Papalis** (modern corso Vittorio Emanuele II). Other marks of papal attention in the city include the sublime **Cancelleria** and its neighboring **Palazzo Farnese**, the papal apartments atop **Castel Sant'Angelo**, the exquisitely decorated **Villa Farnesina**, and Bramante's tiny **Tempietto**. More Renaissance treasures hide within many of Rome's churches—**Sta. Maria del Popolo** houses masterpieces by **Raphael, Caravaggio**, and the divine **Pinturicchio**; **Sant'Agostino** and **San Luigi dei Francesi** boast more Caravaggios; **Sta. Maria sopra Minerva** proudly displays two statues by Michelangelo, while **San Pietro in Vincoli** across town shelters the Florentine master's world-famous **Moses.**

The Renaissance building boom left the popes in command of a richly decorated new city, but some European Catholics weren't too impressed. The crisis of the **Reformation**, incited in part by the church's sale of indulgences to cover the growing construction costs of the new St. Peter's, led Pope Paul III to call the famous **Council of Trent**. The Council's first objective was to reform the church's priestly and monastic orders, but the members also devised new standards for the design of churches. Renaissance interest in classical architecture had inspired a host of circular and Greek-cross churches (like the Tempietto) in which, the Council said, the priest and his altar had been subordinated from their rightful place at the "head" of the congregation. The new plans, first executed in della Porta's famous **il Gesù**, called for a long central nave, with side chapels replacing the traditional basilical aisles, in which every person could have a view of the altar, whose importance was highlighted by a soaring dome and elaborate altar canopy. This model became the pattern for most of the **Counter-Reformation** and **Baroque** churches in the city.

The 17th-century successors to the Renaissance popes took the Council of *Trent's* recommendations to heart, but even the "reformed" churches they built were extravagantly constructed, incorporating Counter-Reformation imagery in monuments of Baroque extravagance. A succession of pontiffs employed the rival talents of **Bernini** and **Borromini** to produce artistic propaganda vaunting not only the triumph of Catholicism but also their own status as absolute monarchs. Bernini's (seemingly ubiquitous) works in the city include the ingenious, oval-shaped piazza **San Pietro**, the elaborate **Fountain of the Four Rivers** in p. Navona, the **Fontana del Tritone** in p. Barberini and the sublime **San Andrea al Quirinale** on the Quirinal Hill. But Bernini's greatest talent lay in sculpture: not even Michelangelo could capture the fleeting expressions of joy, pain, agony and ecstasy in the way this Baroque genius could. His greatest works include the erotic *St. Theresa in Ecstasy* in Sta. Maria della Vittoria, the *Blessed Ludovica Albertoni* in San Francesco a Ripa, and a host of dramatic monoliths housed in the **Galleria Villa Borghese**. In the shadow of such a prolific talent, the cerebral Borromini couldn't help but feel bitter. His lesser-known but equally inspired creations include **Sant'Agnese in Agone** in p. Navona, the celestial **Sant'Ivo** nearby, **San Carlo alle Quattro Fontane** on the Quirinal Hill, the sumptuous interior of **San Giovanni in Laterano**, and the ingenious *trompe l'oeil* perspective at the **Palazzo Spada**. Lesser lights of the Baroque include **Carlo Maderno**, responsible for the façade of St. Peter's,

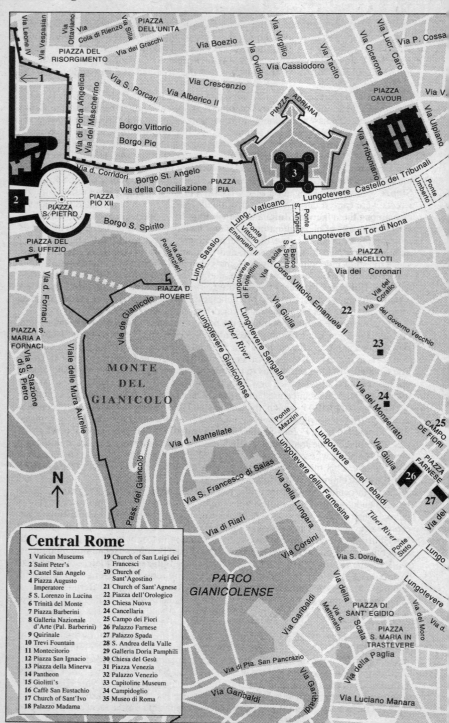

Central Rome

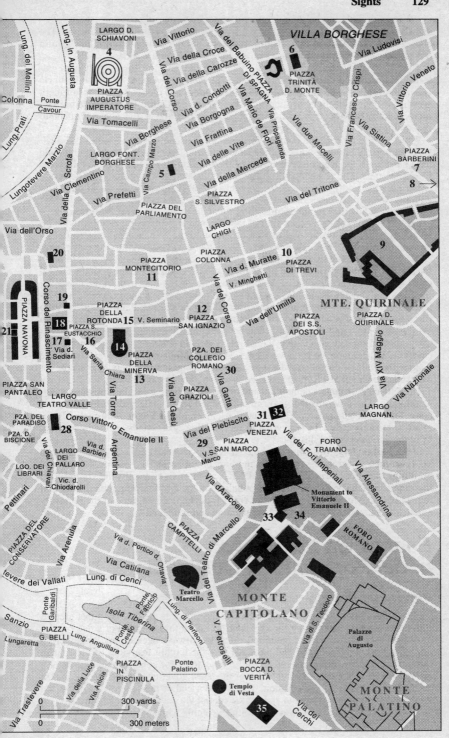

and **Domenico Fontana**, architect of many of Rome's most beautiful fountains. The churches of **Sant'Andrea della Valle, Sant'Ignazio,** the **Chiesa Nuova,** and **Trinita dei Monti** round out the city's roster of Baroque architectural wonders.

The 17th century was also the age of collecting, and many of Rome's **patrician galleries** house collections from the 16th and 17th centuries. Among them the **Galleria Doria Pamphili, Galleria Spada, Galleria Colonna,** and the **Galleria Corsini** merit a visit, for their collections of such Baroque masters as **Guido Reni, Guercino, Domenichino** and others. The Capitoline and Vatican **Pinacotecas** also house 17th-century paintings.

With the 18th century, the political fortunes of the papacy began to wane, as did city's centuries-old building boom. Noble Roman families continued to build and rebuild their palaces, as the **Rococo** confections of the **Palazzo Doria Pamphili** and **Palazzo Colonna** attest. The Rococo style (generally translated as "Baroque-gone-berserk") also graces the frothy interiors of the churches of **Santi Apostoli** and **Santi Giovanni e Paolo.** Some of the city's the last great projects of urban planning date from the 18th century, including the vibrant **Spanish Steps** and the exuberant **Trevi Fountain.**

The excavations of the ancient sites of Pompeii and Herculaneum, along with the intellectual revolution of the Age of Reason, inspired the **Neoclassical movement** all through Europe, but especially in Rome. The aesthetic was essentially a revival of Greco-Roman forms often based on mythology; with it came a newfound interest in **marble statues, tombs,** and **idealized portraits. Antonio Canova** was the period's official papal sculptor, replacing some of the stolen treasures with of his own frigid, Greek-inspired works; three of his technically perfect but rather sterile statues decorate the Vatican gardens, and his seminude portrait of Napoleon's sister, Pauline, sits in Villa Borghese. **Piranesi** produced popular **etchings of Rome.** The German scholar **Johann Winkelmann** initiated a rigorous critique of the clumsily managed archaeological excavations and set new standards—though many remain unheeded—for organizing excavations and curation; he is known as the "Father of Modern Archaeology" (see Love Among the Ruins-General Introduction, above). This period is largely responsible for the extensive Greek and Roman statue collection at the Vatican Museums.

The 19th century counts demolition and overdevelopment among its dubious accomplishments. The now-unified government erected large-scale **public buildings** to house the Italian bureaucracy. The ostentatious, incongruous **Victor Emanuele Monument,** alternately called the typewriter or the wedding cake, stands as blaring testimony to the garish vision of this era.

In the 20th century, Mussolini combined his pomposity and Fascist Nationalism with his reverence for grandiose Imperial monuments to create the horrific **municipal buildings,** the dreary neighborhood of **EUR,** and most significantly, the **via dei Fori Imperiale,** which spews corrosive car-pollution on the city's ancient monuments as it rolls past. The **Museo Nazionale delle Arte Moderne** features some of the relatively unremarkable modern Italian schools of painting and sculpture.

East of via del Corso: p. del Popolo to p. Quirinale

Piazza del Popolo

Piazza del Popolo, the northern entrance to the city, was the first sight that greeted 19th-century travelers entering the city from the north through the Porta del Popolo. The "people's square," as its name indicates, has always been a popular gathering place. Masked revelers once filled the square for the torchlit festivities of the Roman Carnival, and today the piazza remains a favorite arena for communal antics. After a victory by one of the city's soccer teams or the latest government collapse, the piazza resounds with music and celebration. The southern end of the square also marks the start of Rome's famous trident of streets: the central via del Corso, which runs straight for over a mile to p. Venezia (you can see the gleaming white Victor Emanuele Monu-

LET'S GO® Travel

1 9 9 2 C A T A L O G

When it comes to budget travel we know every trick in the book Discount Air Fares, Eurailpasses, Travel Gear, IDs, and more...

LET'S PACK IT UP

Let's Go Supreme

A

Innovative hideaway suspension with parallel stay internal frame turns backpack into carry-on suitcase. Includes lumbar support pad, torso and waist adjustment, leather trim, and detachable daypack. Waterproof Cordura nylon, lifetime guarantee, 4400 cu. in Navy, Green or Black.

A • • • • • • • • • • • • • $165

Let's Go Backpack/Suitcase

Hideaway suspension with internal frame turns backpack into carry-on suitcase. Detachable daypack makes it 3 bags in 1. Waterproof Cordura nylon, lifetime guarantee, 3750 cu. in. Navy, Green or Black.

B • • • • • • • • • • • • • $119

Undercover NeckPouch

Ripstop nylon with soft Cambrelle back. 3 pockets. 6 1/2 x 5". Lifetime guarantee. Black or Tan.

C • • • • • • • • • • • • • $9.95

Undercover WaistPouch

Ripstop nylon with soft Cambrelle back. 2 pockets. 12 x 5" with 30 x 13cm waistband. Lifetime guarantee. Black or Tan.

D • • • • • • • • • • • • • $9.95

B

Let's Go Backcountry

Full size, slim profile expedition pack designed for the serious trekker. Parallel stay suspension system, deluxe shoulder harness, Velcro height adjustment, side compression straps. Detachable hood converts into a fanny pack. Waterproof Cordura nylon, lifetime guarantee, main compartment and hood 6350 cu. in. extends to 7130 cu.

E • • • • • • • • $195

E

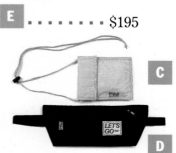

C

D

LET'S SEE SOME I.D.

1993 International ID Cards

Provides discounts on accomodations, cultural events, airfares and accident/medical insurance. Valid 9-1-92 to 12-31-93

F1	Teacher (ITIC)	■ ■ ■ ■ ■	$16.00
F2	Student (ISIC)	■ ■ ■ ■ ■ ■	$15.00
F3	Youth (IYC)	■ ■ ■ ■ ■ ■ ■	$15.00

FREE "International Student Travel Guide."

LET'S GO HOSTELING

1993-94 Youth Hostel Card

Required by most international hostels. Must be a U.S. resident.

| G1 | Adult (ages 18-55) | ■ ■ ■ ■ ■ ■ | $25 |
| G2 | Youth (under 18) | ■ ■ ■ ■ ■ ■ ■ | $10 |

Sleepsack

Required at all hostels. Washable durable poly/cotton. 18" pillow pocket. Folds into pouch size.

| H | ■ ■ ■ ■ ■ ■ ■ ■ ■ ■ | $13.95 |

1992-93 Youth Hostel Guide (IYHG)

Essential information about 3900 hostels in Europe and the Mediterranean.

| I | ■ ■ ■ ■ ■ ■ ■ ■ ■ | $10.95 |

Let's Go Travel Guides

Europe; USA; Britain/Ireland; France; Italy; Israel/Egypt; Mexico; California/Hawaii; Spain/Portugal; Pacific Northwest/Alaska; Greece/Turkey; Germany/Austria/Swizerland; NYC; London; Washington D.C.; Rome; Paris.

J1	USA or Europe	■ ■ ■ ■ ■ ■	$16.95
J2	Country Guide (specify)	■ ■ ■	$15.95
J3	City Guide (specify)	■ ■ ■ ■ ■	$10.95

LET'S GO BY TRAIN

Eurail Passes

Convenient way to travel Europe. Save up to 70% over cost of individual tickets. Call for national passes.

First Class

K1	15 days	■ ■ ■ ■ ■ ■ ■	$460
K2	21 days	■ ■ ■ ■ ■ ■ ■	$598
K3	1 month	■ ■ ■ ■ ■ ■	$728
K4	2 months	■ ■ ■ ■ ■ ■	$998
K5	3 months	■ ■ ■ ■ ■ ■	$1260

First Class Flexipass

L1	5 days in 15	■ ■ ■ ■ ■ ■	$298
L2	9 days in 21	■ ■ ■ ■ ■ ■	$496
L3	14 days in 30	■ ■ ■ ■ ■	$676

Youth Pass (under 20)

M1	1 month	■ ■ ■ ■ ■ ■	$508
M2	2 months	■ ■ ■ ■ ■	$698
M3	5 days in 2 months	■ ■	$220
M4	10 days in 2 months	■ ■	$348
M5	15 days in 2 months	■ ■	$474

LET'S GET STARTED

Please print or type. Incomplete applications will be returned

International Student/Teacher Identity Card (ISIC/ITIC) (ages 12 & up) enclose:

1 Letter from registrar or administration, transcript, or proof of tuition payment. FULL-TIME only.

2 One picture (1 1/2" x 2") signed on the reverse side.

International Youth Card (IYC) (ages 12-25) enclose:

1 Proof of birthdate (copy of passport or birth certificate).

2 One picture (1 1/2" x 2") signed on the reverse side.

3 Passport number

4 Sex: M☐ F☐

Last Name	First Name	Date of Birth

Street — *We do not ship to P.O. Boxes. U.S. addresses only.*

City	State	Zip Code

Phone — Citizenship

School/College — Date Trip Begins

Item Code	Description, Size & Color	Quantity	Unit Price	Total Price

Shipping & Handling

If order totals: . . . . . Add
Up to $30.00 . . . . . . $4.00
30.01-100.00 . . . . . . $6.00
Over 100.00 . . . . . . $7.00

Total Merchandise Price	
Shipping & Handling (See box at left)	
For Rush Handling Add $8 for continental U.S., $10 for AK & HI	
MA Residents (Add 5% sales tax on gear & books)	
Total	

Enclose check or money order payable to: Harvard Student Agencies, Inc.

Allow 2-3 weeks for delivery. Rush orders delivered within one week of our receipt.

LET'S GO® Travel

Harvard Student Agencies, Inc., Harvard University, Thayer B, Cambridge, MA 02138

(617) 495-9649   1-800-5LET'S GO (Credit Card Orders Only)

Prices subject to change

ment at the end), the via di Ripetta, built by Leo X for nonstop service to the Vatican, and the via del Babuino, cleared in 1525 by Clement VII, which leads to the Spanish Steps. The great **obelisk of Pharaoh Ramses II**, restored in 1984, commands the center of the piazza. The obelisk, some 3200 years old, was already an antique when Augustus brought it back as a souvenir from Egypt in the 1st century BC. Outside the Porta del Popolo (with a façade designed by Bernini) is an entrance to the **Villa Borghese Park**.

Nineteenth-century architect Guiseppe Valadier spruced up the once-scruffy piazza, adding the two travertine fountains on the western and eastern sides. Their symmetry jibes with Carlo Rainaldi's **churches of Santa Maria di Montesanto** and **Santa Maria dei Miracoli**, standing guard over the start of the trident (though if you look closely you'll see that the Baroque twins aren't exactly identical). Santa Maria di Montesano— on the left—is the older sibling (1662), with a façade by Bernini (open April-June Mon., Wed., Fri. 6-8pm; Nov.-March 4-7pm). Santa Maria dei Miracoli was completed by Carlo Fontana in 1677. (Open Mon-Sat. 6am-1pm and 5-7:30pm, Sun. and holidays 8am-1pm and 5-7:30pm. Sunday mass at 7pm.)

Behind its simple early Renaissance façade, the **church of Santa Maria del Popolo**, tucked away on the north side of the *piazza* near the Porta del Popolo, contains some of the most important Renaissance and Baroque art in Rome. Immediately to the right as you enter, the **della Rovere Chapel** harbors an exquisite *Adoration* by divine Umbrian master Bernardino Betti, known as Pinturicchio (1454-1513). The delicate coloring of the figures, the fine execution of the fantastic landscape and distant architecture (not to mention two of the more appealing domesticated animals in Italian painting) make the fresco one of the masterpieces of the 15th-century Roman Renaissance. It's complemented by Pinturicchio's sadly faded lunettes depicting the life of St. Jerome, and by the harmonious Renaissance wall tombs, distinguished by their delicately carved *grotteschi* designs. You can find more frescoes, almost as perfect, painted by Pinturicchio's pupils in the third chapel on the right. The gilded relief above the main altar depicts the heroic exorcism that led to the church's foundation. Pope Paschal II chopped down a walnut tree marking the legendary spot of despotic Nero's grave, allowing the terrified neighbors to live free of his ghost, and clearing the ground for the church. The apse behind the altar (sporadically accessible) was designed by Bramante—look for his signature shell-pattern on the walls. The divine Pinturicchio was at work again in the vault of the apse, painting an exquiste cycle of the *Coronation of the Virgin*, accompanied by various saints, sybils and church MVPs, in his own incomparable style. They're illuminated by 16th-century stained glass windows by the Frenchman Guillaume de Marcillat.

The **Cerasi Chapel**, immediately to the left of the main altar, houses two early Caravaggio paintings. *The Conversion of St. Paul* is a rather gruesome portrait of St. Paul being trampled by a horse. In the *Crucifixion of St. Peter*, three faceless men drag the martyred hero, cross and all. Caravaggio's earthy realism, harsh lighting, and psychological intensity heralded the early Baroque style. In both, the main figures are at the forefront of the painting, almost radiating the strong artificial light. Caravaggio shunned traditional iconography, and in the painting of St. Paul, there is no image or sign of God, only a pitying glance from the horse and attendant. Caravaggio's style strikes a great contrast to the comparatively bland, classical restraint of *Assumption of the Virgin* by his contemporary rival, Antonio Carracci, which hangs over the altar of the chapel.

The **Chigi Chapel**, second on the left, was designed by Raphael for the wealthy Sienese banker Agostino Chigi, reputedly the world's richest man. The sumptuous chapel is a triumph of mixed-media design, a riotous symphony of paintings, mosaic, sculpture and precious marbles that foreshadows the theatrical compositions of the Baroque by at least a century. Raphael proved especially ingenious in his designs for the mosaic of the dome. Instead of representing God and the celestial angels as flat figures on the surface of the vault, he used clever tricks of perspective and foreshortening to make them seem to actually stand on top of the chapel, peering down from their gilded empyrean. The virtuoso feat was a breakthrough that would be copied again and again by the illusionistic painters of the Baroque. Raphael also designed the statue of *Jonah* (look for his whale) and the pyramidal tombs, inspired by the ancient Pyramid of Caius Cestius outside the Porta San Paolo to the south of the city. Work on the obscenely expensive chapel ceased in 1520, when both Raphael and Agostino Chigi died within days of each other. It was completed a century later by Bernini for Cardinal Fabio Chigi, the future Pope Alexander VII. Bernini added two hideous medallions to the pyramids and the marble intarsio **figure of Death** in the floor. Outside the chapel, look for more gruesome portraits of Death in the multimedia wall tombs. (Open daily 7am-12:30pm and 4-7:30pm. Mass daily 7am, 8am,10am; holidays, on the hour 8am-1pm and 6:30pm).

One km up the via Flaminia (outside the Porta del Popolo) the small votive **church of Sant'Andrea in via Flaminia** marks one of the high points of High Renaissance architect Jacopo Barocci's (called "il Vignola") long career. Built for Pope Julius III in 1555, the church was dedicated to St. Andrew because it was on that saint's feast day during the 1527 Sack of Rome that Julius, then a cardinal, had escaped from the German mercenaries who were holding him for ransom. The future pope had lost so much weight in captivity that he actually climbed through the chimney to freedom.

Ara Pacis and Mausoleum of Augustus

From p. del Popolo, via di Ripetta leads south toward the Tiber, ending in the Fascist-era **piazza Augusto Imperatore**. The circular brick mound of the **Mausoleum of Augustus** once housed the funerary urns of the Imperial Roman family. Originally, the oversized tomb was crowned by a hill of dirt (in imitation of archaic Etruscan mound-tombs) and planted with cypress trees. The middle ages saw the mausoleum converted to a fortress, an amphitheater, and even a concert hall. (Closed to the public.) Next door, the glass-encased **Ara Pacis** stands as a monument to both the grandiosity of Augustan age propaganda and the ingenuity of modern-day archaeology. The altar, dedicated in 13 BC, was designed to celebrate Augustus's peaceful establishment of a monarchy—a touchy subject for Romans who still cherished the ideals of the old (but shattered) Republic. The reliefs surrounding the marble altar unite allegorical figures from Rome's most sacred national myths with realistic portraits of Augustus and his family. The reliefs on the outer enclosure represent (in part) Aeneas, Augustus's legendary ancestor, sacrificing a white sow as part of his interminable quest to found the city of Rome. On the side walls, Augustus himself appears with members of his family, on their way to perform a sacrifice of their own. Their act becomes, by association with the legendary sacrifice, a symbolic re-founding of the city, thus transforming the establishment of monarchy into an act of service to the state. And, by linking the newly minted Julio-Claudian dynasty with the figure of Aeneas, its legendary patriarch, the altar redefines the upstart Augustus as a near-divine figure, endowed with ancestral authority and quite literally born to rule.

The altar, which originally stood alongside the ancient via Lata (now the via del Corso), was discovered in fragments over the course of several centuries and only pieced together within the last hundred years. The final stages of excavation were almost never completed, as it was discovered that the altar, buried some 30 feet underground, was actually supporting a substantial section of one of Rome's larger *palazzi*. To make matters worse, the water table of the city, having risen with the ground level over the past two millenia, had submerged the monument in over 8 feet of water. Teams of archaeologists and engineers devised a complicated system of underground supports for the palace and, after permanently freezing the water with the help of carbon dioxide charges, painstakingly removed the precious marble fragments. Mussolini provided the colossal aquarium-like display case. (Ara Pacis open Tues.-Sun. 9am-1:30pm; April-Sept. also Tues. and Sat. 4-7pm. Admission L2500). Also, take note of the rear view of the **church of San Carlo al Corso** and of the barrel-toting *Botticella Fountain* erected in 1774 by the Ripetta watermen.

Two blocks south of the *piazza,* the **Palazzo Borghese**, Pope Paul V's (a.k.a. Camillo Borghese) 16th-century abode, contains a magnificent courtyard and garden. Since it's private property, you can only go in as far as the guard will let you. Crane your neck to see the larger statues and lush greenery. (Enter at Largo della Fontanella Borghese, also the site of a colorful rare book and print market; beware the electric gate.)

The Spanish Steps and Piazza di Spagna

Designed by an Italian, paid for by the French, named for the Spaniards, occupied by the British, and currently under the sway of American ambassador-at-large Ronald McDonald, the **Spanish Steps** *(Scale di Spagna)* exude a truly international air as the center toward which most foreigners gravitate. When the steps were first built in 1725, Romans hoping to earn extra *scudi* as artist's models flocked to the steps dressed as the Madonna or Julius Caesar. Today, posers of a different sort abound, most not dressed like virgins or ancient conquerors. Women beware—every eligible man in Rome (usually a self-awarded title) prowls here at night, along with drunken foreigners imitating their Italian counterparts. Recent police crackdowns, including clearing the steps around 1am, have put a damper on the *vivace* atmosphere, but as with most Roman police efforts, the effect may be only temporary.

The Spanish Steps and the **piazza di Spagna** were once quite literally Spanish. The area around the Spanish ambassador's residence, located in the eastern end of the hourglass-shaped *piazza* since 1622, was once granted the privilege of extra-territoriality. Wandering foreigners who fell asleep there were liable to wake up the next morning as grunts in the Spanish army. (Unfortunately, the same fate won't befall the sodden backpacker-casanovas who pass out here at the end of the night.)

The 137 steps were constructed in 1723-1725 to link the *piazza* with important locales above it, including the Pincio hill, the Villa Medici and the Church of Santa Trinità dei Monti. The **Fontana della Barcaccia**, at the foot of the steps, was designed by Gian Lorenzo Bernini's less famous father Pietro. The sculptor was inspired to carve the central basin in the shape of a sinking boat after he saw a barge washed up in the *piazza* after a Tiber flood. The fountain was built below ground level to compensate for the meagerness of the water pressure. The beginning of May heralds the world-famous flower show, when the steps are covered with pots of azaleas and postcard photographers.

Though today you're more likely to see con artists than true artists, the *piazza* has attracted many a creative spirit. Stendhal, Balzac, Wagner, and Liszt all stayed near here; Henry James and the Brownings lived at different times on via Bocca di Leone, a small side street in the area. Above via Frattina, 50, amid the glitter and glamour of chic boutiques, you'll see a plaque commemorating James Joyce's former residence. Another small plaque on the side of the pink house to the right of the Spanish Steps marks the home where Keats died in 1821. The second floor of the house at p. di Spagna, 26, now houses the charming **Keats-Shelley Memorial Museum** (tel. 901 42 46. Open Mon.-Fri. 9am-1pm and 3-6pm. Admission L4000. Discount for student groups). Some morbid curiosities include plaster casts of Keat's face, before and after he was consumed by consumption, a lock of his hair, his deathbed correspondence with his sister, and an urn containing the ashes of Shelley's bones. More scholarly if less titillating exhibits include facsimiles of original manuscripts and an extensive collection of books dealing with the work and lives of Keats, Shelley and Byron. The most precious artifact, touted as "the most famous relic of English literature," is a silver scallop reliquary once owned by Pope Pius V (who excommunicated Queen Elizabeth), which holds locks of Milton's and Elizabeth Barrett Browning's hair. Near the door hangs a list of many famous (and infamous) British and American expatriates and where they lived in Rome. Posters and books are for sale. (See Expatriates in Rome—18th and 19th Century General Introduction section, above.)

On the other side of the steps **Babington's English Tea Room** is an overpriced hangout for anglophiles and ersatz aristocrats. The streets between p. di Spagna and via del Corso are the most elegant in Rome, their plate-glass windows gleaming with gaudy Italian fashions, and the reflections of preening windowshoppers. Boutiques litter **via Condotti** and **via Frattina; via Borgogna** sparkles with jewelry stores; **via della Croce** tempts with sumptuous foodstuffs; and **via del Babuino** and **via Margutta** supply conservative, expensive art fodder. This area was once the Bohemian center of

Rome, as well as the site of numerous brothels, but gentrification has driven out most of the poetasters and ladies of the evening.

Despite its simple design by Carlo Maderno, the rosy neo-classical façade of the **church of Santa Trinità dei Monti** provides a worthy climax to the grand curves of the Spanish Steps, not to mention a sweeping view of the city. The interior is open from 9:30am-12:30pm and 4-7pm, but the upper half is usually blocked by a gate. The whole church opens up only on Tuesdays and Thursdays from 4-6pm. (Mass in Italian at 8:30am. Because the church is connected to the French convent of the Minims, French masses are also held at 11:30am. Vespers are at 5:30pm.) The third chapel on the right and the second chapel on the left contain works by Michelangelo's star pupil, Daniele da Volterra. The last figure on the right of Volterra's *Assumption* is a portrait of his cantankerous grand master. His other painting here, *Descent from the Cross*, was rated by Poussin as one of the three greatest paintings ever created. The fourth chapel on the left was frescoed in the 16th century by the Zuccari brothers; these same siblings built their *palazzetto* at the corner of the *piazza* on via Sistina, endowing it with one of the most imaginative façades in the city. The obelisk in the center of the *piazza* was brought to Rome back in the 2nd century, when its fake hieroglyphics were added, plagiarized from the obelisk in p. del Popolo.

Along viale Trinità dei Monti on the other side of Santa Trinità, the **Villa Medici** houses the **Accademia di Francia** (tel. 676 11). Founded in 1666 to give young French artists an opportunity to live in Rome (Berlioz and Debussy were among the scheme's beneficiaries), the organization now keeps the building in mint condition and arranges excellent exhibits, primarily of French art. Behind the villa's severe Tuscan façade lies a beautiful garden and an elaborate rear façade. (Academy open Nov. to mid-July Wed. and Sat.-Sun. 10am-1pm. Admission L2000 by guided tour only. Villa closed to the public except during exhibits. Opening and exhibition times vary.) The **Pincio,** a public park planted with formal gardens, extends up the hill beyond the villa (see Villa Borghese, below). The paths surrounding its ancient obelisk are one of the city's most fashionable strolling grounds. The **cannonball** in the center of the fountain was shot from Castel San'Angelo by Queen Christina of Sweden when, the story goes, she was late for an appointment with the painter Charles Errard, who was staying at the academy.

At the southern end of the *piazza,* the **Collegio di Propaganda Fide** merits a passing glance. Though it sounds like something left over from the fascist era, the college was actually founded to train missionaries. On December 8, when the pope comes by to pray at the **Column of the Immaculata** out front, Roman firemen climb their ladders to place a wreath on the head of Madonna's statue. The façade along Via di Propaganda is by Borromini.

Outside p. di Spagna to the south you'll find the **church of Sant'Andrea Delle Fratte**, with a funky bell tower designed by Borromini. To get there, take via di Propaganda to its intersection with via Capo le Case (which, incidentally, offers the best view of the tower). Inside near the altar are two angels carved by Bernini which originally decorated the Ponte Sant'Angelo (see Castel Sant'Angelo, below). The interior boasts the usual Rococo excesses. (Open daily 6:45am-12:30pm and 4-7:30pm.)

Piazza Barberini

Indifferent to the modern hum around the square, Bernini's Baroque **Triton Fountain,** with its musclebound figurehead, spouts its perfect stream of water high into the stirring air of p. Barberini. This cascade marks the fulcrum of Baroque Rome. Twisting north is the opulent stretch of **via Veneto,** which has seen its *dolce vita* replaced by a flood of wealthy entertainment-seekers, airline offices, and embassies. This area was once the edge of the city, adjoining the papal Rome of the west with gardens and villas to the east. Pushy real-estate developers and speculators at the turn of the 19th century managed to demolish many of the villas and gardens, including the gorgeous wooded preserve of the **Villa Ludovisi.** The speculator who bought out the Ludovisi built himself a colossal palace in its place, but soon, even he couldn't afford the upkeep and the enormous taxes, and the government repossessed the palace. The U.S. embassy now resides in this immense *palazzo,* traded for tons of war surplus material in 1945. The neighborhood has, ironically, been known since 1885 as the Ludovisi district. The rise of the movie industry and postwar tourism in the 1950's heralded the height of Via Veneto's glamour and fame. The grand *caffè* and hotels attracted movie bigwigs like Roberto Rossellini and Ingrid Bergman, eager *paparazzi*, and wide-eyed American tourists. Via Veneto's prominence has long since faded, though the overpriced *caffè* and restaurants still prey upon ignorant tourists in search of Sophia Loren (hint: she doesn't live in Italy).

Piazza Barberini showcases Bernini's **Fontana delle Api** (Bee Fountain); intended for the "use of the public and their animals," the fountain buzzes with the same motif that graces the aristocratic Barberini family's coat of arms. The 1624 Counter-Reformation **church of Santa Maria della Concezione,** further up via Veneto, is a mausoleum housing the tomb of Cardinal Antonio Barberomo, who also founded the church; the tomb's inscription reads "Here lies dust, ashes, nothing." Head downstairs for a less nihilistic view of death in the **Capuchin Crypt.** The bones of 4000 Capuchin friars (for whom *cappuccino* is named) decorate four chapels, making this one of the most bizarre and elaborately macabre settings in Rome. A French Capuchin monk inaugurated the crypt in 1528, but never saw his brilliant concept brought to its spooky completion because the crypt was not actually finished until 1870. The last chapel features two severed arms with mummy-like skin hanging on the back wall. Angels deck the halls, with the skeletons as heads and the hip bones serving as wings. The bodies of certain more recently dead friars stand, robed and hooded, beneath bone arches. Even the hanging lights are made of bones. The floors are made from dirt shipped in specially from Jerusalem. (Open daily 9am-noon and 3-6pm. Donation requested.) The church makes an excellent haunted house on All Soul's Day (Nov. 2), when the chapels are illuminated. You can earn an extra indulgence by the grace of Pope Paul VI if you visit the crypt on the first Sunday of October.

Museo Nazionale d'Arte Antica

In the other direction from the church, up via delle Quattro Fontane, the sumptuous **Palazzo Barberini,** at via delle Quattro Fontane, 13, houses the **Galleria Nazionale d'Arte Antica** (tel. 481 45 91), a collection of paintings dating from the 13th to 18th centuries. (Open Mon.-Sat. 9am-2pm, Sun. 9am-1pm. During renovation, visits to the apartments are allowed every half hour. Admission to both galleries and apartments L6000.) The *palazzo* was begun in 1624 by Carlo Maderno on a commission from the prosperous Pope Urban VIII. After Maderno's death, it took Borromini and Bernini a decade to finish the palace. Bernini added the theatrical central porch in front, topped by attached columns and shallow pilasters to make the place just that much classier. Borromini worked on the spiral stairs to the right and played around with the building's perspective so that the upper-level windows look the same size as the first floor's. Unfortunately, the main façade is practically invisible beneath a spiderweb of scaffolding which has been up since 1984. Pietro da Cortona's **grand central Salon** is now closed for repairs. Some of the most interesting paintings include Fra Angelico's triptych in **Room 2,** depicting the Last Judgement, the Ascension, and Pentecost. His deep personal faith is visible by the serene depiction and saintly faces of the Last Judgement in the central panel, and by his admiring picture of Jesus in the righthand panel of the Ascension. In the same room, note Fra Filippo Lippi's *Annunciation and Donors,* a sweet Renaissance pastoral. Lippi's curious *Madonna and Child* (1437), depicting the Virgin-Mother cuddling a rather brutish-looking baby Jesus, is significant for its innovative use of architectural elements. Don't stand too close to the paintings, or an embarassing bleep will resound through the gallery.

Room 7 contains two intriguingly dramatic works by El Greco (1545-1614), *L'Adorazione dei Pastore* and *Battesimo di Cristo.* Their deep brooding colors and distorted figures contrast sharply with Raphael's *La Fornarina,* a playful rendering of the artist's scantily clad mistress painted the year of the artist's death. The daughter of a Sienese bakerwoman, she was considered quite lovely in her day. Rumor has it that Raphael died from a fever caused by her unrelenting passion. The *Portrait of a Young Girl* by Guido Reni (1577-1642) hangs in **Room 14.** The subject is supposedly the victimized Beatrice Cenci, though Reni never actually saw her. Along with her brother, Beatrice plotted to kill her powerful, sexually abusive father and was, in turn, gruesomely beheaded. **Room 14** contains Caravaggio's *Narcisso*, captured just before the vain boy is supernaturally transmogrified into a plant. With all this beauty decking the walls, don't forget to look up. Several excellent paintings grace the ceilings of the gallery, including Camassei's *Creation of the Angels* (1630-33) in **Room 6** and Sacchi's *Divine Providence* in **Room 7**. Don't miss Jean François Niceron's bizarre perspective pieces (1613-1646); he toyed with the Renaissance fixation on artificial perspective, creating a series of warped, almost surreal portraits. Pietro da Cortona's grand masterpiece, *Triumph of Divine Providence*, in the Salon, is currently being restored.

The second floor preserves a rather gloomy collection of 18th-century paintings, but the family apartments definitely deserve a peek. In addition to preserving the rooms of the *palazzo* as they were during the height of the Barberini family's influence in the mid-1600s, these galleries display 17th- and 18th-century porcelain, silver, a collection of period gowns and jackets, and even the baby carriage of the Barberini *bambini*.

Trevi Fountain

Taking up most of the tiny *piazza,* the rocks and figures of Nicola Salvi's (1697-1751) famed and now sparkling clean **Fontana di Trevi** mount the back of **Palazzo Poli**. The water for the fountain flows from the **Acqua Vergine** aqueduct, which also supplies the best water in Rome for the spouts in p. Navona, p. di Spagna, and p. Farnese. The aqueduct's name derives from the maiden who allegedly pointed out the spring to thirsty Roman soldiers. She is immortalized in the bas-reliefs above the fountain. Completed in 1762, the present fountain is a grandiose elaboration of an earlier basin. In the most famous scene of Fellini's *La Dolce Vita*, the bodacious Anita Ekberg takes a midnight dip in the fountain with Marcello Mastroanni and a kitten.

Tradition claims that travelers who throw a coin into the fountain will return to Rome, but we urge you to refrain from the practice (and not just for budget's sake). Before the restoration, the fountain was in terrible shape, and though a team full of professionals took several painstaking years to restore it, the fountain is still in danger of further deterioration. At the top of the edifice, one of the arms of an angel was about to fall off, and much of the sculptured edifice contained nicks and scars from the tourists' tossed coins. The fountain was literally black from two centuries of pollution, and the marble was eroding from the rust of coins. Next door, the foundation of the Duke of Poli's *palazzo* settled, shifting the entire weight of the building onto the fountain's back. After the cleaning, the newly white surface reflected into the pool, conjuring up a special kind of algae, though the restorers have now added chlorine. However, the constant deluge of metal coins (especially American, British, and Japanese) is still eating away at the marble and staining the pool. Do the fountain and future generations of visitors a favor; save your pennies to buy a plane ticket to Rome and don't bother with the harmful superstition. Opposite the fountain is the Baroque **church of Santi Vincenzo ed Anastasio**, rebuilt in 1630. The crypt preserves the hearts and lungs of popes from 1590-1903. (Open daily 8:30-noon and 4-7pm.)

Piazza del Quirnale and via XX Settembre

Piazza del Quirinale, at the southern end of via del Quirinale, occupies the summit of the tallest of Rome's seven hills. From the belvedere (reached by steps connecting the *piazza* with the Trevi Fountain below), the view takes in a sea of Roman domes, with St. Peter's—the mother of all domes—in the far distance. In the middle of the *piazza,* the heroic **statues of Castor and Pollux** (mythical warrior twins whom ancient Romans embraced as their special protectors) flank yet another of Rome's many obelisks. The President of the Republic officially resides in the **Palazzo del Quirinale**, a Baroque architectural collaboration by Bernini, Carlo Maderno and Domenico Fontana. Peek through the portals on the *piazza* or on via XX Septembre to see the white-uniformed, silver-helmeted Republican Guards (each of whom must be at least 6ft. tall to get his job), as well as the *palazzo's* lush gardens. The *palazzo* was once the papal summer palace (Sixtus V died there; Pius VII was taken from the *palazzo* by Napoleon and exiled to Elba), and then a royal residence (Victor Emanuele II died there); it's hosted the president since 1947. The neighboring **Palazzo della Consulta** houses the constitutional court.

Straight **via XX Settembre** leaves the *piazza* to the north, passing the modest façade of the **church of Sant'Andrea al Quirinale** (tel. 47 48 01) on the right. One of Bernini's simpler Baroque designs, the oval-shaped interior departs from traditional church plans (the altar is along the long wall, making the nave wider than it is long). Though the building lacks architectural complexity, Bernini's theatrical orchestration of the central altar still deserves a passing glance. St. Andrew, crucified in the painted altarpiece, rises on stuccoed clouds through the vault of his apse, headed for the cherubim-filled space of the central dome. (Open Wed.-Mon. 10am-noon and 4-7pm.) Further along the street, the undulating façade of Borromini's **church of San Carlo alle Quattro Fontane** (often called San Carlino) provides a sharp contrast to Bernini's neighboring work. Borromini, who avoided the kind of mixed-media extravaganzas which Bernini had perfected, preferred to let his architecture do the talking. The head of the religious order which founded this church even bragged, "Nothing similar can be found anywhere in the world." San Carlino, small enough to fit inside one of the pillars of St. Peter's, is a triumph of rhythmical curves and concavities, its narrow interior governed by periodic pairs of pilasters. It also has the distinction of being Borromini's first and last work: though he designed the interior early on in his career, he finished the façade just before his suicide. The church is currently closed to the public during restoration. (When not in restoration, hours are Mon.-Fri. 9am-12:30pm and 4-6pm, Sat. 9am-12:30pm. If the interior is closed, ring at the convent next door.)

The small square formed by the junction of via XX Settembre with **via delle Quattro Fontane** showcases one of Pope Sixtus V's more gracious additions to the city. In an effort to ease traffic and offer greater definition to the city's regions, the 16th-century pontiff straightened many of Rome's major streets and erected obelisks at important junctions. From the crossroads here, you can catch sight of the obelisks at piazza del Quirinale, at the top of the Spanish Steps, and at Sta. Maria Maggiore, as well as (in the distance) Michelangelo's famous Porta Pia. The four reclining figures in the fountains represent the Tiber, Fidelity, Strength, and the Anio. These little spouts recessed into their host buildings have a quiet beauty that is utterly refreshing after the showiness of Rome at large.

After a few more blocks, via XX Septembre opens into the Baroque **piazza Bernardo**, site of Domenico Fontana's colossal **Moses Fountain**. The fountain, recently cleaned but already showing signs of new pollution, was built in 1587 at the point where the Acqua Felice aqueduct enters the city. The beefy statue of Moses was carved by Prospero Bresciano who despite his felicitous name nearly died of disappointment after seeing the finished product. Who could blame him? Across the way, the **church of Santa Maria Della Vittoria** (named for an icon of Mary that "won" a battle near Prague for the Catholics in 1620), harbors Bernini's turbulent, orgasmic *Ecstasy of St. Theresa of Avila* (1652) in the Cornaro Chapel, the last on the left. Bernini's masterpiece of marble depicts the young Spanish saint's cataclysmic vision, in which she felt an angel pierce her heart with a flaming arrow. She later wrote, "The pain was so great that I cried aloud but at the same time I experienced such infinite sweetness that I wished the pain would last forever...It was the sweet caressing of the soul by God." Bernini makes this sculpture dynamic, as much by the figures' disheveled clothing as by the rays beaming down on the two figures, emanating from the frescoed angels and clouds painted directly above. Bernini gives this performance an ersatz audience in balconies that resemble theater boxes on the side of the chapel; the sculpted members of the Cornaro family watch Theresa, and Bernini was supposed to have inserted himself, half-hidden, in the left balcony. (Open daily 7am-noon and 4:30-6pm). The **church of Santa Susanna** to the left has a distinctive Counter-Reformation façade by Carlo Maderno (1603); the inside is closed for restoration.

Baths of Diocletian

Following via della Consulta south from piazza Barberini to via Nazionale, trek east or hop on any of the buses headed to p. della Repubblica, another of Rome's finest fume-spewing *piazze*, and home to the ruins of the **Baths of Diocletian**. Forty thousand Christian slaves took ten years—from 295-305 AD—to build what must have been the grandest community center of the age. The public baths, which could serve 3000 Romans at once, contained gymnasiums, art galleries, libraries and concert halls as well as a 30-person public toilet (don't get the wrong idea—it was done in marble and was even heated), and pools of various temperatures. The cold pool (frigidarium) was open to the sky and the size of a small lake (2500 square meters). The complex fell into ruin in 538 when the water dried up: the supplying aqueducts were destroyed by Witigis. A Sicilian priest had a vision of a swarm of angels rising from the baths, and pestered Pius IV to build a church on the dilapidated site. As a result, the baths came to life again in 1561, when Pope Pius IV ordered Michelangelo, then 86, to convert the ruins into a church as a posthumous thanks to the 40,000 Christians. His original design imitated the architecture of the baths, but was much changed after both he and the pope died three years later. The eventual result is the **church of Santa Maria degli Angeli** (open from precisely 6:55am-noon and 3:55am-7pm). Despite the departure from Michelangelo's plan and years of design screw-ups, the vast interior gives a sense of the magnitude and elegance of the ancient baths. A door marked Sacristy leads to ruins of the frigidarium.

Around the corner on viale E. di Nicola, the **Museo Nazionale Romano delle Terme** (tel. 488 05 30) combines several important patrician collections with sculptures and antiquities found in Rome since 1870. The museum is located in the charterhouse built along with Santa Maria degli Angeli, and utilizes some of the rooms from the ancient baths. Don't miss the **Sala dei Capolavori** (Room of Masterpieces) and the so-called Ludovisi throne, a Greek statue dating from the 5th century BC. Upstairs, the frescoes from the Villa di Livia at Prima Porta, a town north of Rome, remain remarkably vivid. (Open Tues.-Sat. 9am-2pm, Sun. 9am-1pm. Admission L3000.) The Room of Masterpieces contains two 3rd-century BC bronze works, found in 1884. *Pugilist Resting* looks as tired as a turbo tourist after two days in Rome. *Daughter of Niobe*, a 5th-century BC Greek original, is dying of an arrow wound inflicted by Leto, mother of Apollo and Artemis. Niobe ticked off Leto, who retaliated by killing all 14 of Niobe's children.

Vecchia Roma: The Tiber Bend

The via del Corso, running north to south through the center of the city, forms the eastern boundary of the old quarter (*vecchia Roma,* or old Rome) of town, nestled into the elbow-shaped bend in the Tiber. This sprawling labyrinth of ancient streets and alleys is stuffed to the limit with monuments both great and small—proud Baroque churches, ancient marble temples, vast open *piazze,* and shadowy picture galleries. Though there are plenty of attractions to keep an eye out for (among them the ancient Pantheon, Baroque piazza Navona, and medieval Campo dei Fiori), you may have the best time simply wandering, letting the art galleries and antique stores, chic *caffè,* romantic alleyways, and splashing fountains vie with the guidebook sights for your attention.

To help cut a path through these miles of treasure-laden territory, we've devised three routes leading from the Corso and piazza Venezia west to the Vatican. The first covers the northern half of the bend, including patrician art galleries, the Pantheon, piazza Navona, and the streets beyond it leading to the river. The second starts from piazza Venezia and continues along busy Corso Vittorio Emanuele, the express route to St. Peter's. The third starts at Campo dei Fiori, the medieval neighborhood south of p. Navona and leads to the river by way of via Giulia, one of the most tranquil and elegant streets in the historical center. But remember, *Let's Go* never tells its fearless readers what to do; take these suggested routes with a few grains of salt, and strike out to discover old Rome on your own.

Route #1: Via del Corso to Piazza Navona and Beyond

Piazza Venezia to Piazza Colonna

The straight **via del Corso** runs for nearly a mile between p. del Popolo and p. Venezia. Following the line of the ancient via Lata, the Corso takes its name from its days as Rome's premier racecourse, the site of the annual Carnival (see Carnival General Introduction above). Today you'll find a seemingly endless array of boutiques and shoe stores—good window-shopping, if you can survive the apocalyptic onslaught of buses and scooters roaring by inches from the sidewalk. **Piazza Venezia**, anchoring the southern end of the street, is hardly the spot to while away your lazy hours. A deadly expanse of asphalt, where all the aspiring Mario Andrettis of Rome try to hit fourth gear before re-entering the medieval labyrinth of the city proper. The glorified traffic circle is presided over by the bombastic white **Victor Emanuele Monument** (see the Campidoglio section, below). Crumbly **Palazzo Venezia**, on the right of the *piazza* as you face the monument, was one of the first Renaissance *palazzi* built in the city—not hard to imagine, as its plain, battlemented façade shows a healthy attachment to the middle ages. Mussolini occupied the building and delivered some of his most famous speeches from its balcony. One of his nicknames, "The Sleepless One," came from his practice of leaving a light in his study burning into the night, so people would think he worked constantly. Mussolini also had the via dei Fori Imperiali across the *piazza* (see Imperial Fora below) cleared to provide a good view of the Colosseum from his office. (Open Tues.-Sat. 9am-2pm, Sun. and holidays 9am-1pm. Admission L8000.)

The **Museo Nazionale di Palazzo Venezia,** via del Plebiscito, 118 (tel. 679 88 65) maintains a humdrum permanent collection of papal art objects, furniture and ceramics, supplemented by more exciting exhibits announced on banners flying outside. The entrance on via del Plebiscito lies around the left-hand corner from the *piazza* façade. Most of the special exhibits take place in the *Sala del Mappamondo*, which features a mosaic floor and a frescoed map of the world as it was known in 1495. This was Mussolini's office where, along with deviously leaving his light on, he sexually harassed his female workers and intimidated opponents of both sexes. The *loggias* of the interior courtyard and of the **church of San Marco** (next door to the museum entrance) date from the Renaissance. Inside the dark and gloomy church, which was founded in 336 and remodeled in the 15th century along with the *loggias,* Melazzo da Forli's pensive *Portrait of St. Mark* hangs in the chapel to the right of the altar. The mosaic in the apse (set up in 829 AD) depicts Christ and Pope Gregory IV holding a model of the recently restored church (Rome's monuments are perpetually *in restauro*). (Interior open 8:30am-noon and 4-7pm.)

The façades of two soot-blackened churches flank the start of the southern Corso. The **church of Santa Maria in Via Lata**, a spooky little shrine, is open from 5-9:45pm. Inside lurks an ancient well that still gives water generously. Across the street find the **church of San Marcello**; the interior is under restoration. The tomb of Cardinal Michiel dating from 1503 is by the door. The third chapel on the right boasts a 16th-century fresco, while the fourth chapel on the same side contains a 15th-century wooden crucifix that survived a fire in the church in 1519. This crucifix is possibly one of the first **snuff works;** legend has it that the artist killed an unlucky passerby and watched his death throes for inspiration. (Open July-Aug. Mon.-Sat. 7:15am-noon and 4:30-7pm, Sun. and holidays 8:30am-noon and 4-7pm; Sept.-June Mon.-Sat. 7:15am-noon and 4-7pm, Sun. and holidays 8:30am-noon.)

A block behind San Marcello you'll find the *piazza* and **church of Santi Apostoli**, built into a corner of the sprawling **Palazzo Colonna**. Byzantine lions guard the entrance to the church, but the interior is coated in Baroque and Rococo goo. The *palazzo* was built in the 15th century for Pope Martin V, first in a long line of overachievers from an ancient Roman family. The present decoration dates back to the 18th century. Around the back of the *palazzo,* four graceful arches connect the main building with the gardens of the Villa Colonna, closed to the public. The **Galleria Colonna** (tel. 678 43 50), on the other hand, opens its doors every Saturday morning. The rooms, sculpture, and furniture surrounding this patrician collection of paintings are as opulent as the works themselves, having been built in the 17th century for the express purpose of showing off the family goods. The central gallery, lined with ancient statues, is dazzling. The dizzying chaos of the ceiling fresco celebrates the victory of Marcantonio Colonna over the Turks at the Batlle of Lepanto in 1571. Keep an eye out for the ebony desk in the next room with ivory reliefs of Michelangelo's famous *Last Judgement*. The throne room, built for Martin V, preserves a modest portrait of the portly pontiff, as well as his throne. The chair is kept turned to the wall so none but the papal tush might sit in it. (Open Sat. 9am-1pm; Admission L4000.)

Continuing back along the Corso, take a glance at Pasquino's cousin *Il Facchino*, another of Rome's "talking statues," on the southern corner of **Palazzo Simonetti** (No. 307). Covered in *graffiti*, the statue complains to Pasquino and other statues about community and political grievances. *Il Facchino* depicts one of the mischievous water carriers who used to fill their barrels with water from public fountains or the grungy Tiber and sell it to the unsuspecting public.

The frothy façade of the **Palazzo Doria Pamphili** brightens up the left side of the Corso with Rococo frivolity. Turn left at p. del Collegio Romano to see the **Galleria Doria Pamphili** (tel. 679 43 65). The first gallery alone contains two works by Titian and three Caravaggios, including the latter's famous *Rest on the Flight to Egypt*. Rubens's *Portrait of a Franciscan* and several Brueghels grace the rooms of the second gallery, dedicated to Dutch and Flemish painters. Velazquez's *Innocent X* and Bernini's *Bust of Innocent X* compete for attention in the third gallery. (Open Tues. and Thurs.-Sun. 10am-1pm. Admission L4000). Some of the best paintings, tapestries, and sculptures are shown in the private apartments, open only by guided tour. (an additional L3000 and worth it, usually at 11am and noon). The **Room of Andrea Doria** contains not pieces of the shipwreck but two Brussels tapestries and some of Andrea's personal possessions. The **Green Salon** houses a gorgeous cradle from the 18th century, as well as Filippo Lippi's *Annunciation*.

From the entrance to the Galleria Pamphili, via del Collegio Romano leads north into the lovely **piazza di Sant'Ignazio**, a showcase of playful 18th-century Rococo design. The Jesuit church that lends the *piazza* its name demonstrates, by contrast, the Baroque bombast of the Counter-Reformation. The façade (*in restauro* in 1992) is one of Carlo Maderno's greatest designs. Inside, Padre Andrea Pozzo painted his famous *trompe l'oeil Triumph of St. Ignatius* along the vault of the great, aisleless nave. Taking his inspiration from Michelangelo's Sistine ceiling and its intricate, impossible architecture, Pozzo went one step further, exploding the painted architecture itself open to a new vision of clear blue sky. Instead of the Sistine's flat central scenes, the figures on Pozzo's ceiling exist in the same space as the architecture, and the painter's mastery of perspective makes their foreshortened forms seem to actually float in the air above the nave. The dizzying exuberance of the scene is typical of the Baroque era's love of theatrical illusions. The church was originally meant to have a grandiose dome, as magnificent as the one at the Gesù, Sant'Ignazio's sister church. But when the Jesuits ran out of money during construction, Pozzo saved the altar from domelessness by painting a *trompe l'oeil* cupola on the flat ceiling of the unfinished drum. Catch the best view of both the ersatz cupola and the vault of the nave from a gold circle in the middle of the nave. The friendly clergy happily answer visitors' questions. (Open daily 7:30am-noon and 4-7:15pm.)

Just north of piazza di San Ignazio is **piazza di Pietra** and the remaining pieces of the **Temple of Hadrian**, now part of the façade of the *Borsa* (the now-defunct stock exchange). The temple was built to honor the newly deified emperor in 145 A.D. Exit the north side of the *piazza* to reach **piazza Colonna**, named for the colossal **Column of Marcus Aurelius** that occupies its center. Though designed in imitation of the Emperor Trajan's earlier triumphant column (in p. Venezia, see Imperial Fora), Marcus Aurelius's monument actually represents one of the saddest moments in the history of the Empire. Trajan's victories across the Danube in the first years of the 2nd century AD (which his column celebrates) had pushed the boundaries of Roman power to their furthest limit. Only 40 years later, Marcus Aurelius found himself governing an empire so large and far-flung it couldn't be defended. With barbarians encroaching on every frontier, the philosopher-emperor could barely keep his vast armies fed and paid. His campaigns against the Germans and Sarmatians, fought between 169-76 AD, saw the first defeat of a Roman army in over three centuries. Though the spiral reliefs on the column lionize the legions for their efforts, the praise rings hollow and the triumphal monument seems more like a tombstone, marking the start of the 1000-year-old Empire's tragic decline. Sixtus V added the statue of St. Paul to the top of the column in the 16th century.

Across the Corso is the Y-shaped **Galleria Colonna**, an elegant shopping mall done in grand early 20th-century style. The cavernous building is under restoration, but you can still have a *cappuccino* at the *caffè* spilling tables into the shady interior. On the opposite side of the piazza Colonna, **Palazzo Wedekind** grins sheepishly through the *graffiti* on its façade. Now home to the newspaper *Il Tempo*, it was built in 1838 with Roman columns from the Etruscan city of Veio. Check out the clock supported by four strange human figures. **Palazzo Chigi,** built in the 16th and 17th centuries, forms the north side of the *piazza.* Guards hovering around the door prevent public entrance (it is now the official residence of the Prime Minister) but you can peek through into the lovely courtyard. The northwest corner of piazza Colonna flows into **piazza di Montecitorio**, dominated by Bernini's **Palazzo Montecitorio**, now the seat of the Chamber of Deputies. The obelisk in front of the *palazzo* was once the centerpiece of a giant *horologium*, or sundial, which the Emperor Augustus set up in the neighborhood. Several streets lead south from p. di Montecitorio or west from the via del Corso to **piazza della Rotonda**, more commonly known as **piazza del Pantheon**.

The Pantheon

The majestic **Pantheon** (tel. 36 98 31) has presided over its busy *piazza* for nearly 2000 years, its marble columns and pediment, bronze doors, and soaring domed interior (save superficial decorative changes) all unchanged from the day it was erected. While centuries of political chaos and urban neglect corroded most of ancient Rome's great monuments into ruins, the Pantheon has remained whole, a proud but bittersweet reminder of the eternal city's former glories. The temple has drawn visitors for centuries, in large part because it's one of the few Roman ruins that won't strain your imagination; the vast, serene interior not only preserves its perfect architectural proportions, but also retains the power to mystify, inspire, and even terrify as it must have done for the ancients.

The building as it stands today is the product of the Emperor Hadrian's fertile architectural imagination. Though it's unclear whether the emperor actually drew up the plans himself, it's certain that the 2nd century AD philosopher-king, for whom architecture was a favorite hobby, had a hand in its design. (Hadrian also takes credit for the revolutionary design of the Temple of Venus and Rome in the Forum, for the sprawling fantasies of his Villa Adriana at Tivoli, and for his own mausoleum, now Castel Sant'Angelo.) The temple, dedicated to "all the gods," was conceived as a celebration of the abstract spatial harmonies and celestial order which the divine powers had bestowed on the universe. It's a study in (very carefully planned) contrasts and (very cleverly concealed) surprises. The classically proportioned façade, with its traditional triangular pediment, dedicatory inscription, and Corinthian columns, was designed to deceive the first time visitor into expecting an equally traditional interior. (Note the large, functionally useless rectangular brick element that rises behind the pediment: it's only purpose is to hide the dome from the view of those approaching.) If you imagine that the level of the pavement outside in the *piazza* was some twenty feet lower during the Empire (so that the temple was approached by steps), you can see how completely the dome was concealed.

Deceptive too is the inscription across the architrave on the façade. "Marcus Agrippa made it in his third consulship," (27 BC), and indeed he did build a temple here, dedicated to all the gods. Hadrian tore it down and started from scratch in 118 AD, but had the old inscription copied here, apparently to avoid accusations of overweening pride.

Once inside, however, all notions of modesty disappear. Even if you have spotted the dome from outside, the dusky, soaring interior and luminous central oculus come as a shock. The effects of light and shadow on the recessed coffers endow the vast space with an awesome, dizzying power. The dome itself, some 43m across, was constructed entirely out of poured concrete, without the support of vaults, arches or ribs. Archaeologists and architects have puzzled for centuries over how the thing was actually erected, and it wasn't until this century that a larger concrete dome could be built. The central oculus, which provides the only source of light for the entire building, also supports the weight of the dome, as all the inward forces of the sloping concrete are trapped in an eternal ring of tension around the hole. Hadrian saw architecture as a physical manifestation of the philosophical unities he studied and adored: accordingly, the dome itself is as tall as it is wide, making the dome one half of a great sphere that would, if it existed, touch the floor at its very center. (Imagine a basketball in a box.) You can see Hadrian's obsession with spheres and squares played out again in the design of the original marble pavement and in the interplay of rectangular and apsidal spaces in the side chapels. The gleaming floor slopes gently toward the center in order to drain the building; a rainy day in the Pantheon, when the drops fall in great sparkling streams through the airy dome, is a memorable sight (even better are the rare winter days when it snows).

It's not surprising that such an extraordinary building was preserved over the centuries, even as its lesser marble and brick cousins fell into disrepair. It seems that from the beginning the usually lackadaisical Romans knew they had something special on their hands. Though the Senate voted to close all pagan temples during the 5th century AD, the Emperor Phocas (whose column stands in the Forum) gave the Pantheon to Pope Boniface IV for safekeeping in 609 AD. Converted to the church of Sta. Maria ad Martyres (which title it retains to this day), the temple weathered the middle ages with few losses, though it sometimes did double duty as a fortress and even a fishmarket. Later artists and architects adored and imitated the building, which served as the inspiration for countless Renaissance and Neoclassical edifices, including Bramante's Tempietto, Palladio's Villa Rotonda and America's own Jefferson Memorial. Michelangelo, using the dome as a model for his designs in St. Peter's basilica, is said to have designed his own dome 1 m shorter in diameter than the Pantheon's, out of respect for his ancient model. The 17th century wasn't quite so deferential; when the vainglorious Pope Urban VIII Barberini melted down the bronze revetments from the roof of the portico down to make cannon for Castel Sant'Angelo and the *baldacchino* over the altar of St. Peter's, horrified Romans remonstrated, *Quod non fecerunt barbari, fecit Barberini* ("What the barbarians didn't do, Barberini did"). Adding insult to injury, Urban had Bernini add two clumsy turrets on either side of the pediment (visible in the famous Piranesi prints of the temple), which were almost immediately tagged the "ass-ears of Bernini." Saner minds removed the turrets in the last century. Later additions to the interior of the temple include several modest Renaissance frescoes, the tombs of Italy's first two kings, and the simple tomb of the Renaissance master Raphael Sanzio, whose eloquent epitaph reads, "Here lies one by whom, while he was alive, the great parent of all things feared to be conquered, now, as he is dead, she fears she herself will die." (Pantheon open Mon.-Sat. 9am-4pm, Sun. and holidays 9am-1pm; Oct.-June Mon.-Sat. 9am-2pm, Sun. and holidays 9am-1pm. Free.)

In the *piazza* before the temple, Giacomo della Porta's playful late Renaissance fountain (recently restored, and brilliantly so) supports an **Egyptian obelisk**, which was added in the 18th century, when obelisks, popular among ancient Romans, were once again à la mode. Around the left side of the Pantheon another obelisk marks the center of tiny **piazza Minerva**, supported by Bernini's curious, winsome elephant statue. Behind, the unassuming façade of the **church of Santa Maria Sopra Minerva** hides some of Renaissance Rome's artistic masterpieces. To the right of the entrance, six plaques mark the high-water level of floodings of the Tiber over the centuries. Inside the church, stained-glass windows cast a soft radiance on the only Gothic interior in Rome and its celestial ceiling. The chapels in the right hand aisle house a number of treasures, including (in the fifth chapel) a panel of the *Annunciation* by Antoniazzo Romano, a pupil of the divine Umbrian master Pinturicchio, and (in the sixth chapel) a statue of *St. Sebastian* recently attributed to Michelangelo. The south transept houses the famous **Carafa Chapel,** with a brilliant fresco cycle by Filippino Lippi, which was closed off for restoration in 1992. The altar of every Catholic church must house a holy relic or body part, and **Sta. Maria sopra Minerva** got a good one—the body of St. Catherine of Siena, the famous 14th-century ascetic and church reformer, who died in a house nearby. (That's not her under the altar, just a wax copy.) To the left of the altar another medieval great, the painter Fra Angelico, lies under a fenced-off tomb slab. Between the two tombs, Michelangelo's great *Christ Bearing the Cross* stands guard.

To the west of the Pantheon, several streets lead toward Corso del Rinascimento and piazza Navona. Along the way, pause to admire the Baroque treasures of two churches, **San Luigi dei Francesi,** with its Caravaggio paintings and Borromini's intricate **Sant'Ivo.**

Via Giustiniani leads left from p. del Pantheon to the Corso del Rinascimento. Halfway there you'll find the simple white façade of **church of San Luigi dei Francesi**, the French National Church in Rome and home to three of Caravaggio's most famous ecclesiastical paintings. The controversial Baroque artist decorated the last chapel on the left, dedicated to the Evangelist Matthew, between 1597 and 1602. The *Calling of St. Matthew*, to the left of the altar, is rightly the most famous of the three. Here you can see Caravaggio's revolutionary (for the times) attention to everyday detail. While his Baroque compatriots were busy painting up sicky-sweet madonnas on pastel clouds, Caravaggio didn't hesitate to imbue even Biblical scenes with the dark and dirty atmosphere of his own day. Unlike the idealized models of both Renaissance and Baroque painting, the figures in Caravaggio's works seem like plain street people, from their carefully detailed period costumes down to the dirt under their fingernails. But Caravaggio's real brilliance lies in his virtuoso ability to express in oils the play of light on surfaces, from the mellow gleam of a glass goblet to the rough texture of a wooden table, giving every scene a clarity of almost photographic realism. Notice how Caravaggio painted the shaft of light that falls on the bewildered figure of St. Matthew at the moment of his calling to the Christian faith so that it continues the line of the real light pouring in from above the altar. Not surprisingly, Caravaggio's insistence on warts-and-all portraiture wasn't always pleasing to his patrons. His first rendition of the central *St. Matthew and the Angel*, in which an angel helps the aged saint compose his Gospel, is shown on the informative display to the right of the chapel. In his relentless effort to make the most legendary scenes seem real to his viewers, Caravaggio had imagined the apostle as an elderly man, probably illiterate, for whom the task of writing so holy a book was nearly overwhelming. He painted the angel as a symbol of divine grace and inspiration, as Matthew's opposite, a charming, youthful figure who seemed almost to mock the old man's difficulty. The chapel's patrons, on seeing the work, cried foul and demanded a more respectful treatment of the subject, which you can see hanging over the altar. The third painting in the series, to the right of the altar, depicts St. Matthew's agonizing *Crucifixion*. (Church open Fri.-Wed. 7am-12:30pm and 4-7pm, Thurs. 7am-12:30pm.)

The celestial **church of Sant'Ivo** raises its famous corkscrew cupola over the Palazzo della Sapienza, the original home of the University of Rome, founded by Pope Sixtus IV in the 15th century. The entrance to the **cloister** on corso del Rinascimento provides the best view of Borromini's intricate façade and cupola, designed in 1660 and recently restored. Inside, Borromini's obsession with geometry and its perfect, abstract forms climaxes in the hexagonal symmetry of his gleaming white dome. Unlike his rival Bernini, Borromini didn't often incorporate sculpture into his works, preferring to manipulate and decorate his spaces by his mastery of architecture alone. Not surprisingly, when he did choose to use figures, he opted for stark, six-pointed stars and oddly disembodied cherubs, the closest things to terrestrial beings that you'll find in otherworldly Sant'Ivo. (Open Sept.-May daily 9am-noon.)

Piazza Navona

Despite popular belief, Emperor Domitian (81-96 AD) never used his 30,000-person stadium to shred naughty Christians. Instead, he used the site of modern day **piazza Navona** as a racetrack. From its opening day in 86 AD, the stadium witnessed daily contests of strength and agility: wrestling matches, javelin and discus tosses, foot- and chariot races, even mock naval battles. For these seafaring fracases, the stadium was flooded and floated with fleets of convicts. The contests were called the *Agoni Capitolini*, later mutated to *agone*, then *n'agona*, and finally *Navona*.

As the empire fell, real-life battles with maruading Goths replaced staged contests, and the stadium fell into disuse. Resourceful Romans used its crumbling outer walls as foundations for new houses—thus preserving, in careless Roman form, the original outline of the stadium. Large crowds returned to the *piazza* with the Renaissance, and from 1477 to 1869, the space hosted the city's general market. Festivals and jousts were commonplace, as was the contest of the *cuccagna*, in which contestants shimmied up a greased pole to win fabulous prizes. Nowadays the market only comes to the *piazza* between Christmas and Epiphany, during the **Befana** fair (see Festivals Entertainment, below), but caricaturists roost here year-round, joined at night by musicians and roving crowds. Throw money to the wind in the many *caffè* and throw fate to the readers of *tarocchi*. Female travelers will have no problem getting lights for cigarettes or company on strolls, as prowling Romeos vie to test their virility and their English.

One of the great examples of Baroque city planning, piazza Navona owes its beauty and fame to a case of pure one-upsmanship. Innocent X, the Pamphili pope who came to the papal throne in 1644, was only too eager to distract the Roman people from the achievements of his predecessor, the ubiquitous Urban VIII Barberini. Innocent cleared out the old stadium, where his family had had a palace for centuries, and set about constructing a new *piazza* and palace to rival those of the Barberini across town (see piazza Barberini). Innocent's desire to please the people of Rome (and not just his own ego) determined the appearance of the present *piazza*: it was, and is, a place for people to congregate, circulate and celebrate, all under the watchful eye of the Pamphili dove.

Bernini's exuberant **Fountain of the Four Rivers** (*Fontana dei Quattro Fiumi*), commanding the center of the *piazza,* was a crucial element in Innocent's plan. Restoring aqueducts had been one of the Renaissance papacy's great public relations ploys. Innocent didn't find any new aqueducts to restore, but he did manage to divert the flow of a previously repaired channel, which had been supplying (surprise!) the Fontana del Tritone in piazza Barberini. Having stolen old Urban's watery thunder, Innocent commissioned Bernini to make something impressive out of it, and the artist responded with this towering allegory of Pamphili greatness. The fountain "officially" proclaims the triumph of Catholicism over the world, but the master architect included enough Pamphili regalia to remind you that it's really Innocent who's come out on top. Each of the four male river gods represents one of the four continents of the globe (as they were thought of then): the Ganges for Asia, the Danube for Europe, the Nile for Africa (veiled since the source of the river was unknown), and the Rio de la Plata for the Americas. The ancient obelisk they support symbolizes the wisdom of ancient Egypt (i.e. all pagan wisdom), now subordinated to the dove fluttering atop its peak. The dove, symbol not only of the Holy Spirit but also of the Pamphili family, thus commands all knowledge and all known territory—modest enough claims...for a Baroque pope, anyway.

An old story holds that Bernini designed the Nile and Plata statues to shield their eyes from the sight of his archrival Borromini's **Church of Sant'Agnese**. The legend continues that Borromini then made his statue of St. Agnes on the façade look haughtily out beyond the *piazza,* not deigning to drop her gaze to Bernini's work. Unfortunately, the story is probably a load of pole grease, since the fountain was finished in 1651, before Borromini had even started work on the church.

At the southern end of the *piazza,* the **Fontana del Moro** attracts pigeons and small children alike. Originally designed by Giacomo Della Porta in the 16th century, Bernini renovated it in 1653 and added *Il Moro*, the central figure perched on a mollusk (actually carved by Antonio Mari, one of Bernini's pupils). The tritons around the edge of the fountain were moved to the Giardino del Lago in the Villa Borghese in 1874 and replaced by copies. Adding balance to the whole scene is the **Fountain of Neptune**, flowing in the north end of the *piazza*. It too was designed by Della Porta in the 16th century, and spruced up by Bernini, but was without a central figure until 1878. Antonio Della Bitta then added the Neptune from which the fountain takes its name. The ruler of the sea frolics with nereids (mythological sea nymphs), sea horses, and a cock-eyed octopus.

The *piazza* doesn't only have fountains; it was also the site of a genuine *miracolo*, marked by the **church of Sant'Agnese in Agone**. According to Christian legend, Saint Agnes really meant it when she said no to the lascivious son of a low-ranking magistrate; consequently, she was stripped naked in Domitian's stadium. When her hair miraculously grew and covered her sinful nudity, the powers that were tried to burn her at the stake. When the flames didn't even singe her, efficient Diocletian decided to cut her head clean off. This time it worked. The church marks the spot where she was exposed, and houses her severed skull in its sacristy. Girolomo and Carlo Rainaldi reconstructed the now run-down church in 1652, but it was Francesco Borromini who orchestrated the complex façade, with its soaring dome embraced by twin bell towers, between 1653 and 1657. The inside of this Baroque marvel is dominated by the airiness of its tall, frescoed cupola. Statues take the place of paintings on most walls; Maini's monument to Innocent X, who is buried there, is above the entrance. (Open Mon.-Sat. 5-7pm, mass at 6pm; Sun. and holidays 10am-1pm, mass at noon. English masses celebrated here at 10:30am on Sun. by the Parish of St. Susanna (tel. 475 15 10), while their church remains *in restauro*.)

South of the church, **Palazzo Pamphili** was also built by the Rainaldis and Borromini. Now the Brazilian Embassy occupies the *palazzo* and even has a sporadically-open art gallery, **Galleria 'Casa di Brasil' Mostra D'arte**. (Open Mon.-Fri. 5-8pm, Sat. 2-5pm.) The façade of the **church of San Giacomo degli Spagnoli** (a.k.a. **Madonna del Sacro Cuore**), on the southeast side of the *piazza,* hides a pristine Gothic interior, built in 1450 and restored in 1879.

The region to the north of p. Navona, traversed by winding cobbled streets, vaulted alleyways and crumbling ancient arches, harbors some of the most magnificent churches in Rome, well hidden behind ivy-covered walls. Via di Tor Millina leaves p. Navona at its center (past the Caffè Tre Scalini) and opens out after a block into a tiny, romantic *piazza,* filled with tables from the chic Caffè della Pace (see Entertainment: Caffè below). The *piazza's* other main attraction is the charming semi-circular porch of the **church of Santa Maria della Pace**, the product of Baroque architect Pietro da Cortona's playful imagination. His 17th-century facelift made the church so popular among Rome's *haute monde* that the *piazzetta* soon became jammed with carriages of the *crème de la crème* on their way to pray. A nightmare for city planners, commuters, and pedestrians alike, the *piazzetta* was finally expanded to let carriages turn around—an improvement so popular that a Latin inscription was put up, declaring no stone in the *piazza* could be changed thenceforth. At night, the *piazza* brims with less pious crowds of Italian stallions and tourists sipping overpriced *espresso*.

To enter the church, pass through **Bramante's cloisters** (a masterpiece of Renaissance harmony designed in 1504) at vicolo dell'Arco della Pace, 5. The open courtyard and the surrounding buildings are still frequented by crimson-clad nuns. The church is under restoration—and has been since time immemorial—because of humidity in the subsoil, and the dome is blocked off. Still, you can marvel at Raphael's gentle *Sybils* in the Chigi chapel (the first on the right). The painting of the Virgin over the altar supposedly bled when hit by a stone—and the church was built in commemoration. Check out the 15th-century wooden cross, though it's a little hard to see with Jesus in the way. (Open Tues.-Sat. 10am-noon and 4-6pm, Sun. and holidays 10am-noon. No shorts or food allowed.)

To the right of the porch of Santa Maria della Pace, a narrow alley leads under an arch to the cavernous via dell'Anima, home to the **church of Santa Maria dell'Anima**. Don't be deceived by the simple façade of the building—after passing through a small courtyard, you'll find the dark, echoing interior of the church deserted and spooky. Keep an eye out for the bizarre skull-cherub reliefs everywhere, and the statue reclining as if watching TV (actually resting on a tomb). (Open Sept.-June 7:30am-1pm and 3-6pm, Sun. 8am-1pm and 3-7pm).

If you follow via dell'Anima north around the outer curve of p. Navona, you'll see the last remains of Domitian's ancient **stadium** preserved beneath a 20th-century building. Here, cross p. delle Cinque Lune and the wide Corso del Rinascimento to the plain (but now scaffolded) Renaissance façade of the **church of Sant'Agostino**. The interior isn't quite so pristine, as its 15th-century design has been encrusted with the usual layers of Baroque and Rococo stucco and frippery. Still, keep an eye out for Raphael's magnificent *Prophet Isaiah*, painted on the third pillar of the left aisle, and Caravaggio's *Madonna of Loreto*, another striking example of the Baroque artist's insistence on realistic (rather than bombastically sentimental) representation.

Via della Scrofa, to the right of the church, leads north to via dell'Orso, where the Rococo **church of Sant'Antonio dei Portoghesi** (the Portugese national church) is all ashine inside. Artificial bulbs glimmer off the clusters of gilt throughout the church. Antoniazzo Romano (a gifted pupil of the divine Pinturicchio) conveniently gave his 15th-century painting of *Mary, St. Francis, and St. Anthony* a gilded background. To top it off, Canova's somber funeral painting is framed in gold. Animal themes abound along this "street of the pig:" pass by reliefs of lions eating boars and the 15th-century **Albergo dell'Orso** (the "Bear Hotel," a still-famous restaurant) on your way to the **Monkey Tower**. The legend behind this 15th century tower inspired a Nathaniel Hawthorne story: the family living there had a pet monkey who snatched their baby and spirited it off to the top of the tower. They prayed to the Virgin, then whistled, and the monkey brought the brat back home. *Quid pro quo;* a light now burns continuously for the Virgin.

At the end of the street, on the corner of via Zanardelli and Monte Brianza, the **Museo Napoleonico** caters to anyone with a small man complex or fetish. Rooms are dedicated to the vertically challenged emperor and many of his little relatives (most of whom lived in Rome). There's even the couch on which Pauline, his nutty sister, posed naked for the sculptor Canova. Across the *lungotevere,* on the **Ponte Umberto I**, you can catch a breathtaking view of St. Peter's and Bernini's oval *piazza,* with the stern battlements of Castel Sant'Angelo standing guard over the foreground.

Via del Governo Vecchio and Beyond

From p. Navona, make your way west to the Vatican along narrow via del Governo Vecchio, an ancient street now lined with off-beat art and antique galleries, vintage clothing stores and cheap *trattorie*. The street begins in piazza Pasquino off the southwest corner of p. Navona, passes through p. d'Orologio (where it turns into via dei Banchi Nuovi) and ends in p. Banco di Santo Spirito. In **piazza Pasquino**, a scarred torso is all that remains of poor **Pasquino**, a communal bitchboard ever since Cardinal Caraffa put him here in 1501. The "talking statue" was plastered by early activists with satirical comments against city authorities, the pope, and other perennial targets—mass media in the days before CNN. You may still find some *graffiti* on Pasquino (in 1992 he was still blasting Bush over the Gulf War) though present-day authorities try to keep him clean.

Surprisingly, narrow **via del Governo Vecchio** used to be a papal thoroughfare, lined with the townhouses of prosperous bankers and merchants. Though you probably won't be bumping into John Paul II anytime soon, you can still gawk at the medieval mansions overhanging the street, now filled with trendoid boutiques. No. 66, no more than a garage with a room above it, is said to be the smallest building in Rome. Nevertheless, **Palazzo del Governo Vecchio** is right nearby (No.#39), proving it's not a low-rent district after all. Cardinal Stefano Nardini built it in 1473; pass an eye over the ornately carved Renaissance doorway.

Via del Governo Vecchio meanders into **piazza dell Orologio**, where Borromini's Baroque clock-tower (when it's not shrouded in scaffolding) stands guard. Don't miss the beautiful virgin supported by cherubs carved into the rear corner of the **Orotorio dei Fillipini** (see Corso Vittorio Emanuele) on the *piazza*. Listen for the wail of bagpipers who play here in December.

Continuing along via Banchi Nuovi (the extension of Governo Vecchio after p. dell Orologio) you'll end up in **piazza Banco di Santo Spirito**. In the 15th century the *via* and *piazza* were a banking district that attracted moguls from all over Italy. Not only did they change and hoard money, they also acted as bookies, taking bets on anything from Papal behavior to sporting events. The **Palazzo di Banco di Santo Spirito** was a working mint until 1541 and now functions as a regular bank, despite the fact that its ornate façade is crumbling and sprouting weeds. The **Palazzo Niccolini-Amici** (at via dell'Arco della Bontanella) boasts a columned balcony and was built for the Strozzi by Jacopo Sansovino in the 16th century. The **Arco dei Banchi** (on via di Santo Spirito), a grotty little tunnel, leads to the Chigi bank and houses a Virgin and lamp to which Roman passersby say a quick *Hail Mary*. It also shows the height of the Tiber when it flooded in 1277. Via di Santo Spirito opens out onto an amazing view of the Ponte and Castel Sant'Angelo.

Route #2: Largo Argentina and Corso Vittorio Emanuele

Piazza Venezia to Largo Argentina

From p. Venezia, via del Plebiscito leads left around the Palazzo Venezia to the piazza del Gésu and **Il Gésu**, the mother church of the Jesuit Order. The Jesuits, the famous "shock troops" of the Counter-Reformation, were given orders by Pope Paul III at the Council of Trent to combat the growing influence of Protestantism. Their church, begun in 1568 according to designs by Il Vignola (a Michelangelo devotée), encapsulates their new concept of the church's role in the lives of its worshippers. The façade, by Giacomo della Porta, presents a stern and solemn front to the outside world, also drawing from some of Michelangelo's designs for St. Peter's, including the paired pilasters (i.e. the pair of two-dimensional columns). Inside, Della Porta's long, great nave was a deliberate departure from classically inspired circular and Greek-cross churches of the Renaissance which, said the Council of Trent, had subordinated the priest and his altar from their rightful places at the "head" of the church. To combat this architectural corruption, the Council recommended a new set of standards for church design. The aisleless nave firmly directs the congregation's attention ahead to the altar and the towering dome that illuminates it. The lighting here is almost theatrical; the nave remains relatively dark and by contrast, the large windows on the Eastern side of the church (in the drum of the dome) appopriately spotlight the altar with sunbeams. The Gesù became the prototype for endless churches built or rebuilt during the Counter-Reformation. The decoration of the interior, on the other hand, done a hundred years later, expresses the Church's (supposed) triumph over Protestantism. An aggressive array of 17th-century colors highlights Il Baccicia's fresco *The Triumph of the Name of Jesus* in the vault of the nave, no mean testament to the order's ambition. Also look for the **Chapel of Sant'Ignazio di Loyola**, dedicated to the founder of the order, who lies buried under the altar. (Open 6am-12:30pm and 4-7:15pm.)

A few blocks down via dei Cestari (filled with ecclesiastical supply stores and monastic couturiers) the busy **Largo Argentina** sees an unhealthy portion of Rome's bus and taxi traffic scream through in polluted procession. The largo, named for the square *Torre Argentina* (silver tower) that dominates its southeastern corner, was once a center of the medieval quarter of town, filled with similar towers and rustic houses. Mussolini demolished the neighborhood in the 1930s to make way for a grandiose Fascist square, but construction revealed a new obstacle—the **Four Republican Temples** which now repose in the gaping square below the street. Their excavation is as much a testament to *il Duce*'s disregard for the city's medieval heritage as it is a tribute to his monumental love for Rome's antiquities. Archaeologists still don't know for sure to whom the temples were dedicated, but it is known that the four were connected with the larger complex built around the theater of Pompey (near present-day Campo dei Fiori). It was somewhere between the largo and the theater that Julius Caesar was murdered on the Ides of March in 44 BC.

Corso Vittorio Emanuele

Though named for unified Italy's first king, the roaring corso Vittorio Emanuele has a history that extends well past the 19th century. Pope Sixtus IV, the 15th-century pontiff responsible for so much of Rome's Renaissance construction, first widened and straightened the street in the 1470s in preparation for the Holy Year of 1475. Then known as the via Papalis, the *corso* shuttled multitudes of pilgrims between the old basilica of S. Giovanni in Laterano and the pope's new headquarters across the river at the Vatican. From Sixtus's time on, the street has been the favored address of sumptuous *palazzi* and churches, and is still used for papal processions today (see *S. Giovanni in Laterano*), as well as by the infamous #64 bus. From Largo Argentina, the Corso leads west to the **church of Sant' Andrea delle Valle**, begun in 1591 by Grimaldi and completed by Baroque bigwig Carlo Maderno. The church boasts the second-largest dome in Rome after St. Peter's. Rainaldi's recently restored 1665 façade is a surprisingly sober Baroque production, with orderly rows of columns and pediments in place of the usual swirls and curls. Inside, pass by the twin wall tombs of the Piccolomini Popes Pius II and III (on either side of the nave right before the dome) to view Domenichino's colossal 17th-century frescoes of St. Andrew, crucified on his characteristic X-shaped cross. Puccini's opera *Tosca* opens in this church, continues in p. Farnese, and concludes in the prison of Castel Sant' Angelo, across the river at the end of the corso Vittorio Emanuele. Unfortunately, the restoration of this church is purely cosmetic; the funding allowed restorers to clean off the façade—which is now blindingly white—though they didn't clean the interior or reinforce the structure.

Across the street, the soot-blackened facade of the **Palazzo Massimo**, designed by the Renaissance painter Baldassare Peruzzi in 1532, cleverly follows the curve of the *corso*. The street itself, like the via di Grotta Pinta in Campo dei Fiori (see above), follows the line of an ancient theater, the Odeon of the Emperor Domitian. Behind the *palazzo* (accessible from corso del Rinascimento), a solitary column remains from the ancient edifice, which once hosted concerts and theatrical performances. The back wall of the *palazzo* preserves a rare cycle of monochrome painting from the 16th century—most houses in Rome once boasted such intricate decoration, but few have resisted the assaults of wind and rain as well as this one. The palace saw its finest hour when it hosted the first printing press in Rome, set up by migrant German craftsmen in 1467 to serve the newly fashionable humanist tastes of the papal court. Next door in tiny p. San Pantaleo, the **church of San Pantaleo** is usually closed, but dates from 1216. Giuseppe Valadier added the strange façade in 1806.

The Neoclassical Palazzo Braschi, at the back of the *piazza,* houses the **Museo di Roma**. While the museum illustrates the long history of Rome, and the third floor **Modern Art Gallery** (Galleria Comunale d'arte Moderna) mounts excellent exhibits, it is undergoing one of those seemingly never-ending renovations and is closed indefinitely. (Open Tues.-Sun. 9am-1pm. Admission L3500 for adults, L1700 for youth and seniors.)

An imposing stone coat of arms identifies the **Cancelleria**, an early Renaissance *palazzo* on the south side of the Corso. Designed in 1485, it impressed an array popes and cardinals who affixed their insignia to it. Today, the Cancelleria is the seat of the three Tribunals of the Vatican and is legally considered a part of the Vatican City. The building's designer remains anonymous, but its unprecedented size and style have led the architecturally optimistic to suspect Bramante. The courtyard, ringed by three stories of *loggias* supported by Doric columns, resembles his masterful restoration of the adjoining **church of San Lorenzo in Damaso**. No admittance beyond the Cancelleria's courtyard. (Open Mon.-Sat. 7:30am-2pm and 4-8pm. Church open in winter 7am-noon and 4:30-8pm; summer Mon.-Sat. 7am-noon and 4:30-7:30pm, Sun. and holidays 7:30am-12:45pm and 4:30-7:45pm.)

Despite the presence of its imposing next-door neighbor, the plucky **Palazzo Piccola Farnesina** (one block east of the Cancelleria) manages to hold its own. Built in 1523 by Antonio da Sangallo the Younger for Thomas Le Roy, a French diplomat, it gets its name from a case of mistaken identity—of the floral kind. Le Roy's brilliant career in Rome was rewarded when he was made a nobleman and given special permission to add the lily of France to his coat of arms. The lilies were mistaken for similar flowers representing the Farnese and so the *palazzo* got its name, Farnesina, or "little Farnese". To add to the bastardization of Le Roy's castle, it is sometimes called Farnesina ai Baullari; *baullari* refers to the trunkmakers' street which abutted it.

The interior (which was restored in the 19th century) houses the **Museo Barracco** (tel. 654 08 48), a collection of Egyptian, Greek and Roman statues donated to the city in 1902 by Senator Giovanni Barraco (1829-1914). Recently reopened after six years of restoration, the museum houses one of the finest collections of antique statuary in Rome. The museum differs from most in the city in that its small collection is meticulously labelled and exquisitely displayed, over three floors of gleaming Renaissance palace. It's also almost entirely deserted. Once you enter, the din of traffic and tourists on the *corso* outside dies down to a dull roar, and the sun streams through tiled and frescoed *loggias.*

In the entry court, the massive, broken Hellenistic *Torso of Apollo of Omphalos* (#100) presides over the ticket office. On the first floor are Egyptian, Cretan, Cypriot, and archaic Greek sculpture. Look for the serene, 3000-year-old polished basalt *Head of Rameses II* (#19); the *Head of a Bearded Man* (#31) was once thought to be a portrait of Julius Caesar. Carved in Roman Egypt, it shows elements of both cultures' tastes in portraiture. Here you'll also find little Bes, the whip-wielding Phoenician god represented both in sculpture (#60) and relief (#304). In the small room to the left, a mesmerizing painted *Cypriot Head* (#64; 6th-5th century BC) is a rare example of the coloring which once decorated nearly every statue of the ancient world.

On the second floor, Roman and Greek statuary cohabitate. The so-called *Head of Alexander the Great* (#157) is the prototype for most Hellenistic portraiture: you can see the swirling locks of hair, upturned face and vaguely focused eyes repeated on statues around the room. To the left of Alexander, a gallery of well-known Greeks stares ahead: among them Sophocles, Epicurus, Euripides, and Demosthenes. In the small room on the second floor are Roman treasures, including a tiny *Head of a Julio-Claudian Prince* (#194), a funerary urn carved in the shape of a temple (#173), a fresco of a hermaphrodite playing a lyre (#214), and a 12th-century mosaic (#209) taken from the original Constantinian basilica of S. Pietro, showing an allegory of the Roman Church. (Museum open Tues.-Sat. 9am-1:30pm, Sun. 9am-1pm, Tues. and Thurs. also 5-8pm; admission L3750, students L2500.)

A few blocks down the *corso*, the **Chiesa Nuova** has, like most Roman churches, a miraculous history. Although it was originally founded in the 12th century as Santa Maria in Vallicella, it is strongly associated with Saint Philip Neri, one of the leaders of the Counter-Reformation, who used it as the home base for his congregation of Oratorians. He had the place redone, and in 1605 the completed new version was called the "new church" (it was even further restored in the 19th century). During the building process, St. Philip had a vision of the Virgin rescuing churchgoers at a mass-in-progress by supporting a section of the old church that was about to collapse. This mini-miracle is represented in a stucco ceiling painted in 1644 by Pietro da Corona, the man responsible for much of the other art in this Baroque interior. Don't miss the early Rubens (1608) paintings in the chancel. The chapel on the left holds the leftovers of St. Philip Neri and is consequently decorated with bronze, marble, mother-of-pearl, and gold. Next door the **Oratory**, where St. Philip's followers met to make music, is graced by Borromini's intriguing brick façade, a symphony of convex and concave surfaces for which the geometrically-minded architect is rightly famous. It's worth taking a look inside at the courtyard and walkways.

The **Terrina fountain** in front of these structures, in addition to being horribly polluted, has a long history. It stood in Campo dei Fiori until 1899; after an unexplained disappearance, the fountain was placed here in 1925. The basin is from 1590, but the travertine lid with the inscription: "love God, do good and let others talk" came along later.

From the Chiesa Nuova, a five-minute walk across the Tiber will deposit you on the doorstep of St. Peter's. Or head into the welter of medieval alleys around via del Governo Vecchio (to the north; see above) or Campo dei Fiori and the via Giulia (to the south; see below), to see more of the bend in the river.

Route #3: Campo dei Fiori and via Giulia

Around Campo dei Fiori

Across corso Vittorio Emanuele from p. Navona, **Campo dei Fiori** is a haphazard clearing in the middle of a dense medieval quarter. During papal rule, the area was the site of countless executions. A statue marking the death spot of one victim, Giordano Bruno (1548-1600), rises above the bustle, arms folded over his book. Scientifically and philosophically ahead of his age, Bruno sizzled at the stake in 1600 for taking Copernicus one step further: he argued that the universe had no center at all. Now the only carcasses that litter the *piazza* are those of the fish in the colorful **market** that springs up with plenty of fresh fruit and fish every day but Sunday from 7am to 2pm.

The streets around the *campo* are among the most picturesque in Rome and merit a few hours of aimless exploration. The deceptive alleyways may lure you to a cloistered fountain, a secluded *piazza,* a hidden church, or spill you back onto the noisy Corso Vittorio Emanuele.

Several streets lead south from Campo dei Fiori into **piazza Farnese**. The square is dominated by the huge **Palazzo Farnese**, begun in 1514 and considered the greatest of Rome's Renaissance *palazzi.* The Farnese, an obscure noble family from the backwoods of Lazio, parlayed Pope Alexander VI's affair with Giulia Farnese into a clutch of bishoprics for her son Alessandro, a fling at the papal throne, and eventually dukedoms in Parma and Piacenza. As Paul III (1534-1549), the first Counter-Reformation pope, Alessandro Farnese refounded the Inquisition and (more humanely) commissioned the best architects of his day—Antonio da Sangallo, Michelangelo, and Giacomo della Porta-—to design his dream abode. (Unfortunately, the pope selected architects so advanced in their careers that they all died while in his employ.) Although Sangallo's façade and entrance passage are remarkable, the most impressive part of the building is Michelangelo's elaborate cornice, modelled on ancient Roman architectural fragments and running the length of the *palazzo*'s flat roof. Today, the French Embassy rents the *palazzo* for one *lira* per 99 years in exchange for the Grand Opera House in Paris, home of the Italian Embassy. (Palace definitely *not* open to the public.) In the 16th and early 17th centuries, the Farnese family hosted great spectacles in the square and had the two huge tubs (later converted into the present-day fountains) dug up from the Baths of Caracalla to serve as "royal boxes," from which members of the self-made patrician family could look on. While in the *piazza,* peer at the **church of Santa Brigida,** whose ornate portal curiously upstages its *palazzo* façade. Go around the back of the Palazzo Farnese for a glance at the gardens, and to see Michelangelo's beautiful vine-covered bridge over via Giulia. Note the *vanitas* skull motif in the little **Church of Santa Maria della Morte**, on via Giulia.

Galleria Spada

Behind the elaborate Baroque façade of the **Palazzo Spada,** in piazza della Querica to the left of the Palazzo Farnese, you'll find the jewel-like picture collection of the **Galleria Spada** (tel. 686 11 58). Seventeenth-century Cardinal Bernardino Spada bought up a grandiose assortment of paintings and sculpture, then commissioned an even more opulent set of great rooms to house them. Time and good luck have left the cardinal's palatial apartments nearly intact, and a visit to the gallery offers a rare glimpse of the opulent luxury that surrounded Baroque courtly life. The *palazzo* is a treasure in itself. The outer façade and inner court are masterpieces of Baroque stucco work, recently restored to their original creamy-white frothiness. Outside, seven ancient Roman kings, generals, and emperors stand proudly under Latin legends describing their achievements. Inside, the twelve, even less modest Olympian gods surround the court—every last one of them, down to the usually prudish Vesta, here buck naked and proud of it. Plucky Bernardino commissioned the elaborate decoration to make up for the relatively puny size of his palace, but even swaggering stucco couldn't keep the poor cardinal from feeling boxed in on all sides by distressingly banal neighbors. To ease his discomfort, Borromini, the master architectural illusionist, designed an ingenious colonnade beyond the library on the left side of the courtyard. From the court, the colonnade seems to stretch some 50' back through a spacious garden, framing a life-size classical statue. In reality, Borromini manipulated perspective by shrinking the columns and pavement dramatically—the colonnade is only a few yards long, the statue stands three feet tall, and the spacious garden is no more than a narrow alley between the *palazzo* and its next-door neighbor. You can see the colonnade through glass from the courtyard, but if you ask the porter he'll take you round for a tour.

Bernardino proved no less self-serving in assembling his **picture collection**; in the first of the gallery's four rooms he hung no fewer than three portraits of himself, two by Guercino and a third by Guido Reni. The following rooms (each stacked with complete lists of the numbered paintings and furniture) hold more interesting 16th- and 17th-century subjects. In the portrait-studded **Room 2**, look for paintings by the Venetians Tintoretto and Titian, whose somber, restrained colors come as a relief after the gaudy pastels of Roman Baroque. #60 is Titian's pensive *Portrait of a Musician;* #86 a copy of his portrait of the aged Pope Paul III. #75 marks Tintoretto's *Portrait of an Archbishop*. Lavinia Fontana, one of the few women painters whose work has survived from the 16th century, painted the stark *Cleopatra* at #90.

Grandiose **Room 3** houses 17th-century portraits and mythological scenes along its capacious walls—most of the overblown stuff doesn't merit a second look, but stop to take in Guercino's sumptuous *Death of Dido* (#132), in which the Carthaginian queen scorned by Aeneas throws herself simultaneously onto her sword and her funeral pyre. In the distance, Aeneas's ships set sail for Italy and the founding of Rome. In **Room 4**, the father-daughter team of Orazio and Artemisia Gentileschi is represented by three canvases: Orazio's *David* (#155); and Artemisia's *Santa Cecilia* (#149), (the patron saint of musicians, hence her lyre) and *Madonna and Child* (#166).Follow the narrow street further away from p. Farnese past a medieval house built out of an ancient temple—you can still see some weathered Ionic columns plastered into the wall. Via dei Pettinari leads right to the **Ponte Sisto**, one of Pope Sixtus IV's more useful Renaissance erections, which offers pedestrians a handy route to the medieval quarter of Trastevere (see Trastevere below). A left-hand turn on via Arco delle Monte takes you round the **Monte di Pieta**, an architectural collaboration by the Baroque masters Carlo Maderno and Francesco Borromini. Famous for centuries as a pawn shop, the building is now home to a bank and the *carabinieri*. Right across the way stands another relic of the Baroque, the tiny **church of Santissima Trinita dei Pellegrini** (*in restauro*). It was built by Paolo Maggi from 1603-16 and the façade was added in 1723 by Francesco De Sanctis. From here you can pass onto the busy via dei Giubbonari and via dei Chiavari (window-shopping galore). Via dei Giubbonari opens on to p. Cairoli and its **church of San Carlo ai Catinari**, built from 1612 to 1620 by Rosato Rosati. The façade is in the style of the Counter-Reformation and the interior, with its Greek-cross plan, had the same decorating committee as neighboring Sant'Andrea della Valle, namely Domenichino, Lanfranco, and Corona. Via dei Chiavari meanders north to via di Grotta Pinta, a dizzying canyon of curved *palazzi* built over the remains of the semi-circular **Theater of Pompey**. Pompey the Great, one of the power-hungry generals of the first century BC whose autocratic machinations helped destroy the Roman Republic, competed with his rival Julius Caesar both in war and peace. When Caesar's wildly popular victories in Gaul became, well, just too galling for the Rome-bound Pompey, he distracted the populace by building a grandiose theater, the first of its kind in the city. The prudish Senate had outlawed permanent theaters because they feared they would corrupt public morals; Pompey outwitted the censors by building a small shrine at the top of the stands and calling the whole complex a temple. Though Caesar bested the hapless Pompey politically, the old general still got the last laugh: it was in Pompey's portico, built to surround his sumptuous theater, that Caesar (*moxque rex*) was finally assassinated on the Ides of March, 44 BC. Halfway round the horseshoe-shaped street, a dark vaulted passage, half-hidden by ivy, leads back into Campo dei Fiori. (A note to serious archaeology nuts: two restaurants on the back side of the theater, S. Pancrazio and Costanza, have basement dining rooms built out of the 2000-year-old understructure of the theater, and will gladly let you in during off-hours for a dusty peek around.)

Via Giulia

As part of his campaign in the early 1500's to clean up Rome after the "Babylonian Captivity" (when the popes moved to Avignon and the city fell into serious disrepair), Pope Julius II commissioned Bramante in 1508 to construct the long strait leading directly to the Vatican, via Giulia, an elegant, even revolutionary contrast to the narrow and winding medieval streets. Throughout the 16th century this luxurious expanse remained an elegant neighborhood, as later architects built the expensive residences in accordance with Bramante's restrained, classical vision. In the 17th century, however, Innocent X built a prison here in order to down-market this area, and to make the neighborhood that he commissioned himself (around piazza Navona) stand out. Nevertheless, the tony neighborhood attracted popes, Roman nobility and artists, including Raphael, who lived at #85. Today, this street parallel to the Tiber remains one of the most peaceful, elegant, and exclusive in Rome, with well-maintained *palazzi*, antique stores, and art galleries.

Perhaps the most striking of all sights in this area is the ivy-draped **bridge** that spans via Giulia from the Palazzo Farnese and extends to the embankment of the river. Michelangelo designed the bridge, which was originally intended to be the first leg in a longer bridge that would cross the Tiber to connect the *palazzo* with the *Villa Farnesina* on the other side, but the funds dried up and Pope Paul passed away. After passing under it, steal a glance through the iron and glass gate at the lush gardens and Giacomo della Porta's beautiful façade of the Palazzo Farnese. Off the southeast corner of the *palazzo,* just before reaching the end of via Giulia lurks the **Fontana del Mascherone**. The Farnese erected this "gargoyle" fountain; the immense marble mask of the bloated face and the granite basin are ancient Roman.

Continuing along via Giulia, watch carefully for the turn towards the river on via di Sant'Eligio, where it's worth the detour to visit the miniature **church of Sant'Eligio degli Orifici**. Raphael designed this 16th-century Greek-cross church which was continued by Peruzzi, who added the cupola. (Open Sun.-Tues. and Thurs.-Fri. 10am-noon, Sun. mass at 11:30am. Mass cancelled July-Sept. Completely closed in Aug. Ring at via S. Eligio, 9, to get in.) Further down via Giulia intersects with via dei Farnese, where you'll find the **Palazzo Falconieri**, enlarged upon by Borromini; it has been the Hungarian Academy since 1928. The Falconieri is easily recognizable by the giant falcons that roost on each corner. The *palazzo's* neighbor, the **church of Santa Maria dell'Oranze e Morte** was revamped by Ferdinando Fuga from 1733-37 and carries the *vanitas* skull motif. (Open Sun. and holidays for 6pm mass.)

Further along the via Giulia at #66 is **Palazzo Sacchetti**, designed in 1543 by Sangallo the Younger, the Farnese Palace architect. The courtyard features several stone busts and a relief of a Madonna and child illuminated by an enormous candle. In the two blocks between vicolo del Cefalo and via del Gonfalone, giant stone blocks known as the "via Giulia sofas" protrude from the bases of the buildings on the right. They were to provide the foundation for the never-completed law courts of Julius II. Continuing on, note Pope Innocent X's dread **prison** (1655) at #52. The prison was converted into a museum of criminology, reputedly filled with old papal torture instruments, which unsurprisingly, never opened. A quick jaunt one block north to via dei Banchi Vecchi reveals Alexander VI's **Palazzo Sforza Cesarini** with its own little *piazza*.

At the end of via Giulia near the ponte Principe Amadeo, the **Church of San Giovanni dei Fiorentini** has a particularly prestigious history, though in retrospect was not necessarily worth the fuss. Pope Leo X, a Medici from Florence, decided to illustrate the glories of his hometown and build a Florentine church in Rome. All the most famous Renaissance artists competed for the privilege of building it, and Jacopo Sansovino beat out the likes of Peruzzi, Michelangelo, and Raphael. Begun in the 16th century, the work was continued by Antonio da Sangallo and Giacomo della Porta and finally wrapped up by Carlo Moderno in 1614. Two busts were done, one by *the* Bernini (Gian Lorenzo), on the right, and one by his lesser known father (Pietro), on the left. A pupil of Bernini's, Antonio Raggi contributed a set of marble statues. The tombs were designed by Borromini. (Open Mon.-Sat. 7-11am and 5-7:30pm, Sun. 7am-1pm and 5-7:30pm.)

The Ancient City

The Capitoline Hill (Campidoglio)

The physical center, the original capitol, and the most sacred part of the ancient Roman city, the **Capitoline Hill** still serves as the seat of the city's government and is crowned by a spectacular *piazza* of Michelangelo's design. Here you'll also find a rambling complex of museums and some unforgettable views of the Forum and Palatine. In ancient times the hill was dominated by a gilded temple to Jupiter, chief god of the Roman pantheon, along with the state mint and the senatorial archives; with such an officious past, it's not surprising that independent-minded Romans have exploited the site for its aura of republican virtues ever since. In fact the sad truth is that original form of the Capitol is now almost entirely obscured by monuments of medieval, Renaissance, and modern civic construction, all trying to capitalize on the memory of the hill's ancient glories.

The north face of the hill, facing piazza Venezia, has been completely swallowed by the gargantuan **Victor Emanuel Monument,** a colossal confection of gleaming white marble built in the 19th century to commemorate the short-lived House of Savoy, whose kings briefly ruled the newly unified Italy. Around the right of the monument as you face it, a cluster of staircases rises to the top of the hill. The left-hand staircase has 124 steep medieval steps climbing to the unadorned façade of the 7th-century **church of Sta. Maria in Aracoeli.** The right-hand staircase, the curving via delle Tre Pile (1692), climbs toward a small park. In the center rises Michelangelo's magnificent staircase, **la cordonata,** a stepped ramp built in 1536 so that the Emperor Charles V, apparently penitent over his sack of the city a decade before, could ride his horse right up the hill to meet Pope Paul III during a triumphal visit. On your way up *la cordonata,* pause to note a statue of **Cola di Rienzo,** leader of a popular revolt in 1347 which attempted to reestablish a Roman Republic. The statue marks the spot where the disgruntled populace tore the demagogue limb from limb, where only a short while before they had elected him first consul amidst the ruins of ancient republicanism.

At the top of the square, Michelangelo's spacious **piazza di Campidoglio** is fronted on its long sides by the twin **Palazzo dei Conservatori** and **Palazzo Nuovo,** and between them at the back the turreted **Palazzo dei Senatori**. Paul III commissioned Michelangelo to remodel the top of the hill for Charles V's visit and had the famous equestrian **statue of Marcus Aurelius** brought here from the Lateran Palace to serve as the focal point. The gilded bronze, which graced the center of the space until recently, was one of a handful of ancient bronzes to escape medieval melt-down, because it was thought to be a portrait of Constantine, the first Christian Emperor. But the brazen warrior proved too delicate to combat the assault of modern pollution and was removed for restoration ten years ago. The emperor now resides in climate-controlled comfort in the courtyard of the Palazzo dei Conservatori; soon a copy may occupy the vacant plinth at the center of the *piazza*. Michelangelo also set up the imperious statues of the twin warriors Castor and Pollux, protector gods of the Roman populace, along with a set of marble trophies of arms and armor and, at the base of his ingenious split staircase, two reclining river gods converted into fountains and the seated figure of the goddess Roma herself. Note the ingenious geometry of the Florentine architect's pavement—the buildings face each other at just over a 90° angle in order to draw the visitor into the open space—and the gentle slope of the ground to the base of the non-statue: some have called this spot the navel of the world.

The **Musei Capitolini** are housed in the twin *palazzi* on either side of the *piazza*. One ticket covers entrance to both buildings. The museums' collection of ancient sculpture are among the largest in the world, but if marbles aren't your thing you may find the *pinacoteca's* lackluster assortment of 16th-century Italian paintings a bit disappointing. (Museums open Tues.-Sun. 9am-1:30pm; in winter, also Tues. and Sat. 5-8pm, in summer, also Tues. 5-8pm, Sat. 8-11pm. Admission L10,000; L5000 with student ID; free on last Sun. of the month.)

Start at the ticket booth in the **Palazzo Nuovo** (on the left as you enter the *piazza*). In the courtyard, the enigmatic *Marforio*, a colossal river god, reclines beside his plashing fountain. Here Marcus Aurelius rides his stirrup-less horse behind glass, extending his hand in the gesture of imperial clemency. Though he wears civilian dress, the statue was apparently part of a monument to one of the emperor's overseas victories. The rest of the courtyard was being cleaned in 1992, and most of its rooms (containing sarcophagi and inscriptions) are usually closed. A bulky statue of Mars glowers toward the staircase and marks the start of the sculpture galleries. Though the Romans owed much of their artistic culture to their classical Greek forbears, their taste in sculpture often departed quite far from the Greek tradition. Rather than celebrating ideal concepts of form and beauty, Roman sculpture tried to entertain, to amuse, even to horrify. Ugly or charming, grotesque or endearing, Roman marbles were carved to provoke a reaction. The same is true for portraiture—the crusty personalities of the Roman aristocracy liked accurate portraits of themselves, warts and all. Dismiss your expectations of classical perfection, and look instead for a truthful (and not always flattering) picture of ancient Roman taste.

The rooms on the first floor are laid out more like a 17th-century curio cabinet than a modern museum: few works are labeled, and everywhere random heads and limbs have been patched onto bodies, whole sculptures have been placed on alien plinths, and priceless collections of inscriptions and reliefs have been plastered into the walls as decoration. In the first room at the top of the stairs, the morbid *Dying Gaul* heaves through the last moments of life, his chest pierced with wounds and his arm giving way to the heated swoon of death. It's unclear whether the statue portrays a Gaul dying in a Roman arena or in the field of real battle, but whatever the case, the work is testament to the Romans' capacity to view suffering as entertainment, and even as art. Note his intricately carved *torque* (necklace), surprisingly modern mustache, and exquisitely polished physique. From this room you can catch some good views of the Forum and Colosseum.

Next door a vibrant red porphyry *Centaur* cavorts amidst marble masks and sarcophagi. In the large salon, centered round a really awful basalt *Infant Hercules*, more centaurs sport, while on the long wall opposite the windows a pathetic *Drunken Old Woman* spreads a toothless grin. More reserved are the togate *Roman Man and Wife* and fairly puny, recently cleaned statue of Marcus Aurelius (compare with his imposing equestrian pose downstairs). Beyond lie two rooms crammed with busts, a collection which reads like a roll call of Roman and Greek notables. Greek philosophers and writers throng the first room (among them Homer, Demosthenes, Pythagoras, and Epicurus), though they've deigned to admit one Roman to their company—the wholly underrated and much maligned Marcus Tullius Cicero, who secretly exults in the corner. Next door are the lesser Romans, including the Emperor Augustus (by the window), an intricately coiffured Flavian woman, a polychrome bust of the Emperor Caracalla looking angry, a portrait of Lyndon Johnson as the Emperor Vespasian, several bearded soldier-emperors from the 3rd century AD and, finally, an iconic head of Constantine, last of the great emperors. His mother St. Helena reclines coyly in the center. The long corridor outside contains more dusty fragments, funerary urns, and inscriptions. Look for the prudish *Venus Pudens* in her skylit nook, a weird *Winged Psyche*, another *Drunken Old Woman* (this one so far gone she's squatting on the ground) and a cabinet with exquisite mosaics of masks and doves from Hadrian's Villa.

The sculpture collections continue across the *piazza* in the **Palazzo dei Conservatori**. In the courtyard, the fragments of a colossus of Constantine (once mounted on a wooden body in the apse of the Basilica of Maxentius) speak, like Ozymandias, of shattered glory. On a landing before the first floor, four reliefs from a monument to Marcus Aurelius show scenes of the emperor sacrificing, driving a triumphal chariot, bestowing clemency on captives (with the exact same gesture as in his equestrian statue), and receiving the orb of power. The Cavaliere d'Arpino frescoed the giant main room with episodes from the reigns of the early kings; usually there are temporary exhibitions here, of intermittent interest. Two dynamic statues of Popes Urban VIII and Innocent X wave at each other across the room. The small rooms beyond house precious Roman bronzes, including the charming *Spinario*, the stark bronze head of Mar-

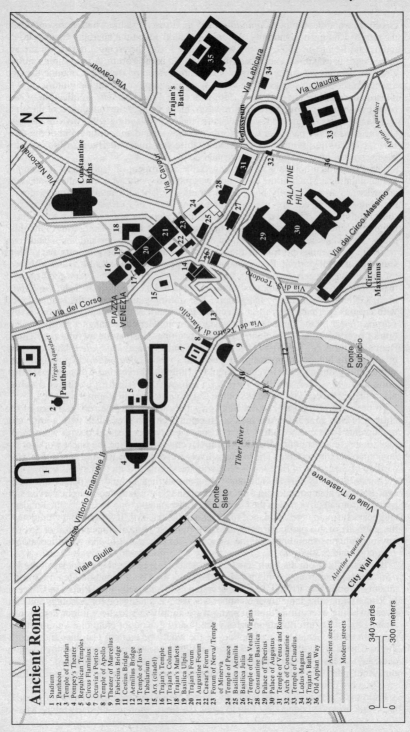

Ancient Rome

1 Stadium
2 Pantheon
3 Temple of Hadrian
4 Pompey's Theater
5 Republican Temples
6 Circus Flaminius
7 Octavia's Portico
8 Temple of Apollo
9 Theater of Marcellus
10 Fabricius Bridge
11 Cestius Bridge
12 Aemilius Bridge
13 Temple of Iovis
14 Tabularium
15 Arx (citadel)
16 Trajan's Temple
17 Trajan's Column
18 Trajan's Markets
19 Basilica Ulpia
20 Trajan's Forum
21 Augustine Forum
22 Caesar's Forum
23 Forum of Nerva/Temple
   of Minerva
24 Temple of Peace
25 Basilica Aemilia
26 Basilica Julia
27 Temple of the Vestal Virgins
28 Constantine Basilica
29 Palace of Tiberius
30 Palace of Augustus
31 Temple of Venus and Rome
32 Arch of Constantine
33 Temple of Claudius
34 Ludus Magnus
35 Trajan's Baths
36 Old Appian Way

— Ancient streets
— Modern streets

340 yards

300 meters

cus Brutus, and the famous *Capitoline Wolf*, an Etruscan statue which has symbolized the city of Rome since antiquity. Antonio Pollaiulo added the cherubic figures of Romulus and Remus in 1509. On the walls are the *Fasti*, the archival records of the ancient Pontifex Maximus, excavated from the Regia in the Forum. A final room exhibits a rare ancient greyhound and Bernini's serpentine *Head of Medusa*. Continue through a room frescoed with scenes of the Punic War (by a pupil of the divine Pinturicchio) to a last gallery of ancient sculpture. Here is another *Venus Pudens*, a collection of rare bronzes, a room of Etruscan red-figure vases, and a view of the foundation of the great temple to Jupiter Optimus Maximus. Stairs lead up to a landing with two vibrant polychrome *opus sectile* panels of tigers (3rd century AD) and an acerbic relief of the *Apotheosis of Sabina*, who rises to heaven while her husband Hadrian looks to his boyfriend Antinous, waiting on the ground below.

The **Pinacoteca** houses a mostly forgettable assortment of 16th- and 17th-century Italian paintings. Much of the collection was pilfered by the Vatican Galleries, leaving an awkward array of badly hung and sporadically labeled canvases. Among the remaining masterpieces are Veronese's stunning *Rape of Europa* and (in the second room) Bellini's *Portrait of a Young Man*, Titian's *Baptism of Christ* and a selection of religious scenes by Domenico, son of the more famous Jacopo, Tintoretto. In the third room van Dyck's portrait of the engravers Pieter de Jode, father and son, stands out, while an anonymous portrait of the aged Michelangelo stares gloomily back. Note Guido Reni's self-portrait. Pass through a collection of second-rate 14th- and 15th-century unknown masters and a room full of bronzes and porcelains (very good ones, if that's your cup of tea). If you missed the original of Caravaggio's *St. John the Baptist* in the Galleria Doria, a copy hangs here. The smiling youth fondles the Lamb of God with curious (perhaps improper) affection. Better still is the recently restored *Gypsy Fortune-Teller* by the same artist, in a nearby room. Here also hangs a ghastly collection of overindulgent 17th-century Baroque painting. Gasp at the awfulness of Guido Reni's *Lucretia, St. Sebastian, Beata Anima,* and *Penitent Madgalen*, but hold your breath for the hideous monstrosity of Guercino's vast *St. Petronilla*. Guercino adds insult to injury during your fevered retreat by flinging *Antony and Cleopatra, St. Matthew and the Angel,* and the *Persian Sybil* at your stinging eyeballs. Feeling masochistic? Proceed to the works of the Carracci brothers in Room 9.

To the right of the Palazzo dei Senatori, stairs lead up to the rear entrance of the **church of Sta. Maria in Aracoeli**, a 7th-century church now filled with a jumble of monuments from every century since. Cross the pavement, studded with worn medieval tombs, to the stunning **Bufalini Chapel**, considered among the finest works of the incomparable Pinturicchio. The master's lively frescoes of the life and death of St. Bernardino of Siena and of St. Francis receiving the stigmata, with four sybils in the vault, are masterpieces of early Renaissance Roman painting. Behind the patchwork medieval-Baroque altar complex, in a small chapel, the Santo Bambino—a relic carved supposedly from an olive tree in the Garden of Gethsemane—reposes in swaddled majesty and bears suspicious resemblance to a Cabbage Patch Kid. If you need an antidote to the schmaltz of this particular venerated object, pause to gaze at the portrait of St. Antony of Padua by the almost divine Benozzo Gozzoli, pupil of Fra Angelico. (Open 7am-noon and 5:30-7pm.)

Down the hill from the back stairs of the Aracoeli are several good views of the Forum (consider returning at night, when the ruins take on a romantic gleam), and the gloomy **Mamertine Prison**, later consecrated as the **church of St. Pietro in Carcere**. In Roman times the dank lower chamber was used as a dungeon for prisoners and captives awaiting execution (though some were simply left to die without ceremony). Among the more unfortunate inmates were Jugurtha, King of Numidia; Vercingetorix, chieftain of the Gauls; the accomplices of the would-be dictator Catiline; and according to Christian tradition, both SS Peter and Paul, to whom the upper church is now dedicated. Steps lead down to the Forum of Julius Caesar and the entrance to the Forum Romanum (see below). (Prison open daily 9am-12:30pm and 2-5:30pm. Admission free but donation requested.)

From the Campidoglio, two parks are accessible and provide great spots for picnicking. Walk around via delle Tre Pile to reach the first; climb up the stairs by the Museo

Nuovo (passing through a *loggia*) to reach the wilder, less-visited second, with views of the Palatine Hill. It's a good idea to avoid these parks at night unless you are a gay man, as they're one of Rome's more-frequented male pick-up spots, and straights may get a less-than-friendly reception.

The Forum Romanum and the Palatine Hill

> Turn all the pages of history, but Fortune never produced a greater example of her own fickleness than the city of Rome, once the most beautiful and magnificent of all that ever were or will be... not a city in truth, but a certain part of heaven.
> —Poggio Bracciolini

In the midst of the countless, scattered stones of the Roman Forum there is a small, truncated column that lies almost forgotten at the foot of the Capitol Hill. This was the **Umbilicus Urbis**, the "navel of the city," set up to mark the geographical center of the ancient urbs, and more than any other monument in this field of broken treasures it represents what the Roman Forum was and still may be—not just the physical center of ancient Rome, the nodal point of all political, economic, social, and religious life, but also the seat from which the Empire was ruled, to which every Roman citizen from England to Persia looked for government, and on which almost every city of Europe, the Middle East, and North Africa was at one time modeled. For a thousand years, these few acres of dusty, low-lying valley were the grandest and most beautiful in existence, the pattern for the ideal European city and the unquestioned center of the Western world.

Today, the vicissitudes of time and neglect have sadly stripped the Forum of its monumental masses, but even the few eroded remains provide daunting testimony to the unparalleled splendor Rome once enjoyed. Though it can be a hot and confusing place on a summer day, there is still no other place on earth like it. (Forum, Palatine, and Forum Antiquarium open Mon. and Wed.-Sat. 9am-6pm, Sun. and Tues. 9am-2pm; winter Mon. and Wed.-Sat. 9am-3pm, Sun. and Tues. 9am-2pm. Admission L10,000.)

The Forum was orginally a marshy valley prone to flooding from the Tiber. Rome's earliest Iron Age inhabitants eschewed its low, unhealthy swampiness in favor of the Palatine Hill, descending only to bury their dead. In the 8th and 7th centuries BC, Etruscans and Greeks using the Tiber Island as a crossing point for their trade brought prosperity to the area, and the forum was used as a weekly market. The early Romans came down from the Palatine, paved the area, drained it with a covered sewer, and built their first religious shrines to the vital natural forces of fire and water. Commercial success went hand in hand with political power, and by the 6th century BC (the traditional date being 510), the Romans had kicked out their Etruscan overlords and established a republic. The Curia (the meeting place of the Senate), the Comitium Well (or assembly place), and the Rostra (or speaker's platform) were built to serve the infant democracy, along with the earliest temples (to Saturn and to Castor and Pollux) dedicated in thanks for the civic revolution.

The conquest of Greece in the 2nd century BC brought new architectural forms home to the city, including the lofty basilica, which was first used as a center for business and judicial activities; the wealthiest Roman families (including Julius Caesar's) lined the town square in front of the Curia with basilicas, to the good of the public and of their own reputations. The Forum was never reserved for any single activity, and it was during these centuries that it was at its busiest, as senators debated the fates of far-flung nations over the din of haggling traders. The Vestal Virgins built their house over a street full of prostitutes, priests sacrificed in the temples, victorious generals led triumphal processions up to the Capitol and pickpockets cased the tourists, as they still do today.

The Forum witnessed the death throes of the Republic in the tumultuous 1st century BC. Cicero's orations against the antics of corrupt young aristocrats echoed off the temple walls, and Julius Caesar's murdered corpse was cremated amidst rioting crowds. Augustus, Caesar's great-nephew, adopted son, and the first Emperor, exploited the Forum to support his new government, closing off the old town square with a temple to the newly deified Caesar and a triumphal arch honoring himself. His successors clotted the old markets with successively grander tokens of their own majesty—the marble temples and arches which still stand are mostly remnants of these later autocrats and their insatiable need to glorify themselves. The Forum still resonated with the ideals of republican liberty, however, and increasingly despotic emperors found it convenient to divert the flow of public life away from its archaic precincts. The construction of the imperial palace on the Palatine Hill and of new fora on higher ground to the north cleared out the old neighborhoods that had surrounded the square, and by the 2nd century AD, the Forum, though packed with gleaming white monuments, had become a cold, cavernous, and nearly deserted ceremonial space.

Barbarian invaders of the 5th century burned and stripped much of the Forum even before the Christian government of the city ordered the pagan temples closed. In the middle ages many buildings were converted to churches and fortresses; what marble remained disappeared into the smoldering lime-kilns of farmers eager for cheap fertilizer. The Forum, its pavements grown over with weeds and its monuments half-sunk in the ground, became known as the *Campo Vaccino*, a cow-pasture, and with the onslaught of the Renaissance the last bits of its marble were quarried by popes looking to revive Roman glories in their own monumental constructions. Excavations, begun in 1803, have uncovered a vast array of remnants great and trivial, but have also rendered the site extremely confusing—the remains of structures built over and on top of each other for more than a thousand years are now exposed to a single view. To really understand the chaotic collage of stone and brick, invest in a copy of Pietro Romanelli's *The Roman Forum* (on sale at the ticket office, L8000); but a morning spent just soaking in the sheer vastness of the decay can be just as instructive-the triumph and collapse of one of the world's great civilizations seeps from every overgrown pile of stones.

The Forum

The best way to see the Forum is to start early in the day, take it slow, and be prepared to be exhausted. It's a big, complicated place, a favorite of slow-moving tour groups, and it gets hot and dusty in the middle of the day. Take a bottle of water. From the entrance gate in via dei Fori Imperiali, a ramp descends, past the Temple of Antoninus and Faustina on the left and the remains of the Basilica Aemilia on the right, to the basalt stones of the **via Sacra**, the main thoroughfare of the Forum and the oldest street in Rome. The via Sacra leads right to the slopes of the Capitol Hill. Refer to our map to orient yourself.

The Civic Center

Turn right at the end of the entrance ramp; you will be on the via Sacra facing the Capitoline Hill. The via Sacra cuts through the old market square and civic center of republican Rome, bordered by the **Basilica Aemilia** and the intact brick **Curia** building to your right. The Basilica, built in 179 BC, housed the guild of the *argentarii*, or money-changers, who operated the first *cambi* in the city, providing Roman *denarii* for traders and tourists. Up the steps of the basilica, the broken bases of columns are all that remains of the great aisled interior. To the rear and right are casts of the decorative frieze, with reliefs of the *Rape of the Sabine Women* and the *Death of Tarpeia*. After Romulus founded his Palatine city, his pioneer Romans needed brides, and so invited their neigbors the Sabines to games and a feast. When the Sabines were drunk enough, Romulus gave the signal and his men hauled the Sabine women back up the Palatine. Later, the Roman girl Tarpeia offered to get the women back for the Sabines, but that chivalrous tribe killed her instead for her treachery. The basilica was rebuilt several times after fires; in the pavement you can see melted bronze coins which the *argentarii* lost during these blazes. The Curia, or Senate House, was one of the oldest buildings in the Forum, although the present structure dates from the time of Diocletian (283 AD); it was converted to a church and only restored in this century. Occasionally the interior is open; you can see an intricate (and very well-preserved) inlaid marble pavement and the steps where the Senators brought their own portable chairs to their meetings.

The broad space in front of the Curia was the **Comitium Well**, or assembly place, where male citizens came to vote. The brick platform to the left of the Curia was the **Rostra**, or speaker's platform, named for the beak-shaped prows of ships which were mounted here after a Roman naval victory at the Battle of Anzio in 338 BC. Senators and consuls orated to the Roman plebs from here, and any citizen could mount to voice his opinion. The hefty **Arch of Septimius Severus** is really an anomaly in this republican square; dedicated in 203 AD to celebrate that emperor's victories in the Middle East, the arch reliefs depict the imperial family. Severus's successor Caracalla grabbed the throne by knocking off his brother Geta, and scraping his portrait off the arch. Halfway up the Capitol Hill, the grey tufa walls of the **Tabularium**, once the repository of senate archives, now serve as the basement to the Renaissance **Palazzo dei Senatori**. Across the square, the **Basilica Julia**, built on the site of an earlier basilica by Julius Caesar in 54 BC, followed the same plan as the Basilica Aemilia but was used by tribunals of judges for administering justice. Look for inscribed grids and circles in the steps where anxious Romans, waiting their turn to go before the judge, played an ancient version of tic-tac-toe.

Archaic Shrines

This part of the Forum, the original market square, was graced by a number of shrines and sacred precincts. Before they built a single bombastic marble temple, the Romans revered the forces of nature with quiet, Italic superstition. Between the Curia and the Basilica Julia, a flat grey stone—the **Lapis Niger**—covers what may have been a *heroon*, or funerary monument, to Romulus, the legendary founder of the city. The shrine was considered ancient even during the Republic, when its statuary and honorific column were covered by the forbidding grey pavement. Below, the oldest Latin inscription around, dating from the 6th century BC, warns against dumping garbage on the shrine. Closer to the Basilica Julia, the **Three Sacred Trees** of Rome—olive, fig, and grapevine—have been replanted. On the other side, a circular tufa basin commemorates the **Lacus Curtius**, an ancient spring where, legend says, a gaping chasm opened in 362 BC, into which the Roman patrician Marcus Curtius threw himself in order to save the city. A relief records his sacrifice.

Temples

The three great temples of the lower Forum (to Saturn, to the Emperor Vespasian, and to Concord) have been closed off during excavations, although the columns of the **Temple of Saturn** are emerging from their shroud of scaffolding at the Capitoline end of the Basilica Julia. At the far end of the Basilica Julia, three white marble columns and a shred of architrave mark the massive podium of the **Temple of Castor and Pollux**, dedicated in 484 BC in celebration of the Roman rebellion against their Etruscan king, Tarquinius Superbus, in 510 BC. Tarquin, who had brutally raped the Roman matron Lucretia, was ejected from Rome by her outraged family. He returned with an Etruscan army and would have defeated the Romans at the Battle of Lake Regillus in 499 BC had the twin gods Castor and Pollux not miraculously routed the enemy. Legend says that immediately after the battle the twins appeared in the Forum to water their horses at the adjacent **Shrine of Juturna**, now marked by a reconstructed marble *aedicule* to the left of the gods' own temple. Across the street is the rectangular base of the **Temple of the Deified Julius**, which Augustus built in 29 BC to honor his murdered adoptive father, and to proclaim himself the son of a god. The circular altar in front marks the spot where Caesar's body was cremated (he was assassinated near Largo Argentina); pious Romans still leave flowers here on the Ides of March. The circular building behind the temple is the restored **Temple of Vesta**, on a foundation dating back to the time of the Etruscans. Built in imitation of an archaic round Latin hut, this is where the Vestal Virgins tended the sacred fire of the city, keeping it continuously alight for more than a thousand years. As long as they obeyed the rules of virginity, the

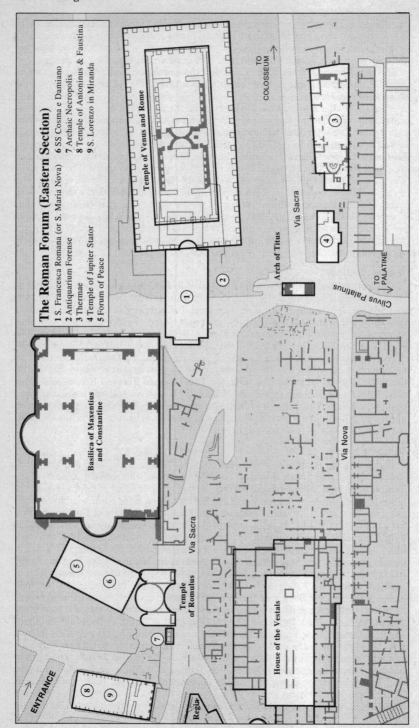

The Roman Forum (Eastern Section)

1 S. Francesca Romana (or S. Maria Nova)
2 Antiquarium Forense
3 Thermae
4 Temple of Jupiter Stator
5 Forum of Peace
6 SS Cosma e Damiano
7 Archaic Necropolis
8 Temple of Antoninus & Faustina
9 S. Lorenzo in Miranda

Temple of Venus and Rome

TO COLOSSEUM

Via Sacra

Arch of Titus

Clivus Palatinus

TO PALATINE

Basilica of Maxentius and Constantine

Via Sacra

Via Nova

Temple of Romulus

House of the Vestals

Regia

ENTRANCE

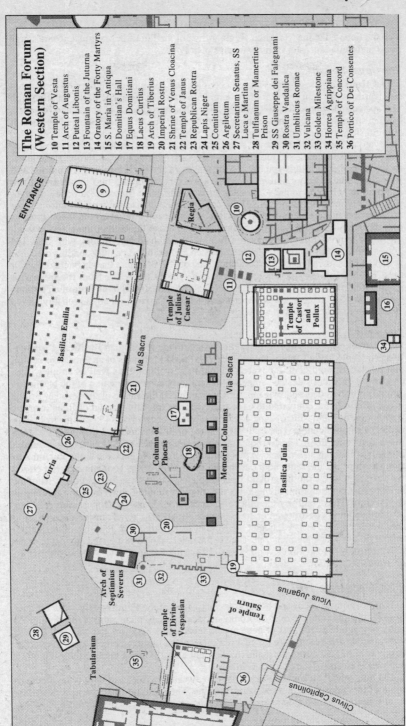

The Roman Forum (Western Section)

10 Temple of Vesta
11 Arch of Augustus
12 Puteal Libonis
13 Fountain of the Juturna
14 Oratory of the Forty Martyrs
15 S. Maria in Antiqua
16 Domitian's Hall
17 Equus Domitiani
18 Lacus Curtius
19 Arch of Tiberius
20 Imperial Rostra
21 Shrine of Venus Cloacina
22 Temple of Janus
23 Republican Rostra
24 Lapis Niger
25 Comitium
26 Argiletum
27 Secretarium Senatus, SS Luca e Martina
28 Tulfianum or Mamertine Prison
29 SS Giuseppe dei Falegnami
30 Rostra Vandalica
31 Umbilicus Romae
32 Vulcana
33 Golden Milestone
34 Horrea Agrippiana
35 Temple of Concord
36 Portico of Dei Consentes

ENTRANCE

Basilica Emilia

Repia

Temple of Julius Caesar

Via Sacra

Temple of Castor and Pollux

Column of Phocas

Memorial Columns

Via Sacra

Basilica Julia

Curia

Arch of Septimius Severus

Temple of Divine Vespasian

Temple of Saturn

Tabularium

Vicus Jugarius

Clivus Capitolinus

Vestals were amongst the most powerful and respected women in Ancient Rome. Behind the temple lay the triangular **Regia**, office of the Pontifex Maximus, Rome's high priest and titular ancestor of the Vatican's own Pope.

The Upper Forum

The **House of the Vestal Virgins** occupied the sprawling complex of rooms and courtyards to the right and rear of the temple to Vesta, in the shade of the Palatine Hill. The six virgins who officiated over Vesta's rites, each ordained at the age of seven, lived in spacious seclusion here above the din of the Forum. Fine living had its price; if a virgin strayed from her celibacy she was buried alive. In the central, fountain-filled courtyard of the vestal's house are statues of the priestesses, including one whose name was scraped away after she turned Christian. A tour through the storerooms and lower rooms of the house brings you back to the via Sacra and the **Temple of Antoninus and Faustina**, whose lofty columns and frieze were incorporated into the **church of S. Lorenzo in Miranda** in the 12th century (its façade dates from the Baroque). Antoninus, one of the "good emperors" of the 2nd century AD, had the temple built in honor of his wife Faustina, who died in 141; the Roman people returned the favor after his own death, and the temple now stands to commemorate the both of them. In the shadow of the temple (to the right as you face it), the archaic **Necropolis**, with Iron Age graves from the 8th century BC, was excavated earlier in this century, lending credence to the Romans' own legendary foundation date of 753 BC. Here the via Sacra runs over the **Cloaca Maxima**, the ancient sewer that still drains water from the otherwise marshy valley. The street then passes what is called the **Temple of Romulus**, a round building that still retains its ancient bronze doors. Not a temple at all, it probably served as the office of the urban praetor during the Empire.

The Velia

The street now leads out of the Forum proper to the gargantuan **Basilica of Maxentius**. The three gaping arches are actually only the side chapels of an enormous central hall whose coffered ceiling covered the entire gravel court, as well as another three chapels on the other side. The emperor Maxentius began construction of the basilica in 306 AD, but was deposed by Emperor Constantine at the Battle of the Milvian Bridge in 312. Constantine converted to Christianity during the battle, and though he oversaw completion of the basilica, some pagan reverence for the Forum kept him from ever dedicating it as a church. (He built the basilica of S. Giovanni in Laterano instead, on much the same plan.) The Baroque façade of the **church of S. Francesca Romana** (built over Hadrian's Temple to Venus and Rome) hides the entrance to the **Forum Antiquarium** (open the same hours as the Forum). Most of the rooms have been closed for years, but a few on the ground floor display funerary urns and skeletons from the necropolis. On the summit of the Velia, the shoulder running down from the Palatine, is the **Arch of Titus**, built by the otherwise ungenerous Emperor Domitian to celebrate his brother Titus's destruction of Jerusalem in 70 AD. The reliefs inside the arch, covered for restoration in 1992, depict the Roman sack of the great Jewish temple, including the pillage of a giant menorah. The via Sacra leads to an exit on the other side of the hill, an easy way to get to the Colosseum. To see the Palatine, follow the street past Titus's arch up the hill.

The Palatine Hill

The flowering gardens and broad grassy expanses of the **Palatine Hill** make for a refreshing change from the dusty Forum—an ideal place to picnic after a morning in the ruins. Though there are lots of ancient remnants to see here too, the cool breezes and sweeping views of Rome are the real reason to make the steep climb from below. The best way to begin is from the stairs (to the right after the street turns at the Arch of Titus) which ascend to the Farnese Gardens.

The hill, actually a square plateau rising between the Tiber and the Forum, contains some of the oldest and "newest" Roman ruins. The first and final chapters of the ancient Empire unfolded atop its heights. The she-wolf that suckled Romulus and Remus had her den here, and it was here that Romulus built the first walls and houses of the city (a legend supported by the discovery of 9th-century BC huts on the southeastern side of the hill). In the republic the Palatine was the city's most fashionable residential quarter, where aristocrats and statesmen (including Cicero) built their homes. Augustus, who was born here, lived in a surprisingly modest house, but his successor emperors capitalized on the hill's prestige by building progressively more gargantuan quarters for themselves and their courts. By the end of the 1st century AD, the imperial residence had swallowed up the entire hill, whose Latin name, *Palatium,* became synonymous with the palace that now dominated it. After the fall of Rome, the hill suffered the same fate as the Forum, though Byzantine ambassadors and even popes sometimes set up house in the crumbling palace. Various medieval families built fortresses and towers out of the ruins, and the Farnese family's gardens still remain partially intact on the side overlooking the Forum.

The staircase from the Arch of Titus ascends through the Farnese Gardens, past a *nymphaeum,* or enclosed fountain room, to a series of terraces with excellent views of the Forum and the city. From the top, take a right through avenues of roses and orange trees until you reach another terrace, with a breathtaking view of the Forum, the Imperial Fora, and the Quirinal Hill. The gardens continue along the western side of the hill, where an octagonal box-hedge maze in the center follows the layout of a real maze excavated from the Palace of Tiberius underneath (this was excavated early in this century, but the practical Romans decided the gardens had really been nicer, and filled the dig back in). At the southwest corner, another terrace looks out over the Capitoline Hill, the republican temples of the Forum Boarium and (across the river) the ridge of the Gianicolo. Steps lead down to covered excavations of the 9th century BC village, wishfully labeled the **casa di Romulo**. The Iron Age inhabitants (who might indeed have included that legendary twin) built their oval huts out of wood, so all that remains are the holes they sunk into the tufa bedrock for their roof-posts. The overgrown lump to the right is the podium of the **Temple of Cybele**, whose cult statue now sits in an arch from the foundation of Tiberius's palace. Further along, the republican **House of Livia** is occasionally open. Livia, Augustus's wife, the first Roman Empress and, according to Robert Graves's *I, Claudius,* an "abominable grandmother," had the house, with its vestibule, courtyard and three vaulted living rooms, connected to Augustus's own house next door (now closed). The three rooms are decorated with rare Roman wall paintings, including trompe l'oeuil architectural motifs and mythological scenes.

Around the corner, the long, spooky **Cryptoporticus** connected Tiberius's palace with the later buildings on this side of the hill. Used by slaves and imperial couriers, it may have been built by Nero in one of his more paranoid moments, as a secret passage. It's easy to imagine the whispers of assasins and informants echoing along its gloomy, stuccoed vaults. The short end of the tunnel brings you up to the vast ruins of the solemn **Domus Augustana**, the imperial palace built by Domitian (81-96 AD) and used by most of the subsequent emperors as the headquarters of the empire. To the left, three (currently fenced-off) brick rooms served as a basilica, throne room, and shrine to the imperial cult. The exterior walls, even in their ruined state, are so high that archaeologists are still unsure how they were roofed over. The broad square to the right was a huge, open-air colonnaded courtyard, graced by an octagonal fishpond in the center. To the south of the court, a sunken **Triclinium**, or dining room, hosted imperial banquets between a set of twin oval fishponds (decorated with niches for statuary). On the other side of the Triclinium, a walkway offers a sweeping view of the grassy **Circus Maximus** and (further off to the left) of the **Baths of Caracalla**. The ground gives way at the end of the terrace, and the multi-layered labyrinth of the central palace gapes below. Arranged around a central court (with yet another fishpond), the private rooms of the Emperor and his household burrow far into the hill-imperial paranoia ran deep. You can't descend into the court, but a few brick rooms are still intact on the surface level. The square holes in the brickwork show where polished marble slabs once lined the palace walls. The **Palatine Antiquarium** remains closed for restoration. The easternmost wing of the palace contains the curious **Stadium**, a sunken oval space once surrounded by a colonnade. Once thought to have been a private racetrack, it seems now that it was used as a garden. From the palace, the Cryptoporticus leads back to the Farnese Gardens; a road leads straight down the hill from the throne room, or you can take a path down from the Stadium to an exit on via di Gregorio Magno, a hundred yards down from the Colosseum.

Imperial Fora

The **Fori Imperiali** sprawl across the street from the old Forum Romanum, a vast conglomeration of temples, basilicas, and public squares constructed by the emperors of the 1st and 2nd centuries AD, partly in response to increasing congestion in the old forum. Julius Caesar was the first to expand the city center in this direction, though he was motivated as much by political reasons as by civic spirit. The forum and temple he built in honor of Venus, his legendary ancestress, seriously undercut the prestige of the Senate and its older precinct around the Curia. Augustus, Vespasian, Nerva, and Trajan all followed suit, filling the flat space between the Forum and the Quirinal Hill with capacious monuments to their own greater glory. In the 1930s, Mussolini, with imperial aspirations of his own, cleared the area of medieval constructions and built the via dei Fori Imperiali to pass over the newly excavated remains. The fora were only partially excavated, and the broad, barren thoroughfare cuts across the old foundations at an awkward angle. The **Forum of Trajan**, the largest and most impressive of the lot, spreads below two Baroque churches at the eastern end of piazza Venezia. The complex was built between 107-113 AD to celebrate the emperor's victorious Dacian campaign (fought in modern Romania). Today you can see the broken columns of his colossal Basilica Ulpia and the nearly perfectly-preserved spiral of his famous **Trajan Column**, the greatest specimen of Roman relief-sculpture ever carved. The 200-meter-long continuous frieze wrapped around the column like a ribbon (which had to be carved *in situ*, after the marble had been mounted) narrates the Emperor's victorious campaigns against the Dacians; from the bottom you can survey Roman legionaries preparing supplies, building a stockaded camp and loading boats to cross the Danube. A statue of the emperor once crowned the column, but was destroyed in the middle ages, and his ashes are kept in the base of the column. "Stretched out" the spiral frieze would be 656 feet long, one of the most dense and ambitious of the ancient world. The sculptor faced several problems in creating this narrative; he had to let the pictures speak for themselves (there were no inscriptions), and they had to flow clearly from scene to scene. Furthermore, the pictures had to be more shallow than normal friezes, because more deeply sculpted figures would produce shadows on the other, lower scenes. Ultimately, the artist had to sacrifice spatial depth and architectural detail, which went against the grain of contemporary relief work. Here, the figures are piled on top of one another, and they stand on rising ground. A door in the base of the column opens into Trajan's tomb. (The Forum itself is closed.) Down the street (but reachable from via IV Novembre, 94, up the steps in via Magnanapoli) the **Markets of Trajan** provide a glimpse of daily life in the ancient city. The semicircular complex, built into the side of the Quirinal Hill, sheltered several levels of *tabernae*, or single-room stores, along cobbled streets. You can stroll along the basalt paving stones and climb to a spectacular view of Trajan's Forum and the Capitoline Hill. (Open Tues.-Sat. 9am-1:30pm, Sun. 9am-1pm; in summer also open Tues.-Sat. 4-7pm. Admission L3750.)

Across the via dei Fori Imperiali, in the shade of the Victor Emanuel Monument, the paltry remains of the **Forum of Caesar** lie beneath one of Rome's largest gypsy enclaves. A few reconstructed columns are all that remain of Caesar's famous **temple to Venus Genetrix** (Mother Venus), but the stone façades of the arcades he built to house Roman shops remain in better repair.

Adjacent to the Markets of Trajan, the great grey tufa wall of the **Forum of Augustus** backs up against the side of the Quirinal Hill. Dedicated by the Emperor in 2 BC in honor of Mars Ultor (Mars the Avenger), the huge complex commemorated Augustus's vengeful victory over Julius Caesar's murderers at the Battle of Philippi, and the founding of his new imperial dynasty. You can still see some of the columns from the porch of the central temple, as well as the roof-lines carved into the back wall. The wall, built to protect the precious new monument from the seamy Subura slums that once spread up the hill behind it, doesn't run exactly straight; legend says that when the land was being prepared for construction, even Augustus couldn't convince one stubborn homeowner to give up his domicile, and the great wall was built at an angle around it.

The aptly named **Forum Transitorium** was a narrow, rectangular space connecting Augustus's forum with the old Roman Forum and with the Forum of Vespasian near via Cavour. Most of it now lies under the street, although new excavations have begun over by the ticket office. The Emperor Nerva built it in 97 AD and wittily gave it a temple to Minerva, a pun on his own name. All that remains to view is a colossal doorway that once led into Vespasian's forum; between two gorgeous Corinthian columns is a relief of Minerva (the Roman Athena) and a decorative frieze. The only remnant of Vespasian's Forum (mostly under the via Cavour) is the **church of SS Cosma e Damiano** across the street, built in 527 AD out of a library in Vespasian's complex. The interior is brightened by a rare set of 6th-century mosaics.

Stairs over the Metro station lead up to an ill-kept park where the remains of Nero's **Domus Aurea** are secreted inside the Oppian Hill (the site itself is completely closed). The "Golden House" once spread over most of the hill, a labyrinthine collection of domed and vaulted passages, each lined in precious mosaic or fresco. The decorations of the palace are rightly famous; the *Laocoon* in the Vatican apparently decorated the fun-loving emperor's dining room, while the wall-paintings, discovered in the Renaissance when the subterranean rooms were thought to be grottoes, inspired the *grotteschi* motifs that are a hallmark of Renaissance decorative art. The few ruins you can see today were only part of the emperor's larger complex—having declared himself a living god, Nero took this whole part of Rome as his private quarters, building a palace on the Palatine to match the Domus Aurea here, with a lake in the valley in between (on the site of the Colosseum) and the Caelian Hill as a private garden. He converted the Forum into a vestibule to the palace and crowned it with a colossal statue of himself as the sun. The party didn't last long, however. Nero was assassinated only five years after building his gargantuan pleasure garden, and the more civic-minded Flavian emperors replaced all traces of it with monuments built for the public good. These included the Flavian Baths, built on top of the Domus Aurea, and the Colosseum, built over Nero's lake.

Colosseum

> As long the Colosseum stands, Rome shall stand
> When the Colosseum falls, Rome shall fall When
> Rome falls, the world shall end.
> —Lord Byron, Childe Harold

The **Colosseum**, named for the colossal statue of Nero that once stood nearby, stands as the enduring symbol of the Eternal City—a hollowed-out ghost of somber travertine marble that dwarfs every other ruin in the city. At its inauguration in 80 AD it could hold as many as 50,000 spectators; the first 100 days of operation saw some 5000 wild beasts perish in the bloody arena, and the slaughter didn't stop for three centuries. Gladiators fought each other here, and the elliptical interior could be flooded for mock sea battles. The outside of the arena, still well-preserved around three quarters of its circumference, provided the inspiration for countless Renaissance and Baroque architectural confections, the triple stories of Doric, Ionic, and Corinthian columns being considered the ideal orchestration of the classical orders. The raw interior comes as a bit of a disappointment; almost all the marble stands and seats were quarried by Renaissance popes for use in their own grandiose constructions, including the basilica of St. Peter's. The floor (now gone) lay over a labyrinth of brick cells, corridors, ramps, and elevators used for transporting wild animals from their cages up to the level of the arena.

When Mussolini created wide, paved roads to circle around the city's ancient monuments in efforts to emphasize their greatness, he also paved the way for their destruction. Today, the Colosseum is facing serious damage and deterioration due to the constant rush of traffic and pollution that tears around the structure. Hundreds of thousands of cars race past the great symbol of Rome each day; the ground beneath it shakes when the subway rumbles by. Homeless people camp under its arches, and young people climb over its iron gates for midnight rendezvous. The Colosseum now serves as a glorified traffic divider, marking the meeting place of several busy streets, despite its grand (if somewhat macabre) past. In 1992, the superintendent of city monuments made an urgent plea to the government to provide funding for its restoration, asking for at least 43 million dollars: ten times more than the minimal maintenance budget which just manages to pay for the clean-up of tourists' litter. The Banca di Roma recently pledged 35 million dollars for rescue work, though that is just a start. For any serious work to be done, the enitre via dei Fori Imperiale would have to be closed off to traffic and its corrosive fumes. For the past quarter century, the government has been considering marking off the entire area, from piazza Venezia to past the Colosseum, as an "archaeological park" closed to traffic. These restrictions would seriously aggravate the already horrible traffic conditions that plague the city, but the park's advocates insist that this is the only way to preserve the ancient monuments from complete collapse. So far, the government has made some minimal efforts to cut down on traffic. Hopefully, the government will start making more serious restoration efforts before we put Harold's prophesy to the test.

The ground level of the Colosseum is open daily; an ascent to the upper floors provides better views of the whole city (and of the nearby Forum). (Upper decks open Sun. and Wed. 9am-1pm, all other days 9am-3pm in winter, 9am-6pm in summer. Closes early on St. Peter's Day (June 29); go in the morning. Admission L6000.)

Between the Colosseum and the Palatine Hill lies the **Arch of Constantine**, one of the latest imperial monuments to grace this area and certainly one of the most intact. Though it straddled the tail end of the Forum's via Sacra since its dedicatation in 315 AD, recent excavations of an earlier garden park have obstructed most access to it. Constantine, after his conversion to Christianity by a vision of a flaming cross, built the arch to commemorate his victory over his rival Maxentius at the Battle of the Milvian Bridge in 312. The triple arch, though well-proportioned, is constructed almost entirely from sculptural fragments pillaged from older Roman monuments. The circular medallions were originally part of a monument to Hadrian and include depictions of his lover Antinous; the rectangular reliefs were taken down from Trajan's Forum and show incongruous scenes of that emperor's defeat of the Dacians.

Circus Maximus, Baths of Caracalla, and the Appian Way

Cradled in the valley between the Palatine and Aventine Hills (a few hundred feet down via S. Gregorio from the Colosseum), the **Circus Maximus** today offers only a dusty shadow of its former glories. Here upwards of 300,000 Romans gathered to watch the riotous, breakneck careenings of chariots round the quarter-mile track. The turning points of the track, now marked by a raised grassy hump, were perilously sharp by design, to ensure enough thrills and spills to keep the crowds happy. The best seats in the house were actually the Palatine palaces themselves, where the emperors built special terraces for viewing the carnage.

At the western end of the circus, **piazza di Porta Capena** marks the beginning of the **via Appia**, built in 312 BC and rightly called the queen of roads ever since. The via once traversed the whole peninsula, providing a straight and narrow path for legions heading to Brindisi and conquests in the East. It also witnessed the grisly crucifixion of Spartacus's rebellious slave army in 71 BC—their bodies are said to have lined the road from Rome all the way to Capua. Some of Italy's modern *autostradas* still follow that ancient path, but a sizeable portion leading out of the city remains in its antique state, with basalt paving stones, avenues of cypress trees, views of the Roman countryside, and crumbling necropoleis of tombs both pagan and Christian. It's a peaceful and evocative change from the more trammeled ruins inside the city. Buses #118 from the

The Appian Way

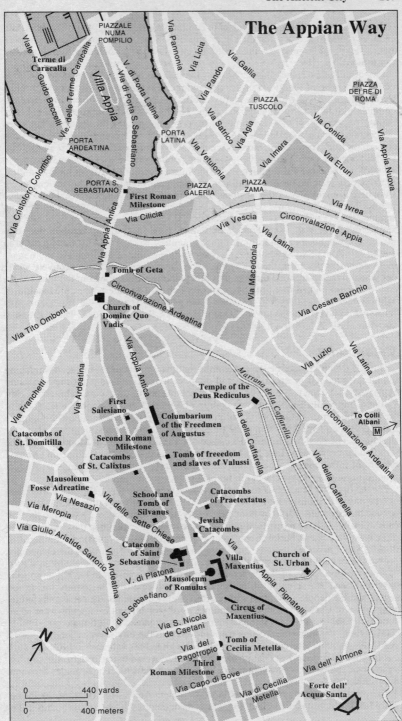

PIAZZALE
NUMA
POMPILIO

Viale di Guido Baccelli

**Terme di
Caracalla**

V. delle Terme Caracalla

Via Pannonia

Via Licia

Via Gallia

Via Pando

Villa Appia

V. di Porta Latina

Via di Porta S. Sebastiano

PIAZZA
TUSCOLO

PIAZZA
DEI RE DI
ROMA

Via Satrico

Via Agia

Via Cenida

Via Etruri

PORTA
ARDEATINA

PORTA
LATINA

Via Vetulonia

Via Imera

Via Appia Nuova

PORTA S.
SEBASTIANO

**First Roman
Milestone**

PIAZZA
GALERIA

PIAZZA
ZAMA

Via Ivrea

Via Cilicia

Via Appia Antica

Via Vescia

Circonvalazione Appia

Via Cristoforo Colombo

Via Latina

Tomb of Geta

Via Macedonia

Circonvalazione Ardeatina

Via Cesare Baronio

Via Tito Omboni

**Church of
Domine Quo
Vadis**

Via Appia Antica

Marrana della Caffarella

Via Luzio

Via Latina

Via Franchetti

**Temple of the
Deus Rediculus**

Circonvalazione Ardeatina

To Colli
Albani
M

Via Ardeatina

**First
Salesiano**

**Columbarium
of the Freedmen
of Augustus**

Via della Caffarella

**Catacombs of
St. Domitilla**

**Second Roman
Milestone**

**Catacombs
of St. Calixtus**

**Tomb of freedom
and slaves of Valussi**

Via della Caffarella

**Mausoleum
Fosse Adreatine**

**School and
Tomb of
Silvanus**

**Catacombs
of Praetextatus**

**Church of
St. Urban**

Via Nesazio

Via Meropia

Via delle Sette Chiese

**Jewish
Catacombs**

Via Giulio Aristide Sartorio

**Catacomb
of Saint
Sebastiano**

**Villa
Maxentius**

Via Appia Pignatelli

Via Ardeatina

V. di Platona

**Mausoleum
of Romulus**

Via di S. Sebastiano

Via S. Nicola
de Caetani

**Circus of
Maxentius**

N

**Tomb of
Cecilia Metella**

Via del
Pagotropio

**Third
Roman Milestone**

Via Capo di Bove

Via di Cecilia
Metella

Via dell' Almone

**Forte dell'
Acqua Santa**

0   440 yards

0   400 meters

Colosseum and #218 from S. Giovanni in Laterano whisk you over the first, traffic-laden miles of the road (get off at the Catacombs of S. Sebastiano to begin a tour on foot). Better yet, consider renting a bike from the city for an afternoon of pastoral (and not too arduous) exercise.

From the Porta Capena, the road passes the hulking remains of the **Baths of Caracalla**, the largest of their kind in the city and the best preserved. Though the ruthless Caracalla wasn't known for his kindly nature, his construction of this monumental complex did do the city some good—some 1600 heat-soaked Romans could sponge themselves off here at the same time. There is an entrance fee for the baths, but when the opera has taken up residence (and covered up much of the ancient site), entrance is sometimes free. The existing remains were once the center of the complex: a huge central hall opening onto a cold-water swimming pool on one side and a round warm-water pool on the other (in summer, under the opera stage). Outside the main complex, remains of a rectangular brick wall demark the outer boundary of the ancient health club; here Romans played sports, sipped juices in snack bars, and exercised their minds in a well-appointed library. (Open Tues.-Sat. 9am-3pm and Sun.-Mon. 9am-1pm; in summer Tues.-Sat. 9am- 6pm. Admission L6000.)

At a fork in the road, via di Porta S. Sebastiano heads out past the **Tomb of the Scipios**, one of republican Rome's most famous families, toward the city walls (closed in 1992). The **Porta San Sebastiano** is a fine example of one of the Romans' more ingenious defensive practices, the killing gate. The outside gate was left deceptively weak, but when invaders stormed through they found themselves trapped in the inner court, where archers picked them off like fish in a barrel. The gate houses a **Museum of Walls**, which lets artillery buffs clamber down a healthy stretch of the 3rd-century Aurelian walls and up into the towers. (Open Tues.-Sun. 9am-1pm; Tues., Thurs. and Sun. also 4pm-dusk. Admission L6000.)

Catacombs

Outside the city proper lie the **catacombs**, multistory condos for the dead, stretching tunnel after tunnel for up to 25km and on as many as five levels. Of the 51 around Rome, five are open to the public; the most notable are those of **San Sebastiano**, **San Callisto**, and **Santa Domitilla**, next door to one another on via Appia Antica south of the city. The Roman catacombs lie shrouded in mystery; no one can adequately explain how persecuted Christians found the time and the means to construct these elaborate structures. The best days to visit the catacombs are Friday through Monday, when the standard three are open. Take bus #118 from via Claudia near the Colosseum (20min.; beware of infrequent service. While admission varies, all the catacombs let student groups accompanied by a teacher in for half-price.)

For the first 200 years of Christianity in Rome, there were no established burial places (the pagan Romans preferred cremation). The Christians took their burial business outside the city walls. Little by little more underground tombs were carved into the volcanic rock beneath the property of philanthropic Romans, explaining the current size of these relatively cheap burial mazes (they had no cost besides labor). As the persecutions of the Christians increased along with the number of martyrs, the catacombs evolved from burial grounds of relatives to pilgrimage sites. At the height of the Christian persecution, some of the catacombs were officially closed down, but at no time were they used as a refuge or as housing. By the 4th century, Christianity was in full swing, and the people's attention shifted from merely expanding the catacombs to creating a city of Christian monuments and places of worship; all catacombs were abandoned with the exception of St. Sebastian's, which remained a pilgrimage site.

Over time, the martyrs' remains were moved into the city (every Catholic church must have its relic, after all) and the tombs were looted for valuables by Rome's various invaders. The long-lost death mazes were rediscovered in the 16th century by Antonio Bosio, but serious excavation didn't begin until the 19th century under Giovanni Baptista de Rossi.

The most impressive is **San Sebastiano**, via Appia Antica, 136 (tel. 788 70 35; fax 784 37 45), which stakes its claim to fame as the temporary home for the bodies of Peter and Paul (or so ancient *graffiti* on its walls suggest). This is the only catacomb that was never abandoned; it provided the derivation for the word catacomb (S. Sebastian's was originally called *ad catacumbus*). Running for 7 miles among three levels, and accommodating 174,000 dead, the tunnels here are eerily decorated with animal mosaics, disintegrating skulls, and fantastic symbols of early Christian iconography, still clearly discernible. In the church above stands Bernini's statue to St. Peter. (Catacombs open Wed.-Mon. 9am-noon and 2:30-5:30pm. Admission L6000, under 10 free.) The **Jewish catacombs** (Appia Antica, 119A) are at a fork in the road between Callisto and Sebastian but are not open to the public. Make a five-minute walk (follow the signs) to **San Callisto,** via Appia Antica, 110 (tel. 512 67 25), the largest catacombs in Rome (almost 22km of winding, subterranean paths) but neither as well-preserved nor as interesting as its smaller neighbors. (Open Thurs.-Tues. 8:30am-noon and 2:30-5:30pm. Admission L6000, under 10 free.) **Santa Domitilla,** via delle Sette Chiese, 283 (tel. 511 03 42), beyond and behind San Callisto, enjoys acclaim for its paintings—a 3rd-century portrait of Christ and the Apostles is still intact—and for its collection of inscriptions from tombstones and sarcophagi. (Open Fri.-Wed. 8:30am-noon and 2:30-5:30pm. Admission L6000.) In all three catacombs, visitors follow a guided tour in the language of their choice, although non-English tours are significantly less crowded (every 20min., free with admission). Santa Domitilla receives very few visitors, so you're almost assured of a personalized tour. Because the catacombs have winding, uneven paths and the tours are conducted briskly (especially in the over-crowded summer), they are not recommended for people who are claustrophobic or have difficulty walking.

If you wish to see another burial place, visit the **church of Sant'Agnese Fuori le Mura,** northwest of the city center at via Nomentana, 349 (tel. 832 07 43). Take bus #38 from Termini. Perhaps the best preserved in Rome, the catacombs here contain skeletons of the saint's Christian followers. Before descending into the catacombs, look above the apse for the extraordinary Byzantine-style mosaic of St. Agnes with a pair of popes. St. Agnes was the 12-year-old who was martyred by Diocletian for refusing to marry—her heart was pledged to God. (see piazza Navona, above, for the whole story on St. Agnes). (Open Sept.-July 9am-noon and 4-6pm. Closed mornings of festivals. Guided tours with admission, L6000.) More 4th-century mosaics await in the **church of Santa Costanza** next door. Originally built by Constantinia (the saintly daughter of Constantine I who was cured of leprosy when sleeping on Sant'Agnese's tomb and therefore converted to Christianity) as a mausoleum for herself, it was transformed into a baptistry and, in the 13th century, a church. Also nearby are the **Priscilla catacombs,** via Salaria, 430 (tel. 83 84 08. Open Tues.-Sun. 8:30am-noon and 2:30-5:30pm; in off-season 8:30am-noon and 2:30-5:30pm. Admission L6000.)

Down the road from the catacombs the **Villa of Maxentius,** Constantine's unfortunate predecessor, lies half-buried in cricket-filled greenery. The Emperor built the villa in the first decade of the 4th century but never got to enjoy it, having been summarily ejected by the newly Christian Constantine at the Battle of the Milvian Bridge in 312 AD. His sprawling circus retains its seats and spina. The **Mausoleum of Romulus,** inside a giant brick portico, housed the remains of the emperor's son, who was named for the city's legendary founder.

At the top of the hill, the proud **Tomb of Cecilia Metella** towers over the road. Built in the 30s BC for the patrician Cecilia, the tomb was preserved by its conversion into a fortress in the middle ages (when its famous crenellations were added). The rest of the medieval complex, including a ruined gothic church, straddles both sides of the road. Beyond Cecilia's tomb, the Appian Way continues about 7km, through progressively more deserted countryside. Here the denuded remains of circular and turreted tombs, commemorative reliefs and steles line the road between the country villas of Rome's glitterati. If you're walking, keep in mind that the bus stops its service shortly after the catacombs.

The Esquiline and Caelian Hills

Horace called the **Esquiline Hill**, sloping south from Termini to the valley of the Colosseum in a gloomy stretch of cemeteries, the haunt of witches and ghosts. Today the hill may seem just as spooky, as its back alleys, churches, and parks are nearly deserted, and many of Rome's homeless and drug-addicted fill its two scruffy parks, piazza Vittorio Emanuele and Parco Oppio. But between ancient and modern disrepair, the Esquiline enjoyed several centuries of prosperity, first as a fashionable neighborhood for imperial villas, then as home to some of the earliest churches in the city. Medieval migration to the banks of the Tiber preserved the hill's ancient state. Like the Caelian Hill to the south, the area offers a glimpse of Rome in its darkest ages, filled with relics of imperial decay and monuments of the Christian Church in its infant centuries.

The **Basilica of Santa Maria Maggiore** (four blocks down via Cavour from Termini) occupies the summit of the Esquiline Hill. As one of the seven major basilicas of the city, it is officially a part of Vatican City. Both its front and rear façades are Rococo works, but its interior, built in 352 AD, is the best-preserved example of a paleochristian basilica in the city. The church has a long, rectangular plan, divided by antique columns into a central nave and two side aisles surmounted by clerestory windows, a flat ceiling, and a semi-circular apse behind the altar lined with gleaming mosaics. The coffered ceiling is believed to have been gilded with the first gold sent back by Columbus from America. The mosaics on the upper walls of the nave and on the triumphal arch before the altar date from the 5th century, when even Christian figures were depicted dressed in togas. The apse mosaic, from the 13th century, glitters with a magnificent scene of the *Coronation of the Virgin*. As with the reliefs on the Column of Trajan, the artisan had to depict biblical scenes to be read by the (mainly illiterate) church-goers, and at a great distance. While the Trajanic reliefs recount historical events, the narration of these mosaics needed to impart ahistorical and "un-eventful" ideals of living Scripture. In imparting these concepts, the mosaics rely more on meaningful glances and gestures than on specific details or dramatic movement, or even the use of three-dimensional form as in the Trajan column. The subterranean *confessio* before the altar contains a relic of the baby Jesus' crib (now sheathed in globs of silver). To the right of the altar, a simple marble slab marks the **tomb of Gianlorenzo Bernini**. In contrast to the medieval simplicity of the central church, the Pauline and Sistine Chapels on either side of the nave are monuments of High Renaissance excess, each lined with extravagant slabs of colored marble pillaged from nearby Roman ruins. (Church open daily 8am-7pm; dress code often enforced).

From p. Sta. Maria Maggiore (anchored by a votive pillar to the Virgin), via dell'Olmata leads, by an alley on the left, to the **church of Santa Prassede**, built in 822 and home to an extraordinary set of 9th-century mosaics. In the apse is the New Jerusalem, a triumphal lamb, and a host of celebratory apostles and elders. The tiny **chapel of St. Zeno** (lit by a coin-operated machine outside the door) in the right aisle is the only chapel in Rome lined entirely in mosaic. The walls are populated by various saints while in the vault four angels hold up a Byzantine Christ floating in a sea of gold. (Open 9am-noon and 4-6:30pm.) If you're hungering after more mosaics, the **church of Santa Pudenziana** (across p. dell'Esquilino, in via Urbana) contains the earliest of all in Rome, dating from 390 AD. The scene shows Christ enthroned with apostles in togas, and the city of Jerusalem represented by Roman basilicas and baths. (Open 9am-noon and 4-6pm.)

Via Merulana leads down the hill to the shabby p. Vittorio Emanuele, home to Rome's biggest food market (known for fish, vegetables, and heroin) or, on the right, to the equally unkempt **Parco Traiano** (or Parco Oppio), where the remnants of giant brick vaults from the Baths of Trajan, the Flavian Baths, and the Domus Aurea of Nero crumble in unmowed grass. Via delle Sette Sale skirts the park to the north, leading through a walled, cobbled, and utterly deserted rural area to the *piazza* and **church of San Pietro in Vincoli**. In the right aisle an unfinished fragment of Michelangelo's *Tomb of Julius II* is testament to the monumental frustration that artist suffered trying to complete his commission. In his original designs, the tomb was to be an enormous, free-standing rectangular structure decorated with over forty statues (among them the unfinished *Captives* in the Academia in Florence). Pope Julius quibbled over the cost, his successor popes stalled out of jealousy, and Michelangelo never found either time or money to finish what he had hoped would be his greatest work. His imposing **statue of Moses**, however, is a masterpiece in itself. The prophet, galvanized by the appearance of the Lord, turns and tenses every muscle in the strain of revelation. The anomalous goat horns protruding from his head are the result of a medieval misinterpretation of the Hebrew Bible. When Moses descended from Sinai with the Ten Commandments, according to Exodus, "rays" (similar to "horns" in Hebrew) shone from his brow. Flanking the Moses statue are Leah and Rachel, who represent the contemplative and active lives, respectively. Julius had wanted this to be the greatest funeral monument ever built; it's either tragic or just that he doesn't even lie in the sarcophagus (his remains were scattered in the 1527 sack of Rome). Under the altar of the church dangle the chains by which St. Peter was supposedly bound when imprisoned in the Tullianum prison on the Capitoline Hill. (Open 7am-12:30pm and 3:30-6pm.)

Though it is adjacent to the south side of the Esquiline Hill, perhaps the easiest way to begin an ascent of the **Caelian Hill** is from the valley of the Colosseum. Via di S. Giovanni leads away from the amphitheater to the multiple **churches of S. Clemente**. True to Roman traditions of building, the complex incorporates centuries of architecture and handiwork. The upper church, encrusted in Baroque stucco but dating from the 12th-century, is built over a 4th-century basilica which in turn rests on the ruins of a 1st-century Roman house and **Mithraeum**, all of which cover a still-operative system of republican drains and sewers, some 30 feet below the current street level. In the upper church are 12th-century mosaics of the Crucifixion, saints, and apostles, and a fresco cycle in the **chapel of Santa Caterina** by Masolino (possibly executed with help from his pupil Masaccio) dating from the 1420s, including scenes of the Annunciation and the Crucifixion. The marble choir enclosure, with its pulpits and candlestick, was originally part of the lower church and dates from the 6th century. In the lower church (admission L2000) the original plan is obscured by newer piers and walls built to support the upper church. With a little imagination, you can trace the lines of the original nave, aisles and apse, all of which retain traces of rare 11th-century frescoes. A second stair leads further underground to the dank imperial ruins and Mithraeum (behind iron bars). According to myth, the Persian god Mithras created the world by slaughtering an enormous bull, out of whose slit throat the universe came pouring. Devotees of Mithras's cult always met in darkened rooms to recreate the slaughter in a festive (and sanguine) banquet. After the Mithraeum, a warren of brick and stone rooms lies over a rushing republican sewer. (Open Mon.-Sat. 9am-noon and 3:30-6:30pm, Sun. and holidays 10am-noon and 3:30-6:30pm.)

Up the street, on via dei Querceti, the solemn **church of Santi Quattro Coronati** lies fortified behind medieval battlements. The church itself is remarkable more for its strange shape and overly wide apse than for any decoration, but the little **chapel of St. Silvester** off the entrance courtyard contains an extraordinary fresco cycle of the life of the Emperor Constantine painted in 1248 (ring the bell of the convent; the cloistered nuns will send you a key on an automated lazy susan). The medieval cloister (ring from inside the church) hides the prettiest, quietest garden spot in the city.

Via dei Santi Quattro Coronati leads up the hill to the grandiose **church of San Giovanni in Laterano**, the cathedral of the diocese of Rome and, as such, the mother church of the entire Catholic faith. The church and adjoining Lateran Palace, accorded the same rights of extraterritoriality as the Vatican City, were the chief residence and church used by the popes until their flight to Avignon in the 14th century. The church itself, though now a confusing jumble of medieval and Baroque decoration, is actually the oldest Christian basilica in the city, founded by Constantine in 314 AD. The traditional pilgrimage route from St. Peter's ends here, and the Pope still celebrates festival masses on occasion. On Corpus Christi, the June 18 commemoration of Christ's Easter sacrifice, a triumphal procession including the College of Cardinals, the Swiss Guard, and hundreds of Italian girl scouts leads the pontiff back to the Vatican after the service. The doors of the main entrance, facing the Porta San Giovanni, were pillaged from the Curia, the Roman Senate House in the Forum. Inside, the old basilical plan (notable for its four aisles) has been obscured by the 17th-century remodeling by Borromini, who encased the antique columns in enormous piers to make niches for statues of the apostles. The giant Gothic *baldacchino* over the altar houses two golden reliquaries with the heads of SS. Peter and Paul inside. A door to the left of the altar leads to the 13th-century **cloister** (admission L1000), a space far more modest and peaceful than the riotous church interior. The twisted double columns are typical of the work of the Cosmati family, who designed them and many other stone projects, including the pavements of inlaid red and green marble that seem to pave every church in the city. (Church and cloister open 7am-7pm; modest dress code rigorously enforced.) Outside the church and to its right the **Baptistery of St. John**, the oldest in the city, maintains its 4th-century character. An octagonal building filled with mosaics and antique columns, it was probably the model for its more famous cousin baptistery in Florence. (Open 8am-noon and 4-6pm). Across the busy piazza di San Giovanni (marked by an Egyptian obelisk from the 5th century BC—yet again, the oldest in the city) the **Scala Santa** houses what are believed to be the marble steps used by Jesus outside Pontius Pilate's house in Jerusalem. Pilgrims earn an indulgence for ascending the covered steps on their knees; if you prefer to walk up to the chapel at the top, use the secular stairs on either side. (Open 6am-12:30pm and 3:30-7pm.)

A Metro stop outside the Porta San Giovanni can take you back to Termini or the Vatican on Linea A, or you can return back across the Caelian Hill to the Colosseum and Circus Maximus. From piazza San Giovanni, **via di S. Stefano Rotondo** passes the church of the same name, an ancient circular edifice which may have been a butcher's market before its conversion. Inside, concentric rings of airy columns and arches make a pleasant change from the gloom of San Giovanni. (Open 9am-noon and 4-6pm.) Across the street is the entrance to the **Villa Celimontana** park, a quiet spot filled with flowers and fountains (open 7am-dusk). On the other side, the ancient **church of Santi Giovanni e Paolo** occupies a small *piazza*. Built over the remains of an imperial Roman house, the church can't quite suppress its ancient foundations. The 12th-century campanile and façade rest on travertine blocks from the temple to the Emperor Claudius, whose podium covers this whole side of the hill. (Open Mon.-Sat. 9-11:30am and 3:30-6pm, Sun. 9-11:30am.) The arch-covered street running down the left side of the church, the **Clivus Scauri**, hasn't changed much since it was built in the 1st century BC; in the wall of the church you can see the bricked-in arches and windows of Roman houses that opened onto the street. The clivus descends to the via di S. Gregorio, in the valley between the Palatine, the Colosseum, and the Circus Maximus.

The Southern City

Piazza Mattei and the Jewish Ghetto

> It was dirty, but it was Rome, and to anyone who has
> long lived in Rome even its dirt has a charm which
> the neatness of no other place ever had.
> —William Wetmore Story (1862).

In p. Mattei, the graceful 16th-century **Fontana delle Tartarughe** (Turtle Fountain) by Taddeo Landini marks the center of the **Ghetto**, the lowland quarter where Jews were confined from the 16th to the 19th century. While Dickens declared the area "a miserable place, densely populated, and reeking with bad odours," today's Jewish Ghetto is one of the most picturesque and eclectic (even chic) neighborhoods, with family businesses dating back centuries and restaurants serving up the tastiest food in Rome. Relatively speaking, Jews have fared better (and certainly longer) in Rome than almost any other place in Europe, but even here they have endured centuries of hostility, prejudice, and segregation.

The **Foro Olitorio** market for oil and vegetables, and the **Foro Boario** for meats made the neighborhood a busy commercial center from the ancient days up until the

18th century, even able to withstand Rome's severe (and rather unpopulated) Dark Ages. It was here that Romans first started networking with Greek traders, and later with the Etruscans. In 160 BC, the Roman senate first sought diplomatic relations with the Jewish community and in 139 BC they signed a treaty of commerce. By 50 BC, the Roman Jewish community was thriving. Cicero wrote of the impressive Jewish influence on the city, and Caesar passed a tolerant edict of religious freedom for the Jews. It was not until the conquest of Jerusalem in 70 AD when Jews were brought back as slaves, that tensions arose. The Arch of Titus in the Forum, under which no pious Jew would pass, commemorates the Jerusalem conquest and the pillage of the Jews.

The Middle Ages proved precarious for Jewish Romans, as their position in the city was dependent on the (frequently unbenevolent) mood of the popes. In the thirteenth century, Jews were forced to wear various accessories to distinguish them from the Catholic citizens—a yellow or orange cap (for men) or a yellow or scarlet scarf (for women). Still, in 1492 Jews from all parts of Europe suffering under the Inquisition escaped to Rome for refuge. Finally, in 1555, Pope Paul IV confined the Jews to the *ghetto*, based on the word "foundries", which was the quarter where Jews lived in Venice. They were forbidden to own land and could only work by operating outdoor markets. Many Jews made their living practicing astrology and fortune-telling. During the Renaissance, Jews were kidnapped and forced to run in cruel races for Carnival (see Carnival and Jews in the Renaissance General Introduction, above).

Galevestro Peruzzi, son of the architect Baldassare Peruzzi (who built Villa Farnese), designed the Jewish Ghetto, paid for by the Jews. It was only 270m long and 150m wide, extending from the Ponte Fabricius to the Portico d'Ottavio, across the piazza Giudea to the vicolo Cenci (excluding the fish market and the Teatro Marcello); this small area was home to 3,500 Jews. Pope Paul commissioned a large, ornamental gate at the Ghetto's main entrance on piazza Giudea to "relieve the misery of the Jews," along with two other gates. The boundaries were enlarged little by little, and eventually, there were eight gates. There were strict curfews for the people inside; the gates were shut promptly at 7pm in winter and 8pm in the summer. The Mattei family, who established sumptuous *palazzi* in the area after being kicked out of Trastevere, served as watchdogs, salaried by the Jews and the Vatican. The Ghetto remained a fascinating, even exotic, place for visitors; Roman ladies frequented the astrologers and the rag shops (for silk). In 1645, John Evelyn visited to witness the "slovenly ceremony" of a circumcision, which he vividly recalls in his published diary. Other visitors came to partake of the fabled artichoke *alla Giudea* or as one less enlightened, 19th-century guidebook writer suggests, to gape at "these poor Hebrews [who] are a dwarfish race with large heads and rickety legs."

Apart from the mystical practices and the sumptuous silk weaving, life in the Ghetto was quite miserable; the area was overpopulated, buildings were in serious disrepair, and the proximity of the Tiber made the entire place swampy and muddy, even malarial. The more illustrious Jews lived on higher grounds, near the via del Portico d'Ottavio. The republican reigns of Napoleon and Mazzini granted Jews more freedom (at least in practice), but it was not until 1870, when Italy became unified and the papacy lost some of its political control, that the Ghetto walls came tumbling down. The government made efforts to integrate Jews into other neighborhoods and to rebuild the neighborhood. However, the community proudly remained (and remains) in its neighborhood—without the humiliating strictures or stigma—and has become an integral part of the city. Even Mussolini denounced anti-Semitism in 1924, though not long after, in 1938, he launched a campaign against the Jews. As with most things in modern Rome, these edicts were hardly followed, and both Italians and Jews were quite shocked by them. During World War II, 85% of Jews in Rome survived, due in large part to the many Italians who hid them in farmhouses, monasteries, and convents despite the horrifying silence of Pope Pius XII. Today, of the 40,000 Jews who live in Italy, 13,000 call the eternal city home. In more recent years, the community has been the target of international terrorism, suffering a bombing of its Synagogue in 1982, as well as more local hatred—there are swastikas graffitied on buildings throughout the city. During the Gulf War, *carabinieri* patrolled the area night and day.

The neighborhood is bounded (roughly) to the west by via Arenula (the trafficked gateway to Trastevere); by the Tiber, Lungotevere Cenci, and the Synagogue to the south; and by via delle Botteghe Oscure and the Palazzo Mattei to the north. The east gives way to the ancient Teatro di Marcello, which leads northward to piazza Venezia, or winds down to the Campitelli and the Aventine Hill. The SIDIC (Service International de Documentation Judeo-Chrétenne, an international library information center for Jewish-Christian relations) offers a half-day **free walking tour** in English of the Ghetto environs on the second Friday of each month. The tours originate at 10am at the center, via Plebiscito 112 (tel. 679 53 07).

There are no less than five Mattei *palazzi* in the area surrounding the Ghetto, traditionally controlled by that (ig)noble family. The **Turtle Fountain** was actually designed by della Porta and Bernini added the turtles when he restored it in 1658. The local story of the fountain goes like this: Duke Mattei, a notorious and incorrigible gambler, lost everything in one night. His father-in-law-to-be was so disgusted by the Duke's flagrantly idiotic behavior that he rescinded his approval of Mattei's marriage to his daughter. The Duke, in a bid to pull his name from the mud of scandal, had the fountain built in a single night to show that a Mattei could pull off anything, even when completely destitute. He got the girl, though she ended up blocking up her window so she would never have to see the fountain that got her married to such a schlemiel.

Leaving the *piazza* on the east along via dei Funari brings you past **Palazzo Mattei**, one of the many Mattei properties which stretch over several blocks. They made much of their money collecting tolls over the bridges to Trastevere, and later, from serving as gate-watchers for the Ghetto. The Mattei constructed their huge expanse of *palazzi*, often called the Island of Mattei, over a period of two centuries (1400-1600s). A papal housing decree in 1574 required all new buildings to be attached in some way, by courtyard or wall, to another; thus the Mattei *palazzi* are actually separated only by styles of architecture, and are not free-standing structures. The Red Brigade kidnappers and murderers of Aldo Moro, the favored candidate for Italy's head-of-state, dumped his body here in 1978, and there are occasionallly flowers and candles for commemoration.

On the next block, the **church of Santa Caterina dei Funari** towers austerely above the street of the same name, titled for the rope-makers who worked here. St. Ignatius founded the church to provide homes for poor and orphaned girls, who were then married off to local artisans. The girls were blessed with a hefty dowry (50 *scudi*) from an endowment by the richest courtesans in Rome. The church is a rare late-Renaissance specimen in Rome, built on the site of a 10th-century monastery, designed in 1554 by Guido Guidetti, one-time apprentice to Michelangelo, while he was re-constructing the Campidoglio. The bell-tower is a sorry addition to the church, and to add insult to injury the recent restoration attempts, which make the top look like a wedding-cake decoration, are now called the sacrilege of St. Catherine.

Down to the right is **piazza di Campitelli,** a lovely and harmonious example of the Counter-Reformation Church's extreme efforts to beautify Rome above all other cities in order to demonstrate the superiority of the Vatican. To create the perfect space for the *piazza,* which is guarded by what were once some of the swankiest *palazzi*, the **church of Santa Maria in Campitelli** had to be moved and rebuilt. Carlo Rainaldi designed and executed the church, which is arguably his best work ever. Like his church of San Andrea delle Valle, this church exemplifies the theatrics of Baroque architecture to an even greater degree by creating a grand sense of space. Hovering ominously over the rest of the church, the front altar seems to give the small interior more depth. The church was built in 1662 to give *mille grazie* to the Virgin. According to the lore, when an image of the Madonna, apparently delivered to the pope by two angels, passed through the plague-infested city in 1656, the epidemic promptly ended. The city decided that the statue deserved a new home and thus the Campitelli church was built. The interior, a variation on the Greek cross plan and full of Baroque art, still houses the miniscule statuette above the central lit altar. Above the first window on the left is a tabernacle to Santa Maria in Porticu, which refers to this protrectress of Rome. Pay L500 for a recorded history and explanation of the church's works. (Open Mon.-Sat. for Mass at 7:30am, 9am, 6pm, and 7pm; Sun. and holidays 7:30am, 10am, 11am, noon, 6pm, and 7pm.) From via dei Funari, take via Sant Angelo in Peschiera towards the river to via Portico d'Ottavia. Several houses on this street, notably #13, 17, and 19, date from medieval times. Note in particular the inscription on the building at via Portico d'Ottavia, 1; after the patriotic invocation *Ave Roma*, it praises the owner for beautifying Rome.

In a city overrun with Catholic iconography and classical designs, the **Sinagoga Ashkenazita** (Synagogue of Rome; tel. 687 50 51) at via Portico di Ottavia and via Catalonia defiantly proclaims its divergent heritage. There were originally several different synagogues (of Spanish, Italian, and Sicilian heritage, to name a few) in the Ghetto reflecting the diversity of the Jewish settlers, and in fact, unsurprisingly, there were tensions even between members of the Jewish community. This synagogue reflects in part, the unity of the Jewish people in Rome. Built between 1874 and 1904, the synagogue incorporates Persian and Babylonian architectural devices, purposefully avoiding any resemblance to a Christian church. The building is topped by a large, metal dome, which, along with the Pantheon's, is visible from the top of the Gianicolo. Now it uses *carabinieri* and video devices to keep terrorists at bay, and all visitors must be searched before entering. The synagogue also houses the **Jewish Museum**, which displays ceremonial objects from the 17th-century Jewish community as well the original plan of the Ghetto. (No cameras. Synagogue open Mon.-Thurs. 9:30am-2pm, Fri. 9:30am-1:30pm, Sun. 10am-noon. Services at 8:30pm. Museum open Mon.-Fri. 10am-1pm and Sat. 10am-noon. Hours fluctuate widely and the administrators advise checking for changes. Admission L4000.) Facing the synagogue on the south, the façade of the **Church of San Gregorio** carries a Hebrew and Latin inscription admonishing Jews to convert to Catholicism.

Also note the **Palazzo Cenci** on a slight rise (Monte Cenci) at the end of via Catalana, named for the Spanish Jews who settled here. The *palazzo* was the scene of a September 9, 1598 scandal when Beatrice Cenci, aided by her brother and her step-mother, succeeded in having her father Francesco Cenci murdered. The whole clan was beheaded a year and two days later at the command of Pope Clement VIII, but the public sympathized with the group's plea of self-defense against the incestuous drug addict Francesco. Every year on September 11, a mass is held in St. Thomas's at piazza di Monte Cenci for the wronged Beatrice. (see Dysfunctional Families General Introduction, above). The *palazzo* now houses a tacky art gallery as well as the Rhode Island School of Design European Honors Program, which sponsors a free, bi-annual art exhibition of its American students' work.

The Velabrum

Back down via Catalana, via Portico d'Ottavia winds to the right through a maze of medieval buildings on its way to the riverbank, site of the ancient Velabrum. The **Velabrum** lies to the south of the Ghetto in the shadow of the Capitol and Palatine Hills. This flat floodplain of the Tiber was a sacred area for the ancient Romans, where they believed Romulus and Remus had been rescued by the she-wolf and Hercules kept his cattle. During the republic the area's proximity to the river made it an ideal spot for the city's cattle and vegetable markets, as well as a port on the Tiber. Civic-minded merchants forested the riverbanks with monuments—temples, arches, and a grandiose theater—dedicated to their gods of trade and commerce. Even after the empire fell, the area remained a populous and busy market center, where medieval Romans continued the tradition of sacred building. Today the remains of the ancient temples and arches stand shoulder to shoulder with some of the best-preserved and most beautiful medieval basilicas in the city.

At the end of via di Portico d'Ottavia in the Ghetto (see above), a shattered pediment and a few ivy-covered columns are all that remain of the once magnificent **Portico d'Ottavia**, one of Augustus's grandest contributions to the architecture of the ancient city. The pediment crowned the side entrance to a long, rectangular enclosure whose 300 columns formed a sacred precinct around two important temples to Jupiter and Juno. Augustus planned this whole area as a monument to his own family, dedicating the portico to his sister Octavia and the nearby Teatro di Marcello (see below) to his nephew and chosen successor, Marcellus. Medieval Romans, in typical carefree style, built around, inside, and on top of the marble portico, then filled the remaining open space with a fish market, which functioned until this century. The market lent its name to the **church of Sant'Angelo in Pescheria**, installed inside the portico in 755 AD. It was here that the Jews of the Ghetto were forced to attend mass every Sunday until the 18th century—an act of aggressive evangelism which they quietly resisted by stuffing their ears with wax. The church is rarely open.

A quick walk around the right of the portico (skirting the fences of never-ending restoration work) brings you to the gleaming white columns of the **Temple of Apollo Sosioanus**, yet another leftover from Augustus's monumental neighborhood. Gaius Sosius rebuilt the temple, one of the oldest in the city, in 34 BC, thus winning the right to attach his own name to it. The three Corinthian columns support a surprisingly well-preserved frieze of bulls' skulls and floral garlands

Theater of Marcellus

If you think the stocky **Theater of Marcellus** (Teatro di Marcello) next door looks like a Colosseum wanna-be, think again. The pattern of arches and pilasters on the theater's exterior, completed in 11 BC, actually served as a model for the great amphitheater across town. You can still make out the classic arrangement of architectural orders, which grows, in accord with ancient principles, more complex from the ground up. Plain Doric pilasters support the bottom story, curved Ionic capitals decorate the middle and (though they're now long gone) elaborate Corinthian capitals once crowned the top tier. Vitruvius and other ancient architects called this arrangement the most perfect possible for exterior decoration, inspiring Alberti, Bramante, Michelangelo, and countless other Renaissance architects to copy the pattern. Sadly, this perfect exterior is all that remains of the theater, as a succession of medieval families used its seats and stage as the foundation for their fortified castles. The Pierleoni first set up shop in the 11th century, using the theater's imposing height to control access to the Tiber and its bridges. The money they made from exacting tolls helped vault the family to social and political power (they had originally been Jews from the Ghetto), culminating in the election of Anacletus I as the notorious "Jewish Pope" (see The Jewish Pope General Introduction, above). The Savelli family, the theater's next occupants, commissioned Baldassare Peruzzi to design the Renaissance castle that crowns the structure's height. The Orsini, the last family to occupy the building, converted it in this century to an apartment complex, making the ancient monument one of the city's most prestigious addresses. Normally closed to the public, the park around the theater hosts classical concerts on summer nights (see Music, above).

Further down via di Teatro di Marcello, the remains of three more Roman temples jut out from the walls of the **church of San Nicola in Carcere** (tel. 686 99 72). The three buildings were originally dedicated to the gods Juno, Janus, and Hope. The most complete temple lies to the right of the church, its Ionic columns littering the tiny lawn and supporting the church's wall. The left wall of the church preserves the Doric columns of the another of the temples. The third temple lies buried beneath the sober little church. The church's name (St. Nicholas in Prison) has two different explanations. One belief is that during the medieval period, this neighborhood was inhabited largely by a Greek population who brought the cult of St. Nicholas to Rome. Another is that the church was built on a prison, in which a girl supposedly kept her father alive by feeding him milk from her breast. The Roman Senate was so touched that they spared the man's life and erected a temple to Piety. (Open Sept.-July Mon.-Sat. 4-7pm, Sun. mass at noon. Visits to the excavations Thurs. 10:30am-noon.)

One block further south lies the **piazza di Bocca della Verità**, the site of the ancient Forum Boarium, or cattle market. Don't miss the little house on the corner of via Ponte Rotto, where the Crescenzi family extorted tolls from hapless travelers crossing the Tiber by the Ponte Rotto. The fragments decorating the façades were snatched from various Roman monuments in the middle ages.

The two ancient **temples** in the Forum Boarium capture one of the most important moments in the history of Roman architecture, the shift from native Italic to imported Greek styles which came hand in hand with Rome's conquest of Greece in the 2nd century BC. The rectangular **Temple of Portunus**, which predates the conquest, follows archaic Italic models with its raised stone base, closed-off back and side walls, and severe front porch. Closely tied to the ceremonial nature of Etruscan religion, the temple focuses all attention on its façade, which was the only part accessible to the people (entry into the holy sanctum was forbidden). The **circular temple** next door shows how different the Greek take on religion was. Built at ground level, its symmetrical shape invites anyone to walk around and through its graceful colonnade. Once thought to be dedicated to Vesta (because of its similarity to the Temple of Vesta in the Forum), the real honoree of the round temple remains nameless to this day. At least it's had the Triton fountain to keep it company since the 18th century.

Across the *piazza* from the temples, via Velabro climbs a short way toward the Capitol Hill. Behind the hulking **Arch of Janus**, built in the 4th century as a covered market for cattle traders, the little **church of S. Gregorio in Velabro** is a typical medieval edifice, with a 9th-century porch and pillars, a simple basilican interior, and a *campanile* (bell tower) built of brick and stone arches. To the left of the church, the eroded **Arch of the Argentarii** was erected by the money changers and cattle merchants who used the *piazza* as a market in the 3rd century AD, in honor of the Emperor Septimius Severus and his family. Caracalla, Severus's son and successor, had his brother Geta's name and image erased from the arch after he had the boy himself rubbed out.

Closer to the river, the exquisite **church of Santa Maria in Cosmedin** harbors some of Rome's most beautiful medieval decoration. The front porch and bell tower, dating from the 12th century, welcome daily mobs of bus-borne tourists, all on their way to see the famous **Bocca della Verità**, in the portico. Originally a drain cover carved as a river god's face, the circular relief was credited with supernatural powers in the middle ages. It's said the hoary face will close shut on the hand of a liar, severing his other fingers. The caretaker-priest used to stick a scorpion in the back to bite the fingers of those little-white-liars. When filming the movie *Roman Holiday,* Gregory Peck put his hand in the mouth. When he yanked it out, he jokingly hid his hand in his sleeve and Audrey Hepburn screamed in shock; the scene wasn't scripted, but they kept it in the movie. The dusky interior of the church brims with Cosmatesque stonework, from the exquisite choir enclosure and pulpits to the intricate, marble-inlaid floor. (Portico open 9am-5pm. Church open 9am-noon and 3-5pm. Byzantine mass Sun. 10:30am.)

From the Bocca della Verità, the hazardous Lungotevere Aventino leads a short way to the Clivio Savello, a lonely, cobbled ramp that climbs between crumbling walls to the spacious gardens of the **Aventine Hill**. In ancient times, the hill was sacred to Diana and crowned with an enormous temple and gardens dedicated to her; today the ramp leads through an iron gate to a park on the same site, where orange trees frame a sweeping view of the Tiber and the southern part of the city, an ideal spot for picnicking. Across the park, another gate opens onto the courtyard of the **church of Santa Sabina**, yet another basilica built in the same style as S. Gregorio and Sta. Maria in Cosmedin, with a porch of ancient columns and a towering campanile. Inside, the wooden doors on the far left date from the 5th century and contain one of the earliest depictions of the Crucifixion. The 24 columns of the nave were pillaged from a pagan temple and are in perfect condition. Over the entrance doors, a colossal mosaic contains seven lines of exquisite Latin lettering. Via Santa Sabina continues along the crest of the hill past the **church of Sant'Alessio** to the **piazza dei Cavalieri di Malta**, home of the ancient crusading order of the Knights of Malta. Piranesi designed the military trophies atop the walls; the keyhole in the gate offers a perfectly framed view of the dome of St. Peter's. The **church of Sant'Anselmo** has a peaceful garden courtyard. From Santa Sabina, via di Valle Murcia descends past a public garden (where an extensive rose show blooms in June and early July) to the Circus Maximus, where you can catch a stunning view of the ruined Palatine palaces and the medieval churches of the Caelian Hill.

South of the Tiber

Testaccio

South of the Aventine Hill, the working-class district of **Testaccio** is known for its cheap and delicious *trattorie*, raucous nightclubs, and eclectic collection of monuments. The #23 bus runs from the Vatican and along the Tiber to via della Marmorata, the northern border of the district. In ancient times the area served as the docklands of Rome, where grain, oil, wine, and marble were unloaded from river barges into giant warehouses. After the goods had been transferred to storage, Roman merchants tossed the left-over terracotta urns into a vacant lot. The pile grew and grew, and today the bulbous **Monte Testaccio** (from *testae*, or potshards) rises 150 feet over the drab surrounding streets. Though grown over with grass, the hill is punctured everywhere by fragments of orange clay amphorae. (Park open sporadically 9am-dusk; no pilfering of potshards, please.)

From the base of the hill, via Nicola Zabaglia turns left onto via Caio Cestio, which runs along the length of the peaceful **Protestant Cemetery**, final resting place for many English visitors to the city (as well as anyone else who wasn't Catholic or Jewish). Ring the bell for admission at number 6; inside, between romantically planted avenues of tombs, John Keats lies beside his friend Joseph Severn. The tombstone itself doesn't mention the writer by name; it merely commemorates a "Young English Poet" and records, "Here lies one whose name is writ in water." On the other side of the small cemetery, Shelley rests in peace, beside his piratical friend Trelawny, under a simple plaque hailing him as *Cor Cordium*, "heart of hearts." Also buried here are Goethe's son Axel Munthe and Richard Henry Dana, author of *Two Years Before the Mast*. Henry James buried his fictional heroine, Daisy Miller, here after she died of malaria. (Open 8-11:30am and 3:20-5:30pm; Oct.-March 8-11:30am and 2:20-4:30pm; admission free but donation requested.)

Outside the cemetery, past the well-preserved **Porta San Paolo** (in ancient times the Porta Ostiense, and still the start of the road to Ostia Antica), the colossal **Pyramid of Caius Cestius** shares a burial plot with the Protestants. Caius Cestius, tribune of the plebs under Augustus, got caught up in the craze for things Egyptian that followed on the Emperor's defeat of Cleopatra in the late 1st century BC. Like the collection of Egyptian statuary in the Vatican and most of the obelisks in the city, there's nothing Egyptian about this pyramid except its inspiration. Though it was built in less than 330 days, the close fit of its marble blocks ensured that it was never pillaged; when the Goths were marauding in the 3rd century, the emperor Aurelian had the pyramid built into his city walls as a bastion; nowadays it's the favored hangout of Rome's impeccably modish transvestite population.

Basilica San Paolo

From the pyramid, grab bus #673, 23, or 170 down the boring via Ostiense to the eery **Basilica San Paolo** (in the Ostiense neighborhood), the third of Rome's extraterritorial basilicas (with S. Giovanni and Sta. Maria Maggiore) and the largest church in the city after St. Peter's. St. Paul, who was martyred near the modern **EUR**, is believed to be buried under the altar (his body, that is; his beheaded head is in S. Giovanni), and the church was, until the construction of the new St. Peter's, the largest and most beautiful in Rome. Completely destroyed by fire in 1823, the present church is a modern reconstruction. It's been called cold and gloomy, but the shiny newness of the marble interior is probably the best representation of how all the paleochristian basilicas of Rome appeared when they were first constructed. The mammoth interior is an Egyptian cross (in the shape of a T) with two aisles flanking the nave on each side. The triumphal arch before the altar and the apse are set with the original mosaics (salvaged and reassembled after the fire) of Christ, angels, saints, and the Virgin. (Open 7am-7pm.) The **cloister** is a peaceful remnant of the original construction, lined with twisted pairs of Cosmatesque columns and enveloping a rose garden. (Open 9am-1pm and 3-6pm.)

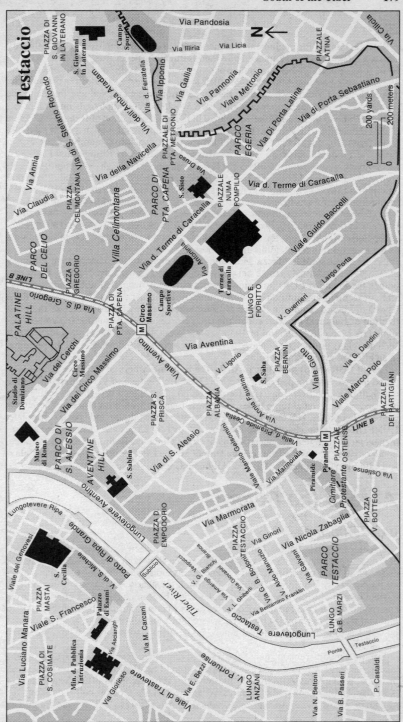

EUR

Rome is famous for monuments that hark back to ancient empires. South of the city stands a monument to a Roman empire that, fortunately, never was. The zone is called **EUR** (pronounced AY-oor), an Italian acronym for Universal Exposition of Rome, the 1942 World's Fair that Mussolini intended to be a showcase of fascist achievements. The outbreak of World War II led to the cancellation of the fair, and wartime demands on manpower and materiel ensured that EUR would never complete its mission of extending Rome to the sea, but the completed buildings house some of Rome's enormous museum overflow. EUR lies at the EUR-Marconi stop off subway line B, or take #93 from Termini to viale della Civiltà del Lavoro. **Via Cristoforo Colombo,** EUR's main street, runs roughly north to south. The **Museo Preistorico ed Etnografico L. Pigorini,** at viale Lincoln, 1 (tel. 591 91 32), off via Colombo, houses an anthropological collection focusing on prehistoric Latium. (Open Mon.-Sat. 9am-2pm, Sun. 9am-1pm. Admission L6000.) The museum features objects from various parts of the Italian peninsula from the Stone, Bronze, and Iron Ages. Artifacts from other parts of the world are exhibited in the ethnographic collection. Located in the same building, through the entrance at p. Marconi, 10, the collection of the **Museo dell'Alto Medioevo** (Museum of the Early Middle Ages; tel. 592 58 06) dates from the Dark Ages. (Open same hours as the Museo Preistorico; admission L2000.)

Up the street spreads **piazza Marconi,** more a highway interchange than a Roman *piazza,* 1959 modernist obelisk notwithstanding. Next, **piazza dei Nazioni Uniti** embodies the intended EUR: imposing modern buildings decorated with spare columns attempt to meld ancient empire with empire-to-come. At the east end of viale della Civiltà di Lavoro stands the **Palace of Congress,** but the awkward **Palace of the Civilization of Labor,** at the west end of the street, serves as EUR's definitive symbol. Designed by Marcello Piacentini in 1938, it anticipates the postmodernist architecture of such designers as Michael Graves, by wrapping archlike windows around the building, in an effort to evoke Roman ruins.

East of EUR stands the **Abbazia delle Tre Fontane,** where St. Paul's head was supposed to have been lopped off. (Take Via Delle Tre Fontane to Via Laurentina, a little over half of a mile from Via Cristoforo Colombo.) The legend says that St. Paul's head bounced on the ground three times, creating a fountain with each bounce. The monks who live here today sell the monastery's own eucalyptus liquor and special chocolate. **LUNEUR park,** on via delle Tre Fontane (tel. 592 59 33), is an old-fashioned amusement center which features cheap thrills like the "Himalaya Railroad" for a hefty price. South of EUR, across the lake (known simply as "the lake" or *il lago*) looms the **Palazzo Dello Sport** designed for the 1960 Olympic Games.

Across the River

Isola Tiberina

The elegant **Tiber Island**, lounging in the Tiber between Trastevere and the historical center, splits the river's unsavory yellow-green flow with banks swathed in marble and brick. It's not surprising that the island seems more like a floating city than a natural landmark—it's been continuously inhabited for nearly 3000 years. According to Roman legend, the island shares its birthday with the Roman Republic: after the Etruscan tyrant Tarquin the Proud raped the virtuous Lucretia, her outraged husband killed him and threw his corpse in the river, where muck and silt collected around it...years passed, Lucretia's family founded a new government, and the Tiber Island grew into dry land.

Tarquin's muddy remains may have deterred republican Romans from settling on the island; the place was first used as a dumping ground for slaves who'd grown too weak or sick to work. Abandoned by their masters, the pitiful slaves attracted the attention of Aesculapius, the Greek god of healing. When the Romans took his cult statue from the sanctuary at Kos, in the Aegean, and dragged it up the Tiber in 293 BC, the god turned into a snake and slithered onto the island. The Romans took it as a sign that this was where he wanted his temple and, with typical architectural overkill, encased the whole island in marble, building its walls in the shape of a boat to commemorate the god's arrival. You can still see traces of the original travertine decoration on the southeast side (look for the serpent carved in relief near the "prow" of the island.) The site has been associated with healing ever since, as the order of *Fatebenefratelli* (do good, brothers) monks established a hospital here in 154 AD. Expectant Roman mothers consider the island the most fashionable place to give birth in the city.

When visiting the Tiber Island, you can't help but participate in its ancient history. The bridge leading from the east bank of the river, the sturdy **Ponte Fabricio**, is the oldest in the city, built by Lucius Fabricius in 62 BC-from the *lungotevere,* you can see the inscription Lucius carved into the bridge to record his public service; it is commonly known as the Bridge of Four Heads *(de Quatro Capi).* As you stroll across the cobbled span, pay your respects to the two stone herms of Janus, four-headed god of entrances and exits, as Romans have done for two millenia. From the bridge, you can also catch sight of the beleaguered **Ponte Rotto** to the south, one of Rome's less fortunate ancient constructions. Built in the 2nd century BC, the poor bridge underwent repair after medieval repair, each time succumbing again to the Tiber's relentless floods. Since its last collapse in 1598, it's been slowly disintegrating. Now all that remains is a single arch planted squatly but proudly midstream.

In the island's one *piazza* the 10th-century **St. Bartholomew's Church** has a Baroque façade and a Romanesque bell tower. The well cover may actually be a relic from the original temple to Aesculapius. The *Fatebenefratelli*'s hospital takes up the northern half of the island. English King Henry I's courtier Rahere reputedly recovered here from malaria, a mostly fatal disease in those pre-quinine days. He was so thankful that he promised to build a church and a hospital in gratitude when he got back to England and, true to his word, he built the structures that are still standing in London's Smithfield district.

The **Ponte Cestio** (built by Lucius Cestius in 46 BC—not quite as old as the Fabricio) links the island to Trastevere. While it may not garner a superlative, the little bridge offers a good view of the Gianicolo Hill on the right and **the bell tower of Santa Maria in Cosmedin** on the left.

Trastevere

> The whole district teemed with ragged, grimy deni-
> zens, children half-naked and devoured by vermin,
> bare-headed, gesticulating and shouting women,
> whose skirts were stiff with grease, old men who re-
> mained motionless on benches amidst swarms of
> flies.
>
> —Zola

Trastevere boasts a proud, independent vitality, only becoming a part of Rome when Augustus insisted on incorporating it. The *Trasteverini* claim to be descendants of the purest Roman stock (*Romani di Roma*)—from Horatius, Scaevola, and others who defended the city from the Tarquinian invasion; some residents brag about never having crossed the river. Augustus Hare once declared the inhabitants to be "more hasty, passionate, and revengeful as they are a stronger and more vigorous race"—undisputed by Romans on either side of the Tiber.

The legendary founder of Ostia, King Ancus Martius, first settled Trastevere not as a residential spot, but as a commercial and military post to protect the valuable salt-beds at the base of the Tiber from numerous competitors. The hill beyond Trastevere also became an important outpost against Etruscan incursions. During the empire, sailors for the imperial fleet inhabited the area, then known as the city of Ravennati. Many of the mud- or clay-based houses were built along the river, accessible by boat. The success of Hadrian's commercial port lured merchants and other ambitious folk to set up camp in the neighborhood, and Eastern and Jewish merchants settled here as early as 2,000 years ago. The maritime business flourished alongside such cottage industries as blacksmithy, tanning, carpentry, milling, and prostitution. In his itinerary of 1617, guidebook editor Fynes Moryson warned readers, "because the aire is unwholesome, as the winde that blows heere from the South, it is onely inhabited by Artisans and poore people." The popes took little interest in this proletarian neighborhood, and rarely extended their wealth to build grandiose churches or monuments here. Instead, their wealth community remained wholly self-sufficient, enough so to develop its own (now-extinct) dialect, popularized by poets G.G. Belli and Trilussa. The exceptions, of course, are the extravagant little villas built by the Roman aristocracy near the river's edge. Despite these bourgeois infiltrators, Trastevere found enough popular support to back several revolutions: Mazzini's quest for a Republic in 1849 and Garibaldi in 1867.

Today, Trastevere attracts hordes of expatriates, bohemians, and artists, but thanks to rent control and centuries of fiery patriotism, the area retains its local *gusto*. To keep the spirit of independence alive, the festival of *Noi Antri* ("We others" in dialect) is still celebrated every July, now filled with junky stalls, an overpriced ferris wheel, and fresh *porchetta* straight from pig heads on display. Take bus #170 from Termini to viale Trastevere, an area packed with ice cream parlors, movie houses, and (dare we mention) a McDonald's. Trastevere's dark maze and medieval quarters, with webs of laundry strung across the buildings, and carefully grungy hippies lounging around the *piazze*, may give you a better sense of a traditional Roman community than any other part of the city.

Right off the Ponte Garibaldi stands the statue of the famous dialect poet, Giacchino Belli, in the middle of his own *piazza,* which spills onto the busy thoroughfare, viale di Trastevere. On the left, the **Torre degli Anguillara**, dating back to the 13th century, stands over a *palazzo* of the same name. The Anguillara family was at the head of Roman activity as priests, magistrates, warlords, criminals, and swindlers. Across the street, the **church of San Crisogno** perpetuates yet another well-known Roman name, Cardinal Borghese's, etched into the façade. Although it was founded in the 5th century, the church has been rebuilt many times through the years. Twenty feet beneath it though, the 5th-century church remains, like an old set of luggage left in the basement. Back upstairs, the canopy over the altar is by Soria and adds an interesting twist to this Mannerist-Baroque pastiche. (Mass, complete with speakers, Mon.-Fri. 7:30am-10am on the hour, and vespers at 6pm.)

A couple of blocks further down the *viale,* the via di Giulio Cesare Santini leads east into via dei Genovesi where the **church of Santa Cecilia in Trastevere** lies half a block away on S. Cecilia. The church is on the site of Santa Cecilia's house. She converted to Christianity and managed to convert her husband and brother-in-law. Unfortunately, her husband and brother-in-law were then beheaded for their refusal to worship Roman gods. Cecilia inherited a considerable fortune from both of them, becoming one of the richest women in Rome, and inciting much resentment, to the point that the prefect of Rome ordered her death in 230. She was locked up in her own fiery steamroom to die, but miraculously survived. They then tried to chop her head off with the three legal lops, but the executioners did a poor job of it and she survived for three days more, slowly bleeding to death and converting over 400 people to Catholicism in the meanwhile; she also bequeathed her palace to build this church. She is the patron saint of music, since she was found singing in the steamroom after her 3-day stint. On November 22, her day of martyrdom, churches hold a special musical service. The National Academy of Music in Rome is also named after her.

Pope Urban I first consecrated the church in her palace, but Pope Pascal I rebuilt it in 821 when, according to one Vatican account, he dreamed of St. Cecilia showing him her burial grounds in the catacombs of St. Calixtus. He had her body exhumed and transferred to the new church. After passing through the spacious courtyard rose garden and into the church proper, you can see the site of the old steamroom, the first room on the right as you enter. The choice artwork, however, is Stefano Maderno's famous **statue of Santa Cecilia** that reclines under the high altar. It is a representation in marble of what she looked like when exhumed from her tomb in 1599, when Maderno was

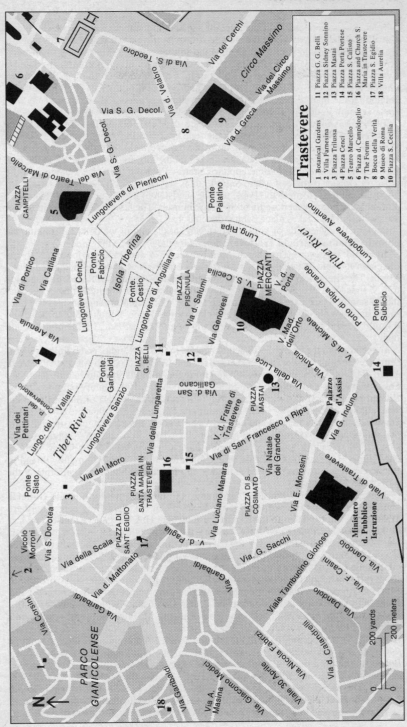

Trastevere

1 Botanical Gardens
2 Villa Farnesina
3 Piazza Trilussa
4 Piazza Cenci
5 Teatro Marcello
6 Piazza d. Campidoglio
7 The Forum
8 Bocca della Verità
9 Museo di Roma
10 Piazza S. Cecilia

11 Piazza G. G. Belli
12 Piazza Sidney Sonnino
13 Piazza Mastai
14 Piazza Porta Portese
15 Piazza S. Calisto
16 Piazza and Church S.
   Maria in Trastevere
17 Piazza S. Egidio
18 Villa Aurelia

present. Rococo restorers wreaked untold damage on the medieval frescoes by Pietro Cavallini which once covered the church. However, there are fragments of his magnificent *Last Judgement,* painted in 1293, in the adjacent cloister. This highly sophisticated work, with unrivaled draftmanship, an extraordinary array of colors, and intense expression, has no contemporary parallel in Italy or anywhere in Europe. Beneath the church are the ruins of Roman buildings and possibly an ancient church. Cardinal Rampolla, the man responsible for the excavations, is memorialized in a wacky perspective tomb in the last chapel outside. (Open 10am-noon and 4-6pm.)

Take via Anicia to piazza San Francesco d'Assisi to find the **church of San Francesco a Ripa,** one of the first Franciscan churches in Rome. Inside, you'll find Bernini's *Beata Ludovica Albertoni,* an erotic (uh, we meant ecstatic) sculpture rivaling his *St. Teresa in Ecstasy* in the last chapel on the left. Ludovica, carved at the moment of her death, lies in some euphoric state—I'll have what she's having. In the adjacent cloister is the cell where Saint Francis stayed in 1219, during his mission to advocate church reform to the Pope; ask the sacristan to let you in. The cell features a 13th-century portrait supposedly of St. Frank himself. The largest flea market in Rome, the **Porta Portese,** takes place behind the church.

Back on the other side of viale di Trastevere, at the end of via della Lungaretta, the **church of Santa Maria in Trastevere** dominates the *piazza* of the same name, and the heart of old Trastevere. The church, built between 337 and 352 by Pope Julius II, has the claim to fame of being the first of Rome's hundreds of churches dedicated to the Virgin. The site is also the spot of the oldest Christian structure in Rome, tracing back to 222 under S. Calixtus. The mosaics lining the outside of the church of the Virgin and the 10 saintly women are only a warm-up for the spectacular mosaics inside. The ones in the apse are phenomenal. If you look closely, the donor, Bertoldo Stefaneschi, had himself worked into the picture. (Open 7am-7pm; Mass at 9am, 10:30am, noon, and 6pm.)

To the north of the church, off via della Paglia in P. Sant'Egidio, is the **Folklore Museum,** celebrating the dialect poets G.G. Belli and "Trilussa" (Carlo Alberto Salustri, d. 1950). This is not the most sophisticated museum, but kids seem to like it. There are hokey waxworks and tableaux of traditional Roman life, 19th-century paintings of the Roman carnival and its fireworks, as well as a ramshackle replica of Salustri's studio. The building also serves as a cultural center and frequently hosts special exhibits. The employees are fairly helpful and can give you a good sense of the city life, past and present. (Open Tues.-Sat. 9am-1:30pm, Sun. 9am-1pm; Tues. also 5-7:30pm. Admission L1500.) Heading down via Lungaretta, hang a right on via di S. Gallicano to check out Filippo Raguzzini's **Ospedale San Gallicano,** an imaginative, mellow blend of Rococo architecture that inspired architects in Florida and Southern California at the turn of the 19th century.

From p. Santa Maria, via della Scala and via Lungara lead north to the **Galleria Corsini,** on the first floor of the Rococo Palazzo Corsini. Sprawling across northern Trastevere from the Tiber to the foot of the Janiculan Hill, the gallery houses one half of the **Museo Nazionale dell'Arte Antica**—the worse half, unless you're a madonna fan. (The other half hangs in the Palazzo Barberini; see above). The gallery's seven rooms boast no fewer than 41 portrayals of the Virgin Mary, with 17 in one room alone, but despite the consistency of theme the collection's haphazard arrangement is uninspiring. If you do visit, concentrate on the second room, with an eclectic assortment of 14th- to 17th-century masters. Here Fra Angelico's triptych of the *Last Judgement,* surrounded by other early Renaissance panels, shares wall space with portraits of the *Madonna and Child* by Andrea del Sarto (two of them), Murillo, and van Dyck. Titian's *Portrait of Philip II* and Pierino del Vaga's *Portrait of Alessandro Farnese* (Pope Paul III) bring the 16th century back to life, but the agonies of Rubens's *St. Sebastian Cared for by Angels* fail to distract Hans Hoffman's memorable (and clearly unperturbed) *Rabbit.* In the third room is a little-known *St. John the Baptist* by Caravaggio and yet another *Madonna and Child,* this one by the early Roman Baroque master Orazio Gentileschi. There's not much else to see along the dim walls of the palace except in **Room 7,** which boasts Guido Reni's sorrowful *Lucrezia* (the Roman matron whose suicide after rape by Etruscan king Tarquinius Superbus inspired the establishment of the Roman

Republic) and pensive *Salome with the Head of John the Baptist.* (Open Mon.-Sat. 9am-2pm, Sun. 9am-1pm. Admission L6000)

Rome's modest **Botanical Gardens** stretch behind the gallery. There's not much in terms of exotic flora, but the shade of the palm trees makes it a great picnic ground. (Entrance off of via della Lungara. Open Mon.-Sat. 9am-7pm, Sun. 10am-7pm; closed Aug. Admission L2000.)

The Villa Farnesina

Across the street from the Galleria Corsini stands the Renaissance **Villa Farnesina**, the jewel of Trastevere. Baldassare Peruzzi built the magnificent suburban villa for the Sienese banker and philanthropist Agostino Chigi ("il Magnifico") between 1508-1511. Thought to be the wealthiest man in Europe, Chigi entertained the stars of the Renaissance papal court in his sumptuously decorated *salone* and extensive gardens. Artists, ambassadors, courtesans, cardinals, and even Pope Leo X partook of Chigi's extravagance, and the stories of his largesse are legendary. He once invited the Pope and the entire College of Cardinals to dinner in a gold-brocaded dining hall, so imposing that the Pope reproached him for not treating him with greater familiarity. Agostino smiled, ordered the hangings removed, and revealed to his astonished guests that they'd only been eating in his stables. At one infamous banquet in his *loggia* overlooking the Tiber, Chigi led his guests in tossing the gold and silver dishes into the drink after every course (no dummy, the shrewd businessman hid nets under the water to recover his sunken treasure). The interior decoration of the villa, with frescoes by Raphael, Peruzzi, il Sodoma, and Giulio Romano, smacks of the same divine decadence. But with the banker's death in 1520, four days after that of Raphael, the villa fell into disrepair and was later bought by the Farnese family, after whom it is now named. Today, the building functions as a center for the *Accademia dei Lincei*, a scientific circle that once claimed Galileo as a member.

Restorations are nearing completion in this Renaissance wonder, though Raphael's pretty *Loggia of Cupid and Psyche* remains under scaffolding. The pendentives depict the long and tortuous courtship of the legendary lovers, while the ceiling is decorated with two scenes of their marriage banquet, painted on tapestries hung across a painted pergola, hung with festoons of fruit and flowers. To the right as you enter the villa you'll find the charming **Sala of Galatea**, painted by the villa's architect, Baldassare Peruzzi, in 1511. The vault displays allegorical and mythological symbols of astrological signs which, taken with the two central panels of *Perseus Decapitating Medusa* and *Callisto* (in a chariot drawn by oxen), add up to a symbolic plan of the stars in the night sky at 9:30pm, November 29, 1466, the moment of Agostino's birth. But the masterpiece of the room is Raphael's fresco of the sea-nymph **Galatea**, plying the seas on a conch-shell chariot drawn by two nasty-looking dolphins. To the right is a Triton hung like a whale. In the panel to left, Sebastiano del Piombo's one-eyed giant Polyphemus gapes at the nymph with gargantuan lust. Del Piombo also decorated the lunettes with scenes from classical mythology, but the giant monochrome head has recently been attributed to Peruzzi. Legend once said that Michelangelo painted it as a dig to Raphael, to show him that his figures were too small.

The stuccoed stairway, with its gorgeous perspective details, is reason enough to visit the villa. The stairs ascend to the *piano nobile*, with its two splendid *salone*, decorated with frescoes to celebrate Agostino's wedding to a young Venetian noblewomen whom he had abducted and kept cloistered in a convent for several years. The **Sala delle Prospettive** is a fantasy room decorated by Peruzzi with views of Renaissance Rome between *trompe l'oeil* columns. In the lunettes are the twelve Olympian gods. The adjacent bedroom, known as the **Stanza delle Nozze**, was frescoed by il Sodoma, who had previously been busy painting the papal apartments in the Vatican, until Raphael showed up and stole the commission. Il Sodoma rebounded with an exuberant scene of Alexander the Great's marriage to the beautiful Roxanne. The side walls have other scenes from Alexander's life, in which you might spot a famous Roman ruin or two. Don't miss the straining Vulcan and three devilish cherubs on either side of the fireplace. (Open 9am-1pm; free, but donations appreciated.)

The Janiculan Hill (Gianicolo)

Though you can reach the Janiculan Hill (in Italian, Gianicolo) by bus #41 from the Vatican, the easiest way to ascend the ridge is from the via della Scala in Trastevere (near the Ponte Sisto). A series of medieval roads and picturesque staircases rises (about a 10-min. walk) to the Spanish **church of San Pietro in Montorio**, built on the spot once believed to be the site of St. Peter's upside-down crucifixion. Now, when visiting hours are over, loyal friends shout messages to inmates in the prison down the hill. The church itself houses a superb *Flagellation* by Sebastiano del Piombo, painted on slate from designs by Michelangelo. Next door, in the center of a small courtyard, is Bramante's tiny but perfect **Tempietto** (1499-1502). A brilliant architectural marriage of Renaissance theory and ancient architectural elements, it was constructed to commemorate the site of Peter's martyrdom and provided the inspiration for the larger dome of St. Peter's, built later in the century at the Vatican. From the belvedere before the Tempietto you'll see a vista of all of Rome; the dome of the Pantheon, Bramante's inspiration, rises straight ahead. Up the road from S. Pietro splashes the lovely **Acqua Paola**, a fountain built by Pope Paul V in 1612 to mark his restoration of the aqueduct from Lake Bracciano. The views from the fountain are even better than those from the church. Up the road from the Acqua Paola is the entrance to the enormous **Villa Doria-Pamphili Park**, about 100m past the Porta San Pancrazio. To the right of the fountain is an entrance to the **Passeggiata del Gianicolo**, Rome's lover's lane (and then some), where a towering equestrian statue of Giuseppe Garibaldi commands the best views of the city yet (and, on clear days, the surrounding mountains of Lazio and the Abruzzi). The northern end of the park descends to the Vatican, past the Renaissance **church of Sant'Onofrio**, with frescoes by Domenichino in the portico, and by the school of the divine Pinturicchio in the apse.

Parks

Rome's many parks provide a well-deserved refuge from the claustrophobic heat and headache-inducing noise of the central city. Here you can stroll, picnic, nap, or join the Romans in a *passeggiata*, the ritual evening stroll. The largest of these parks, the Villa Borghese, houses three of Rome's major museums. All the parks mentioned here are open 7am-dusk.

Villa Borghese

Take Metro Linea A to **Flaminia**, four stops past Termini heading west. Rome's largest splotch of public green, the grounds adjacent to the **Villa Borghese**, occupy a large area north of via Veneto. The cool, shady paths, overgrown gardens, scenic terraces and numerous fountains and statues are a rejuvenating reprieve from the fumes and noise of daytime Rome. Romans have uncharacteristically adopted the American mania for running, and jog the park's car-free, 6km circumference.

Like most property in Rome, the park was at one time connected, albeit remotely, to the Catholic church. Cardinal Scipione Borghese (originally Scipione Caffarelli, nephew of Pope Pius V), in celebration of becoming a cardinal, hired an architect, Flaminio Ponzio, and a landscaper, Domenico Savino da Montepulciano, to build him a private little palace. Completed by Dutch architect Jan van Santen in 1613, the along building with its numerous works of art was bought by the state in 1902. The park's sculptures, reliefs, and knickknacks were mostly looted in the 19th century, but a taste of its former stylish self remains with the sprinkling of Borghese dragons, grotesque masks, dilapidated fountains, and floral reliefs around the park.

Abutting the gardens of Villa Borghese to the Southwest is the **Pincio Hill**, first known as the "hill of gardens" (*Collis Hortulorum*) for the monumental gardens of the Roman Republic aristocracy built on it. This area of Rome contributes its share of macabre historical anecdotes. In the Middle Ages, it served as a necropolis for those bodies (and their souls) denied a Christian burial. Emperor Claudius's third wife Messalina created quite a stir in the nearby **villa of L. Licinius Lucullus** by murdering the owner.

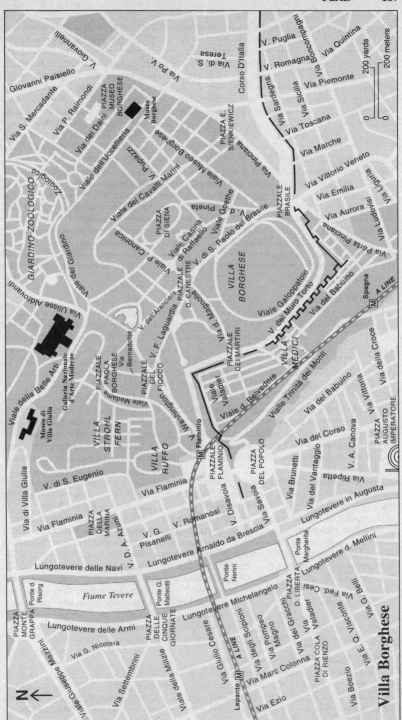

Villa Borghese

When she later ran off with her lover, her infuriated husband sent his troops to kill her. The Pinci family took possession of the villa in the 4th century, giving the surrounding area its present day name. One of the favorite cruising and schmoozing spots of the 19th-century rich and famous, fashionable people would gather on the Pincio at sunset, preferring the view from the terrace of **piazzale Napoleone**. The carriages no longer roll, but the view, which includes St. Peter's, is still one of the best in Rome. The terrace of restaurant and *caffè* **Casa Valadier** offers an even better view, but nothing this good is free. This restaurant has fed an unusual clientele of politicians and celebrities, from Ghandi, Chiang Kai-Shek, Mussolini, and Vincenzo Amato. The north and east boundaries of the Pincio are formed by the infamous **Muro Torto**, or crooked wall, known for its irregular lines and centuries-old dilapidation. Parts of the wall have seemed ready to collapse since Aurelina built it in the 3rd century. When the Goths failed to break through this precarious pile of rocks in the 6th century, the Romans decided St. Peter was protecting it, and refused to strengthen or fortify it.

The park contains three major museums: Museo Borghese, Museo di Villa Giulia, and the Galleria Nazionale D'Arte Moderna. To get to **Museo Borghese** (tel. 854 85 77) without walking all the way from Flaminia Metro stop, take bus #910 from Stazione Termini and get off on via Pinciana. On the northwestern side of the park, along viale delle Belle Arti are the **Galleria Nazionale d'Arte Moderna** (tel. 322 41 54), and the **Museo di Villa Giulia** (tel. 320 15 00). Both are within easy walking distance of the main gate, but the footsore tourist may take tram #19 from via Flaminia to viale delle Belle Arti.

Museo Borghese

Unfortunately, the Museo Borghese is being restored now and is all but covered up by a screen of ugly scaffolding. Only the ground floor is open while repairs are going on. Much of the gallery's painting collection is closed off, but the remarkable sculpture collection is still open and free. There is an extensive collection of Bernini's earliest works, mostly mythological in subject, each sculpture poised in mid-action. **Room 11** contains the other *David*, Bernini's famed Baroque-era representation of the biblical underdog. Sculpted when the artist was a tender 21 years, the handsome but grimacing face is Bernini's own. The differences between Bernini's *David* in the Museo Borghese and Michelangelo's gigantic one in Florence serve as the standard academic comparison for differences between the Renaissance and the Baroque periods of art history. Bernini's *David* is about to release his slingshot; the energy and movement captured in this pose exemplify the intense energy and melodrama of Baroque sculpture. Compare this to the moment of victorious repose in Michelangelo's *David* that typifies the Renaissance.

Room 4 contains another work by Bernini, *The Rape of Proserpine*, possibly a collaboration with his father. The sculpture depicts Pluto, god of the underworld, seizing the terrified virgin Proserpina in the air. This theme reappears in **Room 3** with *Apollo and Daphne* at the moment of Daphne's capture and escape by transforming from a nymph into a laurel tree. Pauline Bonaparte, sister of the emperor and wife of Prince C. Borghese, was one of the villa's more eccentric inhabitants and lives on, naked, in **Room I** as *Venus Victrix* by Canova. When asked by a 19th-century tabloid writer if she felt uncomfortable posing disrobed, Pauline replied, "No, the room was quite warm." Pass through **Room 5**, **Sala Dell'Ermafrodito**, for a titillating glance at something everyone can relate to. The *Salone* contains some rather gruesome 3rd-century mosaics of gladiator scenes by Turronuovo. The closed upper floor contains, among other treasures, Raphael's *Deposition fromm the Cross*, Titian's *Sacred and Profane Love*, Caravaggio's *Boy with a Basket of Fruit*, and Cranach's *Venus and Amore*. (Open Tues.-Sat. 9am-2pm, Sun. 9am-1pm. Ostensible 30-min. time limit; 100 people max.)

Galleria Nazionale d'Arte Moderna

The Galleria Nazionale d'Arte Moderna is housed in the forbidding **Palazzo delle Belle Arti**, designed by Cesare Bazzani in 1911 and enlarged in 1933. The white marble façade incorporates four sets of double pillars, and several large pieces of sculpture sit in the foreground, including Guerrini's primitive *Personaggi* (1974) and Colla's stark *Grande Spirale* (1952) Inside, more than 70 rooms are filled with the best Italian art of the 19th and 20th centuries. Call or check listings for special exhibitions. Stroll through **Rooms 1-30** which concentrate on pieces by 19th-century Italian artists. **Rooms 1-3** present the Neoclassical works of Canova, followed by the Romantics, in particular Francesco Hayez (1791-1882). **Rooms 5-7** feature works from the Neopolitan school, which had ties with the Barbizon School of landscape painting in France. Contemporaries of French Impressionists, the Macchiaioli are best represented in **Rooms 7-8,** though the rooms are being re-organized. Their technique of depicting nature as a series of spots or patches gave them their name (*macchia* means spot), but their work was never as influential or ground-breaking as their French counterparts. Telemaco Signorini (1835-1902), Giovanni Fattori (1825-1908), and Adriano Cecioni (1836-86) are among the best of this school. Other Italian schools represented include the Scapigliati (**Room 16**), started in Milan between 1860 and 1870, celebrating extravagance and dissolution (*scapigliato* means dishevelled). The Divisionists, led by Giovanni Segantini (1858-99) and featured in **Room 18,** aimed for an intense luminosity in their works by juxtaposing primary and complementary colors. The Futurists, covering **Rooms 38-40,** glorify hysteria and turbulence over the staid nature of Neoclassicism and the preciousness of Impressionism.

Artists you'll recognize from the coffee-table books start in **Room 32** with works by Rodin, Manet, Degas, Renoir, Pisarro, and Whistler. Various Rossettis, Klimt's *Three Ages of Man*, Monet's *Lilies*, Degas's *After the Bath*, and Cezanne's *Track Between Rocks* all grace **Room 37**, dedicated to late 19th- and early 20th-century European masters. **Room 57** contains works by Henry Moore, Jackson Pollock and Alberto Giacometti. Don't miss the beautiful garden tucked inside the museum, the lilting sculpture garden, and the riotous, state-of-the-art optical illusions and video flashes on the second floor. (Open Tues.-Sat. 9am-1pm. Closed holidays. Admission L8000.)

Museo Nazionale di Villa Giulia

A short walk towards the river along viale delle Belle Arti takes you to the other temporal extreme: the Museo Nazionale di Villa Giulia, which houses the **Etruscan museum**. The classical building just next to the Museum of Modern Art belongs to the British School, and is not open to the public. It was designed by Sir Edwin Lutyens in 1912. The chap at the foot of the steps is Thorwaldsen, a Danish sculptor who worked in Rome at the beginning of the 19th century. The villa itself was built under Julius III who reigned 1550-55. He was criticized by his contemporaries for leading a rather frivolous life in the middle of the Council of Trent. A poet of the day recorded for eternity the fiasco that erupted when Julius frivolously appointed a 17-year-old monkey trainer to an official post. Julius's playhouse was designed by Vignola, with some input from Michelangelo, in 1551. More conservative popes have stripped away some of the decorative sculpture, though the stairs lead down to the beautiful nymphaeum, designed by Vignola to provide a cool and attractive refuge from the heat. The villa now contains artifacts from pre-Roman civilizations. Every town from here to Florence seems to host an Etruscan museum, but Rome, true to tradition, grabbed many of the best bits, all displayed here with care. Look carefully at the smaller bronzes: modern sculptors like Giacometti owe their inspiration in part to the shapes of the tiny bronze warriors of Todi.

Immediately as you enter, just beyond the left portico two rare, antiquated Etruscan sculptures of a centaur and of a young guy riding a centaur, greet you. Like most of the other Etruscan sculptures, the subject is animated, stylized, and upbeat, though they are funeral relics discovered in tombs. The Etruscans believed that the afterlife was as boring as the present life, and were careful to supply the dead with objects that would keep them amused. Beneath **Room 5** is a reconstruction of a tomb dating back from the 6th century BC, with two funeral chambers, similar to the tomb in the necropolis at Cerveteri.

Room 7 contains strikingly realistic and lively statues of Apollo, one of the little tyke with his mother, and the other of him grown up, done in the 6th century BC. They are set up in their original position, perched atop a temple roof silhoutted against the sky. The sculptures are supposedly the work of Vulca—the only Etruscan sculptor known today—whose reputation was so great that the king of Rome had him build the

Temple of Jupiter on the Capitol in 509 BC. **Room 9** contains a masterpiece of terracotta sculpture: a sarcophagus depicting a deceased man and his wife leaning back happily, as though at a banquet or cocktail party. The artist gave them individual faces, as if they were portraits. Etruscan art has undergone an interesting re-evaluation: in the 18th century, Etruscan sculpture was considered a crude derivative of Greek art, while today Etruscan art is extolled for its elegance, stylization, and expressiveness which has a distinct affinity with modern forms.

The Etruscans took great advantage of their wealth of copper and bronze, fashioning strikingly modern and kitschy pieces, such as chariot-shaped incense burners and urns shaped like huts. **Room 15** holds the much-praised Ghigi Vase (or wine pitcher), an exquisite example of proto-Corinthian handiwork from the 7th century BC, decorated with detailed hunting scenes and the judgement of Paris. Inquire at the ticket office about seeing the extensive Castellani collection of ancient jewelry, dating back to the 8th century BC, in **Room 22.** Just a glance at the painful meticulousness of the designs, like a square inch brooch with 50 golden rams squeezed in, will give you arthritis. In **Room 24,** we get a glimpse of the Etruscan idea of a good time: a large jar depicts two men feasting with a nubile female flute player; another shows Eros seated with a naked lass on (look closely) a panther skin. Also, there are two bowls with the images of Dionysus and Ariadne and a simple message in Faliscan: today I drink wine, tomorrow I shall have none. Villa Giulia hosts evening concerts (usually classical, or classical-jazz hybrid) from mid-June to late Aug.; tickets are L15,000. For concert information and schedules, call 654 10 44 or 678 64 28. (Museo di Villa Giulia open Tues.-Sat. 9am-7:30pm, Sun. and holidays 9am-1pm; mid-Aug. to April Tues.-Sat. 9am-2pm, Sun. 9am-1pm. Admission L8000.)

To see where the mildly wild things are, visit the **Giardino Zoologico,** the Villa's zoo. (tel. 321 65 64. Open daily 8am to 1hr. before sunset. Admission L10,000.) The zoo confines antelope, wolves, a giraffe, and *gabinetti* (toilets). L10,000 seems fairly steep for this little zoo, but admission also gets you to the **Municipal Museum of Zoology,** via Aldrovandi, 18 (tel. 321 65 86). Extensive mammal and bird specimens are on display, though reptiles, amphibians, and fish are poorly represented. We recommend checking out the wolves for free from outside. (Open Tues.-Sun. 9am-1pm.)

Elsewhere in Villa Borghese

If you come to Borghese in the afternooon and find all the museums closed, do not abandon hope; art is rampant even along the paths. In the **Giardino del Lago** (Garden of the Lake), find Jacopo della Porta's Tritons looking suspiciously like the ones in piazza Navona. These are the real thing, moved here in 1984—the ones in piazza Navona are (horrors!) copies. In the lake itself is a classical **Temple of Aesculapius**. Get a close-up from a rowboat if you like. (Rentals 9am-noon and 2pm-sunset; L3000 per person per 20min., with a 2-person min.) Finally, there is an imitation medieval fortress, now known as **Museo Canonica**, just off via Canonica to the east of the lake. The home and studio of artist Pietro Canonica until his death in 1959, it is sporadically open to the public and contains a collection of his sculpture. (Variable hours; ostensibly Tues.-Thurs. 9am-2pm.)

Villa Pamphili

Less known than its Borghese cousin across town, the Villa Pamphili sprawls across the back side of the Janiculan Hill. The park is a favorite among Romans for jogging, dog-walking, and pick-up soccer games, and is dotted with the famous Roman umbrella pines. There are plenty of monuments, gardens, lakes, and statuary, as well as surprising views of the cupola of St. Peter's. Come here to watch the sun set and catch cooling breezes from the Roman countryside. In summer, concerts are held near the gate (where tickets are also sold). From the Vatican (Ospedale San Spirito) take bus #41 to the Porta San Pancrazio; the entrance to the park is 100m down the via Aurelia. From Largo Argentina or Trastevere, take bus #44, 75, or 710 to the city walls, then walk up via Carini to the via Aurelia.

Villa Celimontana

A well-guarded secret, the Villa Celimontana offers a verdant antidote to the dust of the Forum and the cantankerous tourists in the Colosseum. Once a private estate, the villa now welcomes Romans of all ages (particularly children, who come for the playground) to its fountain-filled avenues and flowering stretches of greenery. From the Colosseum or the little-known eastern Palatine exit of the Forum, walk south on via di Gregorio Magno toward the Baroque church of the same name. From here, the ancient Clivio di Scauro ascends to the park entrance.

Aventine Hill

The sacred precincts of the Aventine Hill shelter two formal gardens filled with orange trees and cooled by breezes off the Tiber. A favorite *passeggiata* site on Sunday evenings, the parks offer stunning views of the Capitol and of southern Rome. The Clivio Savello from piazza di Bocca della Verità and the Clivio di Pubblico from the Circus Maximus converge on the gardens and their surrounding churches.

Botanical Gardens

Though you may hesitate to pay for shelter from the summer heat, the Botanical Gardens in Trastevere are well worth the price. Located just north of the Porta Settimiana off the via della Lungara (near the Ponte Sisto) the gardens are filled with well-labeled specimens of trees and flowers. (Open Mon.-Sat. 9am-1pm. Admission L2000.)

Gianicolo

The ridge of the Janiculan Hill is now the favored haunt of sex-starved Roman couples—though the views of the city are spectacular, be prepared to avert your eyes from the quivering Fiats. Still, there isn't a better place in the city to see the sunset, and on clear days you can even glimpse the Alban Hills and the mountains of the Abruzzi. From the Vatican (Ospedale San Spirito), take bus #41; from Trastevere, buses #44, 75, and 710 will take you to the residential district of Monteverde, a 10-minute walk south of the park. Or climb the steps from via della Scala (off via della Lungara).

Campidoglio

Though the *piazza* itself may broil under the summer sun, the Campidoglio actually hides a very pleasant park, the **Belvedere di Monte Tarpeio**—the perfect spot for recovering from a tour of the Forum. With the Palazzio dei Senatori at your back, the via delle Tre Pile climbs left from the front balustrade to the park. The whole southern side of the hill is actually planted with trees and traversed by paths open to the public; at night these are a popular meeting place for Rome's gay population.

Parco Oppio

The Oppian Hill, descending from Sta. Maria Maggiore south to the Colosseum, is almost entirely planted as a park, filled with the crumbling remains of the **Flavian Baths** and Nero's **Golden House**. Fairly scruffy, the greens are often filled with Rome's homeless; for relief from the Colosseum's heat, consider the villa Celimonta instead (see above).

Giardino del Quirinale

A brief stretch of green in the city center, the garden is often filled with lunching bureaucrats from the neighboring Palazzo del Quirinale. Convenient to the Trevi Fountain and via Nazionale, the park lies on the southern side of via XX Settembre.

Parco Adriano

In the shadow of Castel Sant'Angelo, this park offers one of the few green stretches around the Vatican. It was constructed out of the old fortress' moat and outer fortifications, and there are only two entrances (both on the Tiber side of the Castel).

Campo Verano

For those folks with a taste for the macabre (or at least those who have never seen *Poltergeist*), Rome's largest public cemetery makes an interesting stroll, with paths amidst funeral monuments both grandiose and humble. Maybe not the best spot for a picnic, though. Take bus #71 from piazza San Silvestro (off via del Corso) or #11 from the Colosseum; the entrance is to the right of the Basilica San Lorenzo Fuori le Mure, in the San Lorenzo district.

Vatican City

Occupying 108 ½ independent urban acres entirely within Italy's capital, the state of Vatican City is the last toehold of a Catholic Church that once wheeled and dealed as a mighty European power. Under the Lateran Treaty of 1929, the pope remains supreme monarch of his tiny theocracy, exercising all legislative, judicial, and executive powers over the 300 souls who hold Vatican citizenship. According to this agreement, the pope remains neutral in national politics and Roman municipal administration, though the Vatican has generally relied on one or more political parties to fight for its causes at home (albeit with complications). The Vatican state maintains its own army in the form of the Swiss Guards, all descendants of the 16th-century mercenaries hired by Pope Julius II, who wear uniforms designed by Michelangelo. From the Baroque office complex known as the Curia, the priestly hierarchy governs the spiritual lives of hundreds of millions of Catholics around the world.

Recent History

The Church came out of WWII with renewed strength and vigor, and has since spread its message globally, particularly in Eastern Europe and Third World countries. However, in Rome (and in all Italy—especially the North), the Church has lost much of its following; less than 10% of Roman citizens attend Mass. The Church's responses to modernity have been fraught with complications and contradictions. While Pope Pius XII insisted that the Church was not getting involved with politics, in the 1950s, a papal decree forbade all Catholics to associate with the Communist Party (the Partito Comunista Italiano, or PCI) or to publish or distribute any Communist literature. The Church went so far as to pressure (unsuccessfully) the Democratic Christian party to join forces with the far-right party (the MSI) to block the election of the Communist candidates. Interestingly, the Catholic Church in many other Western European countries was directly affiliated with the Socialist parties. Pope John XXIII ushered in moderation in the 1960s. The pope agreed to open dialogue with the Communist party—which represented a new commitment to an amicable dialogue with "non-believers." In the wake of these "liberalizing" efforts, the Church formed Vatican II in 1962. The aim of the ecumenical council was to reassess and improve relations with other religions and to "face the problems of modern society." It disbanded in 1965, and though it didn't modernize the Church, it did produce some material for reformers to work with. One crucial decision took steps to combat clerical anti-Semitism by a "pardoning" of the Jews from the age-old accusation of killing Christ, though the Vatican's continued refusal to recognize Israel as an official country has since strained Jewish-Catholic relations. In the 1970s, the Church stepped into the political ring to fight the passing of divorce legislation—but to no avail. The Church did loosen its collar by abolishing Latin as the official language for rituals, allowing more freedom of interpretation and communication by the laity. The Church has had strong affiliations with the right-wing Christian Democratic Party, or DC, though the intimacy of the relationship has fluctuated over time. Pope John Paul II's international approach to papacy, with his overt use of the media, especially in his constant travels, reflects the Church's intention to establish a more direct relationship with people without the interference of modern politics and parties. This means that the DC party (as well as other Catholic-based political groups) can no longer rely on the Vatican for continual support. The fact that the current pope is Polish also means that the church is even less tied to the vicissitudes of Italian politics and can commit to the pursuit of Catholic ideals at an international level. The Vatican operates a widely popular radio station (which broadcasts news in English daily) as well as publishing a newspaper, *L'Osservatore Romano*.

Getting There

On the western bank of the Tiber, Vatican City can be reached from Rome center by Metro A to Ottaviano (walk south upon exiting station) or by buses #64 and 492 from Termini, bus #62 from p. Barberini, or #19 from San Lorenzo. The country also boasts a train station, St. Peter's. For official use only, trains service Viterbo and La Storta.

Once There

Tourist Offices

Pilgrim Tourist Information Office, piazza San Pietro (tel. 698 44 66 or 698 48 66), to the left of the *piazza* as you face the basilica. Free pamphlets with information on hours and towns, and a well-nigh-illegible map. Money exchange with no commission. Open 8:30am-7pm.

Tours and Sightseeing: Tours of the otherwise inaccessible **Vatican Gardens** (Tues. and Fri-Sat. at 10am, L10,000; you can see them free from the top of St. Peter's cupola) and combining the gardens and the Sistine Chapel (March-Oct. Mon. and Thurs. at 10am, L19,000). Information office open Mon.-Sat. 8:30am-1pm and 2-6:30pm.

Mail

The Vatican Post Office, p. San Pietro, is on the left as you face St. Peter's. A trailer office is set up in the *piazza* in summer. Service from Vatican City is several days quicker and somewhat more reliable than from its Italian counterpart. (Open Mon.-Fri. 8:30am-7pm, Sat. 8:30am-6pm.) No *Fermo Posta* is available. Packages up to 1kg and 90cm, tied with string, can also be sent from the Vatican.

Transportation

Take the Vatican bus from the stop at the tourist information office to the museum entrances via the gardens for L2000 one-way. Buy tickets from the bus driver. Departures every half-hour 9am-2pm. No service Wednesdays and Sundays.

Religious Services

To attend a Papal Audience apply in writing to the **Prefetture della Casa Pontificia,** 00120 Città del Vaticano, or go to the office by the bronze door of St. Peter's (to the right of the basilica; often indoors when its hot or raining) the Monday or Tuesday before the audience you wish to attend (open 9am-1pm; tel. 69 82). Try to arrive early as there is limited seating. Tickets are free. The papal audiences are held Wednesday at 11am when the Pope is in Rome, 10am when he's at his summer estate south of Rome in Castel Gandolfo. During the audience, the Pope gives a message in several languages (Italian, English, French, Spanish, German, and Polish) to about 200-300 people, greets the school groups by name and country, and gives his blessing to all. Crowds of grouchy tourists who realize how far general seating is from the white spot on the stage may leave you feeling less than benevolent. In any case, wear subdued colors; women should wear dresses with sleeves and with their heads covered; men should wear a tie and not wear informal clothing.

Multi-lingual confession is also available inside St. Peter's. Languages spoken are printed outside the confessionals towards the main altar.

Emergencies

Public toilets are to the left of the Basilica, next door to the information office; donations requested.

A hospital, **Ospedale Santo Spirito,** awaits the sick at via Borgo Spirito, while capable nuns on call at via S. Ufficio, to the left of the Basilica, will fix your cuts and bruises. (Open Wed. 8:30am-1pm, Sun. 8:30am-12:30pm.)

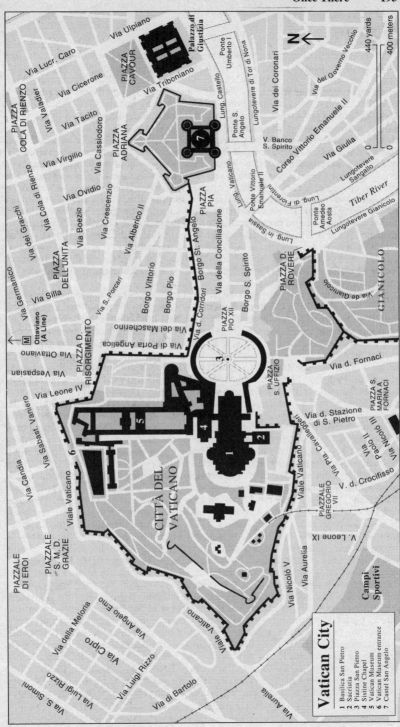

Vatican City

1 Basilica San Pietro
2 Sacristia
3 Piazza San Pietro
4 Sistine Chapel
5 Vatican Museum
6 Vatican Museum entrance
7 Castel San Angelo

Sights

Vastly more efficient and better maintained than any Italian institution (and also just plain vast), the pontiff's incomparable collection of architecture, painting, sculpture, decorative arts, tapestries, books, carriages, and cultural artifacts from around the globe merits enormous amounts of your time and energy, though the official guidebook thoughtfully offers suggested itineraries for the flagging and the faint of heart.St. Peter's Basilica. **Appropriate dress** is always required in the Basilica. No shorts, miniskirts, or sleeveless shirts are allowed.

Begin outside, where Bernini's sweeping, elliptical piazza San Pietro provides an impressive vestibule for the colossal church that dominates its western end. The colonnaded arms were meant to continue around the bottom end of the *piazza;* Mussolini's broad via della Conciliazione, built in the 1930s to connect the Vatican with the rest of the city, opened up a view of St. Peter's that Bernini never intended (he had wanted the spacious marble *piazza* to greet pilgrims as a surprise after their wanderings through the medieval Borgo). This may seem like just another public space, but think of the effect it must have had on people accustomed to the cramped, crowded, dirty streets of medieval Rome that surrounded it originally. The obelisk in the center, originally erected by the Emperor Augustus in Alexandria, is framed by two splashing fountains; round porphyry disks set in the pavement between each fountain and the obelisk mark the spots where, if you stand on them, the quadruple rows of Bernini's colonnades resolve into one perfectly aligned row.

Ascend past the Swiss Guards to the porch of the basilica (you cannot enter in shorts or with bare shoulders); the **Porta Sancta** (holy door), to the left of the central door, can only be opened by the Pope, who knocks in its bricked-up center every 25 years with a silver hammer. The basilica itself rests on the reputed site of its eponym's tomb, and a Christian structure of some kind has stood here since the Emperor Constantine made Christianity the state religion in the 4th century AD. In 1452, with Constantine's original brick basilica showing its age, Pope Nicholas V commissioned Rossellino to rebuild it. Work didn't begin until the more efficient Sixtus IV (of Sistine Chapel fame) acquired the mitre in 1471, and the project continued in fits and starts as a succession of brilliant technicians, including Sangallo, Raphael, and Michelangelo, directed the work. The façade and final shape of the building are the work of its last architect, Carlo Maderno. In 1626, Pope Urban VIII consecrated the building. The overwhelming interior of the basilica measures 186m x 137m along the transepts. (Metal lines in the floor mark the puny-by-comparison lengths of other major world churches.) To the right, Michelangelo's sorrowful **Pietà** is protected by bullet-proof glass, since in 1978 an axe-wielding fiend attacked the famous sculpture, smashing the nose and breaking the hand off the madonna. The sculpture was Michelangelo's first commission in Rome at the age of 25, and the only one he has ever signed, apparently after overhearing some onlookers who thought that it was done by a Milanese artist. Michelangelo intentionally made the proportions slightly imperfect. The madonna's face contains the finest details and expression while her body, actually hidden by the folds of her clothes, is somewhat large: this is both a symbolic sign of her purity and of her ability to hold the powerful figure of Christ. Jesus doesn't exhibit the physical signs of his violent martyrdom; his suffering is evident in the helpless, piteous way he lies in his mother's lap. This sculpture is significant in that it represents marks of pain, suffering and death on a purely incorporeal, sublime level, preceding the ethereal religious art of the Baroque.

Further down the nave a medieval bronze **statue of St. Peter**, seated on a marble throne, presides over the crossing on the right, his brazen foot worn away by the attentions of the faithful. The vertiginous crossing of the vault is anchored by four niches with statues of saints; Bernini's **St. Longinus**, in the northeast niche, represents the centurion who skewered Christ on the cross and then came to have faith, as an allegory of the conversion of pagan Rome to Christianity. To the left of the altar is the **Treasury** (containing sacred paraphernalia and the magnificent bronze tomb of Sixtus IV; open Mon.-Sat. 9am-6:30pm; Sun. 9am-5:30pm; Oct.-March daily 9am-2:30pm; admission L3000).

In the center of the crossing, the **Baldacchino**, another work by Bernini, rises on spiralling solomonic columns over the plain marble altar, which only the Pope may use. The canopy, cast out of bronze pillaged from the porch of the Pantheon, was unveiled on the 28th of June, 1633, by Pope Urban VIII Barberini, whose heraldic bees swarm up the twisting columns toward the cavernous vault of Michelangelo's cupola, built with the same double shell as Brunelleschi's earlier dome in Florence, but made much rounder, on the model of the Pantheon. Out of reverence for that ancient architectural triumph, Michelangelo is said to have designed the cupola a meter shorter in diameter than its predecessor. In the apse, more Bernini treasures gleam in marble and bronze. The convoluted **Cathedra Petri** is a Baroque reliquary which houses the original throne of St. Peter in a riot of bronze and gilt. On either side, the **tombs** of Popes Paul III and Urban VIII slumber in mixed-media (marble, bronze, and gilt, that is) splendor. To the left of the altar, Bernini's last work in St. Peter's, the gruesome **monument to Alexander VII**, is enlivened by the skeletal figure of Death raising an hourglass and proclaiming *momento mori*—don't forget death.

Steps at the crossing lead down to the **Vatican Grottoes**, final resting place of innumerable popes and saints. The passages are lined with tombs both ancient and modern, and though the space is much modernized and well-lit, it's still creepy. The grottoes eject you back at the entrance. From here, you can cross round the left side of the porch to the entrance to the cupola. You can go up by stair or elevatior to the walkway around the interior of the dome, or go up some more fairly hellish stairs to the outdoor tippy-top ledge of the cupola. From here there's an excellent view of the roof of the basilica, the *piazza,* the Vatican Gardens, and the hazy Roman skyline. (St. Peter's open 8am-7pm. Dome closes 1hr. earlier and may be closed when the pope is in the basilica, often Wed. morning. Admission on foot L4000, by elevator (though there's still a hefty climb) L5000. It's worth going up, even at L5000.) Mass is given several times per day in the church, with a particularly beautiful vespers service Sunday at 5pm.

On the left side of the *piazza,* through a gate protected by Swiss Guards, you can descend to the necropolis, one level below the grottoes. A double row of mausoleums dating from the first century AD lies here. Archaeologists believe they have located **St. Peter's tomb** here, in a small aedicule temple located directly underneath the altars of both the Constantinian and modern basilicas. Only small, prearranged tours may enter (L5000). Apply to the *Ufficio Scavi* (excavation office) beneath the Arco della Campana to the left of the basilica (Open Mon.-Sat. 9am-noon and 2-5pm).

Vatican Museums

A ten-minute walk around the Vatican City walls (or the bus that drives from the piazza through the Vatican Gardens) brings you to the **Vatican Museums** (tel. 698 33 33). All the major galleries are open Mon.-Sat. 8:45am-1:45pm; during Easter, and July-Sept. except Saturdays, they are open Mon.-Sat. 8:45am-4pm. The museums are closed on major religious holidays (including Jan. 1, Feb. 11, Easter Monday, May 1, Ascension Day, June 14 and 29, August 15, Nov. 1, Dec. 8, and Dec. 25 and 26). The museums are open the last Sunday of every month from 8:45am-1pm, when admission is free. Otherwise L10,000, L7000 with a student ID, children under 1m tall free.

The Vatican Museums constitute one of the world's great collections of art, a vast storehouse of ancient, Renaissance and modern statuary, painting, decorative arts, and sundry papal odds and ends. The galleries stretch over some four miles of the old papal palace and are stuffed with many more treasures than you could possibly see in one day. Though the entrance price is steep, consider making more than one visit. If you've only got a morning, invest some time planning your tour before you go—the galleries are so crowded and poorly labeled, and the distances between them so long, that simply wandering will leave you more frustrated and exhausted than enlightened. The best known and most noteworthy attractions in the collection are the **Pio-Clementine Museum** with its celebrated masterpieces of ancient sculpture, the brilliantly frescoed **Borgia Apartments** and **Raphael Stanze** (totally worth it for curling up in a window seat and imagining yourself as Lucrezia), Michelangelo's incomparable **Sistine Chapel,** and the eclectic **Pinacoteca,** or picture gallery. From the collections lying off the beaten track, you can choose to see the specialized galleries of Egyptian, Etruscan, Greek or Roman art, each housing world-class collections of antiquities; the more esoteric **Pio-Christian Museum** (with early Christian sarcophagi), the exhibition rooms of the **Vatican Library,** or the intermittently-open **Ethnological Museum** (with artifacts from Third World cultures) and **Historical Museum** (with furnishings and carriages from papal households of the past). The remaining collections (of candelabra, tapestries, maps, and modern religious art) are housed in long corridors leading to the Sistine Chapel. You'll see them if you want to or not—the tapestries are unbelievably large, old, and complex; give them more time and blow past the cheesy amateur-postmodernist renderings of the cross.

In their most basic plan, the galleries function as a conduit for taking visitors from the entrance and the Belvedere Courtyard down to the papal apartments and the Sistine Chapel and back again. Two long, parallel corridors funnel the crowds through; at either end cluster the specialized galleries mentioned above. The museum management has laid out four color-coded tours and tries to make visitors follow one, but it's possible to pick and choose your way through. Just remember that once you have passed a room or gallery, it's difficult to retrace your steps.

The entrance in viale Vaticano leads to a strange bronze double-helix ramp that climbs to the ticket office (where there is also a money exchange, cloakroom, telephones, first aid station, and a booth selling a guidebook (L10,000) that's well worth the price). After the turnstiles a courtyard, with the intricately carved base of Antoninus Pius's column, confronts you with a choice of itineraries. To the right are the entrances to the Pinacoteca, the Gregorian Profane Museum (Greek and Roman sculpture) and the Pio-Christian Museum (early Christian sarcophagi)—for all these, see below; to the left, the Simonetti Stairway marks the start of the official routes. At the top and to the right of the stairs is the entrance to the Egyptian Museum, with ten rooms of Egyptian statuary, painting, coffins, and mummies, as well as an odd assortment of ancient Roman statuary carved in Egyptian style.

A corridor skirts the **Cortile della Pigna** (Court of the Pinecone), the uppermost end of Bramante's **Belvedere Courtyard**, once part of the papal summer palace. Peek out the windows. Steps lead down to the evocative **Chiaramonti Museum**, a 300m long corridor which is really little more than a storeroom for the Vatican's collection of more than 1000 classical busts, statues, altars, and reliefs. Walking through the dusky gauntlet of vacant stares provides eloquent testimony to the grandeur and desolation of a ruined civilization. The **Braccio Nuovo** abuts the midpoint of the corridor. Here, a collection of life-size or larger statues includes the famous Prima Porta Augustus, a portrait of the emperor at the height of his physical and political powers, a bust of Julius Caesar, and the piquant, reclining figure of the Nile, surrounded by crocodiles, sphinxes, and sixteen *putti* representing the sixteen cubits of the river's annual flood. In the far end of the wing are busts of the more famous Roman Emperors.

Retrace your steps through the corridor and back up the stairs; straight ahead is a square vestibule, entrance to the stellar **Pio-Clementino Museum**, the world's greatest collection of antique sculpture. The Octagonal Court opens off the first three small rooms. This is where the Vatican Museums were born when Julius II filled the court, originally the centerpiece of the Belvedere Palace, with his first purchases of classical sculpture, thus beginning the long tradition of papal art collecting. In a niche (since redecorated by Canova), stands the sublime **Apollo Belvedere**, probably the best-known work of ancient sculpture in existence, certainly one of the greatest, and once called "the highest ideal of art." The god's placid features and imperious posture (apparently he was holding a bow in one hand and drawing an arrow from his quiver with the other) inspired innumerable Renaissance copies both in stone and on canvas. Also here is the tortured **Laocoon** group, a sculpture which was famous even in antiquity (Pliny the Elder wrote of his admiration for it) for its convincing grotesqueness. Virgil told the story of Laocoon in his *Aeneid*: the Trojan priest, advising his people against drawing the Trojan Horse into their city, was punished by Athena, the protectress of the Greeks, who sent two sea serpents to devour him and his sons. It's thought that the figures of Laocoon and the son to the left of him were carved from a single piece of marble. Laocoon's raised arm, flexed in a vain effort to escape the serpent, was only

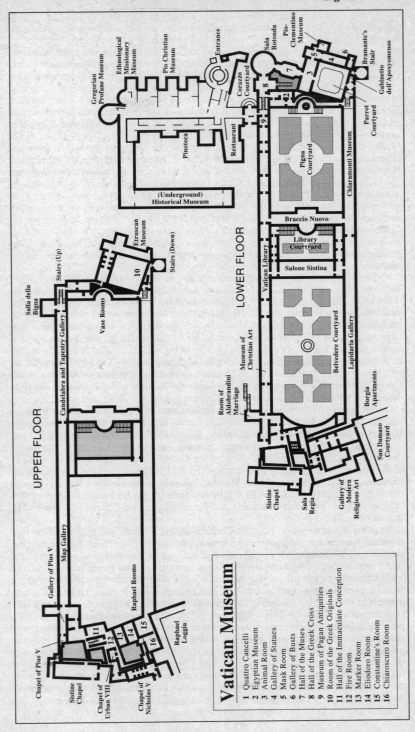

Vatican Museum

1 Quattro Cancelli
2 Egyptian Museum
3 Animal Room
4 Gallery of Statues
5 Mask Room
6 Gallery of Busts
7 Hall of the Muses
8 Hall of the Greek Cross
9 Museum of Pagan Antiquities
10 Room of the Greek Originals
11 Hall of the Immaculate Conception
12 Fire Room
13 Marker Room
14 Eliodoro Room
15 Constantine's Room
16 Chiaroscuro Room

UPPER FLOOR

Chapel of Pius V
Gallery of Pius V
Stairs (Up)
Salla della Bigna
Etruscan Museum
Stairs (Down)
Vase Rooms
Candelabra and Tapestry Gallery
Map Gallery
Raphael Rooms
Raphael Loggia
Sistine Chapel
Chapel of Urban VIII
Chapel of Nicholas V

10

LOWER FLOOR

Gregorian Profane Museum
Ethnological Missionary Museum
Pio Christian Museum
Entrance
Corazzo Courtyard
Sala Rotonda
Pio-Clementino Museum
Bramante's Stair
Gabinetto dell'Apoxyomenos
Parrot Courtyard
Restaurant
Pinoteca
(Underground) Historical Museum
Pigna Courtyard
Chiaramonti Museum
Braccio Nuovo
Library Courtyard
Salone Sistina
Vatican Library
Museum of Christian Art
Belvedere Courtyard
Lapidaria Gallery
Room of Aldobrandini Marriage
Borgia Apartments
San Damaso Courtyard
Sistine Chapel
Sala Regia
Gallery of Modern Religious Art

discovered and reattached in this century. However, many art historians now debate the authenticity of the appendage; if you look closely, the proportions are somewhat off (the arm is smaller than the original body) and the marble seems to be a different color and stock than the rest. Nearby, a plaster cast shows how Renaissance sculptors improvised an arm raised straight into the air; but for expressing the tense horror of Laocoon's predicament, the ancient configuration wins hands down. Two slobbering Molossian Hounds guard the entrance to the **Room of the Animals**, a marble menagerie that reveals a lot about the Romans' predilection for verisimilitude in their art and brutality in their sport. Look for the green porphyry seafood. Three rooms adjacent to the animals, the **Gallery of Statues**, the **Room of the Busts**, and the **Cabinet of the Masks**, were closed in 1992. The **Room of the Muses** opens off the animal room and is anchored by the inscrutable **Belvedere Torso**, a shattered work thought to represent Hercules sitting on his lion skin. Michelangelo worshiped the powerful musculature and tense contortion of this figure; it's said that while he was painting his own colossal nudes in the Sistine Chapel he was once found prostrate before the torso, abasing himself in solitary admiration. In the great **Round Room** beyond are colossal Roman statues, including two of Antinöus, the ill-fated lover of Hadrian, one of the Emperor Claudius dressed in a general's uniform (his reputed obesity, lameness, and drool tactfully forgotten) and a breathtakingly atrocious gilded Hercules. The last room of the gallery contains the enormous red porphyry **sarcophagus of St. Helen**, mother of Constantine.

The next flight of the Simonetti Stairway climbs to the **Etruscan Museum**, filled with artifacts from the necropoli of Tuscany and northern Lazio. Especially noteworthy is **Room II**, with the contents of the splendid **Regolini-Galassi Tomb**, a tumulus found intact and full of treasure outside the necropolis at Cerveteri. In the center are the extraordinary bronze chariot and bed with which the deceased 7th-century BC couple were supplied for their journey to the other side. In **Room III**, the rare 5th-century BC bronze Mars of Todi looks startled. In the rooms beyond are smaller bronzes, terracotta, red-figure, and black-figure vases (imported from Greece by wealthy Etruscan traders), and jewelry. At the end of the Etruscan Rooms you can visit the **Rooms of the Greek Originals**, the **Stairway of the Assyrian Reliefs,** and the **Vase Collection**, though you might do better to conserve your energies for the long haul ahead.

On the landing of the Simonetti Staircase is the usually closed **Room of the Biga** (an ancient marble chariot outfitted with recent wheels and horses) and the entrance to the **Gallery of the Candelabra**, named for the ancient marble candleholders housed here, along with yet more examples of Roman statuary and decorative arts. Here begins the long trudge to the Sistine Chapel, through the **Gallery of the Tapestries,** the **Gallery of the Maps,** (with diverting 16th-century views of Italy and the islands of the Mediterranean), the **Apartment of Pius V** (more tapestries—ere there is a shortcut stair to the Sistine Chapel), the **Sobieski Room** and **Hall of the Immaculate Conception** (with godawful 19th-century murals), and the rather precious **Chapel of Urban VIII**, decorated by Pietro da Cortona.

From the Room of the Immaculate Conception, a door leads into the first of the four **Raphael Rooms**, the sumptuous papal apartments built by Pope Julius II in the first decade of the 16th century. This is the old papal palace proper, just behind and to the right of the great basilica. Julius had abandoned the apartments of his predecessor Alexander VI Borgia one story below, saying he couldn't live under the portraits of the nefarious Spanish pope and his court which had been painted there. Instead, he hired the best painters of his own day, including Perugino, Peruzzi, and il Sodoma, to decorate a new suite of rooms for himself. But though they had already been working for several years, even these geniuses had to make way for the precocious talent of Raphael Sanzio, who arrived at the papal court with an introduction from his fellow Urbinese Bramante, and painted the astonishing **School of Athens** as a trial piece for Pope Julius. The pope was so impressed he fired his other painters, had their frescoes destroyed and handed the entire suite of rooms, with a total of 16 walls to be painted, over to Raphael. The commission marked the beginning of Raphael's brilliant Roman career, and on his untimely death in 1520, his students completed the decoration according to his designs.

A trip through the *stanze* is necessarily confusing, as you must view the rooms in re-verse chronological order (the flow of traffic is now diverted after the Stanza dell'In-cendio through a modern covered walkway to the Sala di Constantino). A further detour from this room takes you to the **Room of the Chiaroscuri**, used by Pope Leo X for various ceremonies, and the Chapel of Nicholas V. The small chapel forms the old-est section of the apostolic palace and was delicately decorated by Fra Angelico be-tween 1447-51, with frescoes depicting events from the lives of St. Steven (in the upper register) and St. Lawrence below. Note in particular St. Lawrence receiving the trea-sure of the church, in which Fra Angelico painted the frail features of Nicholas V him-self on the countenance of St. Sixtus. Although much damaged and repainted, the scene of St. Lawrence writhing on his gridiron admirably recalls the martyr's last words, "Turn me over, this side's done."

Back in the Raphael Rooms, the **Sala di Constantino** (1517-24), mostly painted af-ter Raphael's death, has as its main theme the church's victory over the forces of pagan-ism. On the entrance wall, Constantine addresses his soldiers and sees the vision of the cross; on the wall opposite is the baptism of Constantine; on the window wall, Con-stantine donates the city of Rome to Pope Sylvester; on the wall facing the window, Constantine defeats Maxentius at the Battle of the Milvian Bridge.

Next comes the **Stanza d'Eliodoro** (1512-14). The obscure subjects were chosen by Julius to illustrate the miraculous protection afforded by God to a threatened Catholic Church. The scenes depict, on the right wall, the Biblical story of the expulsion of He-liodorus from the temple; on the left, the miracle of Bolsena. Raphael painted Julius himself in the guise of Pope Urban IV who, after the miraculous appearance of blood on an altar linen at Bolsena, instituted the feast of Corpus Christi (June 14). Note the Swiss Guards kneeling on the right. On the long wall is Leo I repulsing Attila from the city of Rome; on the fourth wall is the gloomy deliverance of St. Peter from the Tul-lianum Prison on the Capitoline Hill.

The **Stanza della Segnatura** (1508-1511), which the pope supposedly used as his office or possibly as his private library, was painted entirely by Raphael and is consid-ered his masterpiece. The four walls represent four branches of learning —theology, law, philosophy, and poetry. On the wall opposite the entrance is the **Disputation of the Holy Sacrament**, in which celebrated doctors of the Church and theologians crowd around a monstrance holding the communion host. On the wall opposite is the splendid **School of Athens**, in which ancient philosophers and scientists (many of whom Raphael painted with the features of his friends and fellow artists) converse as they stroll through an architectural fantasy. In the center Plato, with the features of Le-onardo da Vinci, disputes with Aristotle; Euclid, explaining geometry on the ground, has Bramante's face; to the far right of the composition stand Raphael (in three-quarter profile) and (dressed in white) his friend and fellow artist il Sodoma; in the center, the isolated, brooding figure of Heraclitus is thought to be a portrait of Michelangelo, add-ed as an afterthought when Raphael had been given a sneak preview of the Sistine Chapel. Part of what is so remarkable about this fresco is the rapidity in which Raphael did it. Frescoes (literally meaning "fresh" in Italian), began with an outline, or cartoon. Then, the plaster was added (usually students did these kinds of menial tasks) and se-ries of holes were poked through to illustrate the design. The plaster dried extremely quickly, so a fresco would have to be fully painted in a day; an artist would concentrate on one small section of a fresco for that 15-20 hours. If you look closely at a fresco, you can often see these different sections (i.e. days) where an artist began and ended. In this case, Raphael supposedly drew up the elaborate cartoons in a matter of days. Fur-thermore, it appears that Raphael spent as much time (that is, one day) working on the face of Heraclitus (alias Michelangelo) as he did on the entire left half of the fresco. Part of the reason that painting the Sistine Chapel was so agonizing was that Michelan-gelo had to finish each piece of the fresco within hours of starting.

The remaining two scenes depict Mount Parnassus, peopled by classical and contem-porary Italian poets including Horace, Virgil, Propertius, Dante, Ariosto, Boccaccio, and Petrarch; opposite (over the windows) are the obscure cardinal and theological vir-tues, represented by *Gregory IX Approving the Decretals* and *Justinian Publishing the Pandects.*

The final room is the **Stanza dell'Incendio** (which you passed through before) containing works by Raphael's pupils, including Giulio Romano. By the time of their painting in 1514-17, Pope Leo X Medici had taken up residence in the *stanze,* and portraits of his namesake predecessors dominate the room. The riotous *Fire in the Borgo* depicts a disaster which befell the Borgo, the medieval district between the the Vatican and the Tiber, in 847, but which was miraculously extinguished when Leo IV made the sign of the cross from the *loggia* of St. Peter's. The painting is notable for its depiction of the façade of the old Constantinian basilica, which was pulled down to make way for new St. Peter's. Other scenes represent the coronation of Charlemagne by Leo I in 800, the victory of Leo IV over the Saracens at Ostia, and on the window wall, the oath of Leo III.

Depending on the itinerary you are taking, a staircase leads down to the Borgia Apartments and the Museum of Modern Religious Art or, more directly, to the Sistine Chapel. The **Borgia Apartments**, named after the infamous Alexander VI Borgia, father of the even more infamous Lucrezia and Cesare, comprise six rooms decorated in 1492-95 by the wholly underrated, much-maligned, technically brilliant and unquestionably superb Umbrian painter Bernardino Betti, called Pinturicchio. (*Let's Go* likes Pinturicchio.) Today, all you can see of the decoration here are the lunettes and ceiling vaults, as the walls have been ludicrously smothered by the Vatican's ghastly collection of modern religious art. The staircase descends into the **Room of the Sibyls**, so called by the twelve lunettes which depict pairs of classical sybils and Old Testament prophets, foreshadowing, interestingly enough, Michelangelo's arrangement of the same subjects on the Sistine ceiling. Legend has it that it was in this room that Cesare Borgia had his brother-in-law Alfonso D'Aragone stabbed and then strangled, in order to free up his sister Lucrezia for marriage to Alfonso d'Este, the future Duke of Ferrara. The other rooms depict members of the Borgia court in the unlikely guise of saints and Biblical figures; note particularly in the **Room of the Mysteries (Room IV)** that in the Resurrection there is a splendid portrait of the pope himself, while the central figure of the soldier with a lance may be a portrait of the ruthless Cesare. Above the door leading to the Room of the Mysteries, a *tondo* of the *Madonna and Child* by Pinturicchio may be a portrait of Giulia Farnese, Alexander VI's mistress and mother of the future Pope Paul III.

A brisk walk through the ill-favored collection of **Modern Religious Art** (composed mostly of unwanted presents sent to the Pope by fawning 20th-century artists) is only enlivened by the vibrant copes (church vestments) designed by Matisse, a few hastily-thrown pots by Picasso, and a third-rate Francis Bacon.

The Sistine Chapel

Stairs finally lead to the long-awaited **Sistine Chapel**. One of the few places in the museum outfitted with benches, this sacred chamber consistently overflows with weary, camera-laden tourists (though any any form of photography is strictly forbidden in— and detrimental to— the chapel). Called Sistine after its founder, Pope Sixtus IV, whose nephew Julius II commissioned Michelangelo to decorate its ceiling in 1508-12, the hall serves as a papal chapel but, more importantly, as the chamber in which the College of Cardinals has met to elect a new pope ever since. Its inclusion in the museum tour is somewhat deceiving, since the chapel is really a part of the Basilica of St. Peter's, to which it is attached. The wall by which you enter is the altar wall, while the opposite wall forms the proper entrance, opening onto the official state rooms of the Vatican Palace and the second-story *loggia* of the Basilica. The barrel vault of the ceiling, some 70 feet above the floor, gleams with the results of its recent, celebrated, and hotly debated restoration. Before craning your neck, first prepare yourself by taking in the frescoes on the side walls which predate Michelangelo's ceiling work. On the right wall, scenes from the life of Moses prefigure parallel scenes of the life of Christ on the left wall. The cycle, frescoed between 1481-83, was completed by a team of artists under the direction of Perugino that included Botticelli, Ghirlandaio, Roselli, the divine Pinturicchio, Signorelli, and della Gatta. Down the right wall are the *Journey of Moses* (Perugino), *Flight from Egypt* (Botticelli), *Crossing the Red Sea, Tablets of the Law, Punishment of Korah, Dathan, Abiram* (Botticelli), and the *Testament of Moses* (Signo-

The Sistine Chapel Ceiling

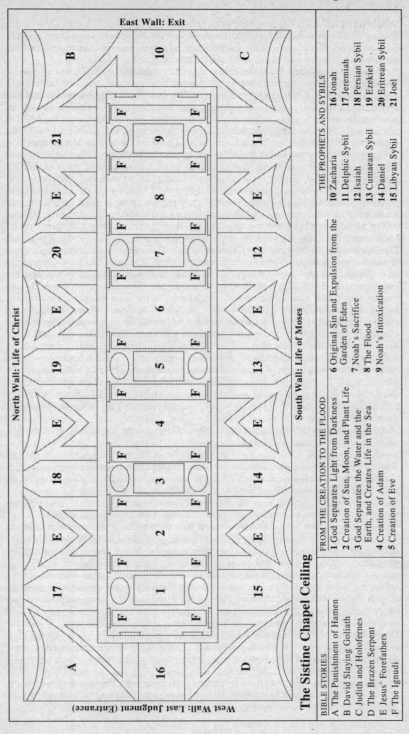

East Wall: Exit

North Wall: Life of Christ

South Wall: Life of Moses

West Wall: Last Judgment (Entrance)

BIBLE STORIES
A The Punishment of Hamen
B David Slaying Goliath
C Judith and Holofernes
D The Brazen Serpent
E Jesus' Forefathers
F The Ignudi

FROM THE CREATION TO THE FLOOD
1 God Separates Light from Darkness
2 Creation of Sun, Moon, and Plant Life
3 God Separates the Water and the Earth, and Creates Life in the Sea
4 Creation of Adam
5 Creation of Eve
6 Original Sin and Expulsion from the Garden of Eden
7 Noah's Sacrifice
8 The Flood
9 Noah's Intoxication

THE PROPHETS AND SYBILS
10 Zacharia
11 Delphic Sybil
12 Isaiah
13 Cumaean Sybil
14 Daniel
15 Libyan Sybil
16 Jonah
17 Jeremiah
18 Persian Sybil
19 Ezekiel
20 Eritrean Sybil
21 Joel

relli); on the left wall, *Baptism of Christ* (Perugino), *Temptation of Christ* (Botticelli), *Calling of the First Apostles* (Ghirlandaio), *Sermon on the Mount, Consignment of the Keys to Peter* (Perugino), and the *Last Supper.* Botticelli and Ghirlandaio painted the series of early popes who stand in the niches between the high windows.

Above stretches the undaunted genius, brave simplicity, and brilliant coloring of Michelangelo's unquestioned masterpiece—some have called these powerful frescoes the greatest works of Western art ever created. The fact that the Florentine sculptor and architect had the commission foisted upon him unwillingly (it's said that Bramante, worried that the genius might take over his own project, the construction of the new basilica, hinted to Pope Julius that Michelangelo should paint the ceiling instead) only makes his brilliant success more impressive. The work is wholly Michelangelo's; though he had never worked in fresco before, he kept his assistants only long enough to learn the technique from them, then settled down to a frenzied four years of solitary painting. He painted, not flat on his back, but standing up and bending backwards, and never recovered from the strain to his neck and eyes. The design of the frescoes is, apparently, Michelangelo's as well. The fledgling painter chose to depict the history of mankind before the coming of Christ, thus linking the ceiling decoration with the stories of Moses and Christ on the side walls. He divided the vault into a monumental architectural scheme, each enclosing a separate scene from Genesis. These are *Separation of Light from Darkness, Creation of the Sun, Moon and Planets, Separation of Land and Sea* and the *Creation of Fishes and Birds, Creation of Adam, Creation of Eve, Temptation and Expulsion from Paradise, Sacrifice of Noah, Flood,* and the *Drunkeness of Noah.* These are framed by the famous *ignudi,* contorted naked male youths who cavort among the decorative vaulting. In the four spandrels are depicted *David and Goliath, Judith and Holofernes,* the *Brazen Serpent,* and the *Punishment of Hanan.* These are surrounded by monumental figures of Old Testament prophets and classical sybils, some pondering the events of Christian history to come, and some holding aloft books of revealed wisdom. The whole expanse of ceiling, each square yard encompassing a masterpiece of painting, fuses into a vibrant testimony to the power of one man's vision of scripture, philosophy, and art. The altar wall, covered by Michelangelo's apocalyptic vision of The Last Judgement (and the ensuing chaos of the last days of time) has been covered for restoration for several years, and probably will be for several more to come. (A paltry Polaroid copy dangles on the scaffolding in the meantime.)

Art historians worldwide debate the wisdom of the most recent work done in the Sistine Chapel: the gradual cleaning of the paintings. The restorations, which will continue for several years, have changed the works from dark and shadowed to bright and pastel—and the art history textbooks are being rapidly rewritten. Opponents argue that the restorers, in scraping off layers of grime as well as paint from previous patch-up jobs, have also scraped off an important second layer that Michelangelo would have added for shadowy details. Frescoes (literally "fresh" in Italian) were layers of plaster which had to be painted within hours before drying. This accounts for some of the agonizing pressure that Michelangelo endured (and for Raphael's remarkable rapidity in *The School of Athens*). One theory is that Michelangelo added an overcoat to his original paint-job to add the finer details, brooding shadows, deeper colors, and outstanding dimension that he is renowned for. Here, the colors are extremely bright, almost saccharine, shadows are non-existent, and the pictures flat relative to pre-restoration days and to his other works. Some purists argue that the work never should have been restored at all, and that it should have just run its course and died gracefully. Of course, the restorers argue otherwise, having used extremely advanced computer analyses (and received hefty funding). One way or another, the ceiling was on the verge of collapse from time and weather, and the fresco was in danger of peeling completely from the ceiling. The restorers, whether they removed a crucial layer or not, reattached the fresco and repaired the ceiling. Refrain from taking flash photos, even if you see others around you doing it; this is detrimental to the fresco; you can buy much better shots (cheaper than using your own film) on professional postcards. The best way to view the ceiling is by using a hand-held mirror, rather than craning your neck to look up (though the giddy feeling of staring straight up at superhuman beauty can be a treat in itself).

From the exit along the left-hand wall of the Chapel, a series of corridors returns you to the Galleries of the Library and the long walk back to the Belvedere. A short way up on the left, the **Room of the Aldobrandini Marriage** houses a series of rare ancient Roman frescoes, including the celebrated wedding scene, set in a flowering park filled with animals and architectural fantasies. On the left wall are frescoes of famous mythological women and the animals they slept with. The corridor continues past cases of unbelievably awful modern religious art (try to miss the *Mute Swans of Peace*) and interesting antique globes and maps. The walls are painted with scenes of Roman tourist attractions. The Sistine Hall on the right is used for exhibits from the Vatican Library's superb collection of books and manuscripts.

Back near the entrance, you can (if you've got the energy left) visit the remaining galleries. The **Pinacoteca**, the Vatican's eclectic picture collection, is entered from the open court immediately after the ticket booths. Unfortunately, you can no longer enjoy an overpriced break at the snack bar, because it is closed. The gallery houses a collection of paintings and tapestries dating from the 11th to the 19th century. The eighteen rooms are 1. Byzantine School and Italian Primitives; 2. School of Giotto and Late Gothic; 3. Fra Angelico and contemporaries; 4. Melazzo da Forli; 5. Various 15th century painters; 6. polyptichs; 7. 15th century Umbrian School; 8. Raphael; 9. Leonardo da Vinci and others; 10. Titian, Veronese and Venetian Art; 11. Late 16th century; 12. Caravaggio and the Caraveggeschi; 13. 17th and 18th century; 14. Flemish, Dutch and German 17th and 18th century; 15. Portraits; 16. 18h century animal subjects; 17. Bernini Maquettes; 18. Icons.

Room 1 houses the oldest picture in the gallery, a curious keyhole-shaped wood panel of the Last Judgement dating from the 11th century, which provides an interesting contrast to Michelangelo's monumental composition of the same subject in the Sistine. In **Room 2**, Gentile di Fabriano's *Scenes from the Life of St. Nicholas of Bari* is a treat. Look for the resurrection of three children who had been found cut up in pieces in a barrel. Stories of the same saint are found in the next room painted by Fra Angelico, along with his *Madonna and Child,* Filippo Lippi's *Coronation of the Virgin* and Benozzo Gozzoli's *Madonna of the Girdle*. **Room 4** contains fragments of a huge fresco by Melazzo da Forli which originally decorated the apse of the basilica of SS Apostoli off the via del Corso. The brightly-colored musician angels are particularly fine. Adjacent is another da Forli fresco, which depicts Sixtus IV conferring the job of librarian on the humanist Bartolomeo Platina. The future Pope Julius II, dressed as a tonsured cardinal, stands at his uncle Sixtus's right hand. **Room 7** contains Perugino's *Madonna and Child* and a *Coronation of the Virgin* by Perugino's exceptionally talented pupil, Pinturicchio. In **Room 8**, three important works by Raphael (the *Transfiguration,* the *Coronation of the Virgin,* and the *Madonna of Foligno*) are surrounded by tapestries copied from the master's cartoons that were meant to hang along the lower walls of the Sistine Chapel. **Room 9** houses Giovanni Bellini's *Pietà* and a mutilated Leonardo da Vinci panel of St. Jerome; prior to its discovery it had been cut in two pieces, one of which had served as a coffer lid, the other as a stool in a shoemaker's shop. **Room 10** provides a refreshing contrast to Roman art with the color and light of the 16th-century Venetian painters. Titian's *Madonna of the Friary* and Veronese's elegant *St. Helena* pose with noble reserve, while Paris Bordone's *St. George and the Dragon* calls to mind the fact that chivalry provided a secular counterpart to religious devotion. **Room 12** brings you into the passionate but cruel world of Baroque devotional art. Here you can see Caravaggio's sensual and sensational *Deposition from the Cross,* Nicholas Poussin's grisly *Martyrdom of St. Erasmus* (who had his intestines rolled out on a winch), and Jean Boulogne's beautifully restored *Martyrdom of SS. Processus and Martinian*. **Room 14** contains a curious series of astronomical observations showing the various phases of the moon, executed for the observatory at Bologna by Donato Cretti, while in **Room 15** Popes Clement VII and Benedict XIV glower down at the bewildered spectator, and Thomas Lawrence's incongruous full-length portrait of King George IV in full coronation robes seems wildly out of place. Animals, icons, and the plaster maquettes Bernini executed as trial runs for the statuary in St. Peter's crossing fill up the remaining three rooms.

The **Gregorian Profane Museum**, called thus for its collection of secular ancient art rather than for any naughtiness on display, is a modern gallery that presents an assortment of Greek and Roman statuary with sensitive moderation. Rarely visited, it makes a peaceful and low-key change from the bustle and bombast of the other museums. Look for the statues of Marsyas, the satyr who dared to play Athena's pipes (and was skinned alive for doing so) and the fragmentary *Chiaramonti Niobid*. Niobe, a mother of 14 children, had taunted Leto for only having given birth to two. Unfortunately, the two were Apollo and Diana, and the outraged gods avenged their insulted mother by shooting down all fourteen of the Niobids. The statue shows one daughter turning to flee the heavenly assault; the crinkled folds of her flowing dress are a superb example of Hellenistic carving. The gallery also contains numerous, finely-carved reliefs from imperial monuments (many of which represent actual buildings of ancient Rome) and, almost hidden in a sky-lit hemicycle toward the back, a breathtakingly noble and sorrowful *Dacian Captive* from Trajan's Forum.

The **Pio-Christian Museum**, with its entrance next door, displays artifacts of a fascinating historical synthesis—the marriage of the Greco-Roman sculptural tradition to the new iconography of the Christian Church. The sarcophagi and statuary here date from the first centuries AD, when the Roman Empire and its artistic vocabulary was still alive and well. Look for the small statue of the Good Shepherd and the many intricately carved sarcophagi.

The **Ethnological-Missionary Museum** (open only Wed. and Sat.) open-mindedly yet subjectively displays representative non-Christian religious articles alongside missionary-inspired works by Third World cultures. The **Historical Museum** (also open only Wed. and Sat., if then) contains fairly recent papal artifacts, including armor, guard uniforms, and carriages.

Near Vatican City: Castel Sant'Angelo

Castel Sant'Angelo, built by the Emperor Hadrian (117-138 AD) as mausoleum for himself and his family, has served the popes of Rome in the centuries since as a convenient (and forbidding) fortress, prison, and palace. The complex, towering over a bend in the Tiber, consists of the original mausoleum, a suite of palatial Renaissance apartments built on top, as well as concentric rings of fortifications including the Ponte Sant'Angelo across the river and the Leonine Wall extending to the Vatican Palace. Hadrian, a dilettante architect as well as emperor, designed the mausoleum in imitation of his predecessor Augustus's more modest tomb across the river. He had the surviving round marble base crowned with an earthen tumulus and planted with cypress trees. But as the city fell to barbarian depredations, panicked Romans quickly converted the imposing structure to defensive purposes. When the city was wracked with plague in 590 AD, Pope Gregory the Great is said to have seen an angel sheathing his sword at the top of the citadel; the plague then abated, and the edifice has been dedicated to the angel, and called by his name, ever since. During the Sack of Rome in 1527, Pope Clement VII ran for his life along the covered wall between the Vatican and the fortress, while the imperial invaders took pot shots at his streaming white papal robes. Pope Paul III used the fortress for more leisurely pursuits, building and decorating a sumptuous suite of apartments over the ancient foundations, which were still used as a prison for heretics and other troublemakers (including the revolutionary astronomer Giordano Bruno and the thieving artist Benvenuto Cellini). The fortress now contains a museum of arms and artillery, but the papal apartments and the incomparable views of Rome seen from them are the real reasons to pay a visit.

From the ticket booth a ramp leads up to the fortress's ramparts and four circular bastions, each named for one of the four evangelists. From the ramparts you can see the massive cement remains of Hadrian's round base and bits of the travertine marble that once completely encased it. A bridge crosses into the base itself, where a ramp (built by Alexander VII; the original mausoleum was ascended by a spiral ramp, now closed) rises over the dismal tomb chamber of the emperor. The **Court of the Angel**, filled with stone cannonballs and the original marble statue of the angel, leads into the **Sala**

di Apollo, whose *grotteschi* frescoes were painted in imitation of ancient Roman designs. Two rooms adjoining the *sala* display 15th- and 16th-century paintings, while from the adjacent semicircular **Courtyard of Alexander VI** you can descend to a dank labyrinth of prison cells and storerooms (including vats where oil was kept for boiling and pouring on besiegers). Upstairs from the courtyard is the **Bathroom** where Clement VII soaked in a tub fit for a Medici prince. Another stair climbs to a **Gallery** that circles the citadel, decorated at intervals with *grotteschi,* stuccos, *loggias* built by Popes Julius II and Paul III, and a bar and souvenir stand. Yet more stairs lead up to the extravagant **Papal Apartments**, including the absurdly overdecorated **Sala Paolina** (with wall paintings of Hadrian and the castle's patron Angel), the **Camera del Perseo** and **Camera di Amore and Psyche** (frescoed and filled with period furniture), and the **Hall of the Library**, frescoed with scenes of cavorting sea gods and lined with an unusual set of stucco reliefs. Keep climbing through some dull exhibition rooms until you reach the broad **Terrace**. Under the watchful eye of the bronze angel, the whole of Rome spreads out below. To the right is St. Peter's and the long wings of the Vatican Museums; to the left, you can see the Pantheon, the Vittorio Emanuele Monument, a dozen or more Baroque domes, the Tiber River and the green parks of Gianicolo. Outside the *castel,* the outer walls of the fort now enclose a large park (good for picnics), while the marble **Ponte Sant'Angelo,** lined with statues of angels designed by Bernini, leads back across the river, and is the starting point for the traditional pilgrimage route from St. Peter's to the Basilica of San Giovanni in Laterano on the other side of Rome. (Castel Sant'Angelo open Tues.-Sat. 9am-2pm, last entrance at 1pm; Sun. 9am-1pm, last entrance at noon; Mon. 2-6:30pm, last entrance at 5:30pm; admission L8000

Entertainment

Since the days of bread and circuses, Roman entertainment has been a public affair—concerts under the stars, street fairs with acrobats and fire-eaters, and Fellini-esque crowds of dippety-do'd Romeos, modern-day minstrels and maestros, yapping dachshunds, and enchanted foreigners flooding *piazze* and *caffè*. Clubs are not necessarily an integral part of the nightlife—the real social scene spills out-of-doors. Those clubs that do exist keep erratic hours and often close in summer. Call before you set out.

Check the various local listings for films, shows, concerts, and special events. On Thursdays, **La Repubblica** comes out with *TrovaRoma,* a comprehensive glossy listing concerts, plays, clubs, and special events. Romans adore summer and hold myriad celebrations. At night, subdued Dionysian revelry claims the streets. Festivals erupt spontaneously in different *piazze.* In **p. della Repubblica**, there's often a Vegas-style crooner, while in **p. S. Maria in Trastevere**, you may run across the last vestiges of the flower children. The **Spanish Steps** host any number of sleazy, ersatz Romeos—you'd do well to skip these festivities. **Piazza Navona** bursts with fortune tellers, caricaturists, soused teenagers, and goggle-eyed tourists, while the **Pantheon** is a favored spot for bachelors to tipple a L15,000 *Campari* and to strut their stuff. **Via Giulia** makes a quiet and romantic evening *passeggiata,* or you can head over to the **Campo dei Fiori** for some low-key schmoozing. **Gianicolo** serves as Lover's Lane, lined wall to wall with shaking Fiats. You'll find the best mix of foreigners and Romans, outdoor strolling, and funky bars in **Trastevere**. Somewhat removed from the historical center, **Testaccio** is renowned for its hip club scene.

Caffè

Coffee is Rome's foremost fuel, and languorous pit stops are *de rigueur.* During the weekdays, most Romans rush in, down an espresso, and leave, but at night, the *caffè* come alive with thunderous cross-table conversations, bustling waiters and shrill cashiers. In most *caffè* you pay one price to stand and drink at the bar and a higher price if you sit down at a table; there is usually a menu on the wall of the bar listing the prices *al bar* (standing up) and *a tavola* (at a table). Check the prices before you get comfy in your seat; especially around the historical center and the major *piazze,* the price of a *cappuccino* can jump from L1500 to L5000 when your tush hits the chair. Still, if you want to lounge for an hour over your coffee, no one will bother you.

Usually you pay the cashier first and present the receipt when you order, along with a small tip (L100). Along with your breakfast cup, you can get a sugar lift from a *cornetto,* a souped-up Italian version of the croissant, usually filled with cream (*crema*), marmalade (*marmalata*), or honey (*mele*). A *maritozzo con la panna* is a sweet roll or *cornetto* sliced open and filled with whipped cream. The number of ways you can get your caffeine fix is remarkable. A *caffè* or *espresso,* a large thimbleful of very strong coffee, is the starting point.

Caffè ristretto (or **alto**): "short" coffee, less water than usual; the Mrs. Butterworth of the Italian coffee world. Not for beginners. **Caffè lungo:** more water than normal; for non-Italian nervous systems. **Caffè macchiato:** literally "stained coffee"; with a spot of milk added, hot or cold (*caldo* or *freddo*). **Caffè coretto:** black espresso "corrected" with a spot of liqueur, usually brandy; one way to start a day of sightseeing. **Cappuccino:** espresso with foamy, steamed milk; ask for a sprinkle of *cacao* (cocoa powder) on top. Generally, Romans only drink it for breakfast, though you can get it anytime. **Caffè latte:** adds an entire glass of hot milk to the thimble of espresso. **Latte macchiato:** hot milk with a spot of espresso; can also be had cold; a favorite with kids. **Caffè americano:** just like your favorite greasy spoon used to serve; only if you really can't cope with the world's best coffee. **Granita di caffè con panna:** a mixture of iced coffee and whipped cream; sublimely refreshing. **Cioccolato caldo:** literally, hot chocolate; they melt a chocolate bar into a mug and douse it with whipped cream.

If all the caffeine has you running up St. Peter's dome in three minutes flat, it's time to switch beverages. Decaffeinated coffee is sometimes available. Fresh-squeezed juice, *spremuta*, is available in three different flavors: orange (*arancia*), lemon (*limone*) and grapefruit (*pompelmo*). If you want lemonade, ask for *spremuta di limone*, not *limonata* (which will get you lemon soda). Ask for a spritz of *acqua gassata* for a little fizz, and don't forget the sugar. You can also get camomile tea (*camomilla*) in any bar, with a little honey (*mele*).

There is no shortage of *caffè* in Rome. We point out some of the most notable, though they are sometimes more crowded and pricier than average. The streets around Campo dei Fiori and Trastevere hide some of the best places. The bars lining the streets (via Condotti, via Frattina, etc.) that lead to the Spanish Steps cater to monied tourists and are often packed and overpriced. Take the few extra steps over towards the river, around via della Scrofa, or head across the bridge to the neighborhood around piazza Cavour, which has many *caffè*, bars, *alimentari*, and *tavole calde*. Avoid the numerous establishments right near the Vatican; the prices are some of the highest in Rome, the quality is poor, and the clientele reads Frommer's; wander a few blocks over to via Cola di Rienzo and environs to find a more authentic and reasonable *caffè*. Discover your own favorite spot and get acquainted with the bartender and the regulars.

Caffè Sant'Eustachio, p. Sant'Eustachio, 82 (tel. 686 13 09), in the *piazza* southwest of the Pantheon. Take via Monterone off corso Emanuele. Rome's coffee empire. Once a favorite haunt of Stendhal and other literary expatriates, now bursting with Romans. Neither the recipe nor the decor has changed since its opening in 1938. Sit out on the *piazza* and nurse a steaming cappuccino (L4000; L2000 at the bar). Open Sept.-July Tues.-Sun. 8:30am-1am.

L'Antico Caffè Grèco, via Condotti, 86 (tel. 678 25 54), off piazza di Spagna. One of the oldest *caffè* in the world, this posh house has entertained the likes of European kings, movie stars, and John F. Kennedy since 1760. Happily, this swank establishment kitty-corner to Gucci has not gentrified their price list. Waiters in tuxedos serve the renowned cappuccino (L1600) in this *caffè*. Pot of tea L1900. Pimm's L6700. Open Mon.-Sat. 8:30am-8:30pm.

Caffè della Pace, via della Pace, 3/7 (tel. 686 12 16). Not just a L5000 cup of cappuccino, but an entire lifestyle. Come prepared with newspapers, books, letters to write, and clever conversations to start up; get the most out of the *a tavola* price hike. Chic, expensive, beneath vines and church façades. Comes alive at night with chic Romans "in the know." Cappuccinos: daytime L2000 at bar, L4000 at table; nighttime L5000 at bar, L10,000 at table. Open 10am-2am.

Tazza D'Oro, via degli Orfani, 84/86 (tel. 679 27 68). No place to sit down, but the best brew around and at fantastic prices (*caffè* L800). Superlative *granita di caffè* (L1500) after a hot day of sight-seeing. Open Mon.-Sat. 6:45am-8:15pm.

Babington's English Tearooms, piazza di Spagna, 23 (tel. 678 60 27). Adjacent to the Spanish Steps, this world-famous tearoom has all of the English trappings, including snooty service and aristocratic prices. Don't buy anything here unless you've got money to burn. Peek in at the parasol-sporting patrons who dish out L20,000 for pancakes with maple syrup. Tea L10,000-12,000. Open Tues.-Sun. 9am-8:30pm. Major credit cards accepted.

Strasté, via della Lungaretta, 76 (tel. 589 44 30). Haiku composers, herbal tea drinkers, and mellow souls rejoice. A mega-artsy *caffè* with floor cushions and soft jazz in the midst of beer-swilling, foot-stomping Trastevere. 22 varieties of tea (L4000). *Torta mimosa* L4500. Wine and beer L4500. Open Tues.-Sun. 7-10pm.

Bar S. Calisto, p. S. Calisto, 4, in Trastevere (tel. 589 56 78). *Il favorito* across the river, where Trasteverean youth, expatriates, and Roman elders socialize outside over inexpensive *cappuccino* (L1200 sitting or standing) and *granita di limone* (L2000). Open Mon.-Sat. 6:30am-3am.

Wine Bars

Many of the best wine bars in Rome are located in clandestine *piazze* or on acutely romantic cobblestone streets. You can nurse a glass of *chianti* for several hours and partake of mellow conversation; don't expect to get roaring drunk, dance on the tables, or play Spin the Bottle with the wait-staff. Since many of these establishments serve food, ranging from small plates of cheese to four-course meals, we have listed some of them in our Food section, under Wine Shops, above.

Vineria, Campo dei Fiori, 15. A chic spot for young Romans to sip wine, exchange meaningful glances, and swap phone numbers. Open Mon.-Sat. 7pm-midnight.

Cul de Sac, piazza Pasquino, 73, off piazza Navona. A quiet little wine bar that also serves home-made paté and other noshies. Better suited to a langorous conversation than a face-stuffing extrav-aganza. Open Tues.-Sun. 12:30-3:30pm and 7:30pm-12:30am. Another branch located at vicolo dell'Ateleta, 21.

Grapperia, via della Lupa, 17 (tel. 687 36 04). Give yourself a few hours (or a few days) here to sample all the different varieties of *grappa* they have, from olive to watermelon. The proprietor won't let you leave until you've tried his fabulous *tiramisù*—and rightly so. Open 12:30pm-1:30am.

Il Piccolo, via del Governo Vecchio, 75. *Molto chic* wine bar for Beautiful People. Try glasses of wines from all over Italy and nibble on an assortment of snacks and pastries. Go with a hot Italian who can purr sweet, incomprehensible nothings into your ear. Open 6pm-2am.

Caffé Settimiano, via Garibaldi, 92, just inside the gate onto via della Lungara. By day a regular Roman bar, by night a bustling *vineria* popular with Trastevere's artsy and expatriate crowd. Wines (L6000 and up), pastries (L2000-8000), and snacks. Open Tues.-Sun. 8am-midnight.

Id Est, vicolo del Bologna, 74. Chatty little wine bar. Open Tues.-Sun. 8pm-1am.

Arc-en-Ciel, via Banco di Santo Spirito, 45. They serve up crêpes along with a variety of coffees and wines. The tiny place is dark and intimate, but that's just so French. Open 7pm-2am.

Crêperie de la Vallée, via Teatro Valle, 64. Crêpes and musique. Tues.-Sun. 7pm-midnight.

La Locanderia, via Sora, 21, off via del Governo Vecchio. Cozy up with your new Italian friend for a cocktail, a snack, and some blasé flirting. Open Tues.-Sun. 8pm-midnight.

Pubs

If you're craving a Guinness, you should no problem finding one. There are numer-ous pubs in Rome, many with some sort of Irish theme. Most of the pubs cater to tour-ists and expatriates. If you want to meet Italians (that is, the kind that don't come to foreign bars to pick up the American clientele), you should probably avoid the pubs and head to a nightclub or jazz bar. The pubs and *birrerie* in Trastevere offer the best mix of foreigners and Romans.

Fiddler's Elbow, via dell'Olmata, 24, right off p. Santa Maria Maggiore. No Zero Mostel here. Rome's oldest pub has an Irish flavor, serving pints for L5000. Large and loud, with lots of anglo-phones. Open Tues.-Sun. 5pm-midnight.

Druid's Den, via San Martino ai Monti, 28. Travelling south on via Merulana from pia Santa Mar-ia Maggiore, take your second right. An Irish hangout where Romans get to be tourists. Pints of Guinness L5000. Open 8:30pm-1am.

Jonathan's Angels, via della Fossa, 16 (tel. 689 34 26). You're in for quite an experience. Jonathan is one wild and ca-rayzee guy, covered in tattoos and sporting a huge gold-like medallion around his neck. He has put strange pictures of himself up all over the walls too. There's live mu-sic and a hip, young crowd, even though the place is listed under "Piano Bar" in *TrovaRoma*. Open Tues.-Sun 11pm-2am.

Melvin's Pub, via Politeama, 8 (tel. 581 33 00), off p. Trilussa in Trastevere. Beer and cocktails to accompany live music. Pints L5000. Open Aug. to mid-July Fri.-Sat. 10pm-4am.

Lucifero Pub, via dei Cappellari, 28 (tel. 654 55 36). Off of Campo dei Fiore. A small, funky joint that serves fondue (chocolate L10,000), as well as cocktails (L8000), beer (L5500), and wine (L7000-12,000). The decor is demonic; so is the crowd. The proprietrix has a cigarette-holder, and knows how to use it. Open Tues.-Sat. 8pm-2am.

Birreria Trilussa, via Benedetta, 19/20 (tel. 71 54 21 80). Behind the fountain across the Ponte Sisto from Campo dei Fiori. A dark, woody pub that hums till all hours. Beer, wine and mixed drinks (L6000-8000), plus *bruschette* (L2500), pasta (L6000-8000) and an *antipasto* spread (L7000). Open 8pm-3am.

Victoria's Pub, via Vittoria. *The* English pub in Rome. God Save the Queen, and all that. Open Mon.-Sat. 8pm-2am.

The Proud Lion Pub, Borgo Pio 36 (tel. 683 28 41). A decent Italian attempt at a Scottish pub—dim light, dark wood booths, plenty of plaid and pints to go around. Open 7pm-1am.

Hungry Bogart, Borgo Pio, 202 (tel. 66 74 88). Brightly decorated with (surprise!) a Bogie motif; serves up drinks, beer, and snacks. Open 10:30pm-2:30am.

The Fox Pub, via di Monterone, 19 (tel. 687 78 89). Take via di Torre Argentina off Vittorio Emanuele; via di Monterone is the first left (near the Pantheon). Once per week this fairly subdued Karaoke palace transforms into a sweaty, English-speaking den. Young Americans and Europeans line up for the Tuesday night special: L10,000 at the door buys you all the beer you can drink from 9:30-11pm. Next thing you know, everybody's singing Italian love songs , some quite soulfully. Beer normally L6000. Open Tues.-Sun. 8:30pm-2am. A sign above the bar claims that nobody leaves without singing at least one song.

Pub 64, piazza Trilussa, 64 (tel. 580 38 89), in Trastevere just across Ponte Sista. Despite strange American artifacts hanging on the walls, mostly Roman clientele. Beer L4000-8000. Cocktails a whopping L10,000. American-ish hamburgers L6000. Open Tues.-Sun. 8pm-2am, but they close earlier if they're not busy and later if they are.

Music Clubs

Rome's music clubs attract a much hipper Italian crowd than the pubs; some even have dancing and are usually much cheaper than discos. Especially if you're getting sick of the meat-market scene at the Pantheon orSpanish Steps or at the foreigner-frequented pubs, these music clubs usually have a friendlier, more interesting, and manageable Italian crowd—not necessarily on the prowl for out-of-towners. There seem to be quite a few "Piano Bars" in the city, but unless you like to mingle with short, balding Italian men with lots of jewelry who want to make you a "big star", many of these will not be particularly enticing; we've listed a few that are not garden variety cheese-n-sleaze joints. Most are officially *associazione culturali,* which means they are private; some require a "membership" which means that you pay a one-time fee (often as little as L1000) for a card. Memberships are usually not exclusive, but on the weekends some of these clubs only allow members to enter (depending on how crowded the place is) and won't sell you a card. These charges sometimes include a drink. Call before setting out; opening hours tend to change seasonally and/or at the manager's whim.

Yes Brasil, via San Francesco a Ripa, 103 (tel. 581 62 69), in Trastevere. Foot-stomping live Brazilian music in crowded quarters. A favorite hang-out of young Romans. Drinks L8000-10,000. No drink, no dance. Open Mon.-Sat. 3pm-2am. Music 10pm-midnight.

Big Mama, via San Franscesco a Ripa, 18 (tel. 581 25 51). On the same street as Yes Brasil in Trastevere. Excellent jazz and blues for the diehard fan. Weekend cover (L20,000) makes it more of a commitment; weeknights are just as fun, although less crowded. Open 9pm-1:30am.

Clarabella, p. S. Cosimato, 39, in Trastevere. Live Brazilian Music. Obligatory first drink about L8000. Open Sept. to mid-July Tues.-Sun. 9:30pm-2:30am.

Alexanderplatz, via Ostia, 9 (tel. 359 93 98), off largo Triunfale near the Vatican. No cover for this true jazz-lovers' club. Drinks L10,000. Good restaurant attached. Monday nights showcase excellent local singers-songwriters; call for special concert dates. Open 9pm-2am.

Caffè Latino, via di Monte Testaccio, 96 (tel. 574 40 20), in the club district of Testaccio. This large fashionable place is built right into Monte Testaccio and the back wall is built out of pottery shards. One room for bands (mostly jazz) and one for videos and dancing. Drinks L5000-12,000. Open Oct.-June 9:30pm-2:30am. Membership fee L2000. **Caffè Caruso,** next door, has an almost identical set-up.

L'Esperimento, via Rasella, 5 (tel. 482 88 88), near p. Barberini. Rome's "alternative" subterranean rock club with a live band nightly. Anything black and a pack of Lucky Strikes seem to be the uniform. Membership L3000 (buy it on a weekday). Open Wed.-Mon. 9pm-4am.

Folkstudio, via Angelo Tittoni, 7 (tel. 589 23 74), at via Sacchi. A small and relatively inexpensive club in Trastevere. Young musicians from all over Europe and elsewhere, and an equally diverse audience. Open Oct.-June 9:30pm-1am.

Tartarughino, via della Scrofa, 1 (tel. 678 60 37). Mixed crowd comes for the music as well as the food. Open June-Sept. 11pm-3am.

St. Louis Music City, via del Cardello, 13a (tel. 474 50 76). An enormous jazz and swing club with a healthy mix of Italians and expatriates. There's a restaurant, a billiards room, live music and so much more. Open Sept.-July 9:30pm-1am.

Music Inn, largo dei Fiorentini 3, (tel. 654 49 34). A heavy-duty jazz bar, long established among self-serious aficionados. Features some of the most important musicians in the International scene. On Mon.-Wed., they show old movies instead of having live music. Open Sept.-July 8:30pm-1am.

Grigio Notte, via dei Fienaroli, 30b (tel. 581 32 49), in Trastevere. When the music is good, this place really heats up. Otherwise, watch Daffy Duck cartoons. Open Sept.-July 10pm-2:30am.

Mambo, via dei Fienaroli, 30 (tel. 589 71 96), next door. A cool piano bar playing a wide variety of your favorite Latino hits. Drinks from L10,000. Open Tues.-Sun. 11pm-5am.

Discos and Dancing

Italians are really not great dancers, but they still pay over L20,000 to get into embarassingly flashy discotheques circa 1984. Occasionally women get in free, but many of those places are gross pick-up scenes. Still, if your feet have to meet the beat, there are some exceptions. The really cool club scene changes as fast as Romans change outfits, so check *TrovaRoma* and ask some Italians where to go. Most places close up shop in the summer and move to the beach, so call before you head out.

La Makumba, via degli Olimpionici, 19 (tel. 396 43 92). One of funkiest places. Hot Brazilian and African music, an old-fashioned mirrored ballroom with palm trees, a thatched roof, and Hawaiian drinks served in kitschy Kon-Tiki bowls. Prices vary. Open 11pm-3am.

Uonna Club, via Cassia, 871. Rock-n-roll of various kinds, from reggae to garage-bands, underground Roman music, and New Wave. Prices and hours vary.

RadioLondra, via di Monte Testaccio, ask someone how to get there. Small—nay claustrophobic—club that plays loud (LOUD!) house music for funk-ay Romans until the wee hours. Mixed crowd of Romans, expatriates, gays, straights, and the occasional androgynatrix in black leather. In the summer, there's a lovely outdoor terrace with umbrellas. The best part—it's FREE. No drink purchase required. Crowded, so get here early. Open 11pm-6am.

Piper Club, via Tagliamento, 9 (tel. 85 44 59). Flashy disco that gets going on Friday nights. Video screens, live concerts, the lingering scent of hairspray and sweat, etc.... Open 11pm-3am.

Gay and Lesbian Entertainment

Rome boasts only a handful of gay and lesbian bars, and these keep late hours (the one exception is the women-only bar). Like straight nightlife in Rome, much happens outdoors, especially in the expatriate pockets of Rome. Gay men gather to socialize and cruise at piazza Navona (around via della Pace), Trastevere, and other busy strolling places. Popular outdoor cruising areas include the Monte Caprino park (a network of paths on the south side of the Capitol Hill) and the via Giulia (north of the villa Borghese near the Museo Villa Giulia). During the day, gay and lesbian Romans crowd the gay beach at "Il Bucco" at Lido di Ostia, especially on weekends. The dunes along the beach are home to an amusing pick-up scene, with many middle-aged Italians standing gopher-like atop mounds of sand; the beach itself accommodates a more relaxed, younger crowd, mostly groups of friends. Take the train from Magliana (Metro A) to Lido di Ostia (L700), then the #7/ bus to the terminus, then walk 1km south along the beach. Check the gay magazine *Babilonia* or *La Repubblica's TrovaRoma* for more information about gay nightlife.

Fruellandia, vicolo dei Piedi, 18, next door to the Pasquino movie theater off p. di Santa Maria. A friendly bar for women only. Beer L5000. Open 5pm-1am.

L'Alibi, via Monte di Testaccio, 44 (tel. 578 23 43), in the Testaccio district. Somewhat removed from the town center. Large, elegant, and diverse, the club's rooms spread over three levels, including a pleasant rooftop terrace. Mostly men, but popular hang-out with women too. The #20N and #30N night buses pass nearby Piramide all night long. Fri and Sat. nights a steep L20,000 cover; all other nights no cover, first drink L10,000. Open Wed.-Sun. 11pm-3am.

Hangar, via in Selci, 69 (tel. 488 13 97) has the advantage of being centrally located (take Metro B to Cavour, or any bus down via Cavour from Termini, or up from the Colosseum). The dark, cavernous (literally—the walls are lined with fake rock) interior is small and often packed wall-to-wall after 11:30pm. Blaring music videos, lots of meaningful eye-contact. Cover L15,000. Open Wed.-Mon. 10:30pm-2am.

Maxi Bar, via in Selci, 83 (tel. 488 22 09), takes the overflow crowd from Hangar. Same throbbing, sometimes aggressive environment. First drink L10,000. Open Thurs.-Sun. 11pm-3am.

Angelo Azzuro, via Cardinal Merry del Val, 13 (tel. 580 04 72) in Trastevere. Forthright atmosphere, but a little slow in getting started (come late). Black lights highlight a vast collection of kitschy statuettes. Mandatory first drink L12,000. Open Tues.-Sun. 10pm-3:30am.

RadioLondra (see Discos, above) has a mixed crowd shaking their thangs to house music.

Music and Theater

Check with the tourist office for upcoming events—consult their free publication *Carnet di Roma,* keep your eyes peeled for posters, and scan the newspaper to keep up with the incessant barrage of events. Concerts are held at the **Foro Italico** (tel. 36 86 56 25), **Stadio Flaminio** (tel. 39 12 39), the **Palazzo dello Sport** (tel. 592 51 07), and the **Palazzo della Civiltà del Lavoro** (the last two in EUR).

Opera

In June, July and August the spectacular stage of the **Terme di Caracalla** (tel. 48 16 01 or 481 70 03) hosts lavish opera productions. Performances last from 9pm-1am, and special buses (L1200) ferry spectators home to various parts of the city. To get to the baths, take bus #90 from piazza Venezia, or the Metro to Colosseo, then bus #118. Tickets start at L5000 and spiral up to L120,000, but since everyone moves down during the first act to empty seats in front, don't waste your cash on a high-end ticket. Informal dress is no problem. Buy tickets at the theater before the show, or at the opera's headquarters in p. Beniamino Gigli, near via Viminale (near Termini, or take the #70 bus from largo Argentina). From November to May, the opera moves back home to its aptly-named **Teatro dell'Opera** (in p. Beniamino Gigli, see above; tel. 48 16 01). Tickets may be bought weeks in advance. **Teatro Valle** sometimes also presents opera (tel. 654 37 94).

Classical Music

The **Accademia Santa Cecilia** performs symphonies and chamber music in its auditorium at via di Conciliazione, 4 (the street leading up to the Vatican). In summer, the company moves outdoors to the *nymphaeum* in the Villa Giulia, a spectacular setting. Special concerts are sometimes also held in p. di Campidoglio. Call their information office at via Vittoria, 6 (tel. 679 03 89).

L'Ippocampo puts on an array of musical events, from Gregorian chants to Bartok, in the ancient Auditorium of Maecenas (tel. 780 76 95). The **Amici di Castel Sant'Angelo** liven up Hadrian's mausoleum with classical music (tel. 854 61 92). **La Risonanza** performs sacred masses in the Basilica di S. Eustachio near the Pantheon Wednesdays at 9pm (tickets at the door). The **International Chamber Ensemble** plays classical music in the Teatro Sala Umberto, via della Mercede, 50 (tel. 86 80 01 25).

Also check with the **Accademia Filarmonica Romana** (tel. 323 48 90), the **Coro Polifonico Romano** (tel. 68 75 95 20), **Euromusica** (tel. 637 22 94), and the **Associazione Musicale Claudio Monteverdi** (tel. 481 48 00) for periodic performances.

In summer, **Concerti del Tempietto** performs symphonic and chamber pieces at night in the shadow of the Theater of Marcellus (tel. 481 48 00).The **Villa Pamphili Park** (tel. 86 80 00 39) hosts a series of nighttime concerts in July. Though tickets are on sale, you can sit on an umbrella pine-covered hill above the seats and hear just fine. To get to the park, take bus #41 from the Vatican or #44, 75 or 710 from largo Argentina and Trastevere to the Janiculan Hill. The entrance to the park (where tickets are sold) is 200m down from the Porta San Pancrazio.

Rock 'n' Roll

Tickets for rock concerts, held primarily at **Palazzo dello Sport,** start at L12,000. The acoustics suck and it's always jammed, but excellent groups perform. For tickets to and information on contemporary music events, visit the **ORBIS** agency at p. d'Esquilino (tel. 48 22 74 03), near Santa Maria Maggiore. (Open Mon.-Fri. 9:30am-1pm and 4-7:30pm, Sat. 10am-1pm.) Check our Clubs section below for lower-scale happenings. The **Stadio Flaminio** (tel. 323 65 39) hosts big-name concerts, like Michael Jackson and Madonna (though no one came to her concert in '91 because there was a big Italian singer playing across town). *Rockerilla* is a popular music magazine that prints concert and ticket information; also check in local record stores for information.

Theater and Ballet

The **Rome Opera Ballet** shares the stage and ticket office with **Teatro dell'Opera** (tel. 48 16 01 or 481 70 03). Call there for information. Tickets run L15,000-35,000. For **theater** listings check again with the tourist office or call the information number at **Teatro delle Arti,** via Sicilia, 59 (tel. 474 35 64), **Teatro delle Muse,** via Forli, 43 (tel. 883 13 00), or **Teatro Ghione,** via delle Fornaci, 37 (tel. 637 22 94), which has both music and theater performances.

Cinema

First-run cinemas in Rome tend to charge about L7000 and, though the movies are often American, they're generally dubbed into Italian. *Cineclubs* and *essais* show the best and most recent foreign films, old goodies, and an assortment of favorites in the original language. To catch the latest Schwarzenegger or Drew Barrymore flick, go to either of the following two theaters. **Cinema Pasquino,** tucked away at vicolo del Piedo, 19/A (tel. 580 36 22) in Trastevere, features undubbed American films. Take via della Lungaretta to p. Santa Maria and turn right at the end of the *piazza*. Their program changes every few days. (Open nightly, closed July 27-Aug. 27. Admission L6000.) **Alcazar,** piazza Merry Del Val, 14 (tel. 588 00 99), also in Trastevere, shows American films *in lingua originale*. Also check out the agenda section in the new, free English-language magazine **Metropolitan**, available at the newsstand next to largo Torre Argentina, 11; the **Economy Book and Video Center,** via Torino, 136; and the **Bookshelf,** via Due Macelli, 23. They list what's showing at Pasquino as well as special showings at other theaters (i.e. art films, outdoor shows, and the like). Finally, **Filmstudio 1 and 2,** at via d'Orti d'Alibert, IC (tel. 65 73 78), in Trastevere off via della Hungara, shows new, prizewinning films. (Admission L800.)

There are a few minor **film festivals** during the year in Rome (see Festivals below), but don't expect to be sharing Goobers with Uma Thurman; Italy's major film festival happens in Venice, in November—and you can probably forget about getting tickets there unless you're a *player*.

Shopping

Food

The cheapest eats in the city can be had at Rome's open-air **markets**, which carry a surprisingly fresh and varied array of produce, dairy, and meat products. The market at **Campo dei Fiori** (Mon.-Sat. 8am-noon) is one of the largest and most colorful, and centrally located, too, off corso Vittorio Emanuele. Near the station, try the market at **p.**

Vittorio Emanuele (on Metro Linea A, a few blocks south of Sta. Maria Maggiore); south of the city, **piazza Testaccio**, in the district of the same name, is where working-class Romans check off their grocery lists; prices here are often much lower than elsewhere. The market in **piazza Cosimato** in Trastevere (three blocks west of p. Sta. Maria) sells fruit, vegetables, and dairy products from 7am-1pm daily. The indoor market at **piazza dell'Unita** off via Cola di Rienzo stocks fruit, vegetables, cheeses, and meats (Mon.-Sat. 8am-2pm). A **watermelon stand** outside Termini on via delle Terme di Diocleziano sells delicious, juicy slabs for L1000 each from June to mid-August; there is another one located right off viale Trastevere, near p. Sidney Sonnino.

The produce available at **supermarkets** costs more and is less fresh than at the markets, but you'll be sure to find the packaged foods and staples you need. **STANDA** is Italy's largest food chain, with clothing and household goods as well, and they take credit cards. At viale di Trastevere, 60 and via Cola di Rienzo, 173.

If you can't face another plate of pasta or slab of pizza, take refuge at **Castroni**, via Ottaviano, 59, near the Ottaviano Metro stop, about 1/4 mile from the Vatican. An oasis of American and other non-Italian goodies and standard junk food (like the magically delicious Lucky Charms cereal), they stock teas, crackers, cookies, and a wide assortment of freshly made baked goods, sweets, and pastries.

Italian delicacies of all kinds are available at specialty stores and make great souvenirs and presents, if you can manage to carry them (and not eat them) over the rest of your trip. **Confetteria Moriondo e Garaglio**, via della Pilotta, 2, packages fresh, homemade chocolates and sweets. **Tazza D'Oro**, via degli Orfani, near the Pantheon, not only serves up one of Rome's best cups of coffee, but also sells bags of their premium beans by the pound. **Ai Monesteri**, at the top of corso del Rinascimento (across from the top of p. Navona) has a bewilderingly arcane selection of liqueurs, wines, chocolates, and other spiritual aids produced by Italian monks. **Enoteca Isabelli**, via della Croce, 76, sells fine wines and olive oils, as well as (expensive) bottles of *grappa*, the potent Roman firewater, and brandies flavored with pickled fruit that's been grown in the bottle.

Clothing

Compared to its more cosmopolitan cousins in the north, Rome is no shopper's paradise—if you'll be passing through Florence or Venice, save your *lire* for a spree up there. Rome's clothing, shoe, and leather boutiques offer a homogenous (and often ho-hum) array of goods. Though prices are often lower than in the states, quality can be rock-bottom too (remember that most Italian clothing is made to be hand washed, and can die a quick death once home in your dryer). The best leather goods made in Italy are exported—you're more likely to find a gorgeous, high-quality Italian wallet in Miami than in Rome. Shopping for clothes in Rome can be a trying experience—most budget stores are reluctant to let you even touch the merchandise, much less try it on, and sizes appropriate for larger-boned bodies are almost impossible to find. Italian shoes, on the other hand, are deservedly world-famous, and you can find excellent values throughout the city, though again, women's larger feet will have a tougher time squeezing into the tiny sizes. Don't be intimidated by pushy salespeople.

For the super-cheap and the die-hard bargain hunter, the **Porta Portese Flea Market** may be the best value (certainly the most chaotic) around. Open every Sunday from 7am-noon, the flea market stretches 4km from the Porta Portese bridge to the Trastevere train station. Bargain, barter or buy used clothing, plastic shoes, t-shirts, bathing suits, watches, as well as fake antiques, used books, bits of broken clocks, used (or stolen) mopeds, illegally cut tapes, beauty supplies, and a myriad of other oddities. Guard your wallet carefully. Traders (and pickpocketers) come here from as far away as Naples; serious shoppers should arrive early. If you want the total bazaar experience (crowds, crowds, and more crowds) wait until about 11am. During the weekday mornings, you can buy clothes more cheaply (and more sanely) at the outdoor markets outside the **Porta S. Giovanni** (Metro A to S. Giovanni in Laterano) or in **p. Vittorio Emanuele** (Metro A to Vittorio). **Used and vintage clothing shops** are the latest rage among trendy Roman teens and carry few bargains (most of the clothes are American, anyway). If you're dying for a pair of faded Levi's, a bunged-up varsity jacket, or a pink chiffon prom dress, the best stores line via Governo Vecchio near p. Navona and the streets around Campo dei Fiori. In a pinch, try selling them your own American duds.

For no-nonsense clothes shopping (if you need something cheap and in a hurry) go to one of Rome's chain **department stores**, where you'll find the kind of reasonably priced (though occasionally godawful-garish) clothing that Romans themselves wear every day. **STANDA** (see Food section, above), **UPIM** (at via Nazionale, 111, p. Santa Maria Maggiore and via del Tritone, 172) and **COIN** at p. Porta San Giovanni (Metro A to S. Giovanni in Laterano) all have extensive clothing sections. For a more upscale selection, try **La Rinascente**, at p. Colonna on the via del Corso and p. Fiume, which comes closer to an American department store (i.e., has fitting rooms) and takes credit cards, though if you're going to pay their prices, you might as well go hunting for a boutique.

You won't have to look far. Rome is filled with **boutiques** selling all kinds of moderately-priced clothing, from the staid to the outrageous. Though you can't help but find stores on the busy via Nazionale and via del Corso, the traffic and crowds may well send you packing. You'll have a better time (and probably find better prices) casing the area around **via Ottaviano** and **via Cola di Rienzo,** near the Vatican (home to many of the same boutiques as in the center) or around p. Bologna, at the end of the #61 and 62 bus routes. In the streets around **Campo dei Fiori,** especially via dei Giubbonari and via dei Chiavari, you'll find innumerable specialty boutiques, many selling hand-tailored or one-of-a-kind fashions at surprisingly good prices. The winding alleys of Trastevere hide similar stores, though not quite as many. Try via di Lungaretta north of viale Trastevere and via di Paglia heading north toward via della Scala.

For the funky and off-beat side of Italian fashion, don't pass up a visit to the **Babilonia-Cantieri del Nord** complex at via del Corso, 185 (tel. 678 66 41), for slick European suits for men and women, platform shoes, patent leather lingerie, an attic full of bell-bottoms and baseball paraphernalia, and even a miniscule discotheque. **Dakota**, at via Seminario, 111 (tel. 679 84 55) east of the Pantheon, or via del Corso, 494 (tel. 361 23 63), lays out piles of new and used clothes of a similar ilk, but at cheaper prices, in the confines of a frescoed former *palazzo*. For more extravagant shoes, check out **Santini e Dominici** at via Frattina, 122 (tel. 678 41 14), also located on via del Corso, right before p. del Popolo. **Lo Scrigno**, via della Lungaretta, 78 (tel. 589 98 28), in Trastevere, has interesting leather bags and belts at prices well below those across the river.

The Romans, always talented in the art of exhibition, have made **window shopping** a supreme performance. The most elegant and expensive shopping in Rome centers around p. di Spagna, especially along via dei Condotti, via del Babuino, and via Borgognona. At **Tagliocozzo** and **Anticoli**, at via Gambero 35 (tel. 678 95 62) and 38 (tel. 678 94 64), you'll find rare bargains on knitwear and sweaters; otherwise, be prepared to gawk rather than buy. Haute Couture (Armani and ilk) surround the Spanish Steps.

Souvenirs and Religious Paraphernalia

You can't turn around in Rome without seeing a souvenir stand. For **sacred objects,** the obvious place to look is the area around the Vatican, where countless booths and stores sell everything from miniscule saintly medallions to life-size plastic crucifixes. The stores on via di Conciliazione and via di Porta Angelica also sell calligraphic blessings; after you pay to have one filled out with someone's name, it's taken to a special audience and blessed by the Pope. There's plenty of papal equipment around too— John Paul II ashtrays, lollipops, thermometers, keychains, bottle openers, etc. **Fabbroni Colombo**, p. del Pantheon 69A (tel. 679 04 83), is a hole-in-the wall stocked with the largest selection of postcards in Italy, including many from other Italian cities.

Sports

The best sources for sporting information (about both participation and voyeurism) are the tourist office and two magazines sold at newsstands (*Corriere dello Sport* and

Gazzetta dello Sport). Otherwise, if you are in Rome between September and May, take in a **soccer** (*calcio*—pronounced cal-cho) game at the **Stadio Olimpico.** Of Rome's two teams, Roma and Lazio, Roma is the favorite, playing in the most competitive *serie A* league. If one of the two teams is playing *in casa* (at home), you'll witness a violent enthusiasm that brings to mind spectacles in the Colosseum. The **Foro Italico** at the Stadio hosts the games (tel. 368 51); admission is L20,000-30,000.

The **Concorso Ippico Internazionale** (International Horse Show) is held at p. di Siena in May. Go to the **Tor di Valle Racecourse** on via Appia Nuova (tel. 799 00 25) for the clay-court **International Tennis Championship of Italy,** held here at the beginning of May, which draws many of the world's top players. Buy tickets for these events at the ORBIS agency (tel. 482 74 03). Or, if you just yearn for the feel of a bowling ball, try **Bowling Roma**, viale Regina Margherita, 181 (tel. 855 11 84).

Lace up your cross-trainers and join the health-conscious Roman set at Villa Borghese park and map out your regular **early-morning run**; the park is cool and pleasant and there's no traffic to contend with. **Villa Ada** also has places to run, a lake with **canoe rental,** and an **exercise course** throughout the park. For a **pick-up soccer game**, hang out at piazza Santa Maria in Trastevere between 4:30-7pm; there's almost always an impromptu match. In the hot summer months, there are over 60 outdoor pools open to the public (some for a nominal fee). Try the **YMCA,** viale Libano, 68 (tel. 592 35 95), or the Tiber-side club, **Circolo dei Lavori Publici,** Lungotevere Thaon di Revel, 7/9 (tel. 39 33 45), opposite the boat dock at the Duca d'Aosta bridge, which has showers, dressing rooms and a snack bar, for L13,000. Look in the yellow pages under *Piscine*, and check our Practical Information for a few more.

Festivals

Rome isn't world-renowned for its festivals; nonetheless, there are plenty of beautiful and sometimes bizarre Italian celebrations to get in on. Most commemorate historical or religious events, and often include elaborate re-enactments. Rome also manages to attract its share of international arts and sports events. For more rural traditions, spend a lot of time in the Italian countryside and you will probably happen upon a few fesitvals without even trying. A food *festa* is rarely well publicized, but if your timing is naturally good, you're in for a treat—local cuisine is celebrated by gorging with the accompaniment of music, dancing, and various other entertainment.

January

1: The faithful light candles and make their way through the **catacombs of S. Priscilla. 5: Epiphany** takes over in p. Navona the night of January 5,culminating the post-Christmas toy fair. The celebrationsincorporate traditions of the witch festival *Befana*. Look out forBefana herself, giving toys to goody-goodies and coal to*enfants terribles*. **17:** Pet owners of Rome celebrate **St. Anthony's Feast Day** bygathering with their best friends for the traditional blessing at**the Church of Sant'Eusebio** (patron saint of animals) in p.Vittorio. **21:** Lambs are ceremonially shorn for wool to adorn bishops at the **Festa di Sant'Agnese**.

February

Shrove Tuesday is the day to disguise yourself for the pre-Lenten **Carnevale** in the city's *piazze*. Onlookers watch precious *daminas* ("little ladies"—eight-year-old girls in foofy L300,000 gowns) parade around town, or get sprayed with shaving cream, confetti, and crazy string by tiny Mutant Ninja Turtle imposters.

March

9: Anyone can buy insurance, but believers can have their cars blessed at the piazzale del Colosseo during the **Festa di SantaFrancesca Romana. 19:** Feast on *bignè* (cream puffs) at the **Festa di San Guiseppe** inthe Trionfale district of the city northwest of the Vatican.

April

Holy Week prompts the Good Friday **procession of the Cross** from the Colosseum to the Palatine and the Pope's Easter Sunday *Urbi et Orbi* blessing in nearly 50 languages. **Civitavécchia** hosts a procession of the dead Christ; repenting sinners follow wearing white robes and dragging chains fastened to their ankles. April's spring festival features the **flower show** at p. di Spagna, with the azaleas in full bloom on the Spanish Steps. Spring, as well as autumn, blossoms with the **Fiera d'Arte,** an art fair in via Margutta. The last week in April there is an **International Horse Show** in Villa Borghese's piazza di Siena.

14-16: Sagra del Carciofo Romanesco (festival of Roman artichokes)in Ladispoli. Pyrotechnics and artifloats. **21:** Theanniversary of **Rome's founding** affords a rare opportunityto see the Palazzo Senatoria in piazza del Campidoglio.Celebrations on the Capitoline Hill, Latin poetry slam, and morepyrotechnics.

May

Antique fair at via dei Coronari; the **rose show** arrives in early May at Valle Murcia, on the Aventine Hill above the Circus Maximus, and lasts through June; the **Italian International Tennis Tournament** gets underway at the Foro Italico in late May.

June

The hills of Rome are alive with the sound of music in the month of June. There is a **Festival of Baroque Music** in Viterbo and the **Pontine Music Festival**, which features concerts in the Caetani castle in Sermoneta and in the abbeys of Fossanova and Valvisciole. Nemi and Genzano, towns in the Castelli Romani district, boast a **Strawberry Festival** and **Corpus Domini** flowers respectively. From mid-June to mid-July, as French performers descend on the capitol for the **performing arts festival** at the French Academy at Villa Medici. June

23: Festi di San Giovanni at San Giovanni in Laterno sponsors agluttonous banquet featuring stewed snails and roast pork. **29:** The **Feast of St. Peter's** takes place, an awe-inspiring religious ceremony in the basilica of the church of the same name for Rome's patron saint.

July

During the first three weeks in July, the Tiber lights up with the sights and sounds of **Tevere Expo,** an annual national exhibition featuring industrial products, crafts, and foods of the various regions of Italy. Civic authorities organize a series of other events under the rubric of **L'Estate Romana.** The **Festa de Noantri** comes to Trastevere for 10 days during the last two weeks in July.

2: Castel Madama near Rome stages the **Palio Madama Margherita**. *Palios* are traditional parades featuring 16th-centurycostumes and horse races.**19:** The *palio* is repeated July 19 for a **Pear Festival.**

August

5: A blizzard of white flower petals represent a legendary out-of-season snow (once deemed a miracle) at the **Festa della Madonna della Neve** at S. Maria Maggiore.

September

An **art exhibition** in via Marguta; piles of grapes and vats of wine at the **Sagra dell'Uva,** in Basilica of Maxentius in the Forum; torchlit **handicrafts fair** from late September to early October in the via dell'Orso.

October

The water in the fountains of Marino (in the Castelli Romani) turns into wine at a **wine festival**, the first Sunday in October. Rome plays host in October to both the **Film Fest Italia** (via Giulia, 00185 Roma, tel. 687 85 56) and the **International Cinema and TV Festival—Eurovision 90** (Academy of France, Villa Medici, piazza Trinita dei Monti, Rome; fax 06 35 34 29).

December

The first week in December is the sentimental, gaudy piazza Navona **toy fair**. Overpriced christmas *tsotchkes* are for sale; a bejewelled Christ-child receives poems and speeches from children.

8: At the **Festa della Madonna Immacolata**, in piazza di Spagna,firemen crown the column's statue with a wreath. **22:** Fish cooked in cauldrons at the **Ciotto del Pesce** at the MercatiGenerali in via Ostiense; free samples. **31:** New Year's Eve is also the **Feast of S.Silvestro**: If you get there by 5pm, you can watch the Pope participate in a ceremony atthe church of the Gésu. New Year's-merrymaking includes sparklers and tossing glass out thewindow. Expand your horizons by sampling the traditional pigs' foot dish, washed down with champagne, of course.

Lazio and Other Daytrips

When the endless frenzy of Rome overwhelms, head for the sanctuaries of rural Lazio. The cradle of Roman civilization, Lazio (*Latium,* originally, "the wide land") stretches from the low Tyhrrenian coastline through volcanic hills to the foothills of the Abruzzese Apennines. North and south of Rome, ancient cities, some predating the eternal city by centuries, maintain traces of the thriving cultures that were born there. Romans, Etruscans, Latins, and Sabines all settled here, and their contests for supremacy over the land make up some of the first pages of Italy's recorded history.

Also known as the *campagna* or *Ager Romanus,* Latium has always been a rich land. Volcanic soil feeds farms and vineyards, and travertine marble quarried from the Latin hills built the Colosseum, St. Peter's, and nearly every other Roman building standing between them. With such resources, the territory attracted the notice of the Etruscan Empire in the 9th century BC, which sent colonies to Tarquínia, Cerveteri, and Veii, while the primitive Latin tribes dwelling in the hills (Colli Albani) around Lake Albano quickly rose to prominence in the south. While Rome was still a collection of mud huts on the bank of the Tiber, Etruscan and Latin towns enjoyed a sophisticated religious, political, and artistic culture.

After centuries of war, Rome emerged as anchor of an empire, and the Latian towns settled down to a peaceful, wealthy existence, providing—as they did in the Renaissance and even today—vacation retreats for Romans wanting some peace and quiet in the country. Follow their example and enjoy a few cool days out of Rome in the Latin towns. Most of the region's famous sights can be seen in a series of day excursions from the capital—few really merit a night's stay.

Trains for Lazio locations leave from the Laziale section of Termini, and one private line serves Viterbo from the Roma Nord Station in p. Flaminio (outside p. del Popolo). **ACOTRAL buses** depart from via Lepanto (outside the eponymous Metro stop on Linea A) for Tarquínia, Cerveteri, Bracciano, and Civitavecchia, from the Anagnina Linea A stop for the Colli Albani and Lake Albano, from the EUR-Fermi stop on Linea B for Anzio and Nettuno, or from the Rebibbia Linea B stop for Tivoli and Subiaco. **Hitchhiking** is not uncommon and rides are generally easy to come by; those who do hitch take a city bus onto the *via* that leads toward their destination. *Let's Go* does not recommend hitchhiking as a means of transportation. **Women in particular should think twice about hitchhiking, and under no circumstances should they do it alone**.

Roman Suburbs

Daytrippers from the city are in good historical company. Roman big-wigs have been weekending in the surrounding towns since they quashed their Latin neighbors in the 3rd century BC. Though the ancient villas declined along with the Roman Empire, their remains inspired countless popes and nobles to build their own pleasure gardens, often on ancient foundations; many villas, ancient and modern, are open to the public in the hill towns listed below. The hill towns are not known for their sights, however, so much as for the cool, slow pace of life. Medieval cobbled streets, belvederes overlooking sweeping views, and the crisp, cold white wines of the region make each Latian hill town an ideal spot for a day of lazing and grazing. However, some of these towns are experiencing the rapid economic growth and construction that encroaches on most of Italy's old towns, and to top it off, many are now besieged by tourists as well. If you really want to escape the crush of modern Italian life, you may have to head further afield to Subiaco or Palestrina, where saints and composers kept quieter court, to the Etruscan ghost towns of Tarquínia or Ceveteri, or to Ostia Antica, the once-bustling, now-deserted port of ancient Rome.

Tivoli

Dramatic Tivoli perches over the boundary between Lazio's hills and plains, providing extensive views of Rome from its hilly streets and gardens. Here, where the Anio River pours over 120m of ravine and cliff on its way to meet the Tiber, water is the inspiration and the attraction. Ancient Roman glitterati came to enjoy the delicious cool of the cascades. Horace, Catullus, Propertius, Maecenas and many others retreated to villas lining the ravine where the River Anio falls, and some of these remains can be seen. Across town, the sparkling Villa d'Este siphons Anio overflow into a hundred spouting fountains lining a Renaissance formal garden, while in between lies a maze of medieval houses, churches, and a fortified castle, as well as two Republican-age temples presiding over one of the most impressive scenes of natural beauty in Lazio. In the valley below, the remains of another Tivoli villa can be visited. Emperor Hadrian, a sophisticated cultivator of art and architecture, built his sprawling **Villa Adriana (Hadrian's Villa)** according to his own unique designs. Some of the best-preserved imperial architecture near Rome is laid out here, amidst gardens and pools of Anio water.

From largo Garibaldi, the cool gardens of the **Villa d'Este** spill over watery terraces from the entrance in piazza Trento. The entrance to the gardens passes through several intermittently frescoed rooms—notable primarily for their views of the gardens. The property was shaped by Cardinal Ippolito d'Este (son of Lucrezia Borgia) and his architect Piero Ligorio in 1550; the idea was to recreate the limpid sumptuousness of ancient Roman *nymphaea* and pleasure palaces. From the bar and gift shop on the first floor of the palace, a terrace offers entrance to the gardens. Immediately below the terrace is the **Fontane del Bicchierone**, a lumpy goblet of Bernini's design. To the left (facing away from the villa) a path leads to the **Rometta**, or Little Rome, a series of fountains including one symbolizing the Tiber (the boat with the obelisk being the Tiber Island) as well as stuccoed miniatures of some principal temples and a statue of Roma herself, accompanied as usual by the suckling Romulus and Remus. Below Bernini's fountain, the **Grotto of Diana** is a fine example of a *nymphaeum*—a stuccoed nook lined with pebbles, statuary, and mosses, filled with the running water which both ancient and Renaissance Romans favored as a shelter from the burning summer heat. The **viale delle Cento Fontane** runs the width of the garden, pouring endless streams of water into its narrow basins. At the other end from the Rometta, the **Fontana dell'Ovato** spurts one great sheet some 50 feet into the air. To the left, the **Fontana dell'Organo Idraulico** once powered a complete water organ, and on some days you can still hear faint musical groans. Below the terraces of fountains, two great **fishponds** stagnate amidst cypress and orange plantings. At the left side, belvederes offer extensive views of the Roman *campagna*. Don't miss the **Fontana della Natura** with its colossal statue of **Diana of Ephesus** and her multiple, egg-shaped breasts, at the very bottom of the garden. The bar in the villa is expensive, but the gardens themselves are a great place to park yourself with some bread and a bottle; buy your picnic fixings before you enter. (Open 9am-6:30pm in summer; Sept.-May 9am to one hour before sunset. Admission L10,000 if water is at full power, L5000 otherwise.)

Across town in via di Sibilla, you can pass through a pricey restaurant (no obligation to eat there) to the two **Republican Temples**, which command a high point overlooking the cascades of the Anio. Archaeologists have been scratching their heads for centuries over which gods were worshipped here, but it's pretty clear that the deities have long since taken their leave. Still, the temples themselves (preserved as churches until this century) are among the best examples of Republican (1st century BC) sacred architecture in Lazio, and the view of the echoing gorge below is awe-inspiring in itself. Bring wine and toast the god of your choice.

The via di Sibilla passes through a dense **medieval quarter**, across the waterfalls, and round to the entrance of the **Villa Gregoriana**, which isn't a villa at all, but a natural park with paths descending through scattered ancient ruins to a series of lookouts over the cascades. The terrain gets wilder and wetter the lower you go; at the bottom of the park a series of grottoes carved out by the rushing water gurgle with eerie light and sound effects. You can climb up the other side of the gorge, but the gate at the top is

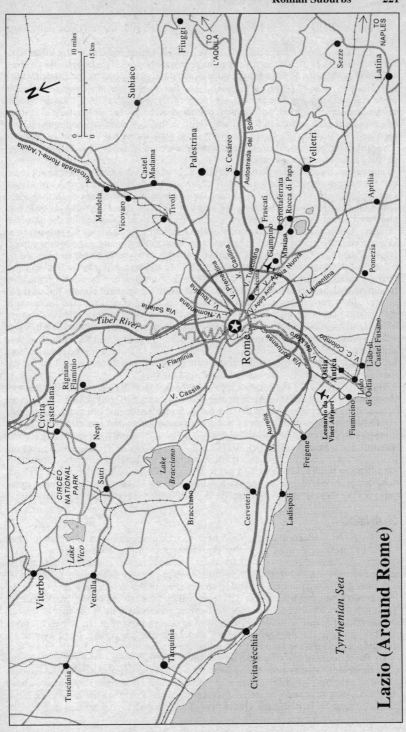

Lazio (Around Rome)

only intermittently open, and you may have to retrace your steps. (Open daily 9am-dusk. Admission L2500.)

In the valley below (take a bus, see above), the intriguing remains of the **Villa Adriana** (tel. (0774) 53 02 03) sprawl over another watery park. The largest and costliest villa ever built in the Roman Empire, it was apparently designed by the Emperor himself. Hadrian came to power in 117 AD, when the empire was at its largest and most powerful, and spent his time judiciously traveling through and enjoying the delights of his possessions. A soldier, philosopher, poet, and architect, the enigmatic and restless emperor built each section of his villa at Tivoli in the style of some monument he had seen before, recalling his varied travels. As you walk through the crumbling remains, the spirit of the cosmopolitan emperor, who treasured his privacy above all else, seems to still pervade his curious retreats.

The entrance gate leads you to the **Pecile**, a great, once-colonnaded court built to recall the famous Painted Porch *(Poikile)* at Athens where Hadrian's heroes, the classic Greek philosophers, once met to debate. Various building complexes open to the left. Don't miss the **Maritime Theater**, the emperor's private circular study and bedroom, cloistered inside a courtyard and protected by its own moat (once outfitted with drawbridges). Underneath the broad **Court of the Libraries** the shadowy **Cryptoporticus** kept the emperor's army of slaves hidden from view as they ran the enormous complex. Beyond the main buildings the **Canopus**, a murky expanse of water surrounded by plasters of the original architecture and sculpture found here, replicates a famous canal near Alexandria in Egypt (note the crocodile). The **Serapeum**, a baroquish semicircular dining hall, anchors the far end of the canal. Here the emperor and his guests dined on a platform completely surrounded by water cascading down from the fountains at the back. It was in the Canopus that Hadrian's beloved companion Antinous drowned himself; afterwards the bereaved Emperor made his lover a god, instituted a cult of him which spread throughout the empire, and subsequently abandoned the villa, unable to bear the memories of happier times—each man, sniff, kills the thing he loves. Before leaving, marvel at the large model of the villa in its prime, next to the bar near the entrance. (Villa open daily 9am-dusk. Admission L8000.)

To get to Tivoli take the Metro Linea B to the last stop, Rebibbia (L700), then exit the station from the ACOTRAL terminal above. Tickets to Tivoli (L4800) are on sale here, and the **buses** leave every 10-15 minutes from Capolinea 1 (30 min.). After passing through smoggy factory areas and travertine quarries, the bus climbs to Tivoli, making a stop at largo Garibaldi. Here a watery park overlooks the sprawling Roman suburbs, and a **tourist office** (tel. (0774) 212 49 or (0774) 29 35 22), which gives out free maps and information on the sights, restaurants and hotels in the city. (Open daily 8am-6pm; in winter 8am-2pm.) To get to Hadrian's Villa, either take the ACOTRAL bus from Rebibbia and get off at Bixio Adriana, about 1.5km from the entrance to the park, or take the orange bus #4 from Tivoli itself, which leaves from largo Garibaldi.

Subiaco

From Tivoli you can trace the Anio back to its source, to the stunning, untouched valley of Subiaco, a rocky town that dominates one of Lazio's emptier up-country quarters. As the road climbs inland, the sheer, forested crags of the Monti Simbruni rise above lush pastures and scattered vineyards; even in summer these nearly alpine meadows manage to keep their cool. Subiaco stands alone in this verdant wilderness, but the few human hands that have touched its rocky valley have left impressive marks indeed. The town owes its origins to Nero, who built an enormous villa at the foot of the hill and diverted the Anio to make a giant reflecting pool in front of it. His armies of slaves needed a place to stay, and Sublaqueum ("under the lake") was born. Nero went down the tubes and so did the lake in 1305, when the last bit of the dam finally broke, and today the remains of his villa are barely visible. The real fame of the town is due to a more humble inhabitant—the young Benedetto di Norcia, a rich wastrel of the 6th century who gave up everything to live a life of penitential contemplation in a cave above the town. After three years of seclusion he emerged and founded a monastery, the birthplace of the great **Benedictine Order**. Though there had been Christian monasteries before Benedict, it was his foundation and Rule, written from atop the craggy cliff, that set the pattern for the great monastic movements that spread throughout medieval Europe. In the following centuries, a building boom of monasteries and convents along the hillside filled the valley with monks and nuns and made Subiaco a center of Christian scholarship. The **Convent of St. Scholastica**, named for Benedict's twin sister, assembled a famous library and in 1465 hosted the first printing press in Italy. The **Convent of San Benedetto**, built over the saint's original cave, is decorated to this day with one of the most extensive assemblages of 13th- and 14th-century painting in central Italy. Though a tour of Subiaco and its precipitous monasteries involves some footwork, the artistic and architectural treasures secreted inside the cliffs are well worth the effort.

ACOTRAL **buses** leave for Subiaco from the end of Metro Linea B (Rebibbia Station) every 50min. (6:20am-8:50pm, 1 ½hr., L4800; return buses 7:30am-7:30pm). The bus terminus is in p. della Resistenza, the center of town. About ½km before, the bus passes the small stone **Ponte di San Francesco**, built in 1358, on the right. Debark here to cross the Anio to the stone **Chiesa di San Francesco,** at the summit of a small hill. The somber interior is filled with notable paintings, including an triptych over the altar by Antoniazzo Romano, *St. Francis Receiving the Stigmata* by Sebastiano del Piombo, frescoes in the third chapel on the left by il Sodoma, and an altarpiece of the Nativity by Pinturicchio, the 15th-century Umbrian genius.

Back over the bridge, the road leads to the town and (on the right) the **tourist office** at via Cadonna, 59 (tel. (0774) 853 97; open daily 9am-1pm). To the left, a winding road climbs to the forbidding **Rocca Abbaziale,** a medieval fortress dating from 1073 and once home to Rodrigo Borgia, later Pope Alexander VI, during his tenure as abbot of San Benedetto. It was here that his famous children Lucrezia and Cesare were born. Only the most energetic need climb the winding streets to view its glowering walls—save your energy for the hike ahead.

In its heydey as home base of the European monastic movement, Subiaco boasted a dozen monasteries, but today only two survive. From p. della Resistenza, the road leads straight out and up to a series of perilous hairpin turns—take the footpaths straight up the hill on the left when you can, though the steep inclines may reduce you to thumbing it (a relatively safe propostion here, as the only cars passing are on their way to the monasteries, though as always *Let's Go* does not recommend that you hitchhike). After 2 ½km, the reconstructed gate of the **Convento di Santa Scholastica** rises on the right. The complex, a massive architectural hodgepodge, encompasses three different cloisters, each planted with its own garden. In the first, a dull reconstruction of a Renaissance design, look for the words "Ave Maria" planted in artichokes. Traveling back through time, the second courtyard features an intricately carved Gothic arch and faded frescoes; the third and earliest court is the work of the 13th-century Cosmati family, whose twisted columns and bright mosaic work found their way into most of the churches in Rome. Off this court a Neoclassical church by Quarenghi (the Italian architect who designed much of Russian St. Petersburg) reposes in white-washed serenity. The library shelters the first two books printed in Italy. (Convent open daily 9am-12:30pm and 4-7pm; a monk leads guided tours every 30 min. Free.)

When Pope Pius II visited the **Convento di San Benedetto**, another ½km up the hill, he likened the Gothic complex, clinging to its perilous cliff, to a giant swallow's nest. Petrarch was more generous (and no less accurate) when he said it seemed like the threshold of paradise. The monastery occupies one of the most spectacular hilltop sites in central Italy: from its honey-colored terraces the peaks and valleys of the Monti Simbruni recede as far as the eye can see. The sights inside the church complex, carved entirely out of its limestone cliff, aren't bad either. The monastery was founded on the site of the **Sacro Speco,** the rocky grotto where St. Benedict lived in penitential solitude for three years. As the fortunes of the convent grew, so did the church—straight up. Each generation of monks carved new chapels out of the rock and plastered them with precious frescoes. A descent through the several levels of subterranean shrines is like a ride on an art-historical time-machine. The *loggia* at the entrance to the upper church is decorated with the newest art in the place, a series of late 15th-century frescoes of the Madonna and Child and the Evangelists by the school of Perugino.

Inside, the first section of the upper church boasts an elaborate cycle of 14th-century frescoes, done by a member of the Sienese school, depicting the Crucifixion and the Biblical events surrounding it. The scenes, including the *Way of the Cross* and the *Kiss of Judas* (on the left wall), the *Crucifixion* (on the central arch), the *Entry into Jerusalem,* the *Visit to the Tomb, Christ with Mary Magdalen,* and *Christ with Doubting Thomas* (on the right wall), are filled with a fascinating cast of medieval men, women, children, and beasts. Beyond, a cycle of less well-preserved 13th-century frescoes decorates the nave and transepts around the exquisite Cosmatasque high altar.

Downstairs, the lower church glows with the colorful paintings of Conxolus, a late 13th-century painter. The walls and vaults depict various scenes from the life of St. Benedict (monks are on hand to explain), including his many miracles. To the right, Benedict's original grotto is decorated only by a 17th-century marble statue of the monk. A small staircase (often locked, but it's worth asking for admission) leads up to the **Chapel of St. Gregory**, where more frescoes by Conxolus depict Pope Gregory IX consecrating the church. Behind the pope stands a pensive, bearded monk, who appears again on the opposite wall. The man is St. Francis, but the inscription, *Frater Franciscus,* suggests that it was painted around 1210, before the famous monk received his stigmata, or sainthood; if that is true, then the painting is the first known portrait of Francis, and possibly the first real portrait painted in Italy. On the left hand wall, Antoniazzo Romano's delicate *Pietà* is an unknown gem—a breathtaking example of the 15th-century Roman artist's quiet (and largely unheralded) technical brilliance.

Fourteenth-century Sienese frescoes of the *Triumph of Death* (including a gruesome skeleton on horseback) line the next staircase down. Here the **Chapel of the Madonna** gleams with winsome scenes from the life of the Virgin—look for her leaning tenderly on Christ's shoulder in the angel-studded *Assumption.* On the lowest level, the **Grotto dei Pastori** is revered as the place where Benedict taught catechism to local shepherds. Fragments remain of a 7th-century Byzantine fresco of the *Madonna and Child,* the oldest painting in this speluncular treasure-house. From the terrace outside you can see more spectacular views of the mountain valleys, as well as a rose bush with its own story to tell. Legend has it that St. Benedict resisted the temptations of Satan by throwing himself on a thorn bush. When St. Francis saw the thorns on his visit (some seven centuries later), he miraculously transformed them into roses, which took root and bloom to this day. (Convent open 9am-12:30pm and 4-7pm. Free.)

Ostia Antica

The romantic remains of ancient Ostia (tel. 565 00 22) offer a cooler, closer, and cheaper alternative to the more famous ruins at Pompeii and Herculaneum. At Ostia, lush greenery and fragrant vines envelop well-preserved traces of a once-thriving Roman city. Even on a hot summer day, the ruins are so sparsely visited you'll have no trouble finding a secluded spot for a picnic, and you'll need to bring one since doing the site justice requires the better part of a day. Bring a water bottle as well.

The city, named for the *ostium* (mouth) of the Tiber, was apparently founded around 335 BC, when Rome was just beginning its rise to power. The growth of Ostia parallels that of its mother city's expansion into the world of Mediterranean trade and politics. First a mere fortified camp established to guard the salt fields of the Tiber delta, the settlement was developed as a commercial port and and naval base during the 3rd and 2nd centuries BC. After Rome won control of the seas in the Punic Wars, almost every bit of food and material imported to the city passed across the docks of Ostia. By 45 AD, the wharves lining the river had reached their capacity, and the Emperor Claudius dredged a huge artificial harbor to the northwest.

Ostia was a city of commerce, and the ruins that remain all speak of the thriving activity the port once saw. Warehouses, shipping offices, hotels, bars, and shrines to the polyglot religious cults of slaves and sailors fill the site. Ostia's fortunes declined as Rome's did. The port fell into disuse during the onslaught of the Goths, and the silty Tiber eventually moved the coastline a mile or so to the west. After the city was sacked by the Goths in the 800s, Pope Gregory IV built a new fortified town (up the road from the entrance gate) and the ancient city receded into malarial swampiness. Happily though, the mud effected a remarkable archaeological preservation. Once boasting a population of 80,000, the site was nearly desolate until papal excavations began in the 19th century; archaeologists continue to dig, and have only uncovered about half of the city. Following ancient tradition, Rome's new arrivals still enter through Ostia: Fiumicino Airport lies only a few miles to the north of the city. Practical Ostia's buildings were built of brick; the site was thus quarried and pillaged far less than the monumental marble precincts of Rome. What remains today is in many ways more impressive. Walking its main streets and narrow alleyways, you can easily imagine the din and flow of ancient city life.

From the entrance gate, the via Ostiensis (the same as the highway that now leads out of Rome), paved with basalt blocks, leads through a necropolis of brick and marble tombs. As at Rome, city law forbade burial within the city walls. The *via* passes through the low remains of the Porta Romana, one of the city's three gates. The road is now the city's main street, the **Decumanus Maximus,** and leads into the center of the city. A few hundred yards inside, the **Baths of Neptune** rise on the right. Climb the stairs for a view of the large entrance hall, paved with a mosaic scene appropriate for a harbor town: Neptune driving his chariot, surrounded by marine creatures. To the left below is the large colonnaded **palestra,** where bathers strolled and played games after their baths.

A street leading off to the right of the baths leads to the **Caserma dei Vigili,** or House of the Firemen, which housed one of Ostia's many trade guilds. The firemen evidently kept a fairly earnest imperial cult, as their main meeting hall is lined with statue bases inscribed to various emperors. Out the back of the firehouse, the **via della Fontana,** a well-preserved street lined with stores and apartment houses, leads back to the Decumanus.

The well-preserved but much-restored **Theater** rises next on the right. Its outside face housed several small stores, now the site of a souvenir stand and bar (closed in 1992). A vaulted passage leads underneath the stands to the semicircular *cavea.* The stage itself was backed by a wall several stories high, which would have been decorated with columns, arches, niches, and statuary; only the low wall of its foundation survives. Beyond the theater, the expansive **piazzale delle Corporazioni** (Forum of the Corporations) extends to the old riverbank. Here importers and shipping agents from all over the Roman world maintained their offices. The sidewalk is lined with mosaic inscriptions proclaiming their businesses, the ancient precursors of modern welcome mats. In the center of the *piazza* are the remains of a temple to Ceres, the goddess of grain—the lifeblood of Ostia's trade.

Back on the Decumanus, the via degli Augustali to the left leads to a **Fullonica,** or ancient dry cleaning shop. The deep pits were filled with clothing and fresh, antiseptic urine, then agitated by the unlucky slaves whose job it was to jump in and splash around. On the theater side of the Decumanus, via dei Molini leads to the **Casa di Diana,** the best-preserved Roman house at Ostia, and among the most complete in the world. Buildings like this, known as *insulae* (apartment blocks), once filled Rome and every city of the Roman empire. The ground floor housed *tabernae* (shops), each with its own opening onto the street. The grooves in the thresholds show where sliding wooden screens served as doors. The entrance to the house leads through a long, dark hallway into the central courtyard. Unlike the large, single-family villas at Pompeii, the *insula* was a collection of apartments and rooms where several dozen people lived together, sharing the courtyard and kitchen facilities. The house gets its name from the terracotta relief of Diana found in the courtyard. At the back of the ground floor, a dark, windowless room holds a **Mithraeum,** a shrine to the Persian god Mithras, whose cult was celebrated by worshippers sacrificing and feasting on sacred banquets on the two low couches. Upstairs there are more apartments and the foundations of stairs that led to as many as three more stories.

Across the street from the House of Diana is the **Thermopolium,** the ancient ancestor of the modern Italian snack bar. Hot drinks were kept in the sunken clay jars and served across the marble bar. The street then opens onto the **Forum of Ostia,** anchored, as at Rome, by the imposing **Temple to Jupiter, Juno, and Minerva.** Behind the Forum is the **Museum,** where a diverse collection of artifacts, both monumental and quotidian, are on display. A colossal statue of Trajan, an intricately carved sarcophagus (**Room 9**), bas-reliefs of various trades and businesses, a statue of Mithras slaying the Sacred Bull, and a spectacular set of polychrome marble panels with an early representation of a haloed Jesus, are among the treasures.

Across the Forum a street leads to (on the first left) a **public latrine**, and (second left) the vast **Terme del Foro** (Forum Baths), with their various hot and cold bathing rooms. The via del Tempio Rotondo runs parallel to the Decumanus and passes the 3rd-century AD **Round Temple**, a miniature Pantheon dedicated to the cult of all emperors. Via Epagathiana, across the Decumanus, leads back into the waterfront warehouse district. The **Horrea Epagathiana** on this street are marked by a delicate pediment and columns constructed entirely of brick.

At the fork in the Decumanus, the via della Foce leads right to the sumptuous **House of Cupid and Psyche**, where the statue of the two lovers now in the museum was initially found. The house, paneled in elaborate polychrome marble, was home to one of Ostia's wealthier merchants. Further down the street, a staircase descends to another eerie subterranean **Mithraeum**, again lined with banquet benches, from where an endless maze of sewers and cisterns spreads beneath the city.

Across the street, the two-story **House of Serapis** has a central atrium with paintings and a relief of the god himself. Climb to the balconied second story for a view of the whole city. The house opens into the **Baths of the Seven Wise Men**, named for a scatological fresco cycle found in one of the rooms. The circular mosaic hall was once heated by a system of hot air ducts and served as an exercise area for the bath. The next building, the **Casa dei Aurighi**, boasts two frescoes of charioteers and an arcaded courtyard. This building complex may have served as a hotel. The **Porta Marina**, where debarking travelers entered the city, lies a few meters down the Decumanus, at the western end of the city.

To reach Ostia Antica, take the Metro Linea B to the Magliana stop (L700; ask for the through ticket to Ostia), change to the Lido train and get off (20min.) at the Ostia Antica stop. The bar outside the train station has the only food or drink before the site. Cross the overpass and continue straight to the "T" intersection. Make a left and follow the signs to the entrance. The site is open daily 9am-6pm in summer, in winter 9am-4pm; admission L8000.

Outside the archaeological park, there's little to see at Ostia. The modern village of **Ostia** (relatively modern—it was founded in 830) has a few bars to slake your thirst. The **Castello**, built by Julius II in 1483-86, while he was still a cardinal, dominates the fortified town (closed in 1992, it may be open in 1993, after a lengthy restoration). Opposite is the small Renaissance **church of St. Aurea.** Growling stomachs should find relief at **Al Monumento**, piazza Umberto I, with pasta dishes at L10,000 (wine L8000, *coperto* L2500; open Tues.-Sun. 12:30-2:30pm and 6:30-10pm). For curiosity's sake, peek in at the hokey **Sbarca di Aeneas** (on the way back to the train), named for the legendary site of Aeneas's landing in Italy. Waiters wear ancient Roman costumes (the maitre d' is the one in centurion's gear) and the garden is filled with prop chariots from the movie *Ben Hur*. More economical is the bar back across the overpass.

Castelli Romani

Overlooking Rome from the volcanic Alban hills, the Castelli Romani are famous for their white wines, Renaissance villas, and annual festivals. The pace of life has slowed since the days when feuding medieval families built the forbidding castles while trading insults across the hills, and today there's not much to do in any of these towns except eat, drink, and wait for the evening *passeggiata* to stroll on past.

All of the *castelli* can be reached by blue ACOTRAL **buses** from the Anagnina Station at the end of Metro Linea A, and most of them are connected to one another by blue buses as well. Buses for Frascati, Grottaferrata, or Marino (all good starting places) leave about every 15 min.; a ticket costs L2800. Service from Termini connects Rome to Frascati and Albano (departures every 1-2hr.; L3200), but takes longer than the bus.

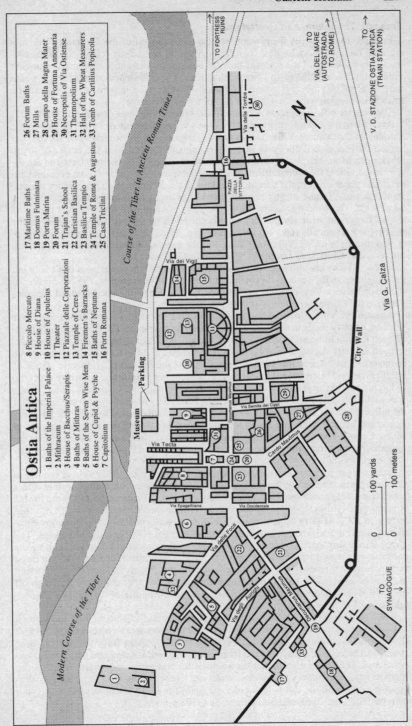

Ostia Antica

1 Baths of the Imperial Palace
2 Mithraeum
3 House of Bacchus/Serapis
4 Baths of Mithras
5 Baths of the Seven Wise Men
6 House of Cupid & Psyche
7 Capitolium
8 Piccolo Mercato
9 House of Diana
10 House of Apuleius
11 Theater
12 Piazzale delle Corporazioni
13 Temple of Ceres
14 Firemen's Barracks
15 Baths of Neptune
16 Porta Romana
17 Maritime Baths
18 Domus Fulminata
19 Porta Marina
20 Forum
21 Trajan's School
22 Christian Basilica
23 Basilica Tempio
24 Temple of Rome & Augustus
25 Casa Triclini
26 Forum Baths
27 Mills
28 Campo della Magna Mater
29 House of Fortuna Annonaria
30 Necropolis of Via Ostiense
31 Thermopolium
32 Hall of the Wheat Measurers
33 Tomb of Cartilius Popicola

Course of the Tiber in Ancient Roman Times

Modern Course of the Tiber

TO FORTRESS RUINS

TO VIA DEL MARE (AUTOSTRADA TO ROME)

TO V. D. STAZIONE OSTIA ANTICA (TRAIN STATION)

Via delle Tombe

PIAZZA DELLA VITTORIA

Via G. Calza

Via dei Vigil

City Wall

Decumanus Maximus

Via Semita dei Cippi

Cardo Maximus

Museum

Parking

Via Tecta

Via Epagathiana

Via Occidentale

Via della Foce

Via degli Aurighi

Decumanus Maximus

TO SYNAGOGUE

0   100 yards
0   100 meters

Frascati, Tusculum, and Grottaferrata

Frascati, famed for its fruity white wines, is the closest of the Castelli to Rome, a mere 20 minutes away by bus. Its lofty position on an ancient volcanic ridge has attracted fugitives from the summer heat for centuries—Frascati's sumptuous patrician villas remain one of the town's finest attractions. The rich slopes outside the town also nurture acres of vineyards where the famed Frascati wine is born, and a visit to the town is incomplete without a taste or two of the local vintage.

The **tourist office** in piazza Marconi (also home to the **bus depot;** tel. 942 03 31) brims with maps and information on the area's villas. Apply here for a free pass to the gardens of the opulent **Villa Aldobrandini,** whose striking Renaissance façade, designed by Giacomo della Porta in 1598, dominates the hill over the center of town. (Park open Mon.-Fri. 9am-1pm.) Frascati's other villas lie on the outskirts and are often closed; ask at the tourist office. In summer, many of the gardens host evening concerts and plays—again, the tourist office knows all. In town, the 17th-century *duomo,* its rough stone façade mostly reconstructed after extensive war damage, stands in p. San Pietro. The winding streets around the *piazza* bustle with restaurants, caffés, and the all-important **wine shops.** Pick up a bottle, then forage for picnic supplies at the **market** at p. Porticella (take via Palestro from p. Marconi, which becomes via Matteoti, and turn right on via Villa Borghese). For the sedentary, reasonable sit-down meals are served at **Club Sara Irma,** via SS Filippo e Giacomo, 12.

If you're lucky enough to be in Frascati in October or November, you can't help but get caught up in the fevered dipsomania of the annual **vendemmia,** the celebration of the grape harvest. Vine-dressers line up their vats to receive the juicy fruits of the vineyards, to the slurred serenade of onlookers.

Beneath the Villa Aldobrandini, the road leading left out of town climbs 5km over winding country roads to the ruins of **Tusculum,** an ancient resort town that once hosted such Roman luminaries as Cato and Cicero along its rocky slopes. The town was destroyed in 1191 during a feud between its residents and the Romans, but the sparse remnants of its ancient foundations spread across the hill amidst romantic stands of wildflowers and olive trees. The climb to Tusculum is a tough one, and many succumb to hitching a ride up the hill. No matter how you get there, it's worth climbing all the way to the top. The citadel of Tusculum, now marked by an iron cross at the summit of the hill, commands a 360° view of southern Lazio, with Rome to the right, the flat *campagna* and beyond it the Tyrrhenian Sea in front, and to the left, the exstinct volcano of Monte Cavo, whose steep slopes are home to the rest of the Castelli Romani. Seize the opportunity for a romantic picnic (and a chance to drink all that wine you've been tasting), even if your only companion is a lump of mozzarella.

From the car park below Tusculum you can walk down the other side of the hill to **Grottaferrata;** alternately, there's frequent bus service from Frascati, as well as direct buses from Anagnina every half hour. Follow Corso del Popolo to its end at the town's Romanesque **Abbey,** founded by the Greek Basilian monks St. Nilus and St. Bartholomew in 1002. History lingers tangibly within the walls of the Greek Orthodox community, from the wizened, white-bearded monks to the 1000-year-old wine kegs. The abbey stands surrounded by an impressive 15th-century moat and fortress, built by the cardinal who would later be Pope Julius II. Inside, the **church of Santa Maria** has a well-preserved medieval portico and bell-tower. In the gloomy interior, the glimmering mosaics boast rare (for Italy) Greek inscriptions. The brighter **chapel of St. Nilus** off the right aisle is famed for its 17th-century frescoes of the life of the saint by Domenichino.

A second gate guards the entrance to the monastery itself. Ring the bell and a monk will take you on a tour of the ancient gardens and the monastery's **Museum** (tel. 945 93 09), where Byzantine mosaics and medieval frescoes taken from the church share space with precious manuscripts and fragments of ancient statuary and pottery excavated nearby. The abbey also maintains a school for Byzantine music and restores rare manuscripts. A few hours a week the monks sell liver-curdling wine from their cavernous wine cellar (to the left as you enter the gate) for about L3000 a liter. Bring your own vessel. (Open Wed. and Sat. 4-6pm, Sun. 10am-noon.)

Head down via XX Settembre or via Cicerone to find cheap *trattorie*. Keep an eye open for *vino produzione propria* (wine made on the premises) signs. Catch the **bus** back to Rome, or on to Lake Albano, on via Santovetti at the other end of Corso del Popolo, until 9pm.

Albano, Genzano and Nemi

A few km across the hills from Frascati and Grottaferrata, the rest of the Castelli Romani cling to the sides of an extinct volcanic crater, now filled with the shimmering blue waters of **Lago Albano**, one of Lazio's cleanest and coolest swimming spots. Lago Albano and its towns are easily accessible from Rome, though as at Frascati, they boast little in the way of sights or entertainments. Crisp wines, clear mountain views, and a taste of Italian country life are the main attractions among the *castelli*.

Buses leave for Marino (for a clockwise tour of the lake) or Castel Gandolfo (to go counterclockwise) and other *castelli* locations every 15 minutes from the Anagnina stop at the end of Metro Linea A (ticket prices vary depending on destination; between L2800-3500). It's not hard to take in several of the *castelli* in a single day; on a complete tour you could see all the towns on both Lake Albano and Lake Nemi, its smaller cousin to the south. Just free of Rome's suburban sprawl, tiny **Castel Gandolfo** owes its fame to the sprawling **Papal Palace** which occupies its volcanic ridge. The current pope comes here every summer to relax and enjoy his famed gardens, which spread down the outer rim of the crater toward the sea. The papal domains are closed to the public, but the town's public street and one tiny *piazza* (dominated by Maderno's early Baroque papal palace, and guarded over by Swiss Guards when the Pope is in residence) offer passing glimpses of the lake views and mountain scenery which have drawn pontiffs here for centuries. The *piazza* also houses the **church of S. Tommaso di Villanova**, an early work by Bernini. Outside the center of town, the lake road opens out to several belvederes, where you can catch better views of the lake and its volcanic outcroppings. A winding road (about 2km) leads down to the lakeshore and a **public beach**, where sailboats and windsurfers are for hire (be careful of the lake's infamous and unpredictable gusts).

The road between Castel Gandolfo and **Albano Laziale**, lined with beautiful and rare specimens of the Italian holm-oak, stretches for a kilometer past more views of the lake and its verdant shores. Albano takes its name from the ancient Latin city of Alba Longa, once the capital of the indigenous Italian Latin League and the parent city of Rome; it's thought that the metropolis (prior to its destruction by the upstart Romans) was sited on this part of the crater's ridge. Albano's one of the bigger *castelli* (that is, it has more than one street), and offers plenty of winding alleys for wandering and exploring. The central **p. Mazzini** is bordered on the right (as you enter from Rome) by a spacious public garden, the **Villa Comunale**, built over the intermittently-visible remains of a villa of Pompey the Great. At the ends of the park's broad avenues you can catch views of the flat Roman countryside. Outside p. Mazzini, Corso Matteotti, the town's main street, leads past the **Palazzo del Comune**, which houses an impressive collection of artifacts left by the Latini and the Romans in the ruins scattered about the town (Open 9:30am-1:30pm and 4:30-7:30pm. Admission L3750).

South of Albano, the same lake road passes the curious **Tomb of the Horatii and Curiatii**, a Republican-age funeral monument believed to mark the graves of the famous triplets whose duel secured Rome's supremacy over ancient Alba Longa. **Aricia**, 1km south of Albano, isn't noted for much beyond the soaring 19th-century viaduct that brings you into town. There's a *piazza* graced by the remains of a Republican temple, the medieval **Palazzo Chigi** (spruced up by Bernini in the 17th century) and another Bernini artifact, the round **Sta. Maria dell'Assunzione**.

From Aricia, the road continues south to the towns of **Lake Nemi**, another flooded volcanic crater. Ancient Romans, marveling at Nemi's placid blue waters, called the lake the mirror of Diana and graced its sloping shores with a famous temple to the goddess. Surrounded by a sacred grove, the temple was presided over by a eunuch priest who could only get the job by killing his predecessor and plucking a golden bough off of one of the grove's sacred trees. Life's a bit less strenuous these days on the ridges surrounding the lake. At **Genzano**, 3km south of Aricia, the sloping streets that radiate from the central p. Tommaso Frasconi host the annual **Infiorata**, a festival of floral extravagance. Artisans spend weeks arranging yards of blossoms in artistic and geometric patterns; on the Sunday after Corpus Domini (June 18), the town deploys them in a frenzy of horticultural pride. Across the lake, tiny **Nemi** clings to its rocky perch over the lake. The vertiginous village boasts more staircases than streets, but its miniature strawberries (*fragolini di Nemi*), grown along the shores of the lake, are the town's real glory. A bowl filled with the tiny fruits and topped with a dollop of fresh *panna* is a specialty at the several bars that line the belvedere overlooking the lake. In late June and early July, the town hosts a **Festival of Strawberries** that lasts several weeks.

Along the shores of the lake, the **Nemi Museum of Ships** lies a 15-minute walk down the road from Nemi. The barn-like museum was built to house two complete Roman barges which were dredged up from the lake in the early part of this century. The barges, made of well-preserved wooden planks and still outfitted with their metal hardware, rope riggings, and marble and mosaic floors, were an incredible archaeological find. Each one was over 230 feet long and 60 feet wide. It's thought that they belonged to the Emperor Caligula, who used the boats as scenes for his favorite debauched orgies. Unfortunately, the ships were torched by the Nazis as they retreated from Italy at the end of World War II—a senseless act of destruction. Today, the museum houses two scale models of the barges and the few bits of lead and bronze that weren't melted in the blaze. (Museum open Tues.-Sun. 9am-2pm. Admission L8000.)

The lake road continues north to the summit of Monte Cavo, where **Rocca di Papa**, the highest of the Castelli Romani, glowers over Lake Albano and the spreading Roman countryside beyond it. The town doesn't offer much in the way of architectural sights, but the views of the lake, of Frascati and Tusculum to the north, and of Rome and the Tyrrhenian Sea to the west, are stunning in themselves. On the other side of Monte Cavo, **Marino** closes the circle of *castelli* to the north. If you're in town on the first Sunday in October, you'll see the town's fountains flowing with wine during the annual **Sagra dell'Uva**; otherwise, Marino's a good place to make ACOTRAL **bus** connections back to Rome.

Viterbo

Heavy Allied bombing shattered Viterbo's old city walls, and reconstruction has been slow. You'll see the results as you step from the station into traffic and rubble. Across the busy highway amid hovering carbon fumes is the forbidding entrance to a city tinctured black. But don't be deterred: the vestiges of Viterbo's eminence warrant a stop.

Viterbo began as an Etruscan center but earned prominence as a papal refuge from Frederick Barbarossa's siege on Rome in the 12th century. The real architectural splurge commenced during the next century, as Viterbo became a Guelph stronghold in the aristocrats' civil war. It was here that the torturous process of papal elections first took shape. The *capitano* (city dictator) locked the cardinals in their palace until they chose a new pope. Threats to cut off food deliveries and to remove the roof from the conference room (so that the cold could creep in more easily) were added incentives for a quick decision. Today Viterbo also serves as an induction point for draftees of the Italian military; its streets brim with an eclectic mix of boys in uniform, punks, window shopppers, and senior citizens. And it still draws many to its sulphurous hot **Bulicane spring** (3km from center), famous for its curative powers.

Orientation and Practical Information

Enter the city through the arched thresholds of the great stone wall, and venture out again at your own risk. Don't chance getting lost in the suburbs—there's plenty to check out within. At first glance, the inner city might intimidate you with its incongruous passages and what seem to be haphazardly scattered yellow signs misleading you down dead-end alleys. But don't worry—do follow the signs. There are few dead ends and several ways of getting to each of the many significant buildings and *piazze*. The town is easily navigated: its walls form a trapezoid with the wide parallel side lining the eastern sector. **San Francesco** and **Santa Rosa** are in the northeast region, **San Sis-**

to and **San Pellegrino** (the historical center) in the southeast, and **San Lorenzo** west of center. **Piazza dei Caduti** is just north of **del Plebiscito** (which is practically dead center). The **bus station** is located just outside the northeast corner. Via Marconi and via Cavour/via Ascenzi converge at the tourist office.

When you arrive at the bus or train terminal, walk right along the city wall to the first opening, Porta Fiorentina, and descend along via Matteotti to p. Verdi at the bottom of the hill. Via Marconi on the right takes you to p. dei Caduti and the EPT; the Azienda di Turismo is on the left, and corso Italia, sloping up to the right, leads to the medieval San Pellegrino district.

Tourist Office: EPT, p. dei Caduti, 16 (tel. 22 61 61). All sorts of printed materials, including a map and self-guided tour of Viterbo. English spoken. Limited hours, but large map displayed outside. Open Mon.-Sat. 8am-2pm. **Azienda di Turismo,** p. Verdi, 4 (tel. 22 66 66). No English, but a helpful wall map. Open daily 8am-1:20pm.

Post Office: via Ascenzi (tel. 23 48 06), between del Plebiscito and the tourist office. Open Mon.-Fri. 8:10am-7:35pm, Sat. 8am-noon. Also p. della Rocca. Open Mon.-Fri. 2-7pm. **Postal Code:** 01100.

Telephones: SIP, via Calabresi, 7. Open Mon.-Fri. 8:10am-7:50pm, Sat. 9am-12:30pm. **Telephone Code:** 0761.

Buses: Tickets can be purchased at the theater/snack bar at viale Trento or at the ACOTRAL on via Sauro (1 block away). All buses board passengers across from the theater. Buses to: Orvieto (1{1/2}hr., L4300); Civitavécchia (1{3/4}hr., L4800); Tarquínia (1hr., L4300); Caprarola (L1500); and Bolsena (L3000) as well as other cities in Etruria. To get to Viterbo from Rome take city transit bus #490 or any bus going to p. Flaminio. At the Flaminio station buy a combination train/bus ticket (L5300) to Viterbo. A train will take you 10min. to Saxo-Rubio (the sticks) and buses bound for Viterbo will be waiting.

Emergencies: tel. 113. **Police: Questura,** località Pietrare (tel. 34 19 55). **Hospital:** via dell'Ospedale, 101 (tel. 23 28 61), at via San Lorenzo. **Red Cross:** tel. 23 40 33.

Accommodations and Camping

Albergo Milano, via della Cava, 54 (tel. 34 07 05). Family-managed hotel located in northeast by San Francesco and not far from the bus station. Stoic but kind grandmother will direct you to a clean room equipped with short-wave radio. Jam to worldwide tunes. Singles L27,000, with bath L35,000. Doubles L40,000, with bath L60,000.

Albergo Roma, via della Cava, 26 (tel. 22 72 74 or 22 64 74). Comfy quarters at 2-star prices. Singles L33,390, with bath L49,350. Doubles L49,350, with bath L71,000.

Pensione Minerva, via della Caserma, 7 (tel. 34 09 90). Clean, cheap, and affable. Singles L23,000. Doubles L34,000, with bath L47,000. Triples L60,000.

Camping: The nearest campgrounds are on the immaculate beach of **Lago di Bolsena,** 30km north. Most accessible by public transport are those in Bolsena itself (ACOTRAL bus, L3000): **Il Lago,** viale Cadorna (tel. 79 91 91), L6000 per person, L4500 per tent, L3500 per car (open March-Sept.).You can find prettier campgrounds near Bolsena off the Cassia in the towns of Capodimonte and Montefiascone. Check with the tourist office for a full list of campgrounds in the province of Viterbo.

Food

Local specialties include the exotic-looking *lombriche* (earthworm-shaped) pasta and a chestnut soup known as the *zuppa di mosciarelle.* Try Viterbo's native *sambuca,* a sweet anise-flavored liqueur. One of the most celebrated local wines exults in the effervescent name *Est! Est!! Est!!!,* with which a duke tippled himself to death. Pope Martin IV experienced a doom of a different sort—the sufferings of purgatory, according to Dante—for his weakness for another local dish, roasted eel from Bolsena. Less exotic, if no less sinful, freshwater fish can be had in the towns surrounding Lake Bolsena. *Alimentari* can be found along via dell'Orologio, or check out the huge **outdoor market** (Saturdays 7am-2pm) in p. della Rocca.

Trattoria del'Archeto, via Cristoforo, 1 , at the open end of a dead end. Dine under the eyes of our patron saint of travel. Outdoor tables rain or shine (*primi* L6000-10,000, *menù* L18,000).

Porta Romana, via della Bontà, 12 (tel. 237 18). You tell her how much you're willing to pay, she tells you how much you're entitled to eat. Provincial specialties lauded by locals. Full meals about L18,000. Cover L2000. Open Mon.-Sat. 7-11:30pm.

Taverna del Padrino, via della Cava, 22. Tasty pizzas and a lively atmosphere. Popular with conscripts. Pizzas average L7000. Cover L2000. Open noon-2:30pm and 7pm-3am.

Sights

At the southern end of town is the medieval quarter's administrative center, **piazza del Plebescito.** The medallion-decked building with the tall clock tower is the **Palazzo del Popolo,** across from the **Palazzo della Prefettura.** Large stone lions, the symbol of Viterbo, guard both. Between them lies the **Palazzo Comunale** in full Renaissance sprawl. The odd frescoes in the **Sala Regia,** painted in 1592, depict the history of Viterbo, mixing in Etruscan, Classical, Christian, and medieval legends. (Open 8am-7pm. Free. Go upstairs to the office on your right and ask to have the Royal Room opened.) Outside, the façade of the church of Sant'Angelo incorporates a late Roman sarcophagus that contains the body of the ineffably beautiful and virtuous Galiana. When she refused to marry an amorous Roman baron, he besieged the city, promising to spare it if she came to the wall. As soon as Galiana appeared, the baron shot her with an arrow, thereby ensuring her fidelity.

Curious *palazzi* line **via San Lorenzo,** which wends its way from p. del Plebescito into Viterbo's medieval heart, p. San Lorenzo. There, in the Siena-influenced bell tower of the **cathedral,** pairs of slender, arched windows climb to a sharp peak. The **Palazzo Papale,** topped by a row of toothlike merlons, fills the far end of the *piazza.* From the *loggia,* enjoy a bird's-eye view of a complex of early Christian churches. This has been the site of three papal conclaves, including the one in which the roof was almost removed to freeze the clergy into a decision. (Open Mon.-Sat. 10am-12:30pm. Free.)

Via San Pellegrino stumbles its way through the medieval quarter of **San Pellegrino.** Churches and towers block the path completely, whittling the sky to a scant strip of blue between the dark *peperino* walls of volcanic rock. At the northwestern boundary of San Pellegrino at the end of v. San Lorenzo is the charming yet unfortunately named **piazza delle Morte** (Square of Death), at the center of which is a vibrant fountain as well as the 13th-century **palazzetto of San Tomaso.** Note the medieval balcony next to the **church of Santa Giacinta,** also on the square. At the northern end of town, the **Basilica of San Francesco** contains the tombs of two popes who died in Viterbo: Adrian V (1276, whom Dante put in hell with the misers) and Clement IV (1265-68). Both mausoleums sport exemplary 13th-century sculpture. At the **church of Santa Rosa** (near the basilica), the 700-year-old corpse of Viterbo's celebrated saint is preserved in a glass case.

Entertainment

At 9pm on September 3, the people of Viterbo honor Santa Rosa. One hundred burly bearers carry the *Macchina di Santa Rosa,* a towering 30m-high construction of iron, wood, and *papier-mâché,* through the illuminated streets. The bearers of the tributary lug it around town and then sprint uphill to the **Church of Santa Rosa** (where the well-preserved remains of the saint lie). In 1814 the *macchina* fell on the *facchini* (bearers), and in 1967 it had to be abandoned in the street because it was too heavy. Several days of frenzied celebration surround this event. The **Festival Barocco** brings excellent classical music to Viterbo's churches in June. Ask at the tourist office about tickets (L12,000) and schedules.

Near Viterbo

Villa Lante, in the picturesque town of **Bagnaia** outside Viterbo, is a particularly enjoyable example of the grandiose villas that were in vogue among 16th-century church bigwigs. The local (orange) bus #6 leaves Viterbo from p. Mártiri d'Ungheria every half-hour for Bagnaia (15 min., L1300, last bus back leaves Bagnaia at 8:30pm).

From the *piazza* where the bus drops you, walk uphill and enter the villa's right-hand gate. Most of the estate now serves as a public park, and you can wander among the fountains and avenues as you please. To enter the gardens immediately adjacent to the villa, however, you must ring at the gatehouse on the left as you enter and wait for a keeper to give you a tour of the verdant glories designed by Vignola in the 1570s. In a manner characteristic of Renaissance gardens, water rushes down the hill behind the villas through a sequence of elaborate fountains before disappearing underground. (Villa Lante open Tues.-Sun. 9am-7:30pm; March-April and Sept.-Oct. 9am-5:30pm; Nov.-Feb. 9am-4pm. Tours of the inner gardens every ½hr, L2000.)

A little farther along the same road lurks a pleasure garden of a different sort: the **Parco dei Mostri** (Park of the Monsters). Blue ACOTRAL buses depart from viale Trento in Viterbo (6 per day, L1300) and drop you off in **Bomarzo,** 1km from the park, 3km from the farmhouse *pensione* outside of town. From where the bus leaves you, walk downhill and follow the signs for Palazzo Orsini (not Parco dei Mostri). Turn left down the stairs marked via del Lavatio, and continue downhill to the park. If the picturesque towns and landscape of this region have left you longing for a tourist trap, this offbeat 16th-century Disney World supplies the diversion. A surreal wilderness of grotesque forms mocks the overly refined aristocratic sculpture gardens of the time (e.g., Villa Lante's). A walk through the mossy paths is anything but pastoral, as you amble into the mouths of snarling beasts and past a giant ripping another apart limb by limb. (Open 8:30am-7pm. Admission L8000.)

The Orsini who commissioned the gardens may also have owned what is now Bomarzo's only lodging, the **Club Agrituristico,** a converted **16th-century hunting lodge.** Its new owners moved from Rome to this idyll, in which they've established two quaint rooms which rent for L60,000 per night per room (each room accommodates up to four people). They also have horseback riding (L15,000 per hr.), their own organic produce, camping (L8000 per person, L3000 per tent), and kitchen facilities. Call ahead and they'll gladly pick you up at the bus stop (tel. (0761) 92 44 66).

The Sabine Hills: Rieti and its Province

Covering the Sabine mountains and the Salto lake basin east of Rome, Rieti province is one of the most naturally verdant in all of Italy, and was coveted long before St. Francis claimed it as a spiritual home. The natives' constant wars against the Romans and Latins (pre-Roman natives of Latium) often turned ugly—the rape of the Sabine women a brutal example—and presaged later invasions by Saracens, French, and the Napoleonic Empire. A brief calm spell under the protection of the Papal State (12th-15th centuries) and the preoccupation with building upon spots where St. Francis slept endowed the tiny mountain villages and countryside with a plethora of medieval and Baroque churches, sanctuaries, and castles. Carved into the promontories on which they perch, these towns peer out over beautiful vistas.

Rieti

Some Romans are better than others. When Curius Dentatus captured this Sabine capital in 290 BC, he did the region a favor and made the land fertile by draining the nearby swamps and diverting the water into what is now Terni's Marmore Falls. The resultant greening later made Rieti a favorite of St. Francis. Easily accessible from Rome, this wee provincial capital makes an excellent base and introduction to the hill country.

Piazza Vittorio Emanuele encloses the **Palazzo Comunale,** which in turn encloses the **Museo Civico.** The museum's collection includes some Iron Age pieces, statues of Diana and Kouros, and the only work signed by Venetian Zannino di Pietro, *Stories of St. Francis.* (Open Tues.-Thurs. and Sat.-Sun. 9am-1pm. Free.) Smack in the center of town at p. Cesare Battisti is the 12th-century **Cathedral of Santa Maria Assunta,** with superb vaulted ceilings and a square bell tower. Inside, the ornate, domed **Chapel of St. Barbara** contains a Bernini statue of the saint. At the end of via Roma, make a left and continue to the 13th-century **Chiesa di San Francesco,** and gaze at the 14th-century copies of Giotto's Assisi frescoes.

Fallone, a calzone stuffed with herbs and olive oil, and *fregracce alla Sabinese,* a pasta dish with black olives, mushrooms, artichokes, tomatoes, and olive oil, are particularly savory Sabine specialties. Try **Al Calice d'Oro,** on v. Marchetti, 10 (tel. 442 71; open Tues.-Sun. 7-11:30pm), or **La Fontanella,** on v. San Francesco, 36 (tel. 456 85), for these and other dishes.

ACOTRAL **buses** run almost every hour from Rome's Castro Pretorio (1hr., L5300). Trains run frequently from Termini to Rieti station (L12,100, round-trip L20,600). The most convenient place for comprehensive **tourist information** is the **Alitalia** office, via Vittorio Emanuele II (tel. 27 07 02), where via Garibaldi ends. Cross p. Mazzini from the train station and walk through the park. Turn right onto via D. Pesheria and make your first left. The office will be on your right as you enter the *piazza.* (Open Mon.-Fri. 9am-1pm and 3:30-7pm, Sat. 9am-1pm.) The **post office** is on via Garibaldi, 283 (to your left). (Open Mon.-Fri. 8:30am-6pm, Sat. 8:30am-noon.) Telephones are also available there. The **postal code** for Rieti is 02100; its **telephone code** is 0746. If you plan to sleep in Rieti while traveling throughout the Sabines, consider doing so at the three-star **Europa,** centally located in the old town on via San Rufo, 49 (tel. 49 51 49), one block south of via Garibaldi behind the Centro d'Italia. (Singles L40,000, with bath L60,000. Doubles L60,000, with bath L80,000. Breakfast L3000.) Or try **Hotel Serena,** on v. della Gioventù, 17/A (tel. 27 09 30), outside the fortified walls off v. Ludovico Canali. The helpful management offers clean rooms with TVs. (Singles L28,000, with bath L55,000. Doubles L47,000, with bath L75,000.)

Near Rieti

The pocket of charming villages in the province are best seen by car, since bus service is infrequent and few excursions are worth an entire day's effort. Among the best spots to stop are **Roccasinibalda,** 23km south of Rieti, a little village with one of the prettiest castles in Italy—a scorpion-shaped edifice fortified and embellished by the Medici Pope Clement VII and Alexander Cesarini. Its hanging gardens and some of the interior are open to the public. Further south **Fara in Sabina** is a village of severe medieval buildings, whose **church of Sant'Antonio** boasts Vignola's **tabernacle,** a stellar exemplar of the Renaissance search for the perfect temple form. Check out the incredible view from the terrace on the square—on clear days you can make out the dome of St. Peter's. Nearby, the itsy-bitsy hamlet of **Roccantica** lies at the base of Monte Pizzuto, its romantic placement a proper tribute to its patron saint, Valentine. You can arrange a free tour of the town by calling the **tourist office** (tel. (0765) 630 15).

Eighteen km west of Rieti is St. Francis's stomping ground, **Greccio.** The convent **Santuario di Greccio,** built right into a cliff, was the saint's private sanctuary for one year in 1217. Francis liked Greccio so much that in 1223 he returned to celebrate Christmas and demonstrated his acumen as a handyman by building a *presipio* (crèche). This crèche, the first ever, earned the convent a reputation as the Franciscan Bethlehem. The convent lies 2km from the town center, a beautiful wooded walk along the main road. Tired pilgrims can rest at the **Hotel della Fonte** (tel. 75 31 10). (Singles L22,000. Doubles L40,000, with shower L60,000.) **Buses** run frequently to Greccio (L4600 round-trip).

North to Umbria

Orvieto

Orvieto's forbidding perch atop a volcanic outcropping and the dark closeness of its streets recall its origin as one of the cities of the Etruscan *Dodecapolis.* However, it is the medieval legacy that colors the city more strongly today. A papal refuge from the Middle Ages through the Renaissance, in the 13th century Orvieto drew Thomas Aquinas to its academies and saw the Crusades planned within its walls. A well-preserved medieval center provides the backdrop for the stunning 13th-century *duomo,* which has rewarded Orvieto's piety with touristic fame and wealth. Sample the product of the other local industry, the excellent white *Orvieto classico* wine.

Orientation and Practical Information

Orvieto lies midway on the Rome-Florence line. From the train station, you cross the street to take the funicular up the volcano. When you reach the top you can walk up **corso Cavour** toward the center or take a **shuttle** to p. del Duomo. The journey takes about 15 minutes and costs L1000. Corso Cavour is the town's backbone, site of most of the city's restaurants, hotels, and shops. Via Duomo branches off c. Cavour and ends at p. del Duomo.

Tourist Office: p. del Duomo, 24 (tel. 417 72). Friendly staff seems frazzled but patient. Get the incredibly complete pamphlet on hotels and restaurants, sights, and practical information. Complete information on trains and buses; city **bus tickets** and **phone cards** for sale. Open Mon.-Fri. 10am-2pm and 4-7pm, Sat. 10am-1pm and 4-7pm, Sun. 10am-noon and 4-6pm. Also has **telephones**. **Telephone Code:** 0763.

Post Office: via Cesare Nebbia which begins after the Teatro Mancinelli, next to corso Cavour, 114 (tel. 412 43). **Stamps** are available at tobacco shops and there are mail drops scattered throughout the town. Open Mon.-Sat. 8:15am-6:40pm. **Postal Code:** 05018.

Trains: To Florence (L13,800); Rome (L10,500); and Perugia (L8800). **Luggage Storage:** L1500.

Buses: ACOTRAL, p. Cahen. 7 per day to Viterbo. **ACT,** p. Cahen, 10 (tel. 442 65). To: Perugia (L10,500) and Todi (L7700). Buy tickets at the shop next to the station.

Emergencies: tel. 113. **Police:** p. della Repubblica (tel. 400 88). **Hospital:** p. del Duomo (tel. 420 71).

Accommodations

Da Fiora, via Magalotti, 22 (tel. 411 19), just off p. della Repubblica through small p. dell'Erba (take minibus B to Erba). The best deal in town. Not technically a hotel; the proprietress rents private rooms. Modest but spotless. Prices go down in winter. Singles L15,000. Doubles with bath L30,000. If it's full, she'll make up beds on the couch or floor for L10,000 per person.

Hotel Posta, via Signorelli, 18 (tel. 419 09), near the Torre del Moro, between corso Cavour and p. Scalza. The location couldn't be better. A leafy garden and pleasant lobby. Curfew 11:30pm. Singles L35,000, with bath L50,000. Doubles L50,000, with bath L70,000. Open March-Dec.

Camping Orvieto (tel. (0744) 95 02 40), on Lake Corbara 14km from the center of town. Call from the station and they'll pick you up. Swimming pool and hot showers included. L7000 per person, L6000 per tent, L2500 per car. Open Easter-Sept.

Food

Most of the fixings will fix you for broke. At least the wine is cheap. An excellent *alimentari* sits below p. della Repubblica at via Filippeschi, 39 (open Mon.-Tues. and Thurs.-Sat. 7:30am-1:30pm and 5-8pm, Wed. 7:30am-1:30pm).

Cooperativa al San Francesco (tel. 433 02), on Cerretti off via Lorenzo Maitani off the front side of p. del Duomo. Follow the large signs, your nose, or the crowd. Extremely popular with locals. A huge restaurant, self-service cafeteria, and *pizzeria* all rolled into one. Dine at outdoor tables on a peaceful *piazza* or indulge in the cavernous interior. Pizza (at night only) and wine L11,000. Full meals L15,000. Open daily noon-3pm and 7-11pm.

Da Fiora, via Magalotti (tel. 411 19). Located just below her rent-a-room residence, Signora Fiora has now established a bustling restaurant enterprise featuring the best deals in town. Pasta, meat, and beer or wine (L12,000) will fill you as you take in a spaghetti Western on TV or enjoy the company of what appears to be the local Boys' Club.

Sights and Entertainment

The shuttle bus drops you off in p. del Duomo. The first glance at the 1290 **duomo** (Orvieto's fervor and pride) promises to be overwhelming: its fanciful façade, intricately designed by Lorenzo Maitani, dazzles and enraptures the admirer with intertwining spires, mosaics, and sculptures. The bottom level features exquisitely carved bas-reliefs of the Creation and Old Testament prophecies, and a final panel of Maitani's realistic *Last Judgement;* the bronze and marble sculptures (1325-1964) emphasize the Christian pantheon, set in niches surrounding the rose window by Andrea Orcagna. The fabulous mosaics provide a day-long performance of light and shadow. Thirty-three architects, 90 mosaic artisans, 152 sculptors, and 68 painters worked for over six centuries to bring the *duomo* this far, and the work continues; the bronze doors were only installed in 1970.

The cathedral's 700th anniversary two years ago provoked a flurry of restoration that has left its masterpieces better than ever, among them the **Capella della Madonna di San Brizio** (sometimes called the **Capella Nuova**) off the right transept. Inside are Luca Signorelli's dramatic **Apocalypse frescoes,** considered to be his *chef d'oeuvre.* Begun by Fra Angelico in 1447, they were supposed to be completed by Perugino, but the city grew tired of waiting and enlisted Signorelli to finish the project. His mastery of human anatomy, dramatic compositions, and vigorous draftsmanship paved the way for the genius of Michelangelo.

On the left wall hangs the *Preaching of the Antichrist.* The prominent Renaissance dandy in a shimmering crimson costume to the left of the Antichrist is the painting's patron; behind the bald man to the patron's left is the red-hatted poet Dante. The woman with the outstretched hand on the other side is Signorelli's mistress; she is seen as a prostitute engaged in the basest act imaginable to a good Catholic of the day, taking money from a Jew. Behind her stand Columbus, Petrarch, Cesare Borgia, and Dante (again). Far off in the corner, Signorelli and Fra Angelico, in black, observe the proceedings. On the opposite wall, muscular humans and skeletons pull themselves out of the earth in the uncanny *Resurrection of the Dead.* Beside it is the *Inferno,* with Signorelli (a blue devil) and his mistress embracing beneath the fiery display.

In the **Cappella del Corporale** off the left transept, Lippo Memmi's *Madonna dei Raccomandati* hangs with abashed pride. In this chapel also sits the gold-encrusted **Reliquary of the Corporale** (chalice-cloth), the *raison d'être* of the whole structure. The cloth inside the box caught the blood of Christ which dripped from a consecrated host in Bolsena in 1263, thereby substantiating the doctrine of transubstantiation, which the papacy was still having some trouble putting over. (The *duomo* is open all year 7am-1pm, but the afternoon hours vary each month—2:30-5:30pm is a safe bet. Free, but bring plenty of L200 coins to illuminate the paintings.)

The austere 13th-century **Palazzo dei Papi** (Palace of the Popes) sits to the right of the *duomo.* Here, in 1527, Pope Clement VII rejected King Henry VIII's petition to annul his marriage with Catherine of Aragón, condemning both Catherine and English Catholicism to a dim prospect. Now the *palazzo* houses the **Museo Archaeologico Nazionale.** Here you can examine Etruscan artifacts from the area, and even walk into a full-size tomb. (Open Mon.-Sat. 9am-1:30pm and 3-7pm, Sun. 9am-1pm. Free.) Across from the *duomo,* the **Museo Claudio Faina,** in the "Museo Civico" building, harbors more Etruscan finds. (Open Tues.-Sun. 9am-1pm and 3-6pm; Oct.-March 9am-1pm and 2:30-4:30pm. Admission L3000.)

A 10-minute walk down via del Duomo and then via Constituente puts you in p. Capitano del Popolo. Here, the 13th-century **Palazzo del Capitano del Popolo** sports the standard motif of Romanesque Orvieto architecture: a checkerboard band surrounding its windows. Return to Corso Cavour and continue through p. della Repubblica into Orvieto's **medieval quarter.** The soils of the verdant slope below p. San Giovanni are enriched by the graves of thousands who perished in the Black Death of 1348. Drop by the small church **San Lorenzo de Arari,** with dozens of luminous frescoes and an Etruscan altar beneath its Christian successor.

On the eastern edge of town, down via Sangallo off p. Cahen, you can descend the **Pozzo di San Patrizio** (St. Patrick's Well). Having fled just-sacked Rome, Pope Clement VII wanted to ensure that the town did not run out of water during a siege, and in 1527 commissioned Antonio da Sangallo the Younger to design the well. (Open daily 8am-8pm; in winter daily 8am-6pm. Admission L6500 includes the Museo Greco.) After cooling off in the clammy well shaft, enter the **Fortezza,** where a fragrant sculpture garden and lofty trees crown battlements overlooking the Umbrian landscape. (Open 7am-8pm; Oct.-March 9am-7pm.)

On Pentecost (42 days after Easter), all Orvieto celebrates the **Festa della Palombella.** Small wooden structures filled with fireworks and connected by a metal wire are set up in front of the *duomo* and the Church of San Francesco. At the stroke of noon, the San Francesco fireworks are set off, and a white metal dove shoots across the wire to ignite the explosives. **Concerts** are held in the *duomo* on August evenings. If you're around in early June, don't miss the **Procession of Corpus Domini,** a solemn parade celebrating the Miracle of Bolsena.

Near Orvieto: Civita

Civita, not just another quaint town teeming with tourists, is slightly off the beaten path but well worth the hike. Literally a one-horse town, Civita is crammed onto the pinnacle of a small mountain. It is accessible via foot bridge from Bagnoregio or foot path through the valley between the two mountain towns. Civita's residents (all 20 of them) will invite you into their backyards or basements where you can see their private collections of Etruscan and Roman relics for a small fee. Take a picnic lunch or dine in the lone café. To get there take a bus from Orvieto to Bagnoregio (30min., L3000 round-trip). Civita is a 15-minute hike from the last bus stop. Buses run throughout the day; the last one returns at 5:20pm.

Beaches

Rome has never been known for its beaches—the marshy flats of the Tiber mouth peter out into fairly dull stretches of polluted Ostia sand—but if you're willing to venture a little out from Rome, the southern coast offers miles of clean and picturesque shoreline, along with some pretty towns and delicious fresh seafood. The further from the city you go, the better your prospects for sunning and swimming in relative peace, but be warned that in August you could go as far as Sicily and still find the beaches packed. Another note: great stretches of the Lazio beaches lie under the thumb of nefarious *stabilmenti balneari*—private companies that fence off the choicest bits of beach and charge admission. The ticket comes with its perks, including towels, beach chairs, the use of showers, etc., but the price is usually pretty steep. Crashing a *stabilmento* isn't a great idea (they have henchmen), but a little polite inquiring will point you to a *spiaggia libera*, the local public beach.

Rome to Anzio and Nettuno

The broad arc of beach stretching south of Rome is a natural extension of the Lido di Ostia, but the President of the Republic's vast seaside compound at Castel Fusano has effectively isolated the southern half of the shoreline. ACOTRAL **buses** (from the EUR-Fermi station at the end of Metro Linea B) skirt inland of the estate before heading seaward to Tor Vaianaca, the first beach town accessible to the public. (Buses depart 5:30am-10pm every ½hr.; L4300.) From here, the road stretches past 25km of *stabilmenti*, beach bars, restaurants, amusement parks and the like—if sand is all you're looking for, hop off at the first appealing stop. Otherwise, continue to the end of the beach, where the twin towns of Anzio and Nettuno occupy a small promontory. The beaches here are prettier and cleaner than to the north, and the diversions are more abundant, but then again so are the people. The two towns were the scene of an Allied invasion on January 22, 1944, and were mostly destroyed by the fighting—today the architecture is strictly postwar reconstruction.

At **Anzio**, despite the present invasion of sun-worshippers, fishing is still the town's main preoccupation, and the busy port is lined with trawlers and the scaly fruits of their daily catch. The bus leaves you off in p. Cesare Battista; walk two blocks down and to the right to the **tourist office** in Riviera Zanardelli (tel. 984 61 19; open daily 9am-12:30pm and 5-8pm) for maps and information on hotels or transport back to Rome. Further north (that is, to the right) of the port stretch the beaches. **Stabilmento Dea Fortuna** offers a clean stretch of beach and a chair for L9500 per day (though in June and Sept. you can haggle), plus use of changing rooms and showers. But a ½km walk along the beach road procures a much better bargain; a well-traveled **hole** in the chain link fence leads to the ruins of the **Villa di Nerone**, a vast seaside complex built by the playboy emperor in the 1st century AD, where tons of ancient statuary, including the Apollo Belvedere, were later discovered. Clamber down through the crumbling vaults and dune-covered terraces of ancient brick to the **public beach,** where the waves lap up against half-sunken arches and Romans sunbathe on slabs of 2000 year-old masonry. Only in Italy.

Nettuno, 3km south of Anzio, sprawls along the coastline with modern bustle. Still, the little town managed to preserve more of its ancient foundations than Anzio did, including a walled medieval quarter and a Renaissance fortress. Both the ACOTRAL bus and the local orange bus from Anzio stop along the beach road, which doubles as Nettuno's main street. Below the gaudy Palazzo Municipale, a busy marina teems with fishing and pleasure boats; the **public beach** lies to the left. The old medieval town, its walls now perforated by several vaulted passageways, preserves its limestone turrets and a miniscule *piazza*, where cheap *trattorie* serve up the morning's catch of seafood beneath an oasis of umbrellas. A few minutes walk to the north brings you to the **Castello,** built in the 15th century by Antonio Sangallo the Elder for the infamous Borgia Pope Alexander VI. The castle's probably been under restoration since Alexander was alive, but the moat is open as a public garden.

Nettuno, like most Italian towns, has done its best to forget its war-torn past. But one somber reminder remains: a ½km inland on via Santa Maria, the **Sicily-Rome American Cemetery** stretches over 72 acres of parkland, donated to the U.S. by a grateful postwar Italian government. The spacious grounds, beautifully landscaped with umbrella pines, holm-oaks, and a sober, cypress-planted island, hold the graves of over 7000 Americans who died during the 1943-44 Italian campaign, which began with the invasion of Sicily and ended with the liberation of Rome from Nazi occupation. The chapel at the top of the park contains a memorial to those whose bodies were lost in the fighting as well as extensive maps and descriptions of the Allied drive up the peninsula. An American custodian remains on duty to provide information and to help locate graves. (Cemetery open Mon.-Fri. 8am-6pm; Sat. and Sun. 9am-6pm. Free.)

Both Anzio and Nettuno are served by the ACOTRAL **buses** running along the coast from EUR-Fermi (see above); a longer ACOTRAL route leaves from the Anagnina stop at the end of Metro Linea A and passes through the hill town of Albano (see Castelli Romani, above), with departures every hour. The **train** from Termini is the fastest way to get down to the beach (in about an hour; 5:25am-11:37pm; return 5:14am-11:03pm; departures every hour; L4800); the train stations in both towns lie one block inland from the beach and bus stops. Anzio is also a point of departure for ferries to **Ponza** (see below).

From Nettuno to Terracina

The next great stretch of Latian shore, from Nettuno to Terracina, is also accessible from Rome by ACOTRAL buses (leaving from EUR-Fermi 6:20am-7pm, every ½hr.; see prices below). **Latina** (L5200 from Rome), the inland provincial capital, sends local orange buses out to the shore towns of Borgo Sabotino, Foceverde, Capoportiere, and Borgo Grappa, all about 20km away. None of these modern beach magnets has much in the way of historic charm, but the sand is clean and the ocean's as wet as anywhere else. Further down the coast, **Sabaudia** (L5800) is a modern agricultural center, founded by Mussolini in the 1930s as part of his (very successful) plan to drain the marshes south of Rome and render them habitable for Roman farmers. Sabaudia is part of the sprawling **Parco Nazionale del Circeo**, a national park named for the imposing promontory of Monte Circeo, which dominates this stretch of sandy shoreline. The town itself is separated from its beach by several modern reservoirs (crossed by bridges), and the mountain lies a few km south across the bay. From Sabaudia's beaches you can walk, take one of the frequent local orange buses, or stay on the ACOTRAL bus from Rome (L6300) to the village of **San Felice Circeo**, which lies on the southern slopes of Monte Circeo. Here the few beaches are pinched between the sheer, corroded cliffs of the moutain, but the scenery is fantastic. From the picturesque medieval village you can climb up to the summit of the mountain, which boasts a bar and some of the more spectacular ocean views in Lazio. **Buses** from San Felice return to Rome every ½hr., 5:25am-8:05pm.

Terracina

South of San Felice, the town of Terracina was a Roman stronghold, sanctuary and stopping-point on the old Appian Way; medieval residents built a walled town over the old forum on the hill, and today a modern beach town occupies the low ground along the sea. The ACOTRAL bus from Rome (departures from EUR-Fermi every hour 6:20am-8:40pm, L6300, 2hr.) deposits you near the beach, where the sheer rock cliff, cut away by Trajan in the 2nd century AD to make room for the Appian Way, dominates the shoreline. Two km up the hill, the medieval town preserves its Roman origins in the pavement of the main *piazza* (once the forum) and its **cathedral**, built out of the ancient Roman *capitolium,* boasts a gorgeous set of inlaid mosaic decorations. The **tourist office** here (off piazza Mazzini; open 9am-noon, in July-Aug. also 5-6pm) provides information on accommodations and transportation back to Rome or elsewhere. A half-hour walk up the hill above town (take via Anxur out of piazza Mazzini), the masonry foundations of the ancient **Temple of Jupiter Anxurus** occupy the highest ground around. The temple, thought to date from the 1st century BC, is long gone, but its vaulted foundations remain and make for a fascinating afternoon of exploring and gaping at vistas.

Gaeta and Formia

Gaeta and Formia dominate their own craggy bay some 60km south of Rome. Here the steep cliffs and rocky promontories are really closer in feel to the spectacular landscapes of the Bay of Naples than they are to the flat shores to the north; the scenery gets more precipitous as you travel south, and in the waters off the shoreline you'll find plenty of stony grottoes, caverns and undersea caves. Only an hour and a half by train from Rome, the area offers a dramatic change of scenery, but one that can get dramatically congested in the height of summer. The train from Termini deposits you in Formia (departures every 2hrs; L10.500), a modern town you'd do best to pass over—though there is a **tourist office** in piazza Mattei (Mon.-Fri. 8am-1:30pm, Sat. 9am-noon). From the station, walk north about ½km to Formia's **public beach,** which stretches beneath a great mounded hill crowned by the 1st century BC **Tomb of Munatius Plancus**, a patrician Roman who picked his final resting place with a good eye for scenery. Around the other side of the mound (accessible by local orange buses from the Formia station), the broader shores of Gaeta offer better swimming and sunning possibilities— though again the *stabilmenti* have swallowed up the choicest spots.

The Pontine Islands

A weekend playground for city-weary Romans, the Pontine Islands are Lazio's most splendid assets. After housing a series of exiles from ancient Rome, this stunning volcanic archipelago with its mountain spines and turquoise water, was given to Bourbon King Charles III of Naples by his mother Elisabetta Farnese in 1730. The Islands' subsequent inhabitation by wood-hungry Neapolitans led to the contemporary landscape of tiny vineyards, fragrant wild herbs, and flowers. Though crowded in July and August, the islands are geared mainly to Italians—a welcome change from the rampaging Germans on Elba and the international mayhem of Cápri.

Getting There

The Pontine Islands can be reached by **ferry** from Anzio, Terracina, Fiumicino and Formia by several ferry lines including **Med Mar** (via Ofanto, 18, tel. 841 90 57; or piazza Barberini, 5, tel. 482 85 79) and **CAREMAR** (in Naples, tel. (081) 551 38 82; in Ponza, tel. (0771) 46 16 00 or 227 10). From Rome the most inexpensive option is CAREMAR from Anzio (L16,700; train to Anzio L4300). The most convenient route is from Fiumicino (prices below). The Terracina-Ponza commute is L10,000 (once daily). If you're on an island spree, consider the journey from or to Cápri and Íschia. (Cápri-Ventotene on Med Mar is L25,000 but only runs June-Sept.)

Fiumicino-Ponza-Ventotene: Med Mar departures daily 9am and 4:15pm, 2{1/2}hr.; L47,000 to Ponza, L44,000 to Ventotene. Free shuttle bus runs from the airport to the port. Make reservations with a travel agent in Rome, especially for weekend travel.

Formia-Ponza: CAREMAR departures 9am and 4:30pm, L16,700. Returns 5:30am and 1:30pm.

Formia-Ventotene: CAREMAR departures 9:10am and 1pm, 3hr., L41,000. Return 5:30pm. If no one is at the information booth at the Ventotene port, inquire at the bar next door.

Ponza-Ventotene: Med Mar departures 11am and 6pm, 30min., L15,000. CAREMAR departure 6:10pm, 35min., L14,500.

Ponza

Orientation and Practical Information

Tourist Office: Pro Loco (tel. 800 31). The office is on your left as you mount the main staircase leaving the dock. Useful brochure available. Open Mon.-Sat. 9:30am-1:30pm.

Post Office: corso Pisacane, 32. Make your 1st right after the tourist office; the sign is on the left. Open Mon.-Fri. 8:30am-1:30pm, Sat. 8:30am-noon. **Postal Code:** 04027. **Telephone Code:** 0771.

Buses: main station Autolinee Ponzesi, via Dante (tel. 804 47). Buses depart from here every 15min. to Le Forna (L1500). On the way back, flag down buses anywhere along via Panoramica.

Emergencies: tel. 113. **Police:** molo Musco (tel. 801 30). **First Aid and Medical Care: Poliambulatorio,** via Panoramica (tel. 806 87).

Accommodations and Camping

Unfortunately Ponza isn't the fishing village it once was. Prices have skyrocketed over the past few years due to the evolution of tourism. Freelance **camping** was outlawed three years ago due to fire hazards. There are two helpful agencies to save you the trouble of searching for a site: **Agenzia Immobiliare "Arcipelago Pontino,"** corso Pisacane, 49 (tel. 806 78), and **Agenzia Afari "Magi,"** via Branchina Nuova, 21 (tel. 80 98 41). They will also help you find a room in *affitta camere* (private homes) that run L40,000 in July and August, less during the off-season.

Pensione-Ristorante "Arcobalene," via Scotti D. Basso, 6 (tel. 803 15). As you ascend the stairs you may be cursing the writer who sent you here. When you reach the summit, however, you will understand why you were sent. Straight up the ramp, follow the street until it ends, then veer right until you pass the Bellavist Hotel. Turn left and follow the signs up, up, up. Wonderful people, the best views in Ponza, and excellent food. Singles L30,000. Doubles L60,000. Off-season L25,000; L50,000. English spoken. Call ahead in summertime.

Casa Vitiello, via Madonna, 28 (tel. 801 17). In the historic part of town, this family-run *affitta camere* has simple rooms in a quiet location. Follow the signs to La Torre dei Borbini and it'll be across the street. Singles L40,000. Doubles L70,000. Off-season L35,000; L60,000.

Food and Entertainment

The Pontine Islands are known for their lentil soup, fish, and lobster. Several comparable restaurants and bars surround the port and spark the island's nightlife. (Be careful if you're staying in Le Forna; Sept.-June the last bus is at 10pm; July-Aug. last bus at 3am.) Most restaurants also rent boats and organize island excursions by day.

Ristorante Lello, strada Panoramica, 10 (tel. 803 95), next door to the bus station. Specializes in regional dishes. Their *zuppa di lenticchie* (lentil soup, L5000) is especially tasty. *Primi* L7000, *secondi* L10,000.

Le Note Blu, via Banchina T. di Fazio (tel. 805 07). Located directly on the waterfront, this "piano bar" with live music nightly is a good bet for jazz and drinks. First drink L5000. Open 10:30pm-5am depending on the crowd.

Sights

Ponza is full of grottoes and hidden **beaches.** Explore either on foot (the best way to savor the breathtaking panoramic views) or by renting a boat (try the jutting pier to the right of the main launch; L80,000 and up for the entire day depending on boat size). For a guided boat tour, inquire at any of the portside resturants that advertise (around L16,000 per person). Most trips visit the **Pilatus Caves,** an ancient Roman breeding ground for Muraena fish. Underwater types should consider going to **Noi e il Mare,** Banchina Mamozio (tel. 80 99 99 or 86 81 40), located right under the ascending ramp from the main disembarkation pier; both **scuba diving** expeditions and lessons are offered. (Equipment rental L40,000. Seven-day certification course L450,000—equipment not included.)

Ventotene

If the crowds of Campania are driving you mad, there's at least one refuge of sanity—tranquil Ventotene. Despite a barren landscape, this tiny island's unexploited charm will rejuvenate your weary traveling bones. Over the centuries, Ventotene has served as a prison in various capacities: ancient Roman women were succeeded in the 18th century by a co-ed clan of convicts (from Naples) sent to the island to reform themselves in arcadian bliss. After four scandalous years of license (1768-72), they were tossed off the island and replaced by farmers.

The tiny **tourist office** is located right on the port and is managed by an affable English-speaking staff. **CSV,** at p. Castello (via Pozzo di S. Candida, 13), will help you find a room in a hotel, *affitta camere*, or private home that costs L30,000 (single) and L60,000 (double) during July and August. Prices drop from September through June. There are two **supermarkets,** one at p. Castello and the other at via Roma. The **Archaeological Museum** is also at p. Castello (open 10am-1pm and 7pm-midnight). Two splendid **beaches** flank either side of the port.

Etruscan Sites

Etruria

> Whoever it is that has departed, they have left a
> pleasant feeling behind them, warm to the heart,
> and kindly to the bowels.
>
> —D.H. Lawrence

The Etruscans, an Italic tribe who may or may not have had roots in Asia Minor (the academic jury's still out on the question), dominated north-central Italy from the 9th to the 4th century BC. Though the wealthiest of their citizens enjoyed trade and communication with Greek colonies in the south of the peninsula, Etruscan culture (as well as its written language, which remains undeciphered) was wholly original—in fact Rome itself owes much of its early artistic and architectural development to this mysterious nation. The Romans weren't feeling too grateful, unfortunately, when they demolished the Etruscan cities during their relentless drive to empire, and in the shadow of the new power to the south, most traces of Etruscan life disappeared. What remains, excavated from their necropolises of tombs, is fascinating. Unlike the stern, superstitious Romans, Etruscans enjoyed life to the fullest; their tomb paintings (at Tarquinia) celebrate life, love, eating and drinking, sport, and the rough, hilly countryside that they called home. Their *tumuli* (at Cerveteri) are carved out of the rock like houses in a friendly neighborhood. Vandalism and theft have forced the government to close many of the tombs, and what artifacts have been excavated now reside in the Villa Giulia and Vatican Museums at Rome and in the Museo Nazionale Etrusco in Tarquinia. Still, a visit to the ancient, rocky landscape of Etruria conjures up plenty of ghosts, and the deserted tombs have a quiet, shadowy appeal that's quite different from the pomp and grandeur that Rome has to offer.

Cerveteri

Outside Cerveteri (ancient *Caere*), the bulbous earthen tombs of the **necropolis** slumber in the tufa bedrock from which they were carved. The tombs are a curious mix—outside, the rock walls and grassy mounds speak of the Etruscans' monumental regard for their dead; inside, the chambers are still and simple, carved to resemble the wooden huts in which living Etruscans resided. Archaeologists have removed the objects of daily life—chariots, weapons, even cooking implements—with which the dead were furnished, but the carved tufa columns and couches remain. As you enter a tomb, small rooms off the antechamber mark the resting place of slaves and lesser household members; the central room held the bodies of the rest of the family, and the small chambers off the back were reserved for the most prominent men and women. A triangular headboard on a couch marks a woman's grave, a circular one indicates a man's. Only some 50 of an estimated 5000 tombs have been excavated, mostly in a cluster of narrow streets at the heart of the ghost town. Don't miss the **Tomb of the Shields and the Chairs**, the smaller **Tomb of the Alcove** (with a carved-out matrimonial bed), and the row-houses where less well-to-do Etruscans rested in peace. Look for the remarkable colored stucco reliefs in the **Tomba dei Relievi**.

ACOTRAL **buses** run to Cerveteri from Rome at via Lepanto (every ½hr., 1hr., L3800; take Metro Linea A to Lepanto, or bus #70 from Sta. Maria Maggiore or Largo Argentina). From the village, it's another 2km to the necropolis along a country road; follow the signs. A **train** from Rome's Trastevere station also serves the city (L3800; round-trip L6400). (Site open Tues.-Sun. 9am-7pm; Oct.-April Tues.-Sat. 9am-4pm, Sun. 11am-4pm. Admission L6000; Maps L1000. Bring a flashlight.)

Also worthwhile is the **Museo Nazionale di Cervéteri**, p. Santa Maria Maggiore (tel. 995 00 03), located in **Ruspoli Castle**, a fairy-tale edifice of ancient walls and crenellations, right next to the bus stop in town. The museum displays those artifacts dug from the Caere necropolis in the last ten years. (Open Tues.-Sun. 9am-2pm. Admission L6000.) Inquire at the **tourist office**, on via delle Mure Castellane, about organized archaeological walks to the necropolis. The last bus for Rome leaves at 9:30pm; if you're stuck, the **Albergo El Paso**, via Settevene Palo, 293 (tel. 994 35 82; ½km out the bottom left side of the main *piazza*) has doubles for L70,000.

From Cerveteri, you can also catch the ACOTRAL bus for **Civitavécchia**, which makes stops at the beaches of **Santa Severa** and **Santa Marinella** (or walk 2km down the hill from the bus stop to the Civitavécchia road, where the blue buses pass more frequently—buy tickets in town, L1200). Treat yourself to excellent seafood (much better than in Rome or Cerveteri) in any of the towns' cheap *trattorie* before catching the bus back to Rome.

Tarquinia

When Rome was no more than a village of mud huts beside the Tiber, Tarquin kings hailing from majestic Tarquinia held the fledgling metropolis under their sway. The tables turned, of course; the Romans came back with a vengeance, and today little remains of the once-thriving Etruscan city or the dynasties that ruled it. But the ravages of neither time nor Romans could wipe out the subterranean **necropolis** of tombs on the ridge opposite the city, and the extraordinarily vibrant frescoes remaining here are worth exploring.

Buses arrive in the Barriera San Giusto outside the medieval ramparts. The **tourist office** here (tel. 85 63 84; open Mon.-Sat. 8am-2pm and 5-7pm) provides a wealth of information and bus schedules. In adjoining p. Cavour stands the **Museo Nazionale** (tel. 85 60 36), one of the best collections of Etruscan art outside of Rome, occupying the huge medieval **Palazzo Vitelleschi**. Inside the entrance loom the sepulchral monuments of many important Tarquinian families. The sarcophagi are crowned by full-length portraits of the dead that lay within; look for the double portrait of a man and woman lying together. On the second floor, the museum's mascot, a magnificent relief of Winged Horses, dates from the 4th century BC. The impressive array of Greek ceramics (imported by wealthy Etruscans and buried with them in their tombs) includes a cup shaped like a woman's head and a huge vase depicting an assembly of the gods. Also on the second floor are several reconstructed tombs with fine frescoes. Don't pass up the second-floor ramparts of the castle, where you can sun yourself and catch great views of the sea. (Open Tues.-Sun. 9am-2pm. Guided evening tours in summer Tues.-Fri.-inquire at the tourist office. Admission L8000.)

The same ticket admits you to the **necropolis** (tel. 85 63 08), Tarquinia's main attraction. Take the bus from Barriera San Giusto (any that go to the "cimitero" stop), or, better yet, walk (15min. from the museum). Head up corso Vittorio Emanuele from p. Cavour and turn right down via Porta. Then take via Ripagretta to via delle Croci, which leads to the tombs. You must wait for a group to form and for a guide to let you into any of the excavated tombs. Because of their sensitivity to air and moisture, only four to six tombs may be seen on a given day (and even then only peered at from behind a metal railing in the doorway). All of the tombs are splendid works of art, decorated with scenes of Etruscan life, including banquets, sacrifices, rituals, and portraits of the dead, as well as animals and geometric designs. (Tombs open Tues.-Sun. 9am-2pm.)

Trip over Tarquinia by day. The site is a popular local stop on the Rome-Grosseto **train** line, and buses run from the station and beaches into town every 30 minutes until 9:10pm. (Trains leave from Roma Ostiense station starting at 7:20am; the last train back leaves Tarquinia at 10:48pm; 1hr; L7200 one-way, L12,200 round-trip). **Buses** also link the town with Viterbo (1hr., L3500), Civitavecchia (45min., L3200) and Rome (8 per day, 2hr., L6300). The bus from Rome leaves from via Lepanto (see Cerveteri, above). For information on Southern Etruria (Provincia di Viterbo), inquire at the Azienda Autonoma di Turismo at p. Cavour, 1 (tel. (0766) 85 63 84), or at the EPT in Viterbo, p. dei Caduti, 16 (tel. 22 61 61). The cheapest hotel in hilltop Tarquinia, **Hotel San Marco**, p. Cavour, 18 (tel. 84 08 13), offers commodious, comfy rooms. (Singles L53,000. Doubles L78,000.)

In **Tarquinia Lido**, a beach 2km from where the train stops, **Albergo Miramare**, viale dei Tirreni, 36 (tel. 880 20), right on the beach, lets beautiful doubles for only L35,000 (with bath L49,500). Camp at **Tuscia** (tel. 88294), and revel in a pizzeria, market, clean bathrooms, and a separate grove for tents (L9000 per person, L11,000 per tent, 4-person bungalow L60,000). Take the bus from the train station (3km), and get off at the last stop along the beach. Eating in Tarquinia is cheap and enjoyable. An absolute must for lunch or dinner is **Trattoria Corneto** (tel. 957826) under the *cucina e pizzeria* sign at via Garibaldi, 12, at via Cavalotti. This nondescript establishment cooks up monumental plates of spaghetti (L6000-8000) and loaded pizzas (L5000-7000).

Veio

The Sanctuary at Veio is particularly fiendish in that it contains the only set of Etruscan ruins that is easy to visit—and the one least worth the bother. Intrepid hikers and Etruscologists are the only ones who need apply. From Rome's p. Ponte Milvio (take the #225 tram from outside p. del Popolo), take bus #201 (8 per day, L1200) to Isola Farnese. The tiny feudal hamlet of Veio surrounds **Castello Ferraioli.** Before the bus goes up to the *castello*, it passes a small dirt road marked "Veio." This path descends to a waterfall where a tiny bridge crosses a babbling stream. On the other side, the path on the right leads up to a large stone gate, the entrance to the excavations. From here, the original Roman road, paved with basalt stones, winds to the summit where temples once stood, with a stunningly romantic view of the surrounding fields and hills. If you're heading to Bracciano (see below), consider stopping off at Veio on the way home; bus #201 and the ACOTRAL bus for Bracciano follow the same road back to Rome.

Northern Lazio Lakes and Towns

The beaches of Lazio, when not polluted by Roman sewage spewing forth from the Tiber or whipped into a frenzy by frequent sandstorms, tend to be packed towel-to-towel during the summer months. Still, you might find a stretch of open beach along the southern coast (see above). For those not pledged to acquiring a sand-flecked tan, some delightful water awaits in Northern Lazio's great lakes. These three round puddles (the craters of extinct volcanoes) see a lot of Roman traffic, but they're large enough to absorb everyone comfortably.

Lake Bracciano

The most convenient place to go swimming near Rome is Lake Bracciano, though even this huge sheet of water has seen some pollution in recent years, and its meager stretches of gritty volcanic sand can be grubby in summer. But the town itself is dominated by an impressive medieval castle, its many *trattorie* serve up fresh lake fish and eel (the local specialty), and a ferry ride across the lake to nearby **Anguillara** or **Trevignano** offers some spectacular scenery. You can take a train to Bracciano on the Rome-Viterbo line (first train leaves Stazione Ostiense 5:47am, last train back leaves Bracciano 10:08pm; L3900 one-way, L6800 round-trip) or an ACOTRAL bus from outside the Lepanto Metro stop (first bus leaves Rome 6:50am, last leaves Bracciano 8:40pm; L3000 one-way). The bus follows much the same route as #201 for Isola Farnese and Veio (see above); consider combining the trips in a day.

The bus lets you off in p. Roma (ask the driver, as it's possible to miss the town entirely); the friendly **tourist office** is via Claudia, 72 (tel. 998 67 82) ½km down via Claudia. You won't have to look hard to find Bracciano's main attraction; the imposing **Orsini-Odescalchi Castle** (tel. 902 40 03) hangs over the medieval and modern quarters of the city with menacing authority. The castle was built in the late 15th century for the Orsini barons, an ancient, independent-minded Roman family who managed to provoke (and withstand) the jealous rages of a succession of autocratic Renaissance popes. Even Cesare Borgia, Alexander VI's Machiavellian son and commander-in-chief, never breached the castle's forbidding tufa towers (the castle only succumbed in the 1670s, when the Odescalchi family tried a more powerful weapon—cash). Inside, a series of great salons and chambers stretches around two picturesque medieval courtyards, their walls and ceilings frescoed with the Orsini arms and with a few stellar cycles by Antoniazzo Romano, the pupil of Pinturicchio, and by Taddeo and Federico Zuccari. The rooms also house an impressive collection of arms and armor, and a substantial number of stuffed wild boars. From the ramparts atop the castle the whole lake and its surrounding towns submits to your view. (Open summer Tues.-Sun. 10am-noon and 3-6pm; winter 9am-noon and 3-5pm; mandatory guided tour (in cheerful, tourist-level Italian, L7000.)

Signs point the way down the hill to the lakeshore, about a 1km walk. There are stretches of sand available in both directions, and stands renting windsurfers, paddle boats and other diversions. *Consorzione di Navigazione* (tel. 6766281) runs a ferry service to the neighboring towns of **Anguilllara** and **Trevignano** (departures at 10am, 11:45am, 4:45pm, 5:45pm as well as 2:30pm on Sundays; L3000 for one stop, L6000 for two, L7500 for a circuit of the lake; follow the signs for the *barchetto*). Neither of these towns has much in the way of sights, but in their winding medieval streets innumerable *trattorie* serve up grilled *coregone* (a lake fish) and delicious *ciriole alla cacciatora* (eels cooked over a slow fire). ACOTRAL runs **buses** between both towns and Bracciano (every hr.) or back to Rome (1 every hr. from Anguillara, 2:30 and 5:05pm from Trevignano; L2500).

Lake Vico

Further away, little Lake Vico is prettier, cleaner, and better supplied with amusements. Take a car down the serpentine road, or get off at the bus stop on top of the hill and walk down 2km from Caprarola. A **train** runs to Caprarola from Stazione Ostiense (leaves 11:03am, change at Orte, arrives 1:40pm; L8800 one-way, L15,800 round-trip) or you can take a **bus** from Lepanto (about every hr.; L4500). Lago Vico is a **nature reserve**, campground, and recreational facility. You must make a reservation to stay at the **campsite** (tel. (0761) 61 23 47; L6000 per person, L5000 per tent, L3500 per car). The campground management also offers **guided tours** of the reserve (mostly in Italian) for a minimum group of four: on horseback (6hr., L75,000 per person); in a jeep (4-8hr., L20,000 per person); on mountain bikes (you must have your own bike; 4-8hr., L35,000); in a canoe (L10,000 per hr.); or by foot (8hr., L18,000 per person). You can also take instructions in canoeing (L15,000 per hr.) and archery (L7000 per hr.). The management is young and eager to show the reserve to visitors.

Pompeii, Herculaneum (Ercolano) and Vesuvius

Mount Vesuvius's fit of towering flames, suffocating black clouds, and seething lava brought sudden death to the prosperous Roman city of Pompeii in 79 AD. The eruption buried the city—tall temples, narrow streets, patrician villas, massive theater and all—under 10 meters of volcanic ash. Archaeologists have worked for centuries to uncover the hidden city, and today a walk through the narrow ancient streets, lined with two- and sometimes three-story townhouses, presents a view of city life largely unchanged by the last 1900 years. Archaeological probes indicate that Pompeii was inhabited as early as the 8th century BC and that during the 7th century BC it fell under the influence of Greek colonists from the south of Italy, who developed it as a commercial center. By the 3rd century BC, Pompeii was a mature city with a prosperous economy, a population of nearly 20,000 and a sophisticated cultural life closely linked to that of the Greek cities in the south. Falling under Roman influence around 180 BC, the city developed further both as a trading port and as an aristocratic enclave, where leading Romans, including Cicero, built lavish country villas.

Life went on as usual on the fateful day of August 24, 79 AD—merchants and shoppers crowded the Forum, farmers completed chores on farms just outside the city walls, and the priests of Isis paused in the middle of their daily rites to eat a quick lunch in their private house. These everyday moments, and countless others, were frozen forever by the sudden eruption, which rained successive layers of ash, dust, pebbles, lava, and rock down on the surprised metropolis. The catastrophe happened so quickly that few residents were able to escape; most took shelter in their homes or in public buildings, where they were quickly asphyxiated by the concentration of deadly volcanic gases. Dust and ash thrown up by the volcano drifted into the town and solidified, encasing not only the buildings but also the bodies of the dead. These decomposed, leaving hollow spaces in the new volcanic rock; when archaeologists found the cavities they filled them with plaster, creating the haunting casts of agonized and panicked figures (including a sadly abandoned dog) which now decorate some of the city's sites.

Herculaneum, on the other side of Vesuvius, endured a harder fate. Laid out along the sea in the shadow of the volcano, the town was swamped by a wall of molten lava and disappeared without a trace. The cataclysm did, however, leave the city nearly intact; when the city went under, it was enveloped in the lava and protected. The townhouses and apartment blocks of the ancient city are almost perfectly preserved, with staircases and ceilings, wall paintings, mosaics, and even furniture still decorating their labyrinthine rooms. The city was discovered by 18th-century farmers sinking shafts for wells. Once scholars grasped the full import of their discovery, digging began in earnest both here and at the site of Pompeii, which had been identified by the analysis of ancient texts.

In both cities, you'll find ample examples of the classic patrician Roman house, known in Latin, as a *domus*, or in Italian as a *casa*. Presenting a harsh and undecorated façade to the outside street, the Pompeian house turns inward on itself, its rooms gathered around one of the three types of open space: the *atrium*, the peristyle court, or the formal garden. The front door (often guarded by a porter's cubicle) leads into the dark and airy *atrium*, the main vestibule of the house, where the family and household gods were kept and where the *paterfamilias* greeted his guests. A rectangular opening in the roof allowed light into the room, as well as rain water, which was collected in the *impluvium*, a stone basin let into the floor. While various chambers and storerooms were arranged around the atrium, the main rooms of the house usually lay beyond, including the *tablinum*, or master's study, across the atrium from the door, and the *triclinium*, or dining room, usually arranged near the back peristyle court. These courts, especially in the more lavish houses at Pompeii, were decorated with colorful frescoes, statuary, formal plantings, and fountains. The most elegant houses also harbored a colonnaded garden at the back of the house, where more greenery and running water provided a sumptuous retreat from the heat of the city. Not all ancients had the luck to live in such style, however; keep an eye out in both cities for the more modest *insulae*, or apartment blocks, where several families lived together in high-rise complexes with shared kitchen and bathroom facilities.

Pompeii

Enter the town near the amphitheater, through the **Porta di Nola** or through the Porta Marina, a short way from the Forum, the center of the ancient town. A comprehensive walk-through will probably take four or five hours; pack a lunch and a water bottle as the two snackbars are rather pricey, though good in a pinch. You can rent a tour guide for L30,000 or save your cash and catch a free ride—a short search is bound to land you in the fringes of an English tour: blend in, bend an ear, and savor the gory details of life and death in Pompeii. The entrances are open 9am-1hr. before sunset (admission L10,000).

From the Porta di Nola, the **Great Palestra** sprawls to your left. The large structure, enclosed on three sides by a colonnade and pine trees, was used by Pompeiian youths for gymnastic exercises and competitions. The **amphitheater** across from the gymnasium, built in 80 BC, is the oldest and best-preserved in Italy. With seating for 15,000, it looms over a vista of Pompeii and the volcano beyond. Next to the gymnasium, the **House of Loreius Tiburtinus** preserves the essentials of a Roman garden—long rectangular pools surrounded by columns and formal paintings. Loreius's house fronts the **via dell'Abbondanza,** one of Pompeii's main streets, stretching 1km from the town's eastern wall to the Forum. It's lined (as it was in antiquity) with small shops and taverns, their plastered walls scrawled with *graffiti* and red-lettered advertisements, some of which extol the virtues of various political candidates. Walking toward the Forum, hang a left on via Stabiana and walk two blocks south. Here you'll find the **Teatro Piccolo**, an exquisite little concert hall built around 80 BC. Next door, the earlier **Teatro Grande**, built around 200-150 BC in the hollow of a hill, hosted larger theatrical productions. In July, August, and September, classical concerts featuring big-name performers are held here (usually Fri.-Sun. at 9pm. Tickets L10,000-30,000). North of the theater stands the well-preserved **Temple of Isis,** testimony to the popularity of the Egyptian fertility goddess's cult among the cosmopolitan residents of Pompeii. To the west, the ruined temples of the **Foro Triangulare** were part of the city's oldest sacred precinct.

Via dei Teatro leads back north to via dell'Abbondanza. Backtrack one block and turn left on via Stabiana; the entrance to the stupendous **Stabian Baths** is on the left. An enormous complex featuring separate facilities for men and women, the baths preserve their hot, warm and cold rooms, as well as a *palestra* where male bathers engaged in contests of wrestling and bowling (yes, bowling). The world's oldest profession claims its own territory one street to the west in the red-light district of **vicolo del Lupanare.** At the top of this street is a small, no-nonsense brothel, in which several stall-like bedchambers are unceremoniously grouped around the central cash-register. The erotic painting over each door advertised with unabashed precision the specialty of the woman inside.

Via dell'Abbondanza ends at the **Forum,** the commercial, civic, and religious center of the city, framing a beautiful but ominous view of Vesuvius. Fragments of the double-decker colonnade that once ringed the entire square survive in the southwest corner.

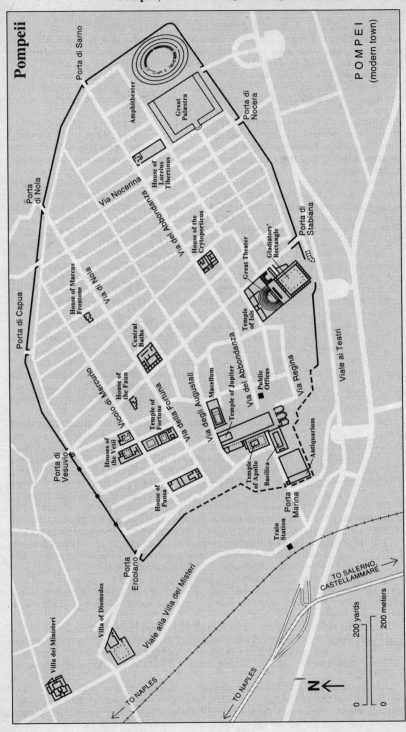

Pompeii

POMPEI
(modern town)

Porta di Sarno

Porta di Nola

Porta di Capua

Porta di Vesuvio

Porta Ercolano

Villa dei Ministeri

Villa of Diomedes

Viale alla Villa dei Misteri

TO NAPLES

TO NAPLES

Amphitheater

Great Palaestra

Porta di Nocera

Porta di Stabiana

Via Nocerina

House of Lorcius Tiberinus

Via della Abbourpanza

House of the Crytoporticus

Great Theater

Gladiators' Rectangle

Temple of Isis

House of Marcus Frontone

Via di Nola

Central Baths

House of the Faun

Vicolo di Mercurio

Houses of the Vetii

Temple of Fortune

Via della Fortuna

Via degli Augustali

Macellum

Temple of Jupiter

Via dell'Abbondanza

Public Offices

Via Regina

Viale ai Teatri

House of Pansa

Temple of Apollo

Basilica

Antiquarium

Porta Marina

Train Station

TO SALERNO, CASTELLAMMARE

200 yards

200 meters

N

TO NAPLES

0

0

The **basilica** (law courts building), which encloses the south side of the Forum, was the largest building in Pompeii and retains parts of its impressive dais in the southeast corner. Three temples also graced the Forum. On the northern side rises the **Temple of Jupiter.** The **Temple of Apollo** sits across the side street from the basilica, almost hidden from the rest of the city (unlike a Greek temple, which usually reigns from atop a hill). The stone in the middle was used as a sacrificial altar. In the **Temple of Vespasian,** on the western side across the Forum from the Temple of Apollo, a delicate frieze on the center altar illustrates the preparation for a sacrifice.

Showcases along the western side of the Forum display gruesome **plaster casts** of some of the volcano's victims, including a crouching pregnant woman and a running boy. The contorted positions of the humans and even a dog support the theory that the inhabitants suffocated from the gases of the eruption rather than being crushed by its ashen discharge.

North of the Forum, rest in the **cafeteria** (go up to its roof for the only aerial view of Pompeii) before starting on a walk to the northwest corner of the site and out to the Villa dei Misteri. Walk up to the massive **Casa del Fauno,** in front of the **Casa dei Vetii.** The Casa dei Vetii contains Pompeii's most remarkable frescoes, all crafted in the latest of Pompeii's styles, involving fantastic architectural designs in grandiose perspective. For a chuckle, follow the halls to a tiny room on the right. This Jesse Helms Special contains a two-and-a-half-foot marble **statue of Priapus** proudly displaying his colossal member. The legendary child of Venus and Adonis is pictured elsewhere in town and phallic images are ubiquitous, but your smirks prove you more dirty-minded than the Romans; phalloi were believed by the ancients to ward off the evil eye. Next to the room a smaller *triclinium* contains some of the most intact examples of the late style of Roman painting.

A short walk from the Casa dei Vetii brings you to **Villa dei Misteri**, a suburban villa just outside the city walls which preserves both its formal living rooms and its rustic storehouses as well as a ram-headed wine press. A renowned cycle of paintings (in the room directly to the right of the entrance) centers around a puzzling religious theme. A young woman is prepared for unknown inititation rites, presided over by the central figures of Dionysius and his bride Ariadne. Especially terrifying is the black-winged female figure to the right, whose whip scars the back of the helpless initiate. (Entrances open 9am-1hr. before sunset. Admission L10,000.)

One km outside the archaeological zone, the second floor of the **Museo Vesuviano** displays Pompeiian threads, while the first floor houses a boring collection of items from the Barto Longo estate. The museum calls Big Bart's old villa home; you can find it on via Colle S. Bartolomeo, 10 (tel. 863 10 41), off the p. Barto Longo, the corner diagonally opposite the road to the train station. (Second floor open daily 9am-1pm.) The **basilica** presides over p. Barto Longo; its crypts hold the remains of rich ol' Barto, Christian Laettner-esque $90 perm and all. (Crypts open daily 9am-1pm and 3-6pm.)

The quickest route to Pompeii (25km south of Naples) is to first take the train to Naples, then take the **Circumvesuviana** train line from Naples's Stazione Centrale (L2500; Eurail passes valid). A less frequent state train leaves from the main track at the Naples station, stopping at Pompeii en route to Salerno (7 per day 7:10am-1:15pm, L2500). Most travelers take the *Circumvesuviana's* Naples-Sorrento line, which lets you off at the Pompeii-Villa dei Misteri stop just outside the Porta Marina gate. An alternative is to take the *Circumvesuviana* from Naples toward Poggiomarino and hop off at the Pompeii Santuario (*not* the Pompeii Valle) stop. Then walk straight from the station, take a right across your first *piazza,* and head about 300m down via Roma to the Porta di Nola gate.

The **tourist office,** via Sacra, 1 (tel. 850 72 55), across from p. Barto Longo on the way to the Porta di Nola, provides free maps and the informative pamphlet *Notizario Turistico Regionale.* (Open Mon.-Sat. 8:30am-1:30pm.) Another tourist office sits near the Porta Marina on via Villa dei Misteri (tel. 861 09 13), to the right of the *circumvesuviana* stop.

Unless you wish to tour Pompeii extensively, there is no reason to stay overnight in the dull modern city. The cheapest alternative is to stay at one of the local campgrounds, all near the ruins. Unfortunately, all are somewhat ruined themselves. **Camp-**

ing Zeus (tel. 861 53 20), outside the Villa dei Misteri *circumvesuviana* stop, boasts a swimming pool and restaurant (L8000 per person, L5000 per large tent, L4000 per small tent). Not far away, on via Plinio, the main road that runs from the ruins, **Camping Pompeii** (tel. 862 78 82), with the same ownership and prices as Zeus, has attractive bungalows for L60,000 for two people and L75,000 for three. You can sack out on the floor of its indoor lobby for L8000 per night. These places yearn for more customers, so you can usually bargain them down at least 25%.

La Vinicola, via Roma, 29, tempts with a pleasant outdoor courtyard and abundant *gnocchi con mozzarella* (potato dumplings with tomato and cheese, L5500). Also try the *zuppa di cozze* for L5000. (Wine L2500 per half liter. Cover L1500. Service 15%. Open daily 9am-midnight; Nov. to mid-July Sat.-Thurs. 9am-11pm.) Gulp down more expensive meals at the **Trattoria Pizzeria dei Platani,** via Colle San Bartolomeo, 8 (tel. 863 39 73), up the street from the Museo Vesuviano, where L7000 buys you a plate of *cannelloni*. (Cover L2000. Service 15%. Open daily 9:30am-7:30pm.)

Herculaneum

Closer to Naples (12km), Ercolano (Herculaneum) would have a sublime seaside view if it weren't 10m underground. Take any *circumvesuviana* train toward Pompeii from Naples's central train station to the Ercolano stop (15min., L1200). Walk 500m down the hill from the station to the **ticket office.** (Open daily 9am-1hr. before sunset. Visitors may remain until half an hour before sunset. Admission L8000.) Before entering, consider purchasing the *Amadeo-Maiuri* guide to Herculaneum, the most comprehensive guidebook, available in the bar across the street (L9000). Neatly excavated and impressively intact, Herculaneum contradicts the term "ruins." Once a wealthy residential enclave on the Roman coast road, Herculaneum doesn't evoke the same sense of tragedy that Pompeii does—all but a handful of its inhabitants escaped the ravages of Vesuvius. In a much less disorienting (and less crowded) tour than those offered in Pompeii, you can wind your way through the 15 or so houses and baths that are now open to the public. There are no colossal buildings, temples, or off-color frescoes to grab your imagination here, but the houses, with their fresh interior decoration, attest to the cultural development of this affluent community. Two-thousand-year-old frescoes, furniture, mosaics, small sculptures, and even wood paneling seem as vital as the day they were made, preserved by a mud avalanche that tumbled off the volcano on a cushion of gas. The **House of the Deer,** so named for a statue of a deer being savagely attacked by greyhounds, is one of the more alluring villas. Probably big partiers, the owners had a statue of a *Satyr with a Wineskin* and an all-too-recognizable statue of the town's patron "saint" Hercules in a drunken stupor trying to take a leak. The **baths,** with their intact warm and hot rooms, as well as a giant vaulted swimming pool, are one of the most evocative ancient sites in Italy. Archaeologists have left some of the lava unexcavated in the *tepidarium:* you can see the imprint of the wooden doors which the lava snapped off their hinges and carried along with it. **The House of the Mosaic of Neptune and Amphitrite** which belonged to a rich shop owner, famous for its mosaic depicting—well, take a guess.

From the Ercolano stop, it's also possible to take a blue bus to **Mount Vesuvius** (round-trip L4500), still the only active volcano on the European continent. Rest assured—it's safe for now; the last eruption occurred on March 31, 1944. You can ramble to the top (1hr.) for a look inside the astounding crater, but you must be accompanied by a guide (L4000). (From the Ercolano stop to Mt. Vesuvius 6 buses daily; Oct.-March 5 buses daily; last return bus 5:50pm.)

Appendices

Language

Modern Italian, a descendant of medieval Latin, was standardized in the late Middle Ages, thanks to the literary triumvirate of Dante, Petrarch, and Boccaccio, who all wrote in the Tuscan dialect. Today, although most Italians still converse at home in local dialects, they can also communicate in "standard" Italian, which is taught and spoken at school, and which reigns though the universal medium of television. There is no dialect in Rome, but a unique cadence. In fact, Roman pronunciation has become the standard for Newscasters . If you don't speak Italian, you'll probably be able to manage with English. More Italians are likely to know a smattering of Frenchor Spanish. Knowing a few basic terms, however, will make your trip much easier, and you'll find that even mangled Italian can evoke enthusiastic appreciation. Take a phrase book (the *Barron's* book is fairly useful; and *Berlitz* has some useful phrases, though the vocabulary is geared toward business travelers) and practice with it before you leave. Better yet, teach yourself with a tape and book set: Barron's provides thorough drilling in basic vocabulary and grammar at a budget price ($75). If you can learn only one complete sentence, learn *Parla inglese?* (PAHR-lah een-GLAY-say: Do you speak English?). When writing numbers, Italians often cross their sevens and use a comma instead of a decimal point (and vice versa). Even more often, what they write is completely illegible to the American-trained eye—once you've learned the numbers, ask the train information people to speak rather than write the time and track you want. Pronunciation is almost entirely phonetic, but remember that no letter (except H) is ever silent.

Reservations by phone

Remember, many proprietors are using to dealing with the minimal Italian of callers; even without any real knowledge of Italian, it is quite possible to get a room.

Pronto! (prohn-toh): phone greeting.

Parla inglese? (PAHR-lah een-GLEH-say): Hopefully, the answer is "Sì," or better yet, "Yes." If not, struggle gamely on ...

Potrei prenotare una camera singola (doppia) senza/con bagno per il due agosto? (POH-tray preh-noh-TAH-ray OO-nah cah-MEH-rah seen-GO-lah (DOHP-pyah) SEHNT-sa/kon BAHN-yoh pehr eel doo-ay ah-GOS-to): Could I reserve a single (double) room without/with bath for the second of August?

Mi chiamo (mee KYAH-moh): My name is ...

Arriverò alle quattordici e mezzo (ahr-ree-veh-ROH ahl-lay kwaht-TOR-dee-chee ay MET-tsoh): I will arrive at 14:30 (remember, Italian use the 24-hour clock, so add twelve to afternoon/evening arrival times).Return phrases to watch out for: *Mi dispiace* (mee dis-PYAH-chay, I'm sorry); *No, siamo completo* (noh, syah-moh com-PLEH-toh, Nope, we're full); *Non si fa prenotazioni per telefono* (nohn see fah preh-no-tat-SYO-nee pehr te-LEH-fo-no, We don't take telephone reservations); *Deve arrivare primo delle quattordici* (DEH-vay ahr-ree-VAH-ray PREE-moh dehl-lay kwaht-TOR-dee-cee, You must arrive before 2pm).

Time

A che ora...?	ah chay orah	At what time...?
Che ore sono?	chay oray sono	What time is it?
Sono le due e mezzo	SO-no lay doo-ay ay MEHT-tsoh	It's 2:30.
È mezzogiorno	eh meht-tsoh-jor-noh	It's noon.
adesso	ah-DEHS-so	now
domani	doh-MAH-nee	tomorrow
oggi	OJ-jee	today
ieri	ee-EH-ree	yesterday

Months (mese) are not capitalized in Italian: *gennaio* (jen-NAHY-oh), *febbraio* (feb-BRAHY-oh), *marzo* (MART-soh), *aprile* (ah-PREE-lay), *maggio* (MAHJ-jo), *giugno* (JOON-yo), *luglio* (LOOL-yo), *agosto* (ah-GOS-to), *settembre* (sayt-TEHM-bray), *ottobre* (ot-TOH-bray), *novembre* (no-VEHM-bray), *dicembre* (dee-CHEHM-bray). Days of the week (*la settimana*) are not capitalized either: *lunedì* (Monday, loo-neh-DEE), *martedì* (mahr-teh-DEE), *mercoledì* (mayr-coh-leh-DEE), *giovedì* (jo-veh-DEE), *venerdì* (veh-nayr-DEE), *sabato* (sah-BAH-to), *domenica* (doh-mehn-EE-cah).

General phrases

Ciao	chow	Hi/So long (informal)
Buon giorno	bon JOR-noh	Good day/Hello
Buona sera	BWO-nah SEH-rah	Good evening
Buona notte	BWO-nah NOHT-tay	Good night
Arrivederci	ahr-ree-vay-DEHR-chee	G oodbye
Per favore	pehr fah-VO-ray	Please
Grazie	GRAHT-zee	Thank you
Prego	PRAY-go	You're welcome/May I help you
Va bene	vah-BEH-nay	Fine, OK
Scusi	SKOO-zee	Pardon
Sì/No/Forse	see/noh/fohr-say	Yes/No/Maybe
Non lo so	non lo so	I don't know
Non parlo italiano.	non PAHR-lo ee-tahl-YAH-no	I don't speak Italian.
Non capisco	non cah-PEE-sko	I don't understand
C'è qualcuno	chay kwahl-KOO-noh	Is there someone
qui chi	qwee kee	here who
parla inglese?	PAHR-lah een GLAY-say	speaks English?
Potrebbe mi aiutare?	poh-TREHB mee iy-oo-TAH-ray	Could you help me?
questo	KWEH-sto	this
quello	KWEHL-lo	that
quale	KWAH-lay	which
dove	DOH-vay	where
quando	KWAN-doe	when
perchè	payr-CHAY	why/because
più	pyoo	more
meno	MEH-noh	less
Come si dice...?	CO-may see DEE-chay	How do you say...?
Come si chiama questo in italiano?	CO-may see KYAH-mah KWEH-sto een ee-tahl-YAH-no	What do you call this in Italian?

Basic Necessities

Vorrei...	VOHR-ray	I would like...
Quanta costa?	KWAN-tah CO-stah	How much does it cost?
Dov'è... ?	doh-VEH	What is...?
un biglietto	oon beel-YEHT-toh	a ticket
solo andato	SO-lo ahn-DAH-to	one way
andato e ritorno	ahn-DA-to e ree-TOR-no	round trip
il gabinetto	eel gah-bee-NEHT-to	the bathroom
il consolato	eel con-so-LAH-to	the consulate
la stazione	la staht-SYO-nay	the station
l'alimentari	la-lee-men-TAH-ree	the grocery store
la chiesa	lah KYAY-zah	church
il telefono	eel tay-LEH-fo-no	the telephone
la spiaggia	la spyahj-jah	the beach
l'ospedale	los-peh-DAH-lay	the hospital
aperto	ah-PEHR-to	open

chiuso	CYOO-zo	closed
l'ufficio postale	loof-FEE po-STAH-lay	the post office
l'ingresso	leen-GREHS-so	the entrance
l'uscita	loo-SHEE-tah	the exit
il treno	eel TREH-no	the train
l'aeroplano	lay-ro-PLAH-no	the plane
l'autobus	LAOW-toh-boos	t he (city) bus
il pullman	eel POOL-mahn	the (intercity) bus
il traghetto	eel tra-GEHT-to	the ferry
l'arrivo	lahr-REE-vo	the arrival
la partenza	la par-TEHN-zah	the departure
il binario	eel bee-NAH-reeoh	the track
il volo	eel VO-lo	the flight
la prenotazione	preh-no-taht-SYOH-nay	the reservation
con bagno/doccia	con BAN-yo/DOCH-CHA	with bath/shower

Directions

Dov'è...?	Doh-veh	Where is...?
Ferma a...?	Fehr-mah ah	Do you stop at...?
A che ora parte...?	a kay o-rah PAHR-tay	What time does the...leave?
vicino	vee-CHEE-noh	near
lontano	lohn-TAH-noh	far
Gira a sinistra.	GEE-rah see-NEE-strah	Turn left.
Gira a destra.	GEE-rah ah DEH-strah	Turn right.
sempre diritto	SEHM-pray dee-REET-toh	straight ahead
dietro l'angolo	dee-AY-troh lan-GO-lo	around the corner
Ferma!	FEHR-mah	Stop!
Aiuto!	iy-OO-toh	Help!

Restaurant Basics

camerierela	waiter/tress
coltello	knife
cucchaio	spoon
forchetta	fork
piatto	plate
l'antipasto	the appetizer
il primo piatto	the first course
il secondo piatto	the second course
il contorno	the side dish
il dolce	the dessert
(prima) colazione	breakfast/lunch
pranzo	lunch
cena	dinner
il coperto	the cover charge
il servizio	the service charge/tip
il conto	bill

Glossary

The following is a glossary of art, architecture, and historical terms used in the book, both Italian and English. Scattered among these terms are a number of Italian words that have appeared in the preceding pages, interesting and mundane.

Abbazia: also *Badia*, an abbey.
Aisle: sides of a church flanking the nave, separated from it by a series of columns.
Apse: a semicircular, domed projection at the east (altar) end of a church.
Atrium: entrance court, usually to an ancient Roman house or a Byzantine church.

Baldacchino: baldachin. A stone or bronze canopy over the altar of a church supported by columns.

Basilica: In ancient Rome, a building used for public administration. Christians adopted the architectural style, a rectangular building with aisle and apse but no transepts, for their churches.

Borgo: A suburb or street leading into a suburb from the center of town (these suburbs are now often just another section of town).

Campanile: a bell tower, usually free-standing.

Camposanto: a cemetery.

Cantoria: choir gallery of a church.

Cartoon: a large preparatory drawing for a fresco or painting.

Chancel: the enclosed space around the altar in a medieval church reserved for clergy and choir; in most Italian churches the space has been opened.

Ciborium: A box or tabernacle that holds the host.

Cloister: a quadrangle with covered walkways along its edges, with a garden

Corso: principal street.

Cupola: dome.

Façade: the front of a building, or any other wall given special architectural treatment.

Forum: in an ancient Roman town, the central square containing most of the municipal buildings.

Fresco: *affresco,* a water-color painting made on wet plaster. When it dries, the painting becomes part of the wall.

Giardino: garden.

Graffiti: *sgraffito* white design scratched on a prepared wall.

Greek Cross: a cross whose arms are of equal length.

Grotesque: painted, carved, or stucco decorations (often heads) on a Roman or Etruscan homes, named for the work found in Nero's buried (grotto) Golden House in Rome.

Latin Cross: a cross whose vertical arm is longer than its horizontal arm.

Loggia: The covered gallery or balcony of a building.

Lungo, Lung: literally "along," so that a *lungomare* is a boardwalk or promenade alongside the ocean; *lungotevere* is the street running alongside the Tiber in Rome.

Lunette: A circular frame in the ceiling or vault of a building that holds a painting or sculpture.

Narthex: the entrance hall before the nave of a church; in a Byzantine church, the portico.

Nave: the central body of a church.

Palazzo: an important building of any type, not just a palace.

Pensione and pension: *Pensione* originally meant a boarding house, but is now used interchangeably with *albergo* (hotel).

Piazza: a city square.

Pietà: a scene of the Virgin, sometimes accompanied, mourning the dead Christ.

Piscina: a swimming pool.

Strada: street.

Transept: either one of the arms of a cruciform church.

Travertine: the chief building material of Rome, ancient and modern, when they weren't using marble. Always light-colored, but sometimes with black speckles.

Triptych: a painting in three panels or parts.

Trompe l'oeil: "to deceive the eye," a painting or other piece or art whose purpose is to trick the viewer with perspectival wit, as in a flat ceiling painted so as to appear domed.

Via: street.

Villa: a country house, usually a large estate with a formal garden.

INDEX

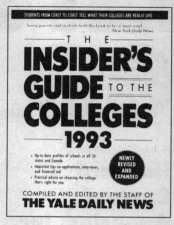